MANAGEMENT

MANAG

William F. Glueck
University of Georgia

EMENT

The Dryden Press
Hinsdale, Illinois

To My Friends
In the Academy of Management
Who Have Been So Supportive In My Work

Copyright © 1977 by The Dryden Press
A division of Holt, Rinehart and Winston, Publishers
All rights reserved
Library of Congress Catalog Card Number: 76-3068
ISBN: 0-03-015491-X
Printed in the United States of America
89   032   9876543

PREFACE

This is a book about management: the effective utilization of human and material resources to achieve the enterprise's objectives.

There are many books on management. Let me explain briefly the approach and emphasis of this one to help you use it more effectively. Note that I will write sometimes in the first person. I know that's not usual. I assure you its not an ego trip. Its just the way we converse most of the time, so hopefully the book will read better that way.

Now let's look at the approach and emphasis in this book on management. First, let's begin by pointing out some special emphases you'll find here.

· Contrasting the managers' job with the job of the entrepreneur, and family business executive
· Contrasting the managers' job in business with the managerial job in government, hospitals, arts organizations, voluntary organizations and others (Chapter 19).
· Contrasting the managers' job in the United States and Canada with the managers' job in many others.

Secondly, the book uses many examples, cartoons, and illustrations to help you understand effective management in the specific, not just in general. It tries very hard to describe the best theory and research on effective management; but then I apply this knowledge to typical managerial situations so you can understand how to use the theory and research.

Thirdly, this management book emphasizes some aspects of management more than many other books. These topics include:

·Contrasting leadership techniques useful in influencing employees with interpersonal influence techniques for colleagues and superiors.

·Effective communication approaches, including effective verbal communication (face to face and on the telephone); effective listening; effective reading skills and others.

·Designing challenging jobs, including the use of job rotation, enrichment, and enlargement.

·Designing a successful career for you.

·Effective management of a manager's time.

·The use of management by objectives effectively.

·The manager's role in managing the environment.

·A contingency approach to organizing and managing. The contingency approach contends that effective managers use one style of managing in one situation, another in a different circumstance. Beginning in Chapter 7, I will simplify the circumstances and begin describing three environments (or situations): the conservative, liberal, and middle of the road. From then on, I'll describe how to apply managerial techniques to these different situations.

Fourthly, the book differs in how it is organized. To give you an overview, I have developed a model of management. It is shown at the start of each of the four parts of the book. These parts are: introduction to management; understanding human behavior; interpersonal skills; and managerial skills. The parts and the topics in them build on the preceding part. For example, what is said in Part 1 about the managerial job is used to help describe human behavior at work in Parts 2 & 3 and the managerial skills in Part 4.

Part 1 is designed to introduce you to management and to give you a good idea of what managers jobs are like. It also explains the jobs of entrepreneurs and family business executives. Finally, it describes what *effective* managers are like and what *effective* enterprises are like.

Parts 2 & 3 are designed to help you understand yourself and employees, superiors, and colleagues (as individuals and as groups) so that you can be a better manager. For management involves getting things done through people. It helps you develop leadership, interpersonal and communication skills of managers.

Part 4 describes the managerial skills used by managers to get the job done: planning and decision making, organizing and organization change, contolling and conflict management, and relating to organizations outside the enterprise.

Lastly, each chapter begins with a list of the chapter objectives and a chapter outline. The objectives are those outcomes you'll receive from reading the chapter. The outline gives you an overview of what you will read. The summary at the end of the chapter reinforces this overview.

The chapters follow this pattern.

· The Meaning of the Section. In this section, I will briefly illustrate a problem managers face and how this section of the book will describe it.

· Specific Definition. The topic discussed is defined *clearly* for you and the definitions are printed in red.

· Reasons for Examining the Topic. This section gives you specific reasons why this topic is discussed and how you'll be a better manager for knowing about this topic.

· What we know about the Topic. This section reviews what managers and management researchers know about the topic; research findings are reviewed. The more important conclusions are placed in red boxes and labeled "Propositions".

· Managerial Meaning. The section is concluded with a section that ties together the problem area with research findings. It is designed to answer the question: How can I use the management research to solve this kind of management problem?

Each chapter provides thoughtful questions and case and exercise material for finding out if you really understood the material. Your instructor may supplement management with one or two volumes:

Study Guide for Management (by Sally Coltrin and myself) also by Dryden Press.

This paperback has a number of materials to help you prepare to read the chapter and to learn if you have mastered it. These include chapter summaries, key terms, and sample examination questions to practice.

Cases, Exercises and Readings in Management (by Lawrence Jauch and myself) also by Dryden Press. This paperback summarizes the chapter, and provides a series of stimulating cases, exercises and field projects and thought provoking readings in management.

Management is an exciting topic. I wrote this book with the hope that you'll get excited over becoming a manager, entrepreneur, or family business executive. I hope you like the book and do choose a career in management.

Acknowledgments

A book is always the product of many people. I have been helped by many of my friends in the Academy including Lawrence Jauch, Southern Illinois University-Carbondale and Sally Coltrin, University of North Florida. The book was reviewed by and helpful comments received from J. Athanassiades, Georgia State University; C. Beavin, Miami Dade Community College; A. Butler, Jr., Santa Fe Community College; R. Donaldson, County College of Morris; E. Duerr, San Francisco State University; M. Lippitt, University of Minnesota; R. Miller, Hillsboro Community College; R. Morey, Western Illinois University; E. Nicholson, Wright State University; S. Scherling, University of North Dakota; J. Seitz, Oakton Community College; W. Thrasher, University of Georgia; B. Weesner, Lansing Community College.

My research assistant Dennis Knapp was helpful in more ways than he realizes. I also wish to thank my colleagues at The University of Georgia, Richard Huseman, Head, Department of Management and Dean William C. Flewellen for their support.

Finally, I wish to thank my children Bill, Lisa, David, and Melissa for the motivation and support they provide me for my work.

Athens, Georgia
January, 1977

William F. Glueck

CONTENTS

Part 1
Introduction To The
Managerial Task

Part 2
Understanding People At Work

Part 3
Interpersonal Skills

Part 4
Managing The Organization's Resources

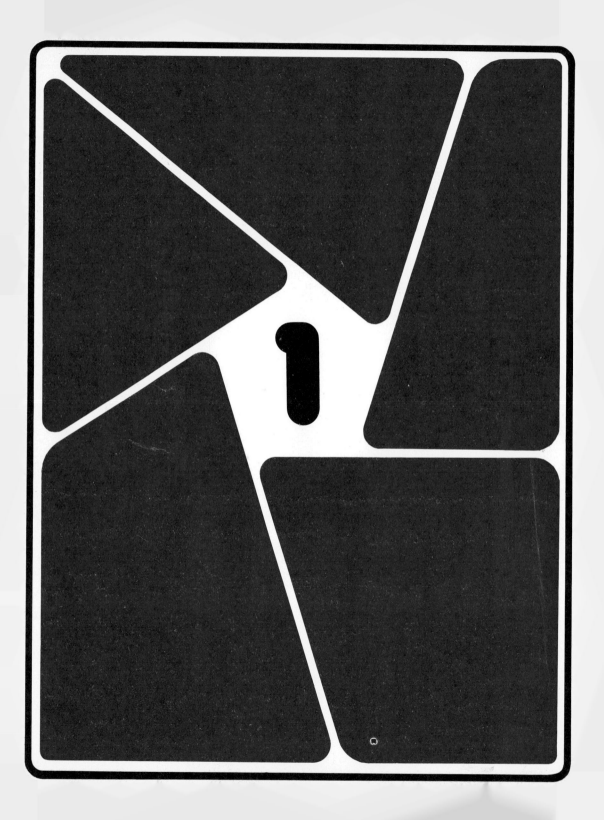

PART 1

INTRODUCTION TO THE MANAGERIAL TASK

This part of the book is designed to introduce you to management—to give you some idea who managers are, what they and their jobs are like, and how knowledge of management can make you a more successful supervisor, middle or top manager, entrepreneur, or family business executive.

Part 1 consists of three chapters. Chapter 1 is an introduction to the book; Chapter 2 introduces you to the world of the manager and the managerial task; and Chapter 3 describes the world of the entrepreneur and the family business executive.

CUSTOMERS

SUPPLIERS

COMPETITORS

COMMUNITY

GOVERNMENT

4
Managerial
skills

- Management of
  environmental relations
- Control and conflict
  management
- Organizing
- Decision making
- Planning

3
Interpersonal
skills of
managers

- Managerial development
- Communicating
- Influencing peers,
  superiors, and others
- Leadership: Influencing
  employees

2
Understanding
people
at work

- Individuals and groups
- Motivation
- Personality
- Attitudes/values
- Perception
- Learning
- Aptitudes and abilities

1
Introduction
to the
managerial
task

- Job of entrepreneur
  and family business
  executive
- Managerial job

Part 1 introduces you to the exciting world of the manager, entrepreneur, and family business executive. It helps you understand what a manager's day is like and how the manager interacts with other people in the enterprise and in the environment. It explains the time and energy expended in managerial and interpersonal skills. Then it contrasts the managerial world with the world of the entrepreneur and the family business executive.

CHAPTER 1
AN INVITATION TO MANAGEMENT

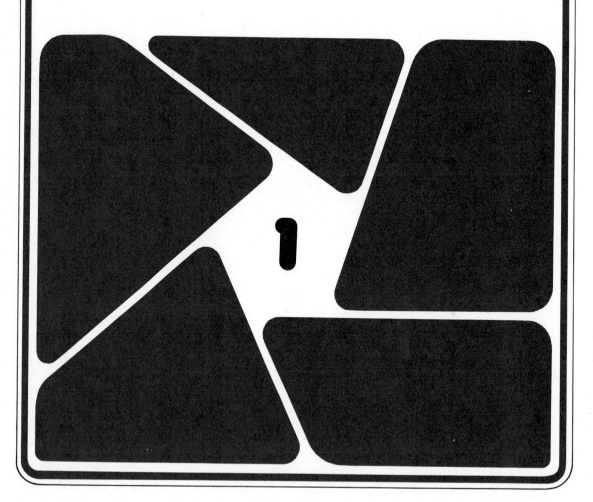

Learning Objectives

1. To introduce you to management.
2. To help you understand the sources of information about management.
3. To describe how this book can help you become an effective manager, entrepreneur, or family business executive.

Chapter Outline

INTRODUCTION

This book is about managers, entrepreneurs, and family business executives: who they are, what they do, and how they succeed. Its objectives are to make you aware of the excitement of a managerial job so you'll want to choose a career in management, and to help you learn how to be a successful manager, that is, to help the enterprise achieve its objectives and to give you a satisfying and rewarding career.

Managers work in all kinds of enterprises. The president of Eastman Kodak is a manager. The operator of Nowell's Supermarket is a manager. The administrator of Valley View Hospital, the director of the Bureau of Labor Statistics, the curator of the Metropolitan Museum of Art, and the president of Indiana University are managers.

There are many similarities among managerial jobs. But there are differences, too. The primary focus of this book is on effective management of businesses. But from time to time I will provide insights into managerial jobs in the nonprofit and government sectors; in fact Chapter 19 discusses in detail the differences between business and nonbusiness enterprises and managerial jobs in each.

This chapter is designed to introduce you to the topic of management.

What Is Management?

Most of us understand what operative employees do. Computer programers write programs in the appropriate computer language to get the data desired by the user. A salesperson calls on customers to get orders for his or her company's products or services and to provide follow-up service to the customer during order processing and after the sale. But not everyone knows what managers are or what they do. Consider the following definition:

MANAGEMENT
Management is effective utilization of human and material resources to achieve the enterprise's objectives.

What does this mean? Generally speaking, managerial tasks include whatever is necessary to make the best use of an enterprise's resources. Over fifty years ago Mary Parker Follett defined management as "getting things done through people."* This makes the point that managers don't do the same things as other employees—at least not regularly. The man-

*Footnotes are not used in this book. However, if you want to know more about a topic you may refer to the references listed in alphabetical order at the end of each chapter under the principal chapter headings. Only the most important sources are cited in the text.

ager's tasks include making good use of the enterprise's employees. Thus managers communicate with and help motivate and develop the potential of employees.

The other managerial tasks are those designed to make the most effective use of the enterprise's financial, material, and ideational resources. These tasks include planning and decision making, building and developing the organization, and creating and monitoring control systems.

So just as you can tell others what a salesperson does, by the time you have finished this book you will be able to tell others what managers do. More important, you will know how to manage and how to manage well in a variety of settings.

The Importance of Management

For enterprises to survive, they must achieve their objectives. All enterprises are responsible to certain groups, such as stockholders, for their performance. The manager is the link to these groups. The manager guides the enterprise, especially in times of trouble. Some writers feel that management is unnecessary—that the employees themselves can do the work of management. But historians and social scientists have yet to find an enterprise that survived very long without developing a hierarchy of management.

On the other hand, many have argued that management—good management—is the key difference between the success and failure of enterprises. Some securities analysts attribute major differences in stock prices to stockholders' evaluation of managers. The great economist Joseph Schumpeter referred to management and entrepreneurs as "the engine of growth." Peter Drucker, a well-known management consultant, says management is the life-giving organ of the enterprise's body. To him management provides the critical difference between success and failure when it performs its four key tasks: achieving economic performance, creating productive work, managing the social impact and responsibilities of a business, and managing the time dimension. And finally, Jacques Servan-Schreiber warned in *American Challenge* that American multinational corporations would overwhelm European business because of the superior skills of American management.

Without managers, it is difficult to get managerial tasks performed effectively. Management contributes to the success of an enterprise in a crucial way. That is why I hope you will think about a managerial career.

The Challenge to Management

Some social scientists would like to wish management away and have society run by self-regulating teams. Others do not like large organizations with their red tape and slow reaction time. They blame these conditions on management and, accordingly, are critical of careers in management.

The 1930s gave rise to the issue of legitimacy of management. If

"I'd like an album praising Management."

Source: Drawing by Drucker; © 1974 The New Yorker Magazine, Inc.

the managers did not own the enterprise and if ownership was distributed among millions of stockholders, to whom was management responsible? Recent revelations of executives using corporate funds for illegal campaign contributions to politicians have led us to ask this question once again. Conflicts of interest also hurt the managerial image. We occasionally hear of corporate managers getting their purchasing agents to place lucrative contracts with firms they secretly own. But look at it this way: An incompetent physician is bad for the medical profession, but does this destroy the profession in your eyes? A shyster who exploits a widow by charging excessive fees for probating and processing a will sickens us, but do we reject a law career because of this? No. American business needs competent, ethical managers who will make enterprises more productive. I hope you will be among them. (In Chapter 20 I describe some systems for controlling the abuse of power by unscrupulous managers.)

CAN YOU LEARN MANAGEMENT FROM A BOOK?

If you are reading this book, you are probably interested in learning what a manager does and how to be a successful manager. Can you do this by reading a book? I think so. To begin with, employers think management courses and books are worthwhile in developing managers. Consider the following:

MORE EFFICIENT FROM A BOOK, BUT EXPERIENCE IS NECESSARY.

Item: Employers continue to pay premium salaries to people who have had courses in management. And they pay even higher salaries to those with graduate degrees in management. Employers do not pay premium salaries because they are generous. This is one of the ways they tell us that you can learn management in the classroom.

Item: Employers give schools of business and management money to encourage the research and teaching of management. Would they do that if it made no sense to teach courses in management?

Item: Employers spend billions of dollars each year in management development programs using books like this one to improve managerial skills.

Item: Professors of management are often told: "I wish I had read your book (or taken your course) years ago. I was appointed a manager but didn't know the job. If only I knew then what I know now. . . ."

There are essentially two ways to learn about management. Reading books about management is one way. The other way is to learn about it on the job. And of course you can combine the two approaches. Lawyers used to get their training by serving as clerks in law offices. It worked; Lincoln learned law that way. Medicine was taught by apprenticing the student to a practicing physician. It worked. Management was learned the same way. But on-the-job training *by itself* is slow and inefficient.

Management courses try to develop the *skills* and *attitudes* of effective, successful managers in their students. Could a person learn these skills and attitudes on the job? Sure. But this process would take longer and wouldn't be as well organized as a management course. After all, on the job the primary emphasis is on getting the job done, not on learning about the job. The managers assume that you know the job—after all, they hired you. But you are not born with management knowledge. And it is not just common sense.

I cannot tell you all you need to know about management in this book. But I can provide information that will give you a head start. You will have to put this knowledge to use to be successful. I hope this book will help you understand what a manager is, how a manager works, and why certain managers are successful.

MANAGEMENT KNOWLEDGE

Knowledge about management comes from the field of management itself and from other fields of study as well. Those who are interested in advancing the practice of management have used the research of organizational psychologists, social psychologists, organizational sociologists, a few social anthropologists and political scientists, and some economists. Those who are interested in quantitative management tools have benefited from the work of engineers, statisticians, and mathematicians. Some managerial insights can be gained from the work of historians and novelists, too.

A BRIEF HISTORY OF MANAGEMENT THOUGHT

Most of what we know about management comes from practicing managers and from scholars who study management. Books on management usually contain a chapter or two on the history of management thought. It seems to me, however, that it makes more sense to introduce historical findings about management throughout the book and to show how they have influenced today's managers. To make this easier later on, a brief preview is given here.

Prescientific Management - RULE OF THUMB

Before 1900 or so, various managers and scholars had given advice on how to manage business enterprises. The Egyptians, the Chinese, the Persians, Greeks, Romans, Germans, and others had provided insights into the management of large enterprises. These insights have been incorporated into later parts of this book.

Scientific Management MEASURED THINGS

At the turn of the century, a group of writers tried to make management more scientific by applying engineering approaches to job design. They were aided by early industrial psychologists, who were applying testing procedures to personnel selection. This group focused on effective design of the employee's task.

Principles of Management

At about the time of World War I, people like French executive Henri Fayol began to reflect on their experiences as managers and to describe what managers did as managerial tasks. Fayol observed that managers performed many functions, including planning, organizing, and controlling. The major emphasis of this group was on effective performance of managerial tasks.

Human Relations

In the 1920s and during the Great Depression, some social scientists, led by Elton Mayo, began to study how employees reacted to managerial incentive schemes, job design, and working conditions. The most significant of these studies was done at Western Electric's Hawthorne Works. This group of theorists emphasized the human side of management and tended to counterbalance the technical engineering emphasis of the scientific management movement. The adherents of this approach believed management should focus on *people*.

Modern Management

The management studies of the past twenty-five years or so have tried to integrate the findings of the scientific management, principles of management, and human relations movements. As Harold Koontz has observed, a "management theory jungle" had arisen because each of these groups had gone off in its own direction and ignored the others. The modern followers of the scientific management movement emphasize scientific decision making, the use of computers, and quantitative decision tools. The current crop of human relations theorists talk about organizational development. The principles people have been succeeded by those who believe one needs to study many managers scientifically before "principles" can be advocated.

Two somewhat overlapping approaches attempt to impose some consistency on what we know about management today. One is the systems approach. Drawing on work from many fields, including biology, systems theorists analyze the functions of the total enterprise in terms of *systems*—inputs, processing, and outputs—with a view toward improving their operations. The other major current emphasis is called the *contingency approach.* Contingency theorists have abandoned the principles-of-management approach. Fayol and his group were looking for effective techniques to manage any kind of business at any time; the contingency theorists believe this is impossible. Their approach (and mine) is to spell out the conditions of the task (scientific management), the people (human relations) the managerial job (principles of management) as parts of the whole management situation (systems emphasis) and integrate them all into an effective management solution. As you will see later, a systematic attempt to spell out the contingency conditions using three different managerial styles makes the contingency approach a bit more specific than "it all depends."

How Scientific Is Management?

But how much do we really know about management? How scientific is this "knowledge"? We often hear the question, Is management a science or an art? This is beside the point. Earlier I mentioned that there are things you can learn in books and some that have to be learned on the job. To a large extent the "science" part of management is what you learn from books. The art comes in trying to apply what you learn to wildly different circumstances. Consider your high school chemistry course. In 999,999 cases out of 1,000,000 when you add one chemical to another you get the same results. That's what we mean by a science: a body of knowledge that will *predict* future happenings. In management, however, the "chemicals" you are working with are people, resources such as money and materials, and products and services. It is a lot harder to make a science out of these constantly changing ingredients. Still, we try. The contingency approach tries to make you an "organization doctor." It teaches you how to look for symptoms of organizational illness and come up with the best prescription for health.

Research about effective management is done in a number of ways. Figure 1.1 illustrates some of the methods used. The lower the level of the method, the less scientific it is. In addition, the lower the level, the more numerous such studies are.

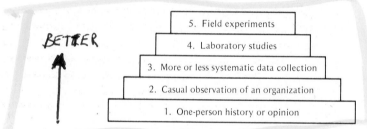

BETTER

5. Field experiments
4. Laboratory studies
3. More or less systematic data collection
2. Casual observation of an organization
1. One-person history or opinion

Figure 1.1
Research methods
in management.

Level 1 One way to learn about management is to listen to a successful manager. We have lots of histories of this sort. For example, Alfred Sloan, former president of General Motors, has told us his feelings about effective management in *My Years with General Motors.* Such histories are helpful, but we are never sure how accurately these management "experts" remember the events. Then, too, how likely is it that your management situation will exactly fit General Motors' in the 1950s? Is your job as important as Sloan's. Are your competitors like his? Are the 1970s like the 1950s?

Level 2 The second kind of information comes from case studies. A management specialist goes into an organization and writes up what he or she sees. This is a little more objective than personal histories, but we have no assurance that the right information was gathered or that it was gathered carefully. Again, too, we have the problem of whether the company studied is typical of the millions of American work organizations. But level 2 research is usually better than level 1 research. (When I use the word *better* here, I mean "more scientific." That is, an objective study by an outside observer is likely to be better than a subjective insider's view. Studies of more rather than fewer enterprises are better. Studies that hold more variables constant are better in a scientific sense than those involving different and changing conditions.)

Level 3 In this type of study the researcher has systematic questions he or she is trying to answer, standardized ways of gathering the information, and scientific ways of analyzing the data. So the research may carefully sample managers or firms, using surveys or multiple research methods. These are clearly better than level 2 studies.

Level 4 In this type of research the researchers try to hold lots of variables constant. They may simulate organizations on the computer or study managerial decision making in laboratory settings. These studies may be better than level 3 studies if their subjects are trained managers and the decisions they are studying are realistic. If not, their value drops to level 2.

Level 5 The best type of research is an experiment conducted in a *real* organization. Suppose we want to learn if older managers are better at dealing with conflict than younger managers. We measure departmental effectiveness before the experiment; then transfer managers of different ages to departments that have been matched by types of employees and problems; then measure the results; then reverse the managers and measure the results again. This is the best kind of research because it controls the variables. However, as you can imagine, there are few studies of this type. Companies won't usually let management specialists shift their managers around.

Finally, a study that lasts over a period of years *(longitudinal)* is much better than a one-time study. Longitudinal studies can take repeated soundings to make sure the results are typical, not unusual.

I wish I could report that more scientific approaches to management research are being used today than twenty years ago. Duncan has found that everyone agrees that this is what is necessary to help managers manage better. But while management scholars have become more scientific in their methods of study, they have not studied the problems that managers feel are most important to their success. This situation is compounded by the factor of change. In the physical sciences experimenters can control some variables and vary others. But a manager's success depends on how well he or she manages the firm's resources and adapts to changes in the environment such as new competitors entering the market, new governmental tax policies, or inventions that make the company's product or service obsolete. How can a management scholar "control" these variables? There are techniques, but it is not easy. And that is why management does not predict as well as chemistry or physics.

As I describe what we know about management I'll try to let you know how sure we are about what we know (and how scientific the findings are). I will use the words "very sophisticated" for level 5 research, "sophisticated" for levels 3 and 4, and "unsophisticated" for levels 1 and 2. But just as chemists occasionally find new elements and astronomers new stars, so management—a discipline so much less developed than chemistry and astronomy that it takes some nerve to mention them in the same sentence—develops its knowledge base further each year. It is important for managers to keep up with management findings by reading journals and going to conferences. The journals in the following list are among those to which you might subscribe in order to keep your management knowledge up to date:

- *Organizational Dynamics*
- *Management Review*
- *Journal of Management Studies*
- *Academy of Management Journal*
- *Academy of Management Review*
- *Harvard Business Review*

·*California Management Review*
·*Business Horizons*
·*Business Week*
·*Fortune*

HOW MANAGEMENT IS APPROACHED IN THIS BOOK

As should be clear by now, there are many aspects to successful management. We begin with a brief overview of managerial and entrepreneurial tasks (Part 1). Chapters 2 and 3 discuss this element so as to introduce you to the world of the manager: what the job is like, what managers are like, and what effective management enterprises are like.

The second element (Part 2) in the manager's world is people. The people in the enterprise are in various jobs that affect the manager; they are subordinates, peers, superiors, and others. Chapters 4 and 5 discuss how and why people behave the way they do as individuals at work. Chapter 6 examines how people in work groups interact with the manager and how the manager relates to them.

Next we examine the interpersonal skills managers need to manage people (Part 3). The managerial skills necessary to be successful with people are leadership skills for employees (Chapter 7); interpersonal skills to influence peers, superiors, and others (Chapter 8); and communication skills (Chapter 9). Finally, we discuss how one selects and develops managers and managerial careers.

Next (Part 4) we discuss the managerial skills necessary to manage people and material resources: planning (Chapters 11 and 12), decision making (Chapter 13), organizing jobs, departments, and enterprises (Chapters 14, 15, and 16), and controlling and managing conflict (Chapter 17). These terms will be used to integrate the traditional research with more recent findings. As will be seen in Chapter 2, not all managers or management scholars view this as the best possible approach.

The fifth element in management is managing the enterprise's relationships with people and organizations (such as competitors) outside the enterprise. This element is shown around the others. Chapters 18–20 discuss this aspect of management. The environment influences earlier chapters too, and these influences are discussed in each chapter. For example, the dependence of the firm on competitors and customers influences enterprise organization; and this is described in Chapter 15.

The pattern of presentation used in each chapter is as follows:

1 Introduction: what the chapter is about
2 Definitions: what we mean by the terms used
3 The importance of the topic
4 What we know about the topic from research and other methods
5 Summary and implications

MANAGEMENT AND YOU This book is designed to stimulate you to think about management: what it is like and whether you can see yourself as a manager. Chapter 10 develops the concept of a managerial career and discusses the practical side of planning career in management.

Each of us must choose a career. This career contributes to the development of our self-image. As Chapter 10 points out, there are many possible career choices: blue-collar jobs (machinist), white-collar/clerical jobs (order processer), gray-collar service jobs (computer repair), technical jobs (medical technologist), and managerial or professional jobs.

Many of us will choose from the latter category. The traditional professions include medicine, law, dentistry, the clergy, and so on. Some writers have argued that management is, or shortly will be, included as well.

Sociologists usually describe a profession as meeting the following requirements:

1 A body of technical and theoretical knowledge
2 A code of ethics
3 Power to discipline and/or remove incompetent or unethical practitioners
4 Provision for specific education and reeducation

Management is developing the first characteristic, as I hope to show. Condition 4 is also met, as can be seen from college courses, associations like the American Management Association and the Academy of Management, and journals like those listed earlier. But management does not fulfill conditions 2 and 3. Lawyers take oaths and can be disbarred. Physicians take oaths, have a code of conduct, and can lose their licenses. Clergymen are ordained and can be defrocked. It is no good to argue that these procedures don't prohibit incompetent lawyers from botching cases and drunken surgeons from killing people. The fact is, management does not even have the rudiments of conditions 2 and 3 and thus cannot be classified as a profession.

But management is a challenging career that can provide you with very rewarding and satisfying experiences. I hope this book will help you make your career choice, and if you choose to be a manager, that it will help you become a successful one.

SUMMARY In this chapter I introduced you to management. I explained that management is effective utilization of human and material resources to achieve the enterprise's purposes, or, in other words, getting things done through people. I tried to convince you that management is important to the success of an enterprise.

The second objective of the chapter was to help you learn where to get information and how to improve your managerial skills. I reviewed basic historical emphases and listed journals you can read to keep yourself up to date. I also gave you a scheme for evaluating what you read, from less sophisticated material (personal histories or casual observations), through sophisticated systematic data collection methods and some lab studies, to very sophisticated lab and field studies.

Finally, I described the pattern in which the material is presented: the format used and a model of managerial elements. I concluded with the hope that you will seriously consider a managerial career.

Questions for Review

1. At a party you meet an artist. She asks you what your major is and you reply "management." She then says to you, half cordially, half in scorn, "What's that? Why would you want to study that?"
2. Later, at the same party, you bump into the owner of a local night spot. He asks you your major and when you give the answer he observes: "What a waste of time! You can't learn management from a book." How do you answer him?
3. Give a brief history of management thought.
4. Describe the various kinds of studies on management. Which are the best? Why do you say that?
5. At the party a business school graduate working for General Electric says to you, "I'm getting behind on what's new in management. What magazines do they suggest you read to keep up these days?" Give her an answer.
6. Outline one model of the management process given in the chapter.
7. Is management a respectable career or just the best way to make a living? Comment.

References

What Is Management?

Bedeian, Arthur, "An Historical Review of the Efforts in the Area of Management Semantics," *Academy of Management Journal,* 17, no. 1 (March 1974): 101–114.

Drucker, Peter, *Management* (New York: Harper & Row, 1974).

Management Knowledge

Davis, Ralph C., "Management: Past, Present, & Future," Mimeographed (Columbus: Ohio State University, n.d.).

Duncan, W. Jack, "Methodological Orientations & Management Theory," *Academy of Management Journal,* 15 (September 1972): 337–348.

Estafen, Bernard, "Methods for Management Research in the 1970's," *Academy of Management Journal,* 14, no. 1 (1971): 51–64.

George, Claude, Jr., *The History of Management Thought* (Englewood Cliffs, N.J.: Prentice-Hall, 1972).

Glaser, Barney, and Strauss, Anselm, *The Discovery of Grounded Theory* (Chicago: Aldine, 1967).

Greenwood, William, "Future Management Theory," *Academy of Management Journal,* 17, no. 3 (1974): 503–513.

Kaufman, Herbert, "Organization Theory and Political Theory," *American Political Science Review,* 58, no. 1 (1964): 5–14.

Kerr, Clark, and Fisher, Lloyd, "Plant Sociology: The Elite and Aborigines," in M. Komarovsky, ed., *Common Frontiers of the Social Sciences* (New York: Free Press, 1957).

Koontz, Harold, "The Management Theory Jungle," in Harold Koontz, ed., *Toward a Unified Theory of Management* (New York: McGraw-Hill, 1964).

Mee, John, *A History of Twentieth Century Management Thought* (Columbus: Ohio State University, 1959).

———, "Management Teaching in Historical Perspective," *Proceedings, Southern Management Association,* 1971, pp. 1–13.

Preston, Lee, and Post, James, "The Third Managerial Revolution," *Academy of Management Journal,* 17, no. 3 (1974): 476–486.

Price, James, "Design of Proof in Organizational Research," *Administrative Science Quarterly,* June 1968, pp. 121–166.

Wieland, George, "The Contributions of Organizational Sociology to the Practice of Management," *Academy of Management Journal,* 17, 2 (1974): 318–333.

Wren, Daniel, *The Evolution of Management Theory* (New York: Ronald Press, 1972).

Management and You

Andrews, Kenneth, "Toward Professionalism in Business Management," *Harvard Business Review,* March-April 1969, pp. 49–60.

Schein, Edgar, "Organizational Socialization and the Profession of Management," *Industrial Management Review,* Winter 1968, pp. 1–16.

CHAPTER 2

MANAGERS, ORGANIZATIONS, AND SUCCESS

Learning Objectives

1. To learn some general characteristics of managers.
2. To understand how managerial jobs differ by task type.
3. To see how managerial jobs differ by level in the hierarchy.
4. To learn what factors lead to managerial success.
5. To understand how managerial jobs differ in different organizational environments.
6. To begin to understand the factors that lead to organizational success.

Chapter Outline

Who Are the Managers?
Knowledge of the Manager's Job
Management by Task Type
Levels of Management
The Supervisor
The Middle Manager
The Top Manager
Summary and Implications
Successful Managers
Managers and Work Organizations
Successful Organizations
Measuring Organizational Success
Summary

Since this book is about management and how to succeed at it, our first order of business is to describe what managerial jobs are like in general and what leads to managerial success. To give you a perspective on the manager's world, there is also a brief section on the organizations managers work in, how they achieve success, and the manager's role in achieving that success. Chapter 3 focuses on the job of the entrepreneur and family business executive.

Before you can learn managerial skills you must understand managerial tasks and how they are similar and different.

WHO ARE THE MANAGERS?

We will look first at who managers are. One way to do this is to look at the overall profile of managers from the 1970 census. The relevant category is "Managers and Administrators." In 1970 there were 6,478,186 managers, of whom 5,394,585 were male and 1,083,601 female. Their median earnings were $11,012 (male) and $5,494 (female). This is a composite group that includes local government officials, bankers, people engaged in trade, funeral directors, health administrators, inspectors, office managers, federal and state government officials, purchasing agents, college administrators, and others. When we separate out business managers (in manufacturing, construction, transportation, communications and utilities, and wholesaling), we find 2,614,103 people (2,342,064 males; 272,039 females). Their median earnings were $11,914 (male) and $5,770 (female); median age, 44 (male) and 45.9 (female). The retail trade category included 664,862 people (576,536 males; 88,326 females); median earnings, $9,332 (male) and $4,937 (female); median age, 41.2 (male) and 46.2 (female).

The racial breakdown is as follows: 5,277,000 white males and 1,023,000 white females; 121,000 black males and 48,000 black females; 102,000 Spanish-surnamed males and 22,000 Spanish-surnamed females; 6,000 Native American males and 1,000 Native American females; and 30,000 males and 6,000 females of Japanese or Chinese descent.

If you look at the age distribution of managers in the private sector, you will find that the largest group was in the 40–49 range; the next-largest groups were in their 30's and 50's, and there were 320,000 managers in their 20's.

With regard to education, the average manager had completed 12.9 years of school; 77.8 percent had completed high school and 20 percent had four years of college or more. Private sector managers typically had a little more education (especially in manufacturing) than public sector managers.

Finally, the typical manager is married. According to the 1970 census, 4,865,394 were married, 344,755 single, 65,362 widowed, and 119,074 divorced. Of course, since these are census figures, a lot of data are obscured by the "median," but these are still the most complete data we have on managers as a group.

Some studies have been made of the backgrounds and lives of managers. Those most frequently studied are the top executives of America's largest corporations. The following is a profile of the typical top executive in 1975.

Age: Four out of five were born between 1914 and 1921; half are between 50 and 60.

Education: Most have college degrees; 33 percent have M.B.A.'s, 33 percent law degrees, and 3 percent Ph.D's; 35 percent have degrees from Ivy League schools, 40 percent degrees from other private schools, the rest degrees from state or public universities.

Sex: Almost all are male.

Politics: About 80 percent are Republican.

Religion: Eighty percent Protestant, 9 percent Catholic, 7 percent Jewish.

Social background: Grew up in small and medium-sized towns in the East and Midwest (especially New York, New Jersey, Pennsylvania, Ohio, Michigan, Indiana, Illinois, and Wisconsin). Most grew up in middle- and upper-middle-class homes, and 45 percent of the parents were founders, chairmen of the board, or presidents of corporations, or self-employed businesspeople. Sixteen percent of their parents are farmers or blue-collar workers. Twenty-two percent started out in mundane jobs such as junior clerk; 14 percent started out at or very near the top.

Life style: Work long hours (9–10 hours per day). Sixty percent own or rent second homes; 40 percent own boats; 85 percent travel outside the United States each year; 50 percent own original art; 10 percent own rare books.

KNOWLEDGE OF THE MANAGER'S JOB

Now that we know something about managers, it is time to look at what they do. It is relatively easy to describe the life style and backgrounds of top managers as I just did. It is not as easy to describe the manager's job. For there are managers at all levels, in direct authority line jobs and support staff jobs. And what they do varies from one job to the next and from one day to the next. Managers spend some time alone thinking, making decisions, writing, reading. They also spend time in communication with others at the office or away from it.

What do we know about managerial jobs? Rosalind Barnett and Renato Tagiuri recently asked 2500 young people aged 9 through 17 what a manager does. They found that in some ways the young people's knowledge was accurate, while in other ways it was erroneous. How would you have done on their "test"?

The young people were first asked to select a career that attracted them and then were asked whether they'd like to be managers. The percentage who chose management increased with age (and increased if their parents were managers), but about 40 percent of the males and 10 percent of the females would like to be managers, preferring high-level management or running their own business. The reasons they gave included leadership opportunity (42%), high salary (25% boys, 12% girls), challenge (14%), responsibility (12%), and the opportunity to work with people (12%).

The young people believed managers are competent, good leaders, honest, thoughtful, understanding, patient, self-assured, and energetic. They had some accurate ideas of how you got to be a manager (such as working for a manager and learning from him or her; going to school; taking over the family business). They also had some inaccurate ideas. Thirty-six percent thought you get to be a manager by employee election; 50% thought you could become a manager by taking a special test.

When asked what a manager does, 54 percent saw the manager as "top man" and 39 percent saw the manager as a supervisor; 15 percent saw the role as including organization of the enterprise; 10 percent saw it as dividing up work; 10 saw it as helping people. Only 6 percent saw the manager as a decision maker.

MANAGEMENT BY TASK TYPE   Managers hold titles that indicate that they are managers. This makes it sound as if they all do the same thing. In some ways they do. They have some problems in common: decision making, communicating, planning. But the amount of each they do, the people they interact with, and many other characteristics of their jobs differ. That is why this book takes the contingency approach. That is, it asks you to examine the factors leading to these differences—the people, the organization, the environment—and helps you decide how to plan, communicate, and make decisions.

This section is designed to make you aware that managerial tasks themselves differ and that this is a factor in how managers behave and what the managerial experience is like. But saying that managers' jobs differ does not tell you much. And of course I cannot describe thousands of different managerial jobs. Writers on management have tried to compromise and have come up with a limited number of different types of managerial jobs. The following list should help you understand differences in managerial role by task:

· staff services manager
· technical supervisor
· business control and coordination manager
· personnel and public relations manager
· large-scale planning and scheduling manager
· top manager
· preservation of assets and maintenance administrator

Thus although they looked at a large number of enterprises, the number of types of managers wasn't too large. However, the nature of their tasks led them to perform differently on their jobs.

Rosemary Stewart has studied managerial jobs in England for many years. She has found that managerial jobs differ along the following dimensions:

1 The extent and nature of contacts with other people on the job

2 The work pattern

   a Self-generating work versus responding to others' work

   b Degree of fragmentation

3 Uncertainty

   a Number of crises

   b Amount of control over problems

   c Amount of valid information to do the job

   d How far ahead the manager can plan

4 Responsibility

   a Direct responsibility for resources

   b Shared or individual responsibility

5 Demands on private life—to be away from home, transfered often, etc.

Stewart has classified the jobs she studied into seven types (excluding top management) as shown in Table 2.1. These differences lead to differing amounts of job pressure, as shown in Table 2.2.

In sum, a manager is not just a manager. The task differs, so the job differs too.

LEVELS OF MANAGEMENT

The president of General Motors is called a manager. He or she supervises hundreds of thousands of employees. The supervisor of ten clerks in an insurance office is also called a manager. But their jobs are not the same. Managerial jobs differ according to how high the manager is in the organization. Although some experts like to look at four levels of management, we will concentrate on three: the supervisor, the middle manager, and the top manager. Our purpose is to look at the *differences* among the three levels.

The Supervisor

Most managers are supervisors. They have various titles: foreman, ward nurse, department chairman, section chief, and so on. The similarity is that the employees who actually perform most of the work in the organization report to them. Supervisors are primarily managers of employees and resources. The supervisor's job is the one most people who enter management start with. In many ways it is an exciting job. It is the "firing line"—where the action is. There is immediate feedback to the supervisor's attention and decisions, and this can be rewarding.

Table 2.1 Managerial Jobs Classified by Task (Stewart) (Excludes top management job where the occupant can largely adapt the role as he wishes.)

Job Types	Relationship, Direction of[1]	Main Characteristics	Subdivisions	Main Characteristic(s) of Subdivisions	Examples of Jobs
I	*Responsibility for separate unit* [Downwards] (Outwards) (Up)	Few or no peer relations. Little or no role conflict. Evaluation possible.	1. Primarily internal contacts.	People management high. Hard information. Responding known contacts.	Retail store manager Same works manager
			2. Entrepreneurial.	External contacts, particularly customers. Can choose balance self-starting responding.	Branch bank managers Some general managers
II	*Field supervision* (area responsibility for separate units) [Downwards & Up]	No interlocking subs. Few or no peer relations. People management high. Known contacts. Demands on private life.	1. Structured.	Responding. Similar tasks. Hard information.	Superintendent, retail chain stores Various area management jobs
			2. Relatively unstructured	High uncertainty. Self-generating.	Regional director of overseas operations
III	*People management* (relatively self-contained dept. or section) [Down] (Up)	People management key relationship. High contact time. Fragmented. Responding.	(Could be subdivided by leadership situation.)		Some administrative jobs. Some production management.
IV	*Work-flow jobs* [Down and sideways] (Up)	Peer dependence. Obtaining co-operation without authority. Role conflict. Meetings. Known contacts.	1. Line management	People management high.	Chief engineer, chief accountant, production manager
			2. SERVICE STAFF a. nonselling-customers come to you.	Time deadlines. Responding.	Some computer management Transport manager
			b. selling.	Self-generating. Role conflict very high.	Training manager Some personnel Some computer mgt.
			c. ext.	External contacts, time deadline.	Service manager
			3. Co-ordinator (non-subs)	Peer dependence very high.	Product manager
			4. Control (over non-subs)	Risk unpopularity. Role conflict very high.	Quality control manager. Some accounting
V	*Solo jobs* [Alone]	Sustained attention. High alone time. Plan work.			Some planning jobs Various specialist jobs
VI	*Consulting and advisory* [Upwards] (Sideways & down)	Sustained attention. Time with senior mgt. Wide contacts.	1. Structured. Continuing.	Known contacts, hard information. Low uncertainty.	Some accounting jobs
			2. Unstructured, often one-shot jobs.	Risk incurring unpopularity. No, or low, people management. Self-generating.	Internal consultancy and special assignments
VII	*External Jobs* [Outwards]	Conflict objectives. External contacts high. Uncertainty high.	1. People management important.	People management high. Demands on private life.	Some sales management
			2. Dealing with specialist contacts.	Conflict job objectives very high. Known contacts.	Purchasing manager Advertising manager
			3. P.R., varied contacts.	Short-term relations. Demands on private life.	Public relations Some general managers

[1] Main direction in [ ], other in ( ).

Table 2.2 Amounts and Kinds of Work Pressure in Various Jobs (Stewart)

HIGH PRESSURE	High	Mild	Low	LOW PRESSURE
WORK PATTERN				WORK PATTERN
1. Self-starting	D	B	A C	Responding
2. Fragmented	C	A B D		Not fragmented
3. Time deadlines		C	A B D	No time deadlines
AMOUNT OF UNCERTAINTY				AMOUNT OF UNCERTAINTY
4. High	D	B C	A	Low
EXPOSED				NOT EXPOSED
5. No one to consult	D		A B C	People to consult
6. Mistakes identified	B D	A	C	Mistakes not identifiable
RELATIONSHIPS				RELATIONSHIPS
7. High contact time	C	A B D		Low contact time
8. Short-term relations		B D	A C	Long-term contacts
9. Conflict objectives (external contacts)		B D	A C	No conflict objectives
10. Role conflict		C D	A B	No role conflict
11. Incur unpopularity		C	A B D	No need to risk unpopularity
DEMANDS ON PRIVATE LIFE				DEMANDS ON PRIVATE LIFE
12. High	D	B C	A	Low
WORK PATTERN				WORK PATTERN
1. Self-starting	F H	G I	E	Responding
2. Fragmented	E	F	G H I	Not fragmented
3. Time deadlines	G	E	F H I	No time deadlines
AMOUNT OF UNCERTAINTY				AMOUNT OF UNCERTAINTY
4. High	H	E F	G I	Low
EXPOSED				NOT EXPOSED
5. No one to consult		H	E F G I	People to consult
6. Mistakes identified		E H	F G I	Mistakes not identifiable
RELATIONSHIPS				RELATIONSHIPS
7. High contact time	E F		G H I	Low contact time
8. Short term relations	F	H	E G I	Long-term contacts
9. Conflict objectives (external contacts)			E F G H I	No conflict objectives
10. Role conflict	F G H		E I	No role conflict
11. Incur unpopularity	G H	F	E I	No need to risk unpopularity
DEMANDS ON PRIVATE LIFE				DEMANDS ON PRIVATE LIFE
12. High	F	H	E G I	Low

A—Job Type I.1—Plant manager, small subsidiary, 50 subordinates, process plant.
B— " " I.2—Branch bank manager.
C— " " II.1—Area manager, retail chain stores.
D— " " II.2—Regional director, overseas operations, four medium-size subsidiary companies, two newly acquired.
E— " " III —Production manager, 6 subordinates, light engineering.
F— " " IV.3—Regional training manager, large company, 8 subordinates.
G— " " IV.4—Management accountant, with an advisory and policing function, reporting to higher management, 3 subordinates.
  " " V —Not illustrated
H— " " VI.1—Internal consultant on special assignment, 3 subordinates.
I — " " VI.2—Group accountant, 2 subordinate accountants, 40 people reporting to them, works mainly with general manager.

Studies indicate that supervisors are busy, experience frequent interruptions, and often have to shift back and forth between tasks. They spend most of their time with subordinates, some with peers, and little with superiors or outsiders.

To bring this home to you, let's look at 11½ minutes of a typical supervisor's day. (See Table 2.3.) Pat is one of 56 supervisors in an auto plant observed by Robert Guest and Frank Jasinski.

Table 2.3	
Time	**Description**
2:15 p.m.	Pat checks with scheduler S. Looks at hourly report of number of cars coming through body shop.
2:16	Walks over to R (repair man) on pickup line and checks to see if earlier repair trouble was corrected.
2:17	Calls over inspection foreman to show him a hole missing in a piece. Inspection foreman acknowledges he will notify the trim department.
2:19	Pat tells repair man to locate the hole by eye until it comes through all right.
2:19½	Pat has a drink.
2:20	Pat walks over to station 5 and asks his utility man how many men he still has to relieve.
2:20½	Moves along the line—stations 5, 6, 7—checking visually on the quality of work.
2:21	Checks a loose nut on a fixture at station 7. Speaks with operator.
2:22	Man at station 3 calls for materials.
2:22¼	Pat tells man at subassembly bench E to make up more material.
2:23	Walks over to MH (stock man). Tells stock man the line is getting low on hinges. They discuss the number short and agree there is enough for tomorrow.
2:25	Pat walks from MH to station 1 and makes visual inspection of the car body to check on the hole discussed earlier at the pickup line.
2:26	Pat sees foreman from preceding section and tells him about the missing hole.
2:26½	A hand signal from welder W.

D. L. Marples' record of the work episodes of a British foreman (Table 2.4) is similar. Marples points out that the episodes involve issues with a foreman on the assembly line, operators 21 and 5, and the assistant foreman. In this sample only three issues were interrelated (during a 45 minute period)—and thus was the *most* coherent part of the foreman's hectic day.

Guest and Jasinski found that their 56 foremen spent 58 percent of the time in personal contact with people: 30 percent with subordi-

Table 2.4

Time	Episode	Occupation
10.45 a.m.	158	Contacted by foreman of assembly line. Assembly line will be stopped in 12 minutes as they have no locking keys. See Jig and Tool fitters, fixture for first miller down now ready.
	159	Inspection says job cannot commence without new cutters promised for 8.00 a.m. (Episode 127).
	160	Contact by operator Op. 21. Pins not cleaning up, instruct him to stop production until I return.
	161	Run to toolroom to check on position of cutters not quite ready. See foreman.
	162	Inspector re: a tin of 100, slightly sub-standard locking keys he had taken in for a final opinion, 1 week previously. Inspection agree to pass them. Arrange dispatch to East Works.
	163	Contact assistant foreman grinding and request his assistance. Re: Op. 21.
11.00	164	Visit tool stores. Cutters not yet arrived for locking key.
11.10	165	Visit locking key section, change arbors from broken down machine to one which is ready to run. Place operator back from web milling onto his own machine (Episode 106). Instruct other milling operator to change roughing cutters on locking key.
11.25	166	Contacted by operator Op. 5. Adjusting nut broken.
11.27	167	Arrange for operator on Op. 17 to cover Op. 31, as no operator available.
11.30	168	Contact progress and inform them that locking keys are back in production.

(It can be seen that episodes 160, 163, and 166 are all interruptions in the foreman's major preoccupation with the provision of locking keys.)

nates, 23 percent with peers and others, and 5 percent with supervisors. The topics of conversation and the time spent on each are shown in Table 2.5.

Studies have found that supervisors think they spend more time than they actually do on planning, writing reports, reading, reflecting, and inspecting. Actually, the auto foremen were occupied as shown in Table 2.6.

In sum, supervisors lead an active, hectic, often interrupted worklife, spending most of their time communicating and caring for the problems of the moment. Note that there have been no observational studies of supervisors of staff activities. These are no doubt different, and it seems reasonable to believe such jobs are less hectic and less active, less splintered, than the line supervisor's job.

Table 2.5 Average Amounts of Time Spent by Foremen on Each Topic

Topic	Percent of Time
Quality	18.2%
Work progress	13.2
Personnel administration	11.2
Personal relations and other non-job-related topics	10.2
Foreman performance of an operation	8.1
Tools, jigs, and fixtures	8.1
Materials	8.0
Employee job performance	7.6
Production schedule	5.2
Grievances	2.0
Injury, illness	1.2
Housekeeping	0.5
Work standards	0.4
Safety	0.2
Meeting	0.1
Miscellaneous	2.4
Topic unknown	2.4

Table 2.6

Activity	Percent of Time
Talks	46.6%
Looks	20.9
Manipulates	9.6
Walks	6.9
Hands, Carries	5.6
Reads	2.9
Telephones	2.4
Writes	2.1
Stands	1.0
Signals	0.8
Listens	0.6
Shows	0.4
Sits	0.2
Total	100.0%

The Middle Manager Middle managers are above the supervisors and below the top manager and those who report directly to the top manager. A typical middle manager is the head of an engineering department (supervising ten engineering units, each with its own supervisor).

The job of middle management is to manage managers—to act as a buffer between the top manager and the supervisors. Middle managers spend most of their time analyzing data, preparing information for decisions, translating top management decisions into specific projects for supervisors, and monitoring the supervisors' results. This is much less hectic than supervisory or top management work.

Many middle managers are writers. Most work on analysis, reporting, and preparation of information for decisions by others. They spend most of their time alone.

Other middle managers spend most of their time on committees. They may spend 80 percent of their time in conversation, mostly with each other (peers) and in their departments. The rest of their time is spent on paper work and reading.

The jobs of most middle managers seem to be almost opposite to those of top managers or supervisors. The differences are apparent not only from their job behavior but also from their own perceptions of their jobs. Lyman Porter and Edwin Ghiselli describe the self-perceptions of middle and top managers as follows:

> Careful planning, thoughtful actions and well-controlled behavior characterize the self perceptions of middle management. . . . Middle management people see themselves as individuals who seldom take rash actions that are not well thought out beforehand. They consider proposed actions from all angles and aspects before they move ahead. They can be counted on not to make hasty or unfounded decisions. They seem to place more reliance on operating within the rules and conditions of the system rather than plunging ahead on their own ideas when these have not been previously tested. They do not appear as willing to take risks or to move ahead where the final outcome is uncertain, and they do not show the same sort of confidence in their own judgment as do members of top management. They seem more concerned about social traits that are especially important in the job situation rather than in general social situations. They indicate they want to avoid giving the appearance of being controversial personalities and of exhibiting self-centered behavior. They want to do nothing that might attract unfavorable comments about their behavior, and they avoid forcing their own ideas on others. In summary, they seem to describe themselves as stable and dependable individuals who try to avoid making mistakes on the job or elsewhere. . . .

> Members of top management perceive themselves as active, self-reliant, and generally willing to take action on the basis of their own faith in themselves and in their abilities, rather than simply on the basis of the weight of the objective evidence. They are willing to take risks when they think they have good, original ideas, and they possess the confidence that their decisions will lead to success. They are not easily discouraged and are able to capitalize on opportunities. In their social relations they are candid and straightforward and show confidence here as well as in the performance of their duties on the job. They picture themselves as behaving in a cultured and refined manner toward others without having to appear to ingratiate themselves.

Middle managers vary by job level, of course. The job of the middle manager directly above the supervisor is more like the supervisor's than the top manager's. And the job of the middle manager just below the top manager is more like the top manager's than the supervisor's.

The job emphasis of the middle manager varies by departmental task, too. Diana Pheysey examined the activities of middle managers in various departments (sales, research and development [R&D], manufacturing, personnel) and found major differences in their managerial skills and activities. (See Figure 2.1.)

In sum, although there are differences by department and level within middle management, the job of the middle manager is less hectic, more reflective, less active, and more frustrating than those of supervisors and top managers. Obviously people who are successful at supervisory jobs will not automatically be successful at middle management jobs.

The Top Manager   If he or she is successful as a supervisor and then as a middle manager, a manager can reach the top. Top managers have job titles like chairman of the board, president, executive vice president, hospital administrator, or secretary of state. The top managers are the chief policy-making officers of an enterprise. Two examples of top managers are Royal Little and Catherine Cleary.

A recent description of a top manager will help you understand what the job can be like. J. Peter Grace, president and chief executive officer of W. R. Grace and Company (1974 sales, $3,470 million; profits, $130 million) is 62 years old and has worked for the family firm for 30 years. He regularly works 80 hours per week, putting in 112 hours per week during the two annual budget months. Here is a description of Grace that appeared in the *Wall Street Journal* on April 2, 1975.

No one says it's easy to work for Peter Grace. Except for infrequent breaks for his beloved horseplay, Mr. Grace hates to waste a single minute that could be used for work. Colleagues say he carries a special key that makes the elevator to his 48th floor office move faster by skipping stops; that saves a minute for work. Mr. Grace spends the 35-minute limousine ride between his Long Island estate and his Manhattan office dictating memos to a secretary (he has eight) who rides with the chauffeur. On frequent business trips via corporate jet, Mr. Grace becomes so absorbed in his work that he sometimes forgets to eat—so underlings don't eat either. (In many ways a softhearted man, Mr. Grace has been known to apologize for such carelessness.)

Underlings are expected to have instant answers to Mr. Grace's numerous questions. "Peter will call me up to ask me the price of corn," says James J. Galvin, a vice president and group executive for agricultural products. "He'll know damn well what the price of corn is, but he'll be checking to see if I do." What's more, Grace executives routinely compile massive

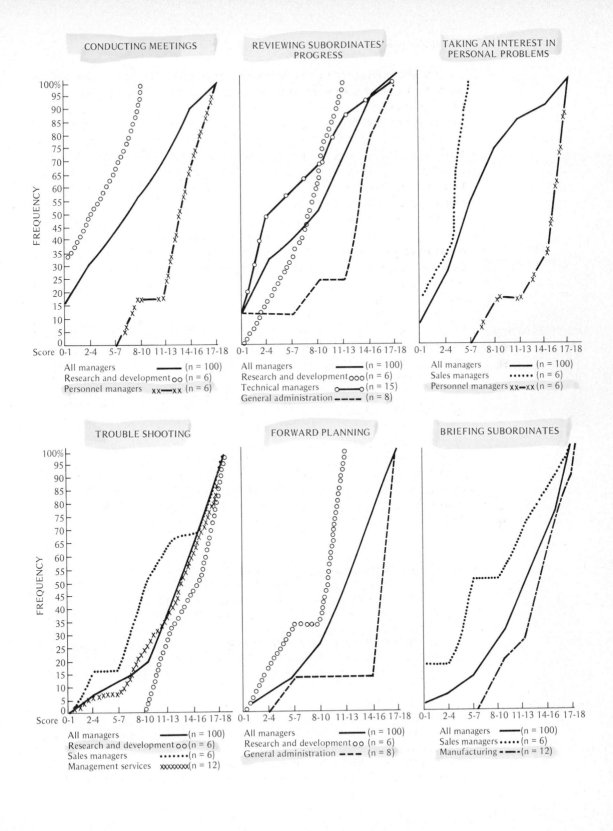

CONDUCTING MEETINGS

FREQUENCY

Score 0-1 2-4 5-7 8-10 11-13 14-16 17-18

All managers ———————— (n = 100)
Research and development oo (n = 6)
Personnel managers xx—xx (n = 6)

REVIEWING SUBORDINATES' PROGRESS

Score 0-1 2-4 5-7 8-10 11-13 14-16 17-18

All managers ———————— (n = 100)
Research and development ooo (n = 6)
Technical managers o——o (n = 15)
General administration – – – (n = 8)

TAKING AN INTEREST IN PERSONAL PROBLEMS

Score 0-1 2-4 5-7 8-10 11-13 14-16 17-18

All managers ———————— (n = 100)
Sales managers ·········· (n = 6)
Personnel managers xx—xx (n = 6)

TROUBLE SHOOTING

FREQUENCY

Score 0-1 2-4 5-7 8-10 11-13 14-16 17-18

All managers ———————— (n = 100)
Research and development oo (n = 6)
Sales managers ·········· (n = 6)
Management services xxxxxxx (n = 12)

FORWARD PLANNING

Score 0-1 2-4 5-7 8-10 11-13 14-16 17-18

All managers ———————— (n = 100)
Research and development oo (n = 6)
General administration – – – (n = 8)

BRIEFING SUBORDINATES

Score 0-1 2-4 5-7 8-10 11-13 14-16 17-18

All managers ———————— (n = 100)
Sales managers ·········· (n = 6)
Manufacturing –·–·– (n = 12)

statistical reports that Mr. Grace scrutinizes from cover to cover (it is said that he rejected one such report because a single punctuation mark was misplaced). . . .

His colleagues say Peter Grace has changed remarkably little over three decades and that he appears to enjoy every minute of his job. Says Mr. Griswold: "Peter gets a hell of a kick out of being a big businessman; he likes the recognition that he isn't just a rich playboy." Mr. Grace himself says that as long as he holds his job he'll continue to work as hard as he does now. There's no point, he says, in working less hard than one is able. Adds D. Walter Robbins Jr., an executive vice president and long time associate: "Peter once told me that when he dies, they can just put on his tombstone, 'I did my best.' "

ROYAL LITTLE (*Fortune* Hall of Fame, January 1975)

In recent years, around Wall Street at least, to be called "the father of conglomerates" is a dubious distinction, like being hailed as the first man to cultivate poison ivy. Nevertheless, "unrelated diversification," as Royal Little prefers to call his offspring, is a development so fundamental that it will probably survive the present overreaction to the speculative overenthusiasm of a decade ago. After all, Little's Textron is flourishing in the hands of a management he picked when he retired in 1962. Several streams of thought converged to carry Little to the Textron experiment. Most obvious was his long experience with cyclical downturns in the textile business. Less obvious but more important is Little's abhorrence of stagnant capital. A well-run conglomerate, he believes, can pick up sound companies and stimulate their return on investment. Roy Little lives very simply on the beach at Narragansett Bay, planning to have zero assets when he dies. He counts thirty organizations and causes in which he is still active. He hopes to reduce the number to twenty when he is eighty, to fifteen at eighty-five, to ten at ninety, and to five at ninety-five.

CATHERINE CLEARY (*Fortune,* April 1973)

"I hope someone hasn't told you she thinks like a man," says a long-time business associate of Catherine Cleary, "because Catherine just *thinks.*" Miss Cleary, fifty-six, an outgoing woman with a keen sense of humor, is president of First Wisconsin Trust Co. (assets under management: $1.25 billion). "I've never had a plan," says Miss Cleary, who once had a passing yen to be in the theatre and taught school for a while before deciding to become a lawyer. After a few years of law practice, she moved, at thirty-one, to the trust company. She rose steadily through trust administration (rather than the investment side of the business) and was named chief executive officer in 1970. Since she took over, the company's earnings have risen sharply. "If I had any sense," she says, "I'd quit right now." She is a member of the board of First Wisconsin Bankshares, parent to the trust company, and of four other corporate giants: A.T.&T., General Motors, Kraftco, and Northwestern Mutual Life Insurance Co. (of which her father was once the president). These boards, and the board committees she sits on, hold over fifty meetings a year, so Miss Cleary sees a lot of the Milwaukee airport (where the photograph shows her).

There have been a number of studies of the top manager's job; these are summarized in Table 2.7. These studies have shown that most top managers' jobs are more like supervisors' in their activity and hectic quality. Top managers spend most of their time with peers, outsiders, and to a lesser extent, subordinates. Some have speculated that one reason top executives often "jump channels" and deal with supervisors rather than middle managers is that the two jobs are similar in activity level and this may lead to similarities in personality.

Top managers' jobs differ for the following reasons:

1 *Time-determined changes.* Preparing a budget is a very different activity from negotiating a labor contract.

2 *Person-determined differences.* The assignments given are fairly broad, with considerable discretion allowed in accomplishing them.

3 *Situation-determined differences.* This category includes differences arising from variety in managerial task (e.g., sales manager vs. personnel manager).

Summary and Implications

What I have tried to do is to describe a "typical" supervisor, middle manager, and top manager. While there's a lot of variety within each of these categories, all managerial jobs require the interpersonal and managerial skills described later in this book. But these skills are required to varying degrees because of differences in managerial task, level, and environmental conditions.

So far we've classified managerial jobs by task and by level. It should be clear by now that:

Source: Reprinted by permission of Newspaper Enterprise Association.

Table 2.7 Studies of Top Managers' Jobs

Author of Study	Carlson	Mintzberg	Copeman Et al	Case	Stieglitz	Connors & Hutt	Business Management
Top Managers	9 Swedish top business executives	5 Canadian top business executives	25 Dutch top business executives	52 American top business executives	240 American & 140 foreign top business executives	4 top administrators, University of Wisconsin Hospital	179 Chicago top business managers
Research Method	observed 4 weeks each	observed 1 week each	observed 5 days each	executives & secretaries recorded events	questionnaire estimates of time	observation over 35-day period	phone questionnaires
Major Finding	hectic job: 44% time away from the firm, 65% away from office; long hours, much of it in consultation, most of time with frequent interruptions	hectic job with frequent interruptions; often out of office; makes informal, unscientific decisions	hectic job: in typical hour 3 visitors, 4 phone calls	time spent as follows: 56% in conference (usually with employees) 12% lunch (usually working lunches) 8% reading & dictating reports 7% reading & dictating mail 5% making decisions & thinking	top management work takes long hours (board of directors did not evaluate their work closely)	Spent their time as follows: 36.0% out of office 25.8% planning; when in office, most of the time was in conference 3.2% alone in office	hectic job: typical executive—worked 63-hour week (10 away from office); attended 2–5 meetings weekly; received interrupting phone calls (typically 2 hours daily); handled mail inefficiently; spent less than 2 hours a day alone and an inadequate amount of time planning, reading

·Managers spend most of their time in verbal communication with other people.

·The frequency of interaction is different in different jobs. Supervisors see the greatest number of people, top managers the next-greatest number, and middle managers the fewest. In other words it's most hectic at the top and at the bottom.

·The length of personal contacts increases as one moves up the management ladder.

·The time focus of managerial problems increases as one moves up in management: Supervisors deal with today's problems, middle managers with short-term problems, top managers with long-term problems.

·The departmental task determines the kinds of problems one deals with and the people one interacts with.

·Managers tend to interact most with their peers at the middle and top levels and with their subordinates and peers at the supervisory level.

·Finally, the organization and its environment affect what managers do. Studies indicate that if the external environment is stable, the manager's job is more routine and less hectic. If it is more volatile, more time is spent in discussion and coordination—in trying to cope.

As I describe each interpersonal and managerial skill I'll focus on how to use that skill effectively in different conditions: (1) when the people are different, (2) when the managers are different, and (3) when the environment is different. In doing this I will use the contingency approach, specifying when to use each style or skill, whether it be communicating organizing, or planning.

SUCCESSFUL MANAGERS The preceding section made you aware of how difficult it is to define and predict success in management, given all the differences in managerial situations. Nevertheless it makes sense to ask the question, What is a successful manager? Let me give you a series of examples and ask you to determine which is the most successful.

Manager 1. Age 58. Born in a slum. Father died when he was 6. Started selling papers at age 7. Paid his own way through college. Graduated in 1929. Held a series of jobs. Joined a major grocery chain. Rose through the ranks to a middle-management job. Liked it and refused further promotions. His unit is rated above average in performance and employee satisfaction.

Manager 2. Age 35. Middle-class background. Head of branch office of H&R Block Tax Service. Branch was losing money when she came two years ago. Since then she has cut the loss in half. Branch rated in bottom 10 percent in terms of performance. Had been in bottom

5 percent when she arrived. Employee satisfaction rating below average for the company.

Manager 3. Age 41. Lower-class background. Graduated with B.S. in nursing two years ago, R.N. two years before that. Took over a hospital ward whose performance was rated much below average, but a "happy ship." Now the ward is rated number 1 in performance. Employee satisfaction is rated below average for the hospital.

Which of these three managers is the most successful? Why? After thinking about these questions, consider the following points:

1 *Success is defined by the person.* If you ask five slum kids what it would take to be successful in a job, you will get one set of answers. Ask five kids at private high schools in Winnetka, Illinois, Darien, Connecticut, or upper-class suburbs elsewhere and you'll get a different answer. Personal success is one measure of managerial success.

2 *Success is defined by the organization and by society.* Organizations usually describe successful managers as those whose units have achieved or exceeded the organization's objectives. These vary, but can be defined in terms of efficiency (e.g., low costs) and effectiveness (e.g., satisfied clients, customers, employees).

3 *A manager can be successful by his or her own definition, but less successful by the organization's or society's definition.*

4 *A manager can be successful in reaching some objectives and less successful in reaching others.* What behavioral scientists call the criterion problem is a serious one: Is success meeting objectives or making progress toward meeting them? Which objectives are the most important: client satisfaction, low cost, employee satisfaction, or profitability?

5 *Many organizations, especially smaller and medium-sized ones, never really define what managerial success is and may not tell the manager when he or she is successful.* To them, success is so vague that they do not want to try to define it.

It should be noted that it is easier to define managerial success for a supervisor than for a middle manager. For example, some organizations equate success for the supervisor's unit with success for the supervisor. In general, the higher one goes in an organization, the harder it is to define success for the individual manager.

So your first problem in trying to become a successful manager is to define success for yourself. Then you need to match yourself with an enterprise whose definition of success fits yours.

Now, the next question is, What does it take to be a successful manager? Figure 2.2 illustrates the factors that I believe contribute to managerial success.

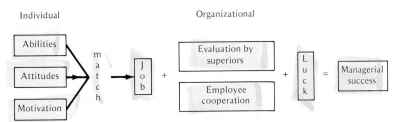

Figure 2.2
Factors in managerial success.

To be successful, managers need certain abilities. These include innate abilities and those developed by education, experience, and training. A successful manager needs technical, interpersonal, and conceptual abilities. The specific abilities necessary for managerial success are discussed in Chapter 4.

Successful managers have certain attitudes and motivations (see Chapters 4 and 5). Naturally, organizational rewards (pay, promotion, etc.) and organizational climate affect the manager's motivation and attitudes.

Note that the model does not say *hard work.* This is assumed under motivation and abilities. Most successful managers work hard. But it does not follow that the harder you work, the more successful you are. Success depends on other factors as well. Too often an employee expects to be successful just because he or she works hard. But will the Oakland Athletics hire the player who bats .350 and practices 2 hours a week or the one who practices 20 hours a week and bats .50? Will the salesperson who sells his quota by working four days a week be kept on over the one who works six days a week and does not make his or her quota? What do you think? The notion that hard work equals success is clearly a myth.

Look now at the interface between the individual and the organization. Success is also a function of the right match between the individual's abilities and the job he or she takes. People are different. A person is successful when his or her strengths are matched by the needs of the job. Some people are more creative than others and are bored by detail. Such individuals will be more successful in jobs that require more creativity than working as, say, a quality control supervisor in a nut and bolt factory. Most psychologists make this point, and Chapter 14 discusses it in more detail.

The next factor is interpersonal influence on success. Other things being equal, if your employees like you and work with you, this will help you succeed. Chapter 7 discusses how to achieve employee cooperation.

Other things being equal, if your superiors like you, this too will help you succeed. Depending on how you interpret this, it will make you a cynic, a realist, or an angry young manager. You just learned that managerial success is hard to define. So two managers are being considered for promotion, if their superiors like one (and that one is a member of the same clubs, goes to the same church, belongs to the same social group, etc.), he or she has an edge.

The Movie "How to Succeed in Business Without Really Trying" and others seem to stress that it's not what you know (or do) that counts—it's who you know. Lots of popular books like William Whyte Jr.'s *Organization Man* imply that all you need for success is to be the right personality type. But just as ability, hard work, and motivation alone don't equal success, so the boss's smile isn't everything either. But believing it does not count at all is going to make an angry young manager of you. Look at it this way: With many professors, whether you get a B or a C when you are on the borderline might be affected by whether he or she likes you. It is the same with managerial success. A professor can't give you an A if you are a D student because he or she likes you. You have got to get close to the success category in terms of results, ability, and so on, but if the professor likes you, you may have an edge. This is discussed further in Chapter 8.

Source: © King Features Syndicate, Inc. 1974.

The last factor, luck, is almost never mentioned in reference to managerial success. Why? Because it is hard to study, and managers would rather believe their own ability propelled them into successful careers. But consider the following:

·You graduated from college in 1950 or 1958; 1962 or 1975. When did you have the best chance of finding a good job?

·If McKinley had not been assassinated, would we have heard much about Teddy Roosevelt? If Franklin Roosevelt had lived to 1948, would Harry Truman have become famous?

·You got stock tips on Xerox and Equity Funding when both were unknown. You could only buy one, so you flipped a coin.

·Your buddy was declared 4F in 1967, got his degree in business, and started his career. You got the "greetings letter" and lost a leg in Vietnam.

The situations I am trying to illustrate are not entirely due to chance or luck. But in part they are. The boss' unexpected heart attack putting you in the home office five years early has little to do with your ability. Your joining a company whose R&D department stumbles onto the formula for cheap gasification of coal when you are just ready for promotion is not entirely a matter of ability either. The fact is, some success results from happening to be in the right place at the right time. I discuss the role of luck in success because it is a factor and because unless you are aware of it you will not be able to fairly assess your prospects for success. If you don't consider the luck factor, you may begin to blame lack of promotion entirely on lack of ability and think, "I don't have it." This becomes a self-fulfilling prophecy. Obviously luck can be over-weighted too. We all know people who blame an F in algebra on bad luck when they did not study for the exam.

How should each of these factors be weighted? Which is the most important? The answer is that you need them all. It is probably impossible to figure out how much less ability you can get by with if you have 10 percent better luck than the next guy. So I will not try to assign weights to the factors that contribute to managerial success.

MANAGERS AND WORK ORGANIZATIONS The preceding section described how managerial jobs are similar yet different because of differences in the departmental task (e.g., personnel vs. marketing) and differences in level (e.g., supervisor of an underwriting department vs. vice president of underwriting). The objective of this section is to make you aware that differences in the work organization's objectives, task, and work climate influence the managerial task and make it different in some ways. This is important. You may believe you can move from one enterprise to another and use the same managerial style in the new job that you used in the old one. But, generally speaking, more effective managers adjust their managerial style (interpersonal and managerial skills) according to the enterprise's objectives, task, and climate.

As a human being you have many characteristics like other people's. These similarities are important. The differences are equally important.

Are work organizations all the same? In some ways, yes. They all have objectives, perform tasks, have a work climate. But these are not all the same. Consider a manager who switches from Exxon to the Orthodox Church of North and South America. (See Table 2.8.) The manager would notice many similarities after the job change. He or she would be paid a salary. The job descriptions might be similar; similar equipment might be used. The manager would probably supervise a work group in both places. But there would be differences—some slight, some significant. The boss' title would be different. The boss' clothing would be different. The traditions of the organization would be different in view of differences in objectives and history. The number of employees would also differ.

It is fairly easy to see differences between two organizations in two different sectors. But there are significant differences between organizations within the same sector. Consider AT&T and Laidlaw Products (a small manufacturer of fly swatters), the largest employer in the United States and one of the smaller ones. There are major differences between them in number of levels of hierarchy, amount of specialization, amount of paper work, formality of communications, and many other factors.

As is pointed out later in the book, organizations are like people in that they go through a life cycle: a lean and energetic youth, a prosperous and vigorous middle age, a fragile and tenuous old age. This makes for further differences among organizations.

Differences in work climate also lead to differences in the managerial jobs. The term *climate* is hard to explain, so let me give you a parallel example you're probably familiar with.

If you looked around to select the college you were going to attend, you probably noticed differences in atmosphere, spirit, or what management people call work climate or character. There are differences of this kind between work organizations too—or, if they are large enough, between parts of organizations. Each organization develops a "culture" of its own, with its own language, ceremonies, and ways of doing things. So when you start to work for an organization, you are entering a different world. This is described in more detail in Chapter 7.

AN ORGANIZATION : I believe work climates develop because of the following factors:

1 *The history and evolution of each enterprise is different.* A coal-mining firm develops in a different way from a cookie factory.

2 *Its crises differ from those of other enterprises.* Fashion design firms face more crises than nut and bolt factories.

3 *The age of the enterprise differs.* The older the enterprise, the more tradition-bound it is. The U.S. Navy (or the Royal Canadian Navy) has a longer history than the Peace Corps (or the Canadian Broadcasting Company).

Table 2.8 Comparison Between Exxon and the Orthodox Church of North and South America

Organizational Element	Orthodox Church	Exxon
A. Objectives	1. solvency 2. satisfied employees and members 3. growth in number of souls saved & depth of spiritual experience 4. survival 5. influence in the world 6. preservation of liturgies & traditions of Christ & the Orthodox Church	1. profitability 2. satisfied employees and clients 3. growth in profits and sales 4. survival 5. influence in the community 6. innovations in marketing and products
B. Time duration	since the time of Christ; established in Orthodox form in 3rd century & in America in 18th century	Since mid-19th century
C. Stable pattern of interactions	yes	yes
D. Hierarchies of managers	council of patriarchs, patriarch of Constantinople, patriarchs or metropolitans, priests, members	board, chairman of the board, president, vice president, middle managers, supervisors, employees
E. Tasks	1. teach Christ's doctrines 2. administer the sacraments 3. conduct liturgies, etc.	1. explore for petroleum 2. refine petroleum products 3. distribute petroleum products, etc.

4 *It has been led by different types of leaders.* These leaders tend to attract other managers much like themselves, who then institutionalize the leader's way of doing things. Consider the Federal Bureau of Investigation and J. Edgar Hoover, IBM and Thomas Watson Sr., the University of Chicago and Robert M. Hutchins.

These values and behavior patterns affect how work gets done in organizations. Eugene Emerson Jennings makes this point very well (also see Table 2.9):

Working at corporation 1 may sound good to you and sound horrid to your neighbor. The point is that some of what J. C. Penney Company stands for results from the founder's concept that he was a "Christian" businessman and he hired and built policies accordingly. Sears is different partially because of what the Woods have believed. When Sewell Avery's vision of the world collapsed, Montgomery Ward lost a leader and a vision. It later was absorbed by Marcor but in many ways is different from Penney's and Sears.

I can list companies that had smoking rooms long before the Surgeon General's report because the founder's wife believed "gentlemen and ladies" did not smoke. Or companies where paternalism is strong partially because the founder was the son of a minister.

To sum up, when you go looking for a managerial job remember that the world of work is a cafeteria of organizations offering a variety of choices. The key is to match yourself to the right organizations, and this takes knowledge of yourself, knowledge of organizations, and some luck. (Finding a job and designing a career are discussed in more detail in Chapter 10.)

SUCCESSFUL ORGANIZATIONS

In this section I will briefly describe organizational success and discuss what makes an organization successful. We regularly make judgments on the success of events, and we also judge the success of enterprises. Most of us would agree that the following businesses were unsuccessful:

Lockheed Airbus Decision
Rolls Royce Engines
Penn Central Railroad
General Electric Computers Division

The following have been listed among the greatest business disasters:

Edsel
Atlantic Acceptance (Canada)

Table 2.9 Definition of a "Good Manager" in Two Businesses

Factor	Corporation 1	Corporation 2
1. Managerial work values	You & the company are one. You & work are synonomous. Therefore good managers take work home, come in on Saturdays & Sundays, skip vacations.	Good managers are well-organized. Therefore they get their work done at the office. If they take work home or skip vacations, they must be inefficient.
2. Money values	Money is something you invest. A good manager is one who uses his budget to achieve the firm's objectives & can make a good case for more funds each quarter because he or she has been so successful.	Money is a scarce resource. It needs to be used carefully. The good manager is one who uses it so wisely that a budget surplus can be returned to the home office at the end of the quarter.
3. Equipment values	Equipment used symbolizes the corporation & its success. Since we are successful, we must always have the latest equipment whether it is typewriters, computers, or company cars.	Equipment is a means to an end. Use it until it is used up. Good maintenance will make it last longer.
4. Manager's personal behavior off the job	You represent your company at all times. You must appear to be reliable & dependable. Therefore you will not get divorced, you will be active in community charities, you will dress formally, you will never drink to excess, you will be active in your church, you will not get into debt, etc.	Your personal life is your own. As long as you stay within the law and do your job during work hours you will be rewarded.

RCA Computers
IOS Ltd.
Equity Funding
National Student Marketing

On the other hand, according to *Dun's,* America's five best-managed companies in 1974 were

American Telephone & Telegraph
Southern Railways System
Merck, Inc.
R. J. Reynolds
Kerr McGee

As a society, we are mesmerized by success. We recognize success in sports (e.g., Super Bowl, World Series), entertainment (e.g., Oscars, Emmys), science, and literature (e.g., Nobel and Pulitzer Prizes). Organizations, too, are granted recognition when they are successful.

Our reasons for being interested in organizational success or effectiveness are both personal and professional. Most of us want to work for and contribute to the results of successful organizations. After all, to some extent one's status depends on where one works: A person tends to be rated higher as part of IBM's success than as part of RCA's failure.

Professionally, we are interested in organizational effectiveness because managers are held responsible for failure and rewarded for success. If we want material rewards (and want to keep our jobs), our interest in this topic should be high.

MEASURING ORGANIZATIONAL SUCCESS

It sounds as if it should be easy to measure success and determine which organizations are successful. In fact, however, it is quite difficult. There is no Nobel prize (yet) for the best-managed company. So when is a company successful? Most writers on this subject do not give complete measures of organizational success.

> **ORGANIZATIONAL SUCCESS**
> An organization is successful if it survives and if it meets its objectives.

The gut measure of success is survival. If you fold, no one will call you successful. No one rushed to declare General Thieu a success; similarly, few would call Kaiser Motors a success, and the same applies to many other long-forgotten enterprises.

Beyond survival, various experts have indicated that there are five categories of success or effectiveness criteria (which may be listed among the enterprise's objectives as well):

·*Production* (or *effectiveness*): the production of goods and services desired by society.

·*Efficiency:* the ratios of benefits to costs, output to input that show that the enterprise uses its resources well.

·*Satisfaction:* of employees, customers, and clients.

·*Adaptiveness:* the extent to which the enterprise can and does respond to changes.

·*Development:* investing in the training and development of employees and managers to help ensure the enterprise's survival.

Each enterprise develops specific measures of these criteria. Examples are presented in the following list:

earnings per share
return on capital
return on equity
market share
percentage growth in sales
expenditures on research and development
days lost per employee because of strikes
days lost per employee because of absenteeism
number of serious grievances per employee
employee turnover
dollar value of gifts to educational and cultural institutions
number of customer complaints per $1000 in sales

The success of an enterprise can be evaluated either objectively or subjectively. Objectively, we can evaluate a business as successful to the degree that criteria such as return on investment or market share get better relative to past performance and/or relative to performance by similar firms. An example of this approach is the *Forbes* rating system. Each year, in its January 1 issue, *Forbes* magazine "measures management" by combining financial and marketing indexes and rating every major company both within its own industry and in comparison with industry as a whole. In the forest products industry, for example, it ranked Louisiana Pacific no. 1 and Georgia Pacific no. 2 in 1976. It rated Boise Cascade 18th (out of 18).

Business Week makes similar ratings each quarter, and *Fortune* rates the "Fortune 1000" firms.

Another approach is to ask "experts" which firms are the most successful. This is a "subjective" approach: Dun's five or ten best-run American companies is an example of this method.

Both objective and subjective approaches to measurement become more difficult when you try to use more than one criterion to rate success. For example, taking two measures of success, efficiency and production effectiveness, we could rate four firms as shown in Figure 2.3.

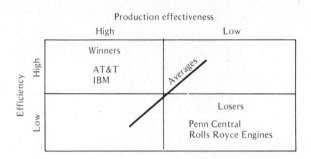

Figure 2.3
Efficiency and production effectiveness.

However, a number of problems are involved in the measurement of effectiveness:

· *Stability of criteria:* A criterion emphasized at one point in time may not be valid later on.
· *Time:* Do we evaluate short-run or long-run effectiveness?
· *Precision and variety of measurement:* Not all measures are easy to compute, and there are different ways of computing them.

It is a lot easier to measure success when a company shows consistent results on most of these measures in most years. In fact the research indicates that there is a high intercorrelation among organizational variables. If you are a "winner" on three measures, chances are you are a winner on all measures.

I would add that to me the most critical problem is the trade-off among measures. Suppose, for example, that you're measuring effectiveness as shown in Table 2.10. Admittedly, success is hard to measure, especially when you have eight measures of success and at the end of 1976 you see three up, three down, and two even. In such a case success is declared if the three measures that are "up" are the most important. Organizations feel that they are successful if the most important indicators are positive. It is easy to recognize success when most indicators are + or −, but very hard when you get results like these.

It appears, then, that successful organizations have the following formula going for them:

| Adequate resources | → | well managed by dedicated and competent managers and employees | → | who meet the changing demands of the environment | → | and are lucky. |

Table 2.10

Criterion	Percentage of Objectives Achieved	
	1975	1976
Production effectiveness		
Production output	110%	105%
Market share	12	13
Efficiency		
Return on capital	6	7
Efficiency in utilization of equipment	95	90
Adaptiveness—		
rate of production innovation	50	65
Satisfaction		
Clients	80	75
Employees	75	75
Development—		
training investments	90	90

SUMMARY   In this chapter you learned that most managers are white, male, 30–55 years old, and usually have a college or at least a high school education. A profile of the "typical" successful manager was given.

You also learned that managerial jobs differ by task, hierarchical level, and other characteristics, including organizational climate. As is stressed throughout this book, all managers use interpersonal skills and managerial skills, but the amount and type of each may vary, depending on the manager's personality, the employees, the task to be done, and the work environment.

Next, the factors necessary to be a successful manager were discussed. These include attitudes, abilities, and motivation; relationships with superiors and subordinates; effective matching of manager to task; and luck.

You learned that just as managerial jobs differ, so do organizations and their work climates. It is vital to match your managerial style and preferences with the right organization for you.

Finally, we examined the factors necessary for organizational success. The criteria used to judge success are effectiveness, efficiency, satisfaction, adaptiveness, and development. The difficulties of measuring success were also described.

By now I hope you have a better understanding of two of the building blocks of managerial success: the managerial job and the organizational environment. Chapter 3 contrasts managerial enterprises with two very special kinds of firms: the entrepreneurial firm and the family business enterprise.

Questions for Review

1. Describe managers as the U.S. census sees them.
2. What are American business leaders like?
3. Contrast the job of a foreman on an assembly line with that of a supervisor of a staff group such as personnel or accounting.
4. Compare and contrast the jobs of top managers, middle managers, and supervisors. How are they the same? How are they different?
5. Are all middle managers' jobs alike? All top managers'? Why or why not?
6. What is a successful manager? Can we measure management success? How?
7. How much does luck influence managerial success?
8. "When it comes right down to it, it's who you know (or get to know) that leads to success." Discuss.
9. "When it comes right down to it, it doesn't make any difference what company you work for. They're all the same." Discuss.
10. Name the five most successful businesses in your city or state. Defend your choices.
11. What makes an enterprise successful?

References

Who Are the Managers?

de Bettignies, H. C., "Leaders Across the Ocean," *European Business,* Summer 1970, pp. 56–63.

Diamond, Robert, "A Self Portrait of the Chief Executive," *Fortune,* May 1970, pp. 180–181; 322–323ff.

U.S., Department of Commerce, Social and Economic Statistics Administration, *Occupational Characteristics,* (Washington, D.C.: Government Printing Office, June 1973).

Price, Karl, "Characteristics of Corporate Executives: A Research Note," *Academy of Management Journal,* 15, no. 3, September 1972: 318–381.

Scientific American, The Big Business Executive (New York: Scientific American, 1965).

Slocum, Walter, *Occupational Careers* (Chicago: Aldine, 1974).

Warner, W. Lloyd, et al., *Large Scale Organizations: Volume 1, The Emergent American Society* (New Haven, Conn.: Yale University Press, 1967), esp. chap. 7.

Knowledge of the Manager's Job

Barnett, Rosalind, and Taguiri, Renato, "What Young People Think About Managers," *Harvard Business Review,* May/June 1973, pp. 106–118.

Mahoney, Thomas, *Building the Executive Team* (Englewood Cliffs, N.J.: Prentice-Hall, 1961).

Management by Task Type

Hemphill, J. K., *Dimensions of Executive Positions* (Columbus: Ohio State University, Bureau of Business Research, 1960).

Stewart, Rosemary, "The Manager's Job: Discretion vs. Demand," *Organizational Dynamics,* 2, no. 3 (Winter 1974): 67–80.

Stogdill, Ralph, et al., "A Factorial Study of Administrative Behavior," *Personnel Psychology,* 8, no. 2 (1955): 165–180.

Stogdill, Ralph, et al., *Patterns of Administrative Performance* (Columbus: Ohio State University, Bureau of Business Research, 1956).

Stogdill, Ralph, "The Work Performance of Leaders," in *Handbook of Leadership* (New York: Free Press, 1974), pp. 156–166.

Levels of Management/The Supervisor

Bhatt, L. J., and Pathak, N. S., "A Study of the Functions of Supervisory Staff and the Characteristics Essential for Success as Viewed by a Group of Supervisors," *Manas,* 9 (1962): 25–31.

Guest, Robert, "Of Time and the Foreman," *Personnel,* 32 (1955–1956): 478–486.

Jasinski, Frank, "Foremen Relationships Outside the Work Group," *Personnel,* 33 (1956–1957): 130–136.

Kay, Brian, "Key Factors in Effective Foreman Behavior," *Personnel,* 36 (1959): 25–31.

Kay, Emmanuel, and Meyer, Herbert, "The Development of a Job Activity Questionnaire for Production Foremen," *Personnel Psychology,* 15, no. 4 (1962): 411–418.

Marples, D. L., "Studies of Managers: A Fresh Start?" *Journal of Management Studies,* 4, no. 3 (1967): 282–299.

O'Neil, Harry, and Kubany, Albert, "Observation Methodology and Supervisory Behavior," *Personnel Psychology,* 12 (1959): 85–95.

Ponder, Quenton, "The Effective Manufacturing Foreman," *Proceedings, Industrial Relations Research Association,* 1957, pp. 41–54.

Roach, Darrell, "Factor Analysis of Rated Supervisory Behavior," *Personnel Psychology,* 9 (1956): 487–498.

Roethlisberger, Fritz, "Foreman: Man in the Middle," *Harvard Business Review,* 23 (Spring 1945): 285–294.

———, "The Foreman: Master and Victim of Double Talk," in *Man in Organization* (Cambridge, Mass.: Harvard University Press, 1968), pp. 37–42.

Sequeira, C. E., "Functions of a Supervisor," *Indian Journal of Applied Psychology,* 1 (1964): 46–54.

Stogdill, et al., op. cit.

Turner, Weld, "Dimensions of Foreman Performance: A Factor Analysis of Criterion Measures," *Journal of Applied Psychology,* 44 (1960): 216–223.

Wallace, W. L., and Gallagher, J. V., *Activities and Behaviors of Production Supervisors* (New York: Psychological Corporation, 1952).

Wikstrom, Walter, *Management at the Foremen's Level* (New York: National Industrial Conference Board, 1967).

Yoga, M., "Patterns of Supervisory Authority," *Indian Journal of Applied Psychology,* 1 (1964): 44–48.

The Middle Manager

Burns, Tom, "The Directions of Activity & Communication in a Departmental Executive Group," *Human Relations,* 7, no. 1 (1954): 73–97.

Burns, Tom, "Management in Action," *Operational Research Quarterly,* 8 (1957): 45–60.

Copeman, G., Luijk, H., and Haneka, F., *How the Executive Spends His Time* (London: Business Publications, 1963).

Dalton, Melville, *Men Who Manage* (New York: Wiley, 1961).

Horne, J. H., and Lupton, Tom, "The Work Activities of 'Middle' Managers: An Exploratory Study," *Journal of Management Studies,* 2 (1965): 14–33.

Katzell, Raymond et al., "Organizational Correlates of Executive Roles," *Journal of Applied Psychology,* 53, no. 1 (1968).

Kelly, Joe, "The Study of Executive Behavior by Activity Sampling," *Human Relations,* 17 (1964): 277–287.

Marples, op. cit.

Nealey, Stanley, and Fiedler, Fred, "Leadership Functions of Middle Managers," *Psychological Bulletin,* 70, no. 5 (1968): 313–329.

Pheysey, Diana, "Activities of Middle Managers: A Training Guide," *Journal of Management Studies,* 9, no. 2 (May 1972): 158–171.

Porter, Lyman, and Ghiselli, Edwin, "The Self Perceptions of Top and Middle Management Personnel," *Personnel Psychology,* 10 (1957): 397–406.

Sayles, Leonard, *Managerial Behavior* (New York: McGraw-Hill, 1964).

Sherwood, Frank, "The R and D Executive and His Time," in Evelyn Glatt and Maynard Shelby, *The Research Society* (New York: Gordon & Breach, 1968).

Stogdill, Ralph, and Shortle, Carroll, "Performance Profiles of High Level Officials," in Stogdill et al., op. cit.

Uyterhoeven, Hugo, "General Managers in the Middle," *Harvard Business Review* March-April 1972, pp. 75–85.

The Top Manager

Beishon, R., & Palmer, A., "Studying Managerial Behavior," *International Studies of Management & Organization,* 2, no. 1 (Spring 1972): 38–64.

Brumback, Gary, & Vincent, John, "Factor Analysis of Work Performed Data for a Sample of Administrative, Professional, and Scientific Positions," *Personnel Psychology,* 23 (1970): 101–107.

Business Management, "How 179 Chief Executives Waste Their Time," March 1968, pp. 12–14.

Campbell, John et al., *Managerial Behavior* (New York: McGraw-Hill, 1970).

Carlson, Sune, *Executive Behavior* (Stockholm: Strömbergs, 1951).

Case, Fred, "An Executive Day," *California Management Review,* Fall 1962, pp. 67–70.

Connors, Edward, and Hutts, Joseph, "How Administrators Spend Their Day," *Hospitals,* 41 (February 16, 1967).

Dalson, M. T., *Progress Report on Pilot Study of Hospital Administrators* (Ithaca, N.Y.: Cornell University, 1963).

Dubin, Robert, and Spray, S. Lee, "Executive Behavior and Interaction," *Industrial Relations,* 3 (1963–1964): 99–108.

Groner, P. N., "Allocating Executives' Time," *Hospital Topics,* 43 (November 1965).

Haas, John, et al., "Actual vs. Ideal Time Allocations Reported By Managers," *Personnel Psychology,* 22 (1969): 61–75.

Hemphill, op. cit.

Hickey, W. J., "Power, Conflict, and the Administrator," *Hospital Administration,* 13, no. 1 (1964):7–25.

Hodgson, Robert, et al., *The Executive Role Constellation* (Boston: Harvard Business School, 1965).

Lamb, Warren, and Turner, David, *Management Behavior* (New York: International Universities Press, 1969).

Lentz, Edith, "Hospital Administrators: One of a Species," *Administrative Science Quarterly,* 1, no. 4 (March 1957): 444–463.

Mahoney, Thomas, et al., *Development of Managerial Performance* (Cincinnati: Southwestern Publishing, 1963).

Mintzberg, Henry, "The Manager's Job: Folklore and Fact," *Harvard Business Review,* July-August 1975, pp. 49–61.

Mintzberg, Henry, *The Nature of Managerial Work* (New York: Harper & Row, 1973).

Sheriff, Don, *Administrative Behavior* (Iowa City: University of Iowa, Center for Labor Management, 1969).

Stieglitz, Harold, *The Chief Executive and His Job* (New York: National Industrial Conference Board, 1969).

Thomason, G. F., "Managerial Work Roles and Relationships," *Journal of Management Studies,* 3 (1966): 270–284; (1967): 17–30.

Wilkie, Ray, and Young, James, "Managerial Behavior in the Furniture and Timber Industries," *International Studies of Management and Organization,* 2, no. 1 (Spring 1972): 65–84.

Summary and Implications

Goodman, Paul, "An Empirical Examination of Elliott Jaques' Concept of Time Span," *Human Relations,* 20, no. 2 (1967): 155–170.

Martin, Norman, "Differential Decision in the Management of an Industrial Plant," *Journal of Business,* 29, no. 4 (1956): 249–260.

Stewart, Rosemary, *The Reality of Management* (London: Hernemann, 1963).

———, "Studies of Managerial Jobs," *International Studies of Management & Organization,* 2, no. 1 (Spring 1972): 7–37.

———, "Management Education and Our Knowledge of Managers' Jobs," *International Studies of Management and Organization,* Summer 1975, pp. 73–89.

Successful Managers

Barnard, Chester, *The Functions of the Executive* (Cambridge, Mass.: Harvard University Press, 1962).

Brooks, Earl, "What Successful Executives Do," *Personnel,* 32, no. 3 (1955): 210–225.

Campbell et al., op. cit.

Cummings, L. L., and Schwab, Donald, *Performance in Organizations* (Glenview, Ill.: Scott Foresman, 1973).

Flanagan, John, "Defining the Requirements of the Executive's Job," *Personnel,* 28, no. 1 (1951): 28–35.

Ghiselli, Edwin, *Explorations in Managerial Talent* (Pacific Palisades, Calif.: Goodyear, 1971).

Harrell, Thomas, *Managers' Performance and Personality* (Cincinnati: Southwestern Publishing, 1961).

Jastram, Ray, "Another View of Business Education Success," *California Management Review,* 16, no. 4 (Summer 1974): 48–49.

Katz, Robert, "Skills of an Effective Administrator," *Harvard Business Review,* 33, no. 1 (November-December 1953): 33–42.

Kay and Meyer, op. cit.

Khandwalla, Pradip, "Style of Management and Environment: Some Findings," McGill University, 1974 (Mimeograph).

Levinson, Harry, *The Exceptional Executive* (Cambridge, Mass.: Harvard University Press, 1968).

McMurry, Robert, *The Maverick Executive* (New York: Amacon, 1974).

Miner, John, "The Real Crunch in Managerial Manpower," *Harvard Business Review,* November-December 1973, pp. 146–158.

Porter, Lyman, & Lawler, Edward, *Managerial Attitudes and Performance* (Homewood, Ill.: Irwin Dorsey Press, 1968).

Sank, Lawrence, "Effective and Ineffective Managerial Traits as Obtained as Naturalistic Descriptions from Executive Members of a Super Corporation," *Personnel Psychology,* 27 (1974): 423–434.

Srinivasan, V. et al., "Measurement of a Composite Criterion of Managerial Success," *Organizational Behavior and Human Performance,* 9 (1973): 147–167.

Williams, William, and Seiler, Dale, "Relationships Between Measures of Effort and Job Performance," *Journal of Applied Psychology,* 57, no. 1 (1973): 49–54.

Managers and Work Organizations

Nadler, Leonard, "The Organization as a Micro Culture," *Personnel Journal,* December 1969, pp. 949–956.

Pace, C. Robert, and Stern, George, "An Approach to the Measurement of Psychological Characteristics of College Environments," *Journal of Educational Psychology.* 49, no. 5 (1958): 269–277.

Trice, Harrison et al., "The Role of Ceremonials in Organizational Behavior," *Industrial and Labor Relations Review,* 23, no. 1 (October 1969): pp. 40–51.

Wright, Robert, "The Application of a Conceptual Scheme to Understand Organization Character," *Academy of Management Journal,* December 1968, pp. 389–399.

Measuring Organizational Success

Barmash, Isidore, *Great Business Disasters* (New York: Ballantine Books, 1973).

Child, John, *The Business Enterprise in Modern Industrial Society* (London: Macmillan, 1969), esp. chap. 5.

Child, John, "Managerial and Organizational Factors Associated with Company Performance," *Journal of Management Studies,* I (October 1974): 175–189; II (February 1975): 12–27.

Child, John, "What Determines Organizational Performance?" *Organizational Dynamics,* Spring 1975, pp. 2–18.

Douglass, Merrill, "How Do You Measure the Effectiveness of a Business?" *Organizational Dynamics,* Winter 1975, pp. 47–50.

Gannon, Martin, "The Measurement of Performance in Multi-Unit Service Organizations," *Proceedings, Midwest Academy of Management,* 1970, pp. 263–272.

Ghorpade, Jai, *Assessment of Organizational Effectiveness* (Pacific Palisades, Calif.: Goodyear, 1971).

Gibson, James et al., *Organizations* (Dallas: Business Publications, 1973), chap. 2.

Heller, Robert, *The Great Executive Dream* (New York: Dell, 1972).

Hersick, Paul, "Organizational Effectiveness and the Institutional Environment," *Administrative Science Quarterly,* 20 (September 1975): 327–344.

Knowles, M. C., "Interdependence Among Organizational Variables," *Human Relations,* 28, no. 5 (July 1975): 431–450.

Ksansnak, James, "Measuring Productivity," *Managerial Planning,* November-December 1974, pp. 15–34.

Mott, Paul, *The Characteristics of Effective Organizations* (New York: Harper & Row, 1972).

Price, James, *Organizational Effectiveness* (Homewood, Ill.: Irwin Dorsey Press, 1968).

Ross, Joel and Kami, Michael, *Corporate Management in Crisis: Why the Mighty Fall* (Englewood Cliffs, N.J.: Prentice-Hall, 1973).

Reimann, Bernard, "Organizational Effectiveness and Management's Public Values: A Canonical Analysis," *Academy of Management Journal,* 18, no. 2 (June 1975): 224–241.

Rushing, William, "Differences in Profit and Nonprofit Organizations: A Study of Effectiveness and Efficiency in General Short-Stay Hospitals," *Administrative Science Quarterly,* 19, no. 4 (December 1974): 474–484.

Steers, Richard, "Problems in the Measurement of Organizational Effectiveness," *Administrative Science Quarterly,* 20 (December 1975): 546–558.

Wahba, Mahmoud, and Shapiro, Harus, "Managerial Assessment of Organizational Components," *Academy of Management Journal,* 16, no. 2 (June 1973): 277–284.

Webb, R. J., "Organizational Effectiveness and the Voluntary Organization," *Academy of Management Journal,* 17, no. 4 (December 1974): 663–667.

Yuchtman, E., and Seashore, S. E., "A System Resource Approach to Organizational Effectiveness," *American Sociological Review,* 32, no. 6 (December 1967): 891–903.

CHAPTER 3

ENTREPRENEURIAL AND FAMILY FIRMS

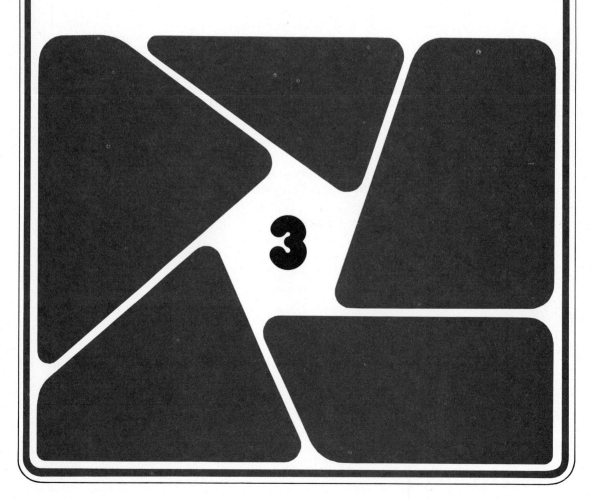

Learning Objectives

1. To understand how entrepreneurs differ from managers.
2. To learn the importance of entrepreneurs to our business society.
3. To understand how the entrepreneural job differs from the managerial job.
4. To understand the family business and how it is similar to and different from entrepreneural and managerial firms.
5. To learn how to be a successful entrepreneur and/or family business executive.

Chapter Outline

Introduction: What are Entrepreneurial and Family Businesses?
Entrepreneurs and Managers
The Significance of Entrepreneurs to Society
Entrepreneurs: Some Examples
The Entrepreneurial Job
Entrepreneurship: Learned or Inherited?
Challenges Faced by Entrepreneurial Firms
The Family Business
The Family Business Executive
Other Relationships in Family Businesses
Family Business Executives: Some Examples
Executives of Family-Influenced Firms
Success in Entrepreneurial Businesses
Entrepreneurial Ability
Entrepreneurial Attitudes, Motivation, and Personality
An Environment Encouraging Success
Adequate Capital
A Genuine Business Opportunity
Entrepreneurship and You
Group Entrepreneurship
Success in Family Businesses
Summary and Implications

INTRODUCTION   Have you ever wondered what it would be like to be your own boss? Or what it is like to work in a family business? In this chapter I discuss this and other aspects of the important economic sector consisting of entrepreneurial and family firms. Some of this material applies to entrepreneurs in the nonprofit and public sectors. But the chapter focuses mainly on the business entrepreneur and the family business executive.

There are essentially three types of self-employed individuals: the entrepreneur, the small-business owner/manager, and the family business executive. Here we will not deal with the small-business owner/manager—an individual running a small business who did not create the business. A typical example is an individual who has worked for a small business (say, a small retail store), purchases it from the owner, and continues to operate it as it has been operated in the past. My purpose here is to introduce you to the world of the entrepreneurial and family business executive in the same way that Chapter 2 introduced you to the world of the manager.

There are three types of entrepreneurial family firms:

ENTREPRENEURIAL FIRM
An *entrepreneurial* firm is one that is directed by its founder.

FAMILY-RUN FIRM
A *family-run firm* is one whose major ownership influence is a family; most or all of its key executives are family members.

FAMILY-INFLUENCED FIRM
The *family-influenced firm* is one whose major ownership influence is a family; some of the key executives are family members.

I believe the distinction between family-run and family-influenced firms is clear. Let me elaborate on the concept of an entrepreneurial firm. Various meanings have been assigned to the term *entrepreneurial firm*. What I mean by this term is an enterprise whose *current head* is the individual who created the enterprise from scratch. Many entrepreneurs create a firm and sell it off only to create another. Such an individual plays an important role in society. But the firm I will focus on is the firm created and still managed by its founder. For this is a significantly different enterprise from the firm run by a manager or, for that matter, by a family business executive.

Almost no major studies have been done on the self-employed individual. Those that have been done are contradictory, alternately showing the self-employed as dissatisfied residues of an earlier era or as individuals who work long hours for not very high pay but are nevertheless satisfied. Given that the entrepreneur and the family business executive have not really been studied adequately, I will try to portray what we know from the few studies we have and from my own experience as the son of an entrepreneur and as a former family business executive. Throughout this book the differences in the jobs and other aspects of the world of entrepreneurs and family business executives are described so that the contingency approach will make sense to you.

ENTRE-
PRENEURS AND
MANAGERS

How do entrepreneurs differ from managers (if at all)? Are entrepreneurs and managers alike? In some ways, yes; in others, definitely not. There is a lot of evidence that managers and entrepreneurs behave differently on the job, especially when making crucial decisions. Entrepreneurs and managers hold different attitudes. They face different problems and choices and, in many cases, come from different social and educational backgrounds. Most researchers agree that entrepreneurs are a different breed from managers.

John Komives, who heads the Center for Venture Management in Milwaukee, has tried to sum up what many researchers have found out about entrepreneurs. If you answer yes to 50 per cent or more of the questions on his Entrepreneurship Test (see Figure 3.1), he believes you should start planning that business venture you've been thinking about.

Joe Mancuso has studied a group of 300 entrepreneurs for several years. He has concluded that the typical successful entrepreneur can be described as follows:

· The entrepreneur was the first-born child in his or her family.
· Is married, with a supportive spouse.
· Began his or her first company at the age of 30 or so (although years ago this happened as late as age 42)
· Entrepreneurial tendencies showed up by the teen-age years.
· Education varies: The technical entrepreneur often has a master's degree. The garden variety of entrepreneur probably has at least a high school and probably a college degree.
· The entrepreneur's primary motivation for becoming an entrepreneur is a psychological inability to work for anyone else.
· The entrepreneur's personality developed mainly in interaction with his or her father's personality.
· The successful entrepreneur is often lucky.
· Entrepreneurs and money providers are often in conflict.
· The entrepreneur seeks advice, if it is needed, from other entrepreneurs, consultants, and college professors.
· Is essentially a doer, not a planner.
· Assume *moderate* risks, not large or small ones.

Figure 3.1
Entrepreneurship
test.

Yes   No

1. *Was your father an entrepreneur?*

   An entrepreneur in the family is the single most telling indicator of the successful entrepreneur. In fact, counting such "businesses" as a law practice, a farm, or a ministership, fully 80% of today's entrepreneurs come from a family heritage of individual business.

2. *Are you an immigrant?*

   There is a high correlation between immigrants and entrepreneurs. *Immigrant* includes not only those who were born outside the United States but also those who moved from farm to city or, say, from the Midwest to the West Coast. A study of 254 technical entrepreneurs on the West Coast revealed that on the average they had lived there only nine years.

3. *Did you have a paper route?*

   Yes? Fine. An entrepreneurial streak shows up early in life. And while rising at 5:30 undoubtedly builds moral fiber, it would have been ever more indicative of entrepreneurial tendencies if you had subcontracted the deliveries to your younger brother and dickered with the news company for an adjoining route. One 12-year-old discovered by Komives has been buying real estate and, through contrivance, getting adult signatures on the papers he needed for his deals.

4. *Were you a good student?*

   The typical entrepreneur was anything but a model student. While there is no indication that he is less well educated than others, the entrepreneur's school record often includes an expulsion.

5. *What is your favorite spectator sport?*

   The best answer would be "none." Entrepreneurs are poor spectators. Says Komives, "They couldn't stand to watch a football game for more than five minutes." Not surprisingly, they excell at individual sports such as sailing and skiing. But not golf. Golf is too slow, involves too much walking.

6. *What size company do you now work for?*

   Statistics show that most entrepreneurs have come from medium-sized companies—those with 30 to 500 employees.

7. *Have you ever been fired?*

   It may not look good on your resume for that job at General Foods, but it indicates that you are entrepreneurial material. Entrepreneurs make poor employees. That's why they become entrepreneurs.

8. *If you had a new business going, would you play your cards close to the vest, or would you be willing to discuss problems with your employees?*

An open communication policy may be good business, but the typical entrepreneur has a secretive streak. If he or she confides in anyone, that person is likely to be another entrepreneur. _____ _____

9. *Are you an inventor? a Ph.D.?*

Not a positive indicator. Inventors fall in love with their products, Ph.D's with their research. They aren't really interested in sharing the fruits of their labors. The entrepreneur is less enamored of his product than of pricing it right and getting it into the market place. _____ _____

10. *How old are you?*

The ideal age for starting a business seems to be 32–35. It takes a certain number of years to build the business self-confidence that will carry the entrepreneur beyond the adversity he or she is sure to encounter in a new venture. It also takes time to develop a critical mass of frustration as an employee. Moreover, by the early 30s a person has "stable" finances and family life, and doesn't yet have college tuition bills to pay. Beyond this age, a person has usually figured out a way of dealing with frustrations and by the age of 40 he will be locked into the corporate pension plan. _____ _____

11. *When do you plan to retire?*

It does not much matter what you answer. If you are an entrepreneur, you will not. "I have never met an entrepreneur who retired," says Komives. "Sure, he sells his business and thinks he is going to retire but pretty soon he takes his money and starts meddling in something new. The real distinction between the entrepreneur and the nonentrepreneur is that no matter what stage of his life you look at him, the entrepreneur is out there starting businesses." _____ _____

This list may be summarized as follows:

Proposition 3.1.
Psychological and developmental differences between entrepreneurs and nonentrepreneurial managers lead to fundamentally different decision-making processes and management techniques.

Until very recently the world of the entrepreneur was almost entirely male. This remains true, but women are entering this world more frequently than in the past, now that the opportunities are greater and societal values have shifted so that it is "normal" for women to want to run their own businesses.

James Schreier recently studied female Milwaukee entrepreneurs who created enterprises in "nonfemale" businesses (that is, he ignored Madge and her beauty shop). He judged them by the characteristics just cited and found the following differences:

·A stronger tendency toward self-employment in the family: 70 per cent of male entrepreneurs come from a family headed by an entrepreneur; 93 per cent of Schrier's female entrepreneurs did.
·Seventy-two per cent of female entrepreneurs liked school, whereas the male entrepreneurs (garden variety—not technical entrepreneurs) did not like it.
·Male entrepreneurs become entrepreneurs because they cannot work for others, as evidenced by prior job history; 50 per cent of female entrepreneurs liked working for others in previous jobs.
·More female entrepreneurs than male ones are divorced or single.
·Less early entrepreneurial behavior was shown, but mainly because of lack of opportunity. For example, the Milwaukee newspapers would not hire female paper carriers.

THE SIGNIFICANCE OF ENTREPRENEURS TO SOCIETY

There are various ways of indicating the significance of a group of individuals such as entrepreneurs to society. One way is to say that entrepreneurs provide most of the new ideas in the business sector. And they do. Another way is to look at some statistics. The following statistics are from the 1970 U.S. census, which mixes entrepreneurs with manager/operators of small businesses. But they make my point. For example,

Only one-tenth of 1 per cent of American businesses employ 2500 people or more.
Among manufacturing firms, 89 per cent employ 100 people or fewer; 70 per cent employ 20 or fewer.
Of all firms, 98 per cent employ fewer than 50 people.
Forty per cent of all firms are in merchandising. Of these, 71 percent have 4 or fewer employees, and 95 per cent employ fewer than 20 people.
Ninety per cent of service businesses (hotels, personal services, business services, repair services) are entrepreneurial or family run.

But, you might say, surely such firms have declined in number in the last 50 years and so are less important. Wrong. In 1900 there were 18 entrepreneurial firms per thousand businesses. Now there are 22 per thousand. What has happened is that most formerly self-employed farmers are no longer self-employed and now work for entrepreneurial or family firms or for major companies.

Today about 9,400,000 of the 10,000,000 American business enterprises are entrepreneurial or small businesses run by owner/managers. The Small Business Administration reports that these firms employ 59 per cent of all private sector employees and that self-employed individuals account for 8 per cent of the private sector.

The 1970 census provides us with the data in Table 3.1. The earnings figures reported in the table are medians in 1970 dollars. In 1970 over 900,000 people were self-employed; probably about a million are self-employed today. About 9 percent earned more than $25,000 per year; about 24 percent earned more than $15,000 per year.

Minorities aren't specifically represented in the table, but of male entrepreneurs, two and one half per cent are black and 2 per cent of Spanish origin. For women, the percentages are three and one third per cent black and two and one half per cent of Spanish origin. Thus minority entrepreneurs clearly get only a tiny piece of the economic pie—but they do get a piece.

ENTRE-PRENEURS: SOME EXAMPLES Examples of entrepreneurs are all around you. They range from the mechanic who opened his own garage and now has three mechanics working for him to that aunt of yours who left the employment agency she worked for to open Maude's Employment Service. Ray Krok (McDonald's), Stephen Bechtel (Bechtel Construction), Gloria Steinem (*Ms.* magazine), and Mary Wells Lawrence (Wells, Rich and Greene) are better known. Other entrepreneurs whom you may have heard about are Walt Disney, Charles Ives, and Tillie Lewis. Among the better-known black entrepreneurships in the U.S. are Johnson Products, Le Roy O. Zane Construction, and fight promoter Don King.

WALTER ELIAS DISNEY (1901–1966)

Drawing, painting, photography, writing, music, acting, architecture—in none of these separate arts did Walt Disney excel. Yet his fanatical quest for excellence wove examples of these arts into innovative shapes that people all over the world applauded. He inspired, stimulated, restrained, and coordinated hundreds of talents brighter than his own into producing at levels of quality that they could not have approached without him. He was quick to see how his studio could use every technological advance. And he built his own patterns of leadership so effectively into the fiber of his organization that the company eight years after his death is more prosperous than ever (1974 revenues: $429,889,000; net income: $48,328,000).

Born into an economically insecure Midwest family, Disney was early

Table 3.1 Characteristics of Nonfarm Entrepreneurs and Small-Business Owner/Managers

	Total	Male				Female			
		Number	Median earnings	Median schooling years	Median age	Number	Median earnings	Median schooling years	Median age
Managers and administrators, n.e.c., self-employed	914 719	772 212	8 878	12.3	49.1	142 507	3 837	12.3	51.9
Construction	142 699	140 640	9 799	12.2	45.8	2 059	7 349	12.4	46.3
Durable goods manufacturing	38 799	36 618	9 698	12.3	48.9	2 181	3 498	12.4	51.9
Nondurable goods, incl. not specified manufacturing	28 900	24 814	10 615	12.7	49.9	4 086	4 319	12.5	51.0
Transportation	20 736	18 563	9 631	12.1	47.6	2 173	5 219	12.7	50.3
Communications, and utilities and sanitary services	2 200	2 031	11 971	12.2	48.7	169	...	...	...
Wholesale trade	56 719	52 585	10 324	12.5	51.0	4 134	5 564	12.5	51.1
Retail trade	436 284	349 368	7 945	12.2	50.0	86 916	3 603	12.2	52.3
Hardware, farm equipment and building material retailing	29 333	27 055	9 398	12.5	51.9	2 278	4 869	12.4	53.5
General merchandise stores	24 123	16 096	8 377	12.5	53.0	8 027	3 618	12.4	52.9
Food stores	117 089	85 244	6 892	11.9	52.5	31 845	3 285	11.2	52.5
Motor vehicles and accessories retailing	24 953	23 847	10 037	12.4	47.5	1 106	5 190	12.4	50.9
Gasoline service stations	101 010	97 547	7 495	12.0	45.2	3 463	3 574	11.4	49.7
Apparel and accessories stores	24 391	14 581	10 738	12.7	54.1	9 810	5 210	12.4	53.1
Furniture, home furnishings, and equipment stores	27 596	23 613	9 616	12.5	48.6	3 983	4 531	12.5	50.7
Other retail trade	87 789	61 385	8 363	12.5	51.7	26 404	3 387	12.4	52.1
Finance, insurance, and real estate	22 903	20 478	14 155	14.5	52.0	2 425	5 235	12.9	55.7
Business and repair services	51 769	46 153	9 448	12.4	47.1	5 616	4 942	12.7	50.0
Personal services	73 259	47 770	8 004	12.3	53.5	25 489	3 938	12.2	52.4
All other industries	40 451	33 192	9 323	12.6	48.7	7 259	3 900	12.7	48.9

inured to hard work. Each success goaded him toward more difficult goals. Mickey Mouse was succeeded by the Silly Symphonies, which broke new technical ground in the coordination of sound and color. (The song from *The Three Little Pigs*, "Who's Afraid of the Big, Bad Wolf?" became a kind of national defiance of the Depression.) Disney gambled boldly in 1938 with the first feature-length cartoon, *Snow White and the Seven Dwarfs*. He then plunged into *Fantasia*, blending color, shape, and motion with classical music played by Leopold Stokowski and the Philadelphia Orchestra.

After World War II, some thought Disney was ready to rest. But Walt told his brother and collaborator, Roy, "If we try to coast, we'll go backward." In the Fifties the studio produced an ambitious program of cartoons (*Cinderella, Alice in Wonderland, Peter Pan*) and live-action movies (*20,000 Leagues Under the Sea*). While most of the movie industry trembled before the advance of televison, Disney mastered the new medium. In theaters and on the tube his *True-Life Adventure Features* made nature vivid to urbanized millions. When he turned his meticulous attention to the design of Disneyland, Walt achieved effects of structural coordination that stirred the imaginations of city planners. All in all, Walt Disney, entrepreneur of images, had a profound and a positive influence on twentieth-century culture.

CHARLES IVES (1874–1954)

Charles Ives was one of the founders of a major New York insurance agency, Ives and Myrick. He was responsible for many breakthroughs in the insurance business such as estate planning and insurance policies for low-income householders and was one of the first to provide professional training for insurance agents. The whole industry used his sales handbook, *The Amount To Carry: Measuring the Prospect*.

In his spare time Ives composed music. He anticipated most of the innovations of twentieth-century music. The music audience of his time (he died in 1954) did not appreciate him; Ives has been quoted as saying, "I have found more open-mindedness in the business world than the music world." But Ives has been called America's greatest composer. In 1947 he received the Pulitzer prize for his Third Symphony.

© Arnold Newman

TILLIE LEWIS

With $10,000 in cash and some tomato seedlings, Tillie Lewis (born Myrtle Ehrlich in Brooklyn) founded what is now a $100-million-plus enterprise. She never had much use for formal education—she dropped out of high school after one semester—but she had an extraordinary entrepreneurial streak, and, as it turned out, a great idea. During a brief marriage in the 1920's to a wholesale grocer, for whom she occasionally took inventory, Tillie began to wonder why so much tomato paste and tomato sauce was imported from Italy. The principal reason was that the main ingredient of these products, a pear-shaped tomato called the *pomodoro,* had never been grown commercially in the U.S. After researching the subject with agricultural experts on the West Coast, Tillie concluded the *pomodoro* could be grown in the San Joaquin Valley. She forthwith went to Italy and sold the idea to a large Italian canner, who provided the financial backing and the seedlings. She later bought out the Italians and named the company Tillie Lewis Foods. When it was acquired in 1966 by Ogden Corp., Mrs. Lewis realized close to $9 million. Now seventyish, she is a director of Ogden.

THE THE ENTRE-PRENEURIAL JOB

In Chapter 2, I described managerial jobs. Now we will look at a well-known entrepreneur's day. In *Working,* Studs Terkel describes Ken Brown, age 26, who is president of four corporations: American Motorcylce Mechanics School, Evel Knievel's Electrocycle Service Centers, Triple A Motorcycle Leasing, and AMS Productions. Some of these are rather large franchises. Ken quit school at 16, worked for a big company for one year, and opened up his own repair shop at 17. He got into the motorcycle business because he felt that it had potential. Now he has all that wealth can buy—two chauffeured Cadillacs, a Corvette, a condominium in Skokie, a house in Evanston, a ranch in Arizona. Ken describes his work habits as follows:

> I usually get out of here at one o'clock in the morning. I go home and eat dinner at two. I do my best thinking at night. I can't fall asleep until seven in the morning. I turn the TV on. I don't even pay attention to it. They got the all-night movies. You actually feel like an idiot. I just sit there in the living room, making notes, trying to put down things for the next day to remember. I plan ahead for a month. Maybe I'll lie down in bed about four in the morning. If something comes in my head, I'll get up and start writing it. If I get three, four hours' sleep, I'm okay.
>
> That's when I come up with my ideas. That's when I put this Electrocycle idea together. I sold Sun Electric on the idea of building them for me. Then I sold Evel Knievel on the idea of putting his name on it. . . .
>
> I'm down at the office Saturdays too. Sundays, about half the time. The other half of the time maybe my wife and I will go horseback riding or visit a friend's house. Even when you're visiting with them, you can't get away from your work. They ask about it. It's kind of a good feeling. There's not too many Sundays like that. I've been traveling more than ever with these franchises. . . .
>
> It wasn't easy. When other people were going out and just having fun and riding motorcycles and getting drunk and partying, I was working. I gave up a lot. I gave up my whole youth, really. That's something you never get back.
>
> People say to me, "Gee! You work so damn hard, how can you ever enjoy it?" I'm enjoying it every day. I don't have to get away for a weekend to

enjoy it. Eventually I'll move out to Arizona and make that my headquarters. I'm young enough. I'll only be thirty-one in five years. I can still do these things—horseback riding, looking after animals. I like animals. But I'll never retire. I'll take it a little bit easier. I'll have to. I had an ulcer since I was eighteen.

[Indicates bottle of tablets on the table. It reads, "Mylanta. A palliative combination of aluminum, magnesium, hydroxide to relieve gastric hyperacidity and heartburn."] I chew up a lot of Mylantas. It's for your stomach, to coat it. Like Maalox. I probably go through twenty tablets a day.

I guess people get different thrills out of business in different ways. There's a lot of satisfaction in showing up people who thought you'd never amount to anything. If I died tomorrow, I'd really feel I enjoyed myself. How would I like to be remembered? I don't know if I really care about being remembered. I just want to be known while I'm here. That's enough. I didn't like history, anyway.

Note some of the characteristics of the entrepreneur's work pattern. Ken works very hard, but he fits his hours to his preferences. He is his own boss.

Entrepreneurs have more time alone than managers. The typical entrepreneur spends 36 percent of his or her time alone, 15 percent doing things like observing or traveling. They spend time talking and listening, too: 9 percent with customers, 4 percent with suppliers, 9 percent with other managers, and 27 percent with other employees. But when asked what they do when alone, they say they spend this time thinking, reading, calculating, or writing.

Note the differences here: much less interruption, much more time to plan, to make decisions alone. Entrepreneurs write their own job descriptions.

ENTREPRENEURSHIP: LEARNED OR INHERITED?

In Chapter 1, I raised the question of whether you can learn how to be a manager from books and in the classroom. The answer I gave was that many managerial attitudes and techniques can be learned in this way. But managerial success also requires the ability to use managerial techniques well and at the right time—the art of management.

Learning to be a successful entrepreneur is similar to learning to be a manager. There is evidence that many aspects of entrepreneurship can be learned. David McClelland has shown that you can even teach entrepreneurial motivation in the classroom. The Center for Venture Management in Milwaukee has much information available on how to become a successful entrepreneur. Some of the most popular courses in business and management schools today are those in entrepreneurship.

Of course some aspects of entrepreneurship are learned best in practice. For example, it is very difficult to teach someone how to create the idea or product that leads to the establishment of a business. But a lot can be taught about how to get going financially and legally, how to organize the business, and the like.

CHALLENGES FACED BY ENTRE- PRENEURIAL FIRMS

Entrepreneurial firms face similar problems to those experienced by managerial firms: They hire and fire people, market goods and services, pay taxes, and so on. But entrepreneurial firms face certain unique problems as well. In describing these challenges I'll use Frederick Webster's analysis of the entrepreneurial venture. This is diagramed in Figure 3.2

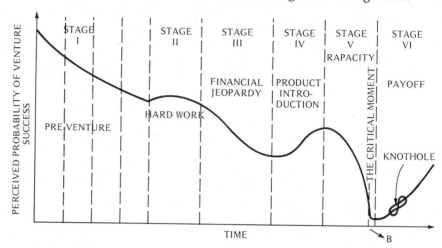

Figure 3.2
Stages in the entrepreneurial venture.

The first stage brings the first crisis, one that few managers face: the start-up crisis. Few managers must face the level of trauma that entrepreneurs experience when they start a business. They must have a product or service they believe they can sell in competition with established giants or other entrenched competitors. Coming up with the idea for a viable enterprise is not easy. And this is the crucial entrepreneurial act: the creation of a new product or service; the creation of new uses for existing products or services; the creation of a new delivery system for existing products or services; the creation of new locations for existing products or services; the creation of a new environment for an existing product or service; or some combination of these possibilities.

The entrepreneur then evaluates his ideas and, if necessary, negotiates with the environment (for example, the inventor) to set the business up.

In stage 2 the entrepreneur spends his time getting the enterprise organized, a process that takes hard work and enthusiasm.

Stage 3 leads to the next crisis: the financial crisis. Getting someone to lend you the funds to take over a franchise or start a new firm is a problem. In effect, the entrepreneur is seeking venture capital, and venture capital firms have been less risk-oriented in recent years than they used to be. Webster calls this the stage of financial jeopardy.

Stage 4 consists of introducing the product, which often includes overdue payables, initial market success, and a lot of hope.

Stage 5 is the next crisis. In Webster's opinion this is *the* time for success or failure. More money problems arise, and the entrepreneur wants to get the financial backers out of the enterprise. Then, if it gets through this "knothole," the enterprise can enter the payoff period.

One of the major problems entrepreneurs have is that of interpersonal relations. Human problems exist in all enterprises. But working for an entrepreneurial firm involves special challenges. In essence, it amounts to this: *Entrepreneurs can be hard to work for.*

Entrepreneurs are hardworking individuals with their own ways of doing things. They tend to look down on people who do not have the courage to be their own boss. So they may be hard on subordinates. It has been argued that entrepreneurs have authority problems because of bad relationships with their fathers. They fear the loss of the business and do not tolerate strong subordinates. According to Robert Bendit, the entrepreneur is characterized by "stubbornness to the point of bull headedness, sullenness, argumentativeness, peevishness, periods of elation and depression, anxiety and insecurity. . . . His insecurities in this high-risk situation are heightened by the uncertainties he faced in the early days of the business. He lives under extraordinary pressures and for this reason, he is likely to overreact. He wants desperately to succeed."

Of course there are difficult bosses in managerial businesses as well, but many entrepreneurs are especially hard to work for. The problem becomes especially acute when the business grows so large that the entrepreneur can no longer effectively make all key decisions himself. This has been called the delegation/leadership crisis: once the firm is off the ground, it is hard to let go of what you have built. Your money and ego are involved. Your name is on the door. Your checking account is paying the bills. It is hard to delegate certain decisions to others—they might ruin the company. Yet if the business grows, the entrepreneur must turn over some authority to others. There are only so many hours in a day, and if the entrepreneur doesn't delegate the least important decisions, or those he knows the least about, the firm will not prosper or grow. Some entrepreneurs "solve" this crisis by stopping growth at the point where they can still control everything. Others go through the crisis and slowly, painfully begin to delegate decisions.

So far we've concentrated on the entrepreneur. Let's turn now to the family business executive.

THE FAMILY BUSINESS EXECUTIVE The family business executive is one who enters a firm founded by a relative while that relative is still running the firm or the ownership of the firm is controlled by his or her family.

There are special relationships involved in a family business that you do not usually find in a managerial firm. Most of the challenges come in the area of interpersonal relations. The key relationships involved are

· those between the entrepreneur and family members working for him or her,
· those between family members working in the firm,
· those between family members working in the firm and nonfamily managers working there.

If the entrepreneur's son, or daughter, or other relative comes to work for him or her, difficult new relationships are established. An organization called the SOBs—Sons of Bosses—meets regularly to exchange experiences about this relationship.

Think about this. You are an employee. Your boss is mean to you that day. You probably curse him and try to forget it. You may learn to hate him. But you live with it and hope you will be transferred. But what if the boss is your father and you aren't going to be transferred? Your frustration can get high, and if you begin to hate your father you face severe guilt feelings.

Look at it from the boss' point of view. You remember your employee when you changed his diapers, spanked him, corrected his algebra, paid his speeding ticket. You know all his weaknesses. Can you trust him with your creation, the extension of your ego, your business?

If it's true that many entrepreneurs had difficult relationships with their fathers, they may have a strong need to show their children that they are competent. They may need to be "the boss" at all times and to continually remind their children who gave them their jobs. This is hardly a prescription for healthy interpersonal relations.

Similar problems can develop if two children enter the business. Rivalry may develop between them, and the entrepreneur, without realizing it, may feed this rivalry. Such rivalries can become intense when the boss has to decide who will take over when he or she dies or retires. This (along with estate taxes) is one of the reasons many entrepreneurial firms sell out.

R. David Yost, himself a boss' son, gives family members who are about to enter a family business some good advice:

· Work harder and longer than anyone else, especially during your first six months.
· Make it a point to work for someone other than a relative in your first job.
· Do not become a spy for the family.
· Refer to your relatives by the same names that everyone else uses.

·Do not bypass the chain of command to get to your relatives.
·Do not make family references on or off the job.
·Do not speak with more authority than you have in your present job.
·Avoid mixing family and business relationships.
·Expect most people to credit your success to being related to the right person.

Of course these problems can be avoided. The Lanes of *Sunset* magazine apparently worked it out. Some parents get along well with their children even under the stressful conditions of a family business. And there is a big advantage in ownership relations *if* the interpersonal relationships can be worked out.

I worked for a family business and left it. Let me give you some advice:

Proposition 3.2.
Never enter the family business directly from school.
Work for another firm for a few years and build your own track record. Then negotiate your way into the business if you are still interested.

The relationships involved are difficult. So you should think carefully before joining the family firm. Consider this: How many sons or daughters succeed at the same jobs as their parents? Think of presidents, pianists, football players, and so on. Generally such a comparison is too hard on the younger person. When just starting out, he or she is compared to a successful, established person. And then if the younger person succeeds at the job there's little recognition. People say, "Of course John made it. His Dad set it up for him."

Thus a crucial variable of success in a family business is family relationships and respect for the newly entering family member.

Other Relationships in Family Businesses

The paternalistic attitude of entrepreneurial and family firms toward their employees is a mixed blessing. Most such firms go out of their way to reward the loyal nonfamily employee who has been with the company a long time. This may mean greater security, benefits, and compensation than are available elsewhere. It often means real human concern for employees' problems and willingness to help out in times of need, a condition rare in managerial firms, especially large ones. On the negative side is the inability to ease out or fire employees who are no longer up to date or doing the job. The entrepreneur or the family members never forget the employee who risked working for them when they started out or in their difficult times. Some employees exploit this feeling and coast for the rest of their lives with little fear of retribution.

A second major challenge for both family and nonfamily executives is intrafamily frictions. In family firms the family may split on key issues, some family executives and board members taking one side, others taking the other side. Managers can be caught in the middle. Harry Levinson describes this situation as follows:

> Perhaps more critical for the health of the business are the factional divisions that spring up in the organization as associates and subordinates choose the family members with whom they want to be identified. (Often, however, those who take sides discover that in a crisis the family unites against "outsiders," including their partisans, who are then viewed as trying to divide the family.)
>
> If the nonfamily employees or board members decide not to become involved in a family fight and withdraw from relations with its members until the conflict is resolved, the work of the organization may be paralyzed. Worse yet, the dispute may eventually embroil the entire organization, resulting in conflicts at the lowest levels, as employees try to cope with the quarrels thrust on them.
>
> Now the business has become a battleground that produces casualties but no peace. Such internecine warfare constitutes a tremendous barrier to communication and frustrates adequate planning and rational decision making.
>
> A business in which numerous members of the family of varying ages and relationships are involved often becomes painfully disrupted around issues of empires and succession. Its units tend to become family-member territories and therefore poorly integrated organizationally, if at all.

Difficulties may also arise when family members who see the business mainly as a source of dividends resist innovations for fear of reducing those dividends. Thus the objectives of the enterprise become opposed to the personal objectives of family members. A final challenge found in the family enterprise is lack of promotion opportunities for the nonfamily executive. He or she knows that certain key positions will never be open to him or her regardless of merit. These positions are reserved for family members, who frequently are younger and less experienced than the nonfamily executive. This is less of a problem when you are working for an entrepreneur—after all, he or she built the business and you respect that. But the entrepreneur's son may not be so easy to respect and in fact may not deserve that respect. The nonfamily executive must not have a strong need for promotional forms of recognition, particularly if the family always practices nepotism.

Some entrepreneurial and family firms become "the employer of last resort" for the whole family. Whether competent or not, hardworking

"... But I'm sure you'll all agree that what our new general manager lacks in ability and experience, he more than compensates for by being my son."

Source: Reproduced by special permission of PLAYBOY Magazine; copyright © 1967 by Playboy.

or not, cousin Charles and niece Mary must be put on the payroll, preferably in high-status, high-paying jobs. This can increase the firm's overhead costs, but even more important, it can disillusion competent employees and cause high turnover.

The special problems just described should not make you think all family firms are unsuccessful. Quite the contrary. This is just another dimension of management. Some examples of successful family enterprises should make this point clear.

Family Business Executives: Some Examples

Family businesses are firms whose ownership control is maintained by the family of the entrepreneur; they are run mostly by family members. Examples include the McIlhennys, the Smuckers, and the Lanes of *Sunset* magazine.

WALTER McILHENNY

Walter Stauffer McIlhenny is president of McIlhenny Company, producers of TABASCO® brand pepper sauce, 50 million bottles of which are sold each year around the world. He is 63 years old and the grandson of the founder. The stock is held entirely by about 55 McIlhenny family members. In 1974 the company, located in Avery Island, Louisiana, diversified the first time in fifty years—into cocktail mix.

The firm is run much as it was fifty years ago. Everyone leaves from 12 to 1 to go home for dinner, and the 6:30 A.M. discussion of the day's work with the foremen is in Cajun patois. Like his predecessors, "Mr. Walter" takes a personal interest in the problems of his employees. The family makes a good living from Walter McIlhenny's management.

THE SMUCKERS

Tucked away in Orville, Ohio, is the headquarters of the J. M. Smucker Company, a $100 million manufacturer of preserves, pickles, and other household products. Paul Smucker heads the firm and is the grandson of the founder. His sons are company executives. A tour through Smucker's plants is enlightening. They are spotless! Large amounts of money are spent to make the product cleaner and more wholesome, even though consumers may not know the difference. Product quality is one of the company's main goals. This quality and cleanliness, together with paternalism toward long-term employees, may be a consequence of the Smuckers' Mennonite heritage.

Many family members are involved in management and are board members, although some stock was sold some years ago. The firm is very conservative in its use of debt. But no one who knows them can help but see the pervasive influence of the Smucker family and its value to the Company.

THE LANES

Bill and Mel Lane are the sons of Laurence Lane, Sr., founder of *Sunset* Magazine. *Sunset* has a circulation of 1,300,000 (1975), mostly in the Western United States. It focuses on gardening, home building, food, travel, and outdoor recreation. Bill Lane runs the magazine, Mel Lane the book side of the business. The firm has annual sales of over $30 million. The stock is held by Bill and Mel Lane, their mother, and their wives and children. The Lanes started working in the business early and were given responsible jobs. Company policies established by the founder, such as refusal to run ads for products such as liquor and tobacco, remain in force.

EXECUTIVES OF FAMILY-INFLUENCED FIRMS

You have probably read that entrepreneurs and owners no longer run large businesses. Large firms are run by professional managers. Just a few years ago Robert Sheehan looked at the *Fortune* 500 firms—the 500 largest in the United States—and found that 150 were influenced in a significant way by a family that provided a few of its executives (often including its president). The family held at least 10 percent of the stock—the largest block. Thus the family had a significant influence on such decisions as dividends, goals, and top executives. Only 1 of the 100 largest firms was controlled by a family or an individual, but 23 family-influenced firms ranked 101–200; 39 ranked 201–300; 38 ranked 301–400; and 37 ranked 401–500.

These firms are likely to continue to have their management tied to the family or family-approved executives. The family is likely to influence company objectives and policies, promotions, and similar issues. These facts make us stop and consider whether managers are all the same. Obviously, if ownership is concentrated like this, they are not. America still provides many examples of individuals who build a business and a legacy for themselves and for their families. A good example is the Watsons of IBM.

THOMAS JOHN WATSON, JR.

All over the world, I.B.M. and the computer have become synonymous. . . . while this was happening, the boss of I.B.M. was the astute, articulate, personable Tom Watson Jr. Like other successors to famous fathers, his achievement tends to be obscured by the assumption that all he had to do was pick the right parents. But Tom Jr.'s I.B.M. was so different from Tom Sr.'s in size, product, and internal character that a lot more than familial descent had to be involved. . . .

Young Tom grew up in New Jersey, got a degree from Brown, and learned to fly. As an officer in the Army Air Corps, one of his jobs was to pilot Major General Follett Bradley on tours of inspection. . . .

The postwar I.B.M. had the brilliant sales staff Watson Sr. had built, but its R. and D. was a minor effort. Tom Jr. remembers that in 1946 his father took him to a part of the I.B.M. building he had never seen before. Behind a door marked "Patent Development" was a scientist with a machine that made calculations electronically a hundred times faster than before. The scientist explained that his computer had no immediate commercial application because the punch cards could not be shuffled mechanically fast enough to keep up. Tom Jr., however, prevailed on his father to produce a few, more for prestige than direct profit.

He remembers a visit a few years later from a friendly vice president of Metropolitan Life, who came with a warning. Several floors of the insurance-company building were filled with company records on I.B.M. cards, and space was getting expensive. The insurance man had heard that there was an electronic tape on which immense amounts of information could be stored. "If somebody gets that tape before you do, I.B.M. will be in trouble."

Young Tom, who was working his way up in the company, redoubled his pressure for the rapid development of electronic calculation. He became president in 1952 and chief executive in 1956, a few weeks before his father's death. His first significant step was to scrap his father's rather autocratic management style, which was retarding decision making. The change was barely in time for the beginning of the computer age, in which I.B.M.'s success would depend not only on its salesmen but even more on a rapidly growing phalanx of scientists and electronic engineers.

By 1956, I.B.M. had opened a clear lead in a market that proved to be far larger than anybody had imagined. But Watson never relaxed. "There never was a day when we thought we were at the end of the road," Watson said. Research teams within the company vied for innovation. "I never felt comfortable," Watson explains, "to have our future depending on one man or one research team." The company learned that competition stimulates scientists as well as salesmen. . . .

Wall Street is awed by the vast wealth Tom Jr. created for his stockholders. The shares were worth $36 billion more when he stepped down than when he took over. By that rough measure, he is the most successful capitalist who ever lived.

SUCCESS IN ENTREPRENEURIAL BUSINESSES

What does it take to be a successful entrepreneur? Most American businesses are entrepreneurial or family businesses. In addition, there is strong evidence that most of the innovations in most businesses come from these firms, and not from managerial firms. You may recall that in Chapter 2, I gave a brief "formula" for managerial success. It is reproduced here in modified form for entrepreneurial firms (see Figure 3.3). Note, first, that the individual factors listed are the same. But there are some differences, too.

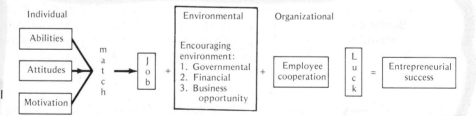

Figure 3.3
Factors in entrepreneurial success.

Entrepreneurial Ability

The first requirement of successful entrepreneurs is managerial entrepreneurial ability. One study of successful entrepreneurs found that they are especially skillful in communication ability and human relations. Another study found that they have the ability to hire and retain excellent employees and the flexibility to change. Other studies have concluded that managerial ability is the key to success. Dun & Bradstreet attributes 91 percent of business failures to lack of managerial ability. Obviously, too, entrepreneurs need the ability to conceptualize and organize a business.

Entrepreneurial Attitudes, Motivation, and Personality

The second requirement is entrepreneurial attitudes, motivation, and personality. Entrepreneurs are different. They work harder and take greater risks. They defer gratification from the present to the future. So entrepreneurial personality and motivation seem to be conducive to entrepreneurial success. Kenneth Lawyer's study of successful entrepreneurs led him to describe them as gamblers, adventurers, people with higher achievement motivation, versatile, self-confident, benevolent despots.

But the entrepreneur also needs an especially helpful environment. Of course managers depend on the environment too, but less so than entrepreneurs. There are three crucial environmental factors.

An Environment Encouraging Success

The third factor in entrepreneurial success is a positive external environment. This includes a government that enacts tax and other policies that allows entrepreneurs to develop, and in some cases provides financial and other forms of encouragement. The helpful government also tries to encourage a successful economic society through the use of modern macroeconomic fiscal and monetary employment and manpower policies. A supportive environment in terms of spouse, family, and friends is also conducive to entrepreneurial success.

Adequate Capital

The fourth factor is capital. No business can succeed without the money to buy materials, hire workers, rent or buy a workplace, pay marketing expenses, and so on. Entrepreneurs are especially vulnerable financially.

A Genuine Business Opportunity

The final success factor is the entrepreneurial idea. Successful entrepreneurs know their markets. Business opportunities exist either in genuinely new opportunities or in competing with ineffective firms. Note that since the entrepreneur has no hierarchical superior, that factor is removed from the model.

Entrepreneurship and You

As a potential entrepreneur, you affect all these factors to some degree. You can develop entrepreneurial personality and motivation. You can also develop managerial ability. You have less effect on government policy, but you can join with others to influence the government. With the right opportunity and business plan, you can get the necessary capital.

Group Entrepreneurship

Much of what has just been said applies to groups of entrepreneurs as well as to individuals. These days, it is not unusual for the employees of a firm to buy it from its corporate owners. For example, in 1975, 500 employees of the South Bend Lathe Company bought it from its owner, Amsted Industries, for $10 million cash. As the *Wall Street Journal* explained,

> They used a vehicle called an Employee Stock Ownership Plan, or ESOP, an employee benefit device similar to a pension or profit-sharing plan. Enjoying many of the same tax benefits of pension funds, the South Bend Lathe ESOP was able to borrow the full purchase price to buy the unit. The $10 million borrowing will be paid back over a number of years out of the enterprise's profits. Thus, the workers eventually will end up with 100% ownership of South Bend Lathe, though they didn't put up any capital in the acquisition. . . .
>
> Under ESOP, principal and interest payments on the debt are tax-deductible, a distinct tax advantage.

The factors I have described as essential to the success of a single entrepreneurship apply equally well to group entrepreneurships. The firm must have enough money, a business opportunity, and the right environment. And it must have managerial talent.

SUCCESS IN FAMILY BUSINESSES What does it take to be a successful family business executive like Paul Smucker or Thomas Watson, Jr.? The family business executive is in a position somewhere between the entrepreneur and the manager. Figure 3.4 makes this clear.

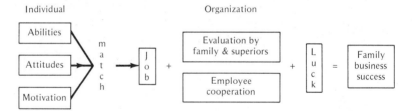

Figure 3.4
Factors in family business success.

A family business needs all the ingredients of managerial success. The main modification is that the entrepreneurial personality of its leaders begins to blend into managerial personality over time. A second major change is in organizational factors. The family business executive must be well evaluated by superiors and/or the family members directly involved in management or ownership of the enterprise. This factor was discussed earlier in the chapter.

SUMMARY AND IMPLICATIONS This chapter was designed to introduce you to the world of entrepreneurs—the individuals who start hundreds of thousands of new businesses each year. Entrepreneurs are more prevalent today than seventy years ago, in spite of the commonly expressed notion to the contrary.

You learned some things about how entrepreneurs differ from managers. In Chapter 4 we will discuss how their personalities differ and in Chapter 5 how their motivations differ.

The chapter revealed some characteristics of entrepreneurs that set them apart from managers: early indication of entrepreneurial thrust, inability to work for others over the long run, self-employed parents, unwillingness to retire, and so forth. These characteristics apply largely to male entrepreneurs. Female entrepreneurs show certain differences; for example, they appear to be able to work for others rather successfully.

Entrepreneurs face different problems from those experienced by managers, such as conceptualizing the business or dealing with start-up problems. The most crucial problems arise when the firm grows too big for the entrepreneur to manage it alone.

The chapter also examined the neglected role of the family business executive and the family executive in a family-influenced business. Such executives are much more prevalent than is commonly acknowledged. The special problems they face include interaction with the nonfamily employee who feels slighted, and interaction with family owners and/or managers in business and personal relationships.

The chapter closed by contrasting the factors that contribute to entrepreneurial and family business success with those discussed in Chapter 2. The entrepreneur does not need to worry about a superior's evaluation, but does need to have a favorable governmental, financial, and business environment. The entrepreneur also needs entrepreneurial attitudes, motivation, and personality.

The family business executive needs the managerial success factors plus the interpersonal skills to deal with family owners and managers.

This chapter completes the introductory section of the book. We turn now to specific managerial abilities and how to develop them. We begin by looking at an important resource: the people at your workplace (including you).

Questions for Review

1. At a party you meet a geologist. She asks you what you do. You tell her you work for your uncle's newspaper chain. She says, "Oh, then you've got it made!" How do you respond?
2. In what ways are managers and entrepreneurs the same? different? Why?
3. Why do men and women choose to become entrepreneurs when it is so risky?
4. Discuss the most successful entrepreneurial and family firms in your city and state. How much longer will they be successful?
5. "Entrepreneurial and family firms have seen their day. They are no longer of significance to our society." Discuss.
6. Back at that party an entrepreneur hears that you are taking a business course and hope to become an entrepreneur. He says, "Why are you going to school for that? Success cannot be taught in class." Discuss.

7. Distinguish entrepreneurial, small-business, family-run, and family-influenced firms. How are they similar? different?

8. Discuss the early phases of entrepreneurial business.

9. What special problems do entrepreneurs face that managers do not?

10. What special problems do family business executives face that managers do not?

11. Would you like to work for an entrepreneurial or family firm if you were

     a. the boss' son or daughter

     b. the boss' nephew or niece

     c. not related to the entrepreneur or family

Why or why not?

12. What are the best predictors of success for entrepreneurial and family firms?

References

Introduction

Cole, Arthur, *Business Enterprise in Its Social Setting* (Cambridge, Mass.: Harvard University Press, 1959).

Eden, Don, "Self-Employed Workers: A Comparison Group for Organizational Psychology," *Organizational Behavior and Human Performance,* 9 (1973): 186–214.

Knoepfel, Rudolf, "American and European Entrepreneurs and Managers," *Managerial Planning,* November-December 1974, pp. 1–14.

Vesper, Karl, "Entrepreneurship, a Fast Emerging Area in Management Studies," *Journal of Small Business Management,* 12, no. 4 (October 1974): 8–15.

Entrepreneurs and Managers

Anyon, G. Jay, *Entrepreneurial Dimensions of Management* (Wynnewood, Pa.: Livingston Publishing, 1973).

Collins, Orvis, and Moore, David, *The Organization Makers* (New York: Appleton-Century-Crofts, 1970).

Deeks, John, "Educational and Occupational Histories of Owner-Managers and Managers," *Journal of Management Studies,* May 1972, pp. 127–149.

Giesbrecht, Martin, "Entrepreneurship vs. Modern Management," *MSU Business Topics,* Winter 1968, pp. 23–31.

Kuhn, James, and Berg, Ivar, "Businessmen: Entrepreneurs or Bureaucrats," in *Values in a Business Society* (New York: Harcourt Brace Jovanovich, 1968), pp. 183–190.

The full issue of *The MBA,* June-July, 1973.

Mancuso, J. R., "What It Takes to Be an Entrepreneur," *Journal of Small Business Management,* 2, no. 4 (October 1974): 16–22.

Nicholson, Edward, Jr., et al., "Social and Attitudinal Differences Between Entrepreneur and Business Hierarchs," *Proceedings, Southern Management Association,* 1973, pp. 182–193.

Schreier, James, *The Female Entrepreneur* (Milwaukee: Center for Venture Management, 1975).

Smith, Norman, *The Entrepreneur and His Firm* (Lansing: Michigan State University, 1967).

Summer, Charles, Jr., "The Managerial Mind," *Harvard Business Review,* 37, no. 1 (January 1959): 69–78.

Susbauer, Jeffrey, *The Technical Enterprise Formation Process,* Unpublished Ph.D. Thesis, University of Texas, 1968.

Zaleznik, Abraham, and De Vrie, Manfred, *Power and the Corporate Mind* (Boston: Houghton Mifflin, 1975), chap. 10.

The Significance of Entrepreneurs to Society

O'Connell, John, "Still a Tiny Piece of the Action," *The MBA,* January 1976.

Robertson, Ross, "The Small Business Ethic in America," in Deanne Carson, ed., *The Vital Majority* (Washington, D.C.: U.S. Government Printing Office, 1973).

Entrepreneurs: Some Examples

Conte, John, "Black is Bountiful," *Wall Street Journal,* January 15, 1976.

Libman, Joan, "Going It Alone: Female Entrepreneurs Like Del Goetz Make Man's Work Pay Off," *Wall Street Journal,* August 22, 1975.

The Entrepreneurial Job

Terkel, Studs, *Working* (New York: Pantheon, 1974).

Wilkie, Roy, and Young, James, "Managerial Behavior in the Furniture and Timber Industries," *International Studies of Management and Organization,* 2, no. 1 (Spring 1972): 65–84.

Entrepreneurship: Learned or Inherited?

Anyon, G. Jay, *Entrepreneurial Dimensions of Management* (Wynnewood, Pa.: Livingston Publishing, 1973).

Baumback, Clifford, et al., *How to Organize and Operate a Small Business* (Englewood-Cliffs, N.J.: Prentice-Hall, 1973).

Durand, Douglas, "Training and Development of Entrepreneurs," *Journal of Small Business Management,* 12, no. 4 (October 1974): 23–26.

Kierulff, Herbert, "Can Entrepreneurs Be Developed? *MSU Business Topics,* Winter 1974, pp. 39–44.

McClelland, David, "Achievement Motivation Can Be Developed," *Harvard Business Review,* November-December 1965.

McClelland, David, et al., *Motivating Economic Achievement* (New York: Free Press, 1969).

Mancuso, Joseph, *Fun and Guts* (Boston: Addison Wesley, 1973).

Roscow, James P., "Can Entrepreneurship Be Taught?" *The MBA,* June-July 1973, pp. 12, 16, 50, 51.

Steinmetz, Lawrence, et al., *Managing the Small Business* (Homewood, Ill.: Richard I. Irwin, 1968).

Vesper, Karl, "A Multidisciplinary Experiment in Management Education," *Proceedings, Academy of Management,* 1973, pp. 284–290.

Challenges Faced by Entrepreneurial Firms

Bendit, Robert, "Working with the Entrepreneur," Periodic Report 47 (New York: Vernon Psychological Laboratory, August 1970): 2–5.

Buchele, Robert, *Business Policy in Growing Firms* (San Francisco: Chandler, 1967).

Camenzind, Hans, "The Agony and Ecstasy of a Startup," *The MBA*, October, 1974.

Filley, Alan, and House, Robert, *Managerial Process and Organizational Behavior* (Chicago: Scott Foresman, 1976), chap. 22.

Henderson, Richard, "The Best of Two Worlds: The Entrepreneurial Manager," *Journal of Small Business Management* 12, no. 4 (October 1974): 4–7.

Klein, Frederick, "Getting Started," *Wall Street Journal*, November 6, 1974.

Lamont, Lawrence, "What Entrepreneurs Learn From Experience," *Journal of Small Business Management*, July 1972, pp. 36–41.

Mayer, Kurt, and Goldstein, Sidney, *The First Two Years: Problems of Small Firm Growth and Survival* (Washington, D.C.: Small Business Administration, 1961).

Perrigo, A. E. B., "Developing Corporate Strategy for Small Businesses," *Journal of Business Policy*, 3, no. 4 (Summer 1973): 57–63.

Webster, Frederick, "A Model for New Venture Interaction," *Academy of Management Review*, 1, no. 1 (January 1976): 26–37.

The Family Business Executive

Bird, Monroe, "Major Problem Areas as Perceived by Presidents of Small Manufacturing Firms," *Academy of Management Journal*, 16, no. 3 (September 1973): 510–515.

Dalaba, O. G., "Lengthening Your Shadow," *Journal of Small Business Management*, July 1973, pp. 17–21.

Donnelley, Robert, "The Family Business," *Harvard Business Review*, July-August, 1964.

Groseclose, Everett, "You Have Problems? Consider the Plight of Nation's SOBs," *Wall Street Journal*, March 20, 1975.

Klein, Howard, *Stop! You're Killing the Business* (New York: Mason and Lipscomb, 1974).

Levinson, Harry, "Conflicts That Plague Family Businesses," *Harvard Business Review*, March-April 1971, pp. 90–98.

Schwartz, Edward, "Will Your Business Die with You?" *Harvard Business Review*, September-October 1954, pp. 110–120.

Sheehan, Robert, "Proprietors in the World of Business," *Fortune*, 75 (June 15, 1967).

Tilles, Seymour, "Survival Strategies for Family Firms," *European Business*, April 1970, pp. 9–17.

Trow, Donald, "Executive Succession in Small Companies," *Administrative Science Quarterly*, September 1961, pp. 228–237.

Yost, R. David, "Family Affair," *The MBA, November 1975, pp. 11–14.*

Success in Entrepreneurial/ Family Businesses

Baumbach, et al., op. cit.

Breman, J. C., "Deferred Gratification, Entrepreneurial Behavior, and Economic Growth in Non-Western Societies," *Sociologica Neerlandica*, 5, no. 1 (Spring 1969): 15–34.

Cochran, Thomas, "The Entrepreneur in Economic Change," *Behavioral Science*, 9, no. 2 (April 1964).

Doctors, Samuel, and Lockwood, Sharon, "New Directions for Minority Enterprise," *Law and Contemporary Problems,* Winter 1971.

Dun and Bradstreet, Business Education Division, *Patterns for Success in Managing a Business,* Business Series no. 2 (New York, 1967).

Friedlander, Frank, and Pickle, Hal, "Components of Effectiveness in Small Organizations," *Administrative Science Quarterly,* September 1968, pp. 289–304.

Ghorpade, Jai, "Organizational Ownership Patterns and Efficiency," *Academy of Management Journal,* 16, no. 1 (1973): 136–148.

Lawyer, Kenneth, Characteristics of Small Business Success," *Journal of Business Management,* 2 (July 1964): 3–9.

Lawyer, Kenneth, et al., "Small Business Success," Washington, D.C.: U.S. Government Printing Office, 1963.

Pickle, Hal, "Personality and Success," Washington, D.C.: U.S. Government Printing Office, 1964.

Redlich, Fritz, "Economic Development, Entrepreneurship, and Psychologism: A Social Scientist's Critique of McClelland's Achieving Society," *Explorations in Entrepreneurial History,* 2d ser., no. 1 (1963–1964), pp. 10–35.

Wainer, Herbert, and Rubin, Irwin, "Motivation of Research and Development Entrepreneurs: Determinents of Company Success," *Journal of Applied Psychology,* 53, no. 3 (1969).

Westfall, Steven, "Stimulating Corporate Entrepreneurship in U.S. Industry," *Academy of Management Journal,* 12, no. 2 (1969): 235–246.

PART 2

UNDERSTANDING PEOPLE AT WORK

In Part 1 you learned something about the work life of the central character of this book: you, the manager or entrepreneur. Now it is time to give you some information on how to improve your knowledge, skills, and attitudes so that you can be successful as a manager or entrepreneur. Part 2 consists of two chapters on individuals' aptitudes, abilities, learning, perception, attitudes, values, personality, and motivation (Chapters 4 and 5), and a chapter on groups and how to understand and manage them (Chapter 6).

CUSTOMERS

SUPPLIERS

COMPETITORS

COMMUNITY

GOVERNMENT

4
Managerial
skills

- Management of
  environmental relations
- Control and conflict
  management
- Organizing
- Decision making
- Planning

3
Interpersonal
skills of
managers

- Managerial development
- Communicating
- Influencing peers,
  superiors, and others
- Leadership: Influencing
  employees

2
Understanding
people
at work

- Individuals and groups
- Motivation
- Personality
- Attitudes/values
- Perception
- Learning
- Aptitudes and abilities

1
Introduction
to the
managerial
task

- Job of entrepreneur
  and family business
  executive
- Managerial job

Part 2 is concerned with helping you understand the people you will encounter at work and your own work behavior as well.

The model highlights these aspects of management. We will discuss employees' abilities and aptitudes, how they learn, how they perceive their work experiences. And we will focus on the attitudes and values they develop about work, how they are motivated, and how all of these factors add up to an individual personality as it is manifested at work. Note that the society and other factors in the environment influence employee attitudes, values, and motivation.

We will also discuss what happens when individuals with different attitudes, perceptions, motivations, values, and personalities interact as a work group—when they work well together and when they do not, when they work with managers and when they work against them. All of this is so you will be a more effective manager, entrepreneur, or family business executive, for most of you will spend most of your time getting things done through other people. Generally speaking, you will get more done, and get it done better, if you understand people.

CHAPTER 4

UNDERSTANDING YOURSELF AND OTHERS AT WORK

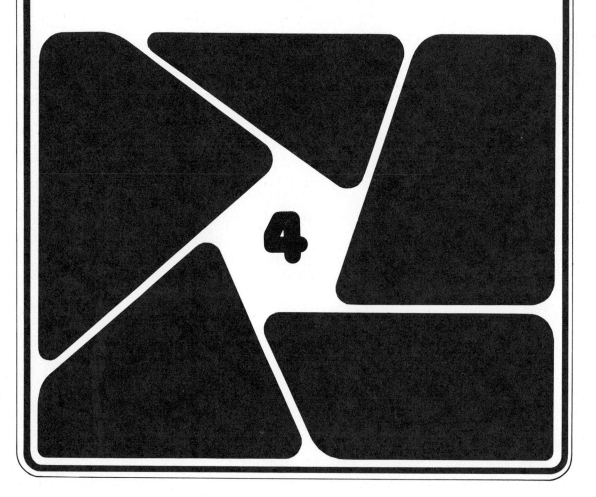

Learning Objectives

1. To learn the different ways people explain human behavior.
2. To understand how the personalities of people differ and how these differences affect the manager.
3. To understand individual differences in ability and aptitude and how managers cope with them.
4. To learn how people perceive work and people at work and how managers are affected by these perceptions.
5. To learn how attitudes and values affect the manager's work life.

Chapter Outline

An Introduction to Human Behavior
Human Nature
Environmental Influences
The Uniqueness of the Individual
Personality and Human Identity
Freud's Theory of Personality
A Freudian Analysis of Entrepreneurial Personality
Jung's Theory of Personality
Kelly's Cognitive Personality Theory
Humanistic Personality Theory
Personality and the Manager
Abilities and Aptitudes
Where Do Abilities and Aptitudes Come From?
Ability, Aptitude, and Management
Learning
Learning and Development
Learning in Adults
Managerial Implications of Learning
Perception
Perception of Objects
Perception of People
Managerial Implications
Attitudes and Values
Work Attitudes
Attitude Conflicts
Managerial Implications
Summary

This chapter is designed to help you understand the people you will work with: employees, superiors, peers, clients, and yourself. This will help you be more successful as an entrepreneur or manager.

For most managers, success or failure depends more on their interpersonal skills than on any other skill. This is because although you need all kinds of resources to get the job done, you spend most of your time with people (as you learned in Chapters 2 and 3) and because people manage the firm's other resources.

Your experiences with people at work can be useful or difficult. This chapter is designed to help you understand some of the problems involved in interpersonal relationships.

For example,

·Mary works for you at the brewery. She has been there for some years. Recently you moved her to a new job. She is not performing well.
·You are thinking about changing the organization structure of your bank. Before you do, you want to know if this will improve the performance and satisfaction of your employees.
·You have a salesman working for you who you believe has great potential. But he does not seem to be working to his potential.

With the information in chapters 4 and 5 you should be able to determine whether Mary's problem is an ability problem, a motivation problem, a learning problem, or another kind of problem. These chapters will also make you aware of the potential impact of perceptual reality on your reorganization plan and the potential motivational impact on the salesman's behavior.

AN INTRODUCTION TO HUMAN BEHAVIOR

Before you can understand how and why human beings behave the way they do in the workplace, you need to understand some basic ideas about human beings. But three basic assumptions should be understood before we go on.

Human Nature

Many models of human nature have been developed by philosophers, historians, theologians, economists, psychologists, psychiatrists, sociologists, anthrologists, and others. In many ways these models are in conflict, and the one you accept will have a lot to do with how you deal with people at work and in your personal life. It is impossible to adequately summarize all of these, but I will sketch some of the major differences among them.

Some theorists see the human being as very rational, a sort of walking electronic calculator. Others view the human being as primarily emotional and intuitive. Some theorists (extreme ethologists) see human beings as animals who respond to situations instinctively. Others view them as having free will to respond or not respond to stimuli.

There are differences in emphasis on the amount of impact the environment has on human actions. According to some, the human being is a piece of clay molded by the environment. Pavlov, Watson, and Skinner talk of environmental conditioning of behavior. Other psychologists imply that the environment is not a significant influence on behavior.

In this book we assume that the human being is both rational and emotional. Centuries before Christ or Moses, Aristotle described the human being as a combination of the rational and the emotional. More recently, a very conservative philosopher, Hegel, and a radical thinker, Marx, elaborated on and supported the view that we are a balance of reason and emotion. As we will see shortly, Freud described human behavior as deriving from conscious motives (rational) and unconscious motives (emotional). In sum, a few choices that lead to behavior might be entirely rational or entirely emotional. But most human choices result from a mixture of rational and emotional influences.

Environmental Influences

We also assume that a person acts in response to his or her own internal inclinations, choices, *and* environmental influences. Kurt Lewin stated this principle as Behavior = F (P, E): behavior is a function of the person and the environment. Sometimes the person's needs and choices predominate and lead him or her to act. At other times environmental forces strongly influence behavior. But all behavior is caused by a *combination* of the personal consent of the actor plus environmental influences.

One of the most significant environmental influences is other human beings. We are all social animals. There are a few people who can develop in isolation—most developed religions can point to mystics who worship, work, and write alone in the desert or on a mountaintop. But most of us develop our abilities, motives, perceptions, and personalities as a consequence of interacting with others. Managers need to remember that although they may believe they are dealing with an individual, this individual will respond partly because of feedback from his or her work group.

The Uniqueness of the Individual

Our final assumption is the belief that each individual is unique. A human being thinks and acts the way he or she does because of

1 the personality he or she has or develops.

2 the abilities he or she has or learns.

3 the attitudes he or she has or develops.

4 the motives he or she has or develops and continues to develop.

Because individuals are unique, understanding human behavior is not easy. Many people are quite complex. Yet a successful manager must try to understand each person he or she works with, looking at that person as an individual with unique abilities, perceptions, learning potential, and personality. The successful manager tries to plan, communicate, and control in the light of these characteristics. And therefore he or she must learn to manage differently in response to differences in employees, superiors, and peers. This is part of the contingency approach to management.

But this is a very general treatment of how and why humans are different. We now turn to an examination of differences in personality, abilities, learning, perception, attitudes, and values and how these affect the manager's job.

PERSONALITY AND HUMAN IDENTITY

Our discussion of human behavior begins with the concept of personality. Surely you know people who have lots of "personality." In this sense the word means something like "outgoing, invigorating interpersonal abilities." But to psychologists and management specialists *personality* means something else.

> **PERSONALITY**
> Personality is a pattern of stable states and characteristics of a person that influence his or her behavior toward goal achievement. Each person has unique ways of protecting these states.

I will be describing many aspects of these "stable states": perception, learning, attitudes, values, motivation. Think of personality as a person's *unifying mechanism*—that which provides identity and allows the person to act to achieve his or her goals.

There is much debate about the development of personality. Various experts have argued that personality is influenced genetically (through heredity); by internal mental development; by interaction with others in the family, in the peer group, and at work; and by the general environment and culture. For example, theorists like Pavlov, Watson, Skinner, Dollar, and Miller emphasize external influences on personality development.

Note that the personality is viewed as more or less *stable* and *consistent* over time. Obviously the personality changes and develops over time, but it tends to evolve gradually.

You will understand yourself and your employees better and thus be a better manager if you understand personality. There are many theories of personality, but only a few of the major ones can be discussed here.

Freud's Theory of Personality
Although some think Freud has gone out of style, he remains the most influential theorist in the area of personality. Freud's theory is very complex; only the highlights can be sketched here.

According to Freud, the mind is composed of the following:

1 The preconscious: items in the mind that can be recognized only through Freud's association method.

2 The conscious: thoughts, feelings, and desires that we can learn about ourselves through introspection.

3 The unconscious: ideas and wishes that cannot be learned through introspection but can be determined from dreams, hypnotism, and Freudian therapeutic techniques.

Freud taught that we act in response to conscious *and* unconscious motives. The conscious is guided by a reasoned reality principle. The unconscious is guided by a hedonistic pleasure principle. Freud and most of the psychoanalytic school teach that the personality of the human being develops out of conflict. At first Freud taught that conflicts took place between the sex instinct and ego instincts (such as hunger and pain). Later he argued that the conflict that influences personality development is between the life instinct (a combination of sex and ego instincts) and the death or destruction instinct.

Various theorists have argued that the personality has levels. In the eighteenth century the Anglican bishop and philosopher Joseph Butler argued that the human being is guided by three levels in the self:

1 primary: instincts

2 regulating/controlling principles: benevolence, cool self-love

3 conscience: the ultimate controlling principle

That is, the self at its "basest" level relies on instincts; as it develops, it begins to regulate the instincts, and conscience regulates the "regulators."

Freud developed a similar organization of the personality. At the base is the *id*, primitive, instinctual, governed by the pleasure principles, greedy. Since the id is not rational, it is childish, never satisfied, demanding, destructive of others and self, often greedy and brutal. Normal adults act in response to the id quite infrequently. When they do, they normally tend to place the id in the third person or explain the act away: "I was not myself" or "It made me angry."

As a person learns to separate unreality from reality in childhood, the *ego* develops. This is the self-oriented "executive of the mind"—rational and logical, but providing for the id's needs, given the circumstances. In essence, the ego is a mediator between the realities of the world and the id's demands. The ego also regulates mental and motor functioning, integrates inner motives and conficting needs, defends the person by using defense mechanisms, and masters the person's goals. The ego develops by creating an effective perceptual system that enables the person to adjust to the *reality principle:* awareness of things, tolerance of tension, expectation of punishment, and the associated inhibition of action. Although the ego contains no energy, Freud contended that it could control behavior by means of the approach-avoidance conflict, turning the energy of the id against itself.

As a child develops and absorbs parental and cultural attitudes and values, he or she develops a *superego* (consisting of the conscience and the ego ideal) that tells him or her what behavior is acceptable. The superego may be quite strict; it may even be committed to the destruction or close control of the id. It operates in terms of what it has been taught to be right or correct and not just out of fear of punishment. If people violate the superego's prohibitions, they may punish themselves (feel guilty).

Freud said that the ego's role was to mediate between the id and the superego. A personality becomes sick when either the id or the superego becomes dominant, a condition that results in a personality disorder. When too much energy is expended by the ego in mediating between the id and the superego, a person's work or personal development will suffer.

The id, ego, and superego are in more or less constant conflict. When the ego feels pressure it adjusts by means of a series of defense mechanisms. In this way it protects the conscious against the unconscious. Four common defense mechanisms are

> **1** *Repression.* One of the less useful defense mechanisms is repression: forcing the concern from the conscious mind, or deliberately "forgetting" the issue. Since problems cannot be solved this way, repression simply postpones them and does not aid personality development. Sometimes a person employs perceptual defenses in the same way.
>
> **2** *Rationalization.* Instead of facing up to the problem in question, the ego may redefine the situation and thus prevent it from reaching the conscious mind. Essentially the ego finds excuses or explains away the problem. Thus this mechanism is not conducive to problem solution or personality development either.
>
> **3** *Reaction formation.* If a person recognizes that the existence of a certain problem is uncomfortable, the ego may repress it and sub-

stitute its opposite. For example, if a person dislikes Germans but is upset by this feeling, he or she may claim to like Germans.

4 *Projection and introjection.* The ego is using projection when a person denies that he or she has a particular emotion or acts in a particular way and "blames" it on something (or someone) else. This normally takes place when admitting the feeling or action would cause the person serious anxiety. Projection is a safety valve, but it does not help the person adjust to personality development. In the opposite function, introjection, the person "takes in" something from the outside, makes it his or her own (*my* country, *my* teacher), and sees it as part of himself or herself. Sociologists call this process *internalization* (especially of values), and it is an important part of the socialization process—growing up.

Freud contended that the person can be understood by understanding how energy affects personality and behavior. Energy is contained in the *libido* (drive), the life-maintaining, pleasure-seeking energy that becomes attached to or withdrawn from various goals or objects. According to Freud, the human personality could be understood by examining the amount of libido attached to or withdrawn from specific objects and activities (likes and dislikes). Tension can arise from the environment or be innate (an impetus). The person seeks the objects necessary to remove tension and restore himself or herself to equilibrium. In an infant, tension requires immediate attention if equilibrium is to be restored. As the personality develops, the reality principle comes into play: the person learns that postponement of immediate gratification may lead to greater gratification later on.

How can this analysis of personality be applied to management? Let's look at one attempt.

A Freudian Analysis of Entrepreneurial Personality

Abraham Zaleznik and Manfred DeVries have written a Freudian analysis of managers and entrepreneurs. They have found that many entrepreneur's fathers had rejected them, left home, or died. This led to a childhood characterized by poverty and deprivation.

In Freudian analysis, the father must be present in order for full development of the personality to take place. For example, the father is a key figure in the development of the superego. With the father gone, the mother often plays a mixed role, threatening the child with a remote or rejecting father or father substitute. The child fears inconsistent or rejecting behavior and feels anxiety or guilt.

Frequently the future entrepreneur fulfills the needs for parental reward in fantasies or uses reaction formation as a strategy for failing to identify with the father. Because of frustrations experienced early in life, the entrepreneur has persistent feelings of dissatisfaction, powerlessness, and rejection leading to rage over loss or abandonment. The lack of integration of the superego and feelings of rejection by the father are translated into inability to relate to superiors (father figures) or difficulty in playing the role of superior (where the entrepreneur must play "father").

The entrepreneur seeks satisfaction and approval in business accomplishments, but such accomplishments never fully replace the social support, esteem, and admiration lost through the father's rejection of the child.

Because the firm is the source of the entrepreneur's status and self-esteem, it's very difficult if not impossible for him or her to retire or delegate authority, for fear of returning to the deprived period of youth. Because of the entrepreneur's early deprivation, Zaleznik and DeVries argue that the entrepreneurial firm is "emotionally charged" because, in effect, the entrepreneur is unsure of himself or herself and needs reinforcement.

This analysis does not have to be accepted in its entirety. But it seems to explain some of the problems many entrepreneurs face early in life and to show why they work so hard and are so "driven" to achieve and hold onto success. It seems reasonable to assume that without parental approval and support during the crucial early period of life, such behavior could result from an effort to compensate for this loss.

Jung's Theory of Personality

Carl Jung, the best known of Freud's students, broke with Freud and developed his own theory of personality and human behavior. Jung's approach is called analytical psychology.

Jung contended that the personality has four functions: thinking, feeling, intuition, and sensation. By *feeling* Jung means the capacity to evaluate others. *Intuition* is the facility that perceives unconscious realities.

People can be classified as *extraverts* (sociable, outgoing, optimistic) or *introverts* (less sociable, absorbed in inner life, withdrawn). Few people are completely extroverts (or introverts)—but one personality type or the other normally dominates. As Alastair MacIntyre puts it,

> The extravert in whom thinking is dominant will be fascinated by facts and concerned to order them rationally, will tend to underrate the emotions and thus be subject from time to time to uncontrolled and perhaps unrecognized bursts of emotion. The introverted thinking type is one in which facts are never of value for their own sake but only in relation to the creative inner theorizing of the thinker. Both types of thinking are accompanied by an undeveloped feeling function, for thinking and feeling are essentially opposite and even inimical. Sensation and intuition are paired in the same way.

Jung used these concepts to explain how the unconscious part of the personality influences us to act. The conscious part of the personality is the extroverted, thinking part. The unconscious part consists of emotions, ideas, and dreams, which Jung called complexes. Complexes are repressed from the conscious because they are too painful to face.

The unconscious develops as a consequence of our own past history plus concepts inherited from human history. Jung argues that our unconscious consists of the *persona* (socially accepted mask for the ego) and the *shadow* (the hidden desires, emotions, and attitudes we experience in dreams as hostile figures). The shadow, when it is unrecognized, can be dangerous to the personality.

In addition to the persona and the shadow, we have the *animus* (the male perception of the female) or *anima* (the female perception of the male). This is an inherited collective image or archtype. To quote MacIntyre again,

> What matters to the child is not merely how his mother treats him; his experience of the mother is produced both by the mother's actual behavior and by the way his anima determines his view of and feelings about her. Jung connected the anima especially with the function of feeling, the animus with that of thinking, supposing that thinking is more likely to be dominant in the man, feeling in the woman.

In sum, each person has an ego (the actual center of the conscious) and a self (the potential center of the unconscious). When both are joined (usually after one is 40), the person has come to terms with himself or herself and the self is the center of the personality.

Kelly's Cognitive Personality Theory

The most prominent of the cognitive theorists is George Kelly. Kelly sees the human being as a scientist who attempts to predict and control future events. The individual experiences events, compares them with other experiences, and formulates *constructs* (ways of looking at events) he or she can use to predict the future. The person is "free" to the extent that he or she can change those constructs, and "determined" in that he or she is guided by those constructs. The human personality, Kelly contends, is a person's construct system, which he or she uses to interpret the world. A person can be understood in terms of that person's view of the world. Kelly's Role Construct Repertory Test, or Rep Test, was developed to determine the individual's world view.

According to Kelly, the basic constructs that form the core of the individual's personality are surrounded by peripheral constructs, which vary by the degree to which the person is willing to change them. All constructs are dichotomous; that is, the person fits the world to a set of opposite (dichotomous) ideas. For example, black-white is a dichotomy including such intermediate positions as slightly black and slightly white. These constructs are verbal (clear words with easily understandable meaning) or preverbal (learned prior to language and hard to explain).

Kelly maintains that a person is constantly trying to expand his construct system so that he or she can operate in the world more effectively. The person examines a number of constructs about a problem, narrows these down to the most relevant alternatives, and then chooses the best one. Anxiety, fear, and threat come into play when the person realizes that his constructs are not accurate pictures of the world and should be changed. When fear or threat is too great, he or she submerges one end of the dichotomy and sees only one way of looking at the phenomenon. This can lead to ineffective performance or, ultimately, to illness. Developed individuals are those with complex construct systems that can deal with change in a complicated world. All have built-in motivation to achieve greater and more useful construct systems.

Kelly's theories systematically explain the internal differences in people's ways of perceiving the world in which they act. His view of why people act and how they grow is not as well developed.

Humanistic Personality Theory
Other theorists such as Rollo May, Gordon Allport, Abraham Maslow, and Carl Rogers have developed a "humanistic" approach to personality. They believe that the conscious is more important than the unconscious and that self-actualization is the highest need of the human being.

Rogers' theory contends that

1 The self is something one can examine. Personality is best understood when one understands the self-concept. The self is formed by interaction with others and with the environment.

2 The ego is the part of the self that protects and organizes it.

3 Several major needs are positive regard for others, self-regard, and self-actualizations—the need for self-fulfillment.

Personality and the Manager
I have just described four somewhat different, somewhat overlapping theories of personality. After reading this section you should see many possible applications of these theories. As a potential manager or entrepreneur, understanding your own and your employees' personalities can make you more competent in the area of interpersonal relations. And this means understanding attitudes, motivation, learning, and other aspects of personality.

Your relationship to your parents (and parent substitutes) is of major significance in personality development. If you are a parent, you should recognize how serious a responsibility this is. To the extent that the personality is influenced by interactions with others such as supervisors, you should recognize how significant an impact you can have on the personality development of employees and peers. Let us move on now to a discussion of an important part of the human personality: abilities and aptitudes.

ABILITIES AND APTITUDES
Abilities are skills. Aptitudes are inclinations and *potential* skills.

ABILITIES AND APTITUDES

Individuals do not all possess exactly the same abilities and aptitudes. You have probably noticed that some tasks come easier for you than for others. Perhaps math comes easily to you and languages come more easily to your friend. Some people seem to grasp mechanical concepts readily. Others never quite understand them. Psychologists call this diversity in abilities and aptitudes individual differences. Just as we differ physically, we differ in relative amounts of ability and aptitudes. We also have similarities—for example, the members of a family may have the same hair and eye color, physique, perhaps the same accent.

Psychologists have spent many years studying similarities and differences in such areas as

Mechanical ability—perception and manipulation of spatial relations; ability to visualize how parts fit together into a whole; comprehension of mechanical relationships.

Motor coordination ability—why some people have excellent motor coordination while others do not.

Mental abilities—general intelligence; logic or reasoning; verbal ability; numerical ability.

Creative abilities—musical and artistic abilities; psychophysical abilities; esthetic judgment.

Psychologists have found that if the group is large enough, the distribution of abilities will fit the "normal curve." That is, about half the people are near average on any specific ability, 25 percent above average, and 25 percent below average.

The question has arisen, Do these differences exist systematically? That is, do women have greater ability in certain areas than men; blacks more than whites; the old more than the young? Various studies allege to have found such differences. But as Norman Maier says,

> Whether or not the distributions of ability between sexes and races differ and whether or not differences reported are due to biological, cultural or educational factors are questions that cannot be answered at this time. For practical purposes, the answers would prove of little value. The differences within a race and whether a sex would show normal distribution and if any differences in shape between these distributions did occur, it would be slight. . . . Race and sex offer no meaningful clues for selection since individual differences are the important variables.

In sum, each of us has abilities and aptitudes. But they differ a great deal from those of others.

Where Do Abilities and Aptitudes Come From?

Various experts have argued about the sources of abilities and aptitudes. On one side are some ethologists, biologists, and psychologists, who argue that aptitudes are transmitted through the genes—that we inherit our abilities from our ancestors. How better to explain the Bachs' musical abilities? At the other extreme are many sociologists, psychologists, and anthropologists, who argue that our abilities are learned. As Ashley Montague put it, "the notable thing about human behavior [and ability] is that it is learned. It is nonsense to talk about genetic determinance of human behavior."

Recently these views have tended to converge. According to the psychologist Lyman Porter and his associates,

> Traditionally psychologists have classified behaviors [abilities] into those that are innate and those that can be altered and learned. This way of thinking seems to be outmoded. . . . Thus it now seems reasonable to think of human response capacities in terms of a continuum. At one end of the continuum are those responses that are relatively uninfluenceable as a result of training and experience (for example, response time and finger dexterity). And at the other end are those that are relatively open to change and not significantly constrained by genetic or physical equal factors (such as interpersonal skills).

The ethologist Theodosuis Dobzhansky explains what appears to be a conflict as follows:

> What is most remarkable of all is that while all other organisms become masters of their environments by changing their genes, man does so mostly by changing his culture, which he acquires by learning and transmits by teaching. Indeed, many animals have become adapted to living in cold climates by growing warm fur or by becoming dormant when the weather is cold; man has conquered cold by building fires and by wearing garments. Adaptation by culture is enormously more rapid and efficient than genetic adaptation; a new thought or a new invention made by one man can become a part of the patrimony of all mankind in a relatively short time. Let us not forget, however, that it is the human genotype that enabled man to invent fire and clothing. Genetic and cultural adaptations are not alternative or mutually exclusive; they are mutually reinforcing. Human genes and human culture are connected by what is known as a circular feedback relationship; in other words, human genes stimulate the development of culture, and the development of culture stimulates genetic changes which facilitate further developments of culture. To say that natural selection has built man's culture is a misleading oversimplification; natural selection has, however, built the genetic endowment that made culture possible.

Thus the answer to the question, What is the source of abilities? is that they come from both heredity and learning from the environment.

Abilities, Aptitudes, and Management
Most of us recognize that people differ in their abilities and aptitudes. In most cases an aptitude can be developed into an ability through training and experience. In some cases it makes more sense to match people with certain abilities to jobs requiring those abilities. Not all people have all the abilities necessary to do a particular job. Nor does a manager always have the time or money to train a person without the needed ability.

As managers, we seek high performance from our employees and enterprises. The following formula shows what goes into performance:

$$\text{Human performance} = \text{ability} \times \text{motivation}$$

Most management experts have found that managers overemphasize the ability side of the equation. That is, they too easily attribute failure to lack of ability. But failure is often a result of lack of motivation. A person who is somewhat deficient in ability can make up for this deficiency in higher motivation leading to harder work.

Because of differences in abilities and aptitudes, managers can best use human abilities in either of two ways:

Selection: Choose people with the abilities needed and match them to the job.
Training and learning: Develop aptitudes into the abilities needed for the job.

LEARNING
Learning is the process by which the individual acquires skills, knowledge, and ability; it results in a relatively permanent change in behavior.

LEARNING
Learning is an important concept for a manager to understand because of its potential impact on the selection, development, and promotion of employees and its role in understanding your own learning process.

In general, individuals have different learning capacities, learn at different rates, and learn in different ways at various stages in life.

The human being begins to learn at birth (and perhaps before) and can continue to learn until death. Where and how we learn influences the kind of person we become. We learn first at home. Family and friends, the neighborhood in which he or she grows up, and local child-rearing practices lead a person to have certain expectations about working conditions. They also affect his or her preferences regarding leadership style, organization practices, and other aspects of management.

Later we learn at school, in church or synagogue, and through work or quasi-work experiences. Again, the kind of school or church attended and the initial work experiences can influence a person's expectations about the world of work.

Learning and Development

Much of what we do at work is affected by the stage of life in which we find outselves. Psychiatrists and psychologists like Jean Piaget, Roger Gould, Daniel Levinson, and George Valliant have divided the human life span into seven phases.

Phase 1: Childhood

The great Swiss scientist Jean Piaget has spent a lifetime observing how children learn. They proceed through four stages of learning (sensory motor, preoperational, etc.), each of which is of increasing complexity. However, since this book focuses on adult life, we will concentrate on the adult life stages.

Phase 2: Leaving the Family (Age 16–22)

The fantasies of youth about what it is like to be an adult begin to meet reality. This is the period during which the family ceases to be the primary influence and is replaced by peers. Peers impose group beliefs, and friendships with peers break easily, usually with feelings of betrayal. Emotions are kept under wraps.

Phase 3: Reaching Out (Age 23–28)

During this period a person tries to discover his or her identity, which includes trying to understand the meaning of work. Deeper relationships develop. Frequently he or she seeks an older mentor or supporter at work. During this period emotional extremes are avoided and commitments rarely analyzed.

Phase 4: The Questioning Period (Age 29–34)

This is the period of crisis. The person begins to question what life is all about and to question his or her relationships personally and at work. Needs such as order versus stability, freedom from restraint versus upward mobility come into conflict. The person begins to want to be accepted for what he or she is—not for meeting others' expectations. According to Levinson, "if a man doesn't start to settle down by age 34, his chances of forming a reasonably satisfying life structure are quite small."

Phase 5: The Unstable Period (Age 35–43)

During this period a person focuses on death for the first time and realizes that his or her life may be half over or more. Some psychologists see this period as a second adolescence. Parents are blamed for unresolved personality problems. At work, the person casts aside his or her mentor. Satisfaction is derived from becoming a mentor to someone else.

Phase 6: Settling In (Age 44–50)

The person realizes that his or her career decisions are settled and must be lived with. Money becomes less important; a few friends and the spouse are focused on as sources of support and sympathy.

Phase 7: Mellowing (After Age 50)

This is the time when a person finally settles down. Emotional issues are avoided. The person focuses on everyday irritations, joys, and triumphs. Little or no attention is given to the past or the future. Parents are no longer blamed for personal problems.

Learning in Adults

American society is learning oriented. Its values are strongly tied to the learning ability of its citizens. You have probably been exposed to economics and the "economic man." This model posits a creature forever thirsting for more goods and services—a thirst that is never satiated. Human potential theorists posit "learning man"—an individual ever thirsting for more learning and thus greater self-development. Psychologists like William James, Maslow, and Rogers believe human beings use only 5–10 percent of their capacity. As Herbert Otto puts it, "the ultimate creative capacity of the human brain may be, for all practical purposes, infinite."

The section on aptitudes and abilities should have made you aware that certain skills and abilities are harder for some of us to acquire than others. So although the learning potential of almost everyone may be very great, all learning is not equally easy or desirable for each of us.

We are not equally motivated to learn all things at all times. So if you are a manager trying to develop abilities of a particular type in a group of employees, some will learn more quickly than others because of differences in aptitudes and motivation. Remember your school experiences: some subjects came easier than others. So does learning on the job.

What conditions are conducive to adult learning? The answer to this question depends partially on how much "learning theory" you accept. If you accept the work of people like Pavlov, who have emphasized *conditioned response,* you concentrate on conditioning people's responses to stimuli the way Pavlov did with his dogs. More sophisticated theories have stressed *operant conditioning*. Operant conditioning involves first stating the goal (terminal response) of the learning and then measuring precisely the individual's behavior prior to learning. Aspects of his or her behavior that are directed towards the goal are rewarded. Other aspects are ignored. Each step that aids him or her in reaching the goal is rewarded (reinforced) over and over, shaping successive approximations to the goal.

Leslie This and Gordon Lippitt have gathered relevant material from learning theorists and other training specialists and have recommended the following ways to improve learning at work:

1 The fact that all human beings can learn must be accepted. Most normal human beings can choose whether they will learn at any time in their lives; people can and do learn.

2 The individual must be motivated to learn. This motivation involves two factors; awareness of the need to learn based on the individual's own inadequacy in this regard, and a clear understanding of what needs to be learned.

3 Learning is an active process. The individual learns better when more of his senses are utilized in the effort and he becomes more involved in the learning process.

4 Normally, the learner must have guidance. Learning is more efficient if it is not by trial and error. Guidance can speed the learning process and provide feedback as well as reinforce appropriate learning and prevent inadequate behavior patterns from developing.

5 Appropriate materials for sequential learning (cases, problems, discussion outlines, reading lists) must be provided. The trainer is an aid in an efficient learning process.

6 Time must be provided to practice learning. Learning requires time to assimilate what has been learned, to accept it, to internalize it, and to build confidence in what has been learned.

7 Learning methods should be as varied as possible. It is boredom that destroys learning, not fatigue. Any method—whether old-fashioned lecture or programmed learning or the jazziest computer business game—will begin to bore some learners.

8 The learner must secure satisfaction from the learning. He must see the usefulness of the material in terms of his own needs.

9 The learner must get reinforcement of correct behavior. As behavioral psychologists have shown, learners learn best with fairly immediate reinforcement of appropriate behavior. The learner must be rewarded for new behavior in various ways—pay, recognition, promotion.

10 Standards of performance should be set for the learner. Benchmarks for learning will provide goals and give a feeling of accomplishment when reached.

11 Different levels of learning are appropriate at different times and require different methods.

Managerial Implications of Learning

You may be wondering how learning relates to management. The point is that a manager must teach. As a manager, you must select people for new jobs that may require training. You must choose people for promotion to jobs that may require a significant amount of learning. And you must decide whether to accept or reject job opportunities that require you to engage in additional learning beyond what you already know.

A manager also influences rewards such as pay and promotion, which can serve to reinforce learning. Moreover, willingness to learn is higher in certain life phases, and so is the ability to serve as a mentor. This relationship is more effective as a reinforcer of learning if the employee is in Phase 3 than if he or she is in Phase 5.

A manager should understand that there are individual differences in ability to learn, too—when and where something is learned and how it is rewarded affect whether a person learns and what he or she learns.

PERCEPTION

This section and the section on attitudes and values that follows are intended to introduce you to other individual differences that affect you as a manager or entrepreneur.

Every day on the job you will realize that somehow other people see things and people differently than you do. It is hard to believe that two people experiencing the same stimuli will behave differently because they do not perceive the "same" thing. But people behave according to what they believe they see, not the "objective reality." To make sense of this experience, a manager must understand how people perceive things. The following definition and sketch may serve as a starting point. Perception of objects will be discussed first, and then, perhaps even more important, we will examine how people perceive each other.

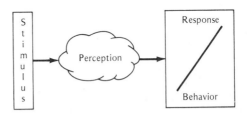

PERCEPTION

Perception is the chief mechanism by which human beings come to know the world outside themselves. Perception "translates" the stimuli received by the senses into impressions of the world.

Perception of Objects

Because of differences in their past experiences as well as physical differences, people perceive physical objects differently. This can be important in such managerial decisions as product design or office arrangement. Certain basic concepts must be grasped for a fuller understanding of how people perceive objects:

1 We respond to perceptual stimuli *selectively*. It is impossible to respond to all the cues we receive from the environment. We focus on selective stimuli and respond to those that are familiar to us, appeal to our internal feelings and attitudes, and fit the situation of the moment.

2 Perceptions result from "filling in" of stimuli to give us *closure*. We do not initially perceive a "car." We see its color, shape, and size, and these "add up" to the perception "car" through closure. Some perceptual differences result from different closures by different people.

3 Grouping and context influence perception. We group objects by similarity or closeness. We contrast light and dark shades (figure and ground). Perceptual differences arise from attention to different parts of objects or from different ways of grouping them.

D. M. Johnson explained perceptual differences as follows:

1 The person may be influenced by considerations that he may not be able to identify, responding to cues that are below the threshold of his awareness. For example, a judgment as to the size of an object may be influenced by its color even though the perceiver may not be attending to color.

2 When required to form difficult perceptual judgments, the perceiver may respond to irrelevant cues to arrive at a judgment. For example, in trying to assess honesty, it has been shown that the other person's smiling or not smiling is used as a cue to judge his honesty.

3 In making abstract or intellectual judgments, the perceiver may be influenced by emotional factors—what is liked is perceived as correct.

4 The perceiver will weigh perceptual evidence coming from respected (or favored) sources more heavily than that coming from other sources.

5 The perceiver may not be able to identify all the factors on which his judgments are based. Even if he is aware of these factors he is not likely to realize how much weight he gives to them.

It is interesting to know that people perceive physical objects differently even though engineers and other scientists can measure these items "objectively." If people can differ in their perceptions of easily measured objects, it is easy to see how they can differ in their perceptions of people.

Perception of People

Psychologists and management experts have studied how people perceive others with a view toward understanding this process and improving interpersonal relations. Although much more time and space should be given to this topic, both are limited. A few of the more significant findings on perception of people will be summarized here.

1 A major difference between perception of objects and of people is that *people affect the observer's perceptions.* A car does not change as it is being observed and perceived; a person can and often does.

2 As we observe another person, we tend to perceive the other as similar to us. We project our characteristics on the observed person.

3 Almost always, we develop a perception of another person based on our first impression of him or her, usually without enough information to do so.

4 Our perceptions of people tend to be consistent. We try to evaluate a person as good or bad, warm or cold, and so on, and stick to that perception.

5 These perceptions (warm-cold, good-bad, etc.) are based on past experiences with the type of person perceived. We combine traits and then they reinforce each other, giving us what psychologists call a *halo effect.*

6 The most recent perception is the strongest impression of a person (other than the first impression).

7 Perception can be biased when we let ourselves be influenced by a peer group. Thus if everyone in the peer group believes unions are bad, a union official will be perceived as bad.

8 The roles we play (such as the department we work for) influence how we perceive others (e.g., those in other departments).

9 The culture we belong to can influence our perceptions. We can base our perceptions on prejudices against whole groups of people of different race, religion, age, or sex.

Managerial Implications

In summary, how a manager perceives people largely determines how he or she behaves toward them. These perceptions are influenced by the manager's personality. The manager's past experiences have sensitized him or her to interpret stimuli (people or objects) and fit them into a perception or picture. There is a strong tendency to be consistent in these perceptions. And these perceptions affect the manager's behavior toward the perceived person or object. For example, if the first time you met a person he was drunk and you are opposed to drinking, you are unlikely to hire him.

The perceptual process affects managerial behavior in many other ways each day. Understanding how perception takes place and why people can view objects or other people differently can help make you a better manager. It also helps us understand ourselves.

ATTITUDES AND VALUES

ATTITUDES
Attitudes are learned predispositions to respond to stimuli in predictable ways.

VALUES
Values are systems of attitudes according to which stimuli are evaluated in positive or negative ways.

Psychologists tell us that attitudes and values influence our perceptions of the world in such a way as to guide these perceptions to a greater or lesser extent over time. Attitudes are learned, and they are influenced by family, peers, church, school, and to a lesser extent, personality.

Attitudes serve a number of purposes:

1 Attitudes and values give order to a person's constructs (to use Kelly's term) and thus help the individual make sense of the many stimuli that are constantly bombarding him or her.

2 Attitudes and values help a person deal with his or her psychological problems and inner conflicts.

3 Values and attitudes contribute to a person's identity

Work Attitudes

Historically, two opposing attitudes toward work have been held by employees:

1 *Work is a means to an end.* It is usually unpleasant, but we must work to reach the ends we desire and to pay our living costs.

2 *Work is an end in itself and is very satisfying.* A person gains self fulfillment through work.

The first view has been the predominant one for most workers throughout history. In early societies work was regarded as degrading, fit only for the masses whose lot it was to be born to it. Workers were slaves or low-caste, ignorant, irresponsible, or unprincipled people. The

Judaeo-Christian view that work was a consequence of ancient sins and a means of expiating those sins is typical of these early attitudes. Later Christianity argued that work was a means of earning one's way in life, but it also was desirable to work to gain wealth in order to serve less fortunate individuals through charity.

Attitudes toward work and a job are developed from the total culture, from the person's experiences, and from attitudes he or she sees in friends and family. In post-World War II America perhaps the dominant attitude of employees has been the instrumental one: We must work to survive. Although bosses bemoan the fact that "people don't want to work any more," some writers wonder if they ever accepted the work ethic once the Industrial Revolution took hold. They feel that when people retire they miss the social side of the workplace but not the narrow jobs they have left. Most of the findings of social science, however, confirm the fact that most Americans regard work as one of the most important parts of life. No major groups of able-bodied males (or, increasingly, females) between the ages of 25 and 65 are without work. Moreover, unemployment for any length of time is regarded as disastrous, even by the unskilled manual workers whose work is least desirable.

Today's employees have varying work attitudes. Some employees identify with work; their attitude is that work is an end in itself. Others, like Leo Garrett, see work as a means to another end.

LEO GARRETT

Leo Garrett, 57, spends as much time in the bowling alley as he does at his University cafeteria job. He belongs to seven leagues and is secretary for two more. Why?

"I got hooked, I guess," Garrett says of his evening passion. He began bowling six years ago with a friend and enjoyed it so much he has belonged to as many as nine leagues at a time.

Garrett explains that his wife works almost every evening and, while his daughter and son-in-law live at home, 4704 Pierre St., he would get bored staying at home watching television.

He has a high game of 254 to his credit and maintains a weekly average of 178 in one of the leagues. He says he doesn't need to practice at his hang-out, Town and Country Lanes, because he bowls in competition so often.

Even if Garrett isn't bowling until 9 P.M., he'll be at the alley by 6:30 to watch others and to socialize. He usually doesn't get to bed before midnight and is up and getting ready for work by 5:30 A.M.

His only regret about bowling is that he didn't start earlier. "I bowled only a little bit when I was younger and didn't keep it up. I wish I had—I'd be a lot better now."

Although work attitudes probably differ by age, sex, race, education, and experience, the attitude that work is a means to an end is probably more widespread among blue-collar workers than among white collar workers. The attitude that work is an end in itself is found among many professional, technical, and managerial people and other white-collar workers.

Attitude Conflicts Many psychologists argue that when people have inconsistencies or conflicts in their attitudes they try to reduce those conflicts or inconsistencies. For example, if an employee sometimes holds attitude 1 toward work and at other times attitude 2, if this conflict is important to the employee, and if he or she is aware of the conflict, the employee will try to develop one consistent attitude. Likewise, if a person likes his or her work but dislikes the supervisor, he or she will try to adjust this conflict. This is so, the psychologists argue, because conflict is unpleasant and most people prefer pleasure to pain. This is why they try to develop a consistent outlook.

Inconsistency or conflict can develop because of conflict in the roles we play, changes in the situation, or new information about the situation.

How do we deal with attitude conflicts? One way is to try to forget about them and repress them. We can do this by convincing ourselves that the problem is not important. We can deliberately distort one of the conflicting ideas so that the two appear to be consistent. Or we can leave the job.

Probably the best-known explanation of how we deal with attitude conflict is Festinger's cognitive dissonance theory. Festinger assumes that people prefer harmony over conflict ("dissonance"). When there is conflict, this creates a need to eliminate it or reduce it. Studies like Festinger's indicate that this drive to reduce dissonance is greater when the conflict comes up often, the issue is important to the person concerned, and the attractiveness of one of the two attitudes or choices is strong.

Most studies have found that what happens is that the person chooses one attitude (or makes a decision). Then he or she selectively hears, reads about, and reinforces the chosen alternative. This reduces the attractiveness of the other alternative and brings harmony. Thus if one chooses to leave one's job, the new job is reinforced, making the old job seem less attractive and eliminating the conflict.

Managerial Implications To manage effectively, managers need to understand employee attitudes and values. For example, if your employees feel that work is satisfying in and of itself, enlarging their jobs and delegating responsibility is more likely to be successful than if the employees believe work is merely a means to other ends. The latter attitude, by contrast, calls for closer supervision and control systems.

Many management programs (job enlargement, compensation, leadership, participation programs) are designed to shift employees from attitude 1 to attitude 2 under the assumption that behavior changes (higher-quality and more efficient work) will follow. Chapters 7 and 14 discuss the impact of attitudes on leadership and job design in more detail.

Attitudes do influence behavior and, thus, performance. But learning, perception, motivation, and abilities affect performance too. So "proper" work attitudes on the part of employees can influence their behavior and performance. Many studies indicate, however, that the results of this relationship are mixed. In general, employees with "good" attitudes (satisfaction with work) are absent less often, quit less often, and have fewer accidents. But in some cases employees with good work attitudes are only average in performance terms. Perhaps they lack ability.

Much has been written on how managers can change employee attitudes. But you should note that most studies on attitude change are laboratory studies. It is a lot easier to change employee attitudes in a laboratory experiment than on the job, with its entrenched work groups (see Chapter 6) and reinforcing environment.

SUMMARY   People are the firm's most important resource, and understanding people, how they behave and why is a significant part of the manager's job. Managers who have not studied human behavior can fall into the habit of stereotyping or oversimplifying people's attitudes and behavior.

This chapter set out to introduce you to individual differences in people and how and why these differences develop. The contingency approach to management is built on individual differences. As you will learn in later chapters, the set of attitudes a person learns in the home, at school, and at work determines management style with which he or she will feel comfortable. This in turn determines when you, as a manager, can most effectively use different styles of leadership, organization, and communication.

The purpose of the chapter was not to make you a sophisticated personality theorist but to provide you with some useful information. Just as an engineer must learn math to perform engineering analysis and just as one must learn a programing language before one uses the computer, so a manager must learn about people before he or she can manage.

Specifically, you should have learned the following:

· Human beings are a mixture of the rational and the emotional, the conscious and the unconscious. Behavior such as learning, attitude development, choice, and motivation results from both these processes in most human beings.

· Each individual develops a unique personality that directs his or her thinking, attitude development, learning, and actions. Factors influencing the development of the personality include internal development and interactions with parents, peers, co-workers, and others. The larger culture influences this development.

· Each of us has aptitudes that can develop into abilities. Each person's set of abilities and aptitudes is different and, moreover, changes over time. It is probably easier for some people to do certain jobs because they have greater aptitude, including intelligence, than others; but most managers exaggerate the impact of abilities on performance relative to motivation and other factors.

· Managers play an important teaching and training role. Understanding the phase of the learner's life span will help the manager improve the learning process.

· Managers should understand how each person filters stimuli (people, information, communications) through his or her perceptual framework. This accounts for different interpretations of actions and communications.

· Work attitudes and values vary from "work is a means to an end" to "work is an end in itself." These and other attitudes significantly affect many managerial processes.

In sum, most managers' most precious resource is their employees. If they are not careful, they will forget a major difference between people and other resources: People differ in abilities and attitudes and thus must be placed and transferred to fit those abilities. Abilities can be increased by learning in the appropriate environment.

How each person behaves is influenced by his or her abilities. More important, people behave differently because of differences in how they see the world around them, differences resulting from attitudinal, value, and personality differences. They also behave differently because of differences in motivation (Chapter 5).

As a contingency-oriented manager, you look at each employee problem and go through a checklist. Is the clerk ineffective because he or she

1 lacks abilities?

2 lacks training?

3 does not understand the situation because of differences in perception, attitudes, or personality?

Once the cause of the problem has been determined, you will know whether you need to transfer, retrain, or counsel the employee.

One conclusion you could draw from this chapter is that dealing with individual differences is a problem. But it is also a challenge. With the information in this chapter you should be equipped to meet that challenge, keeping the following points in mind:

1 *You can welcome individual differences.* They give you the ability to fit a variety of talents to a variety of jobs.

2 *You can listen with understanding to employees and thus reduce conflicts.* You can clarify the nature of the conflict.

3 *You can recognize and accept different views of the causes and solutions of problems* and thus be more effective.

4 *You can indicate the procedures and ground rules you will use* to resolve differences.

One major individual difference needs to be discussed in a chapter of its own, namely, motivating employees. This is covered in Chapter 5.

Questions for Review

1. Explain how some theorists believe people are rational and act entirely rationally, while others assume that people act primarily as a result of emotions and unconscious processes. What are the managerial implications of these two theories, if true?
2. In what way are humans a mix of the rational and the emotional, the conscious and the unconscious? Is it hard to figure people out?
3. Tell me about your personality. What is it? Where did it come from?
4. Give a Freudian explanation of the behavior patterns of entrepreneurs.
5. Choose one of these positions on personality: Freudian, Jungian, cognitive (Kelly), humanistic. How are they the same? Different? Which is best? Why?
6. How can managers manage better by understanding personality?
7. You are in a meeting. Your boss explains an employee's failure by saying, "Oh well, you know Jim. He's just dumb." Explain how she could be oversimplifying.
8. "Effectiveness, when you get down to it, is simply a matter of intelligence." Comment.
9. How does learning change during the various phases of a person's life span. Do we learn different things during different phases?
10. How do adults learn? Is their learning any different from that of a 12-year-old? a 2-year-old?
11. "Managers should understand learning to be effective." Comment.
12. What is perception? attitudes? values? How do we perceive differently? What does this mean to a manager?
13. "No one ever sold more goods or beat the union in a contract negotiations by understanding perception." Comment.

14. Are there differences between perception of objects and perception of people? Why?

15. "People don't want to work any more, what with food stamps, welfare, unemployment compensation, and the unions." Is this true?

16. How might the work attitudes of a mail sorter differ from those of the postmaster?

17. How does understanding human behavior help make you a better manager?

References

Personality and Human Identity

Adler, Alfred, *The Individual Psychology of Alfred Adler,* ed. H & R Ansbacher (New York: Basic Books, 1956).

Allport, Gordon, *Personality* (New York: Holt, 1937).

Carlson, Rae and Levy, N., "Studies of Jungean Typology," *Journal of Personality,* 41 (1973): 559–576.

Carlson, Rae, "Personality," *Annual Review of Psychology,* 1975, pp. 393–414.

Cattell, Raymond, "Personality Pinned Down," *Psychology Today,* July 1973, pp. 40–46.

Dollard, John, and Miller, N., *Personality and Psychotherapy: An Analysis in Terms of Learning, Thinking, and Culture* (New York: McGraw-Hill, 1950.)

Erikson, Eric, *Childhood and Society,* rev. ed. (New York: W. W. Norton, 1963.)

Freud, Sigmund, *The Standard Edition of the Complete Psychological Works of Sigmund Freud,* ed. J. Strachey, 24 vols. (London: Hogarth Press, 1953).

Helson, R., "The Heroic, the Comic, and the Tender," *Journal of Personality,* 41 (1973): 163–184.

Jung, Carl, *Psychological Types* (New York: Harcourt, Brace and World, 1923).

Jung, Carl, *Man and His Symbols* (New York: Doubleday, 1964).

Kelly, George, *The Psychology of Personal Constructs,* 2 vols. (New York: W. W. Norton, 1955).

MacIntyre, Alastair, "Carl Jung," in *The Encyclopedia of Philosophy* (New York: Collier Macmillan, 1967).

Rank, Otto, *The Trauma of Birth* (London: Routledge and Kegan Paul, 1929).

Rogers, Carl, *On Becoming a Person* (Boston: Houghton Mufflin, 1961).

Stagner, Ross, *Psychology of Personality,* 4th ed. (New York: McGraw-Hill, 1974).

Stein, Joseph, *Effective Personality: A Humanistic Approach* (Belmont, Calif.: Brooks/Cole, 1972).

Zaleznik, Abraham, and DeVries, Manfred, *Power and the Corporate Mind* (Boston: Houghton Mifflin, 1975), chap. 10.

Abilities and Aptitudes

Anastasi, Anne, *Differential Psychology* (New York: Macmillan, 1970).

—— *Common Fallacies About Heredity, Environment, and Human Behavior* (Iowa City: American College Testing Service, 1973).

Das, J. P., et al., "Simultaneous and Successive Synthesis," *Psychological Bulletin* 82 (1975): 83–103.

Dobzhansky, Theodosuis, *Heredity and the Nature of Man* (New York: New American Library, 1966).

Godberg, Steven, *The Inevitability of Patriarchy* (New York: Morrow, 1973).

Jolly, Alison, *The Evolution of Primate Behavior* (New York: Macmillan, 1972).

Kefalas, Asterios, and Suojanen, Waino, "Organizational Behavior and the New *Biology,*" *Academy of Management Journal,* 17, no. 3 (September 1974): 514–527.

Maier, Norman, *Psychology in Industrial Organizations* (Boston: Houghton Mifflin, 1973).

Montague, Ashley, ed. *Man and Aggression,* 2nd ed. (New York: Oxford University Press, 1973).

Ornstein, Robert, *The Psychology of Consciousness* (New York: Viking Press, 1973).

Porter, Lyman, et al., *Behavior in Organizations* (New York: McGraw-Hill, 1975).

Rose, Steven, *The Conscious Brain* (New York: Alfred Knopf, 1973).

Tyler, Leona, *The Psychology of Human Differences* (New York: Appleton-Century-Crofts, 1965).

Learning
Fiske, Edward, "Study Ties Child Learning to the History of Science," *New York Times,* June 15, 1975.

Kefalas and Suojanen, op. cit.

Otto, Herbert, "New Light on Human Potential," *Saturday Review,* December 2, 1969.

Phillips, J. L., *The Origins of Intellect: Piaget's Theory* (San Francisco: Freeman, 1969).

Piaget, Jean, *Construction of Reality in the Child* (New York: Basic Books, 1954).

This, Leslie, and Lippitt, Gordon, "Learning Theories and Training," *Training and Development Journal,* 20 (April 1966: 2–11; 20 (May 1966): 1–10.

Perception
Bruner, Jerome, and Tagiuri, Renato, "Person Perception," in Gardner Lindzey, ed., *Handbook of Social Psychology,* 2 (Reading, Mass.: Addison-Wesley, 1954).

Dearborn, D., and Simon, Herbert, "Selective Perception: A Note on the Departmental Identifications of Executives," *Sociometry,* 21 (1958): 140–144.

Haire, Mason, "Role Perceptions in Labor Management Relations: An Experimental Approach," *Industrial and Labor Relations Review,* 8, no. 3 (1955).

Hastorf, A., et al., *Person Perception* (Reading, Mass.: Addison-Wesley, 1970).

Johnson, D. M., "A Systematic Treatment of Judgment," *Psychological Bulletin,* 42 (1945): 193–224.

Leavitt, Harold, *Managerial Psychology,* 3rd ed. (Chicago: University of Chicago Press, 1972).

Secord, P., and Backman, C., *Social Psychology,* 2nd ed. (New York: McGraw-Hill, 1974).

Tajfel, H., "Social and Cultural Factors in Perception," in Gardner Lindzey and

E. Aronson, eds., *The Handbook of Social Psychology*, 2nd ed. (Reading, Mass.: Addison-Wesley, 1969), 3, 315–394.

Zalkind, Sheldon, and Costello, Timothy, "Perception: Implications for Administration," *Administrative Science Quarterly,* 7, no. 3. (September 1962): 218–235.

Attitudes and Values

Aronson, E., "The Theory of Cognitive Dissonance: A Current Perspective," in L. Berkowitz, ed. *Advances in Experimental Social Psychology* (New York: Academic Press, 1969), 4, 1–34.

Festinger, Leon, *A Theory of Cognitive Dissonance* (Stanford, Calif.: Stanford University Press, 1957).

Kiesler, C., *The Psychology of Commitment* (New York: Academic Press, 1971).

McGuire, W., "The Nature of Attitudes and Attitude Change," in Gardner Lindzey and E. Aronson, eds., *The Handbook of Social Psychology,* 2nd ed. (Reading, Mass.: Addison-Wesley, 1969), 3, 136–314.

Wisbett, R., and Valins, S., *Perceiving the Causes of One's Behavior* (New York: General Learning, 1971).

Porter, Lyman, and Lawler, Edward, *Managerial Attitudes and Performance* (Homewood, Ill.: Irwin Dorsey Press, 1968).

Osgood, C., et al., *The Measurement of Meaning* (Urbana: University of Illinois Press, 1957).

Scott, William, "Attitude Measurement," in Gardner Lindzey and Elliot Aronson, eds., *The Handbook of Social Psychology,* 2nd ed. vol. 2 (Reading, Mass.: Addison-Wesley, 1969), 2, 204–273.

Slocum, Walter, *Occupational Careers* (Chicago: Aldine, 1974).

Summary

Schmidt, Warren, and Tannenbaum, Robert, "Management of Differences," *Harvard Business Review,* 38, No. 6 (November-December 1960), pp. 107–115.

CHAPTER 5
MOTIVATING PEOPLE

5

Learning Objectives

1. To understand what motivation is and how it interacts with other human factors to influence effectiveness.
2. To learn that conscious and unconscious motives influence behavior.
3. To understand the major theories of motivation and evaluate their usefulness.
4. To learn how to use motivation theory to understand yourself and your employees with a view toward managerial effectiveness.

Chapter Outline

INTRODUCTION   Motivation is concerned with why people work hard and well or poorly. Consider some examples of employees or managers and their implications in terms of motivation.

Top Managers Remember the description of J. Peter Grace—his long hours, hectic work? Why do top managers work so hard? What is their motivation? A recent cartoon showed the president and vice-president of a large firm talking to each other at the end of the day. The president says to the vice president, "You know, George, we've got hard jobs: long hours, lots of pressure, grind, grind, grind. Why if it weren't for the $200,000 a year plus fringes, I'd hang it up." But many top managers have already made more money than they can spend.

Willy Loman Willy, the central character in Arthur Miller's *Death of a Salesman,* has been brilliantly played by many actors, most recently George C. Scott. Here is a man who is past his prime, a tragic figure. What makes him get up and try each day? How can his boss motivate him to improve his performance?

The Reluctant Bureaucrat You may have encountered the employee who has been on the job long enough to be secure in the job. He or she does just enough to get by, moves very slowly—not slowly enough to be disciplined, but just fast enough to satisfy the boss or client. What motivates this employee? How can a supervisor motivate such an employee to improve?

The Rate Buster The management literature contains lots of examples of employees who constantly outperform their peers. A classic case is Betty Randall. Betty is shunned by her peers, sabotaged by them, even punished by her supervisor. Why does she continue to work so hard with so few extrinsic rewards?

Steve Dubi Studs Terkel describes a Chicago steelworker he calls Steve Dubi, age 59. Steve has worked for the firm since he was 16. This is how he describes his job:

> You're on your feet all day, on concrete . . . oh you get tired. Your feet get tired. Your eyes get tired. . . . They work us twelve days in a row 7–3. . . . You're just a number out there. Just like a prison. . . . A lot of people don't know your name . . . you're just badge 44–065. Of course, there are accidents . . . you eat dust and dirt and take all the things that go with it. . . . The workplace is not inside a building. It's just under a roof. There's no protection against the wind or snow. The roof is so leaky they should provide you with umbrellas. . . . They're forcing you to work harder by making cutbacks. . . . Everyone looks forward to retirement. That's all they talk about is retirement. . . . What have I done in my forty years of work? . . . Here I am almost sixty years old and I don't have anything to show for it. . . . I think I've been a good worker. But they don't appreciate it. They don't care.

What motivates Steve to get up and go to work, to do a good job? In this chapter I try to help you understand what motivates people to act the way they do, with primary focus on motivation at the workplace. We are now relating motivation to our understanding of people at work, especially their personalities, perceptions, and attitudes.

MOTIVATION: WHAT IS IT? *Motivation* has meant many things over the years. In general, it means the process or factors (motives) that influence people to act. Psychologists view motivation as the process of (1) arousing behavior, (2) sustaining behavior in progress, and (3) channeling behavior into a specific course. Thus motives (needs, desires) induce the self (or will) to act, and hence motives cause behavior.

> **MOTIVATION**
> Motivation is the inner state that energizes, channels, and sustains human behavior.

This definition sounds simple enough, but it is anything but simple. First of all, the person changes over time and the environment also changes, influencing his or her motives. Thus a person's motivation is not fixed over time. Consider how important one need (money) might be to a person at various points during a twenty-five-year period.

Age 21. Bachelor, good salary, low expenses, happy-go-lucky, "have-a-good-time" orientation.

Age 23. Gets married, decides to buy home and furnish it.

Age 26. Home furnished, house payments, no money problems.

Age 29. Wife has twins, both severely retarded. Must be cared for in an institution.

Age 31. Wife has normal child.

Age 32. Wife has normal child.

Age 50. Children begin college while retarded children are still institutionalized.

During this period there were times when money was very short, others when it was plentiful. The person's reaction to money as an incentive varied with his need for it at the time, of course. And his other needs and desires could also change over time.

Second, there are many different kinds of behavior. Let me give you several examples:

1 Fingernail growth, growth of hair.

2 Eating, elimination.

3 Driving to work at 7:45 A.M., as you have for the past 22 years.

4 Considering whether to accept a promotion that requires a transfer to Philadelphia.

5 Deciding to leave sales and enter the ministry.

These behaviors are scaled from unmotivated "behavior" (1) through instinctual or semiinstinctual behavior (2,3) to complex behavior (4,5).

Most motivation theories ignore (1); many ignore (2) and (3). But in addition, many theories treat (4) and (5) primarily as rational, consciously motivated behavior. Remember, however, that the human being is a complex blend of conscious and unconscious processes, and these include motivation.

Various theories of motivation are described in this chapter. It is important to understand where these fit in terms of the nature of human beings (see Table 5.1).

Table 5.1 Human Nature and Motivation Theories

Nature:	Instinctual	Mixed	Rational
	Unconscious		Conscious
Theories:	Psychoanalytic	Herzberg's Two-Factor Theory	Consistency
	Behaviorism	Maslow's Need Hierarchy	Equity
		The McClelland/Atkinson Need Theory	Expectancy

At one extreme are those who explain the motivation of behavior as either responses to external stimuli (behaviorism) or responses to unconscious (and possibly unknown) motives. This reduces the rationality of the person (psychoanalytic) or treats the person as an easily programable being. At the other extreme is expectancy theory, in which the person is seen as the rational, hedonistic, predictable being.

In between are a set of theories that, intentionally or not, portray the person as a quasi-rational, quasi-emotional being. Such a theory is likely to provide a fuller explanation of human motivation at work than the extreme positions.

Managers want to understand motivation because together with natural ability, training, and correct job placement it can influence employee performance. Two extreme positions can be taken in considering motiva-

"I used to think I
was highly
motivated. By the
time I found out I
was merely
compulsive, I'd
already made my
pile."

Source: Drawing by Stevenson; © 1975 The New Yorker Magazine, Inc.

tion—that motivation is the key to management or that it should be ignored. The truth lies in between.

Managers seek motivated employees, that is, people oriented to
doing an efficient and effective job. To achieve this, the manager needs
to create a motivating climate. This comes about when the employees'
needs are satisfied by incentives and by the work climate, thus removing
the conflicts that might impede their motivation to work. As a future
manager or entrepreneur, you should understand why employees sometimes work hard and well and sometimes perform poorly, and what you
can do to improve employee motivation.

THEORIES OF MOTIVATION

Behaviorism and Behavior Modification

The first systematic theory to try to explain motivation was *behaviorism,*
which was developed primarily by Clark Hull, from the work of Watson,
Pavlov, and Thorndike. These theorists believed behavior is motivated
by drives. Initially drives were viewed as deprivations of basic needs
such as food. Later a drive was viewed as a tissue deficiency and then
as an intense internal stimulus; finally it was defined as an anticipatory
goal reaction. Drives did not totally determine behavior. The probability
that one drive rather than another would determine behavior was
thought to be the outcome of drive $\times$ habit. Later this was reformulated
as drive $\times$ incentive $\times$ habit reinforcement, and finally as (drive $\times$ incentive) $\times$ habit.

This theory received extensive testing, reformulation, and variation,
often using animals as subjects. The behaviorists placed more and more

emphasis on the external conditions that motivate behavior. Although some psychologists still adhere to classical behaviorism, it appears to be an incomplete explanation of motivation. It has difficulty explaining the simplest behavior such as water and food deprivation, and does not come close to explaining the richness and complexity of human behavior. As Richard de Charms points out, "[the behaviorism theory] is inadequate to explain behavior unless the definition of primary reinforcement is stretched beyond recognition." Moreover, the theory is unable to explain behavior without using internal constructs or circular arguments. It also requires the acceptance of an analysis of man as a kind of machine. It might seem that behaviorism could explain instinctual or semiinstinctual behavior, but it does not even do a good job at that. And it ignores unconscious motives entirely.

"They want me to salivate, but I'll be damned if I'll give them the satisfaction."

Source: Reproduced by special permission of PLAYBOY Magazine; copyright © 1969 by Playboy.

A later variation of behaviorism is *behavior modification,* which was strongly influenced by the work of B. F. Skinner. Skinner argued that behavior is a function of its consequences. He reoriented behaviorism from respondent behavior (that which was reflexive or unlearned) to operant behavior. Operant behavior can be paired with prior stimuli but is not instinctual. As Skinner put it, "Pavlov called all events which strengthened behavior 'reinforcement' and all resulting changes 'conditioning.' . . . In operant reinforcement, behavior is contingent upon a response." Behavior modification was an attempt to apply Skinnerian theory not in a laboratory but in a work organization. The principles of behavior modification are as follows:

1 Deal in terms of specific, observable, behavioral events or responses that have an observable effect on the environment.

2 Measure behavior in terms of response frequency.

3 Because behavior is a function if its consequences, the contingency relationship must be identified.

So behavior modification argues that a particular behavior will occur with greater frequency if positive consequences are tied closely to that behavior. Thus you can get higher performance if rewards (e.g., raises or promotions) are linked directly to the desired behavior.

Behavior modification has been tried in work organizations in training (including self-instruction), performance evaluation, training hardcore employees, quality control, and other settings. The results have been mixed and have rarely been measured scientifically.

Several additional problems are involved in the use of behavior modification. For example, some employees consider it unethical control or "mickey mouse" manipulation. Other problems include the following:

1 Most applications of behavior modification have been in mental health and educational organizations, where the behaviors observed were less complex than in most work organizations.

2 Most of the studies have been in controlled laboratory settings. This neglects many counterinfluences that are present in the workplace.

3 There are too few real-life studies in real organizations that support behavior modification.

It appears to me that the behavior modification approach is oversimplified. It assumes that people will let someone manipulate their environment. But we have too many examples of how human behavior confounds this approach. The problem is that behavior modification assumes away individual differences.

In an uncontrolled experiment, I tried behavior modification on my four children in an attempt to improve their grade performance in school. First I offered money inducements for high grades, with the amount of money increasing significantly the higher the grade. The older son accused me of manipulation, and there was no change in his grades. The older daughter was moderately motivated and improved her grades somewhat. The younger son was totally unimpressed; there was no change. The younger daughter liked the idea, and her grades increased significantly.

Then I tried differential rewards. Instead of money, I shifted the rewards to desired objects. They could pick whatever reward they wanted. Again the sons ignored it. The older daughter wanted a horse, and her grades reached the level desired. I got the horse for her. Then her grades dropped back to "normal." The younger daughter stayed on the money system and kept her grades up.

Obviously this was not a scientific experiment. But it illustrates the problems we have discussed. Peer pressure on the older son led him to ignore grade "manipulation." The younger son ignores my systems most of the time. The older daughter sometimes responded, sometimes shifted her attention elsewhere.

Thus emphasizing the same consequences for everyone behavior modification ignores individual preferences to act in response to the system's rewards. So it sometimes works at very basic levels—instinctual or semiinstinctual behavior. But it appears to be an oversimplified theory to describe the motivation of human beings at work. Perhaps future research will change our present views, however.

Psychoanalytic Motivation Theory

The other "extreme" nonrational motivation theory is psychoanalytic theory, which we encountered in Chapter 4. As we have seen, psychoanalytic theorists believe that

1 All behavior has a psychological cause (psychic determinism).

2 Unconscious mental processes determine thoughts and behavior more significantly than conscious processes do. Most of the true reasons we do things are not known to us.

Flowing from these assumptions are two other points:

3 Since human beings act in such a way as to avoid pain and unpleasantness, and since the actual reasons or causes of behavior can be difficult to accept, these feelings frequently are repressed into the unconscious.

4 When feelings and emotions are repressed long enough, they are expressed in many disguised or symbolic ways.

Freud and others argued that we behave in response to conflicting motives. In his earlier formulation the conflicts were described as sexual drives in conflict with the norms of society (id versus superego). In later formulations life instincts are in conflict with death instincts (suicide and/or outward aggression).

The unconscious is a pool of mainly repressed energies, distorted by frustration and exerting a stress on conscious reasons. These shape the patterns of daily life and behavior. For example, Erich Fromm, a neo-Freudian, argues that much of our behavior at work is aggressive because

we experience boredom at work, even though we may not be aw
of this feeling.

Think about a recent decision you made: buying a car, taking a job,
choosing a mate, what you did Saturday night. Now ask yourself these
questions:

· Did you make these choices rationally? That is, did you have one
end in mind, consider all alternatives, weigh the probabilities of
achieving each alternative, and choose one?
· Or did you consider some factors and make the choice—how, you
are not sure?

The psychoanalytic school contends that the *important, crucial* motives for your behavior are deep in your unconscious, tied to your past
(or, according to Jung, tied to symbols and motives earlier in human
history), and that the conscious motives are less important. This position
in effect rejects conscious motivation as unimportant. But there is evidence indicating that *at least some of the time* there are rational, conscious motives for behavior. And since a manager is unable to use psy-
choanalytical techniques to learn employees' unconscious motives, it is
hard to use this theory *except* in that it helps the manager understand
why some rational systems designed to increase employee motivation
(such as pay and promotion incentive systems) do not always work well
for all employees.

**Herzberg's
Two-Factor
Theory**

We now turn to a discussion of five "middle-of-the-road" theorists who
do not try to explain human motivation as either primarily rational/con-
scious or primarily unconscious/emotional. Instead they try to examine
the motives that seem to have the strongest influence on behavior at
work. The first of these theorists is Frederick Herzberg.

Herzberg developed his theory after asking 200 engineers and accountants what factors at work satisfied them the most. These factors
were then classified as either motivators or hygiene factors.

Hygiene factors—supervisory style, interpersonal relations, salary,
personnel policies, physical working conditions, and job security—must
be present and "satisfied" before motivation can be activated. But these
factors do not motivate greater productivity. People are motivated to
work only when job satisfiers, or motivators, are present in the work
situation. These motivators are (1) the nature of the work itself, (2) the
achievement of an important task, (3) responsibility at work, (4) recognition of work, and (5) opportunity for advancement.

Herzberg's theory is appealing because it is simple. But those who
support this theory and those who oppose it interpret the same data
differently, and as a result their findings conflict. According to John
Campbell and his associates,

> If the empirical studies are examined in total, the negative evidence would appear to have an edge because it has been generated from a wider variety of approaches. . . . On the basis of the data it has generated, it [the theory] appears to be an oversimplification. Repeated factor analytic studies of job attitudes have failed to demonstrate the existence of two independent factors corresponding to motivators and hygienes . . . and the fundamental postulate concerning the independence of job satisfaction has never been tested. The most meaningful conclusion that we can draw is that the two factor theory has served [to stimulate research] and should be altered or respectfully laid aside.

The two-factor theory is another example of an oversimplified explanation of complex human motivation. It is highly unlikely that human beings in many cultures with different abilities, experiences, attitudes, and learning patterns will always be motivated by the same sets of motives.

Maslow's Need Theory Although Maslow originally developed his theory in clinical work, it is the most widely known theory to be applied in management situations. Maslow's theory is a "need" theory of motivation. That is, it argues that we behave in order to satisfy certain desires.

ABRAHAM MASLOW (1908–1970)

Ph.D. University of Wisconsin
President American Psychological Association (1966)
Founded *Journal of Humanistic Psychology*
Author of many books and numerous articles.
Best-known books include
  Motivation and Personality (1954)
  Eupsychian Management (1965)
Early work in mental health area, later extensively in management. Motivation theory introduced in mid-1940s and most influential in 1950s and 1960s.

According to Maslow, there are two kinds of needs:

1 *Innate needs:* inherited or unlearned needs such as the needs for food, water, oxygen, appropriate temperature, and sex.
2 *Acquired needs:* those we learn as we experience life, including the needs for safety, security, social recognition, self-respect, and self-fulfillment/self-actualization.

Maslow theorized that human beings strive to satisfy their needs in a specific order or hierarchy. That is, one set of needs must be satisfied first before the other needs motivate behavior. Thus if a need is not satisfied, it produces a tension that induces us to behave in response to this need in an effort to reduce the tension and restore equilibrium. Psychologists call the state of unfulfilled needs *deprivation.*

Maslow's hierarchy of needs is illustrated in Figure 5.1 and may be explained as follows:

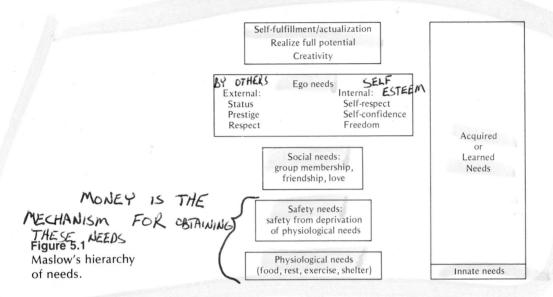

Figure 5.1
Maslow's hierarchy
of needs.

[handwritten annotations on figure: BY OTHERS; SELF ESTEEM; MONEY IS THE MECHANISM FOR OBTAINING THESE NEEDS]

1 *Physiological needs*   Basic to all human beings are the needs for food, water, rest, exercise, shelter (protection from the elements), and sex. If these needs are not satisfied, most people are not motivated by "higher" needs. When you are cold and hungry you cannot afford the luxury of concern about self-actualization.

2 *Safety needs*   Safety needs include freedom from bodily harm or threat of harm. They also include freedom from arbitrary loss of one's job.

3 *Social needs*   After physiological and safety needs are reasonably satisfied, the next motivator likely to become operative is the need for friendship, affection, and interaction with and acceptance by peers. Most people need to be with others at least part of the time when they are at work.

4 *Ego/esteem needs*   The ego or esteem needs include the needs for self-respect and self-confidence and a stable and positive self-evaluation. They also include the need for respect, recognition, and appreciation from others. This results in status and reputation.

5 *Self-actualization or self-fulfillment*   The highest need is the need to realize one's potential, to be what one wants to be, to know one is using all one's talents well, and to be creative.

Maslow argued that these needs are present in this hierarchy in all of us: Physiological needs must always be satisfied before safety needs can influence behavior, and so on. If a need cannot be satisfied, it leads to frustration.

Maslow theorized that once a need is satisfied, it no longer motivates behavior. He recognized that there are individual differences in the strength of each need. For example, workers who have experienced a layoff may have greater security needs than those who have not had such an experience. Deprivation of a particular need for a long time can lead to overemphasis or fixation on this need. Psychologists call the state of satisfaction in which the need no longer motivates behavior *relative gratification.*

Maslow argued that the need for self-actualization is not likely to be satisfied though it is the most important need. He did concede that in a few cases people may be motivated by higher needs such as self-fulfillment even when their lower needs are not satisfied. In such cases the lower needs are suppressed.

People's needs can change with changes in their life circumstances. A person can move back down and start climbing again, like the "happy bachelor" at the beginning of this chapter.

Maslow estimated that only 10 percent of Americans' self-actualization needs were fulfilled, 40 percent of their ego and esteem needs, 50 percent of their social needs, 70 percent of their safety needs, and 85 percent of their physiological needs. Note, however, that he made these estimates some years ago.

Is Maslow's theory the "right" one? Most managers say it makes sense to them. But it is a very hard theory to "prove." Maslow himself said (in 1965),

> I of all people should know just how shaky this foundation for the theory is as a final foundation. My work on motivation came from the clinic, from a study of neurotic people. The carry-over of this theory to the industrial situation has some support from industrial studies, but certainly I would like to see a lot more studies of this kind before feeling finally convinced that this carry-over from the study of neurosis to the study of labor in factories is legitimate. The same thing is true of my studies of self-actualizing people—there is only this one study of mine available. There were many things wrong with the sampling, so many in fact that it must be considered to be, in the classical sense anyway, a bad or poor or inadequate experiment. I am quite willing to concede this—as a matter of fact, I am eager to concede it—because I'm a little worried about this stuff which I consider to be tentative being swallowed whole by all sorts of enthusiastic people, who really should be a little more tentative in the way that I am.

Because it is a hard theory to prove, there have been few studies of Maslow's need theory. Many studies do not support it. Criticisms of the theory vary from questioning the number of need categories to questioning the specific hierarchy. Among the studies that have been made, almost all have found that innate needs must be satisfied before learned needs. But some question the order in which the learned needs must be satisfied. Also, some studies question whether a need is no longer operative once it has been satisfied. There is no evidence to support the statement that once a lower need is satisfied, the next-higher need becomes the crucial motivator.

C.P. Alderfer has attempted to revise Maslow's theory in the light of these findings. He proposes a hierarchy of three levels of needs, as shown in Table 5.2.

Table 5.2

Alderfer	Maslow
Level 3: growth needs	self-actualization and self-esteem
Level 2: relatedness needs	social and status needs
Level 1: existence needs	physiological and some security needs

Alderfer reports some support for this reformulation, but at this point it is too early to say much about it.

Maslow and Management   If Maslow's theory is accepted, it has important managerial implications. If a manager accepts the Maslow theory, he or she will attempt to assess the state of the employee's motivation structure before attempting to induce greater productivity. For example, if the employee is well paid and secure but his or her work space is isolated, the administrator may attempt to determine whether the isolation is contributing to lower performance.

Most managers find Maslow's theory easy to understand, and many have been successful in using it to understand employee motivation. But since it is based on mental health studies and many later studies do not support it, you should look at it with care, try it out, and not be too surprised if it is not always applicable.

DAVID McCLELLAND

Ph.D. Yale 1941
Professor of Psychology, Wesleyan University, 1941–1956
Professor of Social Relations, Harvard University, since 1956
Best-known books include
   Personality (1951), *The Achievement Motive* (1953), *The Achieving Society* (1961), *Motivating Economic Achievement* (1969), *Motivation* (1973).

**The McClelland/
Atkinson Need
Theory**

A somewhat similar perspective to Maslow's can be found in the work of J. W. Atkinson and David McClelland. It is also present in the work of such theorists as George Litwin and Robert Stringer.

Atkinson and McClelland have refined and intensively studied a subset of the needs described by the psychologist Henry Murray in the 1920s. These include the need for achievement, the need for power, the need for affiliation, and minimization of pain or fear of failure. McClelland has studied how these needs are conditioned by early childhood experiences. He contends, for example, that when a society has a high need for achievement the themes of children's stories, fables, and fairy tales are not fatalistic; instead, actions lead to results.

McClelland and others have focused on the need for achievement. They have not studied the need for power to any great extent, though they have studied the need for affiliation. They have found that a high need for achievement (in an individual or a country) usually means a low need for affiliation, and vice versa. This causes certain problems for managers.

The following themes are central to the McClelland/Atkinson theory:

1 Most mentally healthy adults have a large reservoir of potential energy.

2 Most mentally healthy adults have basic motives or needs that channel and regulate the flow of potential energy. These needs or motives are relatively stable and are learned, not innate.

3 There are three major relevant motives in the work situation: (a) the need for achievement—the need to excel, to achieve in relation to a set of standards, to strive to succeed; (b) the need for affiliation —the need for friendly and close interpersonal relationships; and (c) the need for power—the need to make others behave in a way that they would not have done otherwise. Atkinson believes that these motives are simply a name for a group of incentives that result in similar behavior.

4 Within a culture people may have the same needs or motives, but there are major differences in the relative strength of those motives. Litwin and Stringer say that strong needs are like tight, sticky valves that allow only a limited flow of energy to pass through.

5 The trigger that activates a particular motive is the situation with which the person is dealing.

6 Factors in the situation arouse different motives. For example, Litwin and Stringer found the effects of situational variables on arousal of motives in managers to be as shown in Table 5.3. The amount of arousal or reduction varied, depending on the subject studied—for example, students did not always respond the same way managers did. (Remember, managers can change the environment.)

7 Each motive or need leads to a different pattern of action or behavior that results in a different kind of satisfaction. The feeling resulting from achievement is a sense of accomplishment. The feeling resulting from affiliation is warmth, due to being well received by others. Power brings the feeling of being in control, of being influential.

Table 5.3			
Characteristic Present in Organization	**Need for Achievement**	**Need for Power**	**Need for Affiliation**
Warmth	no effect	no effect	aroused
Support	aroused	no effect	aroused
Conflict	aroused	aroused	reduced
Reward	aroused	no effect	aroused
Responsibility	aroused	aroused	no effect

According to the McClelland/Atkinson need theory, the likelihood that a person will perform a task successfully depends on the strength of the motive times the subjective probability of success at the task and the strength of the incentive value of success (the cue that aroused the motive). Atkinson and (especially) McClelland have used this theory to increase job performance by adjusting conditions so that the achievement motive is activated. It appears to be a useful construct for understanding work-related motivation and employee attitudes.

McClelland believes he has identified the characteristics that are typical of achievement-oriented (highly motivated) managers. These characteristics are

1 desire for personal responsibility for decisions and results
2 desire to take moderate risks
3 desire for feedback on results (good or bad)
4 high energy, willingness to work hard
5 tendency to initiate decisions

The research supporting McClelland's theory is strongly positive. There is also strong evidence that his training programs based on this theory are successful in motivating managers to achieve more. Further research is needed, but the theory shows promise.

Consistency Theory

Consistency theory is the first of three theories we will discuss that are toward the rational end of the continuum. The primary mechanisms assumed to be operative in consistency theory are the conscious and rational ones, with the unconscious and emotional ones playing a secondary role.

In its earlier forms consistency theory was a homeostatic, equilibrium, or balance theory. That is, it proposed that people are motivated to keep themselves in a balanced or equilibrium state. The major spokesman for consistency theory in the 1970s is Abraham Korman. He contends that consistency theory is complementary to behaviorism, the Maslow and McClelland/Atkinson need theories, and expectancy theory (to be discussed later).

According to Korman, in our society people must be able to do three things to be effective:

- Achieve in their tasks or jobs
- Keep interpersonal conflicts under reasonable control
- Be creative and adapt to a changing environment

Modern consistency theory is designed to explain how a person can achieve these goals.

Korman hypothesizes that

A Motivational processes are a function of the drive to be consistent with belief systems about the nature of the self, others, and the world.

B Belief systems leading to differing levels of achievement, creativity, and aggression are a function of and develop in the same types of environments.

C Changing environments in certain directions specified by the theoretical model will result in changes in achievement, creativity, and aggression.

Note that in consistency theory the basic motive for all acts (A) is to keep oneself in balance or consistent with one's self-image (developed by the self and others). In effect, we try to maintain that image. This assumes that we want to learn about ourselves and others in order to establish these self-images.

With regard to (B) and (C), Korman makes the following comments:

1 People of high self-perceived competence and positive self-image should be more likely to achieve on task performance than those who have low self-perceived competence, low success expectancy and low self-image concerning the task or job at hand, since such differential task achievement would be consistent with their self-cognitions. This assumes that task performance is seen as valued.

2 People who have beliefs that there is one set of rules to guide behavior in this world and that there is one way of looking at the world are more likely to be opposed to creative change, change in general, and to those people or things that are different or constitute a change from themselves, since such change would be inconsistent with their belief systems.

3 People who have beliefs that people, in general, are not desirable, cannot be trusted, and must be controlled by threats and punishments are more likely to develop aggressiveness toward others and are more likely to engage in generally hostile interpersonal behavior, since such types of behavior would be consistent with their belief systems about people.

The environment described in item 2 of the preceding list leads to what I call conservative management style; item 3 leads to what I call liberal management style later in the book.

In effect, Korman describes the motivational world as shown in the following diagram:

Personal
experience   ↘   Motivation
                               Self-image   →   to be con-   →   Behavior
Others' ex-   ↗   sistent with
pectations   self-image

Korman presents a good deal of research that tends to support his theory. Because of the different effects of different environments (conservative and liberal), consistency theory supports the contingency approach to management. It is also on the rational side, assuming, in effect, that the individual makes a conscious attempt to achieve a single state: consistency of self-image. The theory is promising, but it requires further refinement.

Equity Theory   Another relatively rational motivation theory is *equity theory*. What we call equity theory has been called several other things at other times: social comparison theory, exchange theory, distributive justice theory. It focuses on the theme that rewards such as pay are important motivators of behavior.

In brief, equity theory states that

1 The major cause (motive) leading to job performance and satisfaction is the degree of equity or inequity the employee perceives in the workplace.

2 An employee perceives equity by calculating the ratio of his or her inputs to the outcomes as compared to the ratio (inputs/outcomes) of his or her *reference person* or reference group. Note the emphasis on the *perceived* ratio, not the actual ratio. Examples of inputs include effort, experience and training, seniority, skill, education, and social status. Examples of outcomes are pay, seniority rights, benefits, job status, status symbols and prerequisites, and satisfying supervision. Negative outcomes such as monotony and poor working conditions are subtracted from the positive outcomes.

3 Inequity is a source of tension. The greater the perceived inequity, the greater the motivation to reduce the tension.

4 A person perceives an inequity when he or she is underrewarded.

This perceived inequity is greater than when he or she is overpaid.

5 A person who is overpaid in an hourly pay system will perceive inequity and will produce more than the equitably paid person.

6 A person who is overpaid in a piece rate system will produce higher-quality products than the equitably paid person.

7 A person who is underpaid in hourly system will decrease his or her inputs.

8 A person who is underpaid in a piece rate system will produce a large number of lower-quality products.

9 If a person perceives inequity, he can reduce tension by changing his or her calculations of the ratios.

10 If the magnitude of the inequity is large and there are no other means of reducing it, the person will leave the field.

11 If the inequity is fairly large and there are no other means of reducing it, the person will reduce the inequity through increased absenteeism.

12 Inequity is rarely reduced by changing the reference person or group.

13 The person seeks to maximize positive outcomes and minimize effort.

How well founded is this theory? To begin with, most of its support comes from laboratory studies, not field studies. In Chapter 1 we discussed the shortcomings of such studies. In general, most of the research supports the theory, but not all parts of it have been tested, notably statements 5, 9, 10, 11, and 12.

Equity theory has begun to explain the importance of reward systems in motivating employees at work. Managers have some control over reward systems. To the extent that they try to equitably reward employees for their efforts, this should contribute to employee motivation. Sometimes, however, individual supervisors cannot adequately influence the reward structure (for example, benefits and pay structures are often fixed in spite of various inputs such as education and skill level). This theory helps explain how employees are likely to respond (increase absenteeism, lower the quality of work). Supervisors can try to increase equity by increasing the outcomes that they can control (supervisory style, perquisites, status symbols, lower monotony) in order to offset those they cannot.

Thus this theory provides a manager with significant insights into the relationship between rewards and employee effort. But it is somewhat narrow in its emphasis on visible rewards and probably overemphasizes conscious processes.

Expectancy Theory

The final theory of motivation to be discussed here—and the most complicated—is *expectancy* or *instrumentality theory*. It claims to be compatible with and in fact draws heavily on many of the theories discussed earlier (especially behaviorism, need theories of Maslow and Atkinson-McClelland and to a lesser extent, equity theory).

Philosophically, expectancy theory is based on hedonism (people act to increase pleasure, reduce pain). It is also the most rational of the theories we have discussed, assuming that people act to achieve goals and that they calculate the probabilities that they will be rewarded when they behave in certain ways.

According to expectancy theory, people are motivated to perform at work (1) *if* they believe their efforts will be rewarded *(expectancies) and* (2) *if* the rewards they expect to receive are important to them *(valences)*. This can be expressed in the following formula:

$$\text{Motivation} = E\,(\text{expectancy} \times \text{valence})$$

The expectancy theorists say that expectancies develop from past experiences in the work situation, others' perceptions of the situation, and the employee's level of self-esteem. Valences are developed from the same level of self-esteem, the attractiveness of the outcome, past experiences in the same situation, and how others communicate their perceptions of the situation. In sum, the principal points of the theory are as follows:

1 People have preferences among the outcomes (rewards) that can follow from their behavior. (An example of an outcome is a pay increase or promotion.)

2 People have expectancies (can guess at the probabilities) that their efforts will lead to a particular performance level.

3 People have expectancies that rewards or outcomes will follow their efforts.

4 People are motivated to behave on the basis of these preferences and expectancies.

This appears to be the most popular current motivation theory in terms of amount of research being done. However, the findings of expectancy research are mixed.

·It is based on hedonism, and hedonism is an inadequate basis for explaining human behavior.

·It does not explain individual differences in ability to calculate expectancies and valences.

· It does not explain individual differences in the number and type of consequences people consider when making decisions.

· It ignores unconscious motivations of behavior as well as impulsive and expressive behavior.

· It ignores technical problems: There is no way of measuring valences on a ratio scale, and each valence is explained in terms of all other valences (the infinite regress problem).

Moreover, expectancy theory is overly rational. Not everyone is willing or able to expend the energy to calculate probabilities. Many people respond emotionally to rewards. To the extent that they do, expectancy theory may be an inadequate explanation of their motivation.

If a manager wishes to motivate employees to do more or better work, he or she must be sure that the reward system clearly reinforces hard work or high-quality work. The manager must then make sure this is communicated to the employees so that they are confident that their effort will be rewarded.

The other half of the equation is the "needs" side. The rewards must fit the preferences of the employees, and these vary according to the individual. This is where Maslow, McClelland, and even behaviorism fit into expectancy theory.

But again, managers do not always control all the reward systems. Effective managers try to assess employee preferences and, to the extent that they can, reinforce the links between preferences and rewards. In sum, though it is popular with theorists, expectancy theory needs much more work before it can be accepted as an adequate explanation of motivation.

APPLICATION OF MOTIVATION THEORY TO ENTREPRENEURIAL CHOICE

You may be wondering how motivation theory can help you understand managers, employees, or entrepreneurs. Let me summarize some of what we know about why people are motivated to choose to be entrepreneurs rather than working for someone else. After all, there is considerable psychological and financial risk involved in becoming an entrepreneur. If you work for someone else and things go wrong, you can blame the company. If you work for someone else and the enterprise fails, the company loses the money. But if your business fails, you bear the financial and psychological loss yourself.

Three factors influence a potential entrepreneur in deciding whether or not to become an entrepreneur: (1) the economic, governmental, and home environments; (2) motivation and role models; and the (3) timing of the choice—the triggering mechanism.

With regard to the climate for entrepreneurship, economists like Schumpeter and specialists in entrepreneurship like Arnold Cooper have stressed the importance of economic climate, tax policies, and government policy toward free enterprise to encourage successful entrepreneurs. In addition, the entrepreneur needs encouragement from friends and family.

The third factor affecting the choice of an entrepreneurship or managerial role is its timing or triggering. Many potential entrepreneurs consciously go to work as managers in order to learn the business and build capital, always with entrepreneurship as their eventual goal.

With regard to timing or triggering mechanisms, many entrepreneurs make the choice because they have no other. Big firms reject them as managers because of lack of education or prejudice against their ethnic or social background. Some ethnic groups such as Greeks and Jews are conditioned by a history of prejudice to think primarily of becoming entrepreneurs. On the positive side, an opportunity may present itself and the entrepreneur may seize it while he or she can.

But the second condition is more directly the issue in this chapter. Is there a set of entrepreneurial motives as opposed to managerial motives? Table 5.4 presents a summary and predictions, expressed in terms of McClelland and Maslow's theories.

Table 5.4 Motivations of Managers and Entrepreneurs

Entrepreneurs	Motivations	Managers
	McClelland's Needs	
Desire for high personal achievement with definite feedback	N-achievement	Desire for medium organizational achievement
Higher	N-affiliation	Lower
High need for personal power; desire to be big frog in little pond	N-power	Desire to supervise others
	Maslow's Needs	
High—desire for money initially	A. Physiological	Lower satisfactory level
Lower—trust in own ability to succeed; willingness to take risks	B_1. Security	Higher
	B_2. Risk	Aversion to risk
High	C. Social	High to moderate
High—desire to see own name or business	D. Recognition	High—recognition derived from firm's power and name
High	E. Freedom/autonomy	Low
Through the firm— firm and ego are synonomous	F. Self-actualization	Through rise in hierarchy

The entrepreneurial choice involves consideration of the advantages and disadvantages of both roles: Managers are more secure with a regular income, prestige, less worry away from the job, less risk. Entrepreneurs get more self-expression, freedom of time and action, and if successful, more income and more security against loss of a job. As the table shows, there are some differences between managers and entrepreneurs in the degree to which various needs must be satisfied in each. There are more differences in how these needs are actualized in each case. But both McClelland and Maslow's theories provide a framework for an analysis of differences between entrepreneur and managerial motivations.

SUMMARY   In this chapter I defined motivation as "the inner state that energizes, channels, and sustains human behavior." I pointed out that people and conditions change and therefore motivation may change over time.

The chapter's second objective was to show that motivation can be explained in terms of either conscious, rational processes or unconscious, emotional or instinctual methods. The most useful approach is to assume that both the conscious and the unconscious are involved and that each helps explain certain aspects of behavior.

The third objective was to describe the various motivation theories and evaluate them. First we looked at the instinctual and unconscious end of the continuum. Behaviorism and behavior modification explain behavior in terms of almost instinctual reactions to environmental states and/or inner drives. These theories were found to be too mechanistic and simplistic.

Freud and the psychoanalytic school explain motivation primarily in terms of unconscious if not unknown motives. These clearly play a part in explaining motivation, but again, this is an extreme explanation to apply to *all* behavior.

In discussing the "middle-of-the-road" explanations of motivation we began with Herzberg's theory that only one subset of motives really influences behavior (the motivators), and moved on to Maslow's need hierarchy theory. Maslow's theory can account for both conscious and unconscious motives and appears to be correct in explaining the power of innate or lower needs in determining motivation. The higher needs in his hierarchy have not been fully supported by research. Perhaps Alderfer's reformulation will help.

The McClelland/Atkinson need theory has some interesting and useful applications in attempting to induce achievement motivation in potential managers. It shows promise but needs to be developed further.

Three other theories were discussed. Consistency theory makes an attempt to integrate many other theories and may be useful. Still, it points to a single *basic* motive—consistent reinforcement of the self-image—and this appears to be simplistic and overly rational.

At the rational end of the continuum lies equity theory. This theory tries to explain one facet of work motivation—the relationships between effort, rewards, and effectiveness—and does this fairly well. But the theory may be overly rational and concentrates on a relatively narrow issue.

The most rational of the motivation theories is expectancy theory. Although currently popular with motivation theorists, it is overly rational and has been severely criticized on philosophical and methodological grounds.

In sum, we do not yet have a single, comprehensive, well-supported motivation theory. Behaviorism tells us something about instinctual or semiinstinctual behavior; psychoanalytic theory reminds us of unconscious motivation; Maslow, McClelland, and equity theory each tell us a little about various aspects of motivation. But we are still awaiting a *comprehensive* theory. Consistency theory approaches this goal but does not attain it.

The chapter's fourth objective was to aid the potential manager in understanding motivation—both in the employee and in himself or herself. Every day managers must make decisions on the basis of inadequate information. This applies to motivation, too. Although we do not yet have a comprehensive explanation of motivation, the effective manager will mentally combine the major theories and do the best he or she can to apply them to each situation. Richard Steers and Lyman Porter make the following suggestions about using motivation theory to improve employee performance:

1 If managers want to improve employee attitudes and performance, managers must be active in influencing motivational processes. Shifts toward more positive work attitudes or better motivational climates do not just happen. Managers have to make them happen.

2 Before managers attempt to improve the motivation levels of others, they should have a clear view of their own motives, strengths, and weaknesses and how they themselves are perceived by others at work.

3 Managers should understand that peers, employees, and supervisors' abilities, attitudes, and motives differ; that one set of rewards is not likely to lead to equal effort or performance on the part of everyone.

4 For performance and effort to increase, managers must define superior performance and reward superior performers. At the time of the reward the link between superior performance and reward must be clearly communicated.

5 High performance also requires that employees know what is expected of them on the job and that employees are placed in the types of jobs that will satisfy their needs.

6 Motivation and performance are also affected by supervisory style and social interaction (group dynamics) at work. Managers should determine whether these two factors facilitate performance (more is said about this in Chapters 6, 7, and 8).

7 Work attitudes are important to motivation and performance. Managers need to use attitude surveys more frequently to assess employees' work attitudes and then take steps to improve the less desirable attitudes.

8 The motivation of many employees will be improved if they participate more fully in processes aimed at attaining organizational effectiveness.

Again, remember that managers are busy people. Some, such as supervisors of large sections, will probably have to do the best they can in understanding the motivations of their employees. Others, with smaller sections, will be better able to use their understanding of motivation to help in supervisory, peer, and subordinate relations.

Chapters 4 and 5 concentrated on understanding individual employee behavior. Chapter 6 will help you understand employee behavior as part of a work group or in supervising a work group.

Questions for Review

1. You are attending a training program in a large firm. The sales manager says to the participants, "All I want from you is strong motivation. That's what makes a successful salesperson." Comment.
2. You use the word *motivation* in a management class. The professor says, "What is motivation?" Answer her.
3. Discuss the relative importance of conscious and unconscious motives in influencing behavior in these situations:

   · At work
   · On your first date with someone you are strongly attracted to
   · In considering gifts to your church

   How are they the same? different?
4. Why should you learn about motivation?
5. In what ways do behaviorism and behavior modification explain behavior?
6. How might Freud explain your rejection of a job that pays more money than you make at your present job but is too far from home and would involve more responsibility? How would he explain the equity theory, consistency theory, and expectancy theory?

7. What are the shortcomings of Herzberg's theory? What are its strengths?
8. According to Maslow and Alderfer, what motivates work behavior? How do you explain the popularity of this theory? Does it make sense to you?
9. Compare Maslow's theory to the McClelland/Atkinson theory. Which do you think gives a better explanation of behavior?
10. Examine your study behavior, work behavior, and social behavior during the past week. How would consistency and equity theory explain your choices? Which would provide a better explanation?
11. How does expectancy theory explain motivation?
12. Why do people choose to be entrepreneurs?
13. Which motivation theory is the best? Which ones are compatible? Can you fit them together so that they make sense to you?
14. What use can managers make of motivation theory in its present state of development?

References

Introduction

Terkel, Studs, *Working* (New York: Doubleday, 1975).

Motivation: What Is It?

Alston, William, "Motives and Motivation," *Encyclopedia of Philosophy* (New York: Collier-Macmillan, 1967).

Theories of Motivation/ Behaviorism and Behavior Modification

Alston, op. cit.

Beatty, Richard, and Schneier, Craig, "A Case for Positive Reinforcement," *Business Horizons,* April 1975, pp. 57–66.

Berkowitz, Leonard, "Social Motivation," in Gardner Lindzey and Elliot Aronson, eds., *Handbook of Social Psychology,* 3 (Reading, Mass.: Adddison Wesley, 1969).

de Charms, Richard, *Personal Causation* (New York: Academic Press, 1968).

Hamner, W. Clay, "Worker Motivation Programs," in W. Clay Hamner and Frank Schmidt, eds., *Contemporary Problems in Personnel* (Chicago: St. Clair Press, 1974).

Hull, Clark, *Principles of Behavior* (New York: Appleton-Century-Crofts, 1943).

———, *A Behavior System* (New Haven, Conn.: Yale University Press, 1952).

Luthans, Fred, and Kreitner, Robert, *Organizational Behavior Modification* (Chicago: Scott Foresman, 1975).

Murphy, John, "Is It Skinner or Nothing?" *Training and Development Journal,* 26, no. 2 (February 1972).

Nord, Walter, "Beyond the Teaching Machine: Operant Conditioning in Management," *Organizational Behavior and Human Performance,* 4, no. 4 (November 1969), pp. 375–401.

Schneier, Craig, "Behavior Modification in Management: A Review and Critique," *Academy of Management Journal,* 17, no. 3 (September 1974): 528–548.

Skinner, B. F., *Science and Behavior* (New York: Macmillan, 1953).

———, *Beyond Freedom and Dignity* (New York: Alfred Knopf, 1971).

Sutherland, John, "Beyond Behaviorism and Determinism," *Fields Within Fields,* 10 (Winter 1973-1974).

Weiner, Bernard, *Theories of Motivation* (Chicago: Markham Publishing, 1972).

Psychoanalytic Motivation Theory

Fromm, Erich, *The Anatomy of Human Destructiveness* (New York: Holt, Rinehart and Winston, 1973).

Jung, Carl, *Man and His Symbols* (New York: Doubleday, 1964).

Herzberg's Two-Factor Theory

Campbell, John P., et al., *Managerial Behavior* (New York: McGraw-Hill, 1970).

Dunnette, Marvin, et al., "Factors Contributing to Job Satisfaction and Dissatisfaction in Six Occupational Groups," *Organizational Behavior and Human Performance,* 2, no. 2 (May 1967): 143–174.

Grigalumas, B., and Herzberg, Frederick, "Relevancy in the Test of the Motivator Hygiene Theory," *Journal of Applied Psychology,* 55, no. 1 (1971): 73–79.

Graen, George, "Instrumentality Theory of Work Motivation," *Journal of Applied Psychology Monograph,* 53, pt. 2 (April 1969): 1–25.

Herzberg, Frederick, *The Motivation to Work* (New York: Wiley, 1959).

House, Robert, and Wigdor, L. A., "Herzberg's Dual-Factor Theory of Job Satisfaction and Motivation," *Personnel Psychology,* 20, no. 3 (1967): 369–390.

Pennings, J. M., "Work Value Systems of White-Collar Workers," *Administrative Science Quarterly,* 15, no. 3 (1970): 397–405.

Schwab, Donald, and Heneman, H. G., III, "Aggregate and Individual Predictability of the Two Factor Theory of Job Satisfaction," *Personnel Psychology,* 23, no. 1 (1970): 55–65.

Soleman, H. M., "Motivation-Hygiene Theory of Job Attitudes," *Journal of Applied Psychology,* 54, no. 3 (1970): 452–461.

Maslow's Need Theory

Alderfer, C. P., *Differential Importance of Human Needs as a Function of Satisfaction Obtained in the Organization,* unpublished doctoral dissertation, Yale University, 1966.

———, "An Empirical Test of a New Theory of Human Needs," *Organizational Behavior and Human Performance,* 4, no. 2 (1969): 142–175.

———, *Existence, Relatedness, and Growth* (New York: Free Press, 1972).

Ghiselli, Edward, and Johnson, D., "Need Satisfaction, Managerial Success, and Organizational Structure, *Personnel Psychology,* 23, no. 4 (1970): 569–576.

Haire, Mason, and Gottsdanker, J. "Factors Influencing Industrial Morale," *Personnel,* 27, no. 6 (1961): 445–454.

Hall, Douglas, and Nougaim, K. E., "An Examination of Maslow's Need Hierarchy in an Organization Setting," *Organizational Behavior and Human Performance,* 3, no. 1 (1968): 12–35.

Huizinga, G., *Maslow's Need Hierarchy in the Work Situation* (The Netherlands: Wolters-Noordhoff nv Groningen, 1970).

Lawler, E. E., and Suttle, J. L., "A Causal Correlational Test of the Need Hierarchy

Concept," *Organizational Behavior and Human Performance, 7,* no. 3 (1972): 265–287.

Maslow, A. H., "A Theory of Human Motivation," *Psychological Review,* 50 (1943): 370–396.

———, *Motivation and Personality* (New York: Harper, 1954).

———, *Eupsychian Management* (Homewood, Ill.: Irwin Dorsey Press, 1965).

Mitchell, Vance, "Need Satisfactions of Military Commanders and Staff," *Journal of Applied Psychology,* 54, no. 3 (1970): 282–287.

Payne, R., "Factor Analysis of Maslow Type Need Satisfaction Questionnaire," *Personnel Psychology,* 23, no. 2 (1970): 251–268.

Schneider, Benjamin, and Alderfer, Clayton, "Three Studies of Measures of Need Satisfaction in Organizations," *Administrative Science Quarterly,* 18 (1973): 489–505.

Trexler, J. T., and Schuh, A. J., "Longitudinal Verification of Maslow's Motivation Hierarchy in a Military Environment," *Experimental Publication System* (Washington, D.C.: American Psychological Association, 1969), ms. no. 020A.

Wofford, J. C., "The Motivational Basis of Job Satisfaction and Job Performance," *Personnel Psychology,* 24, no. 4 (1971): 501–518.

Wahba, Mahmoud, and Bridwell, Lawrence, "Maslow Reconsidered," *Proceedings, Academy of Management,* 1973, pp. 514–520.

Wahba, Mahmoud, and Bridwell, Laurence, "Maslow Reconsidered: A Review of Research on the Need Hierarchy," *Organizational Behavior and Human Performance,* 10 (1975): .

The McClelland/ Atkinson Need Theory

Atkinson, J. W., *An Introduction to Motivation* (New York: American Book, 1964).

Atkinson, J. W., and Feather, Norman, eds., *A Theory of Achievement Motivation* (New York: Wiley, 1966).

Atkinson, J. W., and Raynor, J. O., *Motivation and Achievement* (New York: Holt, Rinehart and Winston, 1974).

de Charms, op. cit.

Litwin, George, and Stringer, Robert, *Motivation and Organization Climate* (Cambridge, Mass.: Harvard Business School, 1968).

McClelland, David, *The Personality* (New York: Dryden Press, 1951).

McClelland, David, and Winter, David, *Motivating Economic Achievement* (Glencoe, Ill.: Free Press, 1971).

Wish, Paul, and Hasazi, J. E., "Motivational Determinants of Curricular Choice Behavior in College Males," *Proceedings, Eastern Psychological Association,* 1972.

Consistency Theory

Festinger, L. A., *Theory of Cognitive Dissonance* (Evanston, Ill.: Row, Peterson, 1957).

Heider, F., *The Psychology of Interpersonal Relations* (New York: Wiley, 1958).

Korman, Abraham, *The Psychology of Motivation* (Englewood Cliffs, N.J.: Prentice-Hall, 1974).

———, "Hypothesis of Work Behavior Revisited and an Extension," *Academy of Management Review,* 1, no. 1 (1976): 50–63.

Osgood, C. E., and Tannenbaum, P. H., "The Principle of Congruity in the Prediction of Attitude Change," *Psychological Review,* 62 (1955): 42–55.

Equity Theory Adams, J. Stacy, "Inequity in Social Exchange," in L. Berkowitz, ed., *Advances in Experimental Social Psychology,* vol. 2 (New York: Academic Press, 1965).

———, "Toward an Understanding of Inequity," *Journal of Abnormal and Social Psychology,* 67 (1963): 422–436.

———, "Effects of Overpayment: Two Comments on Lawler's Paper," *Journal of Personality and Social Psychology,* 10 (1968): 315–316.

Evans, Martin, and Molinari, Larry, "Equity Piece Rate Overpayment and Job Security: Some Effects on Performance," *Journal of Applied Psychology,* 54 (1970): 105–114.

Goodman, Paul, and Freedman, Abraham, "An Examination of Adams' Theory of Inequity," *Administration Science Quarterly,* 16 (1971): 271–288.

Homans, George, *Social Behavior* (New York: Harcourt, Brace and World, 1961).

Jacques, Elliot, *Equitable Payment* (New York: Wiley, 1961).

———, *Measurement of Personality* (London: Tavistock Institute, 1956).

Pritchard, Robert, "Equity Theory: A Review and Critique," *Organizational Behavior and Human Performance,* 4 (1969): 176–211.

Weick, Karl, "Reduction of Cognitive Dissonance Through Task Enhancement and Effort Expenditure," *Journal of Abnormal and Social Psychology,* 68 (1964): 533–539.

———, "The Concept of Equity in the Perception of Pay," *Administrative Science Quarterly,* 11 (1966): 414–439.

———, "Dissonance and Task Enhancement," *Organizational Behavior and Human Performance,* 2 (1967): 189–207.

Weick, Karl, and Nesset, Donna, "Preferences Among Forms of Equity," *Organizational Behavior and Human Performance,* 3 (1968): 400–416.

Expectancy Theory Behling, Orlando, and Stark, Frederick, "The Postulates of Expectancy Theory," *Academy of Management Journal,* 16, no. 3 (September 1973): 373–388.

Cummings, Larry, and Schwab, Donald, *Performance in Organizations* (Glenview, Ill.: Scott, Foresman, 1973).

Hackman, J. Richard, and Porter, Lyman, "Expectancy Theory Predictions of Work Effectiveness," *Organizational Behavior and Human Performance,* 3 (1968): 417–426.

Heneman, Herbert, III, and Schwab, Donald, "Evaluation of Research on Expectancy Theory Predictions of Employee Performance," *Psychological Bulletin,* 78, (1972): 1–9.

Lawler, Edward, *Motivation in Work Organizations* (Monterey, Calif.: Brooks/Cole, 1973).

Locke, Edwin, "Personnel Attitudes and Motivation," in *Annual Review of Psychology* (1975): 457–480.

Mitchell, Terrence, and Biglan, Anthony, "Instrumentality Theories: Current Uses in Psychology," *Psychological Bulletin,* 76 (1971).

Pritchard, R., and Sanders, M., "The Influence of Valence, Instrumentality, and Expectancy on Effort and Performance," *Journal of Applied Psychology,* 57 no. 1 (1973): 55–60.

Vroom, Victor, *Work and Motivation* (New York: John Wiley and Sons, 1964).

Wahba, M. A., and House, Robert, "Expectancy Theory in Work and Motivation," *Human Relations,* 27, no. 2 (1974): 121–147.

Application of Motivation Theory to Entrepreneurial Choice

Cooper, Arnold, "Spin Offs and Technical Entrepreneurship," *IEEE Transactions on Engineering Management,* vol. EM 18-1 (February 1971), pp. 2–6.

_____, "Technical Entrepreneurship: What Do We Know?" *R&D Management,* 3, no. 2 (February 1973): 59–64.

Glade, William, "Approaches to a Theory of Entrepreneurial Formation," *Exploration in Entrepreneurial History,* 2nd ser., vol. 4, no. 3 (Spring 1967): 245–259.

Papanek, Gustav, "The Development of Entrepreneurship," *American Economic Review,* 52 (May 1962): 46–58.

"The Entrepreneur as an Innovator," in Joseph Schumpeter, *Business Cycles* (New York: McGraw-Hill, 1939).

Summary

Steers, Richard, and Porter, Lyman, *Motivations and Work Behavior* (New York: McGraw-Hill, 1975).

CHAPTER 6

UNDERSTANDING AND WORKING WITH GROUPS

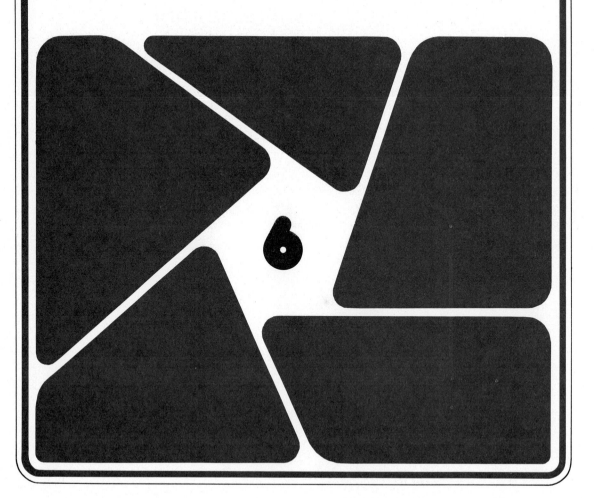

Learning Objectives

1. To understand what a work group is and how groups function.
2. To learn why people join work groups.
3. To understand how groups can help the manager achieve enterprise objectives.
4. To learn that groups can work against managers and when and why this happens.
5. To experience the richness of informal group interactions.

Chapter Outline

The Work Group
Types of Groups
Ways of Studying Groups
What Groups Do for People and Enterprises
The Group's Functions for Its Members
The Group's Functions for the Enterprise
Group Formation and Development
Stages of Group Development
Theories of Group Formation
The Informal Group
Effective Work Groups
Factors in Group Effectiveness
Committees
When Groups Work Against Management
Working with Groups to Achieve Organizational Objectives
Summary

Throughout your life you have been part of a group or groups. If you had brothers or sisters, this was a group. You joined the Scouts or similar organizations, and this was a group. Your class at school was a group. At work, too, we rarely operate alone. In most organizations getting the work done takes a group effort.

Thus far in Part II, I have emphasized the importance of understanding yourself and others *as individuals.* This is very important. But when you become part of a group your behavior is affected by that group. Managing an individual employee requires an understanding of the dynamics of the individual. But most managers manage groups of employees.

One definition of management is "getting things done through people." Almost always, those people are members of a group or several groups. Successful managers therefore must understand the dynamics of group behavior at work. This chapter focuses on human behavior in groups, drawing on your knowledge of individual behavior (covered in Chapters 4 and 5) and expanding it to material specific to group behavior.

THE WORK GROUP

WORK GROUP
A work group is a set of two or more people who see themselves as a group, are interdependent with one another for a purpose, and communicate and interact with one another on a more or less continuing basis. In many cases (but not always) they work closely together physically.

Types of Groups

There are various types of groups. To begin with, groups may be either formal or informal. *Formal groups* are created (usually by managers) to fulfill specific tasks clearly related to the enterprise's purposes. They can be permanent, like departments in an enterprise, or temporary, like committees or task forces. Task forces are formed to achieve a purpose and then disband. But sometimes these "temporary" groups exist for years. *Informal groups* are formed by their members and may either aid in achieving enterprise objectives or serve other needs of the members (such as social needs). There are three types of informal groups (or cliques): the *horizontal clique* (a group of people who work in the same area and are of the same rank and status—for example, all supervisors); the *vertical clique* (a group of people of different rank and status within the same department); and the *mixed clique* (a group of people of different rank and status from different departments in different locations). The latter two types of groups may form because their members have known each other in the past or know each other off the job.

Numerous studies have focused on work groups. One of the most enlightening for the manager is that of Leonard Sayles. Sayles describes how groups differ from each other, but stresses that there is regularity in group behavior. Unlike many studies of groups done in laboratory settings, Sayles observed 300 work groups in 30 companies mostly in the auto and auto-related industries. His findings are diagramed in Figure 6.1.

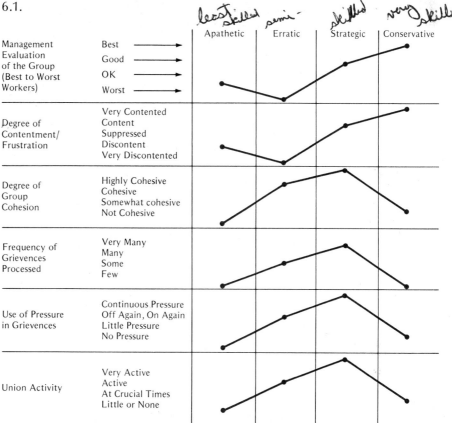

Figure 6.1
Some characteristics of 300 work groups.

Sayles categorized the groups as follows:

1 *Apathetic groups:* relatively low-paid and low-skilled assembly line workers who were interdependent with each other. It was hard to identify the leaders of these informal groups, if they had any.

2 *Erratic groups:* semiskilled workers who worked together in groups doing jobs that required interaction. Essentially, they all did the same job and were homogeneous. They tended to choose as their leaders strong, big buys who were autocratic and tended to centralize power. They also tended to be "loudmouths."

3 *Strategic groups:* skilled employees (such as welders) whose jobs required judgment. Their jobs were not interdependent and were the better or key jobs in the plant. They chose as leaders several people who did their jobs well and represented the group quietly.

4 *Conservative groups:* the most highly skilled workers in the plant (e.g., plant maintenance employees). They worked on their own. Their jobs were such that they could shut the plant if they wanted to. They chose as their leader the most technically competent worker, who led quietly and stayed in the background.

The erratic groups tend to give management the most trouble. They are unpredictable. Sometimes an action by management leads to nothing; the next time it provokes a strike. The apathetic workers tend to be continally and quietly frustrated. The strategic groups have a very rational approach, and managers know where they stand with them. The conservatives are the "elder statesmen" and usually go about their business without any trouble. Management spends most of its time dealing with strategic groups and trying to keep erratic groups in line.

Ways of Studying Groups   There are many ways of studying groups. To some extent, how you study groups—the vantage point from which you look at them—influences what you find out. Most of the research reported later in this chapter is based on three theories or methods: interaction process analysis, sociometric analysis, and systems theory.

Interaction Process Analysis.

Robert Bales has studied groups by observing their behavior and recording (on a moving tape) which people interact with each other and how they do so. He has reduced a list of 87 possible interactions to 12 actions (positive and negative) related to work and human interactions. Positive work acts included:

1 Giving suggestions and directions implying autonomy for others.
2 Giving opinions, evaluations, analyses, expressing feelings and wishes.
3 Giving orientation, information, repetition, and confirmation.

Negative work acts included:

1 Asking for orientation, information, repetition and confirmation.
2 Asking for opinions, evaluations, analyses, and expression of feelings.
3 Asking for suggestions, directions, and possible ways of action.

Positive human interactions included:

1 Showing solidarity, raising others' status, giving help and reward.
2 Showing release of tension, joking, laughing, and showing satisfaction.

3 Agreeing, showing passive acceptance, understanding and complying.

Negative human interactions included:

1 Disagreeing, showing passive rejection, and withholding help.

2 Showing tension, asking for help, withdrawing out of the field.

3 Showing antagonism, deflating other's status, defending or asserting ones self.

By analyzing the percentage of the time each group (and the individuals in it) spends in interaction, Bales' followers can predict problems and analyze a group's operations.

Sociometric Analysis

Sociometric analysis is a way of studying how members of groups prefer to interact. The method, attributed to J. L. Moreno, is most useful in smaller groups. The members are asked to indicate (usually on a questionnaire) the group member they like the least and the one they like the most. When these preferences are totaled, four kinds of individuals can be identified:

1 *Leaders* who accept the group's purpose and norms and provide direction of the group toward its purposes.

2 *Isolates* who do not participate in the group, reject group norms, and do not get along with the rest of the group.

3 *Deviates* who participate in the group but do not accept all group norms; they get along, however.

4 *Members* who typically identify with the group's purpose and norms.

Group preferences can be diagramed as shown in Figure 6.2. In this sociogram John is an isolate; Sally is the leader; Mary, Tom, George, and Angie are members; and Sam is a deviate. Thus sociometric analysis can tell us a lot about healthy intragroup relationships and help identify the problems that are likely to arise in a particular group.

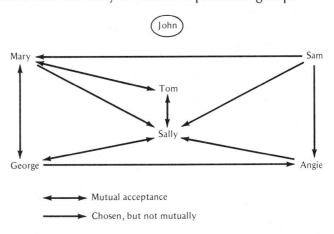

Figure 6.2
A sociogram.

Systems Analysis

The third major approach to studying groups is George Homans' systems analysis. Homans and his followers study groups by analyzing factors that are external to the group (the external system) and those that are internal to it (the internal system). The internal system develops out of the external system, but the two interact after the internal system is well developed.

Factors that Homans considers to be part of the external system include the enterprise's organization structure and control system, the technology of the job and its required communications and interactions (for example, assembly line vs. craft work). He has described the internal system as consisting of three interacting behaviors:

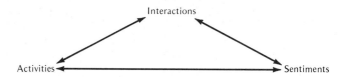

Activities are the things people do with machines or each other as part of their work, such as typing letters or running a punch press. *Interactions* are the ways people relate to each other—for example, one person talks, the other replies. Important here are the person who initiates the interactions, the frequency and length of the interactions, and the person with whom he or she interacts. *Sentiments* include feelings, values, opinions, and beliefs held by an individual or a group. Typical values and sentiments at work include people's feelings about each other (like or dislike), the fairness of reward system, and the like.

Homans has developed theories about the interrelationships among the variables in the external and internal systems. His propositions include the following:

1 The greater the frequency of interaction, the stronger the sentiment of friendship between those who are interacting.

2 The sentiments of group leaders are more influential on the group than those of members of the group.

3 The greater the frequency of interaction, the greater the similarity among the actions of group members.

Research based on Homans' model has contributed many of the findings described later in this chapter.

**WHAT GROUPS
DO FOR PEOPLE
AND
ENTERPRISES**

As we shall see shortly, when you join a group you pay certain costs. There is pressure to conform. And an exchange, a social exchange, takes place. You are expected to contribute to the social and work outcomes of the group. It is difficult to understand why you would be willing to pay these costs unless you get something from the group in return.

Accordingly, we now take a look at the functions groups serve *for their members* and for *the enterprise.*

The Group's Functions for Its Members By becoming a member of a group a person fulfills at least four types of needs:

1 Social and affiliation needs

2 Identity, recognition, and ego/esteem needs

3 Security and power needs

4 Other needs

    a Establish and stabilize work perceptions and norms

    b Serve as information source

    c Relieve boredom

    d Fill in for ill or absent employees

Social and Affiliation Needs

In Chapter 5 Maslow's "social need" was described, as was McClelland's "need for affiliation." Groups serve as the primary mechanism for fulfilling these needs by friendship and support. The work group is the most likely place to find understanding, companionship, and comradeship at work. Job problems can be discussed with group members, and this often applies to personal problems as well. After all, many of us spend more waking hours per day with our coworkers than with anyone else.

Everyone needs someone to take a break with, to have lunch with. The work group provides for these needs, too. At school and at work most of us have had the feeling of acceptance (or rejection) by others. Acceptance by others is a very rewarding experience, and we go to great lengths to acquire acceptance and avoid rejection. The work group is usually the source of acceptance at work. If it becomes a source of rejection, an alternative source of acceptance is sought, often with great difficulty. So employees join work groups and work at being accepted in order to satisfy their need for affiliation (social need).

Identity, Recognition, and Ego/Esteem Needs

The second reason people become involved in work groups is that the group can provide the recognition-ego esteem needs described by Maslow. It can also make a significant input to a person's identity development. As discussed in Chapters 4 and 5, a major part of the identity of those for whom work is important comes from the workplace. Most middle-class and upper-class people (and many lower-class individuals as well) identify themselves as dentists, hospital administrators, personnel managers, or the like. The work group is the primary source of recognition and esteem for these individuals. Other people may not know what a biochemist is or how important he or she is to the lab, but the work group knows and provides the necessary feedback. Thus groups help us train ourselves in psychological adjustment, confirm our identity, and maintain self-esteem.

Groups also give us the feeling of "belonging." It is difficult to get such a feeling in most large organizations. The U.S. military establishment employs millions, the City University of New York thousands, General Motors 600,000. To get a feeling of belonging within organizations like these one must be a member of a small work group.

Security and Power Needs

Groups can provide for other needs of individuals. Specifically, groups help employees satisfy their security needs (Maslow) or their need for power (McClelland/Atkinson). If a group supports an employee against "arbitrary" demands by outsiders (other groups, managers, clients), it gives that employer more control over his or her destiny. It gives the employee a sense of power and, therefore, dignity. The evidence is fairly strong that most employees join unions to protect themselves against what they perceive to be arbitrary or capricious acts by supervisors. Groups provide the employee with similar feelings of security. So by joining groups employees are trying to protect themselves against outside pressures.

Other Needs

Groups serve a series of other purposes in addition to those just discussed. One is to help establish and stabilize perceptions of the workplace. Groups also serve as sources of information, help out when members are sick or absent, and help relieve boredom through mutual interaction.

The Group's Functions for the Enterprise

Some managers have heard horror stories about how groups can work against a particular manager or against the enterprise itself. As a result they may consciously try to prevent the development and operation of groups. Managers can impede group relationships by making frequent transfers, by assigning people who are known to be incompatible to the same work group, or through physical work arrangements (e.g., designing the work area so that people are separated by space, noise, or physical barriers). In extreme cases such measures can be justified. In general, however, it is difficult if not impossible to prevent groups from forming. As we have seen, employees have a strong need for affiliation. And prevention of group formation may backfire in that lack of social interaction is likely to lead to greater turnover, absenteeism, accidents, and lower quality of work if not lower output.

Besides, groups perform at least three functions that are important to an enterprise's success:

payoff for the organization (handwritten margin note)

1 Socialization of new employees
2 Getting the job done
3 Help in decision making

So it makes sense for a manager to learn to work with and through groups instead of trying to prevent them from forming.

Socialization of New Employees

Sociologists describe the process of orienting new employees as *socialization.* By this they mean teaching the new employee the work norms, that is, how to behave at work. In some cases groups "slow down" employees who are "working too hard" and showing up the other members. But they do the opposite, too. If an employee is not working hard enough, the group pressures him or her to "get in line." If an employee is lazy, comes in late, or fools around too much, the output of the whole group goes down. Or the slacker is noticed by bosses or other groups and the word gets around that that group is a "goof-off" group. Few groups want such a reputation. So the group pressures the slacker to meet the group's norms of output, work hours, and the like. This pressure takes the form of talking to the employee, shunning or ignoring him or her, or, in extreme cases, physical pressures. Thus the group orients and integrates the new employee into the enterprise's work rules and norms and keeps the employee under control. After all, the supervisor cannot watch every employee all the time, but the group can.

Getting the Job Done

Although theoretically the enterprise is responsible for training the new employee and getting the work done, this is often accomplished by the work group. Usually the new employee gets some training on how to do the job. But this is rarely enough to get the job done well. The work group really teaches the employee how to cope with the job, how to handle the 1001 variations on the techniques taught in the training program that are needed to get the job done.

Many parts of the job may have to be done by two or more people. Someone in the work group helps out at such times. Thus theoretically, the departmental secretary types and the duplication operator runs the machine. In fact, when the duplication operator has a lot of work the secretary helps out by helping to collate the work. Then the duplication operator helps the secretary proofread the report just typed. They could work separately, but cooperation helps them both. Thus work groups facilitate both training and operations and therefore are beneficial to the enterprise.

Decision Making

Effective decision making is discussed in detail in Chapter 13. Here I will simply point out that some decisions turn out better when several people with different backgrounds and training make them jointly than if one person makes them alone. Again, well-established groups that are operating effectively can make better decisions.

GROUP FORMATION AND DEVELOPMENT

There have been many descriptions and studies of the formation and development of groups.

Stages of Group Development

A typical analysis of group development includes four stages: initial formation, development of goals, elaboration of structure, and development of leaders.

Stage 1: Initial formation A number of people with the abilities necessary to achieve an organizational goal are assembled and assigned a task. At this stage of development it is important that individuals recognize the social need to belong to the group and that they be willing to give and receive friendship and other marks of affiliation, for it is in their self-interest to do so.

Stage 2: Development of goals At this stage the group seeks to establish common task goals. To the extent that these goals are clearly understood, are generally agreed on, and are relevant to the needs of individuals, they are more likely to be achieved.

Stage 3: Elaboration of structure At this stage coordination becomes paramount. Formal leaders are appointed by management, and communication is encouraged in an attempt to reinforce the structure.

Stage 4: Development of leaders To supplement the formal leadership of the supervisor (boss or company executive), informal leaders develop. These are the people group members turn to when they encounter problems. Leadership studies have identified at least two leaders of work groups: the task leader (usually the formally appointed leader), who pays primary attention to formal goal achievement, and the social leader (informal leader), who provides "social maintenance." The informal leaders tend to be those who have the most status both on and off the job—in other words, the "right" education, skill, sex, age, seniority, ethnic background, and social mobility.

A drawback of this analysis of group development is its orientation toward groups formed by the enterprise itself. In reality, smaller groups evolve within formal groups or across them. How do these informal groups evolve? Several theories have been advanced to explain this phenomenon.

Theories of Group Formation

The Demands-of-the Job Theory

Some jobs cannot be done well unless a small, strong group forms and is maintained. Examples are tank and submarine crews. Their lives depend on the group, and this provides a strong motivation for group formation.

Interaction Theory

Informal groups form as a consequence of frequent interaction in common activities. The more frequent the interaction, the stronger the positive feeling toward the group and therefore the greater the likelihood of group formation and maintenance.

The Similarity Theory

Many management specialists believe groups will be formed and maintained to the degree that the members are similar to each other: The more similar they are, the greater the likelihood of group formation. Such similarities may be in the areas of work values, life experiences, education, socioeconomic status, sex, age, religion, ethnic background, and the like.

There are other theories that try to explain group formation on the basis of power manipulation, maintenance or acquisition of status and money, and so forth. But the three just described are probably the most likely explanations of informal group formation. Persistence of groups is discussed later in the chapter.

THE INFORMAL GROUP The material covered thus far in the chapter is theoretically sound and is important in understanding management. But it needs to be illustrated with examples. The following case studies are an attempt to do this.

When a group has really developed, it has become its own society, its own culture. Like a tribe on an island, it has developed its own language, customs, rituals, and ways of doing things. These lead to verbal and physical horseplay, razzing, and practical jokes.

If you watch television regularly, you may have learned something about how the small group "humanizes" the workplace. On M*A*S*H, Hawkeye regularly pulls practical jokes on the overly pompous, rank-conscious Major Burns and Hot Lips O'Hoolihan. The banter you see on the Bob Newhart show, usually with Carol as a central character, is typical. On the Mary Tyler Moore show standard jokes and ceremonies built around Ted Baxter's ego or Lou Grant's gruffness find Mary and Morey playing standard roles to keep the team together. The intermingling of personal lives with work lives is also typical of how the informal organization takes care of the need for affiliation and the ego needs of its members.

Television, however, rarely brings you the work lives of blue-collar or white-collar workers. Therefore I would like to summarize a classic description of how a blue-collar work group can operate for the benefit of all concerned.

Donald Roy was a participant observer of a work group that operated punch presses in an isolated room. It was routine work. It took fifteen minutes to learn to do the job, and Roy worked at it for two months. He worked a twelve-hour day, six days a week. He stood in one spot and "placed the die, punched the clicker, placed the die, punched the clicker" all that time. The work was physically tiring. His legs ached (he was not allowed to sit) and his feet hurt. The work was also, needless to say, very monotonous.

The work group, in addition to filling its members' affiliation and esteem needs, provided for psychological survival by breaking the monotony with episodes of "talking and fooling around." "Management" appeared on the scene only twice, for five minutes, during the two-month period. So although there were many times production could have dropped, it stayed high because *the group wanted it high.* It was not as high as it could be (a night replacement produced a few more items per hour by himself), but still it was higher than management expected.

The work group consisted of Roy and three longtime employees: George (late 50s), an immigrant from eastern Europe; Ike (early 50s), a Jewish immigrant from eastern Europe; and Sammy (late 50s), a Jewish refugee from eastern Europe just ahead of Hitler. All three had held better jobs in the "old country" or had run a business here that failed. George was the senior man, made 5¢ more per hour, and dealt with "the outside"—that is, those outside the room.

Being isolated, unable to "fight" management or other groups, the punch operators created their own world in order to make the job bearable. They did this by breaking the day up with "times" occurring about once an hour. This gave the men a little break, but more important, it showed the passage of the day. At first Roy ignored their banter, but later he realized what was going on. He describes the group's interaction as follows:

> What I saw at first, before I began to observe, was occasional flurries of horseplay so simple and unvarying in pattern and so childish in quality that they made no strong bid for attention. For example, Ike would regularly switch off the power at Sammy's machine whenever Sammy made a trip to the lavatory or the drinking fountain. Correlatively, Sammy invariably fell victim to the plot by making an attempt to operate his clicking hammer after returning to the shop. And, as the simple pattern went, this blind stumbling into the trap was always followed by indignation and reproach from Sammy, smirking satisfaction from Ike, and mild paternal scolding from George. My interest in this procedure was at first confined to wondering when Ike would weary of his tedious joke or when Sammy would learn to check his power switch before trying the hammer.

> But, as I began to pay closer attention, as I began to develop familiarity with the communication system, the disconnected became connected, the nonsense made sense, the obscure became clear, and the silly actually funny. And, as the content of the interaction took on more and more

meaning, the interaction began to reveal structure. There were "times" and "themes" and roles to serve their enaction. The interaction had subtleties, and I began to savor and appreciate them. I started to record what hitherto had seemed unimportant.

Roy then describes the series of "times":

Most of the breaks in the daily series were designated as "times" in the parlance of the clicker operators, and they featured the consumption of food or drink of one sort or another. There was coffee time, peach time, banana time, fish time, coke time, and, of course, lunch time. Other interruptions, which formed part of the series but were not verbally recognized as "times," were window time, pickup time, and the staggered quitting times of Sammy and Ike. These latter unnamed times did not involve the partaking of refreshments.

My attention was first drawn to this times business during my first week of employment when I was encouraged to join in the sharing of two peaches. It was Sammy who provided the peaches; he drew them from his lunch box after making the announcement, "'Peach time!'" On this first occasion I refused the proffered fruit, but thereafter regularly consumed my half peach. Sammy continued to provide the peaches and to make the "Peach time!" announcement, although there were days when Ike would remind him that it was peach time, urging him to hurry up with the mid-morning snack. Ike invariably complained about the quality of the fruit and his complaints fed the fires of continued banter between peach donor and critical recipient. I did find the fruit a bit on the scrubby side but felt, before I achieved insight into the function of peach time, that Ike was showing poor manners by looking a gift horse in the mouth. I wondered why Sammy continued to share his peaches with such an ingrate. . . .

Window time came next. It followed banana time as a regular consequence of Ike's castigation by the indignant Sammy. After taking repeated references to himself as a person badly lacking in morality and character, Ike would "finally" retaliate by opening the window which faced Sammy's machine, to let the "cold air" blow in on Sammy. The slandering which would, in its echolalic repetition, wear down Ike's patience and forbearance usually took the form of the invidious comparison "George is a good daddy! Ike is a bad man! A very bad man!" Opening the window would take a little time to accomplish and would involve a great deal of verbal interplay between Ike and Sammy, both before and after the event. Ike would threaten, make feints toward the window, then finally open it. Sammy would protest, argue, and make claims that the air blowing in on him would give him a cold; he would eventually have to leave his machine to close the window. Sometimes the weather was slightly chilly and the draft from the window unpleasant; but cool or hot, windy or still, window time arrived each day. (I assume that it was originally a cold season development.) George's part in this interplay, in spite of the "good daddy" laudations, was to encourage Ike in his window work. He would stress the tonic values of fresh air and chide Sammy for his unappreciativeness.

Other rituals and ceremonies followed at lunch, pickup time (when the "outside" picked up their work, fish time, Coke time, and closing time.

In addition to the rest break rituals, there were patterns of conversation or "themes." Roy continues:

> Unlike the times, these themes flowed one into the other in no particular sequence of predictability. Serious conversation could suddenly melt into horseplay, and vice versa. In the middle of a serious discussion on the high cost of living, Ike might drop a weight behind the easily startled Sammy, or hit him over the head with a dusty paper sack. Interaction would immediately drop to a low-comedy exchange of slaps, threats, guffaws, and disapprobations which would invariably include a ten-minute echolalia of "Ike is a bad man, a very bad man! George is a good daddy, a very fine man!" Or, on the other hand, a stream of such invidious comparisons as followed a surreptitious switching-off of Sammy's machine by the playful Ike might merge suddenly into a discussion of the pros and cons of saving for one's funeral.

> "Kidding themes" were usually started by George or Ike, and Sammy was usually the butt of the joke. Sometimes Ike would have to "take it," seldom George. One favorite kidding theme involved Sammy's alleged receipt of $100 a month from his son. The points stressed were that Sammy did not have to work long hours, or did not have to work at all, because he had a son to support him. George would always point out that he sent money to his daughter; she did not send money to him. Sammy received occasional calls from his wife, and his claim that these calls were requests to shop for groceries on the way home were greeted with feigned disbelief. Sammy was ribbed for being closely watched, bossed, and henpecked by his wife, and the expression "Are you man or mouse?" became an echolalic utterance, used both in and out of the original context. . . .

> The "poom poom" theme was one that caused no sting. It would come up several times a day to be enjoyed as unbarbed fun by the three older clicker operators. Ike was usually the one to raise the question "How many times you go poom poom last night?" The person questioned usually replied with claims of being "too old for poom poom." If this theme did develop a goat, it was I. When it was pointed out that I was a younger man, this provided further grist for the poom poom mill. I soon grew weary of this poom poom business, so dear to the hearts of the three old satyrs, and, knowing where the conversation would inevitably lead, winced whenever Ike brought up the subject.

Roy also describes other discussion themes, most of them light. But there were serious themes as well:

> Serious themes included the relating of major misfortunes suffered in the past by group members. George referred again and again to the loss, by fire, of his business establishment. Ike's chief complaints centered around

a chronically ill wife who had undergone various operations and periods of hospital care. Ike spoke with discouragement of the expenses attendant upon hiring a housekeeper for himself and his children; he referred, with disappointment and disgust, to a teen-age son, an inept lad who "couldn't even fix his own lunch. He couldn't even make himself a sandwich!" Sammy's reminiscences centered on the loss of a flourishing business when he had to flee Europe ahead of Nazi invasion. . . .

There was one theme of especially solemn import, the "professor theme." This theme might also be termed "George's daughter's marriage theme"; for the recent marriage of George's only child was inextricably bound up with George's connection with higher learning. The daughter had married the son of a professor who instructed in one of the local colleges. This professor theme was not in the strictest sense a conversation piece; when the subject came up, George did all the talking. The two Jewish operators remained silent as they listened with deep respect, if not actual awe, to George's accounts of the "Big Wedding" which, including the wedding pictures, entailed an expense of $1,000. It was monologue, but there was listening, there was communication, the sacred communication of a temple, when George told of going for Sunday-afternoon walks on the Midway with the professor, or of joining the professor for Sunday dinner. Whenever he spoke of the professor, his daughter, the wedding, or even the new son-in-law, who remained for the most part in the background, a sort of incidental like the wedding cake, George was complete master of the interaction. His manner, in speaking to the rank-and-file of clicker operators, was indeed that of master deigning to notice his underlings. I came to the conclusion that it was the professor connection, not the straw-boss-ship or the extra nickel an hour, which provided the fount of George's superior status in the group.

Roy found out how important it was not to interfere in these themes when he accidentally tried to spoof George's professor theme and the work group joined in. George refused to speak to them for two weeks.

The second case is from my own experience. When I worked as a sales manager I noticed that my sales group used similar "themes" and "times" to break up its day and take care of its affiliation and ego needs. The group, consisting of about fifteen men, had some of the problems just described but some different ones too. The salesman called on stores all day. They could not spend much time with their fellow workers. They had to "fight" all the time. The store owners or managers were clearly in positions of power, while the salesmen were "suppliants," always asking for something: an order for their product, a better shelf position, a display or feature. True, they could occasionally offer managers or owners small rewards—a free lunch, tickets to sports events (usually once a year or so). In addition, the salesmen broke the routine for the manager. And the better salesmen were good at story telling, joke telling, community gossip, and the like. But often the owners or managers were busy and did not want to talk to the salesmen. Or they were under competing pressure from "the office" or other salespeople for the same space or order. So they would respond by being gruff with the salesmen, ignoring them, or even humiliating them. On some days, the salesmen felt beaten down and needed to have their self-esteen put back in equilibrum.

The official purpose of the weekly sales meeting (and the annual National Sales Convention) is to introduce the salesmen to new products, new advertising campaigns, price changes, and so forth. But a significant other reason and, in my opinion, a more important purpose was to satisfy their affiliation/esteem needs. The salesmen also met for coffee, lunch, and drinks (after work) for the same purposes. After all, much of the official information (regarding prices, products, etc.) could have been mailed to the salesmen. The purpose of the meetings was recognition. The salesmen were encouraged to tell their success stories at the meetings. This gave them a chance for recognition and also served as training in the mysterious ways of salesmanship.

Like Roy's clicker operators, my salesmen had their themes. In addition to their current success stories, the "classic" sales strategies that each had developed in the past were recounted over and over again. They had a common thread running through them: "how I fooled that SOB (buyer)." Usually these stories were built around an especially unpleasant buyer and how the salesman, by playing on the buyer's weaknesses, had oversold him or her.

The "classic" sales stories would be told over and over. For example, one of Charlie's buyers, representing an independent group of stores, continually humiliated him. I asked him to sell this buyer 500 cases of a new product. In a classic sales strategy, Charlie exploited the buyer's weakness: hatred of chain stores.

> Charlie: Well, Joe, this new product, Kool Pops, is really going to sell. In fact it's on allocation (limited sale). You're entitled to 500 cases, but I'm afraid your small stores couldn't handle that many. I'd hate to see you overloaded, so I suggest you take 250 and we'll give the other 250 to A&P or Kroger.

> Joe: The hell you will! What do you mean my stores aren't big enough. I'm entitled to 500, and by God I get 500. You SOB, don't you dare give any of my cases to those . . . A&P and Kroger.

Each time this story was told there was uproarious laughter. Charlie now had the buyer right where he wanted him. He sold his quota and the buyer could not complain, since he had insisted that he needed all 500 cases. By telling this story Charlie got the recognition he needed, satisfied the group's social needs, and taught new salespeople some "tricks of the trade."

Each of the salesmen was continually reminded of his most outstanding "failings." There was John, a 300-pounder, who was kidded about his eating and his fondness for gardening. He was the straw boss.

Then there was Charlie, who, in spite of his ordinary looks and age of 50, was charged with being a stud and accused of getting his orders by "performing" with the women in the buyers' offices. There was Bill, whose role was to appear befuddled (like a fox) and who always lost "small" orders only to send in bigger ones "by mistake." And there was Roy, who loved fancy cars and always managed to get a "special deal" for extra chrome or options. Though Roy was bald, he was "Curly" to the other salesmen.

The purpose of this section was to show that effective groups create their own cultures with their own language, rituals, and behaviors. More important, informal groups play a vital role in satisfying affiliation and social needs and getting the work done by reducing boredom or restoring psychological equilibrium.

Some managers do not understand the value of groups. When they enter an office or workplace and hear chatter or banter, they scold the employees, telling them to "get to work and cut out this nonsense." This has the effect of *reducing* both employee satisfaction and productivity.

But, you say, group interaction can go too far, so that productivity suffers. This happens in a few cases. But before you react negatively, check the output. If it is high, you know the group is functioning well. If it is low, you may have to point this out to the group and tell them productivity must go up.

As always, remember that there are individual differences in the need for social interaction expressed through chatter, banter, horseplay, and the like. Some people prefer to work alone and produce more under such conditions. It has been argued that southern European people prefer more social interaction of this type than northern Europeans, blacks more than WASPS, and so on. Rather than focusing on supposed ethnic differences in the need for affiliation, it probably makes more sense to realize that some individuals have a greater need for affiliation than others and that some jobs provide for this need better than others. In any case, output quantity and quality, costs, and employee satisfaction are more important than quiet, neat workplaces.

EFFECTIVE WORK GROUPS   The factors influencing group effectiveness may be summarized as follows:

1 Group size
2 Number of members
3 Nature of task
4 Eye contact and location of members
5 Cohesiveness
6 Group norms
7 Other factors

And an effective work group may be defined as follows:

> **EFFECTIVE WORK GROUP**
> An effective work group is one whose members function as a team and participate fully in group discussions; whose goals are clearly developed; and whose resources are adequate to accomplish its goals.

Factors in Group Effectiveness

Let us briefly discuss the factors that can influence group effectiveness.

Size of group The effective group is relatively small. In fact some studies have come up with specific numbers; for example, 7 is the ideal maximum for a decision-making group and 14 is the maximum for a fact-finding group. *NO LARGER THAN 15.*

Theoretically, as a group gets larger it could become more effective. The potential for greater variety of talents is greater. Members have a better chance of finding people they like to work with. But the disadvantages of size more than offset its advantages. More effort must be used to get the group to function. Splinter groups may form. Larger groups take longer to function and may not be able to function at all. As the group gets larger, it becomes less efficient, since most members of necessity participate less. Thus, though the research in this area is tenuous, size is an important variable in group effectiveness.

Number of members Groups with an even number of members make more accurate decisions because they are less likely than odd-numbered groups to resort to the simple process of voting. But odd-numbered groups work faster.

Nature of task Homogeneous groups (those whose members are alike in such areas as age, education, status, and experience) are better when the task or goal requires mutual cooperation and conflict-free behavior and if the task is simple. Heterogeneous groups are more effective when the task is complex, if speed is not important, and if creativity is desirable.

individuals are more creative than groups.

Eye contact and location of members Groups whose members are located close together and can interact frequently and easily are likely to be more cohesive and effective than those whose members are separated by greater distance. This may be due to the ability of the members to maintain eye contact if they are located close together. Eye movement, direction of gaze, and mutual eye contact are important nonverbal interactions that influence group effectiveness. The easier it is to communicate in person, the more likely the group is to be cohesive. Frequency of communication is also important. And, finally, the more isolated the group is from others by distance or physical barriers, the more cohesive it becomes.

Cohesiveness Group cohesiveness is the degree to which group members are of one mind and thus can act as one body. Sometimes cohesiveness is thought of as group loyalty, group solidarity, or group pride.

Cohesiveness results from homogeneity of membership, stability of membership over time (the more stable, the more cohesive), and high status (the higher the status, the more cohesive the group). In general, cohesive groups are more effective. But it is a circular relationship. That is, as James Davis puts it, "there is nothing like success to increase group spirit and cohesiveness. A near universal finding is that cohesiveness generally increases with success."

Cohesion has important managerial implications. A manager must deal with a cohesive group as a unit. Managers can influence cohesion through selection, transfer, location, and other decisions. Cohesion can also be built by threats from "the outside."

Group Norms Group norms are shared values about the kinds of behavior that are acceptable and unacceptable at work. They develop over time and are reinforced by group pressures on the members to conform.

Norms can affect performance positively or negatively. The effects of norms on productivity or performance are affected by cohesiveness. In general, if the group is very cohesive and performance is a group norm, performance will be high. If the group is less cohesive, the norm will be less powerful.

Other Factors Most studies trying to determine whether factors such as greater intelligence, specific abilities, or certain personality traits are correlated with group performance have not come up with significant results.

Committees A committee is a special kind of work group, often a temporary, task-oriented group. Many people have had unhappy experiences on committees and tend to criticize them.

Committees will be more effective if

1 They are composed of five members. If the committee needs technical advice that none of its members can provide, it can invite in an "expert."

2 The members take a cooperative approach instead of competing with each other.

3 They are led by a directive task leader who keeps things moving. If the leader tries to be a social "good fellow," the committee will be less effective.

"There are no great men, my boy—only great committees."

Source: Drawing by Chas. Addams; © 1975 The New Yorker Magazine, Inc.

WHEN GROUPS WORK AGAINST MANAGEMENT

Although the positive aspects of group behavior have been stressed in our discussion so far, groups can also be dysfunctional. People who perceive themselves to be members of different groups can develop tunnel vision, and trouble can develop between groups. It soon becomes a "we" and "they" situation. Perceptual studies have shown how group members perceive themselves as "good" and members of other groups as "bad" if there is no one to act as liaison between the two groups.

Just as groups can organize to achieve organizational goals, they can resist or sabotage them as well, especially if the leaders fail to interpret these goals effectively to the group. Groups that resist organizational goals do not always develop randomly. Sayles' study of 300 work groups, described earlier, indicated that certain characteristics in the technical environment led some groups (which he called erratic and strategic) to cause more trouble than conservative, highly skilled groups or apathetic, unskilled groups. And sometimes there are real conflicts in goals between the group and the organization. For example, management's goal of raising output standards can lead to the fear that jobs will be eliminated. The group may try to protect less competent employees who cannot meet the new standards. These reasons and others can lead to group resistance of managerial goals. One of the challenges of management is to get groups working with the organization rather than against it.

The literature and lore of management contain many examples of groups resisting management and hindering output. Let me describe what a cohesive work group can do to make a point and "fight management." A friend of mine was drafted and sent for basic Army training to the Armor Center, Fort Knox, Kentucky. He was part of a typical tank platoon. The platoon members got along well. Then they got a new commanding officer, an ROTC graduate with a swagger stick, an exaggerated opinion of himself, and a low opinion of the men. He worked them long hours, punished them frequently, and never praised them. The men let their performance drop in order to "send him a message." His response was to berate, punish, and overwork them even more.

The men then decided to "take action." They met for a few beers and planned their strategy. They had observed that the commanding officer (whom they called Little Napoleon) took special pride in the Company Day Room (a place designed for troop relaxation, consisting of pool tables, magazines, bulletin boards, and so on). Generally the Day Room was little used and little noticed, but "Little Napoleon" had privates in there waxing and polishing all the time.

The plan was to "send Napoleon a stronger message." One night after it was dark and Napoleon was gone, the group backed up a truck and emptied the day room of its chairs, card tables, pool tables, and so forth and dumped them in the Ohio River. Napoleon was financially responsible for this furniture. But believe it or not, this produced no change in the commanding officer. He redoubled his efforts to discipline the men.

At about this time the unit was to rotate to Europe. After Napoleon had turned in his equipment, the "crew" slipped into the motor pool and changed the numbers on a tank so that it was sent to the wrong unit in Germany. Napoleon was now out several million dollars. This incident finally convinced him that he was doing something wrong. He began to change, and eventually he got the group working with him toward achieving the objectives of the armor division.

When, then, will groups work against management? Groups can "hurt" management (1) if they are cohesive and (2) if the work norm develops not into "a fair day's work for a fair day's pay" but into "let's do the minimum we can get by with." But why do negative norms develop?

Chapter 5 gives us one explanation of the development of negative norms: equity theory. If the group feels that it is underpaid, overworked, understatused, or in general receiving less than a fair reward (output) for its input (effort, abilities, etc.), trouble is likely to develop. The only way you can stop the group from hurting you and the enterprise is to take the following steps:

1 find out what the perceived inequity is.

2 do something about the inequity (raise pay, increase status, lower negative outputs, etc.).

3 If you feel that the group is taking advantage of you after you have tried to correct the situation seek advice from more experienced managers. Only when you have tried everything else should you try to break up the group.

WORKING WITH GROUPS TO ACHIEVE ORGANIZATIONAL OBJECTIVES

In most organizations work cannot be done without the development of work groups. This is functional for all concerned: the individual, the group, and the organization. Administrators need to be aware that individuals behave in response to internal personal needs and motives, but that they also belong to groups with their own sets of norms, beliefs, and behavior patterns. Many employees will respond by conforming to group norms, but the greatest group conformity is found among younger and less educated workers.

Remember the description of the manager's job from Chapters 2 and 3. Some supervisors have one or more small groups to supervise. Others have a large group of employees to supervise. You should now understand how dealing with groups will vary depending on the number of groups, their size, cohesion, and other factors. To work with groups effectively, the manager must be a politician and a leader. He or she must know when to go along with the group and when to deflect it. This takes leadership ability. And that is the topic of the next chapter.

SUMMARY

This chapter had as its main objective helping you understand what work groups are, how they operate, and what managers need to know and do to manage them.

A work group is a set of two or more people who see themselves as a group, are interdependent with one another for a purpose, and communicate and interact with one another on a more or less continuing basis. In many cases they work together physically. Groups can be formal (created by management to fulfill a specific purpose) or informal (created by group members to serve their own needs).

Studies of groups have tended to follow three approaches: interaction process analysis (observation and recording of all interactions); sociometric analysis (members record their patterns of interaction on questionnaires and a sociogram, or map, is drawn on this basis); and systems analysis (analysis of external and internal interactions, activities, and sentiments).

Next the chapter explained what groups do for members and for the enterprise. People join and support groups and managers generally want work groups to develop and flourish because groups provide for their members' social, identity recognition, ego esteem, and security and power needs, as well as other needs such as providing information, relieving boredom, and establishing work norms. Groups help enterprises, too, by orienting and socializing new employees, contributing to decision making, and getting the job done.

Groups appear to develop in a regular fashion: an initial period is followed by goal development, development of structure, and leadership development. The informal group provides powerful mechanisms for holding the workplace together.

I went on to describe the characteristics of effective work groups. Effective groups are small in size (e.g., 7 members), are located close together, are cohesive, and have norms similar to the enterprise's goals. The number of people in the group and the nature of the task vary according to the goals set by the group and by the enterprise.

Effective committees (one form of group) are composed of five members with the required knowledge who are willing to cooperate and are led by a directive task leader.

Groups can occasionally work against management. This can happen when the group's goals are in conflict with the manager's or the enterprise's goals, and when the group feels that it is inequitably rewarded.

For a manager to be effective in working with groups, he or she needs the interpersonal skill of leadership. This is the subject of Chapter 7.

This chapter completes Part II of the book. It is hoped that you now understand yourself and others better both as individuals and as group members.

Questions for Review

1. Explain how being part of a work group may affect your work behavior.
2. How might your *perceptions* of situations at work differ if you work on an isolated job than if you work a job that is part of a cohesive group? How might your learning differ? Your personality? Your motivation? Your attitudes?
3. What is a work group? In what ways does a work group differ from a crowd? A line of people waiting to get into a concert? Explain the differences between formal and informal groups.
4. Leonard Sayles has explained some differences he found in work groups. What are they? What can a manager learn from this research?
5. What are the three major ways of studying work groups?
6. How might the findings of group studies differ because the researcher used one of the major study methods rather than another?
7. What needs do groups fulfill for their members?
8. Why do managers encourage groups to form? What needs do groups fulfill for the enterprise?

9. Through what stages do groups evolve and develop? What problems would managers face in managing groups in stage 1? How might these differ in stage 3?

10. In what ways do informal groups make the workplace more livable, productive, and satisfying?

11. What is an effective group?

12. What are the major characteristics of effective groups?

13. How can managers encourage the development and continuance of effective groups? How can they hinder them?

14. Can committees be effective? When?

15. Under what conditions do groups work for and with managers; when do they work against them?

16. How does knowledge of how groups work contribute to effective management?

References

The Work Group

Argyris, Chris, "The Incompleteness of Social-Psychological Theory," *American Psychologist,* 25, No. 10 (1969): 893–908.

Bales, Robert, *Interaction Process Analysis* (Reading, Mass.: Addison-Wesley, 1950).

Dalton, Melville, *Men Who Manage* (New York: John Wiley and Sons, 1959).

Moreno, J. L., *Who Shall Survive?* (Washington, D.C.: Nervous and Mental Diseases Publishing, 1934).

Moreno, J. L., et al., *Sociometry Reader* (New York: Free Press, 1960).

Sayles, Leonard, *The Behavior of Industrial Work Groups* (New York: McGraw-Hill, 1963).

Schein, Edgar, *Organizational Psychology* (Englewood Cliffs, N.J.: Prentice-Hall, 1970).

Thibault, J., and Kelly, H., *The Social Psychology of Groups* (New York: John Wiley and Sons, 1959).

Zander, Alvin, *Motives and Goals in Groups* (New York: Academic Press, 1971).

What Groups Do for People and Enterprises

Schein, Edgar, op. cit.

Group Formation and Development

Asch, Solomon, "Effect of Group Pressure Upon the Modification and Distortion of Judgments," in Dorwin Cartwright and Zander, Alvin, eds., *Group Dynamics: Research and Theory* (Evanston, Ill.: Row Peterson, 1953), pp. 151–162.

Caplow, Theodore, *Two Against One: Coalitions in Triads* (Englewood Cliffs, N.J.: Prentice-Hall, 1968).

Chertkoff, J. M., "A Revison of Caplow's Coalition Theory," *Journal of Experimental Social Psychology,* 3 (1967): 172–177.

Collins, Barry, and Raven, Bertram, "Group Structure: Attraction, Coalitions,

Communication and Power," in Lindzey, Gardner, and Aronson, Elliot, eds., *Handbook of Social Psychology.*

Dalton, op. cit.

Delbercq, Andre, "How Informal Organization Evolves," *Business Perspectives,* Spring 1968, pp. 17–21.

Gamson, W., "A Theory of Coalition Formation," *American Sociological Review,* 26 (1961): 373–382.

Gergen, K., *The Psychology of Behavior Exchange* (Reading, Mass.: Addison-Wesley, 1969).

Graham, Gerald, "Interpersonal Attraction as a Basis of Informal Organization," *Academy of Management Journal,* 14, No. 4 (December 1971): 483–495.

Katz, Fred, "Explaining Informal Work Groups in Complex Organizations," *Administrative Science Quarterly,* 10 (1965): 204–223.

Komorita, S., and Chertkoff, J., "A Bargaining Theory of Coalition Formation," *Psychological Review,* 80, no. 3 (May 1973): 149–162.

Reif, William, et al., "Perceptions of the Formal and the Informal Organization," *Academy of Management Journal,* 16, no. 3 (September 1973): 389–463.

Shaw, Marvin, "Why People Join Groups," in *Group Dynamics* (New York: McGraw-Hill, 1971).

Stieglitz, Harold, "What's Not on the Organization Chart," *Conference Board Record,* November 1964, pp. 7–10.

Tichy, N., "An Analysis of Clique Formation and Structure in Organizations," *Administrative Science Quarterly,* 18, no. 2 (June 1973): 194–208.

The Informal Group

Roy, Donald, "Efficiency and 'the Fix': Informal Intergroup Relations in Piecework Machine Shop," *American Journal of Sociology,* 60, no. 3 (November 1954): 255–266.

Effective Work Groups

Bass, Bernard, *Organizational Psychology* (Boston: Allyn and Bacon, 1965).

Berkowitz, Leonard, "Group Standards, Cohesiveness, and Productivity," *Human Relations,* 7 (1954): 505–519.

Bridges, Edwin, et al., "Effect of Hierarchial Differentiation on Group Productivity, Efficiency, and Risk Taking," *Administrative Science Quarterly,* 12 (1967): 305–319.

Cummings, Larry, et al., "The Effects of Size and Spatial Arrangements on Group Decisionmaking," *Academy of Management Journal,* 17, no. 3 (September 1974): 460–475.

Davis, James, *Group Performance* (Reading, Mass.: Addison-Wesley, 1969).

Filley, Albert, "Committee Management: Guidelines from Social Science Research," *California Management Review,* 13, no. 1 (1970): 13–21.

Jackson, J., *Norms and Roles: Studies in Systematic Social Psychology* (New York: Holt, Rinehart and Winston, 1976).

Lorge, Irving, et al., "A Survey of Studies Contrasting the Quality of Group Performance and Individual Performance," *Psychological Bulletin,* 55, no. 6 (November 1958): 337–372.

Stogdill, Ralph, "Group Productivity, Drive and Cohesiveness," *Organizational Behavior and Human Performance,* 8 (1972): 26–43.

Thomas, Edwin, and Fink, Clifton, "Effects of Groups Size," *Psychological Bulletin,* 60, no. 4 (1963): 371–384.

van de Ven, Andrew, and Delbecq, Andre, "Nominal Versus Interacting Group Processes for Committee Decision Making Effectiveness," *Academy of Management Journal,* 14, no. 2 (June 1971): 203–212.

When Groups Work Against Management

Glueck, William F., *Cases and Exercises in Personnel* (Dallas: Business Publications, 1974).

Hampton, David, et al., *Organizational Behavior and the Practice of Management,* rev. ed., (Glenview, Ill.: Scott, Foresman, 1973).

Hickson, David, "Financial Incentives and Group Interests," *Occupational Psychology,* 37, no. 2 (April 1963): 136–142.

Robertson, Leon, and Rogers, James, "Distributive Justice and Informal Organization in a Freight Warehouse Work Crew," *Human Organization,* 25, no. 3 (1966): 221–224.

Sykes, A., and Bates, J., "A Study of Conflict Between Formal Company Policy and the Interests of Informal Groups," *The Sociological Review,* 3, no. 10 (November 1962): pp. 000–000.

Foote Whyte, William, *Organizational Behavior* (Homewood, Ill.: Irwin Dorsey Press, 1969), chap. 8.

PART 3

INTERPERSONAL SKILLS

Part 3 focuses on an analysis of the interpersonal skills the manager and entrepreneur must develop in order to be effective. Development of these skills requires an understanding of the material in Part 2.

In the following chapters we will discuss the exercise of leadership and the interpersonal influence of the manager in dealing with employees (Chapter 7); the exercise of interpersonal influence by the manager in interacting with superiors, peers, and other nonemployee groups (Chapter 8); the use of effective communication skills in interacting with others (Chapter 9); and the development of effective managerial skills (Chapter 10).

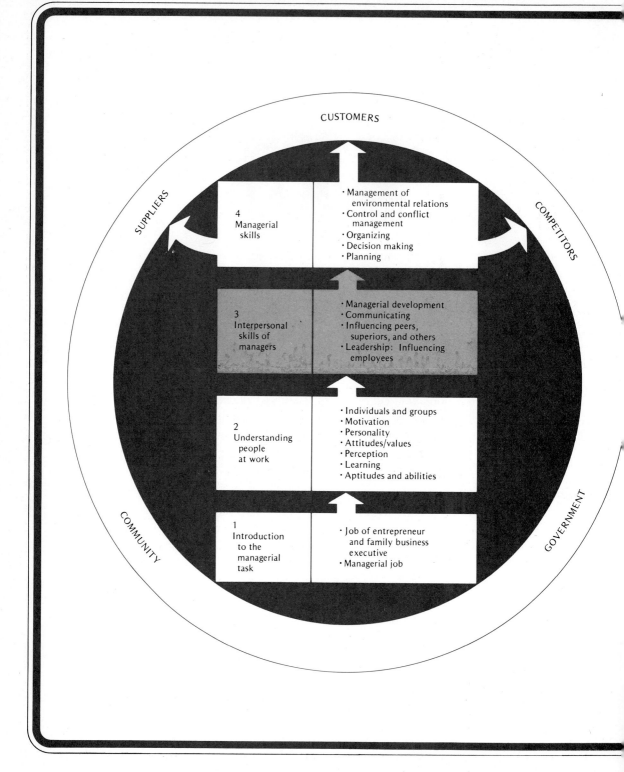

CUSTOMERS

SUPPLIERS

COMPETITORS

COMMUNITY

GOVERNMENT

4
Managerial
skills

- Management of
  environmental relations
- Control and conflict
  management
- Organizing
- Decision making
- Planning

3
Interpersonal
skills of
managers

- Managerial development
- Communicating
- Influencing peers,
  superiors, and others
- Leadership: Influencing
  employees

2
Understanding
people
at work

- Individuals and groups
- Motivation
- Personality
- Attitudes/values
- Perception
- Learning
- Aptitudes and abilities

1
Introduction
to the
managerial
task

- Job of entrepreneur
  and family business
  executive
- Managerial job

Take another look at the managerial model. You learned something about the managerial life in Part 1. You understand people better after reading Part 2. Now it is time to focus on influencing people, something every manager must do to be effective. So in Part 3 you will learn how effective managers, entrepreneurs, and family business executives influence employees, superiors, and peers through direct interpersonal influence and communication, and how effective organizations develop successful managers. Obviously, the community and other groups in the environment influence these aspects of management.

CHAPTER 7
LEADERSHIP OF EMPLOYEES

Learning Objectives

1. To learn the factors involved in leadership.
2. To understand the many sources of leadership influence.
3. To learn different leadership styles and how to use each effectively.
4. To understand three management styles.

Chapter Outline

INTRODUCTION   The word *leadership* is an exciting one. All kinds of people have shown an interest in it—historians, philosophers, psychologists, politicans, executives. Whenever leadership is mentioned, people's names run through your mind. It conjures up images of Lincoln, Jefferson, Truman, and Roosevelt. In the business world, names like Alfred Sloan, James Lincoln, J. C. Penney, Ralph Cordiner, Frederick Keppel, and George Stephen come to mind.

So, too, do other, less positive images: Colonel Nicholson *(Bridge on the River Kwai),* Captain Queeg *(Caine Mutiny),* F. Scott Fitzgerald's *Last Tycoon.* They were leaders too.

Leadership, or influencing people effectively, is a fascinating topic. But if you are looking for a quick, precise explanation of leadership that will give you the influence of a Napoleon over your subordinates, you are going to be disappointed. The topic is more complicated than it appears to be at first glance.

The focus of this chapter is on influencing subordinates. Reflect back on what you learned about the manager's job in Chapters 2 and 3 and about groups in Chapter 6 and consider the leadership challenges facing these executives:

- A busy top manager who has relatively few immediate subordinates, all of whom are after his or her job.
- A less harried middle manager with relatively few employees, all of whom are professional specialists and most of whom have worked for the enterprise longer than he has.
- A busy entrepreneur who is the only manager and "supervises" 75 employees.
- A supervisor of 50 production workers in an auto plant. She was just given the job and was a production worker herself. Some of the men mumble that "she only got the job because of affirmative action."
- A commander of a crack airborne infantry unit, a graduate of West Point and clearly the smartest and most experienced member of the unit.

In these and other situations surrounding leadership, the conditions of leadership vary depending on the leader, the work group, and the leadership task and situation.

The Leader The first factor is the leader: how he or she is chosen, his or her characteristics and personality. Some people try to explain leadership wholly in terms of the leader's characteristics. They tend to argue that leaders are born, not made. Thus Napoleon, Vince Lombardi, and Thomas Watson, Sr., all known for their leadership abilities, were, according to these theorists, born to greatness. This approach is called the *great man theory.* But charisma alone is an insufficient explanation of leadership.

"If God has seen fit to place me in this position for some reason, Hewlitt, and if that reason seems to include sitting in judgment upon you, then so be it."

Source: Drawing by Stan Hunt; © 1974 The New Yorker Magazine, Inc.

The Work Group The second characteristic involved in leadership is the people the leader has to lead. Consider the following three employees:

· Joe (Joan): experienced, dedicated, responsible, hardworking; a good to excellent employee.
· Sandra (Sam): sometimes like Joe (Joan)—sometimes like Tom (Teresa).
· Tom (Teresa): partly experienced; in the job for the money; does only the minimum expected; a barely satisfactory employee.

It should be clear that influence mechanisms that are fruitful for Joe (Joan) may not work with Sandra (Sam) and probably will not work with Tom (Teresa).

Several theorists try to explain effective leadership by emphasizing the interaction between the leader and the members of the group. Ralph Stogdill contends that since groups reinforce their mutual expectations of each other as they work, the individual who exhibits leadership behavior (which he defines as initiating and maintaining the structure of interaction and expectations) will be viewed as the leader. This theory applies primarily to the emergence of the informal leader. Others have argued that as leaders arise in groups an "exchange" of costs and benefits takes place. That is, the group "pays" the leader in status and esteem in exchange for the leader's help in achieving the group's objectives. However, this approach ignores the impact of the leader's personality and the differences among various leadership situations.

The Situation The task and situation constitute a third critical variable. Leadership can exist in times of crisis or in normal times; it is called for in jobs that require standardized work or very creative work. In fact some theorists contend that the situation brings forth the leader. This *situational-environmental theory* is almost the opposite of the great man theory. These theorists argue that leadership arises as a consequence of time, place, and circumstances. The leader emerges to meet these needs and is determined by the situation. But if this theory is true, how does it explain the many occasions when crises arose and no leader appeared? In the business world we can identify numerous occasions of this type. For example, why did no leader come forward to handle the crisis that arose at Curtis Wright in 1945? Why did the firm (the largest builder of planes at the time) eventually leave the business and never again have the impact it had in 1945?

If you think about it, the great man theory is parallel to the genetic explanation of personality and the situational-environmental theory is parallel to the environmental determinists' explanation of personality.

A group of leadership scholars called *person-situation theorists* agree that all three of the factors we have discussed are crucial to understanding leadership. One of these theorists, Cecil Gibb, says that "leadership is an *interactional* phenomenon arising when the group formation takes place." The factors he considers basic to leadership are (1) the traits and motives of the leader, (2) the images of the leader held by the people he or she leads, and (3) the situation in which the leader finds himself or herself.

THE IMPORTANCE OF LEADERSHIP Look at the table of contents of this book. There is hardly a topic in it that is not influenced by if not crucially dependent on the leader at work. The leader's behavior affects the motivation of the work group and how well it is trained. The leader is a crucial communicator to people outside the group as well as to its members. The leader is responsible for seeing that the group's objectives are clearly understood and accomplished. The planning and control mechanisms are designed or modified by the leader. The leader is ultimately responsible for crucial decision making. The leader is critical to the survival of the work group, especially in times of crisis. How the leader behaves strongly influences employee satisfaction and affects the quality and quantity of work performance. All this is to say that the leadership role is very important. As Keith Davis puts it, "leadership transforms the potential [of machines and people] into reality [of organization]."

Thus far the argument for the importance of leadership has been put in the positive. There is a negative side, too. Talk with a business executive about leadership and he or she will tell you that there are not enough *good* leaders around. It is difficult to be a good leader. Some people do not have the ability. Others lose the motivation, or never had it in the first place. How serious is this leadership "shortage"?

WHAT IS LEADERSHIP? Stogdill, who has studied leadership for thirty years, says, "There are almost as many definitions of leadership as there are persons who have attempted to define the concept." I will spare you all these definitions. But it is important to realize that there are two basic approaches to defining leadership:

1 A leader is a person who performs leadership acts. TRAITS ORIENTED

2 A leader is a person who influences others to achieve certain ends. (INFLUENCE) RESULTS ORIENTED — MORE SIGNIFICANT

If we accept the first definition, we are equating leadership with management. But as used here leadership is a *part* of the management process, that is, one of several interpersonal skills. Our definition, therefore, is as follows:

> **LEADERSHIP** (MOTIVATE)
> Leadership is a set of interpersonal behaviors designed to influence employees to cooperate in the achievement of objectives.
> (FOLLOW)

Leadership becomes more understandable if we think of it as the use of many sources of influence and the application of mechanisms of interpersonal behavior that may be labeled "leadership styles."

Formal and Informal Leaders One reason some discussions of leadership seem confused is that there are two types of leaders. The first is the formal or "appointed" leader. In most employment situations the enterprise has chosen a "boss" or "leader." By contrast, the informal leader is chosen by the group itself. This can happen in any social group—youth gang, bridge club, church organization, political party, and so forth.

There are significant differences between how the two types of leaders emerge (come to be) and how they influence the group. This will become clear when we discuss the sources of influence. Most managers are formally appointed leaders. But to many people the "ideal" manager is a person who, in addition to being the formal leader, operates in such a way that he or she is the informal leader as well.

Why Does Anyone Want to Be a Leader?

The motives for leadership include, according to Gibb, economic reward, primitive dominance, power over others, and status needs. In terms of Maslow's hierarchy of needs, esteem-recognition and self-actualization needs seem to be the main motivators of leadership behavior. In the McClelland-Atkinson scheme, the need for achievement and the need for power seem to be the strongest motivators of formal leaders.

Many who chose to be followers and not leaders may be more interested in affiliation or social needs and security needs. Leaders are willing to undergo the stresses and responsibilities of leadership to achieve their goals and to exert power and influence. They are normally reinforced by higher salaries and other organizational rewards.

SOURCES OF LEADERSHIP INFLUENCE

We now know what leadership is and what needs can be satisifed by leadership. But where does leadership come from?

Let us start with the position that to be a leader is to be able to influence subordinates at work. Political scientists, historians, sociologists, management specialists, and many others have discussed the sources of influence available for a manager or leader to use. Table 7.1 presents the seven sources of influence to be discussed here, using the terms each theorist applies to each source.

Legitimate Power

A person exercises *legitimate power* ("authority") if he or she is appointed to a leadership position by a "legitimate" authority. Cultural norms and values in most societies reinforce the idea that an officer has a right to lead troops, a manager to lead employees. This source of power or influence is available to all managers; managers receive legitimate power when they are appointed and retained.

Legitimate power has its greatest impact when employees accept the leader and when their work norms are positive toward the enterprise's objectives. When these conditions are present, legitimate power is a strong influence base for the leader. But note that this kind of power is much more influential if the employees *accept* the leader. If legitimate power is not reinforced by other sources of power, it can be less influential, and the organization's objectives may suffer as a result.

Monetary/Reward Power

A leader can influence some employees by using the pay system to reward or punish them. Employees who accept the objectives of the leader and produce the quality and quantity of output desired receive higher financial rewards (and similar rewards such as better benefits and perquisites). This source of influence is available to most managers and entrepreneurs.

Monetary/reward power taps the physiological and security needs of the employees and the power needs of the leader. For it to be effective, money must be a strongly desired outcome for the employee *and* the reward system must directly tie pay with accomplishment of objectives. It is not always easy to get these conditions to coincide. The work group

Table 7.1 Sources of Power and Influence Available to Leaders

Power Theorists and Their Terms

Source of Influence	Lasswell and Kaplan	French and Raven	Weber	Classical Management Theorists (Fayol, etc.)	Presthus	Bierstadt	Clark	Cartwright
1. Legitimate power		legitimate power	(legal) bureaucratic authority		legitimacy of formal position		legitimate power / constitutional officialdom	
2. Skill/expertise power	skill	expert power		experience, intelligence	authority of expertise	knowledge, skill, competence, ability	knowledge, expertise / power of information	expertise power
3. Monetary power		reward power					power over pay & jobs	positive sanctions
4. Affection power	affection for leader	referent power	patrimonial authority		power of rapport		popularity	
5. Respect (traditional) power			(traditional) patriarchal authority charismatic authority	reputation of leader	legitimacy of deference	prestige of leader	social standing of leader	magnetism
6. Rectitude power				moral worth of leader				
7. Coercive power	physical power	coercive power				dominance		physical power

can offset monetary power by isolating and "punishing" those who respond to it. If the group is cohesive and influential, it can negate the influence of the leader's monetary or reward power.

Skill/Expertise Power

When a person's behavior indicates that he or she really knows how to get the job done (not just the everyday jobs but the tough and tricky ones as well), that person has influence. He or she can help others achieve their objectives. In such a situation group members will defer to the expert.

Ideally the manager has enough competence to have expertise power. To the extent, however, that the manager must depend on another person for expertise, that individual will have power over the manager and the work group.

Affection Power

Surely you have belonged to groups in which the leader was elected because "everyone likes him." When you like people it is easier for them to influence you. Many people become leaders because they develop the ability to get employees to like them. This provides the basis for their influence. Stogdill summarizes the research in this area as follows:

> [Research] suggests that being liked and accepted by group members gives the leader more influence than if he [or she] is not liked or accepted. Leaders high in power are better liked and accepted than those low in power. Members desire acceptance by high power members of the group.

Respect/ Rectitude Power

So if a leader can be not just accepted but liked by employees, peers, and superiors, he or she will have more influence over them.

Some leadership experts do not separate affection power from respect power. But surely you have been influenced by individuals whom you respected but did not like. In many cases you respected them for some of the reasons listed earlier (skill, for example).

In addition to respect power, a few theorists have speculated that some people are influential because they provide a moral example. These two bases of influence have not been studied in much detail, however.

Coercive Power

There are several varieties of coercive power. The first is physical. Anyone familiar with *The Godfather* or *The Longest Yard* knows about this. So did the slave laborers in Hitler's World War II factories or in the Soviet Union's Gulag Archipelago as described by Alexander Solzhenitsyn. The closest equivalent in most work organizations is the power to fire an employee or to suspend him or her without pay. Taking away a person's job has many physical and psychological effects, as we have seen.

Coercive power does tend to induce compliance if the work group is unable to resist it. But even in Hitler's slave labor factories the "workers" sabotaged the output and worked very slowly by taking no initiative and requiring detailed instructions from the supervisors. But then, as Solzhenitsyn has shown, Hitler was ineffective in his use of coercion. The Soviets have perfected the use of coercive power in their prison system; Solzhenitsyn found little resistance to the secret police's methods. In fact in "One Day in the Life of Ivan Denisovitch" the prisoner took pride in his work (bricklaying) and felt guilty if he worked slowly.

In most work situations in the United States and Canada, however, coercive power is the leader's last resort. It should be used sparingly and fairly in order to avoid activating group cohesiveness in opposition to the leader.

Coercive power, then, appears to utilize the leader's need for power and to affect the employees' lower (physiological and security) needs.

The Limits of Power

The discussion so far has centered on how to acquire power or influence. But I cannot leave this subject without making several points.

As Lord Acton said, "Power corrupts; absolute power corrupts absolutely." How right he was! The American Constitution has checks and balances built into it to try to prevent the concentration of power in one branch of government or in the hands of any individual. Despite some close calls, this approach has worked.

Most managers operate without such obvious checks and balances. Some abuse their power. But remember, employees can get back—they can quit, be absent, sabotage your plans, paint the numerals on your tank, report your activities to your boss or to Jack Anderson. This is called "blowing the whistle," and well-known examples include the aircraft brake scandal, the electrical conspiracy, and the Andersonville trial.

Power is an interesting phenomenon. It consumes some leaders. Once they have it, they will do almost anything to keep it. Others seem to be able to handle it. And they are better people to work for and make more long-run contributions to organizational objectives. Really great leaders are able to separate the power associated with the office from themselves. Harry Truman is famous for constantly differentiating between the power of the presidency and his power as an individual. He viewed himself as a temporary occupant of the position (and of the White House) and realized that the deference given him as President was given just for a while. This came home very clearly the day after he left the White House. A reporter asked him, in effect, "What did you do today?" implying that he still had many world-shaking duties to perform. Truman's reply: "I took the suitcases up to the attic."

One of the strengths of our political system is the short tenure of the officeholders. One of the problems of the nonelective officials in many enterprises is that unless there is mandatory retirement they stay on and on and on, and soon the power of the office becomes the power of the person, a situation that can easily lead to abuses of power.

We must develop mechanisms to keep managers aware of the limitations on their power if they are to perform effectively.

Underlying all the bases of social power is the idea that those being led must grant the leader their consent or respect or let the leader influence them. This is a significant point for leaders or would-be leaders to remember.

Managerial Implications

A leader can draw on seven sources of influence. Which is best? Propositions 7.1 and 7.2 try to answer this question.

Proposition 7.1.
The more sources of influence a leader can draw on, the more successful his or her leadership activities will be.

Proposition 7.2.
Some sources of influence tend to be found simultaneously: Legitimate, monetary, and coercive power form a constellation; so do skill, respect, and rectitude power.

Effective leaders draw on as many sources of power and influence as possible and use the source that best fits the situation, the employees, and their personalities.

Our emphasis thus far has been on how a manager acquires leadership. We now turn to the styles various managers use in exercising and maintaining leadership.

LEADERSHIP STYLE
Leadership style is the way a leader uses his or her influence to achieve the objectives of the organization.

LEADERSHIP STYLES

As will become clear as we go along, leaders have many ways of dealing with their employees. The interpersonal influences the leader uses with employees may be characterized as his or her leadership *style*.

Many management experts believe the manager's leadership style is fundamentally influenced by his or her attitudes toward employees and, thus, by the theory of leadership the manager follows, consciously or unconsciously. But before I describe the various styles, what are your attitudes?

Fill in the blanks in Figure 7.1, then score yourself as shown in Table 7.2.

In the section below you will see a series of statements. Please indicate your agreement or disagreement. Use the scale below each statement. For Example:

It is easier to work in cool weather than in hot.

Strongly Agree	Agree	Undecided	Disagree	Strongly Disagree
	X			

If you think it is easier to work in cool weather, put an (X) above "agree"; if you think it is much easier to work in cool weather, put a mark above "strongly agree." If you think it doesn't matter, put a mark over "undecided" and so on. Put your mark in a space, not on the boundaries.

There are no right or wrong answers. We are interested in your opinion about the statements which follow.

1. The average human being prefers to be directed, wishes to avoid responsibility, and has relatively little ambition.

Strongly Agree	Agree	Undecided	Disagree	Strongly Disagree

2. Leadership skills can be acquired by most people regardless of their particular inborn traits and abilities.

Strongly Agree	Agree	Undecided	Disagree	Strongly Disagree

3. The use of rewards (pay, promotion, etc.) and punishment (failure to promote, etc.) is not the best way to get subordinates to do their work.

Strongly Agree	Agree	Undecided	Disagree	Strongly Disagree

4. In a work situation, if the subordinates cannot influence me then I lose some influence on them.

Strongly Agree	Agree	Undecided	Disagree	Strongly Disagree

5. A good leader should give detailed and complete instructions to his subordinates, rather than giving them merely general directions and depending upon their initiative to work out the details.

Strongly Agree	Agree	Undecided	Disagree	Strongly Disagree

6. Group goal setting offers advantages that cannot be obtained by individual goal setting.

Strongly Agree	Agree	Undecided	Disagree	Strongly Disagree

7. A superior should give his subordinates only that information which is necessary for them to do their immediate tasks.

Strongly Agree	Agree	Undecided	Disagree	Strongly Disagree

8. The superior's authority over his subordinates in an organization is primarily economic.

Strongly Agree	Agree	Undecided	Disagree	Strongly Disagree

Figure 7.1 Attitudes influencing leadership style.

Conservative ⟷ autocratic
Liberal ⟷ free lance

Table 7.2

Question	Strongly Agree	Undecided	Strongly Disagree
1.	conservative	middle of the road	liberal
2.	liberal	middle of the road	conservative
3.	liberal	middle of the road	conservative
4.	liberal	middle of the road	conservative
5.	conservative	middle of the road	liberal
6.	liberal	middle of the road	conservative
7.	conservative	middle of the road	liberal
8.	conservative	middle of the road	liberal

Five to eight items in the "liberal," "middle-of-the-road," or "conservative" categories is a strong indication of your managerial style. As you read the next few pages, perhaps you can relate the material covered to your own attitudes and get a picture of what your leadership style is likely to be. As should be obvious, the managerial attitudes that constitute a person's leadership style have a strong influence on how he or she will handle a managerial job.

The crucial managerial attitude or belief that influences leadership style is *the role of the manager versus that of the employees.* If the manager sees the employees as people who do the work under his or her direction, the style is conservative. If the leader sees himself or herself as a colleague of the work group with certain extra responsibilities and different duties, the style is liberal.

Most managers do have a predominant or core style: the one they feel fits them or they are most comfortable with. They will use this style much of the time. *However, all but a few managers have the ability to vary their style to fit varying circumstances or different people.* For example, a liberal leader may become conservative and make all decisions, issue orders, and so forth in a crisis. Or a conservative leader may operate with a liberal style in dealing with some especially trusted employees. This flexibility contributes to a manager's effectiveness.

But this is a very brief description of leadership styles. A number of people have treated this subject in more detail.

Conservative Leadership Style

In spite of the fact that you hear more about the liberal style of leadership, the predominant leadership style now and in the past in the United States, Canada, and around the world is the conservative style. This is admitted by all managerial experts, including those who advocate the liberal style, although the latter often predict that the liberal style will be the wave of the future.

Studies of management have shown that while managers may express support for the liberal style (by agreeing with item 6 of Figure 7.2, for example), they consistently support the assumptions of the conservative style in their beliefs about employee characteristics (by agreeing with items 1 and 5, for example). Thus conservative assumptions may be out of fashion, but most managers nevertheless use conservative leadership styles—or what one of its supporters calls the "benevolent autocratic" style.

How does a conservative leader operate? Basically, the conservative leader believes that he or she is the boss and that the boss is there to make the decisions because that is what the job is about and because many or most employees either cannot or do not want to take the responsibility. So conservative leaders make most decisions themselves. They organize the job, communicate primarily through a chain of command, and pride themselves on designing the job and employment relationship so that the employees know what is expected of them and what will happen if they do not perform.

This does not mean that conservative leaders are unpleasant or mean, though liberals typically stereotype them that way. Douglas McGregor, a critic of the conservative style, has argued that conservative leaders adhere to the following three propositions:

1 Management is responsible for organizing the elements of productive enterprise—money, materials, equipment, people—in the interest of the organization's economic ends.

2 With respect to people, this is a process of directing their efforts, motivating them, controlling their actions, and modifying their behavior to fit the needs of the organization.

3 Without this active intervention by management people would be passive—even resistant—to organizational needs.

McGregor says that managers use the conservative style because they make the following assumptions about people:

1 People are by nature indolent.

2 They lack ambition, dislike responsibility, prefer to be led.

3 They are self-centered, indifferent to organizational needs.

4 They are by nature resistant to change.

5 They are not very bright and lack creative potential.

But accepting McGregor's analysis of conservative leadership style is a bit like asking Yassir Arafat to support Israel or Ronald Reagan to sing the praises of liberal Democrats. Conservative leaders simply feel that the conservative style is best because of the nature of employees, the nature of leaders, and some characteristics of the work situation.

The Nature of Employees

Employees are raised in a society in which most leaders follow the conservative model: parents, teachers, priests, bus drivers—everyone you meet uses the conservative style. So employees expect it at work and work better when they get what they expect.

Moreover, employees can be lazy. It has been estimated that fewer than 25 percent of all employees can operate responsibly with the liberal style. The rest want to know what to do and what is expected of them.

In addition, the conservative style takes care of employees' physiological and security needs. That is, if you do what the boss wants, you get paid well and keep your job. Everyone has basic needs to satisfy. Not everyone wants to exercise the higher needs at work, and the liberal style is oriented to the higher needs.

The Nature of Leaders

The conservative style is very rewarding to leaders. That is why they like it. It takes care of their basic needs, of course, but by making them the center of attraction and power it fulfills their recognition, esteem, and self-actualization needs better than other styles.

Also, the conservative style is the only one that makes sense to the managerial personality. As Robert McMurry puts it,

> [Managers] are more likely to be hard-driving egocentric entrepreneurs who have come up in the business in careers where they had to keep power in their own hands: or they may be the victors in the give and take, no-quarter in-fighting for positions of power. . . . Such men cannot ordinarily bring themselves to use any concept of management other than a purely authoritarian one. . . . I suspect that no more than 10 percent of business executives . . . can use a [liberal style].

To be other than conservative, it would appear, one would have to be manipulative.

It has been argued that managers using the conservative style make better decisions. Only the conservative style provides uniformity of decisions from people who know the "big picture." Less than this leads to chaos or costly repercussions.

The Situation

Many jobs are unpleasant because of technological and cost considerations. Only a conservative leadership style can deal efficiently with employees working on unpleasant jobs.

Moreover, the conservative style is quicker. Decisions made by a good conservative leader will always be speedier than those made in a liberal style.

The conservative style is also simpler and easier to use. The leader plans a structure and the employees follow the plan.

In addition, the conservative style prevents the excessive duplication that always flows from involving more people in decision making, as liberals advocate.

These, then, are the reasons conservative leaders give for using this style. McMurry goes so far as to say that the liberal style is probably more humanitarian, more desirable, but not as practical or workable. Instead, the conservative leader, aggressive, hard driving, self-reliant, gets the work out and does his or her best to use human relations and build employee confidence in the leader. In sum, again quoting McMurry,

> [The conservative leader] structures his subordinates' activities for them; he makes the policy decisions which affect them; he keeps them in line and enforces discipline. He is like a good quarterback, who does not ask the line to decide what plays to attempt or what formations to use, but who tells them—and woe betide the hapless player who fails to follow his orders. He may encourage participation in the planning of a course of action, but much less frequently does he do so in its execution. He encourages participation by his subordinates prior to reaching his decision.
>
> I believe that a proper utilization of these insights and a proper application of the principles which grow out of them will result in the maintenance of nearly as high a level of morale, even under continued pressure for production, as is possible where the liked leadership is available.

Liberal Leadership Style

A liberal leader's behavior is almost the opposite of that of a conservative leader. Liberal leaders involve employees in managerial work such as decision making, planning, structuring the organization, setting goals, and control of the organization.

The liberal pattern of leadership is talked about much more than it is practiced. I suspect that McMurry's 10 percent figure is about right—that only 10 percent of all managers accept liberal assumptions and use liberal leadership style.

According to McGregor, liberal leaders believe that

> The essential task of management is to arrange organizational conditions and methods of operation so that people can achieve their own goals *best* by directing *their own* efforts toward organizational objectives.

Liberals hold to the following three propositions:

> **1** Management is responsible for organizing the elements of productive enterprise—money, materials, equipment, people—in the interest of the organization's economic ends.

2 People are not by nature passive or resistant to organizational needs. They have become so as a result of experience in organizations.

3 The motivation, the potential for development, the capacity for assuming responsibility, the readiness to direct behavior toward organizational goals are all present in people. *Management does not put them there.*

And liberals make the following assumptions about people:

1 People are ambitious.

2 They seek responsibility.

3 They recognize and accept organizational goals.

4 They are dynamic and flexible.

5 They are intelligent and possess creative potential.

To the accusation that people are lazy, lack ambition, and so on, McGregor responded as follows:

> If the "conservative" assumptions approximate human behavior in business organizations, it is not because of man's inherent nature, but rather because of the nature of organizations, of management philosophy, and leadership style practiced therein.

Rensis Likert has diagramed the liberal position as shown in Figure 7.2. The liberal style encourages managers to consult with their employees and involve them in decision making and other managerial work. Liberals believe that today, with more education, employees expect more of their jobs and of their leaders. The liberal style unleashes their abilities and allows them to satisfy more than just their basic needs.

Perhaps I ought to be more specific about what the liberal style consists of. Larry Greiner asked several hundred managers how liberal leaders behave. They believe the liberal leader

· gives subordinates a share in decision making.

· keeps subordinates informed of the true situation, good or bad, under all circumstances.

· stays aware of the state of the organization's morale and does everything possible to make it high.

· is easily approachable.

· counsels, trains, and develops subordinates.

· communicates effectively with subordinates.

· shows thoughtfulness and consideration of others.

· is willing to make changes in ways of doing things.

·is willing to support subordinates even when they make mistakes.
·expresses appreciation when a subordinate does a good job.

(The items listed first were mentioned most often.) Let us now discuss
the most extreme liberal style: industrial democracy.

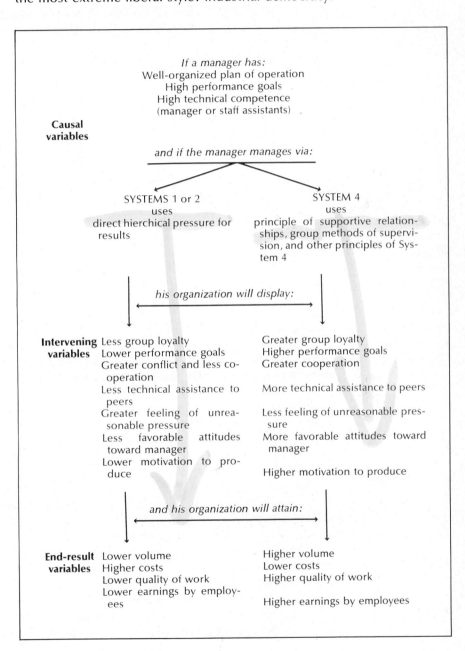

Figure 7.2
Likert's liberal
model.

Industrial Democracy: The Ultimate Liberal Style

The preceding discussion assumed that the individual manager is in a position to decide whether he or she will use a conservative or a liberal leadership style. However, in many leadership situations the employees have a legal right to participate in decisions. This phenomenon is called *industrial democracy*. In its most "liberal" form, the employees actually choose the manager (as in the Yugoslav self-management system). The degree of employee participation in such systems varies, as Figure 7.3 illustrates.

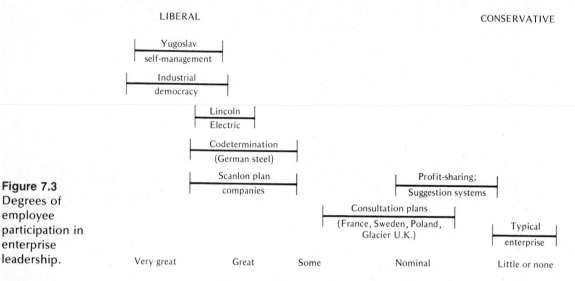

Figure 7.3 Degrees of employee participation in enterprise leadership.

Obviously, if you are the manager of the employee-owned asbestos mine in Vermont or the plywood plant in Oregon or the Yugoslav enterprise, you will be involved in a liberal management style. If you are a manager in a plant with industrial democracy, you are legally required to involve employees in decision making, and this is likely to result in a liberal leadership style.

Some of the participation schemes shown in Figure 7.4 have been around for many years. Whether we will see more of them in the future is anybody's guess.

Middle-of-the-Road Leadership Style

Two quite opposite leadership styles have now been described. The conservative style is by far the most frequently used. The liberal style appeals to some well-educated people. There are, of course, many examples of conservative leaders and some examples of liberal leaders. But there is a position in between. That is, the predominant leadership style is a mixture of both. The manager takes a conservative approach to some aspects of the management job and a liberal approach to others.

One typical approach of the middle-of-the-road manager is to delegate authority. This style is conservative in that it assumes that all authority to make decisions resides in the leader. It is liberal in that it recognizes the contributions dedicated and intelligent employees can make if given the chance. So delegation envisions the leader parceling out his or her authority to make decisions to the employees. Some of these delegators go to great lengths to make sure the amount of authority delegated to specific people to do specific jobs is clear. Thus the middle-of-the-road style attempts to derive the best from both the liberal and the conservative styles.

Contingency Style Models

Five leadership style theorists take a different position (and one that I agree with). They believe there are several effective leadership styles and that good leaders shift their style to fit the needs of the situation and the employees.

Tannenbaum and Schmidt

In 1973 Robert Tannenbaum and Warren Schmidt described a continuum of leadership styles, or what they call manager-nonmanager behavior. This is a revision of their classic 1958 article and is shown in Figure 7.4.

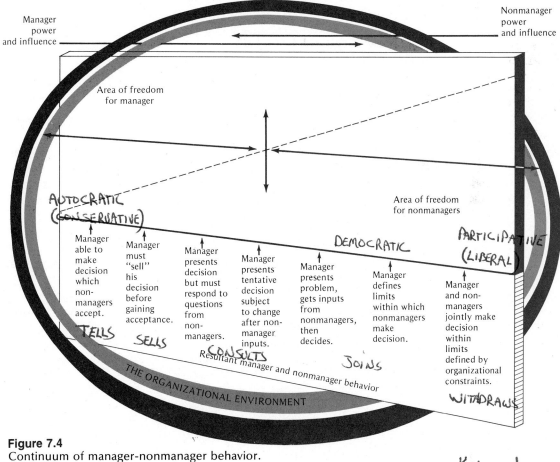

Figure 7.4
Continuum of manager-nonmanager behavior.

Note: They reverse the continuum compared to the presentation elsewhere in the chapter.

KNOW

Tannenbaum and Schmidt's continuum indicates that the leadership style that emerges is influenced by the relationship (they say interdependency) between the manager and nonmanagerial employees. But this relationship is affected by the organizational environment (some call it climate) and the larger society in which the organization operates. The attitudes and values of the organization and the society influence the relationships between managers and employees.

Tannenbaum and Schmidt have tried to advise managers on how to choose a leadership style. As they see it, the choice depends on the situation, the managers, and the nonmanagers. Let me now summarize what they have said, using my terms *conservative* and *liberal.*

The Manager

1 The greater the leader's preference for a particular style, the more he or she should use that style.

2 The greater the leader's belief in the nonmanager's competence, the more likely he or she is to use the liberal style.

3 The greater the leader's need to control the situation, the more likely he or she is to choose the conservative style

The Nonmanager

1 The more competent the nonmanager, the more likely the use of the liberal style.

2 The greater the nonmanager's desire for independence and responsibility, the more likely the use of the liberal style.

3 The more the nonmanagers identify with the objectives of the organization and believe its problems are important, the more likely the use of the liberal style.

The Situation

1 The greater the size of the work group, the more likely the use of the conservative style.

2 The greater the geographic spread of the work group, the more likely the use of the conservative style.

3 The greater the time pressure to make decisions, the more likely the use of the conservative style.

4 The more effective and cohesive the work group, the greater the likelihood of the liberal style.

5 The more complex the problem, the greater the likelihood of the liberal style.

Although there are other style theories (to be discussed), this presentation by Tannenbaum and Schmidt is as good a list of criteria as any that has been developed in the past.

Fiedler's Contingency Theory

Review concepts of TM & RM from Film

Fred Fiedler has spent fifteen years researching leadership in hundreds of work groups. Like Tannenbaum and Schmidt, he says there are three crucial variables to consider in the choice of a leadership style:

1 *Position Power*—the amount of support the leader has from his or her superiors and the power to reward or punish subordinates.

2 *Leader-Member Relations*—how the subordinates feel toward the leader: Do they trust the leader, have confidence in him or her? Are they loyal to the leader?

3 *Task:* Is the task routine or nonroutine? Is it clearly defined or ambiguous?

Fiedler contends that a group's effectiveness depends on the appropriateness of the leader's style to specific situations; that the leadership style that is most effective depends on the degree to which the group situation allows the leader to exert influence; and that since the effectiveness of the leader depends not only on his or her leadership style but also on the group situation, the leader can be made to fit a specific group situation through selection or training.

On the other hand, the group situation can be arranged to fit the leader. Fiedler argues that it is difficult to change the personality and attitudes of a leader, but relatively easy to change the work situation. This leads him to believe in the "organizational engineering" approach to leadership and management development.

Fiedler has developed ways of measuring these variables. The best known of these is the LPC (least preferred coworker) approach.

Fiedler spells out the leadership style to be used in various situations in Table 7.3.

OMIT

Table 7.3 Leadership Styles to Be Used

Situation	Leader-Member Relations	Task	Position Power	Productive Style
1	good	routine	high	conservative
2	good	routine	low	conservative
3	good	nonroutine	high	conservative
4	good	nonroutine	low	liberal
5	moderately poor	routine	high	liberal
6	moderately poor	routine	low	?
7	moderately poor	nonroutine	high	?
8	moderately poor	nonroutine	low	conservative

Fiedler's findings have received a good deal of research support, but more is needed, especially to clarify LPC response. Also, the interrelationship between the leader's behavior and the changing situation in the work group should be examined in greater depth.

The Vroom and Yetton Style

Victor Vroom and Philip Yetton have also tried to systematize Tannenbaum and Schmidt's conditions. They also describe leadership styles as varying from conservative (AI in Table 7.4) to liberal (GII or DI), but they

---

Table 7.4 Leadership Styles According to Vroom and Yetton

Group Problems	Individual Problems
AI. You solve the problem or make the decision yourself, using information available to you at the time.	AI. You solve the problem or make the decision by yourself, using information available to you at the time.
AII. You obtain the necessary information from your subordinates, then decide the solution to the problem yourself. You may or may not tell your subordinates what the problem is in getting the information from them. The role played by your subordinates in making the decision is clearly one of providing the necessary information to you, rather than generating or evaluating alternative solutions.	AII. You obtain the necessary information from your subordinate, then decide on the solution to the problem yourself. You may or may not tell the subordinate what the problem is in getting the information from him. His role in making the decision is clearly one of providing the necessary information to you, rather than generating or evaluating alternative solutions.
CI. You share the problem with the relevant subordinates individually, getting their ideas and suggestions without bringing them together as a group. Then *you* make the decision, which may or may not reflect your subordinates' influence.	CI. You share the problem with your subordinate, getting his ideas and suggestions. Then you make a decision, which may or may not reflect his influence.
CII. You share the problem with your subordinates as a group, obtaining their collective ideas and suggestions. Then you make the decision, which may or may not reflect your subordinates' influence.	GI. You share the problem with your subordinate, and together you analyze the problem and arrive at a mutually agreeable solution.
GII. You share the problem with your subordinates as a group. Together you generate and evaluate alternatives and attempt to reach agreement (consensus) on a solution. Your role is much like that of chairman. You do not try to influence the group to adopt "your" solution, and you are willing to accept and implement any solution which has the support of the entire group.	DI. You delegate the problem to your subordinate, providing him with any relevant information that you possess, but giving him responsibility for solving the problem by himself. You may or may not request him to tell you what solution he has reached.

contend that the choice of style is based on the type of problem being faced. These problem attributes are presented in Table 7.5.

Table 7.5 Problem Attributes (Vroom and Yetton)

A. If decision were accepted, would it make a difference which course of action were adopted?

B. Do I have sufficient information to make a high quality decision?

C. Do subordinates have sufficient additional information to result in a high quality decision?

D. Do I know exactly what information is needed, who possesses it, and how to collect it?

E. Is acceptance of decision by subordinates critical to effective implementation?

F. If I were to make the decision by myself, is it certain that it would be accepted by my subordinates?

G. Can subordinates be trusted to base solutions on organizational considerations?

H. Is conflict among subordinates likely in preferred solutions?

Vroom and Yetton then provide a series of "diagnostic questions" that a leader may use in deciding what style to use. They conclude (as do all the multiple-style theorists) that neither extreme style is effective in all situations. Their theory has received some support, but it is primarily a normative theory ("this is what you should do") that needs much more research before it can be accepted fully.

The Path Goal Theory

Robert House and Terrence Mitchell have developed a theory of leadership that sounds a lot like the expectancy theory of motivation. They argue that the leader's behavior affects the employees' acceptance of him or her, their satisfaction, and their expectation that hard work will lead to rewards.

House says that an effective leader's crucial job is to tell subordinates clearly what they must do to get the rewards they want (path clarification). The leader must reward only if the subordinates accomplish the work goals. If they do so, the effective leader does his best to be supportive (i.e., take care of their needs).

omit

Reddin's Leadership Style Mechanism William Reddin, using Ohio State's two dimensions of leadership (concern for task and concern for people), has developed the 3-D approach shown in Figure 7.5. He takes a position similar to that of Tannenbaum and Schmidt and Reddin. Reddin says that any four of the styles shown are useful in the right circumstances. Used improperly, they are all ineffective.

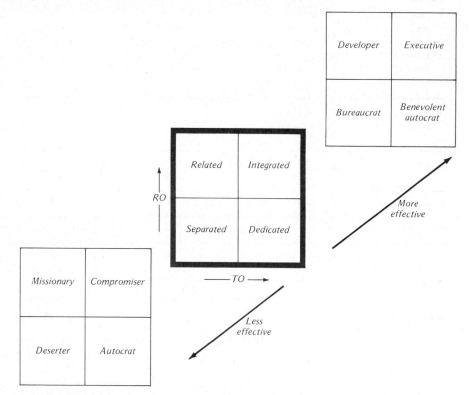

Figure 7.5
Reddin's 3-D style.

When the "dedicated" style (conservative) is used effectively, he labels it *benevolent autocrat.* When the liberal style is used effectively, he calls it the *developer* style. The middle-of-the-road styles he labels *executive* and *bureaucrat.* Again, the conditions in which the various styles should be used are similar to those described by Tannenbaum and Schmidt.

Managerial Implications

We have just been through a lot of theories. Chances are, this discussion has been a bit confusing. Table 7.6 is an attempt to summarize most of the theories discussed along the liberal–conservative continuum.

What does all this mean to you as a manager? I could review for you (and it would take *many* pages) all the conflicting research on the effectiveness of each of these styles. Instead, let me sum it up in propositional form.

Table 7.6 Glueck's Map of the Leadership Style Jungle

Theorist	Liberal	Middle of the Road		Conservative
1. Lewin, Lippitt, and White	democratic			authoritarian
2. Ohio State Studies (Stogdill)	relationship orientated, consideration			task-oriented, initiating structure
3. Tannenbaum and Schmidt	non-manager power and influence			manager power and influence
4. McGregor	Liberal ("theory Y")			Conservative ("theory X")
5. Likert	system 4, participative	system 3, consultative	system 2, benevolent authoritative	system 1, exploitive authority
6. Fiedler	permissive			directive
7. Reddin	developer	bureaucrat or executive		benevolent autocrat

> **Proposition 7.3.**
> Each leadership style is effective if it matches the needs of the situation, the work group, and the leader.

Those who seem to be trying to show that one style is best seem to be heading down the same dead-end road as those who were looking for "the leader's personality." The major difference between the conservatives and the liberals is that the liberals assume that most employees desire responsibility and are capable of participating in most decisions, while the conservatives feel that few employees are sufficiently able or motivated.

Most of the research trying to prove that there is one "best" style is oriented toward the liberal style. Yet studies have shown that most of today's leaders are conservative. This puts the liberals in the position of trying to prove that most current organizations are ineffective, a highly unlikely position.

The more reasonable position appears to be that all styles are effective if the circumstances are right. After twenty years of research the findings remain inconclusive. But proposition 7.4 seems to be a fair summary of the current situation.

Proposition 7.4.
A leadership style is effective if it fits the leader's personality, the subordinates' characteristics, and the situation.

This still leaves you, the manager, in a series of positions where half the conditions point one way, half the other. Obviously, a middle-of-the-road style developed by trial and error would be appropriate here.

Let me add a final proposition.

Proposition 7.5.
Any leadership style that honestly reflects the views of the leader will be more effective than one chosen for manipulative reasons.

There has been a resurgence of writings suggesting that managers should follow the leadership strategy that the employees want even if it contradicts the leader's preferences. I believe most leaders can be flexible in their style. But for those who do hold strong views regarding leadership style it makes more sense to operate accordingly. Your better employees will see through any attempt to use leadership style in a manipulative way.

I have used the terms *liberal, middle of the road,* and *conservative* throughout this chapter—in fact I use them throughout the book. It is very important, therefore, that I make very clear any assumptions regarding the use of these terms:

1 There is nothing good or bad about any of these terms. As I have indicated, *all three styles work.* The word *liberal* may not be your favorite. But here it is simply a *descriptive* term.

2 I have described three leadership styles: liberal, middle of the road, and conservative. Obviously, you can combine liberal or conservative with middle-of-the-road style in a number of ways. To describe more than three would be very cumbersome.

Table 7.7 Three Managerial Styles

LIBERAL	MIDDLE OF THE ROAD	CONSERVATIVE
Participative Management	**Leadership**	**Boss-centered Leadership**
Informal; distant	careful delegation	close; formal

Communications

Informal, multichannel communications "system"	General description of communications	Well-defined chain of command
Much communication encouraged in all directions (up, down, and lateral).	Amount and direction of communication	Little communication encouraged; mostly downward
Adequate; mostly accurate	Quality of communication	Needs supplementary system; somewhat inaccurate

Planning

Manager helped by employees	General description	Performed by the manager
Work group sets the objectives in conjunction with the manager	Setting objectives	A manager's job
Multiple overlapping objectives	Nature of objectives	Clearly defined for the enterprise and for each subunit

Decision Making

Decentralized	General decision description	Centralized
Wherever the knowledge necessary for good decisions is located	Location of most critical decisions	Toward the top of the hierarchy
Responsibility for decisions given to doers	Attitude toward decision-making responsibility	Responsibility for decisions is administrator's
Encourages employees to take reasonable risks	Risk taking	Discourages risk taking by employees
Encourages creative decisions by experimentation, cross-fertilization, and rewards	Creativity (in decisions and tasks)	Expects creativity to come from administrators and filter down from there

Design of Jobs

Enlarged and enriched		Specialized and Simplified
Broadly defined		Narrowly defined
Either not used or very general	Job descriptions	Used, clear and specific

Organization

	Horizontal division of labor	
Used, extensive	Formalization (degree to which documents and forms are used)	Nonexistent or not used
Departmentation by process; not too specialized	Departmentation	Departmentation by function; grouping by function; much specialization
Nonexistent or not used	Standardization of policies, procedures, and rules	Used, extensive
Flat organization, few levels	Vertical division of labor (chain of command)	Tall organization, many levels

Coordination

Informal, unprogramed; performed by work groups	General description	Programed by use of SOPs, individual coordinators, or managers

Control

	Span of control	
Large	Medium	Small
Decentralized	Centralization	Centralized
Few things controlled; general controls	Degrees of control; some general, some specific	Many things controlled; specific controls

Table 7.7 presents these three styles as they will be used throughout the book. It spells out what a leader using each style would do in situations requiring leadership, communication, planning, decision making, organization, coordination, control, and conflict management.

ORGANIZA-TIONAL CLIMATE

Recently it has become popular to discuss organizational climate as a variable tied to leadership. The term *climate* is used in several different ways. For our purposes it is defined as follows:

> **ORGANIZATIONAL CLIMATE**
> Organizational climate is a set of organizational attributes that leads to employee expectations of autonomy, structure, rewards, and warmth and support.

The theory is that certain climates match particular leadership styles and that the manager will be more effective under appropriate conditions. Thus, it is thought, if liberal leadership is practiced, the organizational climate (set of attitudes present) should be one of maximum autonomy and employee responsibility. The opposite is true for the conservative style, which is thought to lead to a more structured or defined climate and a more economically oriented reward system.

Although this concept is appealing, at present there is too much conflict over what organizational climate is and how it operates to reinforce leadership style for it to be useful to most managers.

James van Fleet has written a book entitled *The 22 Biggest Mistakes Managers Make and How to Correct Them.* Seven of those mistakes seem to be related to ineffective leadership style:

- Not setting a personal example for your employees
- Trying to be liked rather than respected
- Failing to give cooperation to your employees
- Failing to ask your subordinates for their advice and help
- Failing to develop a sense of responsibility in your subordinates
- Failing to keep your criticism constructive
- Failing to treat your subordinates as individuals

SUMMARY

It is hard to say how important leadership is relative to other aspects of management. But it should be clear that leadership style is the way a manager makes use of his or her knowledge of people and their role in an enterprise. One can hardly underestimate the importance of an effective leadership style for success as an entrepreneur, family business executive, or manager.

In this chapter you learned that leadership is a set of interpersonal behaviors designed to influence employees to cooperate in the achievement of objectives. You also learned that work groups may have formal leaders (appointed by management) and informal leaders (chosen by the work group).

Leadership is affected by three factors: the leader, the work group, and the leadership task or situation. It is important to remember that although there are explanations of effective leadership that emphasize each of these factors, comprehensive leadership theory probably should include all three.

Next we looked at the sources of influence managers and entrepreneurs can draw on to make their leadership more effective. All managers or entrepreneurs have legitimate power—it comes with the job. Most managers have the power to reward (through pay and other reward systems). Many entrepreneurs and managers have skill and expertise as a source of influence. Managers who develop their interpersonal skills can influence through affection. A few managers can use respect, rectitude, and coercive power. A serious problem exists, however, if the influence or power of a manager is not carefully limited.

We went on to discuss the various ways managers and entrepreneurs can use their power or influence—their leadership style. I described two extreme leadership styles (liberal and conservative) and a combination style (middle of the road). The conservative style is the most frequently used, though many educated employees prefer the middle-of-the-road or liberal styles. The evidence supporting each extreme style is contradictory. Accordingly, a contingency or situational approach seems to make the most sense. The theorists who advocate the contingency approach try to specify the conditions in the leader, the work group, and the task that allow the conservative, liberal, and middle-of-the-road styles to work—some of the time. An overview of the various leadership styles was presented in Table 7.6.

It appears that effective leaders are able to adapt their style to the situation and the subordinates and to mobilize all the sources of influence at their disposal in an honest attempt to reach organizational and individual objectives. This chapter provided you with the basics toward devising an effective leadership style, so important to entrepreneurs and managers. Chapter 8 continues our discussion of leadership and influence, but its focus is on influencing nonsubordinates such as peers and superiors.

Questions for Review

1. What is leadership?

2. How do the leader, the work group, and the task or situation affect leadership?

3. "It is desirable that the formal leader also be the informal leader." What do you mean by formal and informal leaders? Why should one person be both?

4. What sources of influence do entrepreneurs and managers have available to make them effective as leaders?

5. "The more sources of influence used by a manager, the more effective he or she will be as a leader." Comment.

6. How do managers abuse power?

7. What do we mean by a conservative leadership style? a middle-of-the-road style? a liberal style? Which is best?

8. What assumptions about the leader, employees, and work situation do the liberal, conservative, and middle-of-the-road styles make?

9. Compare and contrast these contingency theorists: Tannenbaum and Schmidt, Fiedler, Vroom-Yetton, and House (path goal).

10. What is organizational climate?

References

Introduction　Evans, Martin, "The Effects of Supervisory Behavior on Path Goal Relationship," *Organizational Behavior and Human Performance,* 5 (1970): 272–298.

Fiedler, Fred, and Chemers, Martin, *Leadership and Effective Management* (Glenview, Ill.: Scott, Foresman, 1974).

Gibb, Cecil, "Leadership," in Gardner Lindzey and Elliot Aronson, eds., *Handbook of Social Psychology* (Boston, Mass.: Addison-Wesley, 1969).

Gibb, Cecil, "An Environmental Approach to the Study of Leadership," *Occupational Psychology,* 25 (1951): 233–248.

House, Robert, "A Path Goal Theory of Leadership Effectiveness," *Administrative Science Quarterly,* 16 (1970): 321–338.

Jacobs, T. O., *Leadership and Exchange in Formal Organizations* (Alexandria, Va.: Human Resources Research Association, 1971).

Jennings, Eugene, *An Anatomy of Leadership: Princes, Heros and Supermen* (New York: Harper and Brothers, 1960).

Likert, Rensis, *The Human Organization* (New York: McGraw-Hill, 1967).

McMurry, Robert, *The Maverick Executive* (New York: Amacon, 1974).

Murphy, A. J., "A Study of the Leadership Process," *American Sociological Review,* 6 (1941): 674–687.

Stogdill, Ralph, *Individual Behavior and Group Achievement* (New York: Oxford University Press, 1959).

———, *Handbook of Leadership* (New York: Free Press, 1974).

The Importance of Leadership

Ghiselli, Edwin, *Explorations in Managerial Talent* (Pacific Palisades, Calif.: Goodyear Publishing, 1971).

Leninson, Harry, *The Exceptional Executive* (Cambridge, Mass.: Harvard University Press, 1968).

MacMillan, David, *Canadian Business History* (Toronto: McClelland and Steward, 1972).

Miller, William, *Men in Business* (New York: Harper and Brothers, 1952).

Nash, Gerald, *Perspectives on Administration: The Vistas of History* (Berkeley: University of California, Institute of Governmental Studies, 1969).

Selznick, Phillip, *Leadership in Administration* (Chicago: Row Peterson, 1957).

Stogdill, op. cit.

Waldo, Dwight, *The Novelist on Organization and Administration* (Berkeley: University of California, Institute of Governmental Studies, 1968).

What Is Leadership?

Barnard, Chester, "The Nature of Leadership," in *Organization and Management* (Cambridge, Mass.: Harvard University Press, 1958), pp. 80–110.

Fiedler and Chemers, op. cit.

Gibb, Cecil, "Leadership," in Gardner Lindzey and Elliot Aronson, eds., *Handbook of Social Psychology*

Mintzberg, Henry, *The Nature of Managerial Work* (New York: Harper & Row, 1973).

Stogdill, op. cit.

Sources of Leadership Influence

Bierstadt, Robert, "An Analysis of Social Power," *American Sociological Review,* 15 (December 1950): 730–736.

Blau, Peter, "A Critical Review of Weber's Theory of Authority," *American Political Science Review,* June 1963.

Cartwright, Dorwin, "Influence, Leadership and Control," in James March, ed., *Handbook on Organizations* (Chicago: Rand McNally, 1965).

Clark, Terry, "The Concept of Power," *Southwestern Social Science Quarterly,* 6 (1967): 271–296.

French, J. R. P., and Raven, B., "The Bases of Social Power," in Dorwin Cartwright, ed., *Studies in Social Power* (Ann Arbor: Institute of Social Research, 1959).

Pichler, Joseph, "Power, Influence and Authority," in Joseph McGuire, ed., *Contemporary Management* (Englewood Cliffs, N.J.: Prentice-Hall, 1974).

Presthus, Robert, "Authority in Organization," *Public Administration Review,* Spring 1960.

Weber, Max, *The Theory of Social and Economic Organizations* (New York: Oxford University Press, 1947).

The Limits of Power

Fitch, H. Gordon, and Saunders, Charles, "Blowing the Whistle: The Limits of Organizational Obedience," *Proceedings, Academy of Management,* 1975.

Newman, William, et al., *The Process of Management* (Englewood Cliffs, N.J.: Prentice-Hall, 1972).

Leadership Styles

Haire, Mason, et al., *Managerial Thinking* (New York: John Wiley and Sons, 1966).

McGregor, Douglas, *The Human Side of Enterprise* (New York: McGraw-Hill, 1960).

McMurry, Robert, "The Case for the Benevolent Autocrat," *Harvard Business Review,* January-February 1958, pp. 82–90.

McNair, Malcolm, "Thinking Ahead: What Price Human Relations," *Harvard Business Review,* March-April 1957.

Liberal Leadership Style

Argyris, Chris, *Integrating the Individual and the Organization* (New York: John Wiley and Sons, 1964).

Bennis, Warren, *American Bureaucracy* (Chicago: Aldene Press, 1970).

Greiner, Larry, "What Managers Think of Participative Management," *Harvard Business Review,* March-April 1973.

Likert, Rensis, op. cit.

Lippitt, Ronald, and White, Ralph, "The Social Climates of Children's Groups," in R. Baker, et al., *Child Behavior and Development* (New York: McGraw-Hill 1943).

McGregor, op. cit.

Industrial Democracy: The Ultimate Liberal Style

Bunch, J. D., "How Danish Workers Participate," *Journal of General Management,* 1, no. 4 (Summer 1974).

Eichenberger, J. Y., "Industrial Democracy and the French Board of Directors," *Journal of General Management,* 1, no. 4 (Summer 1974).

Fabricius, Fritz, "Codetermination in Germany," *Journal of General Management,* 1, no. 4 (Summer 1974).

Glueck, William, and Kavran, Dragoljub, "Worker Management in Yugoslavia," *Business Horizons,* February 1972.

Contingency Style Models

Fiedler, Fred, *A Theory of Leadership Effectiveness* (New York: McGraw-Hill, 1967).

Fiedler and Chemers, op. cit.

House, Robert, "A Path Goal Theory of Leader Effectiveness," *Administrative Science Quarterly,* 16 (1971): 321–338.

House, Robert, and Mitchell, Terrence, "Path Goal Theory of Leadership," *Journal of Contemporary Business,* 1974.

Reddin, William, *Managerial Effectiveness* (New York: McGraw-Hill, 1970).

Tannenbaum, Robert, and Schmidt, Warren, "How to Choose a Leadership Pattern," *Harvard Business Review,* March-April 1958, pp. 95–101.

Vroom, Victor, and Yetton, Philip, *Leadership and Decision Making* (Pittsburgh: University of Pittsburgh Press, 1973).

Organizational Climate

Guion, Robert, "A Note on Organizational Climate," *Organizational Behavior and Human Performance,* 9 (1973): 120–125.

Hellriegel, Don, and Slocum, John, "Organizational Climate: Theories, Research, and Contingencies," *Academy of Management Review,* 17, no. 2 (June 1974).

James, Lawrence, and Jones, Allan, "Organizational Climate: A Review of Theory and Research," *Psychological Bulletin,* 81, no. 12, (December 1974): 1096-1112.

Litwin, George, and Stringer, Robert, *Motivation and Organization Climate* (Cambridge, Mass.: Harvard School of Business, 1968).

Pritchard, Robert, and Karasick, Bernard, "The Effects of Organizational Climate on Managerial Job Performance and Job Satisfaction," *Organizational Behavior and Human Performance,* 9 (1973): 126–146.

Summary

van Fleet, James, *The 22 Biggest Mistakes Managers Make and How to Correct Them* (West Nyack, N.Y.: Parker Publishing, 1973).

CHAPTER 8

EFFECTIVE RELATIONSHIPS WITH SUPERIORS AND COLLEAGUES

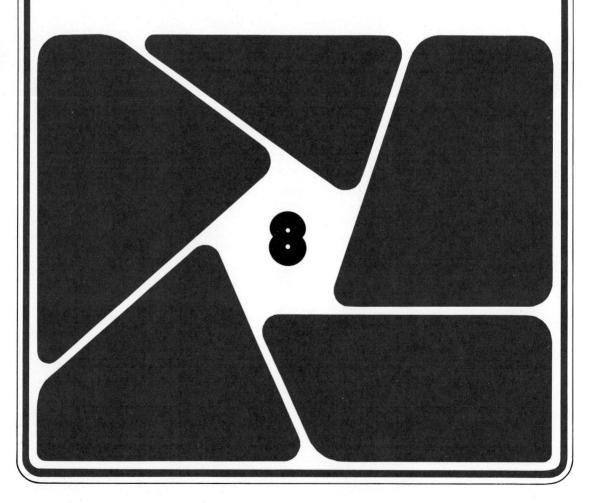

Learning Objectives

1. To understand how to effectively influence your superiors to advance your department's objectives and your career.
2. To learn how to deal effectively with peers who head departments like yours.
3. To recognize the problems and challenges of dealing with staff advisers.
4. To understand the best way to relate to those sent to evaluate you and your department's performance (auditors, for example).

Chapter Outline

Relating to Your Superiors
The Importance of Getting Along With the Boss
Influencing Superiors
Summary
Relating to Colleagues and Peers
Influencing Peers in Workflow Relationships
Influencing Colleagues in Service Relationships
Advisory, Audit, and Line-Staff Relations
Summary and Implications

In Chapter 7 we discussed how a manager or entrepreneur could be most effective as a leader of employees. This chapter is designed to prepare you to deal effectively with two additional groups of people: superiors and colleagues.

Every manager has many roles to play. In private life one plays the roles of parent, spouse, child, and so forth. In work life there are other roles to play: superior, subordinate, and colleague. These roles are defined by people's expectations about how a boss or colleague ought to behave.

This chapter will give you further insight into the differences and similarities between the role of a superior and that of a subordinate or a colleague.

RELATING TO YOUR SUPERIORS

If you read some of the currently popular management literature, you would think all there is to being successful is getting along with and outflanking your boss. In *Management and Machiavelli,* for example, Anthony Jay implies that all you need to do is read Machiavelli's *The Prince* and apply it. And the theme of the musical "How to Succeed in Business Without Really Trying" is that the way to get to the top is by flattering your boss (and key power brokers like the boss' secretary); no talent is needed.

Source: © King Features Syndicate, Inc. 1975.

According to Michael Korda, to get power (from your boss) all you need is a winning, trustworthy smile. His advice for dealing with bosses and peers includes the following pointers:

1 Always arrive late for business lunches so as to make your companion ill at ease.

2 Answer difficult questions with another question.

3 Project an air of mystery.

4 Get a corner office decorated in power colors (blue and touches of red) with low chairs and ashtrays just out of reach.

5 Speak softly with older executives. They will think they are going deaf.

Other writers imply that you can get ahead by trusting no one, maintaining positive mental attitudes, influencing the boss through his or her secretary or spouse, manipulating conferences, or joining the boss in social activities.

There is no doubt that your success depends on effective relationships with your superiors. But surely you do not believe they are so foolish that they cannot see through "intimidation," second-rate power plays, or third-rate fawning. To paraphrase Abraham Lincoln, you can fool some bosses all of the time and all bosses some of the time, but you cannot fool all bosses all of the time.

Relating to a boss is not always easy as the following incident, reported by Studs Terkel, illustrates:

> My father got a phone call. His boss was chewing him out for something—in a tone and language that were humiliating. Here's my father who had worked for this company for thirty years. My father's a dignified man and he worked hard. God knows he's given that company all the years of his life. He doesn't have anything else. There are no hobbies. He wasn't close to any of his children. Nothing outside of work. That was it. He would get up in the morning and leave the house and come home 12–14 hours later, six days a week. That was it. Yet here he is at sixty and here's a guy chewing him out like he's a little kid. I felt embarrassed being there. I felt sorry that he knew I was watching that happen. I could see he was angry and embarrassed. I could see him concealing his feelings, sort of shuffling and scratching his head, in the face of higher authority. We went to lunch. We didn't talk about it at all.

Obviously, superiors are people, so most of them are pleasant most of the time and unpleasant some of the time. A few are unpleasant most of the time.

The Importance of Getting Along with the Boss

> **SUPERIOR**
> A superior (boss) is the individual to whom an employee is responsible for his or her level of performance.

It should be obvious that some of your success as a manager depends on your relationship with your boss—not as much as "How to Succeed . . ." implies, but more than many feel it should. Your superior determines the following:

1 How you are evaluated—which in turn affects your chances of promotion.

2 Your salary and benefits (within limits).

3 Possible transfers, (if positions open up).

4 Your job: whether it is rewarding or not.

5 Your self-esteem (through feedback to you).

6 Your success in your job (through both instructions and feedback).

7 How you relate to others.

Influencing Superiors There has been very little scientific research focusing on the relationship between superior and subordinate. But our discussions of motivation theories (Chapter 5) and influence and leadership theories (Chapter 7) can be applied to this area.

I   **Insights from Motivation Theory**

Superiors are people too. They have needs to be satisfied. You as a subordinate can contribute to the satisfaction of the superior's lower (physiological and security) needs or his or her need for achievement by performing your duties well and thus helping your superior's unit achieve its goals. You contribute to the superior's social or affiliation needs by socializing with him or her, discussing problems, and providing sympathy as you would with any person.

Employees can contribute to the satisfaction of the superior's recognition and esteem needs by recognizing what the superior does for the work group and saying so in word and deed. At one extreme, you can act like Lt. Fuzz. But superiors also have doubts and can benefit from constructive criticism. You can provide such feedback without becoming an insincere phony. When a superior wonders if he or she is getting anything out of the job, you can point out the positive side as well.

> **Proposition 8.1.**
> Managers whose behavior contributes to the need satisfaction of their superiors will influence them and tend to be rewarded by them.

II   **Insights from Influence Theory**

You may recall the seven sources of influence or power listed in Chapter 7:

1 Legitimate – Coercive
2 Monetary –   "

3 Skill/Expertise - non-coercive

4 Affection - ''

5 Respect - ''

6 Rectitude -

7 Coercive

OR LEGITIMATE - coercive
&
CONSENT - non coercive

Which of these do you think a subordinate exerts on a superior?

In general, subordinates do not have legitimate or monetary power over their superiors. In fact the superior usually has this power. But as we learned in Chapter 6, employee coalitions can exert an equivalant of coercive power over superiors. Remember how the soldiers "sent Napoleon a message?" If they all slow down or all work against the boss, the output will drop. Or the employees can "blow the whistle on the boss" in various ways. They can follow the rules to the letter—air traffic controllers are famous for this—or threaten to unionize. Robert McMurry suggests that "the most important strategy of power is for an executive to establish alliances and use passive resistance where necessary."

Thus employees have available (usually as a last resort) the coercive influence of a coalition. Just as the possibility of being fired in the background to make coercive power effective, employee slowdown or "sabotage" provides a source of influence over superiors.

A second, more likely source of influence is expertise (which probably includes some respect). Most bosses do not have the expertise—or the time—to do the job as well as you. So to the extent that the boss needs you, this is a source of influence.

> **Proposition 8.2.**
> To the extent that an employee has important expert knowledge/skill that the superior does not have and to the extent that this expertise is hard to replace, the subordinate will have influence over the superior.

The final source of influence for a subordinate is affection.

> **Proposition 8.3.**
> The more likable a subordinate, the more influence he or she is likely to have on a superior.

As I have mentioned before, if a superior likes a subordinate, he or she is more likely to be favorably inclined toward the subordinate and to be influenced by that subordinate.

McMurry suggests that "the executive should take all the steps he [or she] can to ensure that he [or she] is personally compatible with superiors." He suggests further that the executive become a persuasive person skilled at self-dramatization and radiating self-confidence.

III. Insights from Leadership Theory

If one accepts the interaction theory of leadership, the subordinate who interacts most frequently will be more accepted, better liked, more influential, and better rewarded. If one accepts the premises of leadership style theory, conservative leaders will prefer subordinates who accept their direction and do what they are asked. As McMurry suggests, the subordinate will get a clear, concise, unambiguous statement, in writing, of his or her duties and responsibilities, reporting relationships, and scope of authority. The executive should establish clear communication channels upward.

One would expect that liberal leaders will expect creativity and initiative from their subordinates. The subordinates would do well to act accordingly.

Summary   Motivation theory, influence theory, and leadership theory all provide insights into how to relate better to your boss. A good relationship should contribute to promotions, salary increases, better jobs, and a pleasanter work environment.

> **Proposition 8.4.**
> The more needs of the superior the subordinate satisfies, the better he or she will relate to and influence the superior.

RELATING TO COLLEAGUES AND PEERS   Relating to superiors is crucial to managerial effectiveness. But executives also need to interact with groups other than superiors and subordinates. Within the enterprise, these groups include colleagues and peers.

> **COLLEAGUE**
> A colleague is another person at work of roughly equivalent status or rank who is neither a superior nor a direct subordinate and with whom the manager interacts to achieve enterprise objectives.

There are several kinds of colleagues: peers in the workflow process; managers of service, advisory, or auditing groups. In addition, we will discuss line-staff and committee relations.

Colleagues control expertise and resources without which the manager normally has difficulty attaining his or her objectives. And relationships with colleagues are an important component of organizational success and employee satisfaction. Studies have shown that although lateral relationships (relationships with colleagues) are important in all organizations, these relationships are likely to vary depending on the organizational environment. Thus in stable business environments crucial lateral relations are as follows:

$$\text{Production}\ \diagup\diagdown\ \begin{matrix}\text{Research}\\ \text{Sales}\end{matrix}$$

In rapidly changing environments the crucial relations are as follows:

$$\text{Research}\ \diagup\diagdown\ \begin{matrix}\text{Production}\\ \text{Sales}\end{matrix}$$

Colleague or lateral relations are especially difficult in many organizations because

1 There is no clear-cut set of influence relationships: Who should initiate? When should the other respond?

2 The rewards for performance in the two units (and for the two managers) are likely to be different. Research scientists do not have the same objectives and rewards as salespeople.

3 Lateral relations are likely to be uncomfortable, tension producing, and much lengthier than vertical (superior-subordinate) relations.

Thus lateral relations are important and difficult. In the rest of this chapter, therefore, I will examine them in more detail in order to give you some clues on how to develop effective relationships with colleagues. The following discussion of different kinds of colleagues (workflow, advisory, service, and audit) is based on Leonard Sayles' approach.

Influencing Peers in Workflow Relationships

The first lateral relationship is the workflow relationship. Each manager's section is part of the flow of work and thus has to deal with the units before and after it. The prior units can usually cause more problems for you and your unit than those "downstream" from you. Consider Figure 8.1.

If you are in the brewing business, you are dependent on a number of people and units to order the right amounts of malt, hops, and other ingredients and get them to you on time. The bottling line supervisors, in turn, are dependent on you to get the right amount of beer brewed on time.

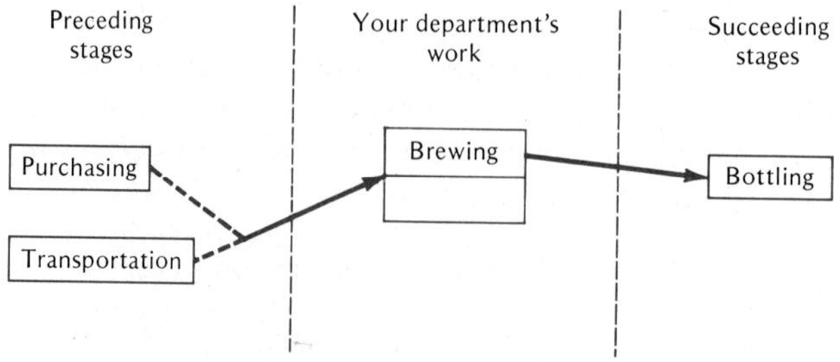

Figure 8.1
Workflow relationships at a beer company.

Sayles studied problems in the relationship between purchasing departments and production departments. The typical problems that arose involved

1 *Timing.*   Much dissatisfaction arises because of mutual pressures to rearrange schedules. If the purchasing department does not order on time, you are behind, and this causes problems both for you and for the bottling department.

2 *Ways of working.*   A second potential problem is the way the preceding department does its work. Does it do it in a way that facilitates yours? In the manufacturing of parts, for example, the preceding group may give you the right number of parts on time, but the quality of the work may be poor, leading to inefficiences in your department.

3 *Information.*   Often the preceding department may not alert you of problems ahead. This prevents you from planning how you will deal with the difficulties, leading to bad feelings between the departments and managers involved.

Thus if you were a department manager in brewing, you would need to interact with the purchasing manager to deal with these kinds of problems. It is natural and necessary for peers and colleagues to relate to each other.

To understand this relationship better, consider the following study by Henry Landsberger. He observed the personal interactions (face to face and on the phone) between production managers, schedulers, stock control, and sales liaison managers in two plants.

The first thing Landsberger found was how important peer relationships were. A large amount of time was spent in these relationships. The sales liaison managers spent the most time in this way (about 60 percent), while the lowest average was for production managers (about 30 percent). The importance of lateral relations could also be measured in terms of suggestions for action: 45–55 percent of these came from peers, not from superiors or subordinates.

Finally, Landsberger found that certain issues came up again and again and had to be resolved. The conflicts usually came down to three issues: flexibility versus stability in production, short-run versus long-run costs, and departmental goal attainment versus plant goal attainment.

How can peer relations be organized and developed? Jay Galbraith suggests that there are several ways enterprises can help organize and develop peer relations at work:

·*Direct contact:* Encourage peers to interact and establish reciprocal relations. There is evidence that peer relations improve when managers' careers include wider experience across departments.

·*Liaison roles/integrating roles:* Create positions whose purpose is to coordinate between peers.

·*Task forces and teams:* Create temporary groups of people from the departments involved whose job is to work out particular problems.

How Not to Do It

There are some ways of relating that work poorly. They include the following:

·Interact directly only infrequently.

·Get rules established at a higher level that favors your department over your peer's.

·Put pressure on your peer's department by going to your boss and getting him or her to pressure your peer's boss.

·Interfere in the peer's department by giving orders to his or her subordinates.

How to Do It

Then what will work? Returning to motivation theory, you and your colleague are likely to work well together if you can help satisfy the colleague's needs:

Physiological/safety: Help get the work out, thereby helping the colleague attain his or her objectives.

Social needs: Interact with the colleague. Get to know him or her.

Esteem: Treat the colleague with respect.

Influence theory would tell you that you have the following sources of power available to you:

Skill/expertise (when you can help the colleague solve problems)

Affection (when the colleague likes you)
Respect (when the colleague respects you)

Leadership theory would tell you that you can increase your influence by interacting with your colleague frequently and developing an exchange relationship ("I'll do this for you, you do this for me"). This is harder the further downstream you are. The last department may depend on six prior departments; the first department depends on none.

Thus some of the methods you can use to influence a colleague effectively include the following:

1 Interact with the colleague frequently. Get to know him or her and understand his or her problems.

2 Share information in an exchange relationship.

3 Try to be open about how quality problems affect the whole relationship.

4 If steps 1–3 do not work, build a coalition of peers around the troublesome colleague and try to exert pressure that way.

5 If step 4 does not work, try to get the workflow rerouted so that you are not so dependent on the troublesome colleague.

6 If all else fails, appeal through the hierarchy (to a mutual boss) and get rules established and hierarchical pressure put on the peer. Again, this is the method of last resort.

A common theme runs through all of this, summarized in Proposition 8.6.

Proposition 8.6.
The greater the uncertainty of the workflow process, the greater the timing, quality, and information problems and the greater the potential of conflict between lateral managers. The greater the potential problems, the more often the managers should interact to solve them.

Influencing Colleagues in Service Relationships

Managers of service departments supervise activities needed by many departments. These activities are centralized for economic purposes. Some examples are specialized machine shops, typing pools, photocopying services, stores, mail rooms, computer services, design engineers, purchasing, maintenance, and hospital laboratories. If you are a manager of a service activity, your job relationships can be diagramed as shown in Figure 8.2.

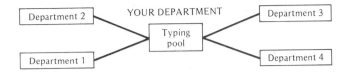

Figure 8.2
Service
relationships.

In this diagram all four departments depend on you for typing service. This creates special problems for the service manager, such as deciding priorities when several departments want service at the same time or deciding how much and what quality of service to provide on a limited budget.

Service relationships actually can be organized in three ways (see Table 8.1).

Table 8.1

	Relationship of Service Unit to Head Operating Executive	Relationship of Head Operating Executive to Service Unit	Relationship of Service Unit to Employees of Operating Unit
1. Service as requested	Offers service if operating units want it.	Same as toward any outside contractor. The "boss" of the staff personnel is their own staff unit head.	Through operating unit's supervisors, issue such requests as required to make service effective.
2. Staff services supplied on a programed basis	Somewhat stronger than (1). Services are rendered on a programed basis approved by higher authority, and cannot be refused by operating unit head.	The direct chain of command of the staff personnel is to the staff unit head. Operating unit head must work.	Same as (1).
3. Auxiliary services routinely supplied	Services are a routine part of operations, not on an "invited" or specially programed basis.	Same as (2).	Service personnel can insist on regular procedures being followed. Routine communications flow directly between staff and operating personnel except in cases of sharp disagreement.

Sayles' analysis of service departments led to the following conclusions:

1 Service functions become scarce resources. Service managers often are unable to satisfy all departments at the same time.

2 When this happens, there is a tendency for the departments to increase their requests for service and shorten the time in which it is needed in order to make sure they get their "fair share." This compounds the problem.

3 Cost and quality then become serious problems.

4 The departments then try to influence the service department manager with gifts, favors, good terms, or mutual protection.

5 This leads the nonfavored departments to use pressure tactics or appeal to the service manager's boss.

6 All this is compounded by the difficulty of predicting service needs ahead of time and planning for them.

George Straus, in his study of a purchasing department, found that the service managers' reactions to the pressure took the form of a series of mechanisms:

1 *Rule-oriented tactics:* appealing to rules, such as written authorizations, to handle problems like priorities.

2 *Rule-evading tactics:* going through the motions of following the rules but doing what they want to anyway.

3 *Personal-political tactics:* working through allies who support their position.

4 *Educational tactics:* persuading the departments to accept their position and explaining why.

5 *Organizational-interactional tactics:* getting procedures changed to fit the patterns they want.

Sayles found that successful service managers did not accept conflict as inevitable but took the initiative and tried educational or organization-interaction methods in planning and scheduling the needed services. The successful service manager also buffered his employees from departmental pressure.

How does the service manager influence the operating department colleague to cooperate and help him or her do the job well and fairly? The manager will use skill/expertise power, affection power, or respect power most frequently and legitimate power or the equivalent of coercive power (losing the service request, etc.) only as a last resort. The manager will increase his or her interactions with operating colleagues, use persuasion and education, and develop an exchange relationship (in leadership theory terms). In this way the manager will help satisfy the achievement and affiliation needs of his or her colleagues.

How does an operating manager influence a service manager? It makes sense to try to influence him or her with affection power, respect power, or skill expertise power. It also makes sense to develop an exchange relationship in order to better serve the needs of both.

A word of caution: The operating manager should be honest when he or she has a real emergency. Then the service manager will try to help. If all jobs are emergency jobs, the service manager will believe (and rightly so) that the operating manager is a poor planner. The exchange relationship also implies that when another department has an emergency and the service manager asks you to accept a delay on a job that is not an emergency, you do so without complaint.

Establishing reciprocity with the service manager makes sense as long as you do not overexploit the relationship. Again, the use of a proxy for coercive power (putting pressure on the service manager through the hierarchy) is risky and should be avoided until all other avenues have been exhausted.

Advisory, Audit, and Line-Staff Relations

The final relationship with colleagues to be discussed is that between line and staff managers or between advisory or audit managers and operating (or other staff) managers.

The Advisory Relationship

STAFF AND LINE

A staff executive is a person whose role is to provide advice, counsel, and expertise to help line operating executives and their units achieve organizational objectives. A line executive is one who is part of a direct chain of command.

This relationship can be diagramed as shown in Figure 8.3.

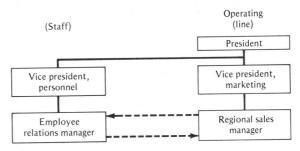

Figure 8.3
The line-staff relationship.

As you will note, if the regional sales manager needs advice on a personnel issue (say, compensation guidelines), he or she will seek advice from the employee relations manager. This is only one of four possible line-staff relationships (see Table 8.2); it is an example of type 1. Staff can be strictly advisory and located at headquarters (type 1). It can consist of separate units located both at headquarters and at field units (type 2). Or staff can be integrated with operating or line units as in types 3 and 4.

The operating-advisory relationship can be a very troublesome one from both points of view. As the line manager sees it, typical problems include the following:

1 *The adviser takes over.*   The adviser starts giving too much advice and says or implies that it is not *advice* but what the manager *must do.* The operating manager views this as taking away the right to make his or her own decisions.

2 *The adviser interferes.*   The line executive observes the adviser bypassing him or her and issuing directives or strongly "giving advice" to subordinates. Again, the operating executive views this as a reduction in his or her influence.

3 *Several advisers cause conflict.*   In some cases, when several advisors or advisory groups are invited in, their advice is conflicting and/or contradictory. This is not viewed as helpful by the operating executive.

4 *The adviser will not help.*   In a few cases operating executives want the adviser to make decisions in his or her area of expertise. Unless the adviser is "Mr. Takeover" (as in problem 1), he or she will avoid this. It is the operating executive's responsibility to make the decision. Yet weaker operating executives want the adviser to make the decision, so they are unhappy with the adviser.

5 *The Adviser takes credit for results.*   Some operating executives believe advisers take credit for their decisions. They believe the optimal role is for the line executive to get credit and blame for all of the unit's results.

Staff advisers often feel that operating executives have too much power and do not pay attention to their advice and new ideas. Their responses may take the following forms:

1 The line executive rejects the advice outright.

2 The line executive "files" the advice after sending a memo praising it (the bottom drawer approach).

3 The operating executive defends "his" or "her" interests against the adviser's by mobilizing support from colleagues or superiors (the political support approach).

Table 8.2 Basic Line-Staff Relationships (Modified from Heyel)

No. Type	Relationship of Staff Unit Employees to Head of Operating Unit	Relationship of Head of Operating Unit to Staff Unit Working in His or Her Department	Relationship of Staff Unit to Employees of Operating Unit
1. Advisory	May only volunteer suggestions, but may not necessarily have to wait to be invited.	May or may not have to avail himself or herself of suggestions.	Do not give or receive instructions.
2. Central staff and counterpart staff unit in operating department.	Advisory and suggestive only, but does not have to wait to be invited.	May or may not have to avail himself or herself of advice and suggestions of central staff unit; through chain of command, head of operating unit is "boss" of the staff unit in his or her department.	"Functional" relationship between central unit and employees of the staff unit in operating department; on matters of professional standards, mode of operation, etc., "suggestions" from the central unit have strong force and are to be disregarded only under special circumstances and with approval of head of operating unit.
3. Personnel assigned to operating unit by staff unit.	Assigned personnel are under administrative command of head of operating unit as to deployment on the job, discipline, hours of work, etc., but their "boss" is the head of the staff unit.	In administrative command of the assigned personnel, head of staff unit may, with notice to head of operating unit, withdraw them from the job if he or she can supply replacements.	Relationships are those of any employees under direct supervision of head of operating unit; they carry on their own activities and work through normal channels within department.
4. A staff unit that is part of an operating organization unit.	Supply information and advise and recommend; decisions are made by operating head, and he or she issues instructions to operating personnel.	Direct relationship through chain of command.	Same as (3). Staff personnel do not issue direct instructions to operating personnel except under unusual circumstances (e.g., a safety or quality inspector shutting down an operation where emergency does not permit working through normal channels.

4 The line executive finds as many errors (including typos) as possible and uses these to indicate that the project is ill conceived and not worth carrying out (the pick-it-to-death approach).

5 The line manager agrees with the specialist's data analysis but argues that future statistics will be different and that the advice therefore is unsound (the future ploy).

6 The line executive simply avoids seeing the adviser by setting up conflicting appointments or using similar evasive tactics (the avoidance technique).

Operating line executives clearly hold most of the cards and, in addition, have legitimate power sources. The staff can try to go along, compromise, or go over the head of the line executive (though the latter is dangerous).

The line-staff problem often leads to frustration. Staff turnover is greater and satisfaction is lower. Since operating executives hold many advantages over staff advisers, most of the advice in the literature is aimed at helping the staff adviser establish good relationships with the line executive. Sayles suggests that such relationships will be better if the following guidelines are followed:

1 Staff advisers should report to their own staff executives (type 1 and 2 relationships in Table 8.2).

2 Staff should be evaluated on their problem-solving abilities, not on the number of projects completed.

3 Staff should try to educate the line employees in staff duties so they can take care of such duties themselves.

4 Staff should respond as soon as possible to requests for help from line executives. The line executives should take the initiative.

5 Staff is successful if it builds support by doing small projects well before undertaking major ones.

6 Managers other than the staff executive should evaluate the staff work performed.

7 Staff should make sure the line manager gets the credit for the results of staff work.

William Whyte suggests that the effective staff adviser

1 Increases the frequency and regularity of interactions and contacts with line executives.

2 Learns the special circumstances of each line department before advising.

3 Builds an exchange relationship.

4 Sees that the line gets credit for the results.

As can be seen from these recommendations, advisory executives will be successful if they utilize influence theory—skill/expertise, affection, respect. Only in extreme cases should they try to use coercive power. From the standpoint of motivation theory, they must be careful of the line's recognition/esteem needs, utilize affiliation/social needs, and contribute to the physiological and safety needs of line executives.

As far as the line executives are concerned, once they realize that the staff executive is there to help, they will be glad to operate on an exchange basis. They should realize that the staff adviser has needs too and try to satisfy his or her social and esteem needs in dealing with the staff adviser.

The Audit Relationship

AUDIT RELATIONSHIP
A staff executive performing an audit appraises and evaluates the extent to which operating managers are meeting objectives, using resources properly, and following enterprise policies.

Sayles believes that the audit relationship developed as organizations grew larger and more complex. No longer could the top managers take the time to gather information on effectiveness and determine whether their policies were being carried out. So specialists with technical expertese were given the task of checking on the operating managers. This, obviously, is a powerful position.

Some examples of the staff specialists involved include accounting auditors (who check on budgets and use of finances) and personnel managers (who check on wage schedules, EEOC requirements, and the like). Figure 8.4 diagrams one such relationship.

Figure 8.4
An auditing relationship.

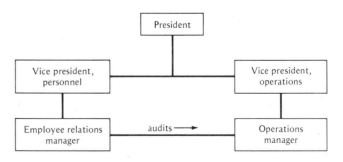

From the operating manager's point of view, the problems in the auditing relationship include the following:

1 Auditors go directly to subordinates and find things the manager did not know.

2 Several auditors give contradictory "orders," so that satisfying the demands of one auditor requires violating the requirements of another. Thus the personnel department's requirement that you hire more handicapped employees may exceed the budget requirements set by the accounting auditor.

3 Collusion can develop between an auditor and an operating manager.

4 The auditor reports the findings to the operating executive's boss without first discussing it with the operating executive.

As with any other relationship, the operating executive can hinder the auditor's work by being unresponsive, not providing information, and so forth. But usually auditors are too powerful for such tactics.

Since much of the power lies with the auditor, most of the "relating" is done by the operating executive. What can he or she do to establish a good relationship with the auditor?

Motivation Theory: The operating manager can help the auditor fulfill his or her needs. Auditors do not have much chance to socialize. They are in different places each week, and they are generally feared. So being friendly and getting to know them can help satisfy their social/affiliation needs. Their esteem needs can be satisfied too if they are called on for advice on how to handle problems in their area of expertise and then the advice is *used.*

Influence Theory: The operating executive's major sources of influence and power are affection and respect. In some cases the operating executive might have skill power as well.

Leadership Theory: It is important to get to know the auditors through frequent interaction. The operating executive should develop an exchange relationship and cooperate fully with the auditors in order to make their job quicker and smoother. In return, the auditors should inform the operating executive of their findings and help them implement changes before reporting back to the home office.

These suggestions may sound like recommendations for manipulating auditors. This is not intended. The point is that auditors are people too. Although it appears that they hold all the cards, operating executives can have an effect and do their job better if they exercise interpersonal skills effectively.

Auditors have most of the sources of influence at their fingertips. They have coercive power and can stop workflow. They can get people reprimanded or even fired. They have legitimate power, too, and they can also use skill, respect, and affection power. But it makes more sense for the auditor to develop a cooperative attitude— "I am here to help you meet your budget"—and then use affection, skill, and respect power to accomplish this. They should rely on legitimate and coercive power only when the others do not work. This is likely to be best for you, for the operating executive, and for the enterprise.

Impossible Relationships

Some enterprises try to combine advisory and auditing relationships in one department and sometimes use the same person to do both. Proposition 8.7 applies here.

> **Proposition 8.7.**
> Combining auditing and advisory duties into one job creates two ineffective relationships.

They don't work Together – people are open with advisors & closed with auditors.

This is so because operating executives never know when the auditor/adviser is auditing and when he or she is advising. Frequently, effective advising requires the operating executives to reveal problems that need to be solved. Many people would be reluctant to do this if they felt that they would be reported on for it. And sometimes that is exactly what an auditor must do.

> **Proposition 8.8.**
> Separate auditing duties from advisory duties. If possible, put them in different departments. If this is not possible, *never* create a job that entails both advising and auditing.

SUMMARY AND IMPLICATIONS

In this chapter I recommended ways of developing effective relationships with your boss. I warned against oversimple fawning ploys, since the boss probably had your job before he or she became the boss and therefore knows all the tricks.

Effective subordinates try to influence their superiors by helping them satisfy their needs. They can also influence their superiors by utilizing skill/expertise power, affection, and if necessary (and only as a last resort), coalition/coercive power.

An important form of human interaction is lateral or peer relations. Fewer mechanisms of influence are available in most lateral relations than in employee leadership situations.

The chapter described a series of peer relationships: workflow, service, audit, and advisory relationships. It recommended using your understanding of motivation (Chapter 5) and leadership (Chapter 7) to make you a more effective executive. Most executives cannot get their jobs done without help from lateral peers.

Peer relations can be handled by direct contact, setting up liaison roles, or teams and task forces. In most cases the direct contact is the method used. In general, it is not fruitful to use hierarchical pressure and rules on peers. Nor is it fruitful to interfere in the peer's needs through expertise power, affection power, or coercive power.

The chapter indicated the differences in emphasis on need satisfaction and influence methods in workflow, service, advisory, and audit relationships.

Chapter 9 discusses the next interpersonal skill needed by managers: communication ability.

Questions for Review

1. "All you need to get ahead in this world is to be 'in' with your boss." Comment.
2. How can superiors affect your career?
3. What forms of power can you use to influence your superiors?
4. Compare and contrast advisory, service, and workflow peers and colleagues.
5. What are the most effective ways to influence workflow colleagues?
6. What are the most effective ways to influence advisory colleagues?
7. How can you influence an auditor?
8. How can you influence an executive who is a peer and heads a service department?

References

Relating to Your Superiors

Jay, Anthony, *Management and Machiavelli* (New York: Holt, Rinehart and Winston, 1968).

Korda, Michael, *Power! How to Get It, How to Use It* (New York: Random House, 1975).

Ringer, Robert, *Winning Through Intimidation* (New York: Funk and Wagnalls, 1975).

Smith, Peter, et al., "Relationships Between Managers and Their Work Associates," *Administrative Science Quarterly,* 14 (1969): 338–345.

Terkel, Studs, *Working* (New York: Pantheon, 1974).

Uris, Auren, and Tarrant, John, *How to Win Your Boss's Love, Approval . . . and Job* (New York: Van Nostrand Reinhold, 1973).

Insights from Influence Theory

Fitch, H. Gordon, and Saunders, Charles, "Blowing the Whistle: The Limits of Organizational Obedience," *Proceedings, Academy of Management,* 1975.

Mechanic, David, "Sources of Power of Lower Participants in Complex Organizations," *Administrative Science Quarterly,* 7 (1962): 349–364.

McMurry, Robert, "Power and the Ambitious Executive," *Harvard Business Review,* November-December, 1973.

Schwartzbaum, Allan, "Lateral Interaction and Effectiveness in Vertical Organizations," *Industrial Relations Research Association Proceedings,* 1967, pp. 360–371.

Thornton, Robert, "Controlling the Technician," *MSU Business Topics,* Summer 1974.

Relating to Colleagues/ Peers

Hall, James, and Leidecker, Joel, "Lateral Relatives in Organization: Theory and Application," in Patrick Conner, ed., *Dimensions in Modern Management* (Boston: Houghton Mifflin, 1974).

Osborn, Richard, et al., "Lateral Leadership, Satisfaction, and Performance," *Proceedings, Academy of Management,* 1973.

Osborn, Richard, and Hunt, James, "An Empirical Investigation of Lateral and Vertical Leadership at Two Organizational Levels," *Journal of Business Research,* 2, no. 2 (April 1974): 209–221.

Influencing Peers in Workflow Relationships

Collins, Barry, and Raven, Bertram, "Group Structure: Attraction, Coalitions, Communication, and Power," in Gardner Lindzey and Elliot Aronson, ed., *Handbook of Social Psychology,* Vol. IV (Boston: Addison Wesley, 1968).

Dowling, William, Jr., and Sayles, Leonard, *How Managers Motivate* (New York: McGraw-Hill, 1971), chap. 9.

Galbraith, Jay, *Designing Complex Organizations* (Reading, Mass.: Addison Wesley, 1973), chap. 5.

Landsberger, Henry, "The Horizontal Dimension of Bureaucracy," *Administrative Science Quarterly,* 6, no. 3 (1961): 299–332.

Sayles, Leonard, *Managerial Behavior* (New York: McGraw-Hill, 1964).

Walton, Richard, et al., "A Study of Conflict in the Process, Structure and Attitudes of Lateral Relationships," in A. Rubenstein and C. Haberstroh, eds., *Some Theories of Organization* (Homewood, Ill.: Richard Irwin, 1966).

Whyte, William, *Organizational Behavior* (Homewood, Ill.: Irwin Dorsey Press, 1969), chap. 18.

Zalesznik, Abraham, "Power and Politics in Organizational Life," *Harvard Business Review,* (May-June 1970): 47–60.

Influencing Colleagues in Service Relationships

Strauss, George, "Tactics of Lateral Relationships: The Purchasing Agent," *Administrative Science Quarterly,* 7, no. 2 (September 1962).

Advisory, Audit, and Line-Staff Relations

Browne, Philip, and Golembiewski, Robert, "The Line Staff Concept Revisited," *Academy of Management Journal,* 17, no. 3 (September 1974): 404–417.

Dalton, Melville, *Men Who Manage* (New York: John Wiley and Sons, 1959).

————, "Changing Line-Staff Relationships," *Personnel Administration,* March 1966.

Efferson, Carlos, "The Line Staff Concept: How to Stay?" Kaiser Aluminium and Chemical Corporation, 1967 (Mimeograph).

Pettigrew, Andrew, "The Influence Process Between Specialists and Executive," *Personnel Review,* 3, no. 1 (Winter 1974).

————, "Towards a Political Theory of Organizational Intervention," *Human Relations,* 28, no. 1 (January 1975).

Sayles, op. cit.

Smith, C. G., "A Comparative Analysis of Some Conditions and Consequences of Intra-Organizational Conflict," *Administrative Science Quarterly,* 10 (March 1966): 504–529.

Stieglitz, Harold, "Staff-Staff Relationships," *Management Record,* February 1962, 2–13.

Whyte, op. cit.

CHAPTER 9

EFFECTIVE COMMUNICATION

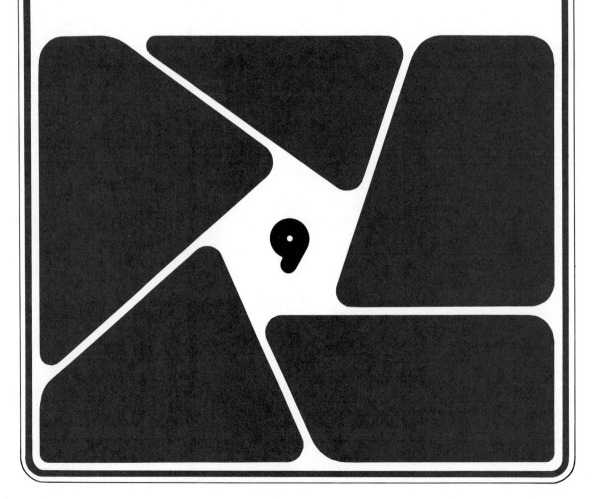

Learning Objectives

1. To understand the various kinds of communication used in enterprises and their role in managerial effectiveness.
2. To learn the relative effectiveness of nonverbal, verbal, and written media.
3. To improve your communication skills.
4. To understand the uses of communication channels.

Chapter Outline

Introduction to the Communication Process
The Importance of Communication
Communication Media
Nonverbal Communication
Verbal (Oral) Communication
Written Communication
Communication Media: Managerial Implications
Communication Channels
Informal Communications: The Grapevine
Formal Communications: The Chain of Command
Research on Communication Channels
Communication: Quantity and Quality
Outward Communication
Summary

INTRODUCTION TO THE COMMUNI- CATION PROCESS

As I said in Chapter 2, most managers spend most of their time communicating. The exceptions are the "writers," whose communications are usually in written form.

Studies of managers at all levels consistently find that most of a manager's time is spent in communication and that most of this is verbal communication. The differences usually involve whom they communicate with and what they communicate about.

Managers are involved in two kinds of communication: interpersonal and organizational.

INTERPERSONAL COMMUNICATION

Interpersonal communication is the process of exchanging information and transmitting meaning between two people or in a small group of people.

ORGANIZATIONAL COMMUNICATION

Organizational communication is the process by which managers develop a system to give information and transmit meaning to large numbers of people within the organization and to relevant individuals and institutions outside it.

Modern communication theorists have added considerably to our understanding of communication. But many of their theories rely on the observations of Aristotle, who lived centuries before Christ. Aristotle thought interpersonal communication consisted of three key elements: the speaker, the speech, and the listeners.

A communication model is given in Figure 9.1 which reflects the modern communication theory. It adds several elements to Aristotle's classic model. First the sender has the idea (thinking) for the message: its purpose. Then he or she encodes the message into the form in which it will be transmitted—words, bodily movements like gestures, or other symbols such as pictures, diagrams, or writing. Then the message is transmitted verbally by a medium (in person, on the phone) or in writing, and then a channel is chosen (formal, informal). Thus the sender has completed the initial phase of communication.

The receiver must first perceive the message: see or hear it with the senses. Then he or she decodes it, and this involves "translating" the message into terms that have meaning for the receiver. Thus comes understanding.

Of course, there is another important element to consider: feedback. In the process of person-to-person communication, cues are sent between the sender and receiver that affect the process of communication at the time of the communication.

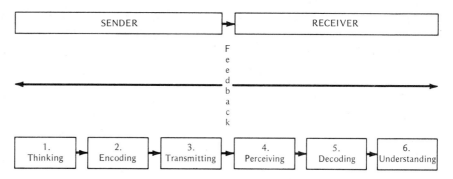

Figure 9.1
A communication
model.

Each of the elements of the model will be discussed in more depth in the rest of this chapter.

THE IMPORTANCE OF COMMUNI- CATION

Communication is important to managers for the following reasons:

1 *Managers spend most of their time communicating.* Many experts contend that 75–95 percent of the manager's time is spent in communicating, as we saw in Chapters 2 and 3. Since as an entrepreneur or manager you will spend most of your time communicating, it follows that improving this skill is crucial.

2 *Communication is needed for managerial effectiveness.* To achieve effectiveness in other managerial functions, one has to be an effective communicator. Look through the table of contents: Almost every subject covered involves communication. According to Mel Grosz, "planning and control, two principal responsibilities of management, are essentially information-processing activities." And it takes communication to make these processes work.

3 *Communication leads to power.* Power is often attained through effective communication. Communication skills are also essential for exercising power or leadership.

· Consider the impact of Franklin Roosevelt's communications on the downhearted, depressed Americans of the 1930s: "The only thing we have to fear is fear itself."
· Remember how Churchill persuaded the almost-beaten British in 1940 to contribute more "blood, sweat and tears" to the war effort.
· Consider how Hitler mobilized a cultured, advanced nation like Germany. You do not have to know German to understand the powerful words and gestures he used to convey the message: "Germany over all."

Executives in business and other enterprises do not usually have the impact that these political leaders did. But J. C. Penney's rejuvenation of his firm after the Depression and AMC's Chapin facing ruin in 1970 and then turning the company around took communication ability of the first order.

4 *Good communication leads to organizational effectiveness.* There is reasonable evidence that if an organization is effective in its communications it will be effective overall. However, as was pointed out in Chapter 2, it is difficult if not impossible to prove that one function, such as communication, is the key to organizational effectiveness.

COMMUNI- CATION MEDIA

There are a number of possible approaches to examining the media for communicating. We will use the following outline:

1 Nonverbal-personal
2 Verbal (Oral)
   a Face to face (dyad or group)
   b Telephone
3 Written-personal
4 Written-group
   a Within the organization
   b Outside the organization

There are other media (for example, verbal communication outside the organization), but these are the major ones that managers use.

Nonverbal Communication

Recently I was a participant in an encounter group. The group leader wished to make the point that we communicate in other ways besides words. We were given several projects to complete without talking to each other. Try it sometime. It is very difficult.

In most situations you can use words to communicate. But Randall Harrison, an expert on nonverbal communication, estimates that no more than 35 percent of the social meaning of a message is conveyed by words used in face-to-face communication. The rest is conveyed nonverbally or is lost. In discussing nonverbal communication I will first briefly mention the forms of nonverbal communication that are used infrequently at work and then describe the more frequently used forms.

Nonverbal Signals

We need not use words to communicate ideas. The sign of the cross sends a message. So does an auto horn or a siren. In baseball, signals are used to send specific messages.

Status symbols are the most frequent application of nonverbal communication at work. They include offices with windows, large desks, and badges of authority. In some workplaces wearing a suit separates a manager from the white-shirt-and-tie clerk and the blue-overalls worker.

Touch and Body Movements

Which is the more powerful way of communicating in a love relationship: saying "I love you" or kissing the lover? Just as touching and body movements are important ways to communicate in one's personal life, so they play a part in communicating at work.

One typical way of communicating is the greeting or farewell handshake. Among southern Europeans and Latin Americans, a hug or "abrazzo" is substituted. The strength of the handshake/abrazzo can communicate very effectively.

The whole body and its movements can communicate. The body can be slumped (dejection), lax (indifference), or tensed (apprehension). A person can walk with stooped shoulders or erect. Tapping of the foot or fingers can indicate boredom. How one applauds indicates degree of enthusiasm; how one nods can indicate extent of agreement. These and other body movements can be important to communication.

Space/Distance Factors

The physical distance a communicator puts between himself or herself and the receiver may influence the communication process. As John Keltner puts it,

> The space factor is particularly noticeable in small-group meetings. I recently worked with a seminar, the first few meetings of which were in a regular conference room, which was so arranged that members of the group sat at long tables arranged in a hollow square. There was open space in the middle, and a number of unused chairs allowed the group to break down into subgroups separated by empty chairs. While the group was meeting under these conditions, there was a very low level of close personal interaction in the sessions. At the suggestion of one of the members, we moved across the street to a dingy little cellar, less than one third the size of the conference room, in which old end-up cable drums had been arranged closely together in a tight circle. There were just enough and all members could gather around the drums only if they sat very close together. Almost immediately after moving to this setting, the tone of the meetings changed from impersonal to a highly personal interactive atmosphere.

Time and Communication

According to Edward Hall, "time talks." How fast we speak and the gestures we use may indicate the intensity of our message. Whether we are on time to a meeting may indicate how important we consider the subject to be discussed. Also, pausing during verbal communication allows nonverbal behavior to reinforce the words spoken.

Facial Expressions

Have you even seen how Marcel Marceau communicates with his face? Among the messages we communicate in this way are the following:

1 discontent (frowning)
2 disbelief (raising the eyebrows)
3 winking
4 antagonism (tightening the jaw muscles or squinting)

Eyes tell a story too. Many managers learn more by "reading" their boss' eyes than by listening to what he or she says.

Nonverbal Voice Communication

How the voice is used sometimes says as much or more than the words used. The following aspects of the voice help get the message across (see Figure 9.2):

Pitch (relative highness or lowness of tone): Variety of pitch leads to interest on the part of the receiver. A high pitch can mean antagonism; a low pitch, complacency.
Quality: The calmer the quality, the greater the clarity of the message.
Volume: The louder the volume, the greater the emphasis.
Rate and rhythm: A very fast rate bores the audience. Faster rates, shorter comments, and more frequent pauses often indicate anger or fear. Too many pauses can mean indecision, tension, or resistance.

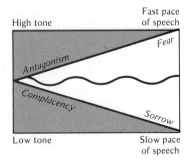

Figure 9.2
Voice inflection and communication.

Managerial Implications

By now it should be clear that nonverbal behavior is a very important part of oral communication. It should be used to reinforce the words spoken. Most nonwritten communication is a mixture of verbal and nonverbal "signals." Some varieties of mixed communication are illustrated in Figure 9.3. In effect, nonverbal communication reinforces the verbal message. So managers need to communicate through both verbal and nonverbal media. For example, suppose a supervisor asks a new employee if he understands the job. The employee nods and says yes. But an examination of his facial expression and body tension may indicate that the right answer is "no."

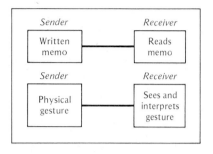

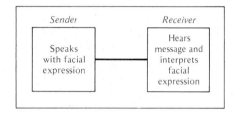

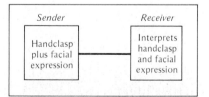

Figure 9.3
Examples of mixed verbal/nonverbal communication (Porter).

Verbal (Oral) Communication

We come now to the most frequent form of communication used by managers: oral or verbal communication. As stated earlier in the chapter, this is what most managers do with most of their time. In Fritz Roethlisberger's words, "the executive's environment is verbal."

Although verbal communication between individuals appears to be a simple process, Raymond Ross' model of the process indicates how complicated it can be (see Figure 9.4). As Ross points out, interpersonal verbal communication is a process of *mutual* influence, "a transactional process involving cognitive sortings, selecting, and sharing of symbols in such a way as to help another elicit from his own experience a meaning or response similar to that intended by the source."

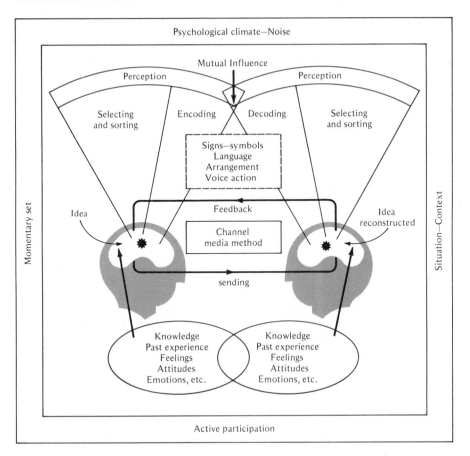

Figure 9.4
Ross' transactional communications model.

Figure 9.5 illustrates some ideas that we have already encountered. In Chapter 4 we discussed how individuals differ in their attitudes, perceptions, and emotions; in Chapter 5, differences in motivation and participation; in Chapter 7, leadership and organization climate. Earlier in this chapter factors like voice quality were discussed. Differences in communicators' backgrounds (experience, education, upbringing) can cause difficulties in communicating accurately. I do not intend to review all this information. Instead, I will concentrate on a topic that is included in the Ross model but that we have not discussed before: how language (signal symbols) influences communication. Later in the chapter I will describe channel media methods.

Oral communication can be of two types: face to face and by telephone. Face-to-face communication can involve more nonverbal communication methods than telephone communication. This is why many people find the telephone a less desirable method of verbal communication. You have to be especially careful in your choice of words and tone of voice to get your meaning across.

One other point should be made before we discuss the impact of language. Sometimes the primary purpose of communication is to persuade the other person to do something. There is evidence that some people are easier to persuade than others. In general, studies show that women are easier to persuade than men, people with low self-esteem are easier to persuade than those with a very positive self-image, and less aggressive people are easier to persuade than aggressive people. You are even more likely to be persuasive if

BECAUSE THEY HAVE A LOW SELF-IMAGE (ei. 'JUST A HOUSE WIFE')

1 you appear to know what you are talking about
2 you appear to believe what you are saying
3 your message is attuned to your listeners' needs
4 your ideas are arranged logically
5 your presentation is interesting

Language as a Tool of Verbal Communication

A reasonable conclusion from the models presented earlier in this chapter would be that for verbal communication to be effective a number of conditions must be met (see Figure 9.5). For the sender to achieve the goal of conveying the message correctly, (A) he or she must encode it in words (and nonverbal cues) that will convey the message effectively to the sender; (B) the message content must be well organized, well thought through; (C) there should not be too many "noise" factors in the environment obscuring the message; and (D) the receiver must be able to decode the message and willing to listen to and accept it.

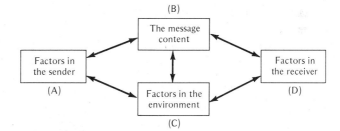

Figure 9.5
Conditions for effective verbal communication.

Encoding the Message Effectively

"Encoding" means, simply enough, using the "right" words to reach the receiver. There is an old anecdote about the boys at a British school sitting in the chapel pews listening to an Anglican missionary talk about his missionary work in Africa. After a few sentences in English the missionary shifted into Swahili for the rest of the talk. This missionary could have been effectively communicating to his parishioners in Africa but had ceased to communicate in England.

> **Proposition 9.1.**
> The effective communicator encodes the messages in words that are meaningful to the receiver.

Words have many meanings. One expert has pointed out that the 500 most often used words in the English language have *an average* of 28 different meanings. English is not different in this respect from the 3000 other languages used on the earth.

The meanings of words are determined by dictionary meanings, the way they are used in the sentence, the context in which they are used, and the setting in which they are used. Figure 9.6, the "triangle of meaning," shows how the meanings of words develop over time.

We learn the meanings of words the way we learn other things. In Chapters 4 and 5 we reviewed how influences such as parents, friends, school, and jobs give meaning to attitudes. This is how we learn words as well.

The meanings of words change, too. The slang from my college days is meaningless today; "getting my act together," "that's where it's at," and other current expressions will someday be equally meaningless.

An American who travels in England finds that hundreds of our words have no meaning there. To communicate, the traveler has to learn the equivalent British words. Here are some examples:

North American Word	British Word
hood (of car)	*bonnet*
trunk (of car)	*boot*
windshield	*windscreen*
vacation	*holiday*
clothes pin	*peg*
blue book (for exam)	*script*
truck	*lorry*
elevator	*lift*

Just as the American in England must ask to get on the *lift* and watch out for the *lorry,* so the manager must communicate with words understandable to the board of directors, the vice president, the janitor, or the Xerox operator. Each may speak a different language. The following points should be kept in mind by anyone who wants to communicate effectively:

1 Words mean different things to different people.

2 Words vary in degree of abstraction.

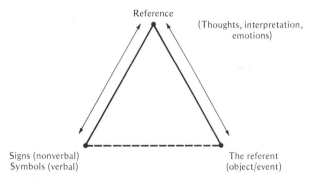

Figure 9.6
Triangle of
meaning (Ogden
and Richards).

3 Language, by its very nature, is incomplete. It should be supplemented with nonverbal cues, and the idea expressed in several ways.

4 Language reflects not only the personality of the individual but also the culture of his or her society.

5 Language creates a social reality.

Guidelines for effective encoding include the following:

1 Communicate with the right degree of intensity for the message.

2 Avoid rambling. Have the message thoroughly encoded beforehand.

3 Do not deliver the message too quickly.

4 Use some redundancy of wording for important concepts to make sure the receiver gets the message.

5 Watch for feedback cues showing lack of understanding and repeat the message when such cues are received.

6 Use simple and direct wording.

7 Phrase the message in such a way as to tap the receiver's needs (see Chapter 5).

Environmental Factors in Communication

Now we know some of the factors the *sender* must keep in mind as he or she encodes the message. The second imperative in effective communication is expressed in Proposition 9.2.

Proposition 9.2.
Effective communicators consider factors in the environment to make sure their message is received.

Sometimes environmental barriers to effective communication are called *noise*. Noise factors include the following:

1 *Interruptions* by other people or stimuli during the communication. Sometimes one can avoid some of this—for example, by stopping phone calls during an interview.

2 Problems with the *communication channel:* The path the message follows may be wrong.

3 *Time pressures:* Sometimes there is not enough time to communicate as thoroughly as one would like.

4 *Status and power differences:* Sometimes the receiver is so aware of these differences that he or she focuses on them instead of on the message.

This last point needs amplification. The differences between the president of General Motors and the janitor, Chicanos and Anglos, satisfied WASPs and alienated blacks, union leaders and management, the middle-aged executive and the teenager may be so great as to make communication difficult if not impossible. In general, if the sender is higher in status or power, he or she would do well to communicate in a setting designed to reduce these differences—say, talk to the janitor in the hall instead of in the office. Conscious attempts to be friendly and speak in the janitor's "language" also might help reduce the status barrier.

Receiver Barriers and How to Overcome Them

There are four factors controllable by the receiver of the message that can hinder or help communications. The sender must be aware of these and try to offset them.

1 *Decoding-translating problems* (discussed earlier).   The receiver may misunderstand or mistranslate the message. If the sender is alert and encourages feedback, he or she can send the message again (redundancy), using different verbal and nonverbal media.

2 *Evaluative/contrary attitudes.*   Some receivers evaluate certain concepts negatively or may be contrary toward certain topics. You cannot discuss unions easily with some people or religion with others. Again, the sender tries to offset this problem by recognizing it, being sensitive to it, and utilizing his or her knowledge of motivation in trying to influence the communication process.

3 *Lack of interest.*   The receiver may not get involved or may listen only partially (selective perception) to the sender's message. This is a difficult problem. Sometimes you can pick it up in the feedback. When you are communicating to groups of people, some of the receivers will be getting the message, others not.

The best you can do about this is to try to make your communication interesting by building in messages that contribute toward satisfying the receiver's needs. Try to show why the receiver should be listening—how he or she can benefit from the message.

4 *Distrust of the sender.* One of the most difficult barriers to overcome is distrust of the sender. Before you can communicate, you must be perceived as knowing what you are talking about, considered honest, and viewed with good will (again according to Aristotle).

Trust (a combination of honesty and good will) develops out of rapport. The sender starts by establishing some common basis for beginning the discussion. Then the sender's qualifications can be introduced. Then, slowly, a trustful reciprocal relationship can be built up. Without it, communication is difficult.

So far we have discussed how a sender can communicate more effectigelz by using language well and understanding how the sender, environment, and receiver must work together. But the emphasis has been on the *sender's* side of communication. A manager often plays the role of sender. But the manager can be a receiver too. He or she may ask for help or counsel, receive instructions from superiors or complaints from clients. Accordingly, we will now focus briefly on effective listening.

Effective Receivers Are Good Listeners

For communication to be effective when you are the receiver, you must listen with understanding. Researchers have found that listening is only about 25 percent effective. And it is a complicated process. Some of the difficulties preventing good listening include the following:

1 Faking attention while considering the topic uninteresting [lack of interest]

2 Allowing diversion because of emotional words or topics [evaluative/contrary attitudes]

3 Inefficient note taking—getting bogged down in details

4 Allowing environmental noise to continue [interruptions]

5 Bad listening techniques—listening only for facts and letting the mind wander. Since we can think faster than others can speak, the mind will wander if we let it.

The following are guidelines for effective listening:

1 *Stop talking.*

2 Establish rapport with the sender: Put the speaker at ease.

3 Indicate willingness to listen. Look interested. Do not engage in other activities. Show empathy.

4 Cut distractions. Hold telephone calls and choose a quiet place to communicate.

5 Allow time for discussion. Listen patiently to the full message.

6 Keep your emotions in check. Do not get angry or lose your temper. Recognize your emotional involvement in some topics and try not to argue or criticize.

7 When you are not sure of part of the message, restate what you think you heard in the form of a question. When you feel that something is missing (after noting what you did not hear), ask simple, brief, direct questions to get the information needed.

A Note on Telephone Communications

Many executives spend a great deal of their communication time on the telephone. Communicating on the phone entails the elimination of all supplementary nonverbal communication methods except for speed of communication and tone of voice. So it is a more difficult communication medium, although most executives preferred it to written communication.

Many managers make very inefficient use of the telephone. And much of the hectic pace of the manager's day described in Chapters 2 and 3 is due to lack of telephone management. Here are some suggestions for more efficient telephone use:

1 Call other executives after 10:30 A.M.

2 Use the phone efficiently.

  a Answer it promptly.

  b Identify yourself at the beginning of the conversation.

  c Speak distinctly, keeping the receiver close to your mouth.

3 Use a secretary to save time. Block your phone calls and make them all together. Have the secretary place the next call while you are completing the first one.

4 Control interruptions by having a secretary take messages. If you have no secretary, use a recorder on the phone to say you are out or in conference and get the return message.

These are commonsense ways to save time and interruptions in telephone use. The key point about telephone communication, however, is that your use of words, communication speed, tone, and so forth must compensate for the lack of nonverbal means of communication. The phone is quick, but it is a tricky medium.

Written Communications

The alternative to verbal communications is written communications. Managers prefer to communicate verbally because verbal communication gets there quicker. But the main reason they prefer verbal communication is that they can supplement the words with nonverbal clues more easily than in the case of written communication.

Still, many forms of written communications are used in business. Examples include reports, memoranda, letters, and enterprise newsletters and news magazines. The following are some suggestions for good written communications:

1 The written message must be drafted with the receiver and his or her needs clearly in mind.

2 The facts of the message must be thought through *ahead of time.*

3 The message should be as brief as possible. Eliminate all unnecessary words and ideas. Important messages should be prepared in draft first, then corrected.

4 If the message is long, place a summary of the report on the first page. This summary should make the main points clear, with page references for details on each item.

5 The message should be carefully organized. State your most important point first, then the next most important point, and so on. This way if the receiver reads only the first few points, the main message will get across.

6 Make the subject clear by giving the message a title.

7 Use simple words. Make the message more readable by using short, clear sentences.

The Company Publication

Many organizations try to communicate with their employees by publishing newsletters, newspapers, magazines, and the like. Generally these publications present a mixture of personal news (new employees, retirements, bowling league news, etc.) and enterprise news (new officers, changes in the pension plan, and the like). Often they are expensive and time-consuming to prepare, their readership low and their impact lower. Employees prefer oral communication. It is cheaper, quicker, and more rewarding to most employees.

Effective Reading

From the sender's point of view, effective listening is required if oral communication is to be effective. Similarly, written communications require effective reading to get their messages across. Three kinds of reading can be of value to the manager for various purposes:

Inspectional reading (also called skimming or prereading). The focus is on completing the reading in a limited amount of time, and the goal is to examine a book (report, etc.) in a superficial way in order to find out what it is about.

Analytical reading. This is a thorough, complete reading. The purpose of analytical reading is an in-depth understanding of the content of the communication.

Syntopical reading (comparative reading). In this method the reader examines several books simultaneously and relates them to each other. The purpose is a systematic comparison of the works read.

Most reading improvement programs focus primarily on reading speed. In fact, the effective reader reads at several speeds: quickly for less important items, slower for more difficult or significant material.

Most ineffective readers *subvocalize;* that is, they move their lips with the words. Poor readers also *fixate*—that is, go over and over certain words or passages—sometimes as often as five or six times. Thus the way to improve their reading speed is to get the eye to move as fast as the brain can. Mortimer Adler and Charles Van Doren suggest the following method for increasing your reading speed: "Place your thumb and first two fingers together. Sweep this 'pointer' across a line of type, a little faster than it is comfortable for your eyes to move. Force yourself to keep up with your hand. You will very soon be able to read the words as you follow your hand." This can triple your reading speed.

But there is more to effective reading than increasing your word-processing speed. Since executives encounter almost no reading of the third type (syntopical reading), I will concentrate on the first and second types (inspectional and analytical reading).

Inspectional (Skim) Reading All written material received by a manager should be given an inspectional reading. In this way the manager can determine whether it should be given an analytical reading as well. Adler and Van Doren give the following suggestions for effective skimming:

1 Look at the title page and preface of the book or report. Read each quickly. Note subtitles. This gives the scope and angle of the work.

2 Study the table of contents to get an idea of the structure of the work. This is like looking at a road map before taking a trip.

3 Check the index and estimate the range of topics covered and the authors or (reports) referred to.

4 Look at the sections or chapters whose titles sounded most useful. Read their summary statements (usually on the opening and closing pages) carefully.

5 Turn the pages of these chapters or sections, dipping in here and there. Read a paragraph or two, but never more than several pages in sequence. This will give the flavor of the relevant material.

This quick skimming should give you an idea of whether the book or report is worth reading in more detail. If a more thorough reading seems warranted, read the book or report through quickly without stopping to look up words, ponder the material, or understand it. Adler and Van Doren call this superficial reading.

To make most effective use of the report or book, use the following techniques:

1 Answer the following basic questions:
   a What is it about?
   b What was said (in detail) and how?
   c Is it true (in whole or in part)?
   d What is its significance?
2 Read with a pencil (pen)
   a Make sure you understand major points (circle key words and phrases).
   b Mark the margin beside very important points or sections that are too long to underline.
3 For the ten or so most important items in the book (report), place a star in the margin.
4 Keep track of a sequence of items by numbering them in the margin.
5 Write comments on key points in the margins.

Analytical Reading A few reports or books are important enough to be read analytically, understood, and pondered. In addition to the suggestions just given, the following steps will improve your analytical understanding of written material:

I Finding Out What a Book Is About
   1 Classify the book (report) according to kind and subject matter.
   2 State what the whole book (report) is about with the utmost brevity.
   3 Enumerate its major parts in order; outline these parts as you have outlined the whole.
   4 Define the problem or problems the author has tried to solve.
II Interpreting the Book's Contents
   5 Come to terms with the author by interpreting key words.
   6 Grasp the author's leading propositions by dealing with the most important sentences.
   7 Know the author's arguments by finding them in, or constructing them out of, sequences of sentences.

8 Determine the problems the author has solved and those he or she has not; of the latter, decide which ones the author knew he or she had failed to solve.

III Criticizing a Book (Report) as a Communication of Knowledge

   A General maxims of intellectual etiquette

   9 Do not begin criticism until you have completed your outline and interpretation of the book (report). (Do not say you agree, disagree, or suspend judgment until you can say "I understand.")

   10 Do not disagree in a cranky way.

   11 Demonstrate that you recognize the difference between knowledge and personal opinion by presenting good reasons for any critical judgment you make.

   B Special criteria for points of criticism

   12 Show where the author is uninformed.

   13 Show where the author is misinformed.

   14 Show where the author is illogical.

   15 Show where the author's analysis or account is incomplete.

Note: Of these last four, the first three are criteria for disagreement. Failing in all of these, you must agree, at least in part, although you may suspend judgment in the light of the last point.

COMMUNI-CATION MEDIA: MANAGERIAL IMPLICATIONS

So far this section has focused on the media managers use and how they can improve their use of those media. The question is, Although managers prefer to communicate verbally, are there specific types of communication that *should* be used? The following are the findings of a survey of 72 supervisors by Dale Level:

I Oral communication by itself

   A Oral communication is *most* effective

   1 to reprimand an employee for work deficiency

   2 to settle a dispute among employees about a work problem

   B Oral communication (by itself) is *least* effective

   1 to communicate information requiring future employee action

   2 to communicate information of a general nature

   3 to communicate a company directive or order

   4 to communicate information about an important company policy change

   5 to communicate with your immediate supervisor about work problems

   6 to promote a safety campaign

II Written communication by itself

    A Written communication by itself is *most* effective

        1 to communicate information requiring future employee action

        2 to communicate information of a general nature

    B Written communication (by itself) is *least* effective

        1 to communicate information requiring immediate employee action

        2 to commend an employee for noteworthy work

        3 to reprimand an employee for work deficiency

        4 to settle a dispute among employees about a work problem

III Oral communication, then written communication

    A Oral, then written communication is *most effective*

        1 to communicate information requiring immediate employee action

        2 communicate a company directive or order

        3 to communicate information on an important company policy change

        4 to communicate with your immediate supervisor about work problems

        5 to promote a safety campaign.

        6 to commend an employee for noteworthy work.

    B The supervisors did not feel that any of the ten messages would be ineffective if they used oral, then written communication.

IV Written, then oral. The supervisors did not view this as a frequently used method of communicating.

In summary, Level's study indicates that supervisors see oral, written, and oral-plus-written communication as useful for various purposes.

COMMUNI-CATION CHANNELS Now that we have covered the sender and the receiver in the communication model, we turn to an examination of the path of transmission: the channels of communication.

> **COMMUNICATION CHANNEL**
> A communication channel is the route through which a message passes, that is, the chain of personnel who pass the message on.

There are two kinds of communication channels: formal and informal. Organizations establish formal communication channels when they set up structural relationships. In other words, when they create boss-employee relationships and departments (i.e., an organization chart). They in effect tell the employees that they should communicate according to this structure. In large organizations these channels are carefully defined. Lists of people who should receive information and the order in which they are to receive it are established. (Sometimes these are called *routing lists.*) A great deal of information passes through these formal channels of communication.

In addition to the formal channel and established order of communication, there are informal channels, usually called *the grapevine.* The grapevine exists at the same time as the formal channels. Note that the formal channel moves directly down (and up) the chain of command. The informal channel moves in several directions.

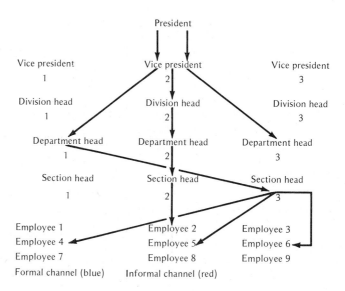

Figure 9.7
Formal and
informal channels
of communication.

Table 9.1 excerpts from Table 7.7 to show how communication channel usage differs with liberal, middle-of-the-road, and conservative managerial style.

All organizations need communication to survive, but it is probably true that some organizations are more dependent than others on upward communication and employee advice. A few propositions may specify these conditions more clearly.

Table 9.1		
Liberal	**Middle of the Road**	**Conservative**
Informal, multichannel communications "system"	General description of communications	Well-defined chain of command
Much communication encouraged in all directions (up, down, and lateral).	Amount and direction of communication	Little communication encouraged; mostly downward
Adequate; mostly accurate	Quality of communication	Needs supplementary system; somewhat inaccurate

Proposition 9.3.
The larger the organization, the greater the need for upward communication and employee advice and counsel.

Proposition 9.4.
The greater the complexity of the organization's services and/or products, the greater the need for upward communication and employee advice and counsel.

Proposition 9.5.
The greater the volatility in the technological and environmental conditions affecting the organization, the greater the need for upward communication and employee advice and counsel.

Proposition 9.6.
The greater the geographic dispersion of the organization's units, the greater the need for upward communication and employee advice and counsel.

From these propositions it can be seen that although all managers need information, advice, and counsel from all members of the organization, this is more crucial to the success of a large conglomerate in the electronics and computer industry than to a small manufacturer of washboards.

Thus all managers need to know how to communicate. All organizations need to have communication systems. But communication is not all there is to management, and some managers need communications less than others.

Informal Communications: The Grapevine

Every organization has grapevines because they serve several purposes and fulfill a number of needs. Consider the following points:

1 *Grapevines are fast.*　Grapevines exist because they get information to people much faster than formal channels. Most people prefer to know important information sooner rather than later.

2 *Grapevines are accurate.*　Studies indicate that the grapevine is 80–95 percent accurate. The "inaccuracy" normally takes the form of incompleteness rather than wrong information.

3 *Grapevines are efficient.*　Grapevines selectively handle a lot of information. Formal channels have a way of sending information to people who do not need it. The unwanted information may sit on one desk for a long time before it is passed on. Almost never is the formal system faster or more efficient than the grapevine.

4 *Grapevines fulfill people's needs.*　Grapevines are based not on hierarchy but on need or desire to communicate: they are made up of people who like each other and *want* to communicate. Thus they serve social needs, and through speed and accuracy they help fulfill security needs as well. In a way they satisfy recognition needs too. The "communication center" gets recognition when people call him or her to find out "what's going on."

How Grapevines Work

Generally the grapevine is a verbal channel. But Keith Davis has shown it can become "written" when a grievance covers more than one location (see Figure 9.8).

In other research Davis has studied how the channels of the grapevine work. Figure 9.9 illustrates four such patterns: the single chain, the probability chain, the gossip chain, and the cluster chain. By far the most frequent is the cluster chain. In the cluster chain pattern A tells several others (B, R, F) the message. Only some of these employees pass the information on (F, C), and some of these, in turn, will tell others. As more people learn the information, the grapevine quiets down. Davis calls this pattern a cluster because each link leads to another cluster of people (not just one). Research to be discussed shortly supports Davis' finding that only a few employees are in a "liaison" role—those who start the clusters. Most people learn the information but do not spread it. In Davis' study, 68 percent of an executive group heard the information but only 20 percent spread it; in another study, 81 percent of the execu-

Figure 9.8 Actual transcript of a teletypewriter grapevine over a company private wire between two warehouse clerks in separate cities.

IS JOE* THERE GA[1]

YES

PUT HIM ON TELEX PLS[2] GA

THIS JOE

THIS SUE AND I AM A LITTLE CURIOUS ABOUT UR[3] TELEX
YESTERDAY   COAST CLEAR NOW   SO WHAT DO THEY ASK YOU GA

THE FIRST STUPID QUESTION WAS THEY WANTED TO KNOW WHAT
HAPPENED TO CERTAIN ITEMS THAT WERE ON THE INVENTORY ONE
MONTH AND NOT ON THE NEXT MONTH   I TOLD THEM IT WAS ONLY
LOGICAL TO ASSUME THEY WERE SOLD   SO THEY ASKED TO
WHOM   TOLD THEM TO LOOK IT UP ON THEIR COPIES OF THE DR'S[4]
GA

UR ANSWER WAS PRETTY GOOD   UR RIGHT   THINGS LIKE THAT
COME UP ALL THE TIME BUT UNFORTUNATELY I HAVE TO FIGURE OUT
MOSTLY FROM HERE   WHAT ELSE JOE GA

THEY SAID MY INVENTORY WAS SHORT 25 TONS AND WANTED TO
KNOW WHY   I ASKED THEM FOR THE FIGURES THEY USED AND I
CHECKED IT OUT ONLY TO FIND THEY CANT EVEN COPY THE RIGHT
FIGURES DOWN GA

WELL SOMETIMES I GUESS THEY MAKE BOBOS[5] LIKE THAT BUT UR
LUCKY ONLY BEING OFF 25 TONS   WE WERE OFF 400 TONS AND IT
TOOK ME AWHILE TO FIND IT   WHAT ELSE

THIS IS PROBABLY THE FUNNIEST   I PAY THE LOCAL PAPER HERE EVERY
MONTH FOR ADVERTISING AND WHEN OUR STATEMENTS COME HERE
FROM CHICAGO THEY NEVER HAVE ANYTHING CHARGED TO
ADVERTISING WHICH AMOUNTS TO A FEW THOUSAND A YEAR   I
ASKED ABOUT IT AND THEY WERE SURPRISED   I GUESS THEY DONT
LOOK AT THE COPIES OF THE CHECKS THAT I MAKE OUT GA

WELL THEY SURE LOOK AT OURS BECAUSE THEY CONSTANTLY ASK US
WHY AND TO WHOM AND WHAT FOR WE PAID THIS AND THAT   THE
ONLY ONE WHO KNOWS ABOUT CHECK COPIES IS MAX SMITH AND
I THINK HE KEEPS GOOD TRACK OF IT BUT U[6] ARE RIGHT THAT IS
FUNNY   OH GOOD GA

ANYWAY I REMEMBER GEORGE TELLING ME ABOUT UR PROBLEM AND
I JUST WANTED TO LET U KNOW U WERE NOT THE ONLY ONES THAT
KEEP IN DAILY COMMUNICATION WITH CHICAGO GA

I THINK IT WAS VERY NICE OF U AND AS FAR AS I CAN SEE I HAVE IT
WORSE THAN U SO MY COMPLIMENTS TO YOU AND THANKS AGAIN
FOR UR CONCERN GA

THATS ABOUT ALL FROM HERE GA

OK JOE BIBI[7]

Key: *All names are disguised.
        [1]Go ahead.
        [2]Please.
        [3]"Your" or "you are," depending on the sentence.
        [4]Delivery receipts.
        [5]Errors; "boo-boos."
        [6]You.
        [7]Bye bye.

tives knew the information but only 11 percent communicated it to others.

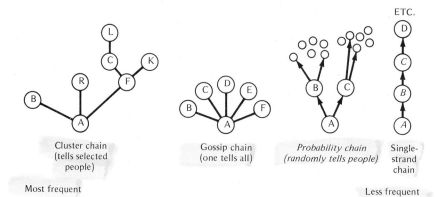

Figure 9.9
Davis' grapevine patterns.

Cluster chain (tells selected people)

Gossip chain (one tells all)

Probability chain (randomly tells people)

Single-strand chain

Most frequent

Less frequent

Employees become active on the grapevine when they have news that is fresh and is likely to be "hot." Jay Knippen studied the grapevine in a large grocery store employing 170 employees (because of turnover he actually studied 216 employees over time). Here are his findings:

1 *Amount of information known:* Managers knew about 79 percent of grapevine information. Employees knew only 42 percent.

2 *Source:* Managers got a bit more than half the information from outside the store. Employees got 78 percent from inside, 22 percent from outside.

3 *Location:* Employees heard the grapevine in their departments and spread it primarily within the department. Managers heard the information from outside and inside, but spread it primarily in their own departments.

4 *Active grapevines:* Although managers accounted for only a few of the 170 employees, they initiated almost 50 percent of the grapevine information. On average, they told almost eight other people. The typical employee told four other people.

Many management books report cases of managers who try to suppress the grapevine. But Knippen found managers active in its use.

Managers and the Grapevine

Since grapevines are ubiquitous, speedy, and accurate, managers should think of them as a good communication channel. It is ineffective to try to eliminate them. Instead, the manager should learn who the "liaison" people in the informal network are. Then he or she should give those people the information to be communicated. This is especially necessary when the grapevine has been spreading incomplete or inaccurate information.

Sometimes a manager may go too far to find out what the grapevine is saying. I know an executive who was being interviewed for a top job. The top executive interviewing him was called to a side door several times during the morning. The interviewer whispered a few minutes, then gave the person at the door some $20 bills. When the applicant asked what was going on, the interviewer said, "Look: I have to know what's going on out in the plant. So I have my communication network for finding out." Few executives need a network of paid spies to find out what is going on in their workplace. The grapevine helps them find out.

As Table 9.1 indicates, the manager who uses a conservative leadership style will discourage the development and use of grapevines and use the formal communication channels. The liberal manager will use the grapevine frequently and the formal channels rarely. The middle-of-the-road manager will use both.

Formal Communications: The Chain of Command

Most large organizations establish chains of command through which communication of an official nature is expected to flow. Most written communication follows these formal channels. As Figure 9.8 indicates, the formal channel follows the superior-subordinate hierarchy. Formal channels often need help from the informal channels because of a series of typical problems. First, formal channels often become overloaded, get clogged up, and slow down, especially in times of crisis. Second, as the organization gets larger, these channels have to be used to communicate lengthy rules, regulations, policies, and the like. In many ways, then, the formal channels *supplement* the grapevine or serve the purpose of communicating *official* communication. Third, formal channels are often very bureaucratic. People who do not want to allow certain information to enter the informal network often tell the sender to "Go through channels," assuming that this will slow it down or kill it.

The following story may give you an idea how bureaucratic and bogged down official channels can get. In the days before bug sprays the Army tried to keep down the number of flies in the kitchen tents by hanging strips of flypaper over each table. The flies would fly into the paper, get stuck, and die there.

In 1945, after the war was over and before he could be sent home, a frustrated second lieutenant stationed in the Philippines decided to "get the Army." He designed an official-looking report and routed it to his company commander, the division commander, and several headquarters up to and including the Pentagon. Naturally he did not identify himself as the sender.

The lieutenant's report was entitled "The Fly Report." In neat columns he reported the number of flies on each strip of flypaper ("table

1: 12 flies; table 2: 14 flies; table 3: flypaper just replaced," etc.). He sent the report up through channels. He expected immediate repercussions (which would have made him feel good). The second, third, and fourth weeks went by and he sent in more fly reports. No results.

The lieutenant was sent home, and of course the fly reports stopped going up the chain of command. But two weeks after he had left, the unit received a request for the missing fly reports!

RESEARCH ON COMMUNICATION CHANNELS

The preceding story illustrates some of the problems of formal communication channels, but it is hardly research. Research on communication channels has been approached in several ways. In the laboratory, for example, the researcher can control all aspects of the setting except the dependent variables: speed, accuracy, satisfaction, and effectiveness. A number of studies of this nature were conducted in the 1950s and 1960s. Their major conclusion was that each type of channel has some good points and some bad points. No one type of channel is best. You have to match the kind of communication you need with the right kind of channel. Three possible channel patterns are presented in Figure 9.10.

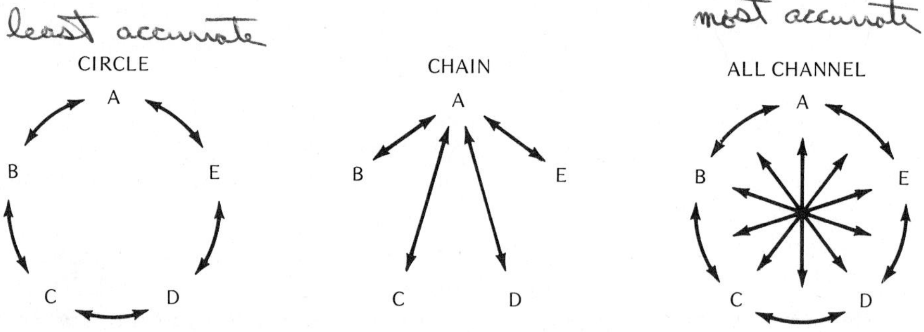

least accurate   *most accurate*

Figure 9.10
Three communication channels.

The circle is slow; its accuracy is poor; a leader either does not emerge or emerges later; the group's satisfaction is low; and structure arises slowly if at all. It is not a preferred pattern of communication.

The chain is preferred by conservative leaders. It is fast and accurate, has a strong leader, and is slowly changing in structure. The leader is satisfied with this approach, but members may not like it. It is not good for unstructured or fast-changing problems.

The all-channel approach is very fast and fairly accurate. No specific leader is present, nor does much structure develop. Liberal theorists prefer this approach and claim that it is more effective for unstructured, fast-changing problems.

In sum, the all-channel pattern is good for unstructured problems needing a lot of creativity when time is not of the essence. For routine day-to-day communication the chain is more effective.

Although the research design for these studies was good, as with all lab studies the people studied were not members of work groups who interacted regularly. Unlike the situation in real organizations, the messages and channels were controlled. Whether these studies reflect reality is not known.

A second approach to studying communications is *sociometry,* in which people record their interactions—their frequency, purpose, and so forth. This method shows promise, though it has not been used very often. A good example is Albert Wickesberg's Minneapolis/St. Paul study. Wickesberg asked 35 executives to keep a record of all their communications during a different day each week over a five-week period. The following are some of his findings:

1 *Purpose:* Fifty-three percent of the communication was for informational purposes, 22 percent took the form of instructions, 11 percent involved problem solving, 7 percent was scuttlebutt, and the rest consisted of official approval of requests.

2 *Direction:* About one-third of the communication was vertical, one third lateral (colleagues), and one-third diagonal (a cross between vertical and horizontal). (Note the importance, again, of relationships with peers). Most managerial communication was with people outside the manager's unit.

3 *Formal versus informal:* The formal channels were rarely used on a day-to-day basis. This finding might have been biased by the 35 executives' jobs, however; many were staff executives.

A third approach to studying communication is *message flow analysis.* In this approach the researchers send a message and follow the channels by which it is spread, its speed, and any resulting distortion. This is a very new type of research.

In sum, conservative managers prefer to control the communication channels. They can do so to some degree through the use of reward power and by channeling the information they receive only through formal channels. Liberal managers utilize both formal and informal channels and encourage communication in all directions. Conservatives prefer downward and upward communication.

**COMMUNI-
CATION:
QUANTITY
AND QUALITY**

In Table 9.1 it was suggested that liberals prefer a great deal of communication and that the open communication style leads to adequate amounts of rather accurate communication. It was further suggested that conservatives, by restructuring the communication channels, have problems of accuracy, so that the grapevine has to work overtime to supplement the formal channels.

There is some research to support this contention. For example, studies have found that a superior must trust and be trusted by his or her subordinates before complete and accurate communication will take place. Liberal managers usually meet this requirement. But so do many middle-of-the-road managers. And managers can be conservative in their decision making but encourage and reward truthful and complete communication.

Liberal managers also tend to encourage more lateral communications, and to the extent that this is necessary to get the work done, it leads to greater effectiveness.

Thus for your vertical communication to be effective you must reward employees who tell the truth and the *whole* truth. If you do not, you will hear only what you want to hear. And one day you will find out that you are the only one who does not know the bad news.

OUTWARD COMMUNI- CATION

In this chapter I have focused on communicating *inside* the enterprise. Obviously the enterprise also communicates with other entities outside itself: the general public, competitors, the government, and so forth. Persuasive communications of this type are normally part of the organization's marketing or public relations activity. They are touched on very briefly in Chapter 20.

SUMMARY

At the beginning of the chapter I defined interpersonal communication as the process of exchanging information and transmitting meaning between two people or within a small group of people. Organizational communication is the system managers design to give information to large numbers of employees and key outsiders.

Communication is important because managers spend much of their time communicating, because it can increase managerial influence, and because almost all managerial behavior and decisions must be communicated.

The second objective of the chapter was to understand the relative effectiveness of the three communication media: nonverbal, verbal, and written. The section also contained information designed to help you improve your communication skills. We discussed how the use of voice quality, facial expressions, time, space/distance, body motion, touch, and the like are important aspects of communication. You learned that most managers prefer face-to-face communication over telephone or written communication because they can pick up nonverbal cues.

Oral or verbal communication was described next. The challenges of language encoding, environmental factors such as time pressure, interruptions, and status power affect the verbal communication process.

There are several barriers to effective verbal communication: translation problems, evaluative attitudes, lack of interest, distrust of the sender. Some suggestions for overcoming these barriers were given. The section concluded with a discussion of good listening and effective use of the telephone.

The section on written communication consisted of a brief discussion of effective writing and a longer discussion of methods of reading written communications.

The section on managerial implications compared the usefulness and effectiveness of written and verbal communications. Here I specified when oral communication by itself is effective (in counseling employees regarding work deficiencies and in settling disputes between employees). The written form is most effective in communicating information about future action as well as general information. Sometimes it is best to combine written and oral media. The best way is to use oral, *then* written, communication, particularly for information requiring immediate action, a new company directive, or an important policy change. Other effective ways to use oral and then written communication are to contact your supervisor about work problems, to promote a safety campaign, or to commend an employee.

The final objective of the chapter was to help you understand the nature of informal and formal channels and how to use each well. First the informal grapevine was described. It was shown to be an accurate, useful channel that most liberal and middle-of-the-road managers and entrepreneurs use often. It is usually misunderstood by conservative managers and entrepreneurs.

The formal channel (chain of command) has problems but can carry a great deal of information. I described formal channels as they exist in reality as well as some experimental research indicating the relative speed, accuracy, and satisfaction of several patterns of communication channels. It was shown that liberal, middle-of-the-road, and conservative managers and entrepreneurs tend to use different patterns.

By now you should have learned that communicating is how most managers and entrepreneurs spend a lot of their time. Communication is important, but not equally important to all managers or entrepreneurs. Nor are all messages equally important. So effective managers and entrepreneurs concentrate on effective communication of the most important messages.

In dealing with important messages effective communicators will follow these guidelines:

1 Clarify ideas before communicating. Be careful in choice of words and symbols—choose them with the receiver in mind.

2 In really important communications the sender will test the message before delivering it.

3 At the time of communication the sender will try to establish rapport with the receiver and will try to eliminate environmental barriers such as status differences.

4 The sender will use more than one medium to convey the message. For really important messages face-to-face verbal communication carefully coordinated with nonverbal symbols will be used. In many cases following up with a written summary of the verbal communication is a good idea.

5 Reinforce words with actions. Support the words and other symbols in the message.

The next chapter completes Part 2. It describes what a managerial or entrepreneurial career can be like and discusses how to develop a career plan.

Questions for Review

1. Distinguish between interpersonal and organizational communication. In what ways are they similar? different?
2. Outline a model of the communication process.
3. Is communication the essence of all managerial problems? Why or why not?
4. Describe some of the ways of communicating nonverbally.
5. Which are the most powerful and frequently used nonverbal media at work?
6. Explain Ross' transactional communications model and what it means to managers.
7. Under what conditions are you likely to be persuasive?
8. What are the crucial issues in the use of language in effective verbal communication?
9. How do environmental factors influence communication?
10. How can a manager be a good listener?
11. How can you be an effective telephone communicator?
12. Are company publications useful?
13. How should a manager read important reports? general reports? In what ways will the methods differ?
14. What kinds of messages are most effectively communicated verbally? What messages should be in written form? verbal, then written? written, then verbal?
15. Which channel patterns are most effective and when?
16. Is the grapevine a good way to communicate? When? What kinds of information are best communicated in this way?
17. How do conservative, liberal, and middle-of-the-road managers differ in their communication styles?
18. Under what conditions is the need for upward communication greatest?
19. When should you use formal channels of communication alone? the grapevine alone? both?

References

Introduction to the Communication Process

Aristotle, *Rhetorica,* in *The Works of Aristotle* (New York: Oxford University Press, 1946), vol. XI.

Berlo, David, *The Process of Communication* (New York: Holt, Rinehart and Winston, 1960).

Korzybski, A., *Science and Sanity,* 4th ed. (New York: Institute of General Semantics, 1962).

Shannon, Claude, *Communication Theory* (Urbana: University of Illinois Press, 1949).

Shannon, Claude, and Weaver, Warren, *The Mathematical Theory of Communication* (Urbana: University of Illinois Press, 1949).

Stewart, Rosemary, *The Reality of Management* (London: Hernemann, 1963).

The Importance of Communication

Gibb, Jack, "Communication and Productivity," *Personnel Administration,* January-February 1964.

Grosz, Mel, "General Theory of Management Communication", (Providence, R.I.: Institute of Management Sciences, Research Committee on Management Measurements, October 3, 1969).

Nonverbal Communication

Giffin, Kim, and Patton, Bobby, *Fundamentals of Interpersonal Communication* (New York: Harper & Row, 1971).

Gunther, Bernard, *Sense Relaxation: Below Your Mind* (New York: Collier, 1968).

Hall, Edward, *The Silent Language* (New York: Doubleday, 1959).

Harrison, Randall, "Non Verbal Communication," in J. H. Campbell and H. W. Harper, eds., *Dimensions in Communication* (Belmont, Calif.: Wadsworth, 1970).

Keltner, John, *Interpersonal Speech Communication* (Belmont, Calif.: Wadsworth, 1970), chap. 6.

Porter, George, "Non-Verbal Communications," *Training and Development Journal,* June 1969, pp. 3–8.

Ruesch, Jurgen, "Non-Verbal Communication and Therapy," in A. Smith, ed., *Communication and Culture* (New York: Holt, Rinehart and Winston, 1966).

Ruesch, Jurgen, and Kees, Weldon, *Non-Verbal Communication* (Berkeley: University of California Press, 1956).

Watzlowick, Paul, et al., *Pragmatics of Human Communication* (New York: Norton, 1967).

Verbal (Oral) Communication

Fritz, Roethlisberger, "The Executive's Environment Is Verbal," in *Management and Morale* (Cambridge, Mass.: Harvard University Press, 1941).

Ross, Raymond, *Persuasion* (Englewood Cliffs, N.J.: Prentice-Hall, 1974).

Language as a Tool of Verbal Communication

Berlo, op. cit., chaps. 7 and 8.

Griffin and Patton, op. cit., chaps. 5–7.

Keltner, op cit., chap. 9.

Ogden, C., and Richards, I., *The Meaning of Meaning* (New York: Harcourt Brace and World, 1956).

Effective Receivers Are Good Listeners

Nichols, Ralph, "Listening Is Good Business," *Management of Personnel Quarterly,* 1 (Winter 1962).

Nichols, Ralph, and Stevens, Leonard, *Are You Listening?* (New York: McGraw-Hill, 1957).

Nichols, Ralph, and Stevens, Leonard, "Listening to People," *Harvard Business Review,* November-December 1957, pp. 35–42.

A Note on Telephone Communications

Cooper, Joseph, *How to Get More Done In Less Time* (New York: Doubleday, 1962), chap. 10.

Written Communications

Burack, A. S., *The Writer's Handbook* (Boston: The Writer, 1972).

Fleach, Rudolph, *The Art of Reasonable Writing* (New York: Harper & Row, 1949).

Lindauer, J. S., *Communicating in Business* (New York: Macmillan, 1974).

The Company Publication

Kindre, Thomas, "Corporate Policy Programs and Communications Media," in Joseph Famularo, ed., *Handbook in Modern Personnel Administration* (New York: McGraw-Hill, 1972), chap. 72.

Seybold, Geneva, "Employee Communication: Policy and Tools," *Studies in Personnel Policy,* no. 200 (New York: National Industrial Conference Board, 1966).

Effective Reading

Adler, Mortimer, and Van Doren, Charles, *How to Read a Book* (New York: Simon & Schuster, 1972).

Communication Media: Managerial Implications

Dewhust, H. Dudley, "Influence of Perceived Information Sharing Norms on Communication Channel Utilization," *Academy of Management Journal,* 14, no. 3 (September 1971): 305–315.

Level, Dale, Jr., "Communication Effectiveness Method and Situation," *Journal of Business Communication,* Fall 1972, pp. 19–25.

Melcher, Arlyn, and Beller, Ronald, "Toward a Theory of Organization Communication: Consideration in Channel Selection," *Academy of Management Journal,* March 1967, pp. 39–52.

Communication Channels

Davis, Keith, *Human Behavior at Work,* 4th ed. (New York: McGraw-Hill, 1972), pp. 261–273.

French, Cecil, "Some Structural Aspects of a Retail Sales Group," *Human Organization,* Summer 1963.

Hershey, Robert, "The Grapevine: Here to Stay but Not Beyond Control," *Personnel,* 43, no. 1 (January-February 1966).

Knippen, Jay, "Grapevine Communication: Management Employees," *Journal of Business Research,* 2, no. 1 (January 1974): 47–58.

Marting, Barbara, *A Study of Grapevine Communication Patterns in a Manufacturing Organization,* unpublished D.B.A. thesis, Arizona State University, 1970.

McCleery, Richard, "Communication Patterns as Bases of Systems of Authority and Power," *Policy Change in Prison Management* (East Lansing: Michigan State University, Governmental Research Bureau, 1957).

Simon, Herbert, *Administrative Behavior* (New York: Macmillan, 1947), pp. 160–162.

Smith, Dorothy, "Front Line Organization of the State Mental Hospital," *Administrative Science Quarterly,* 10, no. 3 (December 1965): 381–399.

Suttona, Harold, and Porter, Lyman, "A Study of the Grapevine in Governmental Organizations," *Personnel Psychology,* 21 (Summer 1968): 223–230.

Walton, Eugene, "How Efficient Is the Grapevine?" *Personnel,* March-April 1961.

Formal Communications: The Chain of Command

Katz, Robert, and Kahn, Robert, *The Social Psychology of Organizations* (New York: John Wiley and Sons, 1969), chap. 9.

Maier, Norman, et al., *Superior-Subordinate Communication in Management,* AMA Research Study 52 (New York: American Management Association, 1961).

Research on Communication Channels

Allen, Thomas, and Cohen, Stephen, "Information Flow in Research and Development Laboratories," *Administrative Science Quarterly,* 14, no. 1 (March 1951): 12–19.

Bavelas, Alex, and Barrett, Dermot, "An Experimental Approach to Organizational Communication," *Personnel,* 27, no. 5 (March 1951): 366–371.

Berkowitz, Norman, and Bennis, Warren, "Interaction Patterns in Formal Service Oriented Organizations," *Administrative Science Quarterly,* 6 (June 1961): 25–50.

Farace, Richard, and McDonald, Donald, "New Directions in the Study of Organizational Communications," *Personnel Psychology,* 27 (1974): 1–15.

Guetzkow, Harold, "Communication in Organization," in James March, ed., *Handbook on Organizations* (Chicago: Rand McNally, 1965).

Lawson, Edwin, "Change in Communication Nets, Performance and Morale," *Human Relations,* 18, no. 2 (1965): 139–147.

Leavitt, Harold, and Knight, Kenneth, "Most Efficient Solutions to Communication Networks," *Sociometry,* 26, no. 2 (June 1963).

MacDonald, Donald, *Communication Roles and Communication Content in a Bureaucratic Setting,* unpublished Ph.D. thesis, Michigan State University, 1970.

Schwartz, D. F., "Liaison Communication Roles in a Formal Organization" Fargo: North Dakota State University, Department of Communication, 1968, mimeograph.

Shaw, Marvin, et al., "Decision Progress in Communication Nets," *Journal of Abnormal and Social Psychology,* 54 (1957): 323–330.

Wickesberg, Albert, "Communications Network in the Business Organization Structure," *Academy of Management Journal,* 11, no. 2 July 1968, pp. 253–262.

Communication: Quantity and Quality

Athanassiades, John, "The Distortion of Upward Communication in Hierarchical Organizations," *Academy of Management Journal,* 16, no. 2 (June 1973): 207–226.

Boyd, Bradford, and Jensen, J. Michael, "Perception of First Line Supervisor's Authority: A Study of Supervisor-Subordinate Communication," *Academy of Management Journal,* 15, no. 3 (September 1972): 331–342.

Burke, Ronald, and Wilcox, Douglas, "Effects of Different Patterns and Degrees of Openness in Supervisor-Subordinate Communication on Subordinate Job Satisfaction," *Academy of Management Journal,* 11, no. 3 September 1969, pp. 319–327.

Roberts, Karlene, and O'Reilly, Charles, III, "Failures in Upward Communication in Organizations: Three Possible Culprits," *Academy of Management Journal,* 17, no. 2 (June 1974): 205–215.

Outward Communication

Otto Lerbinger, *Designs for Persuasive Communication* (Englewood Cliffs, N.J.: Prentice-Hall, 1972).

Ross, op. cit., chaps. 4–10.

Summary

Davis, Keith, "Success of Chain of Command Oral Communication in a Manufacturing Management Group," *Academy of Management Journal,* 10, no. 4 December 1968, pp. 379–387.

Ference, Thomas, "Organizational Communications Systems and the Decision Process," *Management Science,* 17, no. 2 (October 1970): B83–B96.

Greenbaum, Howard, "The Audit of Organizational Communication," *Academy of Management Journal,* 17, no. 4 (December 1974): 739–754.

CHAPTER 10

MANAGERIAL CAREERS

10

Learning Objectives

1. To understand how enterprises develop their management teams.
2. To learn why managers need to perceive their work lives as managerial careers.
3. To determine how to develop your own career plan for greater success and satisfaction as an entrepreneur or manager.

Chapter Outline

Personnel for the Management Team
Planning for Managerial Needs
Recruiting Managers
Selecting Managers
Orienting New Managers
Evaluating the Manager's Performance
Compensating Managers
Developing a Management Team
Managerial Obsolescence
Personnel for the Entrepreneurial or Family Business
Managerial Careers
Effective Career Management
Problems in Managerial Careers
Your Career Plan
Joe, Fred, and Carol
How to Plan a Managerial Career
Career Planning for Family Business Executives and
    Entrepreneurs
Career Planning for Women and Members of
    Minority Groups
Summary

This chapter completes our discussion of interpersonal skills of managers and entrepreneurs by focusing on

1 how enterprises plan for, acquire, orient, evaluate, counsel, develop, and compensate managers—in other words, personnel administration for managers.

2 how managers develop their careers and the problems they face—conflicts in personal and professional life.

3 A self-development plan for your career as an entrepreneur or manager.

The emphasis of the chapter is on the full development of a management team for the enterprise. This is an especially important aspect of personnel administration, since managers or entrepreneurs make the important decisions that determine the future success or failure of any enterprise.

PERSONNEL FOR THE MANAGEMENT TEAM

Managers are like any other resource. For an enterprise to have the right number of the right quality at the right time, it must plan for its needs and then carry out these plans effectively. Unlike nonhuman resources, managers expect to be rewarded through pay and in other ways (such as personal development). The following flow chart illustrates the personnel process for managers.

Planning the demand for managers $\longrightarrow$ Recruiting candidates $\longrightarrow$ Selection $\longrightarrow$ Orientation $\longrightarrow$ Evaluation

$\rightarrow$ Counseling
$\rightarrow$ Compensating $\longrightarrow$ Retirement
$\rightarrow$ Developing

Planning for Managerial Needs

To make sure it has the managers it needs to staff it, an enterprise needs to plan for a management team. In essence, this planning consists of estimating the number of managers needed at a future point in time (say, in one year). Then the enterprise looks at the number of managers expected to be present (the "supply": present supply less retirements and expected losses through firings, quittings, and deaths). The difference is the number of managers the enterprise needs to hire (or let go).

Forecasting Managerial Needs

There is no "demand" for managers as such. The demand for managers is a result of the increases and decreases in the demand for products and services that an enterprise offers its customers and clients. Enterprises plan in either of two ways: They may try to estimate the overall demand for products or services (and, hence, the demand for managers); or they may ask each unit to forecast its demand for services or products (and thus for managers) and add these up. The total is the firm's demand for managers.

An enterprise can try to predict the total demand in several ways:

1 *Estimate by "experts"*   The top manager asks an expert on personnel needs how many managers will be needed. The expert gives his or her best guess. This is the method used by most entrepreneurs, family businesses, and small enterprises, and by many middle-sized enterprises.

2 *Trend projection*   Many middle-sized and some large enterprises use more than expert estimates. They plot on a graph (or on a computer) the relationships between a factor like sales and the number of managers needed. The trend line gives the forecast of managerial demand. This method works well if the fundamentals behind the relationship have not changed recently.

3 *Unit forecasts*   A third way to forecast demand for managers is to have each unit project its demand and then sum these up at headquarters. One way to do this is to have each unit develop a management replacement chart (See Figure 10.1). The manager in charge (e.g., manager of sales, household fan division) knows who is promotable, who is leaving or retiring, and the unit's sales trends. On this basis he or she projects the unit's needs. The vice president for personnel sums these up to get the total demand. This is a frequent approach to forecasting.

4 *Less frequently used methods*   A few large enterprises forecast their needs by using multiple-trend projections (e.g., plotting managerial needs not just against sales but also against profits, GNP, industry trends, etc. as well). A very few firms have developed mathematical models of their operations, and the computer forecasts their needs.

Matching the Forecast with the "Supply" of Managers

The other half of planning managerial needs is examining the supply of managers available within the organization. In general, the effective organization (middle-sized or larger) keeps a management skills inventory. The most sophisticated of these are computerized. Less sophisticated inventories are kept on file cards or cardex cards, which can be easily indexed. Vital information on each manager is contained in the inventory. This information may include age, date of employment, present position, length of time in that position, other experience, education, languages known, and managerial strengths and weaknesses. Figure 10.2 is an example of a management inventory card.

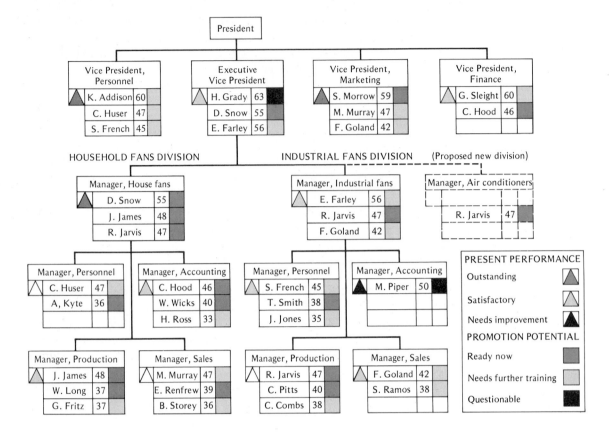

Figure 10.1 Management replacement chart.

Name	Age	Date This Card Updated	Employed
Harley Blackburn	49	1/3/77	1/24/61

Education—B.S. Public Administration, Syracuse University

Experience Outside the Federal Civil Service
1949–1950 City of Syracuse: Public Works Department
1950–1953 U.S. Army: Korean War
1953–1961 State of New York Department of Health

Experience in Federal Service
1961–1977 Department of Health, Education and Welfare: Contract Administration

Present Position: Contract Administrator IV

Present Performance: Outstanding. Performance Evaluation in top 10% of HEW Employees

Potential: Contract Administrator V. Anytime soon

Figure 10.2
Management
inventory card.

The personnel experts will search the management skills inventory for potential candidates for all new management jobs needed (depending on the forecast). If there are not enough managers available, the personnel experts will seek out promotable nonmanagerial staff members and recurit managers from outside the enterprise.

Recruiting Managers If the firm is unable to fill its need for additional managers from within the enterprise (and most organizations prefer to promote from within), then it must recruit managers from schools or other enterprises.

Another reason for recruiting managers outside the organization is to meet the federal requirements for equal employment opportunity. Under the Civil Rights Act of 1964 and several later acts, government agencies have been examining enterprises to see if they have discriminated against potential managers because of their race, color, national origin, sex, age, religion, or physical condition.

Many enterprises hire few women or members of minority groups. Others eliminate older managers (to save pension money) or refuse to hire some managers because their religion is different from the top manager's. Systematic discrimination of this kind is illegal. And government agencies like the Equal Employment Opportunity Commission and the Office of Federal Contract Compliance can order top management to hire managers who have the characteristics the entreprise has discriminated against in the past.

When an enterprise decides to recruit managers, there are a number of factors involved—the nature of the recruiting choice, the sources investigated, and the media used.

Recruiting Choice

The recruiting choice process involves two sets of expectations: those of the enterprise and those of the managers to be recruited. The enterprise has a list of ideal characteristics it is seeking in the manager, and the applicants looking for jobs have their own lists of preferences. The applicant might have strong preferences for a particular location, pay and benefits, challenge in the job, and working conditions. The applicant may have to compromise his or her preferences for several reasons. For example, if the economy is poor, few jobs may be available. Or the available jobs may meet only some of the applicant's preferences. So the recruiting–job choice process can be thought of as a mutual matching and trading off of preferences from the firm's and the applicant's lists of ideals.

Obviously the preferences of the applicant are influenced by his or her perceptions, attitudes, and motivation (Chapters 4 and 5). The enterprise manager's preferences are based on his or her experiences and attitudes toward managing people (and therefore the kind of people he or she wants to hire—see Chapters 6 and 7).

Recruiting Sources and Media

When an enterprise seeks to recruit managers from outside the firm, it can investigate several sources:

1 personal contacts

2 specialized employment agencies (executive search firms)

3 professional associations and their meetings (e.g., the American Marketing Association)

4 organizations of retired military officers

5 college and universities

If the job is at the supervisory level, the enterprise is likely to use source 5 and possibly source 4. For middle managers, sources 1, 2, 3, and 4 might be used. For top managers, sources 1, 2, and possibly 3 would be used.

The media used in recruiting include the following:

1 print media: newspapers, journals, magazines

2 electronic media: television and radio

3 computer matching services (used infrequently)

4 friends and acquaintances of current employees

5 special events (job fairs, etc.)

6 college placement services

Selecting Managers

Before an organization can select recruits it must develop selection criteria. In effect, these criteria are the characteristics on the "ideal recruiting list" such as education, experience, and personality, ranked in order of desirability. That is, if you cannot find an applicant who has all the education and experience you want, would you rather have one with more experience and less education or the reverse? Thus the recruiter must compute the trade-offs between the desired factors. This computation should be based not on the preferences of the present managers but on a systematic examination of the characteristics of successful managers already working for the enterprise.

When the enterprise has assembled a list of recruits it must select "the best." Sometimes there is a selection "problem": ten recruits and five jobs. How is this "problem" handled?

There are a number of methods of making effective selection decisions. The methods most frequently used are interviews with the applicant, examination of the information on the application form, and a check of the applicant's references, especially prior employers. If a large number of managers are to be selected, a scientific way to handle the application form data is to create a weighted application form—a method of systematically determining the trade-offs mentioned earlier. In this method personnel experts examine the application forms of successful managers. They determine which items seem to predict managerial success and assign weights to these criteria. Selections are then made on the basis of this weighted application form.

Tests have not been very successful in selecting good managers, and their use is declining. Especially poor results have been obtained from the use of personality "tests."

Thus, selection of managers is a tough job. Leadership styles enter into these choices. And if more systematic ways (like those just suggested) are not used, the present managers will have a tendency to choose applicants whose personalities they like (i.e., those most like themselves). This can lead to the hiring of less than adequate candidates. In general, you will do a better selection job if you follow these rules:

1 Have more than one manager interact with the applicants and evaluate them.

2 Use more than one selection method: use the interview, the application form, and reference checks if possible.

More selection methods and more people doing the selecting usually lead to better selection.

Orienting New Managers

Just as you have to learn your way around, when you start in a new school, so beginning a new management job will be more effective if you receive a well-planned orientation.

The orientation should, of course, include the technical side of the job: hours of work, where to work, what to do. But often neglected is the social side of orientation: what your new supervisors and coworkers are like and how to get along with them. It has been demonstrated that good social orientation reduces a new employee's anxiety about success on the job and increases employee satisfaction and performance.

Many experts have shown that the beginning of a person's career is critically important to his or her later success. Probably the most significant part of the orientation process is getting to know the supervisor. If you work for a thoughtful, understanding, and talented supervisor who knows your potential and understands your shortcomings, your chances of success are higher than if you work for an unsympathetic supervisor.

Most studies indicate that new managers prefer on-the-job training —informal if possible. They do not like classroom training or observation of others working.

Supervisors of new trainees should avoid anxiety-creating situations in orienting new managers. New employees are already concerned about their ability to do the job. The following approaches are especially poor:

1 *Sink or swim:* Introduce the new manager and let him or her find the way. Do not offer any help. If the new manager is any good, he or she will figure it out.

2 *Upending experiences:* Find a hazing experience, a way to embarrass the new employee because of his or her lack of knowledge of the enterprise or the job.

A good social and technical orientation or management training program pays dividends in increased satisfaction and performance. And the key to this is the choice of supervisors for new managers.

Evaluating the Manager's Performance

After a manager is on the job the superior will begin to evaluate his or her performance. Why? Because the enterprise must determine whether to keep the manager in the job, whether the manager should get that new opening in Honolulu, and whether he or she should get a raise and/or promotion.

Evaluation also allows the enterprise to assess the manager's present knowledge and shortcomings. This will help him or her improve if a program of counseling and training is designed with this goal in mind. So the two primary purposes of performance evaluation are (1) to counsel the manager in order to improve his or her performance and satisfaction and (2) to allocate rewards such as promotions and raises among the better performers.

Evaluation consists of rating a manager against a set of criteria. The criteria for effectiveness in managerial jobs are a lot harder to develop than in blue-collar jobs.

Since managers work primarily through others, they can be evaluated on the performance of their employees, on the development of their employees' potential, on their handling of client complaints, and many other criteria. There are a number of ways of setting these performance criteria. One popular method (to be discussed in more detail in Chapter 12) of handling criteria is *management by objectives.* In this approach the manager and his or her boss jointly agree on goals for the future—increase sales by 3 per cent, increase new customers by 2 per cent, conduct 10 sales training clinics, reduce customer complaints by 1 per cent. Then if the manager achieves these objectives he or she is rewarded. But for this method to be effective the manager must know the basis for the evaluation.

There are many techniques used to record and report evaluations. Three frequently used ones are the graphic rating scale, simple ranking of the managers, and the critical incident technique. In the *graphic rating scheme,* the manager is assessed by assigning a number (e.g., 5 - excellent) to each criterion (e.g., develops his/her employees). These are summed (simple sum or weighted), and a score is assigned. *Ranking* involves listing the managers from best to worst according to overall performance or by each criterion. The *critical incident technique* requires the manager's boss to keep a record of his or her best and worst performances and use this to assign a rating and for counseling purposes.

One technique being used by some large employers to evaluate managers most likely to be promoted is the *assessment center.* In this approach candidates for promotion are given a series of simulations, case studies, and projects to do and are observed by expert assessors. Those scoring the highest are selected.

The final step in evaluation is the review session between the supervisor and the manager. This is the most crucial aspect of the evaluation. The supervisor begins by discussing the manager's rating, giving reasons for the rating and reviewing the manager's many good points. Then the supervisor discusses where the manager should improve, stressing future behavior and the willingness of the supervisor to help the manager succeed even more in the future. Properly done, this can be a rewarding and motivating experience for the manager.

Compensating Managers
Like anyone else, managers are compensated for their work. Compensation satisfies several needs. In Maslow's terminology, compensation takes care of physiological and security needs. In addition, pay and other forms of compensation can satisfy recognition needs. A raise helps pay the manager's bills. It also lets him or her know that the job being done is appreciated. Managers will work harder for higher compensation if there is a strong need that pay can satisfy and if pay is seen as a way of satisfying that need.

Managers are paid in one of three ways: (1) salaries based on time (monthly or yearly salaries), (2) salaries based on output (e.g., commissions), or (3) a base salary plus incentive pay if objectives are met (e.g., $12,000 per year and a $1,000 bonus if sales objectives are met). Most executives receive salaries alone; a few receive bonuses. The number of executives paid on commission alone is very small and is declining.

How executives are paid is partly a function of the tax laws at various times. Before 1969, for example, there were tax advantages in giving executives *stock options* (a chance to buy company stock below the market price and then sell it, taking the profit at capital gains rates instead of regular tax rates). Since then, however, the tax advantages of stock options have not been as great.

A later variation of the stock option is the *performance share.* In this method executives are given company stock for reaching particular objectives. They receive the dividends but not the stock for some years (perhaps after retirement). *Bonuses* (sometimes invested and not paid until retirement) are another form of incentive compensation for executives.

In addition to pay, bonuses, and stock options, most managers receive a large part of their compensation in the form of *benefits.* Usually one-third of the compensation takes the form of company-paid (or shared-cost) life insurance, health insurance, and/or pensions. Other benefits include reduced-cost education for the manager and his or her family, vacations, club memberships, financial and legal advice, company cars, and similar services. Most of these benefits are tax free or tax sheltered.

All of these programs are designed to attract highly productive executives, keep them working for the enterprise, and motivate them to do a good job. Of course managers remain and do well on their jobs for many reasons, compensation being only one.

Developing a Management Team

Once a manager is at work, he or she will need updating as new techniques develop. Some relearning of the fundamentals of management is also needed. The process of improving a manager's knowledge in order to increase the competence of an enterprise's management team is called *management development*. An important aspect of management development, career planning, is discussed later in the chapter.

Self-Development

There are three approaches to management development. One is to encourage each manager to develop himself or herself to the fullest, providing funds to enable him or her to attend conferences, courses, and the like, and emphasizing that it is the individual manager's responsibility to develop. This is the approach most small enterprises take. Many middle-sized enterprises use this approach, and a few larger ones do too.

There are many positive aspects to this approach. One is that in many cases the person best able to determine a manager's need for development is the manager. And because of individual differences (described in Chapters 4 and 5), no one program is best for every manager.

But there are problems with the self-development approach too. First, the managers who need development most may be least willing to develop their own programs. They may not know how to do it, put it off, or never "get around to it."

Second, what economists call economy of scale can be lost in this approach. In many cases it is cheaper and more efficient to hire a consultant to come in and train your executives in the latest techniques than for the various managers to take a number of different courses. So as enterprises get larger there is a tendency to formalize some parts of the management development process.

On-the-Job Management Development

The second approach to management development, and the one most likely to arise after the informal self-development approach, is planned on-the-job experience. In this approach the enterprise plans a series of ways to develop managers while they are working. Three techniques are used:

1 coaching and counseling programs
2 transitional experiences
3 rotation and transfer programs

Coaching and counseling The first method is simple enough in theory and can be effective if well run. The manager receives regular coaching and counseling on how to do the superior's job. This makes sense because the manager must do the superior's job when the superior is on vacation, on site visits, or out of the office. The superior takes the manager into his or her confidence, shows how the job is done, encourages the manager to make recommendations, and allows the manager to make some of the decisions and handle some of the problems.

For this system to work the superior must have confidence in the manager's ability and be moderate to liberal in managerial style. Also, the enterprise must reward the superior for taking this approach. Many organizations will not promote the superior unless he or she has a well-trained replacement ready to take over. This is one kind of reward system. Another kind is a system of formal rewards (raises, promotions) tied to the development of subordinates. If this system is used, the performance evaluation criteria must clearly include development of subordinates as a factor to be evaluated.

If these two conditions are not present, the coaching counseling system will work primarily when the manager's motivational needs are satisfied by helping others (social and recognition/esteem needs could be satisfied in this way).

Transitional experience The second technique is transitional experience. In this method, instead of transferring a superior and appointing a replacement the same day, the enterprise announces the change in advance. For a specified period the manager does the superior's job with the help and advice of the superior. The first time through a difficult experience the superior does the job with the manager watching; then the roles are reversed.

This concentrated, realistic coaching and counseling works well when the superior is willing to share his or her methods with the manager, when the superior is knowledgeable, and when an enterprise is willing to expend extra time and money to pay two managers to do the job (for weeks, sometimes months, depending on the level of the job). This approach removes many of the potential problems of coaching and counseling discussed earlier.

Rotation and transfer The third method is to develop a rotation and transfer program so that all managers who are perceived to have potential for promotion receive a variety of experiences in terms of both function and location. This method is similar to career planning.

Off-the-Job Management Development

In the discussion of self-development programs I mentioned that the enterprise might pay for courses, conferences, and so forth. Many larger and some medium-sized enterprises try to develop their managers' ability and attitudes through off-the-job programs. For example, they may establish a program with a university so that at a particular point in their careers executives receive training in certain abilities or have an opportunity to examine certain attitudes. If it is large enough, the enterprise's own staff may run these programs, sometimes supplemented by university faculty or consultants.

Managerial Obsolescence

Management development programs are designed to improve managerial abilities and to prevent managerial obsolescence. In a fast-changing world managers can easily fall behind. If a manager's skills and abilities become obsolete, he or she can severely retard the progress of the enterprise or of a unit within the enterprise. This is an increasingly common problem today, and studies indicate that it is especially difficult in the 31–40 and over-55 age groups. Effective management development and selection practices will minimize the effects of managerial obsolescence resulting from limited abilities, low motivation, and low self-esteem.

PERSONNEL FOR THE ENTRE-PRENEURIAL OR FAMILY BUSINESS

In this section I will not repeat the information presented in the preceding section. But it should be noted that entrepreneurial and family businesses are different from managerial firms, especially in their personnel and managerial practices. Some of these differences were described briefly in Chapter 3.

When planning for its executive team the. entrepreneurial/family firm will use the tools of similar-sized managerial firms. An additional consideration for these firms, however, is the extent to which the family will supply executives for the firm. This aspect must be planned, especially if the family wishes continuity or wants always to have family members in certain key positions. Sometimes few or no family members are interested in the firm. This often happens when the grandchildren or great-grandchildren of the founder are due to take charge. In such cases the family may pressure some of its members to enter management.

A more frequent and more difficult problem arises when there are more family members who wish to manage the firm than there are positions available. Usually the firm tries to maintain a balance between family and nonfamily executives. If there are four family members interested in two positions, some difficult personal and political decisions must be made. Often these decisions are made in family councils.

Sometimes the decisions are based on abilities alone. In other cases trade-offs develop. For example, if one branch of the family has furnished an executive fairly recently, it is the other branch's "turn." This can play havoc with family relationships.

Sometimes decisions of this kind can be institutionalized to prevent difficulty. At *Sunset* (see Chapter 3) one brother runs the magazine, the other the book company. But what happens when their children decide to enter the business?

Often such problems are handled by education. One heir is urged to become a lawyer and head one end of the business; another is urged to get an M.B.A. in marketing. Or one child is designated to run the business, another given stock but encouraged to become an independent professional.

The career paths of family executives are different too. Although a family member may start in the mail room and rotate through jobs like other trainees, it is clear to most employees that better things await him or her. Just as Prince Charles is given a series of minor ceremonial duties to prepare him to be King of England, so the family executive is oriented and developed in such a way that he or she will be ready to take over at the appropriate time.

It is obvious that a family executive is evaluated differently. Evaluation by his or her superior is less important than how the family executives view his or her progress. This is complicated by personal relations within the family: "You know, I never liked cousin George when we went to St. Paul's together." As I pointed out in Chapter 3, it is not always pleasant to be evaluated in this way.

Finally, the compensation of family executives differs significantly from that of nonfamily executives. Perhaps the family executive is paid more than similar managers. More likely, the compensation includes in addition to pay and benefits, partial payment in voting stock of the concern, in amounts and combinations that are usually carefully planned by tax lawyers and accountants. This, again, may be complicated by family politics. Should the family members be treated "equally" even if one makes a greater contribution to the enterprise's success? Who gets control of the firm? Alliances can be formed to dislodge a relative who is generally disliked. In short, sometimes it is almost impossible to separate family and business life.

MANAGERIAL CAREERS

As we discuss various aspects of personnel development we keep coming back to the concept of a career in management. We will now focus more directly on this idea.

> **MANAGERIAL CAREER**
> A managerial career is a sequential set of work roles or jobs in an enterprise or a series of enterprises.
>
> **CAREER DEVELOPMENT**
> Career development is the process by which an enterprise plans the development of employees in order to meet its needs and, at the same time, fulfill their need for a satisfying work life.

In some lines of work, such as the older professions, the typical career pattern is clear-cut. In others, like management, the career can consist of a series of unrelated job experiences.

The enterprise can develop a career plan that fits together logically, fully develops the individual, and provides for the management needs of the enterprise. Unfortunately, however, at present very few enterprises engage in career development planning.

Effective Career Management

For career management to work it must mesh with the individual's life cycle (see Chapter 4). Most enterprises do not get involved in phases 1 and 2 (ages 0–22). They tend to recruit and orient new managers in phase 3 (ages 23–28) and retire them after phase 7 (age 51 and over).

An example of a fully developed career plan is given in Figure 10.3. At this company, first-level management (and introductory work experience) lasts 15 years, middle management 10 years, general management 15 years, and top management 5 years. General management is a transition from the middle level to the vice presidential and presidential level. Note the mixture of job experience, management development, and transfers in this plan.

If it is properly worked out, career development takes into consideration the life cycle of the employee. Thus in Figure 10.4 first-level management covers phases 3 and 4. Middle management covers phase 5, general management phases 6 and 7, and top management phase 7.

Problems in Managerial Careers

Most managers face a series of problems during their careers. These tend to correspond to periods in the manager's life cycle.

The Young Manager's Career Problems

Managers just starting their careers face a number of problems. An understanding of these problems may put them in perspective and help reduce some of the turnover that is prevalent in the early years.

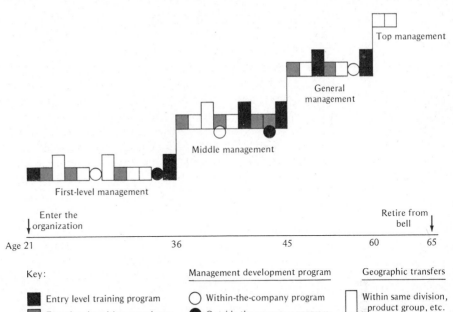

Figure 10.3
Career plan for
general manager at
a telephone
company.

Key:

■ Entry level training program

▨ Functional position experience

□ Rotation of function experience

Management development program

○ Within-the-company program

● Outside-the-company program

Geographic transfers

□ Within same division,
product group, etc.

■ To different division,
product group, etc.

Anxiety Typically, the young manager is anxious over whether he or she will be successful, can hold the job, and is in the right job. This is a problem that many younger managers hide from each other. They are afraid that admitting it would indicate immaturity. In fact, however, it is quite normal. As discussed earlier in the chapter, the proper orientation program can help reduce such anxiety to manageable dimensions. An understanding superior and peers can help. If you find very competitive peers and a supervisor who expects high confidence and lack of anxiety, this can accentuate the problem. Too much attention to these anxious feelings will reduce your chances of success: Psychic energy that could be channeled into job behavior is used to control the anxiety.

A variation of this problem is concern over whether you are in the right job. If you had few job offers, the job may appear to be your only choice. You may not be happy about it and may long for other choices. If you had several offers, you may wonder whether you made the right choice. Chances are that if you gave serious thought to the matter you made the right choice. An understanding of cognitive dissonance may help reduce anxiety.

The expectations problem Some young managers come out of college with the expectation that they will shortly earn per year what their parents took twenty years to get, and that although they will spend a short time "learning the business" (say, a year or two) they will soon be making significant managerial decisions. This problem is compounded if the recruiter promised more than he or she could deliver.

These expectations are found especially in people who have not worked before, and often in graduates of the most prestigious schools. In addition, new managers may expect that their supervisor's main job is to give them frequent feedback (normally glowing), just as they could expect grades at frequent intervals while they were in school.

If instead they are put in a standardized job, with little or no exposure to big decisions and an indifferent supervisor who may "review their progress" only annually (if that often) and on unknown criteria, they may develop an acute case of the expectations problem. This may be compounded if the manager's supervisor is much older—a situation that can create variations of the parent-child problem (which the young manager may have been through only recently).

The expectations problem varies in intensity. In most cases young managers are anxious. But consider the two managers in Table 10.1. It should be easy to see that Mary might have a slight expectations problem, but Constantine is likely to be seriously bothered by it. To the extent that your conditions approach Mary's, you will be better able to cope with the expectations problem.

Table 10.1

Manager 1 Mary	Factor	Manager 2 Constantine
Low	1. Income of family	High
Worked way through with little or no parental help	2. College financing	Parents paid
Community college	3. College attended	Harvard
Supervisor, small firm	4. Parent's position	Vice president, large firm
	5. First supervisor	
32	a. Age	50
Middle of the road	b. Leadership style	Very conservative
Up the ladder	c. Future	Present job
MBO, critical incident method, frequent feedback	d. Performance evaluation method	Annual cursory graphic rating scale
Varied	6. First job	Standardized in hierarchy

In fact young managers must think carefully to determine whether they have an expectations problem or whether they have been put in a "dead-end" job—one with no future promotion possibilities. In the latter case the manager should become a "mobile manager," as discussed later in this chapter.

The political environment One of the biggest problems the generally idealistic young manager runs into is the political game. In some enterprises, as we have seen, it is "who you know" that gets you ahead. If you hook yourself up to a sponsor who is powerful and become loyal to him or her, you make it. The sponsor tells you what the hidden performance criteria are, which clubs to join, whom to impress, whom to invite to parties. He or she helps you get through the political jungle. If you belong to certain clubs, attend a certain church, have a certain ethnic background, vote a certain way, know certain people, and so on, your success in some companies is assured. The sponsor teaches you how to be ruthless, and you prosper.

Many people cannot tolerate an environment that is almost totally political. Some young managers exit in disgust. Others "go along to get along" and become cynical.

Is this really the way it is? Yes, in some organizations. There are no organizations where politics is not part of the picture. But some firms are much less political than others. Top management may make personnel decisions using several advisers, not just one, thus partially negating a single-sponsor system. Or it may rotate executives often and press for evidence of competence, not just opinions. Thus the most obvious political choices are eliminated. Still, politics may operate at the margin, and this can disillusion the young manager. But unless one opts for, say, choice by lot between two equal candidates for promotion, how else can a decision be made? In any case, enterprises that want to hold and promote competent managers and to keep politics "in its place" will do well to try to minimize its influence.

Now let us turn our attention to another troublesome period in the manager's career: phases 5 and 6, the mid-life crisis.

The Mid-Life Middle-Manager Crisis

Phase 5 of the life cycle (ages 35–43) is an unstable, troubled time for anyone, even outside the workplace. But since we spend most of our waking hours at work, this condition sometimes manifests itself at work more than at home. It is important for managers to understand this mid-life crisis because it helps them understand their superior's problems, their parents' problems, and a period that they will experience themselves.

The great Italian poet Dante wrote, "Midway on the path of life I found myself in a dark woods." He expressed the mid-life crisis well. Studies indicate that everyone or almost everyone in the work-force experiences the mid-life crisis. Dr. David Morrisson of the Menninger Clinic has examined thousands of men and has found that they have all experienced it. Lee Stockford of California Institute of Technology has found that five out of six managers and professionals experience it and that one out of six never recover.

The experts point out that although it is frequently denied, it is necessary to experience this crisis. Otherwise the person feels weighed down and does not go through the later phases of life.

What is the mid-life crisis like? In a word, *depression*. This does not mean merely "feeling down." This depression leads to insomnia and vulnerability to illnesses. In the more serious cases it leads to abandonment of one's career, alcoholism, mental illness, marital difficulties, divorce, and suicide. The mid-life crisis is likely to be most serious when the person is under job stress and is vulnerable because of problems at home, and when the job or economic environment is antagonistic. In its least severe form the manager has trouble concentrating on the job, has trouble doing it well, and cannot see any meaning to the job or to life itself.

Why does the mid-life crisis hit managers? Four sets of factors seem to come together at this period. Each can cause the problem, and they may reinforce each other to make it worse.

Problems in personal life At age 40 a person is at least halfway through life (the American male tends to live 67–72 years, the female a few years longer). At this point the manager realizes that he or she is on the downside, especially since his or her parents may die during this period. The manager's children begin to leave home, and marital problems may develop. Aging has set in: vision becomes less sharp; hair grays and/or thins; weight is hard to lose; sexual activity declines. The fact of human mortality becomes abundantly clear.

Broken dreams Most of us, but especially managers, have dreams or expectations of reaching certain job, status, and money goals. Rarely are these dreams or expectations met. Often these goals are set to be reached by age 40. But they are rarely met, because the more ambitious a person is, the higher the goals and the harder it is to reach them. So the manager suddenly realizes that he or she "didn't make it." Feelings of failure arise, and the manager asks, "What's the use?" These feelings are compounded when the manager compares himself or herself to the few people who have achieved much more, a very unfavorable comparison indeed.

Broken relationships Many managers receive help during their early years from a mentor—man executive higher up in the hierarchy. This relationship tends to be broken at this stage because the mentor is older and less influential, or perhaps retired. It may also be broken when the manager decides that "it's time I grow up and achieve on my own." This break has been compared by psychiatrists with the break from one's parents. The mid-life crisis thus may be considered a second painful adolescence.

The competition seems worse Job competition seems especially tough at this stage. Everyone seems to be after your job. There is a terrible feeling of rivalry, the feeling that you have no friends and must constantly defend yourself and your job. In many companies this feeling may be compounded by the naming of a younger president. If the new president is 41 and you are 42, what future do you have?

Overcoming the Mid-Life Crisis

The first step toward overcoming the crisis is awareness. This should be coupled with the realization that for the majority who survive the crisis, although life (and work) is different, it is not over. After Dante went through the dark woods he wrote his masterpiece, *The Divine Comedy*. In a few fields (notably the sciences) major contributions are made before age 40. But in most jobs, including management, a person's highest output comes during his or her 40s.

In addition to facing the crisis, managers should be aware that life will be different. Erik Erikson points out that after the crisis the dominant mode becomes caring. The manager's leadership style begins to change. He or she becomes a mentor. The enterprise's management development programs should emphasize updating and mentor skills (counseling, etc.). Also, the enterprise should build in opportunities for discussing the manager's feelings during performance evaluations and should provide other counseling opportunities.

The manager's personal life should be enriched by "renegotiating," renewing the marriage and making new and closer personal friendships. Almost all research indicates that we survive life's traumas better with friends. People without friends literally die of loneliness—sometimes immediately, but in most cases a little at a time.

The mid-life crisis is serious. But with the right steps it can be conquered, and the manager will go on to a very rewarding phase 6.

The Mobile Manager

In this section we will discuss briefly two kinds of mobility: voluntary job changing by managers and geographic mobility (transfers). In the early phase of a managerial career, especially the first few years, quite a few job changes are usually made. This happens for two reasons:

> **1** The manager is looking for the right niche.
>
> **2** The manager has unreasonable expectations. He or she changes jobs several times before realizing this. Eventually the manager realizes that there is no perfect job and chooses one with problems he or she can live with.

Our society has only recently accepted this early job changing as normal. This was not always so. If a manager moved around, he or she was considered a bit unstable. Now this is no longer a serious problem. However, it seems to me that managers today are making fewer job changes than in the 1960s.

The second type of mobility is job hopping later in the career. Some managers are quite willing to quit one enterprise for another if they think they are getting a better deal. In some cases they can speed up their movement through the hierarchy and increase their salary by doing this. But this is true mainly in special cases—for example, if the manager's superiors are close to him or her in age and promotions are likely to be slow, or if the enterprise is in trouble and has stopped growing and a fast-growing enterprise offers the manager a job.

Although it is difficult to prove the following proposition, the studies done so far support it:

Proposition 10.1.
Managers in growing enterprises will usually be rewarded better, get promoted faster, and reach the top sooner by staying with one enterprise than by job hopping.

The third mobility question is, How much transferring around should you expect as a manager? In the 1950s and especially the 1960s, American enterprises went on a "kick," transferring numerous managers each year. The military is notorious for this. In the private sector, the costs of this policy finally came home in the early 1970s. The actual financial costs were high. But the psychological cost in terms of uprooted families, lost friends, and isolated relatives hit harder, and many more managers quit or refused to transfer. This brought the companies up short; they began to reexamine their rationales for the transfers and found them wanting.

So if you work for a bigger company, the number of transfers should be limited to perhaps three in your career. This will vary, however, depending on the characteristics of the enterprise. If the enterprise has only three sites, the chances of transfer are fewer than if it has 300 or 3000. Moreover, effective self-development and management development programs can reduce the number of transfers an enterprise needs to make.

Spouse and Career

As is often pointed out, work life overlaps with personal life. This means that if the manager is married, his or her work life affects the spouse's life.

In an earlier period *spouse* usually meant *wife*. The literature focused on how the enterprise affected the manager's wife. This is still generally true, although the situation is changing.

I can recall hearing Army officers' wives talking about the social events conducted by the commander's wife. The wives were assigned seats according to their husbands' ranks. They were expected to defer to the wives of their husbands' seniors. They were also expected to perform menial duties that corresponded to their husbands' ranks (for example, lieutenants' wives washed dishes while colonels' wives chatted). It was alleged that if the wife did not butter up the boss' wife, the husband's career would be seriously hurt.

This pattern could be seen in many large corporations as well. Upwardly mobile husbands asked their wives to become "friendly" with bosses' wives and conform to their wishes. In some enterprises the wife was interviewed and evaluated along with her husband. These enterprises expected the wives to be extensions of their husbands' careers. They were given public service and community relations duties to perform, sometimes by the boss' wife.

The wife was also expected to be ready and willing to move each year, for this meant greater success for the husband. Of course a career for her was out of the question. It implied that her husband was not successful and she was not sufficiently devoted to her husband's employer.

These factors, plus a husband away at work most of the time, led to serious problems. Corporate wives often turned to drink, the consequence of loneliness and enforced conformity. There has been a reaction to this attitude in recent years. Wives simply refuse to be considered as merely extensions of their husbands.

Sometimes the executive and his wife attend seminars in which they explore their mutual role relationships. Or the wife pursues her own career.

This whole issue is declining in importance as more enterprises face the loss of good executives if they try to manipulate their wives. In effect, these executives say, "You hired me, not my wife. Keep her out of my job considerations." But the fact is that many enterprises still expect their executives' wives to conform and perform. If you are a male manager in such a situation, you and your wife must decide whether you want to play the game this way. If not, it may mean a job change.

Husband-wife relationships in the entrepreneurial or family business are more difficult than in the managerial firm, as indicated earlier. Whereas it is possible for the spouse to ignore the manager's business associates, it is much harder to avoid the manager's family. Business and family affairs are intermingled. Jealousies and conflicts are carried back and forth between the business and the home. Some distance and privacy are necessary to keep these relationships from becoming impossible. Anyone who has had family or in-law problems can understand what a mess they can become.

Working Partners

With more couples composed of two employed people, a quite different career problem is faced by the couple and their employers: conflicts in the career advancements of husband and wife.

Each year the percentage of the labor force made up of women increases. In the past there were a few managers whose wives had separate careers. But it was assumed that the wife's career was secondary to the husband's and that if he was transferred, she went along.

Today we see more couples like the Lawrences. Harding Lawrence is president of Braniff Airways. Mary Lawrence is president of Wells, Rich and Company. I suspect that Mr. Lawrence does not have to worry about being transferred out of Dallas. But we also find couples like these:

> ·*Mary and John.* Mary is a manager for a large retail firm. John is a college professor.
> ·*Howard and Sally.* Howard is a manager for an insurance company. Sally is the head nurse at a local hospital.
> ·*Jerri and Sandy.* Jerri is a lawyer working for a large corporation. Sandy is a manager for another corporation.
> ·*Bob and Marlyn.* Bob and Marlyn are both executives with one firm. *Business Week* recently reported many examples like Bob and Marlyn.

What happens if Mary, Howard, and Sandy are asked to transfer? If their children are sick, who stays home with them? Who does the housework if help is not available? These problems are difficult, but they can be worked out between the spouses.

How do two working partners go about job selection? One pattern that is developing is as follows: The couple agrees on minimum conditions each partner would accept. And they agree to look in locations where there are possibilities for both. The first one to get an acceptable job takes it; then the other must find a job in that area.

Once jobs have been found, the question of how to deal with mobility arises. Several approaches have been used by dual-career couples:

1 Both spouses declare that they are going to stay in a particular city and will not move.

2 Managers ask for different career paths than the old transfer system and sometimes get them with the right enterprises.

3 Before one partner accepts a promotion elsewhere, a suitable improvement for the other partner must be found. Sometimes the transferring company helps, but not usually.

This is a relatively new issue in management development. Few enterprises have faced up to it yet. But old rules like "you move when we tell you, where we tell you, or your future is zero with us" are being modified. And enterprises are relaxing their rules on marrying a coworker or hiring couples within the same company.

The Manager and Health

What you do at work affects your health, how long you live, and how you live. Meyer Friedman and Ray Rosenman have shown that heart attacks are caused *not* by lack of exercise, *not* by cholesterol, *not* by cigarette smoking, but by behavior patterns (including behavior at work). And as you know, more Americans die of heart attacks than any other cause. According to Friedman and Rosenman, if you are or become a "Type A," you will have a heart attack in your 30s or 40s, not in your 70s. Type A behavior is partly a matter of personality and partly a result of the way some enterprises work. If you want to live longer and if the enterprise wants your services longer, examine the following Type A checklist and determine what you must do to modify your behavior. Enterprise personnel policies can be adjusted to help managers become Type B's—successful, healthy individuals—as shown in the Type B checklist.

Type A Characteristics

1 You *always* move, walk, and eat rapidly.

2 You feel impatient with the pace of things. You almost cannot restrain yourself from hurrying others.

3 You do several things at once. For example, you listen to someone else while thinking about another matter.

4 You feel vaguely guilty when you relax or do nothing for several hours or days.

5 You attempt to schedule more and more in less and less time. You have a chronic sense of urgency.

6 When meeting another "A," you want to challenge him or her.

7 You believe you are successful because you do things faster than others.

8 You evaluate everything in terms of numbers.

9 You use "Type A" nervous gestures (clench fist, bang hand on table, etc.).

10 You always bring the conversation around to topics that interest you.

11 You express the last few words of a sentence much more rapidly than the first few words, and you overlap and accentuate key words more than necessary.

12 You do not have time to enjoy life.

Type B Characteristics

1 You are completely free of Type A characteristics.

2 You never suffer from a sense of impatience or urgency.

3 When you play, you do so for fun, not to exhibit your superiority.

4 You relax without guilt and work without agitation.

5 You feel no need to display your superiority or discuss your accomplishments.

Just as work patterns affect physical health, mental health is affected by work. Pushed too far, the pressures of work can lead to suicide.

Generally, frustrations lead to mental and physical health problems more for people who feel that they have failed than for those who feel successful. A recent study showed that there is a direct relationship in the United States, England, and Sweden between unemployment and mental health hospital admissions. This is also true for homicides, suicides, and heart attacks.

Organizational policies that lead to stressful work environments influence mental health of employees and managers. Managers need to take positive steps to reduce stress through vacations and antistress exercises like the "relaxation response"; they need to become Type B executives.

YOUR CAREER PLAN

This section concentrates on the planning of your future career in management or as an entrepreneur. Career planning is not a science. But the consensus of research (and common sense) is that planning for the future is more likely to lead to the achievement of your goals than not planning. Of course luck is a factor, as I pointed out in Chapter 2. But if you have a plan, you are more likely to be able to exploit the opportunities that luck presents. As you read the rest of this chapter, keep in mind the following axioms of career planning:

· Each individual must assume primary responsibility for his or her career planning.
· With a well-thought-out career plan you have a better chance of having a rewarding career.
· Career planning does not guarantee success, but it allows you to take advantage of circumstances.
· Once you have made a career plan, it takes courage to carry it out.

Joe, Fred, and Carol

Joe is about to graduate from State U with a degree in business. He has heard that the job market is tough, but he does not start worrying about it until November. He interviews at the placement office and in his home town. He takes the first job offer he gets: a job in a bank. Years later he vaguely hates the job and wishes he had never gotten into banking.

Fred was going to graduate in six months. He visited one of his professors and got some career advice. Together they planned a career with a nearby sports organization. Fred loves his job.

Carol was thinking about taking a job with a large financial institution. She consulted with her professors, and they convinced her that big business was not for her. Instead, they helped her get a job with a promising entrepreneurial firm. Carol loves her job.

Most students drift into a career instead of planning it, with predictable results. Career planning can help you become a Fred or a Carol and not a Joe.

How to Plan a Managerial Career

Career planning consists of the six steps, presented in Figure 10.4. The first step is to prepare a list of what you are looking for in a career. This is the "ideal list" described earlier in the chapter. Crucial questions include the following:

1 How hard do I like to work?

2 Do I like to be my own boss, or would I rather have someone else take the responsibility?

3 Do I like to work alone, with a few others, or with large groups?

4 Do I work evenly or in bursts of energy?

5 Do I want to work near home? in warmer climates? ski country? Does location matter? Am I willing to be mobile?

6 How much money do I want? Am I willing to work for less if the job is interesting?

7 Do I like to work in one place or many, indoors or outdoors?

8 How much variety do I want in my work?

The list of questions is potentially limitless. What you must do first is rank the more important ones so that you know the trade-offs, since you will not find them all in one job.

Questions about the potential employer might include the following:

1 Do I have a size preference: small, medium, large, none?

2 Do I have a sector preference (private, nonprofit, public sector)?

3 What kinds of industries interest me? (This is usually based on interests in their products or services. Do you like mechanical objects, counseling people? This is a crucial question.)

4 Does the sector or product or service have a good future that will lead to greater opportunity?

At this point suppose you have determined that what you really want is the following:

1 a job near home

2 in a small firm

3 in the toy industry

4 that you can buy out someday

STEP 1. Realize that you're looking for a career objective and the sequence of jobs you'll use to achieve it.

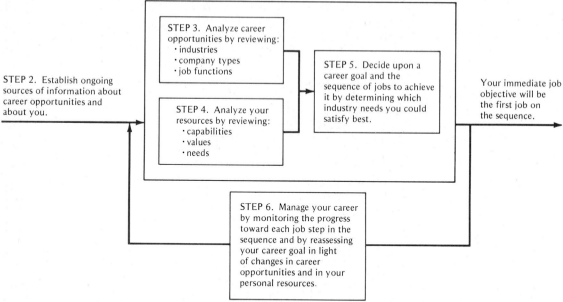

Figure 10.4 Career decision strategy (Greco).

That will narrow your choices. Next you prepare a list of your comparative advantages to help you sell yourself to the employers you have chosen. You also prepare a resume (a sample is shown in Figure 10.5).
Your advantages are as follows:

1 *Education*
grades
courses
skills developed

2 *Experience*
variety
relevance to company
amount
skills developed

3 *Personality and personal characteristics*
interpersonal skills
conscientious/ambitious
leadership skills

4 *Contacts with company*
businesspeople
bankers
professors

PERSONAL   John Roerger   Born: December 12, 1955
INFORMATION   2745 Artis Rd.   5' 8", 170 lbs.
                    Chicago, IL 60600   Health: Excellent
                    (314) 476-8765

EDUCATIONAL EXPERIENCE

Sampson High School, 1969–1972
Chicago Junior College, 1972–1974
Northern Illinois University, 1974–1976
   B.S. (Business Administration)
   Gradepoint Average: 3.1 (4.0 system)

Extracurricular Activities and Honors

   Member, S.A.M.; President, 1975–1976
   Beta Gamma Sigma Business Honorary
   Dean's List, 1974–1975, 1975–1976
   Delta Sigma Pi Fraternity
   Northern Illinois Debate Team, 1974–1976

WORK EXPERIENCE

Part-Time Jobs: (1) Sales: J. C. Penney and Company, 1972–1974
                (2) Computer Programer, Northern Illinois University, 1974–1976
Summer Jobs: 1972, 1973, 1974, 1975: J. C. Penney and Company

I earned 75% of my college expenses.

POSITION DESIRED

Management Trainee, Sales, Finance, or Operating Supervisor leading to challenging career. Location, company size open.

REFERENCES

Mr. Samuel Logan, J. C. Penney and Company, Chicago, IL 60600—supervisor
   of my work at Penney's, 1972–1974 and summers.
Dr. Henry Higgins, Computer Center, Northern Illinois University, DeKalb, IL—
   supervisor of my work, 1974–1976.
Dr. Eileen Jones, Department of Marketing, Northern Illinois University, DeKalb,
   IL—my adviser at Northern Illinois University.

Figure 10.5
Sample resume for
college graduate
seeking
management job.

Establishing Your Career Objectives

For career planning to be successful you must have specific goals or
objectives. These are usually stated in terms of

1 the number of people you want to supervise by a certain age (e.g.,
500 by age 35).

2 a target salary per year by a certain age (e.g., $35,000 per year
by age 35).

3 a specific title by a certain age (e.g., vice president by age 40).

4 a colleague goal (e.g., to be working with at least four compatible colleagues by age 25).

5 whether you wish to run your own business or not.

As should be clear by now, because of individual differences these objectives will vary. What is important is setting your goals precisely.

A word of caution: Do not become inflexible. If your goal is to become a millionaire by age 35 and you are close at 35, be willing to wait until you are 36.

Guidelines for Successful Career Planning and Development

Recently *Business Week* summarized the success stories of several fast-moving young managers in large companies. They tended to have the following characteristics:

1 They get experience in several fields, including finance. They become generalists early.

2 After a few years of experience (and before age 30) they get an M.B.A. This helps in career advancement. A recent study by The Association of M.B.A. Executives found that:

·upon graduation, the average starting salary for an M.B.A. is $3304 per year higher than that of his or her counterpart with a bachelor's degree.
·over a working lifetime, an M.B.A. degree will yield $511,378 more than a bachelor's degree.

3 They do not leave the company when their promotion progress slows down a bit. But if it definitely slows, they change jobs, especially in their 20s and 30s.

4 They realize that career goals like "make your age in salary" are guideposts, not inflexible requirements.

5 They do not want to spend too much time in any single job. Rule of thumb: two years in early jobs, five years as a vice president. When they stop learning they push for transfer or promotion.

6 They switch from line to staff and back to line jobs, with line predominating.

7 They work in such a way as to make their boss look good.

8 They get a reputation as an innovator by taking jobs that give them exposure. They develop their style so that they are noticeable.

Eugene Jennings has studied successful managers for years. His nine career success rules (many similar to *Business Week*'s) are as follows:

1 Maintain the largest number of job options possible.

2 Do not waste time working for an immobile manager.

3 Become a crucial subordinate to a mobile superior.

4 Always favor increased exposure and visibility.

5 Be prepared to nominate yourself for jobs that come open. Define your corporation as a market of jobs.

6 Leave a company when your career has slowed too much.

7 Rehearse quitting. It is a crucial act.

8 Do not let success in your present job preempt your career plan. You will stop moving up.

Many of these rules imply that a career plan is only useful to the upwardly mobile. This is not the case. Any career will be more effective if it is well planned and if you are lucky.

Career Planning for Family Business Executives and Entrepreneurs

What about the person who plans to become an entrepreneurial or family business executive? It is a good idea, if possible, for the future family business executive to acquire experience in at least one other firm before entering the family business. Preferably, this should be a successful firm in a similar business in another location. This allows the executive to become successful independently of the family (which is very important psychologically) and provides perspective for the family experience. A good career plan for a future family business executive is the following:

Experience with
nonfamily business ⟶ Family business
2–5 years ⟶ Career period

An entrepreneur or future entrepreneur can follow one of two patterns: direct entry or postponed entry.

The most frequent pattern is postponed entry:

Work for others ⟶ Open own firm
10 years or so ⟶ Career period

In this pattern the potential entrepreneur learns the business and develops his or her capital (and entrepreneurial plan) while working for another firm in the same business. This can be a successful firm or a competitor. The entrepreneur builds capital by saving his or her salary and making a believable case with a bank (or friends) so he or she can borrow the rest later. Many times the entrepreneur fails several times before making it. If the capital is used up, the entrepreneur goes back to working for someone else and tries again.

In the direct entry pattern the entrepreneur borrows from relatives, friends, or businesspeople to start the business directly after finishing school. This is a much less frequent pattern, but with luck the entrepreneur can succeed more quickly using this approach.

Career Planning for Women and Members of Minority Groups

You may recall the statistics from Chapters 2 and 3. To date very few women and members of minority groups have become successful managers or entrepreneurs. Since 1964 there has been pressure from the federal government to change this situation. The number of women and minority group members in management has been increasing since then. But these groups are still a long way from being represented in numbers comparable to their percentages in the total population.

Very little has been written about American Indian, Hispanic, or Oriental managers, but there has been some research on black managers. John Fernandez, in "Black Managers in White Corporations," writes that blacks do not have much influence because of what he calls "neoracism." He argues that since managers (especially at upper levels) are promoted and rewarded rather informally and are recruited through contacts and friends, blacks are usually excluded. According to Fernandez, selection criteria are biased against blacks. He feels that this will change only if blacks continue to pressure the government and corporations to place more blacks in positions of power. Too often blacks are given staff jobs rather than line jobs, or jobs visible to the community, so the firm can call itself an equal opportunity employer.

Blacks do not have a tradition of entrepreneurship. On one list of the 100 largest black-run firms, many of the last 25 had sales well under $5 million. Still, before 1964 or so you probably would not have found more than 25 medium-sized black-run firms (and a few large ones) in the United States.

The minority manager must recognize that he has a special problem. He should accept only jobs that give him a piece of the action—significant *line* jobs. He should be aware that prejudice exists and that he will be criticized (and maybe sabotaged) unless his performance is outstanding. But until a few years ago he was locked out; today his chances of becoming a manager are better.

Hispanic American men have a strong entrepreneurial history. Cuban exiles in Florida have been especially successful. But the Chicanos in California and the Southwest have had some success. Today's minorities should be aware that earlier minorities built up economic power through entrepreneurship. Usually this came about because they were not hired by the majority ethnic groups of the time. This pattern is still open to minorities, and the pattern of working for a big firm to learn the business and build capital for your own business is still a good idea.

Women have had similar problems. Although women account for a fairly large percentage of the work force in many industries, the managers are normally male. Exceptions are found primarily in the fields of retailing, banking, personal care, advertising, and a few others.

In spite of all the talk about equal opportunity, women hoping for careers in management are having similar problems to those faced by minority males. The standards set for them tend to be higher. And like minority males, women have been given jobs that are more visible than valuable in order to meet equal opportunity requirements.

Employers who are negative toward female managers always have ample reason for not hiring or promoting a woman:

·She might get pregnant.
·She does not have the experience.
·Her spouse (lover) might move.
·Men do not like to work for women.

Under such conditions it is harder for a woman to be a successful manager or entrepreneur than for a man. The woman must work harder to establish her credentials and to build rapport with subordinates, superiors, and peers.

As society accepts the fact that normal, intelligent women want to run or own banks, airlines, and toy factories (as well as secretarial services, retail outlets, and nursery schools), it will be easier for women to enter management. Unfortunately for women, however, it will be some time before they are no longer evaluated differently from male managers.

SUMMARY The first step in personnel administration is to forecast the number of managers needed by the enterprise in the future. This is done by means of expert estimates, trend projection, unit estimates, or more sophisticated tools like multiple-trend or computer-modeling techniques. The enterprise compares its needs with its present supply (its management inventory) and thus determines how many managers it can promote from within and how many it needs to recruit from outside the company. If managers need to be recruited, the enterprise determines the criteria to be met in terms of education, experience, and personality. Then it seeks out applicants through personal contact, employment agencies, and colleges and universities. It can use advertising, computer matching, recruiting visits, and special event recruiting.

Selection of new managers is based on interviews, weighted application blanks, reference checks, and possibly tests.

Once the manager is hired, he or she must be oriented to the new job. This is crucial to early success and to lower the excessive turnover among new managers. The key to orientation success is the new manager's supervisor.

Once on the job, the manager's progress is evaluated in order to provide feedback and help him or her develop in the job. Compensation plays an important part in motivating and rewarding managers.

Enterprises also use various methods to develop their managers' abilities and attitudes in order to improve their performance and reduce the impact of obsolescence. These include self-development and on- and off-the-job management development techniques. The chapter contrasted the techniques used for planning, recruiting, selecting, orienting, evaluating, compensating, and developing managerial personnel in entrepreneurial and family business firms and in the managerial enterprise.

I then went on to discuss managerial careers and career planning. Career planning is a process by which an enterprise (or a manager) plans a career designed to achieve the manager's objectives and increase his or her satisfaction. Several major career problems were discussed.

A young manager faces anxiety on the first job, has to deal with disappointments because of the expectations problem, and must learn how to cope with the political realities at work. Managers in the mid-career stage must face crises due to changes in personal life, broken dreams and relationships, and competition.

Also discussed were the problems of the mobile manager and the role of family relationships, especially when both husband and wife have careers. Ways of reducing stress (and the possibility of a heart attack) were described as well.

The final section of the chapter was designed to help you plan your career and select your first job. Career planning for managers, entrepreneurs, and family business executives was discussed. The difficulties faced by female and minority managers were described.

This chapter completes Part II of the book. Chapter 11 begins Part III: Managing the Organization's Resources.

Questions for Review

1. Describe how enterprises plan their need for managers and how they decide how many managers are to be recruited from outside the enterprise.
2. Describe how managers are recruited from outside the enterprise.
3. How important is a manager's orientation experience to his or her early success on the job? What part does the supervisor play in this orientation?
4. Describe some methods of evaluating and improving managerial performance.
5. How are managers compensated? How does compensation affect managerial motivation?
6. Describe typical self-development, on-the-job, and off-the-job management development techniques. Which are best?
7. In what ways do entrepreneurship and family business personnel techniques differ from managerial personnel practices?
8. What is a career? How can an enterprise (or a manager) plan a career for the manager?

9. What problems does a young manager face? How can he or she deal with them?
10. What problems does a manager in mid-career face? How can he or she handle them?
11. What are the major issues faced by mobile managers?
12. What problems does the executive's wife face in some entreprises? How do you think you would deal with these problems?
13. If both husband and wife have careers, how do they come to grips with conflicts in their career progress?
14. In what ways does work influence a manager's health? How can a manager reduce the possibility of a heart attack?
15. How will you plan your career as (1) a manager, (2) an entrepreneur, or (3) a family business executive?
16. What problems do women and members of minority groups face in managerial, entrepreneurial, and family business careers?

References

Personnel for the Management Team

Glueck, William F., *Personnel: A Diagnostic Approach,* 2nd ed., (Dallas: Business Publications, 1977).

Planning for Managerial Needs

Burack, Elmer, and Walker, James, *Manpower Planning and Programming* (Boston: Allyn and Bacon, 1972).

Coleman, Bruce, "An Integrated System for Manpower Planning," *Business Horizons,* 13 (October 1970): 89–95.

Geisler, Edwin, *Manpower Planning: An Emerging Staff Function,* AMA Management Bulletin 101 (New York: American Management Association, 1967).

Vetter, Eric, *Manpower Planning for High Talent Personnel* (Ann Arbor: University of Michigan, Institute of Industrial Relations, 1967).

Recruiting Managers

Behling, Orlando, et al., "College Recruiting: A Theoretical Base," *Personnel Journal,* 47 (January 1968): 15–25.

Behling, Orlando, and Rodkin, Henry, "How College Students Find Jobs," *Personnel Administration,* 32 (September-October 1969): 35–42.

Glueck, William F., "Decision Making: Organization Choice," *Personnel Psychology,* 27, no. 1 (Spring 1974): 77–93.

Hawk, Roger, *The Recruitment Function* (New York: American Management Association, 1967).

Lopresto, Robert, "Recruitment Sources and Techniques," in Joseph Famularo, ed., *Handbook of Modern Personnel Administration* (New York: McGraw-Hill, 1972), chap. 12.

Selecting Managers

Bray, Douglas, and Moses, Joseph, "Personnel Selection," *Annual Review of Psychology,* (Palo Alto, California, 1972): 545–576.

Hardesty, D., and Jones, W., "Characteristics of Judged High Potential Management Personnel, *Personnel Psychology,* 21 (1968): 295–322.

Orienting New Managers

Gomersall, Earl, and Myers, M. Scott, "Breakthrough in on the Job Training," *Harvard Business Review,* 44 (July-August 1966): 62–71.

Habbe, Stephen, "College Graduates Assess Their Company Training," *Studies in Personnel Policy,* no. 188 (New York: National Industrial Conference Board, 1963).

Hall, Douglas, "A Theoretical Model of Career Subidentity Development in an Organizational Setting," *Organizational Behavior and Human Performance,* 8 (1971): 50–76.

Patten, Thomas, Jr., "The College Graduate Trainee," *Personnel Journal,* 48 (August 1969): 581–592.

Schein, Edgar, "The First Job Dilemma," *Psychology Today,* 1 (March 1968): 27–37.

Evaluating the Manager's Performance

Byham, William, "Assessment Center for Spotting Future Managers," *Harvard Business Review,* 48 (July-August 1970): 150–167.

Finkle, R., and Jones, W., *Assessing Corporate Talent* (New York: John Wiley and Sons, 1970).

Cummings, L. L., and Schwab, Donald, *Performance in Organizations* (Glenview, Ill.: Scott, Foresman, 1973).

Dunnette, Marvin, "Managerial Effectiveness: Its Definition and Measurement," *Studies in Personnel Psychology,* 2 (1970): 6–20.

Lopez, Felix, *Evaluating Employee Performance* (Chicago: Public Personnel Association, 1968).

Miner, John, "Management by Appraisal," *Business Horizons,* 11 (1968).

Quinn, James, "Bias in Performance Appraisal," *Personnel Administration,* 32 (1969): 40–43.

Tosi, Henry, et al., "Setting Goals in Management by Objectives," *California Management Review,* 12 (1970): 70–78.

Compensating Managers

Belcher, David, *Compensation Administration* (Englewood Cliffs, N.J.: Prentice-Hall, 1974).

Hettenhouse, George, "Cost Benefit Analysis of Executive Compensation," *Harvard Business Review,* 48 (July-August 1970): 114–124.

Lawler, Edward, Jr., *Pay and Organizational Effectiveness* (New York: McGraw-Hill, 1971).

Salter, Malcolm, "Tailor Executive Compensation to Strategy," *Harvard Business Review,* 51 (March-April 1973).

Tosi, Henry, et al., *Managerial Motivation and Compensation* (East Lansing: Michigan State University, MSU Business Studies, 1972).

Developing a Management Team

Glueck, William F., "Managers, Mobility, and Morale," *Business Horizons,* December 1974, pp. 65–70.

Hague, Hawdon, *Executive Self Development* (New York: Halstead Press, 1974).

Kaufman, Herbert, *Obsolescence and Professional Career Development* (New York: Amacon, 1974).

Levinson, Harry, "A Psychologist Looks at Executive Development," *Harvard Business Review*, 1967, pp. 69–75.

Mahler, Walter, and Wrightnour, William, *Executive Continuity* (Homewood, Ill.: Dow Jones Irwin, 1973).

Peter, Lawrence, and Hill, Raymond, *The Peter Principle* (London: Pan Books, 1969).

O'Meara, Roger, "Off the Job Assignments for Key Employees," in Elmer Burack and James Walker, eds., *Manpower Planning and Programming* (Boston: Allyn and Bacon, 1972).

<table>
<tr><td>Managerial
Careers</td><td>

Alfred, Theodore, "Checkers or Choice in Manpower Management," *Harvard Business Review*, January-February 1967, pp. 157–169.

Becker, Howard, and Strauss, Anselm, "Careers, Personality, and Adult Socialization," *American Journal of Sociology*, 62, no. 3 (November 1956): 253–263.

Ferguson, Lawrence, "Better Management of Managers' Careers," *Harvard Business Review*, March-April 1966, pp. 139–152.

Glueck, William F., "Career Management of Managerial, Professional, and Technical Personnel," in Elmer Burack and James Walker, eds., *Manpower Planning and Programming* (Boston: Allyn and Bacon, 1972), pp. 239–255.

Mahler and Wrightnour, op. cit.

Moment, David, and Fisher, Dalmar, *Autonomy in Organizational Life* (Cambridge, Mass.: Schenkman, 1975).

Schein, Edgar, "The Individual, the Organization, and the Career: A Conceptual Scheme," Working Paper 326–368 Cambridge: Massachusetts Institute of Technology, Sloan School of Management, 1968), Mimeograph.
</td></tr>
<tr><td>The Young
Manager's Career
Problems</td><td>

Dalton, Melville, *Men Who Manage* (New York: John Wiley and Sons, 1961).

Hughes, Everett, "Queries Concerning Industry and Society Growing Out of Study of Ethnic Relations in Industry," *American Sociological Review*, 14 (April 1949).

Moore, M. L., et al., "Predictors of Managerial Career Expectations," *Journal of Applied Psychology*, 59, no. 1 (1974).

Phillips, Victor, Jr., *The Organizational Role of the Assistant To* (New York: American Management Association, 1971).

Ward, L. B., and Athos, Anthony, *Student Expectations of Corporate Life* (Cambridge, Mass.: Harvard Business School, 1972).

Webber, Ross, *Management* (Homewood, Ill.: Richard Irwin, 1975), chap. 30.

Zaleznik, Abraham, "Power and Politics in Organizational Life," *Harvard Business Review*, May-June 1970, pp. 47–60.
</td></tr>
<tr><td>The Mid-Life
Middle-Manager
Crisis</td><td>

"Executives and the Mid-Life Crisis," *Dun's Review*, June 1975, pp. 48–51.

Fried, Barbara, *The Middle Age Crisis* (New York: Harper & Row, 1976).

Kay, Emmanuel, *The Crisis in Middle Management* (New York: Amacon, 1974).
</td></tr>
</table>

Levinson, Harry, "On Being a Middle Aged Manager," *Harvard Business Review,* July-August 1969, pp. 51–60.

Pearse, Robert, and Pelzer, Purdy, *Self-Directed Change for the Mid-Career Manager* (New York: Amacon, 1975).

The Mobile Manager

Albrook, Robert, "Why It's Harder to Keep Good Executives," *Fortune,* November 1968, pp. 136–139.

Dressel, Wayne, "Coping with Executive Mobility," *Business Horizons,* August 1970, pp. 53–58.

Glueck, "Managers, Mobility and Morale," op. cit.

Papier, William, "Push, Pull and Brain Drain," *Personnel Administration,* November-December 1968, pp. 43–49.

Rosenthal, Edmond, "Greener Pastures," *Personnel,* 46, no. 1 (January-February 1969): 22–30.

Spouse and Career

Bralove, Mary, "Working Partners," *Wall Street Journal,* May 13, 1975.

Business Week, "The Corporate Woman," August 2, 1976.

Gunther, Max, "Your Wife Is None of Your Company's Business," *True,* January 1970.

Hacker, David, "Where Couples Learn to Mix Job and Family," *Wall Street Journal,* April 20, 1974.

Lovelady, Steven, "A Mind of Her Own," *Wall Street Journal,* December 5, 1968.

Schermerhorn, John Jr., et al., "Women in Management," *Proceedings, Academy of Management,* 1975.

Scott, Donald, *The Psychology of Work* (London: Duckworth, 1970), chap. 11.

Seidenberg, Robert, *Corporate Wives: Corporate Casualties* (New York: Amacon, 1973).

Stoess, Alfred, "Conformity Behavior of Managers and Their Wives," *Academy of Management Journal,* 16, no. 3 (September 1973): 433–441.

The Manager and Health

Benson, Herbert, "Your Innate Asset for Combating Stress," *Harvard Business Review,* July-August 1974, pp. 49–60.

Friedman, Meyer, and Rosenman, Ray, *Type A Behavior and Your Heart* (New York: Alfred Knopf, 1974).

Levinson, Harry, et al., *Men, Management, and Mental Health* (Cambridge, Mass.: Harvard University Press, 1966).

Meyer, Herbert, "The Boss Ought to Take More Time Off," *Fortune,* June 1974, pp. 140–142, 229–230ff.

Your Career Plan

Association of MBA Executives, *The Master of Business Administration* (1975).

Boeles, Richard, *What Color is Your Parachute* (Berkeley: Ten Speed Press, 1972).

Crane, Donald, "An Experimental Program in Career Planning," *Proceedings, Academy of Management,* 1975.

Dill, William, et al., *The New Managers* (Englewood Cliffs, N.J.: Prentice-Hall, 1962).

Career Planning for Women and Minority Managers

Greco, Benedetto, *How to Get the Job That's Right for You* (Homewood, Ill.: Dow Jones Irwin, 1975).

Gutteridge, Thomas, "The Hardest Job of All: Career Planning," *The MBA*, October 1973.

Haldane, B., *Career Satisfaction and Success: A Guide to Job Freedom* (New York: American Management Association, 1974).

Jackson, T., "Turned Off by Your Job? Knowing Yourself Is Essential," *Industry Week*, 176, no. 7 (February 12, 1973).

Jennings, Eugene, "Success Chess," *Management of Personnel Quarterly*, 9, no. 3 (Fall 1970): 2–8.

———, *Routes to the Executive Suite* (New York: McGraw-Hill, 1971).

Johnson, M., "Plan Your Career—Or Wing It?" *Industry Week*, 182, no. 14 (September 14, 1974).

Kellogg, Marion, *Career Management* (New York: American Management Association, 1972).

"Plotting a Route to the Top," *Business Week*, October 12, 1974.

Schoonmaker, Alan, *Executive Career Strategy* (New York: American Management Association, 1971).

Vance, Charles, *Manager Today, Executive Tomorrow* (New York: McGraw-Hill, 1974).

Fernandez, John, *Black Managers in White Corporations* (New York: John Wiley and Sons, 1975).

Higginson, Margaret, and Quick, Thomas, *The Ambitious Woman's Guide to a Successful Career* (New York: Amacon, 1975).

Loring, Rosalind, and Wells, Theodora, *Breakthrough: Women into Management* (New York: Van Nostrand Rheinhold, 1972).

Lynch, Edith, *The Executive Suite: Feminine Style* (New York: Amacon, 1973).

PART 4

MANAGING THE ORGANIZATION'S RESOURCES

Part 4 is the longest section of the book. The chapters in this section are designed to improve your skills in the management of resources and people. Chapters 11, 12, and 13 cover planning and decision making; Chapters 14, 15, and 16, organizing and coordinating; Chapter 17, control and conflict management; and Chapters 18, 19, and 20, environmental relations.

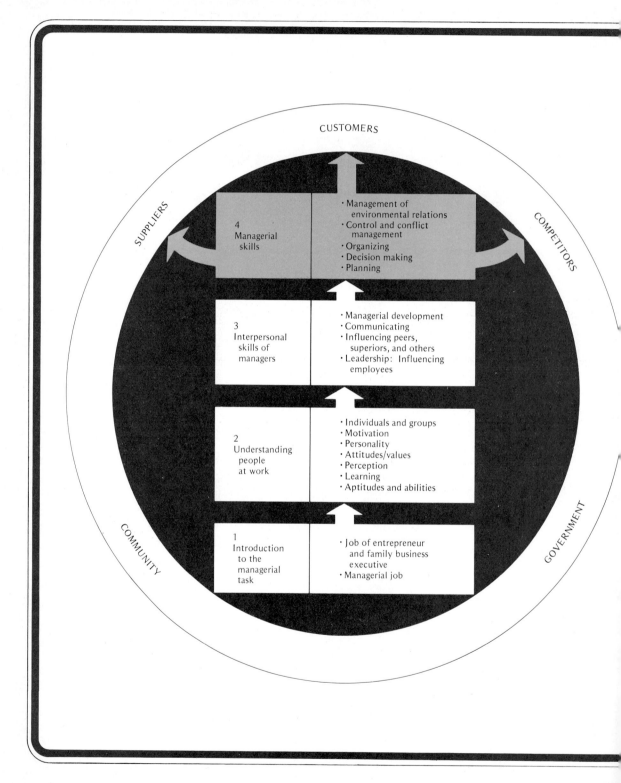

CUSTOMERS

SUPPLIERS

COMPETITORS

COMMUNITY

GOVERNMENT

4
Managerial
skills

· Management of
  environmental relations
· Control and conflict
  management
· Organizing
· Decision making
· Planning

3
Interpersonal
skills of
managers

· Managerial development
· Communicating
· Influencing peers,
  superiors, and others
· Leadership: Influencing
  employees

2
Understanding
people
at work

· Individuals and groups
· Motivation
· Personality
· Attitudes/values
· Perception
· Learning
· Aptitudes and abilities

1
Introduction
to the
managerial
task

· Job of entrepreneur
  and family business
  executive
· Managerial job

As the highlights on the model indicate, we have arrived at the point where we can discuss effective practice of managerial skills themselves. These skills—planning and decision making, organization, control and conflict management, and environmental relations—are what managers do each day. And these are the tasks that managers use their interpersonal skills and knowledge of people to accomplish.

This is the longest section of the book. The model should help you understand managerial skills and how the environment affects these skills. One of the most important managerial skills is the ability to represent the enterprise to others in the environment (the government, customers, etc.) as shown on the model. As will be made clear in each chapter, however, the influence runs both ways: The environment influences how the managerial skills are performed.

CHAPTER 11
MANAGERIAL PLANNING

Learning Objectives

1. To learn what planning is.
2. To learn why managers should plan even though they may not like to.
3. To understand how planning may differ according to managerial style.
4. To learn what kind of planning is done by top managers, middle managers, and supervisors.
5. To understand the planning process and how its steps are interrelated.

Chapter Outline

Planning and the Manager's Day
Why Plan?
Planning Leads to Success
Planning Helps the Manager Cope with Change
Planning Helps Employees Focus on Enterprise
  Objectives
Planning Is Necessary for Effective Control
Planning in Perspective
The Time Dimension in Planning
Planning and Managerial Style
Which Managers Plan?
The Planning Process
Determining Enterprise Objectives
Examining the Environment and Forecasting of
  Changes
Developing Plans to Ensure Achievement of
  Objectives
Feedback and Planning
Evaluation of Planning
The Human Side of Planning
Summary

With this chapter we begin a three-chapter section on planning and decision making. So far we have talked about the people side of the enterprise and how to manage it. But managers manage more than people: They manage resources as well—money, equipment, services, and products. In doing so they perform three kinds of duties: planning and decision making, organization and coordination, and control and conflict management.

In Chapters 11 and 12 we discuss the first of these tasks: planning. Chapter 11 focuses on the planning process, Chapter 12 on planning techniques. We discuss planning first because it normally precedes the use of controls and often precedes organization as well. But these skills are interrelated, as will become clear in later chapters.

PLANNING AND THE MANAGER'S DAY

In Chapter 2, I described what managers do all day. In each description of a manager or entrepreneur were items that can be considered planning activities. Consider the following definition:

> **PLANNING**
> Planning is a set of managerial activities designed to prepare the enterprise for the future and ensure that decisions regarding the use of people and resources (the means) help achieve enterprise objectives (the ends).

A number of management experts believe that planning consists of several interrelated phases:

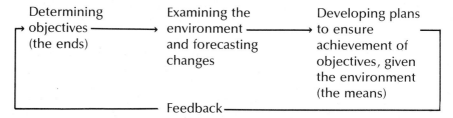

Determining objectives (the ends) → Examining the environment and forecasting changes → Developing plans to ensure achievement of objectives, given the environment (the means)

Feedback

Determination of objectives is a vital part of planning, as we shall see, as is enviromental search and development of the plan. Feedback is usually part of the control system, described in Chapter 17.

What is remarkable about planning activities can be summarized in two statements:

· The human being is the only creature we know that can understand the concept of "future" and anticipate it if he or she cares to.

·Yet many managers with the skills and foresight needed for planning resist such activity.

This ironic situation is due to the following conditions:

·Managers have a lot to do. Planning is only one of several activities competing for the manager's attention.
·Managers prefer to act on immediate problems because they generate immediate feedback. If a customer makes a rush order and the manager helps out, the customer's thanks is given *now*. Planning deals with future events (will they ever come?), and the rewards (if any) are deferred into the future. Most of us prefer to take our rewards now rather than later.
·Planning, good planning, is hard work. Plans can be used to measure results (control). Sometimes managers do not want anyone else to know that their plans were poorly thought out or could not be accomplished.
·Planning often involves thinking, paper work, and time alone—activities most managers do not like or have precious little of. Managers tend to prefer to be doers, not thinkers. The evidence we have is that *effective* managers are more than doers: They are thinkers and planners as well.

WHY PLAN? If planning is so hard to do and most managers would prefer to do other things, why should managers plan? Many managers never plan effectively in spite of the advantages of doing so. But there are good reasons for planning.

Planning Leads to Success Planning does not guarantee success. But studies have shown that planners consistently outperform nonplanners. Before citing these studies, however, let me make a commonsense argument for planning:

·If two football teams of equal ability are going to meet two weeks hence, which do you think will have the best chance of winning: Team 1, which has scouted the other team, trains its players on Team 2's strengths and weaknesses, and prepares plans to exploit its weaknesses and isolate its strengths, or Team 2, which ignores its opponents?
·Two salespeople are competing for an order. One studies the client's organization and determines its needs and how the purchasing agent operates. The other comes to the enterprise with a standard pitch. Assuming that their products are about equal in value, who gets the order?

I am making this argument at length because managers tend to put off planning or never do it at all. Let us turn, therefore, to six studies that illustrate the importance of planning.

The Ansoff Study

H. Igor Ansoff and his associates looked at top-management planning by 93 companies over a 20-year period. Concentrating on the planning that took place before merger decisions, they found that managements that went through a formal planning process before the merger (1) out-performed the nonplanners on all measures of performance (sales, earnings, growth, stock price, etc.) and (2) were able to predict the future better and hence anticipate problems better.

The Eastlack-McDonald Study

Joseph Eastlack and Philip McDonald studied 105 of America's largest companies and 105 middle-sized and smaller firms. They found that the companies with a formal planning process had the fastest growth rates.

The Stagner Study

Ross Stagner studied 217 top executives of 109 large American companies. He found that the companies headed by executives who planned had the best results (as measured by profit as a percentage of capital and profit as a percentage of sales).

The PIMS (Project of Institute of Marketing Sciences) Study

Sidney Schoeffler and his associates studied 620 major business units of 57 very large American corporations. Although they were not directly studying planning as such, their findings led to the conclusion that planning pays off.

The Thune and House Study

This is probably the most "scientific" study to be described here. Stanley Thune and Robert House matched 18 sets of firms for size, industry, and other characteristics. The industries studied were machinery, drugs, food, steel, oil, and chemicals. In each pair of companies neither firm did any formal planning. Then one in each set started planning. Thune and House observed the companies for seven years. The results: The companies that planned outperformed their own past performance and the performance of the nonplanning companies on *every* measure of success, including return on equity, growth in earnings per share, return on investment, and many others.

The Herold Study

David Herold followed up on Thune and House's study. He took the companies in the drug and chemical industries and watched them for four more years. The planning companies not only outperformed the nonplanners on every measure of success but also *widened* the margin of their success. That is, the planners' performance got much better much faster than the nonplanners' performance.

Conclusions

These and other studies indicate that, other things being equal, planning pays off in terms of greater success. But not only is the company's success greater; the manager's ability to *predict* is better. Among other things, this helps him or her deal with bankers and security analysts effectively. The latter become favorable toward the company when the manager knows what he or she is about. And this helps the enterprise get the resources it needs.

Although the "proof" cited has been from the business sector, planning has been shown to pay off in other sectors as well. Military historians attribute much of the success of the world's greatest generals to effective battle plans. Many hospitals could have greatly improved results if they instituted planning procedures. The Church of England is trying, with some success, to solve some of its troubles through planning. But there are fewer "scientific" studies of planning in the public and nonprofit sectors than in the business sector.

Planning Helps the Manager Cope with Change

The second reason for planning is to deal effectively with change. No doubt you have run across lots of articles about how fast the world is changing and how the speed of the changes is accelerating. There is change in all sectors. Consider technological change. We hear about chemical, physical, and material changes occurring every day. The economy changes too: A full business cycle ran its course between 1972 and 1976. Governments fall and government policies change. As firms get larger, the amount of money it takes to enter a business increases. Longer lead times are necessary to make decisions. Social norms and attitudes also change. Consider how the attitudes toward large and small cars or attitudes toward cigarettes have changed over the past ten years. Finally, competitive structures change. Each year about 15 percent of all businesses fail. The number and types of competitors change. An example is computer manufacturing: In 1972 this industry included firms like General Electric, RCA, and Xerox. By 1976 these companies had left the industry, and only two of the present computer firms may be left by 1980.

Enterprises, like civilizations, rise, stabilize, decline, and disappear. So managers have to cope with a changing environment. This is best done through planning. The manager has a feeling of being in control if he or she has anticipated some of the possible changes and planned for them.

Source: Reprinted by permission of Newspaper Enterprise Association.

Planning Helps Employees Focus on Enterprise Objectives

The third reason for planning is this: Without it, employees do their work without seeing the results. The activities they perform become ends in themselves, and when a particular adapation or change is needed the employee resists. We all need meaning in our work. Knowing the objectives of the enterprise helps employees relate what they are doing to meaningful outcomes (ends). The planning process requires managers to define the enterprise's objectives. If employees are involved in this process, they can more effectively tie what they are doing (the means) to the firm's objectives (the ends). Many studies indicate that this process of defining objectives leads to greater performance and employee satisfaction.

Planning Is Necessary for Effective Control

The final reason for planning to be discussed here is that the rest of the process of managing resources is impossible or ineffective without it. For example, we discuss the control and evaluation process in Chapter 17. Control involves holding employees accountable for resources and evaluating whether they have used them well or poorly so that rewards can be distributed accordingly. How can we evaluate employees' effectiveness if we do not tell them what they are expected to accomplish with the resources they control? The design of standards for evaluation is in fact the setting of objectives (part of the planning process). Without definite objectives, managers will be evaluated too subjectively. (A superior can always find some reason to criticize a junior manager.) Thus effective planning enables managers to design good control and evaluation systems for their enterprises.

Planning and nonplanning are actually two different managerial philosophies. Nonplanners blame the things that are always happening to them on bad luck. They are a bit like the student who does not make out a course schedule and then finds out that the accounting course meets at the same time as the computer-programing course.

I once worked for a food business that did not do much planning. When the salespeople wanted to spend time planning, they were berated for wasting time in the office instead of calling on customers. But which customers? Which products should get the most attention? Which new accounts should be accepted? No one knew, and the sales staff went through a series of crises because the wrong orders were taken, customers did not get the right amount of the right product at the right time, and so forth. After planning was initiated, the salespeople's work life settled down and goals were met.

PLANNING IN PERSPECTIVE

This section is included to make sure you understand that planning does not necessarily equal success. As I hope is clear by now, lots of factors contribute to success. One is having enough resources; another is luck. Planning *contributes* to the success of an enterprise. But planning alone is not sufficient to *ensure* success.

Moreover, planning is more important to some enterprises than others. These relationships can be stated in propositional form.

Proposition 11.1.
The larger the enterprise, the more significantly planning contributes to its effectiveness.

Proposition 11.2.
The more volatile the enterprise's environment, the more significantly planning contributes to its effectiveness.

Proposition 11.3.
The more complex the enterprise's product or service line, the more significantly planning contributes to its effectiveness.

It is conceivable that an energetic entrepreneur running a small, single-product-line business in a slowly changing industry can be effective with a minimum of planning. Thus the Ace Washboard Company, employing 50 people and making a product that has hardly changed in forty years, can be successful without much planning. General Electric has to plan.

Sometimes no planning is better than bad planning. Bad planning can consist of preparing too many policies and standardizing the planning process; this leads to inflexibility and wastes time and money. But since most managers do not spend much time planning, few enterprises involve themselves in this kind of planning.

In sum, planning usually contributes to managerial success, though it is not a guarantee of success. The need for planning varies from one enterprise to the next.

THE TIME DIMENSION IN PLANNING

Managers are involved in various kinds of planning. They need to plan what the salespeople will do this week, how the department will reach its quotas this year, what new accounts will be taken on, and where the firm's income will come from five years from now. The first of these problems leads to daily or weekly planning schedules, the last to strategic planning; yet all are referred to as planning.

The lead time needed for planning varies according to the resources involved. Table 11.1 gives some examples.

Table 11.1 Planning Horizons (Koontz and O'Donnell)	
Resources	**Lead Time (Years)**
Planning for materials procurement	$1/2$
Planning for operating expenses (budget)	1
Planning for capital expenditures (budget)	$1\frac{1}{2}$
Planning for recruiting engineers	2
Planning for major financial needs	$2\frac{1}{2}$
Planning for new-product development	$3\frac{1}{2}$
Planning for new production facilities	5

As a general rule of thumb, managers use the following time horizons:

Short-range planning—1 year or less
Intermediate planning—more than 1 year, less than 5 years (average: 3 years)
Long-range planning—5 years or more

But these are *averages.* One study of planning in larger companies found that the actual time horizons for planning ahead depended on the following factors:

· Lead time for the item or industry
· Length of time required to recover capital funds invested in plant, equipment, and personnel training
· Expected future availability of customers
· Expected future availability of raw materials and components

With regard to the first factor, the lead time to prepare for a new series of computers may be three to five years. The lead time for a new line of women's dresses may be six months to a year. Capital recovery in petrochemicals takes much longer than in most service industries.

The lead time for customers of machinery and equipment firms like Cincinnati Milacron is much longer than in most consumer goods industries. And it takes 99 years to replace some trees but much less time to replace other components.

So the short-range plans of some firms are shorter than those of others. Utilities may have to plan new generators 10 to 25 years in advance. The < 1, 1–5, > 5 guideline is simply a rule of thumb.

Proposition 11.4 summarizes the time horizons involved in planning according to size of enterprise.

Proposition 11.4.
All but the very smallest enterprises prepare short-range plans. Some medium-sized and most large enterprises prepare long-range plans.

Large companies can and often do prepare all three types of plans.

PLANNING AND MANAGERIAL STYLE

Table 11.2 is an excerpt from Table 7.7 and focuses on how managers differ in their approaches to planning.

Table 11.2 Three Planning Styles

Liberal	Middle of the Road	Conservative
	Planning	
Manager helped by employees	General description	Performed by the manager
Work group sets the objectives in conjunction with the manager	Setting objectives	A manager's job
Multiple overlapping objectives	Nature of objectives	Clearly defined for the enterprise and for each subunit

The most basic difference between the three types of managers lies in *who* is seen as responsible for doing the planning. The conservative manager views planning as a manager's job: something the manager and only the manager must do. The middle-of-the-road manager may delegate parts of the planning process (probably the least significant parts) to subordinates. The liberal manager views planning as a joint responsibility of the employees and the manager.

These attitudes carry over into the setting of objectives. With regard to the number and clarity of objectives, conservative managers tend to prefer precisely defined objectives in order to establish responsibility and exert control. Liberal managers recognize the difficulty of setting precise objectives and calculating trade-offs, so they tend to operate with more general goals.

THE PLANNING PROCESS

Earlier in the chapter you learned that the planning process involved several interrelated steps. We will discuss these steps separately for the sake of clarity. In reality, however, they influence each other and feed into each other, and it would be nearly impossible (or at least very artificial) to separate them in the world of work. The steps (or phases) of the planning process are as follows:

·Determining objectives (the ends)
·Examining the environment and forecasting changes
·Developing plans to ensure achievement of objectives, given the environment (the means)
·Feedback and control (discussed in Chapter 17).

Determining Enterprise Objectives

ENTERPRISE OBJECTIVES
Enterprise objectives are the goals the enterprise seeks to accomplish through its operations.

In Chapter 2, in the section on organizational effectiveness and success, I pointed out six kinds of objectives:

·survival
·production of goods and services desired by customers
·efficiency in use of resources
·employee satisfaction
·adaptiveness to changing circumstances
·employee development

All enterprises are started for a reason or set of reasons. These are the firm's original objectives. Its current objectives may be the same or may have been modified over time. Note that the six sets of objectives just listed are not equally important in all businesses. In very competitive industries like food canning, for example, efficiency must predominate because of the cutthroat competition in this industry.

Formulating objectives is the first stage of the planning process. We determine objectives in order to achieve the results we expect of the planning process, including setting standards and providing coordination and direction for employees. This leads to greater organizational effectiveness.

Do All Organizations Have Objectives?

All organizations have objectives, at least at one point in time. Many smaller organizations might have trouble specifying their goals. But I believe that once a manager realizes the importance of objectives, he or she begins to formulate them consciously or unconsciously. This process seems to evolve over five steps:

1 No formal objectives
2 Formulation of general objectives, usually not in written form
3 Formulation of general objectives in written form
4 Formulation of specific objectives
5 Ranking of specific objectives in terms of importants.

Step 2 is the stage in which the manager becomes aware of his or her objectives in a general sense. The next step is to put these objectives on record. They might appear in the company's annual reports, for example. The enterprise usually is relatively large and well established when it gets to this stage.

The hurdle that appears at step 4 is that of getting the management to specify the firm's objectives, such as "increase return on investment," in greater detail—for example, "increase return on investment to 6 percent."

The final and most difficult step is that of asking management to compute trade-offs between objectives. This entails determining whether return on investment is more important than market share, whether market share is more important than satisfied employees, and so forth. This step is found only in the most sophisticated firms—perhaps less than 1 percent of the firms in the United States and Canada.

There are various techniques for moving the firm through these steps. One of the more popular at present is management by objectives (MBO). MBO attempts to develop an enterprise philosophy by requiring top managers to proceed through step 5 in formulating objectives. Then middle- and lower-level managers are expected to translate these objectives into specific targets and plans for each unit. More is said about MBO in Chapter 12.

Robert Schaffer recommends that the objectives with the highest priorities should be short-run, measurable goals. And the following proposition applies here:

> **Proposition 11.5.**
> As time goes on, objectives tend to get more specific.

I would add that unspecified objectives allow less effective managers to get by with lower performance. So they tend to resist planning too.

A difficult question is, How specific should objectives be? The answer is that they should be as specific as possible. Generally, the lower the level of the unit in the enterprise, the more specific its objectives should be. They thus become meaningful goals for the employees to work toward in a specified period.

Where Do Objectives Come From?

There are two basic answers to this question, which I will refer to as the "trickle up" and "trickle down" answers. The "trickle up" theorists believe that employees' objectives are somehow summed up and thus become the enterprise's objectives. The opposite position with which I agree is that managers formulate the objectives and they "trickle down" to the employees. These choices of objectives are influenced by three factors:

1 The realities of the external environment and external power relationships.

2 The realities of the enterprise's resources and internal power relationships.

3 The value systems of the top executives.

The first factor is *forces in the environment.* The managers may wish to maximize profits but must modify this objective because of pollution control, excess profits, antitrust, consumer labeling, and other regulations. Trade unions may require higher than market wage rates, featherbedding, fringe benefits, more holidays, and the like. Competitors may sell other products or services at unrealistically low prices and spend excessive amounts on advertising. Suppliers may become monopolized and charge outrageous prices.

The second factor restraining top managers in setting objectives is the *internal resources* of the firm. American Telephone and Telegraph may be able to deal more equally with big government, big labor, or big suppliers than Sandy's Bar and Grill. This affects the objectives chosen by management.

Running through both these factors are the political realities of management relative to other groups involved. Does management have the full support of the stockholders? Has management developed the support of employees and key employee groups such as the professional employees or lower and middle management? If so, it can set higher objectives that employees will help achieve. Or it can act to force the employees to meet its objectives and receive support from the owners if they wish to take drastic sanctions to ensure success.

The third factor influencing the choice of objectives is the *values and preferences of the managers*. These develop out of their education and experience, as described in Chapters 4 and 5. But enterprises with strong value systems or ideologies will attract and retain managers whose values are similar. These values are essentially a set of attitudes about what is good or bad, desirable or undesirable.

Some characteristics that may affect the choice of objectives are combativeness, innovativeness, risk orientation, and individuality. With regard to combativeness, some executives believe that to be successful a firm must be aggressive in the marketplace. Others believe that "you go along to get along." With regard to innovativeness some executives believe that to succeed a firm must innovate, while others say, "let someone else make the mistakes first." The value of dynamism varies too. Some executives prefer fast-changing, dynamic environments, others stable, quiet ones.

Risk is an important element in setting objectives. Some executives feel that to "win big" you must take big risks. Others comment that "risk runs both ways." Thus it is easy to see how executives with certain values emphasize one set of objectives, while another group stresses another set.

Management does not set new objectives each year. It begins from the most recent set of objectives. These may have been set by strong leaders in the past. The managers consider small, incremental changes from the present set of objectives, given the current environment and the current demands of conflicting groups within the enterprise. They have developed ideas about what the firm's objectives ought to be. But they choose the current set of objectives to satisfy as many demands as they can and then "muddle through." Proposition 11.6 summarizes some of the points just made.

Proposition 11.6.
Objectives are formed for an enterprise when its top managers react to the complex interplay among the demands of groups in the environment and within the enterprise. The managers adjust the firm's objectives incrementally, considering these demands as well as their own values and aspirations.

Organizational objectives change as a result of the following factors:

1 Increased demands from coalition groups within the enterprise.

2 Changes in the expectation levels of managers. The managers begin to extrapolate past achievements and expect the enterprise to do more. Or they look at what relevant competitors or other enterprises have achieved and decide to match that level of achievement. Objectives also change when executives perceive a gap between desired ends and the current achievement level.

3 Objectives can change as a result of a crisis. Such a crisis occurred at the National Foundation for Infantile Paralysis when a cure was found for the disease. NASA went through a crisis after men had finally been placed on the moon. When such a crisis arises objectives must be changed, and in successful organizations they are.

On this subject James Thompson gives us the following proposition.

Proposition 11.7.
Objectives change more frequently in firms whose task environment and technology are more volatile.

Studies of Business Objectives

It is not always easy to determine what an enterprise's objectives are. Most organizations have many objectives. Ideally an analyst can categorize these into primary and secondary objectives. But objectives change in response to pressures from inside and outside the enterprise. They can be concretely spelled out or very vague. And many organizations drift along with little or no clear direction in the form of objectives.

In spite of these difficulties some analysts have studied business objectives. All have found that businesses have *many* objectives. Before discussing these studies, however, an important distinction needs to be made. In interpreting the studies and in listening to businesspeople talk about objectives, one must distinguish between official objectives and operative objectives.

OFFICIAL OBJECTIVES
Official objectives are those vague, general objectives that firms invoke in annual reports, public statements by top management, the company charter, and the like.

OPERATIVE OBJECTIVES
Operative objectives are goals actually sought by an enterprise as measured through the actual behavior of the organization.

Sometimes the two types of objectives are the same. But often you must examine the behavior of the firm to see which is which.

What objectives do businesses pursue? At one time it was thought that businesses existed mainly or only to maximize profits. This was a doctrine of traditional economists: a normative objective. But even such prominent economists as Baumol, Williamson, and Grabowski/Mueller have argued that this is not so. In fact the evidence supports Proposition 11.8.

Proposition 11.8.
No sizable firm exists for more than a very short time if its only objective is profit maximation.

Table 11.3 summarizes the findings of the two major studies of business objectives. James Dent studied 145 businesses in the 1950s, and George England studied over 1000 executives in the mid-1960s. As you will note, many potential objectives are not ranked at all. Profit is the leading objective, but *not the only one.* Next often mentioned was public service in the form of good products or services and employee welfare.

Dent found that larger businesses stressed public service more than small businesses. If the firms were unionized, they stressed employee welfare more than nonunionized firms. Also, if the firms had more white-collar than blue-collar workers, they were less profit oriented than the heavily blue-collar firms. Finally, Dent points out that more successful firms focused *outward* to stress meeting the competition and producing good products. Less successful firms focused on *internal* efficiency.

Table 11.3 Business Objectives (Dent and England Studies)

Potential Objectives	Dent Study	England Study
Maximize net profit over a short period	A	A
Maximize the company's net assets and reserves	—	—
Maximize net profit over a long period	A	A
Maximize the dividends for the shareholders	C	—
Maximize the company's prestige	—	—
Be influential in local community decisions	—	—
Survive	—	—
Maximize the rate of innovation of products or service	—	—
Be of service to the community	C	C
Be the leading innovator in the industry	—	B
Be a socially responsible company	C	C
Provide high rewards and benefits to the employees	A	C
Create a friendly and pleasant workplace	A	C
Have satisfied employees	A	C
Prevent unionization or further unionization	—	—
Provide income or jobs for owning family members	—	—
Keep government out of this business	—	—
Keep tax payments to a minimum	—	—
Maximize the market share	—	—
Maximize the company's rate of growth	B	B
Increase sales growth	—	—
Provide the best-quality products or services possible	A	—
Be a market leader, e.g., first in market with new products or services	B	B
Have the most satisfied customers	—	—
Be the most efficient firm in the industry	C	A
Run a stable organization	B	B

A=Most important third of objectives ranked.
B=Middle third of objectives ranked.
C=Least important third of objectives ranked.

England did not find the differences in ranking of objectives based on organizational differences that Dent found. His differences were explained as individual managerial differences.

In comparing these studies we see only a few major differences, and some of these are due to the fact that the two researchers did not provide the executives with the same list of objectives. The major differences are these: Dent's executives ranked employee welfare objectives considerably higher than the later England study. And England's executives put much more emphasis on efficiency than Dent's executives did. There appears to be remarkable consistency in objectives, however, considering differences in time, sample, and list of objectives.

What About Social Responsibility?

The recent management literature abounds with articles and books indicating that businesses are or ought to be making social responsibility a major objective. Social responsibility is defined very broadly and includes everything from producing safe products to giving a portion of the firm's profits to welfare organizations or the arts. Checklists and social audits have been drawn up, presumably for managers to use in measuring themselves.

Few advocates of irresponsible profiteering are heard these days. But as the Dent and England studies indicate, businesspeople do not really agree with the social responsibility ethic. Some businesspeople always were more socially responsible than others. They had stronger religious or moral values. Many others are pressured by citizen lobbies and the government to modify their objectives so as to include some elements of social responsibility. But much of the talk seems to be lip service. As some elements of the coalition press for social responsibility, a few executives respond. But social responsibility is not a major objective of most businesses, though it appears to be modifying the standard objectives listed earlier. Chapters 18 and 19 discuss social responsibility at greater length.

Summary

Objectives are the starting point of the planning process. Useful objectives are measurable, attainable, and consistent with the organization's resources.

Effective objectives are measurable by those who are expected to reach them. They may be stated as follows (for example):

3% ROI   (not "maximize ROI")
2% sales growth   (not "maximize sales growth")

And they are attainable; that is, they are not set so high as to have employees give up because they appear unattainable.

Once objectives are formulated by top management, the rest of the planning process (examining the environment, forecasting changes, and developing plans) can proceed more meaningfully. Planning will take place whether objectives are well formulated or not. But it will be much less effective without well-thought-out objectives.

Examining the Environment and Forecasting Change

The second step in planning is gathering information and forecasting the future. Objectives are modified by the forecast. Before making plans for the next year (or five years) it makes sense to know or try to determine what the future holds. This forecast may also modify next year's objectives. As indicated earlier, these steps are interdependent and influence each other.

Managers need to search the environment in order to determine (1) what threats to achieving the enterprise's objectives are developing and (2) how changes in the environment present opportunities for greater achievement of those objectives. Unless a manager keeps up with change, he or she will become self-satisfied and get left behind. Self-satisfaction is a good way to start an enterprise on a decline. Look what happened to the film companies when TV came in, to the steam locomotive companies when diesels came onto the scene, to A. B. Dick when Xerox grew. One manager who searched the environment and persuaded his enterprise to anticipate the future was David Sarnoff.

DAVID SARNOFF (1891–1971)

At 12:18 A.M. on April 15, 1912, a smart young radio operator working for the Marconi company in New York picked up a CQD signal (predecessor of the SOS) sent out by the S.S. *Titanic*. David Sarnoff alerted the world to the most shocking maritime disaster in history. Four years later Sarnoff picked up another kind of signal. He wrote a memo to his superiors saying he had a "plan of development which would make radio a 'household utility' in the same sense as the piano or phonograph." After the Radio Corp. of America bought out Marconi, Sarnoff became its general manager. His "radio music boxes," put on the market in 1922, grossed $83.5 million in the first three years. He formed the National Broadcasting Co. to help feed the box with news and entertainment. As early as 1923 his interest turned to television; he was to spend $50 million of RCA's money toward its development before a dollar came back. This gamble was to be overshadowed by another. RCA spent $130 million on a color televison system that for years looked like a loser. The Federal Communications Commission had approved a different system sponsored by RCA's rival, CBS. Doggedly, Sarnoff fought on and finally won a reversal from the FCC. This intense, opinionated, driving man, who loved to be called "General" (he had served on Eisenhower's staff), had been born near Minsk, Russia. Like a million other Jewish immigrants, he knew poverty on New York's Lower East Side. At his funeral in 1971, John D.'s grandson, Governor Nelson Rockefeller, delivered Sarnoff's eulogy in Temple Emanu-El: "In David Sarnoff, the word 'visionary' meant a capacity to see into tomorrow and make it work."

Management uses three methods to search the environment: information gathering, spying, and forecasting/modeling. Information gathering involves reading written material from company, industry, and government sources to determine potential changes. But managers prefer to gather information verbally from the media (radio and TV), employees, clients, competitors, industry channel executives (e.g., wholesalers), consultants, bankers, and stockbrokers.

A second source of getting information is by using spies. These individuals can be the enterprise's employees, an employee of a competitor, a supplier, a customer, or a "professional" spy. The third method of information gathering is formal forecasts and models of the future. The forecaster can be an enterprise employee, a forecasting service, or a consultant.

These are the three sources. But which is used when, and how are they used? There have been a few studies of managers' information-gathering activities. Francis Aguilar studied how the executives in 41 chemical companies in the United States and Europe gathered information to be used in forecasting the future. He found that the primary way of gathering information is verbally, usually from subordinates and friends in the industry. What written data are used come mostly from newspapers. Usually any information gathered by executives from subordinates is solicited. Information from outside often comes unsolicited, and it has greater impact.

We know little about spying that is not mere sensationalism. But Jerry Wall, having studied 1200 companies, argues that spying has not increased much since the late 1950s and that most of what took place then was not of the professional variety. It usually consisted of questioning clients and competitors' salespeople.

What Managers Search For

A businessperson usually looks for three factors: general environmental factors, supplier factors, and market factors. In the general environment the manager looks for changes in areas like government structure, laws affecting his or her business, social attitudes toward the firm's products and services, the business cycle, and population. With regard to suppliers, the business manager looks for major technological breakthroughs, changes in the number of suppliers offering raw materials or components, and price changes in components or raw materials. The businessperson also examines the market for the entry of new, powerful competitors (or their exit), changes in consumer preferences for products or services, and new product or service entries.

I have just listed the factors the businessperson *could* look for. But what does he or she actually look for? The four studies summarized in Table 11.4 give us some idea (though there are great variations from one company to another). All four studies indicate that managers believe market factors are very important. Most studies find supplier factors least important, with general factors in between. My own study indicates that businesspeople are almost as interested in the future of the business cycle (a general factor) as they are in market factors.

Table 11.4 The Relative Importance of Environmental Factors Searched for by Executives

Factor	Studies			
	Aguilar	Collings	Wall	Glueck
General environment	least important	least important	least important	next most important
Supplier	next most important	next most important	next most important	least important
Market	most important	most important	most important	most important

Proposition 11.9.
The greater the power of the enterprise relative to its competitors, the less it will focus on the competitive sector of the environment.

Proposition 11.10.
The less dependent the enterprise is on one or a few customers, the less it will focus on the customer sector of the environment.

Proposition 11.11.
The less dependent the enterprise is on the government for subsidies and the less it is regulated by the government, the less it will focus on the political sector of the environment.

Proposition 11.12.
The less dependent the enterprise is on one or a few suppliers, the less it will focus on the supplier sector.

Proposition 11.13.
The greater the volatility of the technological environment, the more the manager will focus on the technological sector.

Proposition 11.14.
The smaller the geographic area served by the enterprise, the less widely it will search the environment.

Managing the Environmental Search

Most experts provide managers with a long list of factors to check up on. It is just about impossible to keep up to date on all of these factors. So managers reduce the number of factors they follow closely to the ones that are most important for them. Several propositions will make clear which factors they should watch.

To supplement these propositions, consider the example of Ace Hardware. Figure 11.1 portrays graphically the reduced focal zone of an executive at Ace Hardware. The industry is not regulated much, nor are there government subsidies. So the managers at Ace Hardware focus only slightly on information about the government. They watch only a few key suppliers, only certain geographic areas. They do, however, have a few key customers that they watch. There have been some technological changes of concern to them. As a small firm, Ace's major worry is its competitors, so the managers focus most of their search and prediction activities on this sector. Thus they concentrate on the important problem areas.

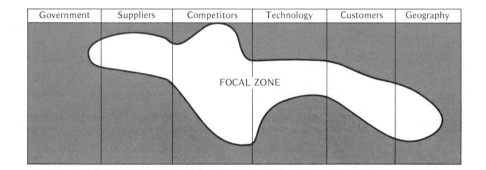

Figure 11.1
Environmental
search and
prediction at a
hardware store.

**Developing Plans
to Ensure
Achievement of
Objectives**
The final step in planning to be discussed in this chapter is the development of plans to help achieve the firm's objectives, given the likely environmental opportunities and threats. To make the planning process complete, the firm's managers institute a multilevel set of plans. As can be seen in Table 11.5, each level of management prepares its own set of plans, derived from the higher levels and fitting the needs of that level's employees (and employees at lower levels).

Top management sets objectives and makes decisions on how the enterprise will respond to environmental threats and opportunities. Middle management translates these decisions and plans into specific financial and organizational terms. It sets up a system of quarterly and yearly targets and budgets based on top management's long-range plans. Lower middle management factors these plans into monthly plans. The supervi-

Table 11.5 Types of Plans Prepared by Three Levels of Managers		
Management Level	**Type of Plan**	**General Content**
Top: 　board of directors, 　president, operating 　division vice 　presidents Middle: 　staff departments, 　department heads, 　regional executives, 　etc. First level: 　supervisors, foremen, 　etc.	strategic planning top-level budgets policies, rules, 　procedures, 　intermediate-level 　budget Schedules, programs, 　short-run budgets	· objective of enterprise · basic mission · basic strategies · total budget · quarterly plans · standing plans · subdivisions of budget · daily and weekly plans · unit budgets

sors then make daily, weekly, and biweekly (possibly monthly) plans, monitered by middle management.

Let us look a bit more at the specific plans of each of these management levels. The description so far implies that plans flow only downward. Obviously, however, adjustments and recommendations flow upward as necessary.

Top Management's Strategic Planning

STRATEGY

A strategy is a unified, comprehensive, and integrated plan designed to ensure that the basic objectives of an enterprise are achieved.

Strategies are designed by the top management of an enterprise. They come to be as a result of the strategic planning process. This process is modeled in Figure 11.2. As you can see, strategic planning involves development of objectives (step 1 in the planning process). Next the top managers search the environment and seek to learn what opportunities and threats they face. For example, a consumer goods manufacturer may face increasing populations in the key age group along with increasing income: This provides an opportunity for sales growth. A threat perceived by the leather companies several years ago was DuPont's Corfam leather substitute.

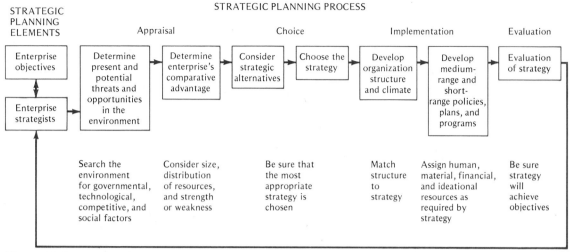

Figure 11.2 A model of strategic planning.

The enterprise's top managers also look inside the firm and try to determine their comparative advantages and weaknesses. Thus Procter and Gamble's comparative advantages include very strong consumer marketing, while Lockheed's weaknesses include inadequate financing.

The managers then try to match up the opportunities and threats with the strengths and weaknesses and, on this basis, choose one of several strategic alternatives. Among the typical alternatives are the following:

Stable growth: continuing to serve the same or similar product service sectors; pursuing the same or a similar level of objectives.
Growth: significantly increasing the level of objectives sought and/or increasing the number of product/service sectors served.
Retrenchment: significantly reducing the level of objectives sought and/or the number of product or service sectors served (e.g., cutting back, becoming a "captive" company, divestment, liquidation).
Combination: simultaneously pursuing two or more of the grand strategies (stable growth, growth, retrenchment) in different parts of the enterprise; or using two or more grand strategies over time (e.g., stable growth for two years, then growth).

Next management weighs the advantages of the several strategies considered and chooses one. It outlines the general organizational and policy changes necessitated by its strategic choice. It then delegates detailed planning and implementation activities to its staff and middle management. Top management also sets budget levels and indicates general usage of funds; detailed budgeting is done by middle management.

Strategic planning is exciting. It involves decisions like Xerox's decision to enter (and leave) the computer field, Textron's decision to get out of textiles and become a conglomerate, and Hershey Chocolate's decision to become Hershey Foods. Strategic planning decisions are the most important ones any manager can make.

Middle-Management Planning

Now middle management takes over. It breaks the big decisions down into meaningful parts for divisions, departments, and units. The plans developed by middle managers include policies, procedures, rules, intermediate-level budgets, and organizational changes. Some specific ways of developing these plans are discussed in Chapter 12. Here I will describe them in general terms.

Policies *Policies* are guides to decision making and action for enterprise employees. Of the kinds of plans developed by middle management (policies, procedures, rules), policies are the most general. A policy is not a specific directive. It provides general guidance for middle and supervisory executives and their employees in a particular decision area.

Suppose top management has made a strategic decision in favor of growth. To implement this decision the middle managers develop policies to make this decision a reality. Typically policies are developed in these areas:

- operations
- finance/accounting
- personnel
- marketing/logistics
- research and development

For each of these areas middle management develops policies to make growth a reality. Here are some examples:

Personnel Policies

1 *Promotion policy*   As the enterprise grows, managers will be promoted from within. Normally the enterprise will hire only supervisory managers from the outside.

2 *Managerial selection policies*   In selecting potential supervisory managers the firm will normally hire college graduates.

Marketing Policies

1 *Internal growth policy*   Normally the major avenue of growth will be to increase the sales of present products. Merger will be used rarely.

2 *New-product policy*   Normally new products will fit the firm's current product line by increasing the number of sizes or quality levels of the product offered.

As you can see, an enterprise could develop hundreds of policies to cover the important areas of the business. Note that a policy does not tell the manager how to handle a specific promotion or add a specific product. It is a general guide to action. It limits the choices of managers in most cases (for example, do not expect to lure the new vice president from another firm; do not expect to get new products out of a merger). But it does not limit them entirely. It serves as a guide to middle and supervisory managers in making certain choices.

Policies are developed to ensure that

1 the strategic decision is implemented.

2 there is a basis for control.

3 there is relative consistency and coordination of work.

4 the amount of time executives spend making decisions is reduced.

In smaller and many medium-sized enterprises, the policies are generally understood and verbal. In larger and some medium-sized firms, they are often in written form and are distributed to managers. Without policy development managers would make the same decisions over and over again. And different managers might choose different directions (e.g., on promotion from within), and this could create problems. On the other hand, policies should never be so inflexible as to prevent exceptions for good reasons.

To give you an example of the significance of policy development to managerial success, I reprint *Fortune* magazine's article on Theodore Vail, policy developer extraordinaire and one of the top managers of all time. Without his policies this country's communication systems might be much less successful today.

THEODORE N. VAIL (1845–1920)

All over the world, telephone companies have long since been nationalized, many becoming branches of the postal service, where they languish on the border between stagnation and chaos. Probably this would have happened in the U.S. too, if the leading telephone company had not early recruited a brilliant and farsighted organizer in (of all unlikely places) the U.S. Post Office. Theodore N. Vail had a hard time finding work that interested him. After some drifting, he became a Western Union telegraph operator, then shifted to the postal service, soon rising to head the railway mail division. In 1878 he joined the troubled Bell Telephone Co. and began to develop distinctive policies that shaped today's A.T.&T. On the one hand, he believed that a "universal" telephone system would serve the public better than would a host of companies in direct competition. On the other hand, he took seriously the danger that a monopoly would stagnate. All his great creative policies came out of his efforts to solve that dilemma. To his subordinates he preached service to the public, rather than profit maximization. He insisted that the company accept—and even try to strengthen—public regulation. He laid the groundwork for Bell Laboratories, from which over decades gushed forth a stream of technological progress. His financial policies were perhaps his greatest contribution. Vail foresaw—and the company still relies upon—a huge securities market of little investors who wanted a relatively safe stock with the hope of gradually increasing dividends. In 1916, Alexander Graham Bell remembered that he had once "dreamed of wires extending all over the country and of people in one part of America talking to people in another part. Mr. Vail has made it come true. . . . He has accomplished the dream of my youth."

Procedures and rules After the broadest policies are developed, some enterprises push the planning process further and develop procedures or rules. These are more specific plans that limit the choices of middle and supervisory managers still further. Procedures and rules are developed for the same reasons as policies in areas where problems have been severe in the past or in potential problem areas that management considers important enough to warrant this kind of attention.

A procedure or rule is a specific guide to action. It tells a manager how to do a particular activity. In larger organizations procedures are collected and put into manuals, usually called Standard Operating Procedures (SOPs).

Procedures or rules or methods (all mean approximately the same thing) exist to make sure policy decisions are carried out. Recall the policies just described to implement top management's growth strategy. Among them was the following: "In selecting potential supervisory managers the firm will normally hire college graduates." If management feels that this is an important area in the company's growth strategy, it will develop procedures based on enterprise experience to get the best managers. Here are some examples:

Procedure 1 Only graduates of business and engineering schools should be hired.

Procedure 2 All potential managers should have a full-day site visit and be interviewed by at least five supervisory and middle managers.

Procedure 3 Preference should be given to veterans.

Procedure 4 Preference should be given to individuals who worked their way through school.

Procedure 5 Preference should be given to individuals in the top 5 percent of a graduating class.

If you stop and think about procedures for a moment, you can readily see how the overconscientious manager could soon develop procedures for every conceivable thing and then barely be able to find them, much less remember or effectively use them. If you have had a government job, been in the military, or worked for a very large organization, you know how procedures can slow you down. A balance must be struck between initiative and consistency. In my opinion formal procedural plans should be drawn up only in really serious decision areas.

I do not mean to imply that procedures and rules serve only to restrict managers' actions. In many cases they also free managers from having to make decisions in areas in which they have less competence or on matters they do not want to become involved with. In this way rules and procedures enable managers to concentrate on more important issues or on decisions for which they have greater competence.

A Note on Corporate Planning Staffs Some very large corporations (as well as government and military organizations) hire staff officials whose main job is to develop plans for top management. Normally these specialists are highly trained individuals with graduate degrees. As was indicated in Chapter 8, jurisdictional disputes can develop between key line officers (e.g., vice presidents) and the staff's well-detailed and documented plans.

Positions on corporate planning staffs are highly valued. But a planning staff can be particularly frustrating to the manager who is a "doer." For the staff can almost never make decisions itself; it must persuade line managers to accept its plans. Nevertheless the use of corporate planning staffs is an important planning tool in large enterprises.

Supervisory Planning

Obviously, not all enterprises have middle-management planning. They may have no middle management. But in almost all enterprises supervisors must plan in order to get the work done. Where upper-level planning is done, the supervisor's planning takes top management's plans one step further, keeping the enterprise's objectives in view.

Essentially, supervisors have two types of planning to do: routine planning and project planning. The methods used are similar. A project is a special job that needs to be done within a specified period. Routine jobs are those that the unit normally performs. Some of the tools and techniques used in supervisory planning are described in Chapter 12.

Feedback and Planning Throughout this chapter I have argued that planning leads to effectiveness. But no matter how good the plan and the planners, there are times when the environment changes, unanticipated events occur, or the plan simply does not work.

Managers need feedback in order to know when to redirect their plans. One way to fill this need is through the use of feedback and control systems (described in Chapter 17). Another is to prepare several plans or sets of plans based on the most likely future events (not one future possibility but several contingencies). An example of this kind of planning is the Apollo moonflight backup plans.

In effect, contingency plans are prepared as follows:

If A happens, follow Plan A.
If B happens, follow Plan B.
If C happens, follow Plan C.

This kind of system requires good feedback to let management know whether A, B, or C is happening—or A and B, in which case a hybrid Plan AB may be prepared.

The crucial point is that planning in most enterprises is a dynamic event. You should not get the idea that one plans at point 1 in time and then simply follows the plan to the letter at points 2, 3, and 4.

EVALUATION OF PLANNING

In an enterprise with a completely developed planning system the managers review the success or failure (or both) of their plans several times a year with a view toward improving future plans and the planning process itself. Although this is desirable, we know little at present about how such an evaluation is done, how frequently or how effectively. Sometimes this step is integrated into the control process.

THE HUMAN SIDE OF PLANNING

Thus far I have described planning without commenting on the human problems involved. Remember, however, that plans can have a tremendous impact on people. They can determine whether a unit will grow or be closed down, and this in turn can affect employee promotions, salaries, and terminations.

Plans can also affect how people will work, where they will work, and for how long. If employees do not have some say in the planning that affects their future, this can lead to anxiety, dissatisfaction, or lowered performance. A middle-of-the-road or liberal manager will try to solve this problem by involving employees in the planning process.

There is some evidence that managers who involve employees in planning get better results. Why? Because often several heads are better than one. Employees may find problems in a particular plan and help avoid those problems. And research indicates that in general employees will try hard to accomplish plans that they helped formulate. So a manager would do well to prepare a preliminary plan and ask key employees for their comments, suggestions, and recommendations before implementing it.

SUMMARY Planning takes time and effort. It is best done as a separate activity when few interruptions are likely to occur. This is another reason why managers do not like to perform planning activities. Effective managers find hideaways and private moments in which to do their planning. Otherwise they become fire fighters, spending all their time putting out fires instead of preventing them from occurring.

In this chapter you learned that planning is a set of managerial activities designed to ensure that decisions regarding people and resources are made in accordance with the enterprise's objectives. The planning process consists of several interrelated phases or steps: determining objectives; examining the environment and forecasting change; developing plans; and developing feedback, control, and evaluation systems to ensure success. The last step overlaps with control (see Chapter 17). You also learned that although planning is useful for all enterprises, it is more vital for larger, more volatile, more complex enterprises.

We next asked why managers should plan. There are four main reasons: planning leads to success; it helps the manager cope with change; it helps employees focus on enterprise objectives; and it is vital to the development of effective control systems.

A manager's style can affect how he or she plans and with whom. The liberal manager involves employees in the planning process and sets multiple overlapping objectives. The conservative manager tends to do his or her own planning and to set precise objectives for each unit.

We went on to discuss the planning process and how it differs by level (top, middle, and supervisory). First we looked at the setting of objectives, which is done at the top-management level. Objectives tend to fall into six categories: survival; choice of goods and services to offer the public; efficiency; employee satisfaction; adaptability; and employee development.

Objectives are not always clearly known and formally written up. In fact formality usually evolves as the enterprise grows in size. Objectives are normally chosen by top managers, who consider both internal and external pressures on the enterprise. The value systems of these managers influence this process significantly.

Studies indicate that all but a very few enterprises have many objectives, not just one. Social responsibility, a much-talked-about objective, is not the primary goal of most enterprises.

The second step in the planning process is examination of the environment for threats and opportunities. This too is the primary responsibility of top management. Often these managers get some help from middle managers in the form of detailed studies of the environment.

The next step is the development of detailed plans by middle and supervisory managers. Examples of such plans are policies, procedures, and rules.

In fully developed planning systems regular meetings are held to evaluate the plans made and the planning process itself. Today the dynamics of most enterprises require contingency planning, and progressive enterprises are using this approach.

Chapter 12 describes some of the most common and useful planning tools and techniques.

Questions for Review

1. What is planning? What interrelated phases or steps does it involve?

2. Why should managers plan? Does it really pay?

3. In what ways (and why) do larger enterprises need to plan more than smaller ones? volatile ones more than stable ones? simple ones more than complex ones?

4. What are short-range, intermediate-range, and long-range plans? How do their purposes differ? How are they related?

5. Does managerial style affect planning? If so, how?

6. What are objectives? How formal are they in most enterprises?

7. Who formulates an enterprise's objectives? What factors influence their choices?

8. What is an official objective? an operational objective? What are the usual objectives of American businesses today?

9. How do managers search the environment? What are they looking for? How do they decide where to concentrate their search?

10. How are objectives implemented by middle managers, corporate planners, and supervisors?

11. What is a policy, procedure, or rule?

References

Why Plan?/Planning Leads to Success

Adair, John, "Formulating Strategy for the Church of England," *Journal of Business Policy*, 3, no. 4 (1973):3–12.

Ansoff, H. Igor, et al., *Acquisition Behavior of U.S. Manufacturing Firms, 1946–65* (Nashville: Vanderbilt University Press, 1971).

Eastlack, Joseph, Jr., and McDonald, Philip, "CEO's Role in Corporate Growth," *Harvard Business Review*, May-June 1970, pp. 150–163.

Fromm, Erich, *The Anatomy of Human Destructiveness* (New York: Holt, Rinehart and Winston, 1970).

Herold, David, "Long Range Planning and Organizational Performance: A Cross Validation Study," *Academy of Management Review*, March 1972, pp. 91–102.

Reimnitz, Charles, "Testing a Planning and Control Model in Non-Profit Organizations," *Academy of Management Journal*, 17, no. 1 (March 1972):77–87.

Schoeffler, Sidney, et al., "Impact of Strategic Planning on Profit Performance," *Harvard Business Review*, March-April 1974, pp. 137–145.

Stagner, Ross, "Corporate Decision Making," *Journal of Applied Psychology,* 53, no. 1 (February 1969): 1–13.

Thune, Stanley, and House, Robert, "Where Long Range Planning Pays Off," *Business Horizons,* August 1970, pp. 81–87.

Wheelwright, Steven, "Strategic Planning in the Small Business," *Business Horizons,* August 1971.

The Time Dimension In Planning

Koontz, Harold, and O'Donnell, Cyril, *Principles of Management* (New York: McGraw-Hill, 1976).

Thompson, Stewart, *How Companies Plan* (New York: American Management Association, 1962).

The Planning Process/ Determining Enterprise Objectives

Glueck, William, *Business Policy: Strategy Formation and Management Action,* 2d ed. (New York: McGraw-Hill, 1976), chap. 2.

Hamner, Clay, "Goal Setting, Performance and Satisfactions in an Independent Task," *Organizational Behavior and Human Performance,* 12 (1974): 217–230.

Latham, Gary and Yubl, Gary, "A Review of Research on the Application of Goal Setting in Organizations," *Academy of Management Review,* 18, no. 4 (1975): 824–845.

Do All Organizations Have Objectives?

Eilon, Samuel, "Goals and Constraints," *Journal of Management Studies,* 8, no. 3 (October 1971):292–303.

Schaffer, Robert, "Putting Action into Planning," *Harvard Business Review,* November-December 1967.

Where Do Objectives Come From?

Cyert, Richard, and March, James, *Behavioral Theory of the Firm* (Englewood Cliffs, N.J.: Prentice-Hall, 1963).

Hickson, D. J., et al., "A 'Strategic Contingencies' Theory of Intraorganizational Power," *Administrative Science Quarterly,* 16, no. 2 (June 1971).

Sills, David, *The Volunteers* (Glencoe, Ill.: The Free Press, 1957), pp. 253–368.

Simon, Herbert, "On the Concept of Organizational Goals," *Administrative Science Quarterly,* 9, no. 1 (1964):1-22.

Thompson, James, *Organizations in Action* (New York: McGraw-Hill, 1967).

Studies of Business Objectives

Baumol, William, *Business Behavior, Value, and Growth* (New York: Harcourt, Brace and World, 1966).

Dent, James, "Organizational Correlates of the Goals of Business Managers," *Personnel Psychology,* 12, no. 3 (1959):365–393.

England, George, "Organizational Goals and Expected Behavior of American Managers," *Academy of Management Journal,* 11, no. 2 (June 1967): 107–111.

Grabowski, Henry, and Mueller, Dennis, "Managerial and Stockholder Welfare Models of Firm Expenditures," *Review of Economics and Statistics,* 52 (1972): 9–24.

Perrow, Charles, "The Analysis of Goals in Complex Organizations," *American Sociological Review,* 25 (1961): 854–866.

Williamson, Oliver, *The Economics of Discretionary Behavior* (Englewood Cliffs, N.J.: Prentice Hall, 1963).

What About Social Responsibility?

Ackerman, Robert, "How Companies Respond to Social Demands," *Harvard Business Review,* July-August 1973:88–98.

Adizes, Ichak, and Weston, J. Fred, "Comparative Models of Social Responsibility," *Academy of Management Journal,* 16, no. 1 (March 1973):112–128.

Andrews, Kenneth, "Can the Best Corporations Be Made Moral?" *Harvard Business Review,* May-June 1973. pp. 57–64

Butler, E. A., *The Big Buck and the New Business Breed* (New York: Macmillan, 1972).

Carrol, Archie, "Corporate Social Responsibility: Its Managerial Impact and Implications," *Journal of Business Research,* 2, no. 1 (January 1974):75–88.

Davis, Keith, "The Case For and Against Business Assumption of Social Responsibilities," *Academy of Management Journal,* 16, no. 2 (June 1973):312–322.

Examining the Environment and Forecasting Changes

Glueck, op. cit.

Aguilar, Francis, *Scanning the Business Environment* (New York: Macmillan, 1967).

Collings, Robert, *Scanning the Business Environment for Strategic Information,* Unpublished D.B.A. thesis, Harvard Business School, 1968.

Keegan, Warren, *Scanning the International Business Environment,* Unpublished D.B.A. thesis, Harvard Business School, 1967.

Taylor, Robert, "Age and Experience as Determinants of Managerial Information Processing, Decision Making and Performance," *Academy of Management Journal,* 18, no. 1 (1975):74–81.

Wall, Jerry, "What the Competition Is Doing: Your Need to Know," *Harvard Business Review,* November-December 1974.

Developing Plans to Ensure Achievement of Objectives/Top Management's Strategic Planning

Glueck, op. cit., chaps. 1, 4, 5, 6.

Drucker, Peter, *Management* (New York: Harper & Row, 1974), chap. 7.

Henry, Harold, *Long Range Planning Practices in 47 Industrial Companies* (Englewood Cliffs, N.J.: Prentice-Hall, 1967).

A Note on Corporate Planning Staffs

Denning, Basil, "Organizing the Corporate Planning Function," *Long Range Planning,* 1, no. 4 (June 1969): 67–71.

Pettigrew, Andrew, "Strategic Aspects of the Management of Specialist Activity" (Brussels: European Institute for Advanced Studies in Management, 1975), Mimeograph.

Ringbakk, K. A., "Organized Planning in Major U.S. Companies," *Long Range Planning,* 2, no. 2 (1969): 46–57.

Taylor, Bernard, and Irving, Peter, "Organized Planning in Major U.K. Companies," *Long Range Planning,* 3, no. 4 (1971): 10–21.

Thompson, op. cit.

CHAPTER 12

TECHNIQUES FOR EFFECTIVE PLANNING

12

Learning Objectives

1. To improve the planning performance of managers.
2. To learn some useful planning techniques.

Chapter Outline

Planning the Use of Time
Determining How You Use Your Time
Analyzing How You Use Your Time
Setting Priorities and Developing a Time Use Strategy
Hints on Effective Time Management
Management by Objectives
What is MBO?
Why Does MBO Work?
Problems Encountered in the Use of MBO
Effective Implementation of MBO
Forecasting
What Do Enterprises Forecast?
Forecasting Techniques
Who Does the Forecasting?
The Reality of Forecasting
Quantitative Planning Tools
Break-Even Analysis
Scheduling
Inventory Planning
Programing: Mathematical, Linear, and Nonlinear
Managerial Implications of Quantitative Tools
Summary

This chapter continues our discussion of planning. It gives more specific information on various techniques used to complete the three major planning steps: formulation of objectives, environmental analysis and forecasting, and implementation. From the standpoint of formulation of objectives the chapter describes a frequently used planning technique: management by objectives (MBO). The best-known forecasting tools are also described, and the use of quantitative tools in the implementation process is discussed. First, however, we look at an essential factor in the planning process: the manager's use of his or her time.

PLANNING THE USE OF TIME

There is clear evidence that managers do not like to plan. One of the reasons for this is that planning takes time. Managers never seem to have enough time to plan. Often this is because they do not plan the use of their most valuable resource: their own time on the job. In this section I will tell you how to get control of your time so you can spend more time planning. The precepts discussed here apply to your off-the-job life as well.

To make more effective use of your time you need to do the following four things:

· Find out how you spend your time.
· Analyze how you use your time.
· Set priorities and develop a time use strategy.
· Implement an effective time plan.

Determining How You Use Your Time

Studies of how managers use their time are not very helpful if they ask managers to estimate their own time usage. Such studies are notoriously unreliable. Managers are doers, not thinkers. So asking them to describe their past managerial behavior in specific terms is not useful. They consistently overestimate the time devoted to production and underestimate the time spent on other matters such as employee problems.

The first step toward better use of your time is to *know how you use your time now.* Only recording and observational methods can do this effectively. The recording can be done by you or by your secretary, although you usually can be more thorough. One way of keeping such a record is by using a device leased by Extensor Corporation for $200 per week. The device beeps randomly during the day. At each beep you punch a button on a keyboard to indicate what you are doing at that moment. Extensor recommends a five-week study period.

Another approach is to use the work-sampling method just described during a shorter but *typical* period such as one week and record how each block of time is used. Assuming that you can find a typical period to study, getting the study done now will get you started on your time management program sooner.

A third approach to time use study is to keep a log. This log will vary according to the type of managerial job being studied. The more standardized the job, the more abbreviated the symbols used. Figures 12.1 and 12.2 are examples of logs for a supervisor and for a top manager.

Date _____
Time _____

Start	End	Total	Activity	With Whom	Initiation	Action/Notes
8:00	9:00	60	M	Region 1 Salespeople	S	Discussed entry of Smith Brothers Region 1 Market. Action: discuss with boss our reaction.
9:00	9:05	5	TP	Arthur's Wholesale	S	Set up appointment.
9:05	9:50	45	TR	John Artis (Salesperson)	S	While on way, Artis briefed me on Smith Brothers problem at Arthur's.
9:50	10:00	10	WT	Artis	—	Waiting for appointment.
10:00	10:30	30	C	Artis; John Arthur (Buyer)	S	Discussed Smith Brothers campaign with buyer and how we should respond.

Initiation	Activity	Functional Code
O = Other	I = Individual discussion	P = Personal Activities
S = Self	C = Conference	F = Financial and accounting problems
	TP = Telephone	M = Marketing/customer relations/logistics
	W = Writing correspondence, reports	E = External/public relations
	R = Reading	O = Operating problems
	T = Thinking	PP = Personnel problems

Figure 12.1 Time Log For Top Manager

Date _____
Time _____

Start	End	Total	Activity and Purpose	With Whom	Initiation	Activity	Function	Action/Notes
8:00	8:45	45	Morning orientation meeting	Sec'y, Bob, Joe, Mary	S	C	F PP	Planned day; set up meeting.
8:45	8:48	3		Sam—Red Cross	O	TP	E	Refused committee assignment.
8:49	9:00	11	Rest room	—	S	P	—	—
9:00	9:20	20	Mail	—	S	W	M O	Answered mail.

Initiation	Activity	
O = Other	I = Individual conference	W = Writing reports or correspondence
S = Self	C = Customer call	R = Reading
	M = Sales meeting	T = Thinking
	TP = Telephone	P = Personal time
	TR = Travel	WT = Waiting time

Figure 12.2 Time Log For Marketing Supervisor

For this system to work well the following hints should be kept in mind:

- Carry your log with you at all times.
- Note your comments immediately or you will forget the details.
- Make your entries short, but be specific.
- Record the *smallest* uses of time, *especially interruptions.*
- Subdivide long periods. (For example, a meeting may cover three areas: finance, accounting, and marketing.)

Now that you have a record of your activities during a typical period you are ready for step two.

Analyzing How You Use Your Time

Time analysis can be done in several ways. The first way is to total the categories and see how much time you spend in various areas such as personal time, telephone calls, conferences, and individual discussions. Then you can examine how you allocate time to functional areas, and you can analyze the flow of activities. This includes a study of the time taken up by interruptions.

Next your time can be divided into four categories: creative, preparatory, productive, and overhead:

- *Creative time* is time devoted to planning future activities, new product ideas, and the like.
- *Preparatory time* is time spent in setup activities such as gathering facts in preparation for a conference.
- *Productive time* is time spent actually doing the job.
- *Overhead time* is time spent on correspondence and reports, paperwork, public relations, and so forth.

In analyzing your use of time you should ask yourself the following questions:

1 *Should anyone be doing this activity at all? Does it serve any purpose?* For example, suppose you always start the day by meeting with three assistants. Is this conference really needed? What purpose does it serve? Maybe it should be eliminated.

2 *If the activity needs to be done, should I be doing it?* If a subordinate can do it equally well (with a little experience), then you should not be doing it. But if you decide to delegate the activity, do not oversupervise.

3 *If I should do it myself, can it be done in less time? How?*

4 *Do I keep punctually to my time schedules or do I waste subordinates' time?*

5 *Do I keep a pile of overhead duties (correspondence to be signed, etc.) at my elbow to be done while waiting for telephone callers to get on the line or visitors to show up?*

Setting Priorities and Developing a Time Use Strategy

The preceding step serves the purpose of getting you to realize how you spend your time. The next step is much harder: deciding what to do with your time.

Your time is divided into several categories: work, pleasure, sleep, personal hygiene, self-development, travel. You set personal priorities among these categories. Some people become "workoholics" and eliminate the pleasure category, maybe self-development, and sometimes sleep. Only you can set priorities like these, and your allocation of time is a reflection of your life style, beliefs, and attitudes.

But how do you set priorities within the work category? The story is told of a top executive who asked a consultant to make his time use more efficient. He paid the consultant $25,000 for the following advice: At the end of each day make a list of the important things you did not get done today. The next day use it as your job list. Do the jobs in the order of their importance, starting with the most important or difficult ones.

To take advantage of this advice you must be able to set your priorities—to come up with that list, then rank the items in order of importance. The list should be shorter as a result of step 2. Still, if there are six items on the list, which three should you do first? It is frequently pointed out that 80 percent of your results come from the vital 20 percent of your activities. Thus the importance of setting priorities should be evident.

Hints on Effective Time Management

A basic element of effective time management is developing a time budget for the week. This may be made easier by the following hints:

- Assign substantially long periods of continuous time (without interruptions) to major tasks (production time). Control interruptions during crucial periods by accepting no visitors or phone calls.
- Next block out time for creative planning, preparation, and overhead activities. Creative planning and preparation time should be used in a quiet place away from your desk, if possible.
- Group together related kinds of work to save starting and stopping time. Put all phone calls together and get your secretary to dial the next call when you signal that you are almost through with the current one.
- Schedule top-priority projects early in the week.
- Budget decision times to reduce procrastination.
- Reserve an average amount of time for unanticipated crises and time over which you have no control (e.g., conferences initiated by others).

·Schedule your least interesting jobs at your peak energy periods so they will get done.

·Postpone shorter projects until you have started long ones. This will motivate you to complete the long ones once they are started.

·Make better use of meetings. Prepare an agenda with time allocated to each topic. Schedule meetings so that they will be naturally cut off by lunch time or the end of the work day.

MANAGEMENT BY OBJECTIVES

In this section we discuss a technique that is frequently used to translate objectives into useful goals for divisions, departments, units, and individuals. This technique is management by objectives (MBO). It helps management make the first step in planning more effective in businesses, hospitals, and other enterprises. In its "Greatest Managers" sequence *Fortune* described George Washington, an exacting planner, as if he had been oriented toward MBO.

GEORGE WASHINGTON (1732–1799)

GEORGE WASHINGTON, Gilbert Stuart, National Gallery of Art, Washington, Andrew W. Mellon Collection.

A surfeit of other "firsts" has obscured the fact that George Washington was one of the first in business leadership. His shrewd bets were mostly placed on the asset that he, a surveyor and farmer, knew best and deemed of "permanent value," namely land. After buying and selling land for years, he owned at his death some 64,000 acres, scattered from Mount Vernon to the upper reaches of the Ohio and even the Mohawk Valley. When he acquired a 1,200-acre tract near Pittsburgh, he noted that under it were coal deposits of "the very best kind." His account books tell more about him than many a romanticized portrait. In managing Mount Vernon, he made careful observations of yields per acre. He got out of tobacco, which he knew depleted the soil, and was one of the first in his area to plant alfalfa. He told his neighbors that, for farm work, mules were more efficient than horses. He worked out an elaborate system for the division of labor during a wheat harvest. His flour achieved brand recognition in the West Indies market; one grade he advertised as "Superfine." As a commander his success was largely attributable to the transfer of methodical habits he had learned as a civilian. On his arduous horseback rides into the Appalachians he not only sensed the westward destiny of the country but also concluded that trade among Americans was the best means of binding East and West together. Indeed, it was his attempt to develop water routes to the interior that prompted efforts toward a stronger national government, efforts that led to the Constitutional Convention of 1787, and to his own businesslike presidency.

What Is MBO?

The ideas behind MBO sound new, but they have been around for some years. Peter Drucker first used the term in 1954, but the ideas that led to MBO were contributed by Donaldson Brown and Alfred Sloan in the

1920s and Edward Hagen in the 1930s. Since then literally thousands of books and articles have been written about MBO. Although they use conflicting terminology, they describe MBO as having the following three characteristics.

1 MBO requires a manager to formulate measurable objectives for his or her job or unit.

2 Development of objectives is a joint project of the manager and his or her supervisor.

3 A system of information must be provided to ensure implementation.

Table 12.1 reports on the percentage of management authorities agreeing with various aspects of MBO.

Table 12.1 Characteristics of MBO Systems According to Various Management Authorities	
Characteristics	**Percentage of Authorities Agreeing**
1. Objectives should be defined in terms of measurable results.	100%
2. The indicator of the result or the method of measuring the result should be specified as part of the objective.	94
3. The time period for accomplishing the result should be specified.	88
4. Objectives should be in writing.	82
5. Objectives should be reviewed two to four times a year.	73
6. A set of objectives should include regular or routine goals and new development goals.	73
7. A set of objectives should have priorities or weights assigned to each one.	67
8. A set of objectives should include personal development goals.	55
9. Objectives should include a plan of action for accomplishing the desired results.	55

Note that all the authorities agree with characteristic 1, but only about half feel that characteristic 8 is important.

There is considerable evidence (pro and con) on what MBO can accomplish. Here we are discussing MBO as a planning technique. In reality it is also a control technique that has an impact on motivation and rewards, job design, and many other aspects of management, as will become clear in later chapters. Table 12.2 summarizes the major studies of MBO.

Table 12.2 Studies of the Effectiveness of MBO Programs

Study	Factors Examined (see list on p. 357)	Conclusions
1. Meyer, et al. (General Electric)	A1, A3, A4, A5, A6 B1, B2, B3, C2, C3,	The experimental group using MBO achieved the benefits claimed much more than a control group using the standard performance appraisal methods.
2. Carroll and Tosi (Black & Decker)	A1, A2, A7, B2, B3, C1, C2, C3	When used properly, MBO developed higher performance, improved superior-subordinate relations, and more favorable attitudes toward enterprise objectives.
3. Ivancevitch ("Palos" Mfgr. Co.)	A1, A2, A3, A7, B2, B3, C2, C3	The experimental plant that introduced MBO improved production and sales; the control plant did not. The experimental plant then reinforced the method with letters of support from top executives, group meetings about MBO later in the program, and personnel department offers of help. This led to large improvements in achievement of marketing and production objectives.
4. Sloan and Schrieber (Hospital)	A1, A4, A5, B1, B2, C1, C2, C3	Like Meyer, Sloan and Schrieber found that MBO helped improve performance appraisal and goal clarification.
5. White (Mental Retardation Hospital)	A1, A2, A4, B1, B3, C1, C3	MBO improved planning and utilization of resources and interpersonal communications. Mixed results otherwise. Goal achievement improved only if managers and superiors are strongly pro-MBO.
6. Shetty and Carlisle (University)	A1, A2, A4, A6, B3, C2, C3	Mixed results. Those who felt that MBO achieved better planning, awareness of goals, communication, performance, and performance appraisal were the younger, untenured, lower-ranked professors who had been there a shorter time and whose departments supported it. MBO was also favored by professors whose departments gave them frequent feedback and involved the professors in the process.
7. Other Favorable Studies (Chesser, McConkey, Migliori)	Various	Generally favorable to MBO program results.

Advocates of MBO claim that it provides the following advantages:

A. Benefits for the Enterprise

1 Focuses managers' efforts on the right objectives.

2 Improves the potential for achieving objectives such as profits.

3 Provides the data to reward managers "objectively."

4 Helps pinpoint human development needs.

5 Helps identify promotable managers.

6 Facilitates the enterprise's ability to change.

7 Helps coordinate the enterprise's efforts.

B. Benefits for Superiors

1 Helps the superior coach the subordinate.

2 Helps eliminate vague performance appraisal tools.

3 Motivates subordinates to perform better.

C. Benefits for Employees (and Lower-Level Managers)

1 Increases employee job satisfaction.

2 Clarifies what is expected of the employee.

3 Provides measurable objectives that the employee is expected to achieve.

Of course not everyone agrees with this opinion. Several studies have indicated that MBO does not always work wonders. But most of them conclude that "MBO must be implemented properly or it will not work." (Proper implementation will be discussed shortly.) In sum, the evidence that properly implemented MBO programs can be effective is very positive at present.

MBO is being used in many enterprises. In January 1974 the *Management by Objectives Newletter* estimated that 83 percent of the companies it had surveyed were using it. Other, more detailed studies indicate that a much smaller percentage use it *fully and successfully.* So MBO is well known and growing in use, but is more likely to be used in large and medium-sized enterprises than in smaller ones.

Why Does MBO Work? According to Stephen Carroll and Henry Tosi, MBO works because, when it is properly done, the employee participates in the process and therefore accepts the company's goals and becomes committed to achieving them.

This point was discussed in Chapter 7 on leadership style. Participation (liberal style) motivates many (but not all) employees to work for goals they help choose. Even conservative employees are motivated by the process because it makes clear what is expected of them. They know what they need to do to be rewarded.

MBO also works because the communication system ensures that employees know how they are doing and what remains to be accomplished. This can improve their performance. In addition, clearly set goals direct employees' attention to the results of their work. They lead to higher levels of achievement by preventing arbitrary judgments of performance and improving the ability of all concerned to predict results. Many studies indicate that MBO goal-setting sessions, properly done, result in achievable goals and that motivation is positively affected when these goals are achieved: in other words, success breeds success. The employee sets the goal, reaches it, everyone knows it, and he is rewarded for it; this keeps the success momentum going.

Problems Encountered in the Use of MBO

When MBO fails or does not work well the enterprise has one or more of the following problems:

1 inadequate top-management support
2 inadequate explanation of MBO
3 poorly defined objectives
4 conflicting personalities
5 insincere commitment by managers
6 inadequate reinforcement of MBO
7 overemphasis on paper work

Inadequate Top-Management Support
Time and again top managers see MBO as a panacea for all their problems. So they decide to go ahead with it but delegate its operation to someone else. MBO will not work well without the participation and strong support of top management at the beginning and regularly during the year.

Inadequate Explanation of MBO
Some enterprises get off on the wrong foot and assume that the employees know and understand MBO. They provide only a short, cursory explanation. If employees and supervisors do not understand the system and why it was introduced, it should be no surprise to learn that it will not work.

Poorly Defined Objectives
MBO works when important, measurable objectives are jointly agreed upon. It works less well if the objectives are too narrow or when, in an attempt to quantify every aspect of the job, the objectives chosen are short-term, unimportant ones that may be hard to measure. To the extent that the objectives are *measurable* and *important* to the enterprise and to the employee, MBO works. Objectives may be hard to develop in very volatile environments. They are also hard to develop if the position's job description and responsibilities are vague.

Personality Conflicts

It is difficult to set up an MBO system between superiors and subordinates whose personalities conflict. MBO requires *joint* development of objectives. This is hard to do when the participants do not get along.

Insincere Commitment by Managers

For MBO to work, the superior must use a liberal or moderate leadership style. It will not work if a conservative leader goes through the motions and, at the "joint" meeting, simply tells the subordinate his or her objectives. This turns MBO into a sham; the employee will resent it and view it as "playing games."

Inadequate Reinforcement of MBO

MBO works better when progress meetings are held frequently to provide feedback. Refresher training in the principles and techniques of MBO is also needed, and rewards must be tied to the achievement of objectives. What you learned about motivation in Chapter 5 and communication in Chapter 9 makes this obvious.

Overemphasis on Paper Work

A good way to kill MBO is to convert this approach (which is in essence a philosophy of management) into costly, technique-oriented paper work. The essence of MBO is getting managers and employees together to agree on objectives. Some enterprises design lots of paper work to provide evidence that MBO is being used: forms to be filled in (in several copies) at the beginning, after objective-setting and reinforcement meetings, at end-of-year reviews, and so forth. This increases the time necessary to operate MBO. Employees and managers will resist this "paper mill" and, thus, MBO itself.

Effective Implementation of MBO

Having told you how to get into trouble running an MBO program, I will now focus on how to handle MBO more effectively.

Starting an MBO Program

Top managers must take the initiative in starting the MBO program, making it clear why they believe in it and indicating over and over that they are very interested in it.

An adequate training program in MBO is necessary for all employees. All parts of the organization must participate. This means that MBO cannot be implemented overnight.

In setting up an MBO system the following steps should be taken:

1 Specify the objectives of the program.

2 Name the departments and units that will participate.

3 Clarify relationships between departments that are affected by MBO.

4 Assign responsibility for MBO activities at each level; make sure job descriptions are clear.

5 Establish time deadlines for each stage of MBO and check back to see that these are met.

Setting Measurable Objectives

A crucial next step is to insist that *realistic, important, measurable* objectives be set at all levels of the enterprise. These objectives must meet five criteria:

1 They must be clear, concise, and unambiguous.

2 They must be achievable by the person concerned.

3 They must be interesting, motivating, and challenging.

4 They must be consistent with organizational policies, procedures, and plans.

5 They must be accurate in terms of what is actually desired by the enterprise.

The objectives should also be team oriented rather than stimulating competition between employees in the same unit.

To meet these criteria a "cascade" approach is necessary. That is, before lower-level objectives can be set, clear, concise top-management objectives must be set, cascading down to long-range objectives, short-range objectives, and then unit objectives throughout the organization.

Thus the statement of organizational purpose includes precise definitions of the firm's business, the strategies chosen, the organizational structure, the markets to be served, and measurable objectives (e.g., return on investment, market share, etc.). The following should also be defined:

profitability (specific measures)
markets (share of market, dollar volume, etc.)
productivity (outputs per employee)
facilities (square feet, etc.)

This process continues down to the departmental level, where objectives are specified for each unit. Examples of specific objectives include the following:

·Sales volume (X total dollar revenues for 1977–1978)
·Share of market (15 percent of total dollar volume of industry sales in Y countries)

·Market penetration (5 percent increase in the number of sales out-
lets carrying our product) by January 1, 1978
·Reduction in sales costs (3 percent less newspaper advertising by
January 1, 1979)

The final step, then, is to set the objectives of each job in a conference between the employee and the supervisor. These objectives should
be set in the following areas:

·Routine activities in key areas—for example, to limit waste to 3 percent of raw materials; to reduce the grievance rate by 5 percent.
·Creative activities—for example, to introduce a new computerized
billing system by January 1, 1978, and thus reduce accounts receivable to 10 days of sales on average.
·Personal development activities—for example, to learn FORTRAN
by June 15, 1977; to use transcendental meditation daily in order
to reduce stress by July 30, 1977.

Next the objectives should be assigned priorities in case all cannot
be accomplished. One possible weighting system is the following:

1 Critical objectives: must do

2 Necessary objectives: should do

3 Desirable objectives: need to do

Objectives that are most useful in MBO systems are measurable,
relevant and important, challenging, and attainable. Thus they must be
above the average level of achievement of pre-MBO days (assuming no
serious changes in the environment), but not excessive. If the company
has improved its market penetration 1 percent, 1½ percent, 2 percent,
2½ percent, and 3 percent in the past five years, 3½ percent is not
challenging and 6 percent is probably unattainable. Four and one-half
percent may be just right.

Negotiating Objectives

It is important for the superior to take MBO seriously. This means he
or she must do the following:

·Come prepared for the MBO meeting. Have objectives in mind.
·Put the employee at ease.
·Facilitate discussion by listening, summarizing progress at various
points, minimizing criticism, and rewarding insight and self-criticism.
·List disagreements and work them out.
·Summarize in writing the objectives that have been agreed upon.

A good checklist for the objective-setting interview is presented in Table 12.3.

Table 12.3 Checklist for Objective-Setting Interview (Slusher and Sims)

Checklist 1—Before the Interview

What the Subordinate Should Do

Develop preliminary objectives that have a clear performance standard and completion deadline.

Provide the superior with a copy of the preliminary objectives prior to the interview.

Prepare supporting data for each objective.

Decide what resources and coordination will be necessary.

List questions and problems for discussion with the superior.

What the Superior Should Do

Decide whether each preliminary objective represents a priority need.

Check for technical completeness of objectives. Is there a clear performance standard, completion deadline, and method of checking results?

Judge whether performance standards are realistic (not too easy, not too difficult).

Decide if the subordinate has sufficient authority in the objective area.

Specify any required personnel coordination needed to achieve an objective.

Determine if needed resources can be provided.

Note whether foreseeable contingencies should be recognized.

Consider the extent of personal support that the subordinate will require for improved performance.

Examine the subordinate's other job responsibilities to see if any are being neglected.

Determine whether additional objectives are appropriate.

Insure that there are neither too few nor too many objectives in total.

Checklist 2—During the Interview

What the Superior Should Do

Select a convenient interview location and stress the meeting's importance. Be prompt and allocate sufficient time for an uninterrupted discussion.

Begin with small talk to set the subordinate at ease; tailor the approach to the individual.

Request that the subordinate explain each objective. Provide ample opportunity for developing insight into the objectives. Listen with interest and understanding.

Ask questions based on prior preparation and new information. Encourage subordinate to respond and ask his [or her] own questions.

Ask how superior can help subordinate do an even better job. Take notes on agreed support.

Avoid placing the subordinate in a defensive position. Keep advice to a minimum. Avoid clashes over personality differences, weaknesses, and past mistakes; avoid arguments.

Provide positive comments whenever possible. Be open about ideas. Seek self-awareness and mutual understanding. Help him [or her] gain insight into his [or her] behavior and its consequences. Concentrate on anticipated performance. Future improvement should be the focus.

See that final objectives meet technical requirements (clear performance standard, completion deadline, and method of checking).

Remember that setting objectives is a joint process. Compromise when possible. Be willing to change viewpoints.

Table 12.3 (continued)

Be willing to resolve serious controversies (in the final analysis, there must be a boss).

What the Subordinate Should Do

Present objectives vigorously.

Be thorough and confident in discussing each objective.

Accentuate the positive by emphasizing what should be done.

Checklist 3—After the Interview

What the Subordinate Should Do

Set up a method for regularly reviewing progress toward objectives.

Renegotiate objectives when major changes occur.

Let the superior know when progress is lagging.

Let the superior know when a lack of co-ordination or resources requires action.

Listen carefully to the superior's responses, both positive and negative. They are important indications of his [or her] priorities and perception of career development.

Insist on final agreement. Do not leave questions hanging in the air. Use the opportunity to bring differences out into the open and resolve them.

What the Superior Should Do

Maintain a historical and current file on each subordinate's objectives.

Develop checks and reminders for using with each subordinate to insure continuous progress.

In a timely and informal way, let subordinates know that he [or she] is interested in week-to-week progress (however, avoid nagging).

It has been pointed out that MBO is not MBO if the supervisor sets the objectives: They must be *jointly* set. Research indicates that a large majority of employees will set higher objectives than their supervisors if given the chance.

Reinforcement of MBO

Research in MBO and behavioral science in general shows that any program works better if it is reinforced regularly. If you receive feedback once a year, it is less effective than quarterly or monthly feedback, as can be easily seen by considering the advantages of weekly grades over a single grade per term.

Reinforcement can take several forms:

·Letters from top executives thanking supervisors for carrying out the MBO program.

·Group meetings during which managers express renewed support for MBO.

·A letter from the president telling employees about MBO's great future.

·Memos from the personnel department offering refresher courses in MBO.

·Periodic performance reviews.
·Counseling sessions when objectives are behind schedule.

Evaluation and Reward

The final step necessary to make MBO work is the review session in which objectives are matched against performance. Guidance on future achievements is given, and the employee is rewarded verbally and in other ways (pay, promotion, etc.) for achieving particular objectives. This is essential to employee motivation.

FORECASTING   The next planning tool to be examined here is forecasting. Forecasting can help managers in performing step 2 of planning: examining the environment for changes.

> **FORECASTING**
> Forecasting is the formal process of predicting future events that will significantly affect the functioning of the enterprise.

As indicated earlier, all the steps in the planning process are interrelated. Setting achievable and challenging objectives requires some knowledge of future events. If the economic forecast predicts depression, does it make sense to raise the firm's sales objectives? Formal forecasting leads a manager to think ahead, to anticipate future threats and opportunities, and this helps improve the quality of his or her planning.

What Do Enterprises Forecast?   In theory an enterprise could (some would say *should*) forecast the future of every aspect of the enterprise, including the following:

·The governmental and economic environment: political climate, economic conditions, new laws and regulations
·Public taste and values affecting the enterprise
·Availability of natural resources and the money supply
·Technological changes
·Demand for the company's product or service
·What the competition is likely to do
·Implications in terms of personnel needs

An enterprise needs to know what the government is doing that may influence it economically. It can get some clues by learning what the government's policy is or is going to be in the areas of taxation (fiscal policy), budgetary actions, monetary policy, and incomes policy (wage and price controls), and in general how the government is influencing business activity. Managers can get this information by listening to government officials and reading periodicals. They can determine its potential by observing key economic indicators: gross national product, unemployment rates, interest rates, and legal changes.

Government policy affects the future availability of money. Various periodicals and reports can provide some insight into the long-term availability of raw materials like petroleum. But it is difficult to predict the availability of substitutes that perhaps have not yet been discovered.

Technological changes can be predicted by monitoring technical publications and making reasonable assumptions about the feasibility of new technologies. The most crucial forecast, however, is the probable future demand for the firm's products and/or services. All the other items depend on this. If whale oil is no longer demanded because people are using Kerosene, its availability is of secondary interest.

Population change can be a major factor in the demand for a product or service. Thus as the number of births has declined relative to the total population, the need for elementary school teachers, books, and classrooms has also declined.

Finally, as a consequence of these various predictions the firm can forecast its need for employees.

Forecasting Techniques

In a formal forecasting procedure the forecaster essentially decides what to forecast, does the necessary research using various techniques, prepares a forecast, and then compares the forecast to later actuality and modifies his or her premises or techniques accordingly. Note that the output of the process is a forecast of future events. This forecast is then used to plan the enterprise's operations.

In more sophisticated forecasting systems several forecasts are prepared. This is called *contingency forecasting.* The forecaster prepares several forecasts with explicit assumptions about major future events. For example, forecast 1 may assume that OPEC will not shut off the supply of oil and that it will raise prices 7 percent per year. Forecast 2 may assume a 12 percent annual rise in oil prices.

Forecasting techniques can be categorized as qualitative, historical/predictive, technological, or causal.

Qualitative Techniques

The qualitative approach uses an informed expert to predict some future occurrence. Sometimes the opinions of many "experts" are summed or weighted to arrive at a single forecast. But whatever quantitative techniques are used, the qualitative approach is always used by the decision maker. He or she must decide to accept, modify, or reject a prediction.

When a decision maker rejects or modifies a quantitative forecast, in effect he or she substitutes his or her judgment for the expert's findings.

Many enterprises have found that certain informed, savvy salespeople can make better predictions of future demand than experts using sophisticated computer models. The salespeople know the customers and their recent product decisions, and these can be adjusted more quickly than an econometric model can be rebuilt.

A more formal qualitative forecast can be prepared by using the Delphi technique. Delphi was originally developed by the Rand Corporation to forecast possible military events. The unit seeking a forecast identifies the experts whose opinions it wants to know. Each expert does not know who the others are. A coordinator mails a description of the subject of the forecast to each expert. The experts make their forecasts and the coordinator summarizes their responses, indicating the average (median) response and the range of the middle 50 percent of the answers. The experts are then asked to reconsider their predictions; if a prediction was not in the middle 50 percent, the expert is asked to give reasons for making that particular forecast. Even without this kind of feedback, studies indicate that these second responses tend to be closer together than the first group of predictions. This process continues (probably through three or four sets of predictions), and then the forecast is made on the basis of the median responses. Sometimes the "extreme" prediction on round 1 becomes the final forecast if the reasons are good. Otherwise (and most frequently) the predictions get closer with each round. The Delphi technique is used to reduce the "crowd effect" in which everyone agrees with "the expert" when they are in the same room.

The key to the success of a qualitative forecast is the choice of experts. It is important to choose people who know the field and who have a history of making good forecasts.

Another type of qualitative forecast is the market survey. The enterprise can poll (in person or by questionnaire) customers or clients about expected future behavior. The University of Michigan asks people about their probable future purchases of cars, for example; political polls ask people about their probable future usage of government services, among other things. Forecasts based on such surveys are effective if the right people are sampled in enough numbers; if those sampled know what they want to do; and if the sample is taken close enough to the time at which the purchase would be made (or the service used, etc.). This method amounts to asking a set of "experts"—consumers or potential consumers—what they will do. If they are indeed "experts," the forecast will be a good one.

Trend Projection

A second approach to forecasting is quantitative projection of historical patterns into the future. The simplest way of using this approach is to project past data into the future. This can be done in a table or put on a graph. For example, if you want to predict future usage of the Xerox machine, examine past usage. If the machine has been used 60 times per day with an average load of 600 pages per day for the past week, you can confidently predict 60 uses and 600 pages per day for tomorrow.

Xerox usage is rarely exactly the same from day to day, however. You can make the forecast more sophisticated by examining the variations around the average. A closer look may indicate a pattern (see Table 12.4). The previous forecast was based on Week IV alone. But a quick look reveals that usage is increasing. So computing *moving* averages is better than taking a simple average. This can be made more sophisticated by using weighted moving averages or exponential smoothing. As you get more data to work with, it becomes easier to visualize if it is incorporated into a graph (see Figure 12.3). The extension of the trend line (which I have drawn in arbitrarily) is the forecast of future usage.

Table 12.4 Xerox Usage				
	Week I	**Week II**	**Week III**	**Week IV**
Monday	54/540	55/560	57/578	64/640
Tuesday	52/510	54/546	53/525	58/560
Wednesday	53/535	53/537	55/560	59/590
Thursday	50/490	51/500	54/540	57/570
Friday	55/570	56/565	58/580	62/635

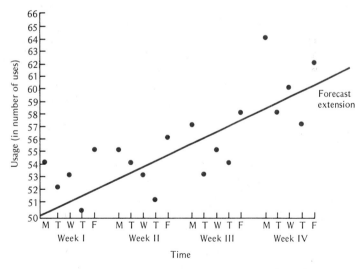

Figure 12.3
Xerox usage.

Look again at Table 12.4. It is clear that Monday and Friday are the busiest days, Wednesday somewhat less busy; Tuesday and Thursday are slower. In predicting things like sales, patterns of this type develop too. They are called *seasonal variations.* In sales of cranberry sauce these variations are dramatic, in soap sales less so. In forecasting the future the period for which the forecast is made can be adjusted to take seasonal variations into account. In really sophisticated trend projections long-run changes such as business cycle changes can be considered as well. Such projections are called *time series analyses.*

There is a big assumption behind trend analysis: that future conditions will be similar to past conditions. This is truer in some businesses (e.g., demand for telephones) than in others (e.g., demand for high-fashion merchandise). The historical method is less useful in cases in which this assumption is less justified.

Technological Forecasting

Some enterprises try to predict changes in technology—for example, what are the possible future uses of the minicomputer? This is called *technological forecasting.* The enterprise can use techniques like Delphi or simply extrapolate present technological trends. For example, if you examine the data on lumens per watt from the first lightbulb in 1880 to the fluorescent bulb in 1940, the trend is almost a straight line upward.

Technological forecasting has not been very successful. Many experts can predict that a change is coming, but predicting *when* it will come is more crucial, and technological forecasting has done a poor job in this area.

Causal Modeling

The most technically sophisticated forecasts use statistical techniques and econometric modeling to forecast the future. This method involves studying the statistical relationship between the factor under consideration (e.g., demand for our product) and another factor (e.g., gross national product). In statistical terms this relationship is called a *correlation.* The closer the correlation comes to "perfect" (1.000), the better we can forecast. If the correlation is good (say, 0.95) and we know the other factor, we can make our forecast on this basis. More sophisticated techniques that involve more than two factors can be used (multiple correlation or multiple regression). Again, the better the predictors and the closer the correlation, the better the forecast.

The most technically sophisticated forecasting technique is mathematical/econometric modeling. Specialists develop a series of equations that relate the essential functions of the enterprise. Once this is done, they can forecast the future by putting the model through a series of "what if" changes. This works *if* the model is accurate and *if* the rest of the environment does not change (and *if* you can afford it).

Thus there are a number of possible forecasting techniques. How do you choose the right one, considering cost, accuracy, and other factors? The information presented in Table 12.5 may serve as a starting point for such a choice.

Who Does the Forecasting? This is a relatively easy question to answer. With regard to qualitative forecasting (but not the Delphi technique), the top managers of most enterprises are expected to forecast the future as it affects the enterprise. In smaller enterprises and most medium-sized ones we find the top executives making qualitative forecasts based on their knowledge of the industry and the economy. Quantitative forecasts are used (along with Delphi) by the largest enterprises and some middle-sized ones.

> **Proposition 12.1.**
> The larger the enterprise and the more complex and volatile its environment, the greater the probability that it will use quantitative forecasting tools.

In the largest and most sophisticated enterprises corporate staff specialists execute the forecasts. Often these forecasters are trained in statistics and economics. In the same enterprises the top executives of decentralized divisions are frequently expected to forecast future sales, personnel needs, and facilities needs, leaving the forecasting of governmental, economic, and money market conditions to corporate forecasters. These forecasts at the division level are usually done by a combination of qualitative and quantitative methods.

The Reality of Forecasting The previous sections on forecasting tended to be normative (i.e., what *ought* to be done). Specifically, I suggested that forecasters have several tools available to make their forecasts more scientific. In fact, however, there is evidence that at present forecasters rely more on qualititive tools than on quantitative ones, and that forecasting is not taken seriously by many top managers because the forecasts have often been wrong or in conflict with each other. This attitude may be seen in the following quote from the *Wall Street Journal:*

> However useful or useless their predictions may be, this can be said unequivocally about economic forecasters: They manage admirably to disagree with one another. A year ago, for example, there was much squabbling over the timing of the business recovery. Optimists correctly forecast that by mid-1975 business would be on the rise. Pessimists wrongly saw no upturn before late in the year. Now with the recovery indisputably under way, forecasters have come up with a new matter to disagree about—the outlook for inflation. Some say that inflation will be relatively moderate and others predict a return to double-digit inflation rates. While imponderables becloud the picture, we suspect that once again the optimists may prove correct.

Table 12.5 Basic Forecasting Techniques (Chambers et al.)

| | A. Qualitative methods | | | | |
	1. Delphi Method	2. Market Research	3. Panel Consensus	4. Visionary Forecast	5. Historical Analogy
Description	A panel of experts is interrogated by a sequence of questionnaires in which the responses to one questionnaire are used to produce the next questionnaire. Any set of information available to some experts and not others is thus passed on to the others, enabling all the experts to have access to all the information for forecasting. This technique eliminates the bandwagon effect of majority opinion.	The systematic, formal, and conscious procedure for evolving and testing hypotheses about real markets.	This technique is based on the assumption that several experts can arrive at a better forecast than one person. There is no secrecy, and communication is encouraged. The forecasts are sometimes influenced by social factors, and may not reflect a true consensus.	A prophecy that uses personal insights, judgment, and, when possible, facts about different scenarios of the future. It is characterized by subjective guesswork and imagination; in general, the methods used are nonscientific.	This is a comparative analysis of the introduction and growth of similar new products, that bases the forecast on similarity patterns.
Accuracy					
Short term 0–3 months	Fair to very good	Excellent	Poor to fair	Poor	Poor

Medium term 3 months–2 years	Fair to very good	Good	Poor to fair	Poor	Good to fair
Long term 2 years and up	Fair to very good	Fair to good	Poor	Poor	Good to fair
Turning point identification	Fair to good	Fair to very good	Poor to fair	Poor	Poor to fair
Applications	Forecasts of long-range and new-product sales, forecasts of margins.	Forecasts of long-range and new-product sales, forecasts of margins.	Forecasts of long-range and new-product sales, forecasts of margins.	Forecasts of long-range and new-product sales, forecasts of margins.	Forecasts of long-range and new-product sales, forecasts of margins.
Data required	A coordinator issues the sequence of questionnaires, editing and consolidating the responses.	As a minimum, two sets of reports over time. One needs a considerable collection of market data from questionnaires, surveys, and time series analyses of market variables.	Information from a panel of experts is presented openly in group meetings to arrive at a consensus forecast. Again, a minimum is two sets of reports over time.	A set of possible scenarios about the future prepared by a few experts in light of past events.	Several years' history of one or more products.
Cost	$2,000+	$5,000+	$1,000+	$100+	$1,000+
	Yes	Yes	Yes	Yes	Yes
Time required to develop forecast	2 months+	3 months+	2 weeks+	1 week+	1 month+
References	North & Pyke, "'Probes' of the Technological Future," HBR May-June 1969, p. 68.	Bass, King & Pessemeier, Applications of the Sciences in Marketing Management (New York, John Wiley & Sons, Inc, 1968).	—	—	Spencer, Clark & Hoguet, Business & Economic Forecasting (Homewood, Illinois, Richard D. Irwin, Inc., 1961).

Table 12.5 Basic Forecasting Techniques (Chambers et al.) *(continued)*

	B. Time series analysis & projection (Quantitative)			C. Causal methods (Quantitative)	
	1. Moving average	**2. Exponential smoothing**	**3. Trend projections**	**1. Regression model**	**2. Econometric model**
Description	Each point of a moving average of a time series is the arithmetic or weighted average of a number of consecutive points of the series, where the number of data points is chosen so that the effects of seasonals or irregularity or both are eliminated.	This technique is similar to the moving average, except that more recent data points are given more weight. Descriptively, the new forecast is equal to the old one plus some proportion of the past forecasting error. Adaptive forecasting is somewhat the same except that seasonals are also computed. There are many variations of exponential smoothing: some are more versatile than others, some are computationally more complex, some require more computer time.	This technique fits a trend line to a mathematical equation and then projects it into the future by means of this equation. There are several variations: the slope-characteristic method, polynomials, logarithms, and so on.	This functionally relates sales to other economic, competitive, or internal variables and estimates an equation using the least-squares technique. Relationships are primarily analyzed statistically, although any relationship should be selected for testing on a rational ground.	An econometric model is a system of interdependent regression equations that describes some sector of economic sales or profit activity. The parameters of the regression equations are usually estimated simultaneously. As a rule, these models are relatively expensive to develop and can easily cost between $5,000 and $10,000, depending on detail. However, due to the system of equations inherent in such models, they will better express the causalities involved than an ordinary regression equation and hence will predict turning points more accurately.
Accuracy **Short term** **0–3 months**	Poor to good	Fair to very good	Very good	Good to very good	Good to very good

Medium term 3 months–2 years	Poor	Poor to good	Good	Good to very good	Very good to excellent
Long term 2 years and up	Very poor	Very poor	Good	Poor	Good
Turning point identification	Poor	Poor	Poor	Very good	Excellent
Applications	Inventory control for low-volume items.	Production and inventory control, forecasts of margins and other financial data.	New-product forecasts (particularly intermediate- and long-term).	Forecasts of sales by product classes, forecasts of margins.	Forecasts of sales by product classes, forecasts of margins.
Data required	A minimum of two years of sales history, if seasonals are present. Otherwise, less data. (Of course, the more history the better.) The moving average must be specified.	The same as for a moving average.	Varies with the technique used. However, a good rule of thumb is to use a minimum of five years' annual data to start. Thereafter, the complete history.	Several years' quarterly history to obtain good, meaningful relationships. Mathematically necessary to have two more observations than independent variables.	The same as for regression.
Cost	$.005 Yes	$.005 Yes	Varies with application Yes	$100 Yes	$5,000+ Yes
Time required to develop forecast	1 day–	1 day–	1 day–	Depends on ability to identify relationships.	2 months+ Yes
References	Hadley, *Introduction to Business Statistics* (San Francisco, Holden-Day, Inc., 1968).	Brown, "Less Risk in Inventory Estimates," HBR July-August 1959, p. 104.	Hadley, *Introduction to Business Statistics* (San Francisco, Holden-Day, Inc., 1968); Oliver & Boyd, "Techniques of Production Control." Imperial Chemical Industries, 1964.	Clelland, de Cani, Brown, Bush & Murray, *Basic Statistics with Business Applications* (New York, John Wiley & Sons, Inc., 1966).	Evans, *Macro-economic Activity: Theory, Forecasting & Control* (New York, Harper & Row, Publishers, Inc., 1969).

Why, then, are we discussing forecasting here? Because I believe formal forecasting procedures will grow in importance. As predictions become more accurate, forecasting will develop into a useful tool for managers involved in planning. Qualitative methods will always be crucial in interpreting data, but in complex situations only quantitative forecasts can provide a useful basis for planning.

QUANTITATIVE PLANNING TOOLS

This final section of the chapter concentrates on some tools and techniques used to develop plans and on the implementation of plans to ensure the achievement of enterprise objectives (step 3 of planning).

Many of the tools described here are also useful in the control function, and some of the tools used in control have implications for planning. In Chapter 17 I describe budgets and budgeting systems such as PPBS. The tools described here are break-even analysis, scheduling, including PERT/CPM, inventory planning, and mathematical, linear, and nonlinear programing.

Break-Even Analysis

One type of plan almost every manager must make is a profit plan. Before going ahead with a decision to add a product, for example, it should be clear that the product will meet the profit objectives of the division or enterprise. One way to develop the profit plan is through break-even analysis.

To understand break-even analysis you need to know the following accounting terms:

Total revenue: the price of the product or service × quantity sold.
Fixed cost: a cost that remains the same regardless of total revenue. Examples include rent, real estate taxes, and insurance on fixed assets.
Variable cost: a cost that increases or decreases along with the number of units produced. Examples include the costs of materials and direct labor.
Total costs: fixed costs + variable costs.

In planning for profits a firm expects to at least break even. That is, total costs must not exceed total revenue. One can compute the break-even point mathematically, or it can be shown graphically. Figure 12.4 is an example of a break-even chart. The company breaks even when it sells 50,000 units; if its sales go above this quantity it makes a profit.

This is a very simple break-even chart. But it portrays the data. Using this chart management can determine whether the firm can sell enough units to break even and plan accordingly. In more sophisticated break-even analyses the cost and revenue lines are not straight lines: They curve to more closely represent the "real world." This may lead to several break-even points as the lines cross several times. Contingency break-even analyses can be prepared for each possible combination of costs and revenues.

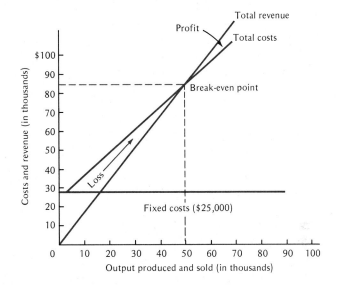

Figure 12.4
Break-even chart.

Break-even charts are rather widely used for a variety of planning purposes. They have several major shortcomings and are more useful for short-range than for long-range planning, since they assume unchanging cost and revenues (which is obviously unrealistic). But they can be helpful planning tools when properly prepared and interpreted by experienced managers.

Scheduling A second frequently used planning method is the *schedule.* Schedules are used at various levels, but I will focus on supervisory scheduling. Essentially, the supervisor divides up the total output he or she needs to produce by time period, then divides that up by the people available to determine the daily or weekly output.

Scheduling methods vary from simple to more or less complex. Among the tools used in scheduling are variations of the chart shown in Figure 12.5. As you can see, the sales supervisor has scheduled the sales staff to cover all four products each week. The salespeople tend to specialize, however; for example, Sam concentrates on products 2 and 3. All products receive some emphasis each week, but during some weeks, because of sales patterns and contests, some products receive greater emphasis (for example, product 3 during week 3). Plans of this nature help the supervisor reach his or her sales objectives, guide the salespeople's efforts, and allow the salespeople to plan their calls and prepare their presentations and materials more efficiently.

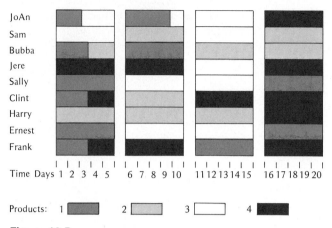

Time Days 1 2 3 4 5   6 7 8 9 10   11 12 13 14 15   16 17 18 19 20

Products: 1 ▒▒▒   2 ▒▒▒   3 □   4 ■■■

Figure 12.5
Sales department schedule.

Although it is an important tool, this kind of scheduling is not very complicated. Another tool, used in more complicated scheduling, is *network analysis.* The best-known network methods are PERT (program evaluation and review technique) and CPM (critical path method). Both use similar approaches, except that CPM relies on one estimate of the time required to get an activity done, while PERT uses more than one estimate. These scheduling aids were developed to help plan complicated projects in which coordination is necessary to get the project completed on time. They are used primarily for complicated planning of nonrepetitive projects.

A PERT plan is prepared as follows:

I Prepare a list of all activities necessary to complete the project.

II Design the PERT network (see Figure 12.6). Relate all the activities to each other in the proper sequence. Perform as many activities concurrently as is practicable.

Figure 12.6
PERT scheduling
plan.

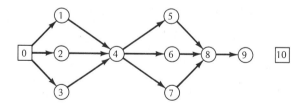

III Estimate the time between "events" (how long will it take to get activity 1 completed before it can link up with activity 4?).

A Three people most familiar with the activity should make three estimates:

1 Optimistic time (the shortest time it could take if everything ran perfectly).

2 Pessimistic time (the longest time it could take if everything went wrong, as Murphy's law predicts).

3 The most probable time.

B Compute a weighted average of these times and insert it into the PERT network. The 10 in the box in Figure 12.6 indicates that the project is expected to take 10 weeks.

IV Carefully monitor the times for each activity, paying special attention to crucial events, such as four and eight, that can prevent later activities from being completed.

Inventory Planning

A technique that has long been used for inventory planning is the economic order quantity (EOQ) model. Its purpose is to ensure adequate inventory on hand at the lowest total cost to the enterprise. It is one of the oldest management science models in use, and it is rather widely used. In effect, this model tries to trade off ordering costs against inventory carrying costs. It does not really consider effectively the cost of orders lost when the company is out of stock.

The EOQ formula involves the following factors:

· *Ordering costs (OC):* the clerical and administrative costs necessary to place an order. They include purchasing agents' time, typists' time, mailing or telephone costs, the paper work involved in getting the order placed, computer time, and the like.

· *Inventory costs (IC):* the direct costs of keeping inventory on hand: spoilage, theft, obsolescence, insurance, cost of space (rent), inventory taxes, and interest on money tied up in inventory rather than in the bank.

· *Demand (D):* the number of items needed per year.

· *Quantity (Q):* the quantity ordered in each order.

OC and IC have opposite cost patterns. The fewer orders you place per year, the lower the OC. The more inventory you carry (because of fewer orders), the higher the IC.

The EOQ formula is

$$Q = \sqrt{\frac{2 \times D \times OC}{IC}}$$

This planning model is helpful to managers to the extent that (1) the manager knows the demand; (2) OC and IC can be computed realistically; and (3) the manager can anticipate delays that may require placing an order earlier than usual—strikes, transportation breakdowns, availability from normal suppliers, and so forth. So EOQ should be used judiciously by an experienced manager.

Programing: Mathematical, Linear, and Nonlinear

A technique developed primarily by the U.S. military after World War II is *linear programing,* which allows the manager to solve planning problems graphically or mathematically. But for this technique to be effective several characteristics must be present:

> **1** The variables we are trying to plan for must be linearly related. That is, if we graph them (A on one axis, B on the other) the relationship is a straight line (thus the term *linear*). This means that we are dealing with *proportional* relationships.
>
> **2** We must be trying to maximize one objective, such as profits, when the variables are scarce or in short supply.
>
> **3** There must be several ways to accomplish the objective—for example, by substituting more of A for B.

The mathematical technique used allows for the solution of several unknowns in a number of simultaneous equations. When a linear relationship is not present, more sophisticated nonlinear techniques such as dynamic programing can be used.

Typical applications of linear programing include scheduling alternative products for production and solving transportation problems. Its usage is limited not only by the costs of calculation but also, and more significantly, by the lack of useful data to plug in for some variables and by the fact that many important variables are nonlinear.

Managerial Implications of Quantitative Tools

The management science tools I have described, as well as many others (queuing theory, simulation, econometric models, etc.), have each burst onto the managerial scene with advocates claiming that they hold great promise for the solution of difficult planning problems. But, as Peter Drucker has repeatedly pointed out, the promise has invariably exceeded the performance. Several groups are to blame for this. Many management scientists are so technical in their orientation that they cannot communicate with the managers who are expected to use these tools. Many managers are afraid of quantitative tools and ridicule them rather than trying to use them. When they do use these tools, they tend to apply them to mundane situations. But the biggest problem of all is that the real-world data frequently are unavailable or do not fit the mathematical functions necessary for the tool to work.

Nevertheless quantitative techniques do hold great promise. As computer usage increases and enterprises develop what Barbara Weaver and Wiley Bishop call effective corporate memories, these techniques will be used more frequently. It is important, therefore, that you learn more about these tools from specialized books or courses.

SUMMARY

In this chapter I described the various tools that can be used by managers and entrepreneurs to plan and make decisions more effectively. The first tool described was effective time management. Time management requires you to take the following steps:

· Find out how your time is spent now (usually by keeping a log or having someone observe your time use).
· Analyze how that time is used by function (personal, telephone, conferences), and analyze activity flow.
· Set priorities and develop a time use strategy by ranking items in order of importance. It is important to block out time for planning.

The next tool described was management by objectives, which is used in steps 1 and 3 of planning. Research studies indicating the conditions under which MBO can be effective were described, as were typical problems often encountered in using MBO. These include inadequate support or communication, inadequate implementation, and insincere commitment by managers.

Forecasting is the formal process of predicting future events that will significantly affect the enterprise's effectiveness. It consists of a set of tools that take care of step 2 of the planning process. The techniques used vary from the qualitative Delphi method to historical analogy to trend projection (extending past trends into the future) to quantitative forecasting using causal models or multiple regression analysis. The more sophisticated forecasting approaches are used—when they are used—by staff experts, and managers are not enthusiastic about them.

The chapter closed with a brief introduction to break-even analysis, scheduling, inventory planning, and programing.

Questions for Review

1. What does a manager gain by planning his or her time?
2. How do you manage your time effectively?
3. What is MBO?
4. How is MBO used in planning?
5. Describe the MBO process.
6. Under what conditions is MBO effective? Why does it work?
7. What are the problems often encountered in using MBO?
8. What is forecasting? What do enterprises forecast?
9. Describe some of the techniques used to forecast future events.
10. Describe what each of the following are and how they might be used to help managers plan:

    break-even analysis
    PERT/CPM
    scheduling charts
    programing

References

Planning the Use of Time

"Teaching Managers to Do More in Less Time," *Business Week,* March 3, 1975.

Cooper, Joseph, *How to Get More Done in Less Time* (New York: Doubleday and Company, 1962).

Lakein, Alan, *How to Get Control of Your Time and Your Life* (New York: Wyden, 1973).

Moore, Leo, "Managerial Time," *Industrial Management Review,* Spring 1968, pp. 77–85.

Sayles, Leonard, *Managerial Behavior* (New York: McGraw-Hill, 1964), chap. 4.

Management by Objectives

Bass, Bernard, and Eldridge, L. D., "Accelerated Managers' Objectives in Twelve Countries," *Industrial Relations,* May 1974, pp. 158–171.

Brady, R. H., "MBO Goes to Work in the Business Sector," *Harvard Business Review,* March-April 1973, pp. 65–74.

Byrd, Richard, and Cowan, John, "MBO: A Behavioral Science Approach," *Personnel,* March-April 1974, pp. 42–50.

Carroll, Stephen J., and Tosi, Henry L., *Management by Objectives: Applications and Research* (New York: Macmillan, 1973).

Chesser, Rodney, *MBO as a Behavioral System,* unpublished D.B.A. thesis, Michigan State University, 1971.

Drucker, Peter F., *Management: Tasks, Responsibilities, Practices* (New York: Harper & Row, 1973), chap. 34.

Hand, Herbert, and Hollingsworth, Thomas, "Tailoring MBO to Hospitals," *Business Horizons,* February 1975, pp. 45–52.

Ivancevich, J. M., "Longitudinal Assessment of Management by Objectives," *Administrative Science Quarterly,* 17 (March 1972): 126–138.

————, "Changes in Performance in an MBO Program," *Administrative Science Quarterly* (1974): 563–574.

Kirchoff, Bruce A., "MBO: Understanding What the Experts Are Saying," *MSU Business Topics,* Summer 1974, pp. 17–21.

Mali, Paul, *Managing by Objectives: An Operating Guide to Faster and More Profitable Results* (New York: Wiley, 1972).

McConkey, Dale D., "MBO—Twenty Years Later, Where Do We Stand?" *Business Horizons,* August 1973, pp. 25–36.

————, "20 Ways to Kill Management by Objectives," *Management Review,* October 1972, pp. 4–13.

Mendelson, Jack, *Management Goal Setting,* unpublished Ph.D. thesis, Michigan State University, 1967.

Meyer, Herbert, French, Emanual, and French, John R. P., Jr., "Split Roles in Performance Appraisal," *Harvard Business Review,* January-February 1965, pp. 125–129.

Migliore, R. Henry, *A Study of Management by Objectives in the Banking and Selected Manufacturing Industries,* unpublished Ph.D. dissertation, University of Arkansas, 1975.

Muczyk, Jon, "A Controlled Field Experiment Measuring the Impact of MBO on Performance Data," *Proceedings, Academy of Management,* 1975.

Schuster, Fred E., and Kindall, Alva F., "Management by Objectives: Where We Stand—A Survey of the Fortune 500," *Human Resource Management,* Spring 1974, pp. 8–11.

Shetty, Y., and Carlisle, Howard, "Organizational Correlates of MBO Program," *Academy of Management Journal,* March 1974, pp. 155–160.

Simon, Herbert, "A Study of MBO in a Professional Organization," *Journal of Management Studies,* February 1975, pp. 1–11.

Sloan, S., and Schrieber, D. E., *Hospital Management: An Evaluation* (Madison: University of Wisconsin, Bureau of Business Research, 1971).

Slusher, Allen, and Sims, Henry, "Commitment Through MBO Interviews," *Business Horizons,* August 1975, pp. 5–12.

White, Donald D., "Factors Affecting Employee Attitudes Toward the Installation of a New Management System," *Academy of Management Journal,* 16, no. 4 (December 1973): 636–646.

Winning, Ethan, "MBO: What's In It for the Individual?" *Personnel,* March-April 1974, pp. 51–56.

Forecasting   Fulmer, Robert, "Forecasting the Future," *Managerial Planning,* 21, no. 1 (July-August 1972).

Kahn, Herman, and Wiener, Anthony, *The Year 2000* (New York: Macmillan, 1967).

Trend Projection   "Forecasting," 1CH9-036, Gen. Mdt., 127R, Intercollegiate Case Clearinghouse, Harvard Business School.

Causal Modeling   Coyle, R. G., "Systems Dynamics: An Approach to Policy Formulation," *Journal of Business Policy,* 3, no. 3 (Spring 1973): 40–48.

The Reality of Forecasting   Chambers, John, et al., "How to Choose the Right Forecasting Technique," *Harvard Business Review,* July-August 1971, pp. 45–74.

Jantsch, Erich, "Forecasting and Systems Approach: A Frame of Reference," *Management Science,* 19, no. 12 (August 1973): 1355–1367.

Simister, L. T., and Turner, J., "The Development of Systematic Forecasting Procedures in British Industry," *Journal of Business Policy,* 3, no. 2 (Winter 1972): 42–54.

Thurstone, Philip, "Make TF Serve Corporate Planning," *Harvard Business Review,* September-October 1971, pp. 98–102.

Managerial Implications of Quantitative Tools   Drucker, Peter, *Management* (New York: Harper & Row, 1974), chap. 40.

Grayson, C. Jackson, "Management Science and Business Practice," *Harvard Business Review,* July-August 1973, pp. 41–48.

Weaver, Barbara, and Bishop, Wiley, *The Corporate Memory* (New York: Wiley, 1974).

CHAPTER 13
DECISION MAKING

13

Learning Objectives

1. To help you understand how decisions are made.
2. To make you a more effective decision maker.

Chapter Outline

What Is a Decision?
Why Study Decision Making?
The Decision-Making Process
Recognition and Definition of the Problem
The Search for Information and Alternatives
Choice
Implementation
Factors Affecting the Decision-Making Process
Factors in the Decision Situation
Significance of the Decision
Time Pressure
Factors in the Decision Environment
Factors in the Decision Maker
The Decision Mode
Individual versus Group Decisions
The Power Dimension of Decision Making
Summary
The Decision
The Decision Maker
Effective Decision Making

Most aspects of management have decision making at their core. Indeed some management experts equate management with decision making.

WHAT IS A DECISION?

> **DECISION**
> A decision is a choice between two or more alternatives.
>
> **DECISION MAKING**
> Decision making is the process of thought and deliberation that leads to a decision.

Each day of your life you make decisions, both personal and professional. For example,

- You decide to go to work rather than sleeping in.
- You decide to hire Sam and not John.
- You decide to purchase item X instead of manufacturing it in your factory.
- You decide to introduce product A into the line instead of product B.

All of these are decisions: choices among alternatives. The process by which you make the decisions is called decision making. Let us briefly review why we are looking at decision making. Then we will examine the who, what, when, where, and how of decision making.

WHY STUDY DECISION MAKING?

There are many reasons for learning about effective decision making. I will discuss only two:

- Managers spend a great deal of time making decisions. Thus if you want to improve your managerial skills you need to learn how to make effective decisions.

- Like it or not, a manager is evaluated and rewarded on the basis of the number and importance of his or her decisions.

The object of learning about decision making is to make better decisions. A decision can be judged as good or bad by either of two standards: (1) it fits the general criteria of a good decision at the time it is made; (2) it turns out to be right later on. It fits the general criteria of a good decision if it shows the following characteristics:

·It is action oriented and pragmatic, clearly indicates what will be done about a problem, and can be communicated.

·It is designed to help achieve the unit's or enterprise's objectives in a reasonable way.

·It was made efficiently. That is, the decision-making process was followed and the resources used (manager's time, computer time, etc.) were reasonable given the potential benefits to the enterprise.

Many managers believe they should be rewarded on the basis of the first standard only (a good decision at the time). But sometimes luck intervenes and decisions that were "right at the time" turn out to be wrong later. And sometimes managers make "wrong" decisions that through luck turn out to be right later. You will be evaluated on the rightness of your decisions by both standards.

Source: © King Features Syndicate, Inc. 1966.

THE DECISION-MAKING PROCESS

Since decision making is in many ways a subcategory of problem solving, we will treat it accordingly. It is generally agreed that the decision process involves the following overlapping and interacting stages:

·Recognition and definition of the problem
·Search for information and decision alternatives
·Choice among the alternatives
·Implementation of the decision

Let us briefly discuss each of these stages.

Recognition and Definition of the Problem

Decision making is hard work. It also exposes the manager to direct evaluation. And managers have other things to do. So a very important question is, When does a decision situation arise, and when is a manager willing to make a decision?

A decision situation arises when the following conditions exist:

·There is a gap between the desired level of achievement and the existing level.

·The gap is large enough to be noticeable and thus deserving of attention.

·The decision maker is motivated to reduce the gap.

·The decision maker believes he or she can do something about the gap.

With regard to the first condition, the gap must be some sort of performance inadequacy in terms of enterprise objectives. For example, if the enterprise objective is a 10 per cent return on investment and it is getting a 6 per cent return, there is a gap.

With regard to the second condition, it must be a large, noticeable gap. A gap between a $9^{1}/_{2}$ per cent ROI and a 10 per cent ROI may not lead to a decision. Some theorists describe minimum thresholds (or gaps) that must be reached before decisions arise. But these minimum thresholds will be influenced by each decision maker's perceptions of what a "large" gap is.

With regard to the last two conditions, the gap must exist in an area that the manager considers important and feels he or she can do something about.

William Pounds' study of 50 managers found that three sources of information led to decisions:

·*Historical data.* When the firm's or unit's performance declined relative to past performance, a decision was likely.

·*Planning data.* When the results did not meet the planned objectives, a decision was likely.

·*Criticism.* When outsiders pointed out problems or when the results were compared unfavorably to those of other similar enterprises, a decision was likely.

Problem finding, as Pounds sees it, is a matter of identifying variances from objectives and defining their causes. The decision maker looks first for single, then for multiple causes.

Problems may be defined in either of two ways:

·Working forward versus working backward. The most common approach is to work forward and project the results that are likely if the problem is not solved; this projection becomes the basis for the decision.

·Means-ends factoring. The manager breaks the problem down into subproblems and solves each one individually. This method is useful only when there are not too many interrelationships among the parts.

Thus the first stage in decision making is to recognize that a problem exists and to define it in terms of probable causes.

The Search for Information and Alternatives

This next stage begins to address the issue of what can be done about the problem. Of course managers begin to think this way *as they are* defining the problem. But the thought and the actions are different. Suppose the problem has been identified as failure to meet profit objectives. Beginning with problem definition, we note that the spread between costs and selling price is beginning to narrow. This can be caused by higher costs or price pressure in the marketplace or both.

At this point we begin to gather more information to determine the cause or causes of the problem and consider alternatives. If after some information is gathered it appears that costs are the culprit, some possible alternatives might be the following:

- Reduce raw material costs through better purchasing methods.
- Reduce raw material costs by producing our own raw materials.
- Reduce production costs by using more efficient machinery.
- Reduce production costs by hiring cheaper labor.

As indicated in Chapter 11, the information search is likely to be verbal, centering on subordinates and friends and acquaintances in the industry. The amount of search necessary depends on whether the problem is a recurrent, routine one or a new one. If it is an old problem, the manager is likely to reinstitute successful past programs and focus on past patterns. If it is a new problem, he or she will search more widely and generate enough alternatives to fit his or her *decision mode.* The decision modes (to be described shortly) are *satisficing* and *maximizing.* A satisficer will look until he or she finds a solution that satisfies his or her needs. Maximizers will generate more alternatives and pick the best one.

Choice

The decision maker then chooses one of the alternatives that have been considered. The choice process may be rational, quasi-rational, intuitive, or some combination of these. (These are discussed later in the chapter.)

Implementation

The effective manager makes sure that he or she has communicated the decision, organized support for it, and assigned resources to implement it. The manager also designs a feedback system to ensure that he or she will be alerted if the decision is not being implemented (a control system) and/or can respond if the desired results do not flow from the chosen alternative.

FACTORS AFFECTING THE DECISION-MAKING PROCESS

This four-step description of problem solving and decision making provides a background for more specific information on how to understand decision making. Obviously, decision making varies; that is, managers make decisions differently depending on several factors:

· Factors in the decision situation
· Significance of the decision
· Time pressure
· Factors in the decision environment (stability vs. volatility)
· Factors in the decision maker
· Decision mode
· Individual versus group decisions
· Politics of decision making

FACTORS IN THE DECISION SITUATION

There are two aspects of the decision situation that affect how managers make decisions: the relative significance of the decision and time pressure.

Significance of the Decision

Thus far we have been discussing decisions as if they were all similar. But this is not the case. All managers make a series of decisions, some very significant, others insignificant, some in between. President Truman's decision to proclaim "National United Appeal Week" and his decision to drop two atomic bombs on Japan could both be called decisions, but, as you suspect, the decision-making process was not exactly the same in each case. The four steps in the process were probably covered in both cases, but the time and methods used certainly varied.

The relative significance of a decision is measured in three ways:

1 *Number of people affected.* For an enterprise with 250 employees a very significant decision might affect 150 or more people; a significant decision could involve 50–149; and minor ones would affect 1–49.

2 *Relative impact of dollar amounts involved.* A decision is significant if it affects the survival or profitability of an enterprise. A $99,000 decision may be minor to a big corporation, but to most family restaurants it would mean the difference between survival and failure.

3 *Time needed.* Significance can also be measured by how long it takes to be educated to make good decisions (in school or on the job). Insignificant decisions might take a week, significant ones ten years.

Some theorists also look at decision significance in terms of the frequency with which the decision must be made. The frequently made decision (such as buying milk) is routine; the infrequently made decision (like getting married) is nonroutine. Routine decisions can have quantitative tools like EOQ or linear programing applied to them.

It seems reasonable to conclude that effective managers will give more time, care, and attention to significant decisions than to insignificant ones. For example, they may not consider more than one or two quickly generated alternatives in making an insignificant decision. But they will consider more alternatives, take more time, and make more detailed calculations in making significant decisions.

Time Pressure A second factor affecting the decision process and the quality of the decision made is how much time the decision maker has in which to make the decision. The deadlines are often set not by the manager but by others. Consider the following decision situations:

> ·You are trying to decide whether to take a job at Enterprise A or at Enterprise B. A's job offer will expire before you know whether B will make you an offer, much less whether it will be a good one.
> ·Firm C offers your enterprise (a job shop foundry) an order that is not very profitable. You think you will get a more profitable offer from D, but C wants to know now whether you want the order or not.
> ·Bank E offers you a loan with a less than ideal set of conditions, but has a taker waiting if you do not accept now. Bank F has not decided whether it will give you a loan or what conditions it will require.

As you can see from these examples, the manager must make decisions in time frames *set by others.* In other cases he or she has more time to seek alternatives and choose among them.

When time pressures are significant, managers or entrepreneurs may be unable to gather enough information or to consider an adequate number of alternatives. Time pressures also affect the decision-making process itself. For example, one study found that managers under time pressure put more weight on negative evidence than on positive evidence and considered fewer factors in making decisions.

Of course these results could differ, depending on the alternatives being considered. For example, several studies indicate the following:

> **1** In making difficult decisions managers take longer to select from two good alternatives and two poor ones than when all four alternatives are good.
>
> **2** In making easy decisions managers take longer to select from four good alternatives than from two good ones and two poor ones.

Perhaps in the first case the job looks difficult when there are four good alternatives and they impulsively pick one, whereas with two bad alternatives they feel competent rejecting two and take their time choosing one of the remaining two. In the second case they feel capable of deciding that it takes longer to compare four alternatives than two.

FACTORS IN THE DECISION ENVIRONMENT

The environment in which the decision maker operates affects how he or she makes a decision. Various terms have been used to describe the environments—*certainty-uncertainty, static-dynamic.* Here I will briefly define these terms and then apply them to show how decision making can vary depending on environmental conditions.

One way to categorize the environment for decision making is to scale it from *certain* to *uncertain* (see Figure 13.1).

Figure 13.1
The certainty-uncertainty continuum.

In a *certain* environment the decision maker knows all the alternatives and the outcomes of each. The decision consists of choosing the alternative that maximizes the outcome desired by the decision maker. In such an environment linear programing, inventory models, and break-even analysis can be used effectively.

In an environment of *risk* we can detect the outcomes of various alternatives. What we do not know is the *probability* of each outcome. So we must appraise the likelihood of each outcome and decide on this basis, taking into account the kind of outcome desired. In risk situations PERT (Chapter 12) and other tools such as statistical quality control and game theory could help in making the decision.

In *conflict-competition* some of the outcomes are under the control of competitors or other groups. Some normative decision theorists believe that game theory might help here, but game theory has not often been used successfully by real-world managers.

In an *uncertain* environment the probabilities of the various outcomes are not known.

There are many other ways of scaling the environment. Robert Duncan, for example, uses two continua: simple-complex and static-dynamic (see Table 13.1):

1 *Simple-complex*   A simple decision environment is one in which the factors to be considered are few in number and located in a few units. A complex environment includes many environmental factors and/or many decision units.

2 *Static-dynamic*   In a static environment the factors to be examined remain basically the same over time or change very predictably and gradually. In a dynamic environment the factors change or the degree of change is drastic.

Table 13.1 Duncan's Scale of the Environment	
Simple	**Complex**
Cell 1: low perceived uncertainty	Cell 2: moderately low perceived uncertainty
Static (1) Small number of factors and components in the environment (2) Factors and components are somewhat similar to one another (3) Factors and components remain basically the same and are not changing	(1) Large number of factors and components in the environment (2) Factors and components are not similar to one another (3) Factors and components remain basically the same
Cell 3: moderately high perceived uncertainty	Cell 4: high perceived uncertainty
Dynamic (1) Small number of factors and components in the environment (2) Factors and components are somewhat similar to one another (3) Factors and components of the environment are in continual process of change	(1) Large number of factors and components in the environment (2) Factors and components are not similar to one another (3) Factors and components of environment are in a continual process of change

Duncan identifies four decision environments (Cells 1–4). He has found that the amount of uncertainty *perceived* by decision makers increases from Cell 1 (least) to Cell 4 (most). He has also found that the static-*dynamic* factor is a more important influence on the decision maker than the simple-*complex* factor. Duncan emphasizes that these are *perceived* differences. What is dynamic to some managers (e.g., in slowly changing fields like heavy metals extraction) might be static to others (e.g., truly dynamic fields like electronics).

Although the concepts are not exactly the same, we will review here four types of environments influencing decison making:

1 *Certainty (Cell 1)*   These decisions are easy to make. The decision maker simply applies the most sophisticated tools described in Chapter 12 and looks at the results. The trouble is, few significant problems fit these characteristics, so managers rarely get involved in them.

2 *Risk (Cell 2)*   A few decisions of this type are made by managers. The manager relies on past experience and tries to draw conclusions from problems that appear similar, then uses the best decision tools available. The number of such decisions made by the manager varies according to the kind of enterprise he or she works for and how he or she perceives the environment. If the manager so desires, these decisions can be made more or less "rationally."

3 *Conflict-Cooperation (Cell 3)*   Many managerial decisions fit this category. Again, the number varies according to the type of enterprise. In fashion merchandising and electronics managers make many decisions of this type; in social security check processing, few. Sophisticated decision-making tools are almost worthless in such cases, but having more than one decision maker may help.

4 *Uncertainty (Cell 4)*   This type of decision requires intuitive decision making, drawing on experience and creative abilities. Some managers contend that most of their decisions fall into this category, since they lack information, time, or the ability to rationally "decide too often." Again, more than one decision maker may be necessary in cases like these.

With regard to the last three categories, decision makers use several strategies to deal with uncertainty:

·*Avoid uncertainty:* Ignore the sources of uncertainty and hope for the best—an uncommon strategy.
·*Reduce uncertainty to certainty:* Pretend that the future will be like the past and decide as in the past. This is a frequent strategy.
·*Reduce the uncertainty in the environment:* Negotiate with the source of uncertainty. Thus if supplies are uncertain the manager may sign a long-term contract (to reduce the uncertainty of future prices, etc.).

By now it should be clear how the degree of uncertainty affects decision-making style and accuracy. We turn next to factors in the person making the decision.

FACTORS IN THE DECISION MAKER

The factors in the decision maker that affect the decision-making process include the decision mode, group versus individual decision making, and the politics of the decision situation.

The Decision Mode

There appear to be three decision styles or *modes:* rational (maximizing), quasi-rational (administrative/satisficing), and intuitive/heuristic.

Rational Decision-Making Theory

This theory has been put forth by some economists, mathematicians, and management scientists. It may be summed up in two statements:

1 The decision maker is a unique actor whose behavior is not only intelligent but rational. The decision is the choice this actor makes, in full awareness, among all feasible alternatives, in order to maximize his or her advantages.

2 The decision maker therefore considers all the alternatives as well as the consequences that would result from all the possible choices, orders these consequences in the light of a fixed scale of preferences, and chooses the alternative that procures the maximum gain.

Those who accept this model believe that individuals are thorough in making decisions and that these decisions are always directly related in a *conscious* way to achieving a particular objective. If you are familiar with the economist's "economic man" seeking to maximize profits, you know this model. The decision maker is said to be "rational" because he or she knows the objectives and makes decisions systematically in order to achieve them.

To make decisions "rationally" a decision maker must

·know his or her objectives and rank them in order of importance.
·know all possible alternative solutions to the decision problem.
·know the relative pros and cons of each alternative.
·always choose the alternative that maximizes attainment of the objective.

This theory is the oldest of the decision theories. It has been criticized on the following grounds:

·The decision maker often is not a unique actor but part of a multiparty decision situation.
·Decision makers are not rational or informed enough to consider all the alternatives or to know all the consequences.
·Research evidence indicates that multiple objectives are involved in decision making. How do you maximize multiple objectives *simultaneously?*

The theory is inadequate philosophically, too. If you accept this theory, you must believe that everything you do is done to maximize pleasure and minimize pain. Philosophical and psychological evidence contradicts this. And no one has ever been able to construct a set of decision rules on the basis of this theory.

The maximizing theory ignores the evidence that decision makers rarely fulfill *any* of the conditions of the theory, much less all four. Decision makers rarely are intelligent enough, have enough time, or take an exclusively rational approach to decision making. Certainty in the environment is also necessary in this theory. So this is an infrequent decision mode.

When decisions are made this way, the management science tools described in Chapter 12 are used. Ultimately, of course, if management decisions can be made fully rational they can be made by computers.

The Quasi-Rational Administrative Satisficing Decision Maker

Many theorists have pointed out the shortcomings of the maximizing theory. They propose that managers make decisions "administratively" or *satisfice*. This decision mode takes the following forms:

· The manager has a general idea of his or her objectives but does not rank these objectives because they are multiple and the ranks are subject to change.
· The manager investigates alternatives only until he or she finds a *satisfactory* solution, that is, one that satisfies the objectives minimally.
· The manager knows some of the pros and cons of the various alternatives but lacks the knowledge, information, and time to learn them fully.
· The manager chooses the first alternative he or she discovers that meets the objectives set. This choice is limited by the decision maker's values, attitudes, abilities, and experience.
· If the manager finds no alternatives that satisfy his or her minimum objectives in a reasonable time, he or she reduces the level of objectives sought and accepts the first alternative that satisfies the new level of objectives.
· The manager adapts his or her decisions from the present decision situation, making small, incremental changes from the present.

Thus the administrative decision maker operates with a simplified model of the world because of *bounded rationality,* or limitations in terms of ability, and time.

The Intuitive-Emotional Decision Maker

The opposite of the rational manager is the intuitive manager who makes decisions based on hunches, gut feelings, ESP, and other creative mechanisms. The intuitive manager may make decisions this way because he or she feels that this is the best way or because the decision problem seems to call for this decision mode. This mode has been called "sudden reorganization"; it has also been referred to as "heuristic." The methods used in intuitive decision making include thinking in analogies, word association and concept association *(synectics),* extrasensory perception, and unfocused thought.

Essentially, in intuitive decision making there is no systematic approach to the decision process. The mind is allowed to focus *generally* on the topic or else is deliberately taken away from the topic by means of analogies and other mechanisms. It is just the opposite of the rational management science approach.

There is evidence that this mode of decision making is often used by creative individuals. Research indicates that the characteristics of these individuals tend to include strong need for independence, high aspirations, very strong ego, high intelligence, self-control, and wide-ranging interests.

This is not to imply that only intuitive decision makers are creative. They just make decisions differently than "rational" decision makers do. Judging from the nature of the theory you would not expect much empirical support for it. This assumption is correct, though case studies of decision effectiveness provide some support.

The ultimate form of intuitive decision making is to let the decision be made by chance. The Coptic Orthodox Church chooses the Patriarch of Alexandria by preselecting several reasonable choices, placing their names in a cup, holding a liturgy, and having a blindfolded child (called the Hand of God) choose one.

The acceptable decision mode in Western business is the rational or administrative mode. In reality, however, many more decisions than managers may care to admit are made using the intuitive mode. "Executive dart boards" have sections labeled "yes," "no," "study it," "merge," "sell out," and so forth. Managers joke about making decisions by throwing a dart at the board, flipping a coin, praying, and the like. So do not be surprised when you find managers making decisions on the basis of hunches—intuitive decisions—especially on very uncertain, volatile questions.

It is likely that most decisions are made using a mix of the rational and intuitive modes. After all, as we saw in Chapter 4, the human decision maker is a mix of these two elements. It appears highly unlikely that most *important* decisions can ever be made entirely rationally or entirely intuitively and be effective in the long run. Three different modes of strategic decision making are described in Table 13.2. The terms *entrepreneurial, adaptive,* and planning correspond to *intuitive, administrative,* and *rational,* respectively. As can be seen, the decision mode chosen leads to major differences in the decision-making process.

Individual Versus Group Decisions   Who should make the decision: an individual or a group? There are several possible patterns:

1 The manager can make the decision alone.

2 The decision can be made by the manager after consulting with others involved.

Table 13.2 Characteristics and Conditions of Three Decision Modes

Characteristic	Entrepreneurial Mode	Adaptive Mode	Planning Mode
Motive for decisions	proactive	reactive	proactive and reactive
Goals of organization	growth	indeterminate	efficiency and growth
Evaluation of proposals	judgmental	judgmental	analytical
Choices made by	entrepreneur	bargaining	management
Decision horizon	long-term	short-term	long-term
Preferred environment	uncertainty	certainty	risk
Decision linkages	loosely coupled	disjointed	integrated
Flexibility of mode	flexible	adaptive	constrained
Size of moves	bold decisions	incremental steps	global strategies
Vision of direction	general	none	specific

3 Those affected by the decision can make the decision as a group (with the manager as one of the group members).

If one pattern of decision making is followed consistently, chances are this is highly correlated with the manager's leadership style. Pattern 1 fits the conservative style, 2 the middle-of-the-road style, 3 the liberal style.

Other managers, especially middle-of-the-road managers, will vary their decision-making patterns according to the nature of the decision and the environment. For example, if the decision is minor and affects few people directly, the manager may follow pattern 1. If the decision is critical but not controversial, the manager may follow pattern 3. The manager may use pattern 2 for critical decisions that are so value and conflict laden that a group may be unable to decide them effectively. Table 13.3 is an excerpt from Table 7.7 showing how leadership style affects decision making.

Since the manager responsible for the decision is always involved, we will first contrast group decision making with individual decision making and then consider consultative decision making.

The topic of group decision making is one of the most emotion laden in the management literature. It follows some of the same arguments that are found in leadership theory, and it has political overtones as well. Those advocating group decisions claim that they are modern and democratic and characterize individual decision making as "reactionary" and "autocratic." This conflict is compounded by a split in research findings. In general, many experiments support group decision making. But many managers' experiences with group decision making and committees in the "real world" do not correspond with the findings of experimental research.

Table 13.3 Styles of Decision Making

Liberal	Middle of the Road	Conservative
Decision making		
Decentralized	General decision description	Centralized
Wherever the knowledge necessary for good decisions is located	Location of most critical decisions	Toward the top of the hierarchy
Responsibility for decisions given to doers	Attitude toward decision-making responsibility	Responsibility for decisions is administrators'
Encourages employees to take reasonable risks	Risk taking	Discourages risk taking by employees
Encourages creative decisions by experimentation, cross-fertilization, and rewards	Creativity (in decisions and tasks)	Expects creativity to come from administrators and filter down

How can we make some sense out of these conflicting findings? To begin with, let us examine the positive case for group decision making. By this we mean that the decision is made by the group, not by the manager consulting with the group and then making the decision. For example, the Roman Catholic Church is headed by a Pope who may consult with his Cardinals but who makes the decision himself. The Orthodox Churches operate differently. Their decisions are made by a Council of Patriarchs. The group spokesman is the Patriarch of Constantinople, whose title is First Among Equals. The Patriarchs of the Greek, Russian, and other Orthodox Churches make decisions *jointly*. The Patriarch of Constantinople explains these decisions to the press, but he is acting as spokesman for the Council.

Advocates of group decision making contend that group decisions have the following advantages:

·*Increased acceptance by those affected* Decisions made by a group more often than not are accepted by the group's members, and they help implement those decisions more readily.

·*Easier coordination* Decisions made by groups reduce the amount of coordination necessary to bring the decision into play.

·*Easier communication* Decisions made by groups reduce the amount of communication necessary to implement the decision.

·*Greater variety of alternatives and solutions considered* Since "several heads are better than one," more different solutions are discussed in a group situation.

·*More information processed* Because many individuals are involved, more data and information can be brought to bear on the decision.

These advantages lead the advocates of group decision making to conclude that group decisions are better—usually defined as *more accurate*—decisions. But group decisions have their negative side, too. The following characteristics are usually cited as disadvantages of group decisions:

·*Group decisions take longer*   There seems to be little doubt that groups are slower to arrive at decisions. One study found that groups took 50 per cent longer than individuals to make decisions. Others have found that most executives believe group decisions waste time.

·*Groups can be indecisive*   Some research indicates that groups may drag on and on and never make decisions because they can always blame other members of the group for lack of progress.

·*Groups can compromise*   Groups can make decisions by compromising. This can lead to decisions that satisfy the "lowest common denominator." It can lead to "groupthink" or conformity to peer pressure.

·*Groups can be dominated*   The highest-status individual, if he or she chooses, can influence the group so that it ratifies his or her choices. This negates the advantages of group decision making.

·*Groups can play games*   Some individuals may use groups to increase their self-image by playing off factions and trying to win "points." This too can negate the advantages of group decision making.

Certain characteristics of group decision making appear to be present at some times and not others. They include:

·*Risk taking*   Some laboratory research indicates that groups are more willing to make risky decisions than individuals. Most executives feel, however, that individuals make more "hard" or "risky" decisions than groups. It appears to me that risk is a function of the values of the decision maker(s) at the time. Some individuals are averse to risk, while others prefer it.

·*Conflict and disagreement*   Sometimes groups cannot make decisions because of internal conflict and disagreements—something that is avoided in individual decision making.

Group decision making can be improved if these guidelines are followed:

·Make sure that the higher-status individuals in the group are secure enough so they will not dominate the group's decision processes.

·Coach the group to avoid personalizing conflicts.

·Make the group uneven in number (preferably five or seven).

·Include specialists from relevant areas.
·Clearly explain the objectives of the decision.

When, then, can groups be effective as decision makers? As indicated at the beginning of the section, group decision making can be functional for some problems, less so for others. If you are convinced that groups can make good decisions, it appears that they are best used when the following conditions are present:

·When accuracy is particularly important. Speed is more important in some situations, accuracy in others. The group is usually more accurate than the individual decision maker.
·When the group is cohesive and works well together with a reasonable amount of conflict.
·When the coordinator facilitates the achievement of group objectives and keeps meetings on schedule.
·When the decision requires a number of skills and experiences unlikely to be present in one person (when *in fact* several heads are better than one).
·When the group is rewarded for making good decisions.

Finally, we have the consultative, middle-of-the-road decision maker. Somewhere between the group and the individual decision maker is the individual who consistently seeks the advice of good advisers before making a decision. The individual recognizes the need for advice and consultation and knows how to pick good advisers for the decision in question. Good advisers combine the technical abilities needed with broad perspective and common sense. Sometimes the best technician is the worst adviser.

But note that the manager then makes the decision alone. This pattern parallels the middle-of-the-road leadership style and is likely to be the most frequently used decision style. But little research has been done on this approach to decision making.

The Power Dimension of Decision Making

If you read the newspapers regularly you realize that politicians and government officials do not always make decisions on the "facts of the case." Sometimes they are influenced by how the voters feel. Decisions in all enterprises may be influenced by what others think. These others can be your boss, peers, stockholders, board members, and the like. Harlan Cleveland, a man with vast experience in making decisions in business, government, and universities, explains this factor as follows:

This increase in the extent to which each individual is personally responsible to others is most noticeable in a large bureaucracy. No one person "decides" anything; each "decision" of any importance is the product of an intricate process of brokerage involving individuals inside and outside the organization who feel some reason to be affected by the decision, or who have special knowledge to contribute to it. The more varied the organization's constituency, the more outside "veto-groups" will need to be taken into account. But even if no outside consultations were involved, sheer size would produce a complex process of decision. For a large organization is a deliberately created system of tensions into which each individual is expected to bring work-ways, viewpoints, and outside relationships markedly different from those of his colleagues. It is the administrator's task to draw from these disparate forces the elements of wise action from day to day, consistent with the purposes of the organization as a whole.

It should be obvious that a manager is not left alone to make decisions. Rather, his or her decisions affect other members of the organization (boss, subordinates, peers, customers, etc.), and these others will sometimes try to influence the manager's decisions.

Management experts have pointed out that elements *outside* the enterprise influence managerial decisions in three ways:

1 They are constraining forces: They limit the number of choices managers consider when making a decision.

2 They interact as individuals with the manager and with the enterprise.

3 The environment is a social system. Other enterprises put pressure on the manager's enterprise and thus influence his or her decisions.

But there are influences *inside* the enterprise too: superiors, peers, and others. How do these forces influence managerial decisions? Enterprises have been described as coalitions of interest groups and individuals. In a *coalition* two or more people or social units seek to maximize their portion of the payoff from a particular decision. No single alternative will maximize the return to all participants; no one has sufficient power to control the outcome unilaterally; and no one must be included in every winning combination. This concept stresses the political aspects of decision making. Members of the enterprise do not participate equally in this process. Managers are the most powerful members of the coalition, but some managers are more powerful than others.

In a coalition government two or more political parties share power and the government stays in office as long as they get along. Enterprises are like that. The manager needs the cooperation of others to do the job. These others therefore influence his or her decisions. And the more power the others have, the more they influence those decisions.

Sometimes it is not a good idea to give in to political influences. There are times when a certain action is politically undesirable. In such cases the effective manager makes his case, tries to persuade others, and then makes the best decision possible under the circumstances. In other cases fundamental issues are not involved, so the manager does the politically desirable thing in order to build support that can be drawn upon when conflicts arise.

But you do not avoid "politics" by working only for nongovernmental enterprises. Politics exists in all organizations, though some are more political than others. Managers should seek the enterprise with the amount of politics they can live with (some managers thrive on it and seek out the most politicized enterprises). In any case political realities influence some managerial decisions, and the typical manager has to live with this fact.

SUMMARY   In this chapter I defined a decision as a choice among two or more alternatives. Decision making was defined as the process of thought and deliberation that leads to a decision. Decision making is important because managers spend much of their time making decisions and because they are evaluated on the effectiveness of their decisions.

The decision-making process consists of four overlapping and interacting stages: recognition and definition of the problem, search for information and decision alternatives, choice, and implementation of the decision. Decision making is complicated by three sets of factors: the decision situation (significance and time pressures); the decision environment (stability vs. volatility, uncertainty vs. certainty); and the decision maker (mode, politics, and individual vs. group decisions). No real understanding of the decision-making process is possible unless entrepreneurs and managers realize the significance of these factors.

We also discussed briefly the styles of decision making, ranging from liberal, group-oriented, decentralized decision making to conservative, individual decision making. It is clear that as conditions vary along these dimensions the decision-making process takes different forms. This variability is illustrated in Table 13.4. The most challenging decisions are in Cells L, I, and K (in that order). The least difficult ones are in Cells A, B, and D. These rankings will vary according to the ability of the manager to deal with time pressures, political pressures, or uncertainty. The decision-making process will differ correspondingly. With regard to decision-making mode, although it is interesting to speculate on the relative effectiveness of the rational maximizing style versus satisficing and other styles, it appears more useful to recognize that the effective manager adapts his or her style to the decision under consideration, as stated in Proposition 13.1.

> **Proposition 13.1.**
> The effective decision maker chooses a decision-making mode to fit the decision environment, and the decision maker's abilities and personality. Rarely will effective decision makers use the same decision style for all decisions.

In effect we now come across the contigency approach again. In this approach decision-making patterns vary according to the decision and the decision maker.

The Decision As discussed in earlier sections, there are all kinds of decisions and decision environments. A contingency theorist would say that the effective decision maker will use rational decision making for routine operating problems, quasi-rational decision making for administrative problems, and creative or intuitive decision making for strategic problems.

The irony of decision making is that the more significant the decision, the more likely it is to be nonroutine, which means the harder it is to use the rational/maximizing mode. Usually the best that can be done is to gather more information, seek more advice, and think more about the decisions in an *attempt* to be rational.

The Decision Maker The second point a contingency theorist would make is that the decision approach varies with the decision maker. As we saw in Chapter 4, some managers have greater ability (innate and learned) than others, and managerial attitudes and personalities also differ. Those who are oriented toward management science make decisions differently than those who are more intuitive in their outlook. Bayard Wynne and Gary Dickson showed that the decision styles of 32 middle managers were related to personality differences. There are also cultural differences in how decisions are approached, as Bernard Wilpert and Frank Heller showed in their study of British and German companies.

Finally, there are differences between older and younger, experienced and inexperienced managers. Ronald Taylor studied 79 Canadian managers in 80 units. He found that

·older executives sought more information before making a decision.
·older executives took longer to make their decisions.
·older executives were more accurate in their decisions.
·older executives were more willing to change their decisions if conditions warranted a change.

Table 13.4 Impact of Four Decision Factors on Decision Making

Degree of Time Pressure and Lack of Timely Information

	Light	Medium	Heavy		
Certainty (Cell 1)	A	B	C	Light	
					SIGNIFICANCE OF DECISION
Risk (Cell 2)	D	E	F	Moderate	
Conflict/ Cooperation (Cell 3)	G	H	I	Heavy	
				Very Heavy	
Uncertainty (Cell 4)	J	K	L	Heavy	

(Left vertical axis: Degree of Certainty)

Light   Medium   Heavy

Degree of Political Pressure

The same conditions were true of more experienced executives: the more experienced they were, the slower, more accurate, and more flexible they were. Thus they came closer to the rational model than younger, less experienced managers.

Effective Decision Making

The following guidelines are intended to help you make decisions more effectively:

·*Avoid crisis decisions.* Some of the worst decisions are made in crisis conditions. If at all possible (and it is not always possible), try to anticipate a future crisis and decide ahead of time what you will do if that crisis comes up. If you could not anticipate the crisis, try to put the decision off to a time when you are less emotionally involved than at the time of the crisis. Many people would still be married if they had not decided to divorce during a fight. Some managers would still be working if they had not quit in the middle of a crisis. Upon reflection, these may have been the right decisions —or they may have been very wrong.

·*Set a time limit for making decisions.* More failures result from no decision at all than from making the wrong one. Making decisions is not easy. One way to avoid indecisiveness is to allocate a reasonable amount of time for thinking about gathering information for a decision. For some decisions this may be half an hour, for others a year.

·*Once you have made a decision, stop worrying about it.* If you have gathered the necessary data, thought about it, and consulted with advisers, make the decision and go on to other important matters. You have other decisions to make. If you worry about each decision you will never make the next one, and you will become indecisive. As we will see in Chapter 17, you can set up control and feedback systems to alert you if problems develop.

·*Do not expect to be right all the time.* Some potentially good decision makers fail because their expectations are too high. They expect to be right 100 per cent of the time. When they are wrong once, they are paralyzed the next time they have to make a decision.

This completes our three-chapter unit on planning and decision making. We turn now to another managerial skill: organization.

Questions for Review

1. What is a decision? Give some examples of decisions you have made lately.
2. What is decision making? What are the steps in the decision-making process?
3. Why is decision making important?
4. What are the factors in the decision situation? Give examples of each and explain how they affect the decision-making process.
5. What are the factors in the decision environment? How do they affect decision making?

6. What are the decision modes? Describe each in detail. Which is best? When?

7. In what ways do the politics of the situation affect decision making?

8. "Individuals make better decisions than groups. A camel is a horse designed by a group." Comment.

References

What Is a Decision?

MacCrimmon, Kenneth, "Managerial Decision Making," in Joseph McGuire, ed., *Contemporary Management* (Englewood Cliffs, N.J.: Prentice-Hall, 1974).

Oldenquist, Andrew, "Choosing, Deciding, and Doing," *Encyclopedia of Philosophy* (New York: Collier Macmillan, 1967).

Shull, Fremont, Delbecq, Andre, and Cummings, L. L., *Organizational Decision Making* (New York: McGraw-Hill, 1970), chap. 1.

Why Study Decision Making?

Shull, et al., pp. 12–18.

Thompson, Victor, *Modern Organization* (New York: Alfred Knopf, 1961).

The Decision Making Process

Eilon, "What Is a Decision," *Management Science,* 16, no. 4 (December 1969): B172–B189.

Hyman, Ray, and Anderson, Barry, "Solving Problems," *Science and Technology,* September 1965, pp. 36–41.

MacCrimmon, op. cit.

Pounds, William, "The Process of Problem Finding," *Industrial Management Review,* Fall 1969, pp. 1–19.

Factors in the Decision Situation

Kiesler, Charles, "Conflict and Number of Choice Alternatives," *Psychological Reports,* 18 (1966): 603–610.

Pollay, Richard, "An Experiment into Factors Affecting Decision Difficulty as Measured by Decision Time" (Lawrence, Kans.: TIMS College of Organization, October 1, 1969), Mimeograph.

Wright, Peter, "The Harrassed Decision Maker," *Journal of Applied Psychology,* 59, no. 5 (1974): 555–561.

Factors in the Decision Environment

Duncan, Robert, "Characteristics of Organizational Environments and Perceived Environmental Uncertainty," *Administrative Science Quarterly,* 17, no. 3 (September 1972): 313–327.

Jurkovich, Ray, "A Core Typology of Organizational Environments," *Administrative Science Quarterly,* 19 (1974): 380–394.

MacCrimmon, op. cit.

Morris, W. T., *Management Science: A Bayesian Introduction* (Englewood Cliffs, N.J.: Prentice-Hall, 1968).

Tersine, Richard, "Organization Decision Theory: A Synthesis," *Managerial Planning,* 21, no. 1 (July-August 1972): 18–24, 40ff.

Factors in the Decision Maker/Rational Decision-Making Theory

Gremion, Catherine, "Toward a New Theory of Decision Making," *International Studies of Management and Organization,* 2, no. 2 (Summer 1972): 125–141.

Kepner, Charles, and Tregoe, Benjamin, *The Rational Manager* (New York: McGraw-Hill, 1965).

Miller, G. A., "The Magical Number Seven, Plus or Minus Two: Some Limits on our Capacity for Processing Information," *Psychological Review,* 63 (1956): 81–97.

Peterson, C. R., and Beach, L. R., "Man as an Intuitive Statistician," *Psychological Bulletin,* 68 (1967): 29–46.

The Quasi-Rational Administrative Satisficing Decision Maker

Bailey, John, and O'Conner, Robert, "Operationalizing Incrementalism; Measuring the Middles," *Public Administration Review,* January-February 1975, pp. 60–66.

Clarkson, Geoffrey, "A Model of Trust Investment Behavior," in Richard Cyert and James March, eds., *A Behavioral Theory of the Firm* (Englewood Cliffs, N.J.: Prentice-Hall, 1963).

March, James, and Simon, Herbert, *Organizations* (New York: John Wiley and Sons, 1958), esp. chap. 6.

Newell, Allen, and Simon, Herbert, *Human Problem Solving* (Englewood Cliffs, N.J.: Prentice-Hall, 1972), esp. pp. 789–867.

Simon, Herbert, *Administrative Behavior* (New York: Macmillan, 1961), esp. chaps. 1, 4, 5.

Soelberg, Peer, "Unprogrammed Decision," *Proceedings, Academy of Management,* 1966, pp. 3–16.

Soelberg, Peer, "Unprogrammed Decision Making," *Industrial Management Review,* 8 (1966): 19–29.

The Intuitive-Emotional Decision Maker

Bolen, James, "Interview: Al Pollard," *Psychic,* December 1974, pp. 12, 14–18, 56ff.

Crosby, Andrew, *Creative Thinking as a Process* (London: Tavistock, 1968).

Dean, Douglas, "Testing for Executive ESP," *Psychic,* December 1974, pp. 21–25.

Durkin, H. E., "Trial and Error, Gradual Analysis, and Sudden Reorganization," *Archives of Psychology,* no. 210 (1937): 44–84.

Ghiselin, Brewster, *The Creative Process* (Berkeley: University of California Press, 1961).

Gordon, William, *Synectics* (New York: Harper & Row, 1961).

Guilford, J. W., *The Nature of Human Intelligence* (New York: McGraw-Hill, 1964).

Mintzberg, Henry, "Strategy Making in Three Modes," *California Management Review,* 1975:44–53.

Osborn, Alex, *Applied Imagination* (New York: Charles Scribner's Sons, 1953).

Reynolds, William, "Problem Solving and the Creative Process," *MSU Business Topics,* Autumn 1967, pp. 7–15.

Torrance, E. P., "The Minnesota Studies of Creative Behavior: National and International Extensions," *Journal of Behavior,* 1 (1967): 137–154.

Individual Versus Group Decisions

Collaros, P., and Anderson, L., "The Effects of Perceived Expertness Upon Creativity of Members of Brain-Storming Groups," *Journal of Applied Psychology,* 53 (1969): 159–163.

Davis, James, *Group Performance* (Reading, Mass.: Addison-Wesley, 1969).

Delbecq, Andre, et al., *Group Techniques for Program Planning* (Chicago: Scott, Foresman, 1975).

Hall, Jay, et al., "The Decision Making Grid," *California Management Review,* 7, no. 2 (1964): 43–54.

Janis, Irving, *Victims of Groupthink* (Boston: Houghton Mifflin, 1972).

Lorge, Irving, et al., "A Survey of Studies Contrasting the Quality of Group Performance and Individual Performance, 1920–1957," *Psychological Bulletin,* 55, no. 6 (1958): 337–372.

Maier, Norman, *Problem Solving Discussions and Conferences* (New York: McGraw-Hill, 1963).

Marquis, Donald, "Individual and Group Decisions Involving Risk," *Industrial Management Review,* Spring 1968, pp. 69–75.

Webber, Ross, "The Relation of Group Performance to the Age of Members in Homogeneous Groups," *Academy of Management Journal,* 17, no. 3 (1974): 570–574.

The Power Dimension of Decision Making

Blankenship, L. Vaughn, and Elling, Ray, "Organizational Support and Community Power Structure: The Hospital," *Journal of Health and Human Behavior,* 3 (1962): 257–269.

Boddewyn, Jean, "External Affairs," *Organization and Administrative Sciences,* 5, no. 1 (1974): 67–111.

Cleveland, Harlan, "Dinosaurs and Personal Freedom," *Saturday Review,* February 28, 1964.

Cyert, Richard, and March, James, *A Behavioral Theory of the Firm* (Englewood Cliffs, N.J.: Prentice-Hall, 1963).

Gerwin, Donald, "Towards a Theory of Public Budgetary Decision Making," *Administrative Science Quarterly,* 14, no. 1 (March 1969): 33–46.

Hage, Jerald, "A Strategy for Creating Interdependent Delivery Systems to Meet Complex Needs," *Organization and Administrative Sciences,* 5, no. 1 (1974): 17–43.

Hall, Richard, and Clark, John, "Problems in the Study of Interorganizational Relationships," *Organization and Administrative Sciences,* 5, no. 1 (1974): 45–65.

Mindlin, Sergio, and Aldrich, Howard, "Interorganizational Dependence," *Administrative Science Quarterly,* 20 (September 1975): 382–392.

Sayles, Leonard, *Managerial Behavior* (New York: McGraw-Hill, 1964).

Van de Ven, Andrew, et al., "Frameworks for Interorganizational Analysis," *Organization and Administrative Sciences,* 5, no. 1 (1974): 113–129.

Zeitz, Gerald, "Interorganizational Relationships and Social Structure," *Organization and Administrative Sciences,* 5, no. 1 (1974): 131–139.

Summary

Glueck, William, "Decision Making: Organizational Choice," *Personnel Psychology,* 27 (1974): 77–93.

McKenney, James, and Keen, Peter, "How Managers' Minds Work," *Harvard Business Review,* May-June 1974, pp. 79–90.

Mintzberg, op. cit.

Nystrom, Harry, "Cognitive Styles in Management and Reaction to Organizational Stagnation" (Uppsala: University of Uppsala, September 1974), Mimeograph.

Taylor, Ronald, "Age and Experience as Determinants of Managerial Information Processing and Decision Making Performance," *Academy of Management Journal,* 8, no. 1 (March 1975): 74–81.

Wilpert, Bernard, and Heller, Frank, "Decision Making in German and British Companies" (Brussels: International Institute of Management, 1974), Mimeograph.

Wynne, Bayard, and Dickson, Gary, "Experienced Managers' Performance in Experimental Man-Machine Decision System Simulation," *Academy of Management Journal,* 18, no. 1 (March 1975): 25–40.

CHAPTER 14

ORGANIZATION: DESIGN OF JOBS

Learning Objectives

1. To help managers understand how job design affects productivity and employee satisfaction.
2. To realize the different characteristics that lead to a variety of jobs.
3. To understand how different job designs affect employees differently.
4. To learn the different strategies of job design.
5. To help managers choose a job design strategy that fits the characteristics of the enterprise, its employees, and the environment.

Chapter Outline

A Job is Not Just a Job
Why Do Jobs Differ?
How Do Jobs Differ?
Styles of Job Design
Specialized Jobs
Job Rotation with Specialized Jobs
Job Enlargement
Job Enrichment
Job Design Combinations
Which Strategy Should You Use?
Job Rotation and Combination
Job Enlargement Versus Work Simplification
A Contingency Approach to Job Enlargement
Job Enrichment Strategy
Summary

With this chapter we begin a three-chapter unit on effective organization of work. Chapter 14 introduces this unit by focusing on the basic building block of organization: the job. Essentially, this chapter describes what a job is and how it can be designed. Chapter 15 discusses the factors that affect organization structure and coordination such as environmental factors (e.g., volatility) and other factors such as size. Chapter 16 concentrates on effective structuring and coordination.

JOB DESIGN
Job design consists of specifying the content of the job, the methods used on the job, and how the job relates to other jobs in the organization.

Topics important to understanding effective job design have been discussed earlier in the book and will be referred to in this chapter. You learned something about job design for managers and entrepreneurs in Chapters 2 and 3. This chapter focuses on job design by managers for employees.

Note that effective job design includes technical aspects (the work to be done) and human aspects (the employees who do the work). So references will be made to individual differences in attitudes, abilities, and motivation (Chapters 4 and 5) as these affect job behavior. And since employees rarely work alone, the work group (Chapters 6 and 9) affects job behavior too.

A JOB IS NOT JUST A JOB
We can and often do place people in categories to help in making decisions. But we are aware of differences *within* the categories. Likewise, we can and do categorize jobs. For example, the government classifies jobs into the following categories: professional and technical, managerial, clerical, sales, craftspeople, operators, service, laborers. But there are many differences *within* these categories. Look at Table 14.1, which is an excerpt from the government's *Dictionary of Occupational Titles*. Did you know there were so many different food-processing jobs?

You may believe that most employees work on assembly lines where the machine controls the pace of work. Perhaps you see these jobs as Charlie Chaplin stereotyped them in *Modern Times*. In fact, however, only 2–5 percent of the labor force works at such jobs, and the percentage is dropping.

But it is not enough to tell you that jobs differ. The sections to follow will examine why and how they differ. Let us look at the whys first.

Why Do Jobs Differ? The ways jobs are designed vary because of at least five factors:

·The employees available to do the task
·The economic resources of the enterprise
·Technology and working conditions
·The influence of unions and government agencies
·The managerial philosophy toward job design

First, jobs cannot be designed to require greater ability than the employees or potential employees can offer. For example, if the only people available for the job are unskilled, the job must be simplified to meet their skill levels or the employees must be trained to meet minimum skill levels. Thus if the present job design requires a skilled carpenter and none is available, the manager can train an unskilled person to do the whole job or break the job down into steps that a partially trained carpenter can perform. The opposite situation will be discussed in some detail later in the chapter. That is, if the job design has reduced the job skill level so far that it does not fully utilize the employee's abilities, redesign of the job may be called for. Some jobs require strong, positive work attitudes to be done well. Others require less positive attitudes. If few people with training and positive work attitudes are available, this may cause more difficulty in educational job design than it would for toy assemblers. In sum, the supply of people available for jobs can affect job design if there are major differences between abilities and job requirements.

Second, the resources available to the enterprise and the economic environment also affect job design. Managers in some organizations have all the resources they need and the best equipment and working conditions available. Other managers must make do with very little. A manager of a research lab at IBM's research facility in New York has a different set of job design challenges than a foreman in one of the old steel factories in Gary, Indiana, or an almost-played-out coal mine in eastern Kentucky. Thus if new equipment is available to improve job design but the enterprise cannot afford it, job redesign will not take place. Maybe the enterprise cannot afford the services of a well-trained job design engineer. Other enterprises can. In theory we could improve the design of every job. But in practice the money may not be available.

Third, job design is affected by the technology of the enterprise and/or its industry. The technology consists of the equipment, work flow, tools, techniques, and procedures used to complete the work. The technology of a government office may include forms and typewriters. The technology of an oil refinery includes complicated automated machinery and computers as well as typewriters and forms.

Generally we can scale technology from craft work to machine tending to assembly lines to automation. The craftsperson pursues his or

Table 14.1 Machine-Tending Job Titles: Selected Industries

52
520. **Processing, Food and Related Products Mixing, Compounding, Blending, Kneading, Shaping, and Related Work**
520.885 Batter Mixer (bake. prod.)
Batter Mixer (food prep., n.e.c.)
Blender (bake. prod.)
Blender-Machine Operator (oils & fats)
Blender, Snuff (tobacco)
Blending-Line Attendant (tobacco)
Blending-Tank Tender (flav. ext. & sirup)
Brine-Mixer Operator, Automatic (can. & preserv.)
Broth Mixer (bake. prod.)
Cake Former (oils & fats)
Cake Stripper (oils & fats)
Candy-Maker Helper (confection.) I
Candy Puller (confection.)
Casing-Fluid Tender (tobacco)
Casting-Machine Operator (confection.) I
Casting-Machine Operator (daily prod.)
Tray Casting Machine Operator (dairy prod.)
Chopping-Machine Operator (slaught. & meat pack.)
Churn-and-Milk Man (oils & fats)
Churner (oils & fats)
Cocoa-Powder Mixer Operator (choc. & cocoa)
Confectionery-Drops-Machine Operator (choc. & cocoa; confection.)
Cooker, Casing (tobacco)
Cooler Man (sugar)
Dividing-Machine Operator (bake. prod.)
Dough-Brake-Machine Operator (bake. prod.)
Dressing-Machine Operator (tobacco)
Feed Blender (corn prod.)
Feed Mixer (grain & feed mill.)
Feeder Operator, Automatic (grain & feed mill.)
Flaking-Roll Operator (cereal)

Sausage Maker (slaught. & meat pack.)
Sausage Mixer (slaught. & meat pack.)
Sirup Maker (flav. ext. & sirup)
Snuff-Blending-Machine Operator (tobacco)
Spice Mixer (food prep., n.e.c.)
Starchmaker (corn prod.)
Starch-Treating Assistant (corn prod.)
Stuffer (slaught. & meat pack.)
Bulk-Sausage-Stuffing-Machine Operator (slaught. & meat pack.)
Molder, Meat (slaught. & meat pack.)
Sweet-Goods-Machine Operator (bake. prod.)
Tumbler Tender (food prep., n.e.c.)
Yeast Cutter (food prep., n.e.c.)

521. **Separating, Crushing, Milling, Chopping, Grinding, and Related Work**
521.885 Almond-Blancher Operator (nut process.)
Almond-Cutting-Machine Tender (nut process.)
Almond-Grinding-Machine Operator (nut process.)
Almond Huller (agric.)
Bleacher, Lard (oils & fats; slaught. & meat pack.)
Bolter (grain & feed mill.)
Breaking-Machine Operator (chew. gum)
Brine-Tank-Separator Operator (can. & preserv.)
Cellarman (vinous liquors)
Centrifugal-Station Operator, Automatic (sugar)
Centrifuge Operator (can. & preserv.; oils & fats)
Centrifuge Operator (corn prod.)
Centrifuge Operator (dairy prod.)
Centrifuge Operator (food prep., n.e.c.)
Clarifier (corn prod.; oils & fats)
Clarifier (vinous liquors)
Clarifier Operator (sugar)

521.885 Con.
Grinder Tender (grain & feed mill.)
Hasher Operator (slaught. & meat pack.)
Honey Extractor (food prep., n.e.c.)
Hopper Attendant (sugar)
Hop Strainer (malt liquors)
Hot-Wort Tankman (malt liquors)
Key Washerman (can. & preserv.)
Laboratory Miller (grain & feed mill.)
Linterman (oils & fats)
Liquor-Bridge Operator (sugar)
Liquor-Grinding-Mill Operator (choc. & cocoa)
Lye-Peel Operator (can. & preserv.)
Mash-Filter Operator (malt liquors)
Meat-Grading-Machine Operator (nut process.)
Meat Grinder (slaught. & meat pack.)
Milk-Powder Grinder (dairy prod.)
Miller (malt liquors)
Millman (sugar)
Millman Helper, Distillery (distilled liquors)
Mill Operator (corn prod.)
Monitor-and-Storage-Bin Tender (grain & feed mill.)
Nut-Grading-Machine Operator (nut process.)
Panman (oils & fats)
Peanut Blancher (nut process.)
Potato-Peeling-Machine Operator (food prep., n.e.c.)
Powder-Mill Operator (sugar)
Pressman, Head (corn prod.)
Pressman, Head, Feed House (corn prod.)
Press Operator (distilled liquors)
Processor, Grain (grain & feed mill.)
Pulper Tender (can. & preserv.)
Pulp-Press Man (sugar)
Raisin Washer (food prep., n.e.c.)
Riddler Operator (tobacco)
Rough-Rice Tender (grain & feed mill.)
Saccharate-Filtration Man (sugar) I

Flour Blender (grain & feed mill.)
Flour Mixer (grain & feed mill.)
Grain Mixer (grain & feed mill.)
Green-Coffee Blender (food prep., n.e.c.)
Icing Mixer (bake. prod.)
Kettleman (chew. gum)
Lozenge-Dough Mixer (confection.)
Lump-Machine Operator (tobacco)
Mash Grinder (dairy prod.)
Mill Feeder (grain & feed mill.)
Mingler Operator (sugar)
Mixer (food prep., n.e.c.)
Mixer-and-Blender (food prep., n.e.c.)
Mixer, Chili Powder (food prep., n.e.c.)
Mixer, Dry-Food Products (food prep., n.e.c.)
Mixer Operator (choc. & cocoa)
Mixer Operator (flav. ext. & sirup)
Mixer Operator (salt production)
Mixer, Whipped Topping (food prep., n.e.c.)
Mixing-Machine Operator (can. & preserv.)
Mixing-Machine Operator (food prep., n.e.c.)
Mixing-Tank Operator (oils & fats)
Pellet-Mill Operator (grain & feed mill.)
Plug Shaper, Hand (tobacco)
Potter (tobacco)
520.885 Presser (corn prod.)
Con. Pressman (macaroni & rel. prod.)
Press Operator, Meat (slaught. & meat pack.)
Pretzel-Twisting-Machine Operator (bake. prod.)
Refined-Sirup Operator (sugar)
Rolling Machine Operator (confection.)

Clean-Rice Grader and Reel Tender (grain & feed mill.)
Cocoa-Bean Cleaner (choc. & cocoa)
Cocoa-Butter Filter Operator (choc. & cocoa)
Cocoa-Room Operator (choc. & cocoa)
Coffee Grinder (food prep., n.e.c.)
Corn Grinder (food prep., n.e.c.)
Corn-Grinder Operator, Automatic (corn prod.)
Cracking-and-Fanning-Machine Operator (choc. & cocoa)
Crushing-Machine Operator (vinous liquors)
Cutter, Frozen Meat (can. & preserv.)
Cutting-Machine Operator (confection.)
Egg-Breaking-Machine Operator (slaught. & meat pack.)
Electric-Sorting-Machine Operator (nut process.)
Extractor-Machine Operator (flav. ext. & sirup)
Feed Grinder (grain & feed mill.)
Filterman (vinous liquors)
Filterman, Head (corn prod.)
Filterman Helper (corn prod.)
Filterman Helper, Head (corn prod.)
Filterman, Jelly (can. & preserv.)
Floorman (grain & feed mill.)
Fruit-Press Operator (can. & preserv.; flav. ext. & sirup)
Gluten-Settling Man (corn prod.)
Grader Man (agric.)
Granulating-Machine Operator (tobacco)
Granulator Man (sugar)
Grated-Cheese Maker (dairy prod.)
Grinder Operator (cereal)

Sand-Screen Operator, Automatic (tobacco)
Screen-Room Operator (sugar)
Separator Man (corn prod.)
Separator Operator (glue)
Separator Operator, Shellfish Meats (can. & preserv.)
Sheller (nut process.) II
Sieve-Grader Tender (can. & preserv.)
Slice-Plug-Cutter Operator (tobacco)
Slicing-Machine Operator (bake. prod.)
Slicing-Machine Operator (slaught. & meat pack.)
Smoking-Tobacco-Cutter Operator (tobacco)
Snuff Grinder (tobacco)
Snuff Screener (tobacco)
Soft-Sugar Operator, Head (sugar)
Sorting-Machine Operator (can. & preserv.)
Spice Cleaner (food prep., n.e.c.)
Spice Miller (food prep., n.e.c.)
Stemmer, Machine (tobacco)
Stem-Roller-or-Crusher Operator (tobacco)
Strip-Cutting-Machine Operator (tobacco)
Stripper-Cutter, Machine (macaroni & rel. prod.)
Sugar-Chipper-Machine Operator (corn prod.)
Sugar Grinder (sugar)
Sugar-Mill Operator (tobacco)
Sugar Presser (corn prod.)
Thresher (tobacco)
Tipple-Machine Man (corn prod.)
Utility Man (grain & feed mill.)
Winterizer (oils & fats)

her work with simple tools. The machine tender services the machine. (This can develop into trouble shooting and emergency jobs.) The assembly line employee helps keep the line moving. The employee in an automated factory reads gauges, services the machine, and handles emergencies. To the extent that the job design is determined by technology, there is less flexibility in job design. It is easier to redesign craft work than assembly line work; it is easier to redesign order processing in a restaurant than at an automated factory.

Fourth, organizations outside the enterprise can affect job design. Although you might expect unions to influence job design, they have not done so as yet. The government, however, influences job design by requiring that minimum safety standards be met.

The final factor influencing job design is managerial philosophy. Some managers do not feel that this is an important area of responsibility. This attitude affects how much time and effort they put into it. If they do little in this area, jobs will simply evolve, sometimes more or less efficiently, sometimes poorly. On a plant visit, for example, I observed several poorly designed jobs on the assembly lines. Some workers were working too hard because of poor placement of tools. When I pointed this out to the management, the response was, "It's always been that way. Besides, it's not an important job." To the degree that management's philosophy is to try to design effective jobs for all employees, job design will be reexamined frequently.

How Do Jobs Differ? On many of the dimensions of job variance we can measure objective differences (e.g., the number of tools used to do the job) as well as *perceived* differences (some employees perceive more variety in the *same* job than others do). Let us consider the factors leading to job variance.

Variety

Jobs differ in the degree of variety within the job. A job has variety if the number of motions performed is great and/or if the number of operations performed is great. A job is narrow and routine if just a few things are done over and over. Variety allows more creativity; requires more education, training, and experience; and provides more prestige.

One can design the job of processing welfare claims so that one person interviews the client, another checks the form, and another fills out vouchers: This provides little variety. Another way to design the job is to have a single official handle the whole claim process: This offers more variety. Greater variety contributes to the fulfillment of Maslow's recognition and self-actualization needs (and McClelland's need for achievement). Recent technological changes often provide greater opportunity for job variety.

Wholeness

A job can provide a meaningful, whole experience or a very fragmented experience. Consider salad cooks. You can design the job so that one cook washes the materials, another chops them up, a third mixes them, and a fourth puts them in bowls. Or all four cooks can wash, chop, mix, and bowl them. The latter is a "whole" job and is more meaningful. The cook can receive feedback: "We got a lot of compliments on your salads today." Whole jobs take more training and experience and provide more prestige.

Erich Fromm contends that without variety and wholeness in their work people become destructively aggressive because splintered jobs lead to boredom. His argument is that boredom (a state of insufficient inner productivity) leads people to provide themselves with substitute satisfactions. For many people leisure is no substitute for work satisfaction, Fromm says, so they turn to sadistic or destructive behavior. Fromm's analysis and others provide the rationale for job rotation, job enlargement, and job enrichment (to be described shortly). Wholeness helps fulfill Maslow's recognition and self-actualization needs and McClelland's need for achievement.

Human Interaction

Some jobs are designed so that people work closely together and can enjoy social interaction and develop friendships (remember "peach time" in Chapter 6). Other jobs are designed so that people must work in teams. For example, you can design the painter's job so that one painter works on one side of a house and another on the opposite side. Another way is to team them up and paint the same side at the same time. (The equipment available can affect this aspect of job design.) Thus jobs can be designed to help fulfill the need for affiliation (social need), or this need may be ignored.

Freedom and Control

Jobs vary in the amount of freedom an employee has in doing the job. Some jobs give the employee the freedom to decide what to do, when to do it, and how to do it as long as the job gets done by a set time and within cost and quality limits. Thus the employee controls job pace, tools used, and other factors as long as he or she does not hold up another person's work and serves the clients in a reasonable time.

On the other hand, a job can be programed. A salesperson, for example, can be told when to start work, which calls to make when and in what order, what sales pitch to use, and so on. Or you can say, "Sue, by Friday you need to call on your customers in Arkansas. Here's the sales budget. If you need help, call me." One design uses control; the other, freedom. Freedom on the job helps fulfill the need for power and for achievement.

Responsibility/Autonomy

Closely related to freedom is responsibility. If the employee is given freedom he or she must be made responsible for the results. This is often called *autonomy.* Freedom does not work unless Sue knows that if she does not call on the Arkansas customers by Friday there will be adverse consequences. This serves the same motivational needs as freedom.

Degree of Physical Exertion/Fatigue

Jobs differ in the amount of physical effort they require. In a series of jobs ranging from bookkeeper to mail carrier to automobile assembler to ditch digger, each requires a greater expenditure of physical energy. The fact is that although many people believe job fatigue is not a problem today, this is not the case. In many factories heavy physical labor is done *without rest periods.* Or there are "assigned" rest periods but breakdowns "use them up." In one restaurant I studied recently the dishwashers worked from 2 P.M. to midnight. Their "rest periods" consisted of taking out the garbage twice during the evening. This kind of work leads to great fatigue. Many workers say they come home so exhausted that all they can do is flop down in front of the TV and fall asleep at 8:30 P.M. Thus too much fatigue at work reduces the satisfaction of physiological needs.

Job Environment

Certain physical conditions on the job may be unpleasant for workers, and their absence can make the work more pleasant. These conditions include excessive heat, particles in the air, noise, darkness, smells, and the like. The more of these that are present, the less pleasant most workers will find the work.

Location of Work

Work can be performed outside or inside. Construction workers, for example, work outdoors. This is not pleasant when it is 28 degrees and snowing. Work can also be performed in one place or many. Many people work in a single work location, even a small area (assembly line workers, bank tellers, medical technologists). Others move about for social and other reasons (outside salespeople, weights and measures supervisors, union business agents, entertainers).

Times of Work

There is great variety in work times. Some jobs call for long hours of relatively less taxing work, others for shorter periods of intense work. Some provide for continuous work (auditors), and in others the work is intermittent (tax accountants).

There has been much experimentation recently with hours of work. Some firms have shifted to a four-day week of ten-hour days and a three-day weekend, although unions may oppose this plan as a violation of overtime patterns. Other enterprises are experimenting (generally successfully) with "flexitime." Under this system everyone is at work during a "core" time (say, 9–3) and can choose when to start and stop before and after that time (7–9, 3–5, etc.).

Sex Stereotyping

An aspect of job variance that is largely a thing of the past is sex stereotyping. For example, primary school teachers were women; nurses were women; college professors and doctors were men. Even in jobs that were less sex stereotyped, certain jobs (often managerial jobs) were reserved for men. For example, in a study of travel agencies, which supposedly are not sex stereotyped, Lewis Mennerick found that managers were male and sales people female. Men ran the most prestigious agencies, women the least prestigious ones.

I hope sex stereotyping will continue to diminish. For surely we need more male teachers as role models for fifth-grade boys. And women make good physicians, as is evident in the Soviet Union. Of course some jobs will probably continue to be performed primarily by one sex because of physical differences. Few women are likely to prefer consistent heavy physical labor (coal mining, ditch digging) or work in conditions that might be difficult for women (selling insurance in clients' homes at night). But most jobs would benefit from the elimination of sex stereotyping so that those who choose to "break the mold" will not be considered odd.

Summary

Figure 14.1 profiles the differences between two jobs: receptionist and traveling salesperson. Note the substantial differences between these jobs: They are almost opposites. Employees should be matched with jobs that fit their abilities and preferences. Imagine the difficulties that would arise if a person whose qualifications and characteristics fit the salesperson's job was placed in the receptionist's job!

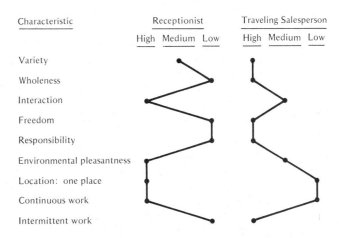

Figure 14.1
Differences
between jobs.

STYLES OF JOB DESIGN

In this section I will describe four job design styles: specialized jobs, job rotation with specialized jobs, job enlargement, and job enrichment. I will also discuss how these styles can be combined.

Specialized Jobs

Jobs get more specialized by a process called *work simplification.* Those who design jobs in this way break complete jobs down into small, "simplified" subparts. We have already encountered the welfare employee whose job is to check forms, the salad cook who washes the lettuce, and the salesperson whose day is programed. Now suppose that your enterprise makes chairs. The production jobs could be designed as follows:

1 Each worker makes the entire chair.
2 Each worker makes a major subpart (the arms, the seat, the back).
3 Each worker makes one complete part (the left leg).
4 Each worker performs a few operations on one subpart (runs the sanding machine on left legs).

The work simplification approach tends to design jobs like job 4. This is not a matter of random choice, however. Job design engineers believe this kind of design yields production efficiencies such as the following:

· Less skilled (and lower-paid) workers can perform these jobs.
· More workers are available to do these jobs.
· As a person does the same job over and over, he or she gets better at it and can produce more products of sufficient quality in the same time.
· The work gets done sooner. (Can you imagine one man producing a missile guidance system?)
· Productivity increases because the employee does not lose time shifting from one task (and pattern of action) to another.

The job design engineer uses time and motion study, ergonomics, and other tools to find the best way to do these specialized jobs. (*Ergonomics* is the study of ways to make work less taxing physiologically.) The engineer designs the total workplace, including tool design and arrangement, conveyors, and the like. He or she designs jobs using appropriate movements and the best man-machine engineering to reduce fatigue and improve output. The engineer also fits the job to the employee, taking into consideration the employee's physical and mental characteristics.

Job Rotation with Specialized Jobs

Job rotation is not a way to design a job but a system of arranging work, usually designed by the work simplification method. In the job rotation system each employee has a simplified job to which he or she is normally assigned. Periodically the employee shifts to a different job. Job rotation has several advantages:

> · *Flexible assignments.*   Employees learn other jobs so they can fill in for absent employees. Thus this system requires more training than work simplification. It also requires more complex scheduling than work simplification.
> · *Easier staffing.*   Jobs that involve heavy physical exertion or exposure to unpleasant working conditions may be difficult to staff if the job is held by the same person for eight hours a day. A person might be able to stand it for only four hours. Maybe two employees could rotate jobs every two hours.
> · *Less boredom and monotony.*   Simplified jobs can become boring, and this sometimes reduces productivity and satisfaction. Rotation of jobs provides some variety and is less costly to implement than job enlargement.

An example of this approach to job design is provided by Alcan Aluminium of Canada, which enhances its white-collar jobs by rotating people onto task forces, using several promotional ladders, (one for managers, one for scientists, etc.) and experimenting with career planning that includes extensive job rotation as part of the plan.

Job Enlargement   A number of management specialists are disturbed by the work simplification approach to job design. They believe that the better-educated workforce of the 1970s and 1980s deserves better jobs, which they define as jobs that are meaningful to educated workers in democratic settings. These analysts attribute work alienation, which they believe leads to poor-quality work, absenteeism, turnover, and low productivity, to work simplification. Their solution: *job enlargement.* Job enlargement reverses the flow of work simplification. Jobs that are redesigned using the job enlargement approach find the employee performing more tasks of the same nature and with a lengthened work cycle. This leads to greater diversity in the job. Thus in work simplification 25 workers perform repetitive tasks, each taking 30 to 60 hundredths of a minute. In job enlargement the tasks are regrouped. For example, each worker may assemble a motor in 14 minutes. The operations may still be rudimentary, but job enlargement gives the work variety, wholeness, and meaning or significance.

It is not easy to enlarge a job *well*. The tasks that are combined must be of different types so as not to overtax some parts of the body. And one must not combine so many tasks that the employee cannot remember them all. To use this approach successfully job designers must combine varied operations with task stability and moderate use of memory.

In effect, job enlargement attempts to increase the variety and wholeness of the job. Later in the chapter we will evaluate the studies of job enlargement. Note, however, that although job enlargement has received a lot of attention, fewer than 20 percent of the largest companies use it, and the percentage of other firms using it is probably much lower.

Job Enrichment

Some job redesigners advocate *job enrichment.* Job enrichment tries to increase responsibility/autonomy and freedom. In this approach employees are given enough information so that they can make decisions about the job—the pace of work, for example. This can be reinforced by eliminating supervisory jobs so that employees know *they* must make these decisions. The employees become responsible for functions done by others in work simplification jobs. In the more advanced forms of job enrichment "autonomous" crews are responsible for organizing the work of the crew as well as for the unit's results. This movement ultimately leads to employee participation and industrial democracy, as discussed in Chapter 7. Its advocates contend that job enrichment activates the employee's need for achievement and for power.

Source: Reprinted by permission of Newspaper Enterprise Association.

Job Design Combinations

Thus far the four job design systems have been described separately. As indicated earlier, a major factor in the choice of a job design approach is managerial preferences and leadership style. Thus it seems reasonable to scale the methods as follows:

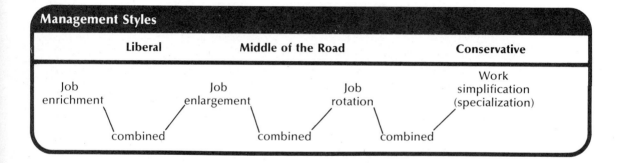

Table 14.2 (excerpted from Table 7.7) illustrates how job design is affected by leadership style.

Table 14.2 Job Design and Management Styles		
Liberal	**Middle of the Road**	**Conservative**
Design of Jobs		
Enlarged and enriched		Specialized and simplified
Broadly defined		Narrowly defined
Either not used or very general	Job descriptions	Used; clear and specific

Thus conservative leaders who are not getting optimum results from specialized jobs may add job rotation. It is unlikely, if not impossible, to combine work simplification with job enrichment. If the results of job rotation are positive, the manager may become "middle of the road" and begin to combine job rotation with job enlargement.

Advocates of job enlargement, if they find it useful, often begin to combine it with job enrichment. The beliefs and styles of the manager influence job design style if technology and cost considerations are conducive to movement toward job enlargement and job enrichment.

WHICH STRATEGY SHOULD YOU USE?

The first issue we encounter in answering this question is that of the criteria to be used in deciding on a strategy. If the criterion is costs/efficiency, you may make one decision. If it is job satisfaction and product quality, you might make another. Probably most of us want low costs and *reasonable* job satisfaction. With this in mind, let us look at the results of the research in this area.

Job Rotation and Combination

With regard to two possible design strategies it is hard to answer the question of which to use when. There is no good study on combination strategies and only one study on job rotation of which I am aware. F. G. Miller and his associates studied a small manufacturing plant. They examined five employees who were rotated through several jobs. Sometimes an operator worked the same job eight hours a day for several days in a row. At other times he was rotated through several jobs in the same day. Miller examined the productivity of the employees for two nonconsecutive months using sophisticated statistical techniques. The data indicate that job rotation was more productive than working the same job all the time. In fact from the data one can determine how long the employee should work each job before being rotated to maximize efficiency.

The authors also claim that the employees were more satisfied when they were rotated, but they provide no data to support this claim. Moreover, there is no background on the workers themselves (age, education, background, etc.), so it is difficult to determine whether these characteristics were important. Job rotation appears to offer good opportunities for variety and flexibility. But too little research has been done to say much on this subject.

Job Enlargement Versus Work Simplification Most of the research on design strategy has concentrated on work simplification and job enlargement (see Table 14.3). The following conclusions can be drawn from these studies:

Table 14.3 Summary of Research Studies on Job Enlargement/Work Simplification

Factor	Pro-Work Simplification or Anti-Job Enlargement	Anti-Work Simplification Pro-Job Enlargement
Employee attitudes/ job satisfaction	Hulin; MacKinney, et al.; Levitan; Smith and Lemm; Vroom; Blood and Hulin; Hackman and Lawler; Kennedy and O'Neill; Wyatt, et al.; Hall; Kahn; Smith; Rizzo, et al.; House; Larke; Ivancevitch and Donnelly	Gooding; Terkel; Walker and Marriott; Sheppard and Herrick; Shepard; Davis (1966); Mahler; Goldthorpe, et al.; Stewart; Janson; Ford; Jacobs; Herrick; Richleff; Walton; Walker; Biggone and Stewart
Quantity of output	Marks; Schoderbek; Maier; Wyatt, et al.; Kennedy and O'Neill; Hackman and Lawler; Blood and Hulin; Vroom; Smith and Lemm	Walton; Biggone and Stewart; Walker; Ford; Richleff; Jacobs; Herrick; Elliott; Guest; Goode; Plisson; Kilbridge
Quality of output		Stewart; Ford; Richleff; Jacobs; Walton; Biggone and Stewart; Walker; Herrod; Kilbridge
Absenteeism		Davis; Mahlin; Ford; Richleff; Jacob; Herrick; Walton; Biggone; Walker
Turnover	Turner and Michlette	Davis; Walker; Kilbridge; Mahler; Sheppard and Herrick; Ford; Walton; Biggone and Stewart; Richleff; Jacobs; Herrick
Accidents/safety (mental and physical)		Weintraub

1 The evidence both supports and detracts from work simplification and job enlargement. Work simplification is by far the more frequent method of job design. Sometimes it leads to good results, sometimes not. Job enlargement does not always lead to good results either.

2 In general, the studies supporting job enlargement are less well done in terms of research methodology than those whose results are unfavorable to job enlargement.

3 The best way to explain the pro and con results is to attribute them to individual differences in employees.

4 It is not known what percentage of employees really desire job enlargement. There is much evidence on both sides. For one thing, there are cultural differences in employee preferences. Given a choice of more variety, more responsibility, and more autonomy, different groups of workers indicate different preferences. No one factor accounts for the biggest increases in satisfaction.

5 It is impossible to say at present who gains most from job enlargement: employees or management. There is not enough evidence.

It is interesting to consider what has *not* been studied as well as what has been studied. There is little research on the result of job enlargement among employees with different abilities. Do semiskilled workers react differently to job enlargement than unskilled employees? One would suspect from the research thus far that their attitude would be more positive, but this is not known for sure.

Little research has been done on the external factors influencing job design. Studies have found, however, that American and Norwegian unions oppose job enlargement and that Swedish unions support it.

Most research indicates that managers are quite pragmatic: They will use job enlargement if it works. But so far the research is mixed. Very little research has been done on other factors—such as economic resources, technology, and working conditions—that may influence this decision. It has been argued that these factors probably operate against job enlargement. Among the reasons given are the following:

1 Managers are likely to find that the results of job enlargement are short-lived. Just as better wages may produce short-run increases in productivity, so job enlargement results are likely to drop off after a while.

2 Technology limits job enlargement. Most successful experiments with this approach have involved products with small components, few tools, and fairly lengthy assembly times. Job enlargement is very difficult to do in cases involving larger products such as cars, refrigerators, and engines. In such cases the most efficient method is a moving assembly line.

3 The unions and most employees are not excited by job enlargement, and this keeps managers from using it.

4 Most jobs that are increasing in number are not easy to enlarge.

These include secretarial, retail sales, restaurant, bookkeeping, and office-cleaning jobs. Most applications of job enlargement are in declining sectors.

The major early studies of job enlargment were very encouraging. Companies like Maytag, IBM, Sears, and Detroit Edison, as well as civil service workers, seemed to respond to job enlargement. Usually, however, the response was higher job satisfaction and lower turnover, less absenteeism and higher product quality. Rarely did productivity *really* improve over the long run. An exception to this was at Maytag, but even there the cost savings were not great. Other researchers found *lower* productivity after job enlargement, and even in cases with positive results it could rarely be proved that the gains were not caused by factors other than job enlargement. There is good reason to believe the "Hawthorne effect" was responsible for some of these results. After all, job design is only one of the possible influences on job satisfaction. Moreover, there is little evidence that work simplification *always* leads to monotony or boredom and thus to dissatisfaction. And studies have shown that some aspects of job enlargement increase employee satisfaction and some aspects lead to *decreased* satisfaction. Finally, job enlargement can also lead to problems of role conflict and ambiguity, and this helps explain why relatively few employers have embraced job enlargement.

A Contingency Approach to Job Enlargement

When, then, should you consider using job enlargement? Since job enlargement can cost more, is not supported by the unions, and can be difficult in view of technological considerations, when can it be used effectively?

To begin with, job enlargement should not be the only change that occurs. If you enlarge the job, the employee will see it as more important and will expect other rewards (such as a raise or promotion) to reinforce the job enlargement.

Several earlier researchers tried to answer the question, Which employees should be offered job enlargement? Their research revealed that the results were best for employees working in rural areas or those trained in rural areas. But this is an insufficient answer.

Other experimenters have found that job enlargement is likely to work for employees who subscribe to the Protestant ethic attitude that work is important. They respond well to both job enlargement and job enrichment.

Two groups of researchers have tried to specify *when* job enlargement is likely to work on the basis of individual differences and organizational and job characteristics. William Reif and Robert Moncza summarize the research to date (including their own studies). They present no new evidence, but they do present a comprehensive list of the conditions in which job enlargement is feasible. Table 14.4 summarizes this information, using terms introduced earlier in the chapter. Unfortunately, the authors do not discuss factors outside the enterprise such as union and government influences. They also broaden the term *managerial philosophy* somewhat. Nevertheless they have provided us with a useful summary of the factors operating for and against job enlargement.

J. Richard Hackman and his associates have also attempted to put job enlargement into proper perspective. They spent three years trying to determine *when* job enlargement works in order to offset the propaganda implying that "job enlargement will solve all your problems." They experimented with 1000 employees on 100 different jobs in firms like Travelers Insurance and Roy Walters and Associates and found that the following conditions must be present for job enlargement to work:

1 The cause of the productivity problem must be low motivation and job satisfaction, not something like poor production control.

2 The job must be low in motivation potential. The authors computed a "motivation potential score" (MPS). If this score was low, the next step was taken. The score was computed using the following formula:

$$MPS = \frac{(\text{skill variety} + \text{task identity} + \text{task significance})}{\times \text{ autonomy} \times \text{feedback}}$$

Note: Autonomy is in fact a job enrichment factor, Hackman's work deals with both job enlargement and job enrichment.

3 The next step was to analyze which factors were causing the low score: variety, identity, significance, autonomy, or feedback. It was determined how costly it would be to redesign for this factor.

4 The employees had to be ready for job enlargement. This factor is diagramed in Figure 14.2. Again we come across individual differences. Only if the employee is "high-growth" oriented should job enlargement go foreward.

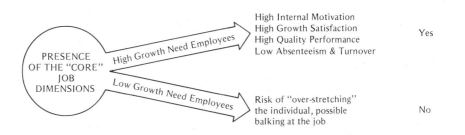

Enlargement: Individual differences

Job enlargement

Figure 14.2
The go-no go decision.

[1]Skill variety, task identity, task significance, autonomy, feedback.

PRESENCE OF THE "CORE" JOB DIMENSIONS

High Growth Need Employees

Low Growth Need Employees

High Internal Motivation
High Growth Satisfaction
High Quality Performance
Low Absenteeism & Turnover

Yes

Risk of "over-stretching" the individual, possible balking at the job

No

Table 14.4 Conditions Favorable and Unfavorable to Job Enlargement (Reif and Moncza; rearranged by author)

		Favorable	Unfavorable
A. Employees available to do the task	1. Personality	Workers are self-confident and achievement oriented.	Workers lack self-confidence and have low achievement drives.
	2. Work attitudes, values, and beliefs	Workers are positively oriented toward the work ethic and willingly accept change.	Workers do not readily identify with the work ethic and fear change.
	3. Position in need hierarchy	Workers are concerned primarily with fulfilling higher-level needs (esteem, autonomy, and self-actualization).	Workers are concerned primarily with fulfilling lower-level needs (physiological and security).
	4. Knowledge and skills	Workers are capable and motivated to develop their talents to the fullest.	Workers have little interest in developing new knowledge and skills or lack the capacity to do so.
	5. Work group characteristics	Younger, more highly educated.	Little education, unsatisfying work experiences.
B. Resources and economics of the enterprise	1. cost	Low dollar investment in technology.	High dollar investment in technology.
	2. State of technology	Technology is available to improve the quality of work life.	Technology is not capable of dealing with problems of worker dissatisfaction.
	3. Organization's ability to apply technology	High, in both a technical and a managerial sense.	Low.
C. Technology and working conditions	1. Technical dominance	Workers, not technology, are primarily responsible for output and quality levels.	Emphasis on equipment, machines, and systems in job design; technology primarily dictates the quantity and quality of work.
	2. Variety	Little variety exists because of the way jobs are structured, but there is potential for variety because there are a large number of parts, tools, and controls that can be manipulated, and the work pace, physical location, and prescribed operations can be modified to meet individual requirements.	The work environment is such that little potential for increasing variety exists.
	3. Autonomy	Inputs to the job and methods of doing the job (procedures, sequence, pace, etc.) do not have to be totally dictated	The production/operation system defines work flow, methods, pace, and sequence, and changes cannot be made

Factor	(Positive)	(Negative)
	to the worker by the production/operation system.	without seriously affecting scheduling, line balance, worker efficiency, and output levels.
4. Interaction	The opportunity exists for people to work together as a team; that is, the job naturally requires the coordination of tasks or activities among several workers.	The job can be performed best by an individual working alone.
5. Knowledge and skill	The job can be made more challenging by adding additional or more complex tasks, and workers are capable of meeting more demanding job requirements.	It would be inefficient to incorporate new tasks into the existing job structure and/or increase worker proficiency.
6. Responsibility	It is feasible to reduce reliance on the "only one way to do the job" approach to performing work and making work-related decisions.	It would be economically or technically unrealistic to allow variability in the way job situations are handled.
7. Task identity	The job can be redesigned so that the worker can see the value of his or her work in terms of its contribution to the total work effect.	An increase in the scope of the job would reduce the likelihood that the individual could complete the task efficiently.
8. Feedback	It would not be difficult to redesign the control system to provide workers with information about their job performance on a regular basis.	Information cannot be readily provided to workers because of cost and data collection problems.
9. Pay	The wage payment plan is not based solely on output.	Workers are paid under a straight piece-work wage plan.
10. Working conditions	Working conditions, along with other hygiene factors, are perceived as satisfactory by most workers.	Working conditions are considered to be unsatisfactory by most workers.
11. Cycle time	Short, with potential for expansion.	Longer cycle times would interfere with other, interrelated work activities.
D. Managerial philosophy toward job design		
1. Management philosophy	Concerned with the utilization of human resources to the mutual benefit of the individual and the organization.	Concerned primarily with production; view job enrichment only as a means of increasing output.
2. Attitude toward change	Positive.	Negative.
3. Leadership style	Democratic, employee centered.	Authoritarian, task centered.
4. Superior-subordinate relationships	Built on liberal set of assumptions about work behavior.	Built on conservative set of assumptions about work behavior.
5. Union-management relationships	Open, supportive.	Closed, antagonistic.

If these four conditions are met, then job enlargement should be implemented, as Hackman suggests in five "implementing concepts" (see Figure 14.3).

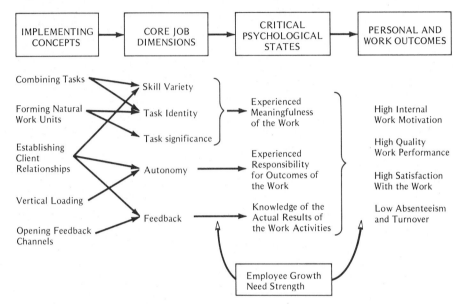

Figure 14.3
How implementing concepts can lead to positive outcomes (Hackman et al.).

Job Enrichment Strategy The final strategy is job enrichment: increasing the responsibility and autonomy of the employee. Much less direct research has been done on this concept, but so far the findings are more consistent. The results can be summarized briefly as follows:

> **1** If the employees feel that work is important, job enrichment will reduce turnover, absenteeism, and accidents and improve employee performance and satisfaction.
>
> **2** If the employees do not have a positive attitude toward work, job satisfaction will decrease, especially among blue-collar workers.

Although not much research has been done in this area, it appears that job enrichment affects primarily supervisors and some white-collar workers. Hackman's four-step procedure is useful in examining job enrichment as well as job enlargement.

SUMMARY Job design consists of specifying the content of the job, the methods used on the job, and how the job relates to other jobs in the system. Once a job is designed, the manager (at least in larger enterprises) writes up job descriptions and job specifications. These are used in hiring employees to fit the jobs.

It was shown that jobs differ because of perceptual and environmental differences such as variety, wholeness, amount of human interaction, amount of freedom or control, responsibility and autonomy, amount of fatigue, environmental unpleasantness, location of the work, and time of work.

Four job design styles were described: work simplification/specialization (at one extreme), rotation of specialized jobs, job enlargement, and job enrichment (at the other extreme). Certain combinations of these four styles are possible. The contingency approach indicates that conservative managers tend to prefer simplified jobs or job rotation, liberal ones job enrichment and/or job enlargement.

Next the research on the effectiveness of job enlargement versus work simplification was presented. The small amount of research on the other styles was also noted. A major conclusion of this research is that no style is clearly superior to all the others.

People are always looking for simple solutions to complex problems like productivity. One "easy way" is job enlargement or job enrichment. After all, one look at some jobs shows that the employees are bored, and this sometimes accounts for lower productivity.

In this chapter we examined the factors that can influence job design. Most enterprises have gained a great deal in efficiency from the use of work simplification techniques. Properly used, these techniques can reduce employee fatigue and speed up output without damaging the employee physically.

Work simplification becomes a necessity in competitive industries like textiles. Sometimes the expensive technology required to do the job gives management no alternative but to use work simplification. Sometimes unions prefer it and management knows no other way or does not wish to change its ways. This can lead to boredom (which results in higher turnover, absenteeism, and similar consequences of low job satisfaction). Normally this occurs when the employee considers his or her work to be very important and/or desires to satisfy his or her recognition, ego, and self-actualization needs *at work*.

Table 14.5 attempts to show that when there is no particular economic or technological reasons for job enlargement or work simplification management should shift the job design method from work simplification to job enlargement or vice versa, depending on the kinds of workers available. When work simplification is determined by technology or economics, management should try job rotation and/or choosing employees with the attitudes needed to work satisfactorily in simplified jobs.

Job enlargement and job enrichment appeal to the humanistic employer. I have tried in this chapter to indicate the likely outcomes of these job design strategies.

This completes the discussion of job design. Next we will move on to organization design: how to group jobs into organizational units effectively.

Table 14.5 Job Design Strategies

Present Status	Employee Attitudes	Likely Result	Likely Managerial Action
Work simplification (historical reasons)	nonwork ethic-instrumental workers	good to satisfactory outcomes	none
Work simplification (technologically or economically determined)	low to moderate work ethic values	moderate to low outcome	A. job rotation B. hiring preference for instrumental workers
Work simplification (historical reasons)	A. some high-work-ethic employees	A. low outcomes	A. job enlargement/job enrichment
	B. some low-work-ethic employees	B. good to satisfactory outcomes	B. none
Job enlargement (historical reasons)	A. some high-work-ethic employees	A. good to satisfactory outcomes	A. none
	B. some low-work-ethic employees	B. moderate to low outcome	B. work simplification

Questions for Review

1. What is job design?

2. Why is it important to study job design?

3. In what ways do jobs differ? Why do they differ?

4. What job design styles can managers use?

5. What job design strategies do liberal managers prefer? Conservatives?

6. Which job design strategies are best? Under what conditions?

7. Which kind of job design strategy would you prefer to be used on your job? Are you typical of most employees in this matter? Why or why not?

References

A Job Is Not Just a Job

Blauner, Robert, *Alienation and Freedom* (Chicago: University of Chicago Press, 1964).

Calame, Byron, "Wary Labor Eyes Job Enrichment," *Wall Street Journal,* February 26, 1973.

Faunce, William, "Automation and the Division of Labor," *Social Problems,* 13, no. 2 (Fall 1965): 149–160.

Hodge, Robert, and Siegel, Paul, "The Classification of Occupations: Some Problems of Sociological Interpretation" (Washington, D.C.: American Statistical

Association, Social Statistics Section, 1966–1969), pp. 176–192.

Scoville, James, "A Theory of Jobs and Training," *Industrial Relations,* 9, no. 1 (October 1969): 36–53.

Walker, Charles, *Toward the Automatic Factory* (New Haven, Conn.: Yale University Press, 1957).

White, Bernard, "Union Response to the Humanization of Work," *Human Resource Management,* Fall 1975, pp. 2–9.

Whyte, William, *Human Relations in the Restaurant Industry* (New York: McGraw-Hill, 1948).

How Do Jobs Differ? Anderson, B., et al., "Status Classes in Organizations," *Administrative Science Quarterly,* 11, no. 3 September 1966, pp. 264–283.

Davis, Louis, and Taylor, James, "Technological Effects on Job, Work and Organization Structure," in Louis Davis and Albert Cherns, *The Quality of Working Life* (New York: Free Press, 1975).

Dubin, Robert, et al., "Implications of Differential Job Perceptions," *Industrial Relations,* 14, no. 3 October 1974, pp. 265–273.

Filley, Alan, et al., *Managerial Process & Organizational Behavior,* 2nd ed. (Glenview, Ill.: Scott, Foresman, 1976).

Fromm, Erich, *The Anatomy of Human Destructiveness* (New York: Holt, Rinehart and Winston, 1973).

Mennerick, Lewis, "Organization Structuring of Sex Roles in Nonstereotyped Industry," *Administrative Science Quarterly,* 20, no. 4 (December 1975): 570–586.

Wisner, Alain, "Work Content and Work Load," *International Studies of Management & Organization,* Fall 1975, pp. 16–40.

Styles of Job Design/ Specialized Jobs Folker, David, "Does the Industrial Engineer Dehumanize Jobs?" *Personnel,* July-August 1973, pp. 62–67.

Konz, Stephan, "Fitting the Job to the Man," *Industrial Engineering,* 3, no. 1 (January 1971): 10–15.

Maier, Norman, *Psychology in Industrial Organizations,* 4th ed. (Boston: Houghton Mifflin, 1973), chap. 11.

Job Rotation with Specialized Jobs Champagne, Jean, "Adapting Jobs to People: The Alcan Experiment," *Monthly Labor Review,* April 1973, pp. 49–52.

Job Enlargement Durand, Claude, "Employer Politics in Job Enrichment," *International Studies of Management & Organization,* Fall 1975, pp. 66–86.

Herzberg, Frederick, Hackman, J. Richard, et al., "A New Strategy for Job Enrichment," *California Management Review,* 17, no. 4 (Summer 1975): 57–71.

Jenkins, David, *Job Power: Blue & White Collar Democracy* (New York: Doubleday, 1973).

Schoderbek, Peter, "The Use of Job Enlargement in Industry," *Personnel Journal,* November 1968, pp. 796–801.

Work in America (Cambridge: M.I.T. Press, 1971).

Which Strategy Should You Use?

Biggane, James, and Stewart, Paul, "Job Enlargement: A Case Study," in Louis Davis and James Taylor, eds., *Design of Jobs* (Baltimore: Penguin, 1972).

Blood, M., and Hulin, C., "Alienation, Environmental Characteristics, and Worker Responses," *Journal of Applied Psychology,* 51 (1967): 284–290.

Calame, op. cit.

Conant, E., and Kilbridge, M., "An Interdisciplinary Analysis of Job Enlargement," *Industrial & Labor Relations Review,* 18 (1965): 377–395.

Davis, Louis, "The Design of Jobs," *Industrial Relations,* 6 (October 1966): 21–45.

———, "Readying the Unready," *California Management Review,* 13, no. 4 (1971): 27–36.

Donaldson, Lex, "Job Enlargement: A Multi-Dimensional Process," *Human Relations,* 28, no. 7, 593–610.

Durand, op. cit.

Elliot, J., "Increased Office Productivity Through Job Enlargement," *The Human Side of the Office Manager's Job* (New York: American Management Association, 1953).

Emery, F. E., and Thorsrud, E., *Form & Contention in Industrial Democracy* (Oslo: Oslo University Press, 1964).

Ford, Robert, *Motivation Through the Work Itself* (New York: American Management Association, 1969).

———, "Job Enrichment Lessons from AT&T," *Harvard Business Review,* January–February 1973.

Geijer, A., and Hauser, V., *Democratie Industrielle* (Stockholm: Lands Organizationen I Sverige, 1971).

Goldthorpe, J. H., et al., *The Affluent Worker: Industrial Attitudes & Behavior* (New York: Cambridge University Press, 1969).

Goode, C., "Greater Productivity Through the Organization of Work," *Personnel Administration,* 27 (1964): 34–49.

Gooding, Robert, "Blue Collar Blues on the Assembly Line," *Fortune,* July 1970.

Gordon, Michael, and Arvey, Richard, "The Relationship Between Education and Satisfaction with Job Content," *Academy of Management Journal,* 18, no. 4 (December 1975): 888–892.

Guest, Robert, "Job Enrichment: A Revolution in Job Design," *Personnel Administration,* 2 (1957): 13–15.

Hackman, J. Richard, and Lawler, E. E., Jr., "Jobs and Motivation," unpublished paper, Yale University, 1970.

Herrick, Neil, "The Other Side of the Coin," Invitational Seminar of Profit Sharing Research Foundation, Evanston, Illinois, November 17, 1971.

Herzberg, et al., op. cit.

Hulin, Charles, "Individual Differences and Job Enrichment: The Case Against General Treatments," in John Mahler, *New Perspectives in Job Enrichment.*

Ivancevich, John, and Donnelly, James, Jr., "A Study of Role Clarity and Need for Clarity for Three Occupational Groups," *Academy of Management Journal,* 17, no. 1 (March 1974): 28–36.

Jacobs, Carl, "Job Enrichment at Xerox Corporation," International Conference on the Quality of Work Life, New York, September 24–29, 1972.

Janson, Robert, "Job Enrichment in the Modern Office," in John Mahler, *New Perspectives in Job Enrichment.*

Kahn, Robert, et al., *Organizational Stress* (New York: John Wiley and Sons, 1964).

Kennedy, J., and Neill, H. O., "Job Content and Worker's Opinions," *Journal of Applied Psychology,* 42 (1958): 372–375.

Kilbridge, M. D., "Reduced Costs Through Job Enlargement," *Journal of Business,* 33 (October 1960): 357–362.

———, "Do Workers Prefer Larger Jobs?" *Personnel,* 37, (1960): 45–48.

———, "Turnover, Absence, and Transfer Rates as Indicators of Employee Satisfaction with Repetitive Work," *Industrial & Labor Relations Review,* 15 (1961): 21–32.

Levitan, Sar, and Johnston, William, "Job Redesign, Reform, Enrichment: Exploring the Limitations," *Monthly Labor Review,* July 1973, pp. 35–41.

MacKinney, A. C., et al., "Has Specialization Reduced Job Satisfaction?" *Personnel,* 39, no. 1 (January-February 1962): 8–17.

Mahler, John, *New Perspectives in Job Enrichment* (New York: Van Nostrand/ Reinhold, 1971).

Marks, A. R. N., *An Investigation of Modification of Job Design in an Industrial Setting,* unpublished Ph.D. thesis, University of California, Berkeley, 1954.

Miller, F. G., et al., "Job Rotation Raises Productivity," *Industrial Engineering,* 5 (1973): 24–26.

Reif, William, and Monczka, Robert, "Job Redesign: A Contingency Approach to Implementation," *Personnel,* May-June 1974, pp. 18–28.

Richleffs, Roger, "The Quality of Work," *Wall Street Journal,* August 21, 1972.

Rizzo, John, et al., "Role Conflict and Ambiguity in Complex Organizations," *Administrative Science Quarterly,* 15, no. 2 (June 1970): 150–163.

Schoderbek, op. cit.

Shepard, H. L., and Herrick, N. Q., *Where Have All the Robots Gone?* (New York: Free Press, 1972).

Simonds, Rollin, and Orife, John, "Worker Behavior Versus Enrichment Theory," *Administrative Science Quarterly,* 20 (December 1975): 606–612.

Smith, H. R., "From Moses to Herzberg: An Exploration of Job De-Enrichment," *Proceedings, Academy of Management,* 1973.

Smith, Patricia, "The Prediction of Individual Differences in Susceptibility to Industrial Monotony," *Journal of Applied Psychology,* 43 (1959): 322–329.

Smith, Patricia, and Lemm, C., "Positive Aspects of Motivation in Repetitive Work," *Journal of Applied Psychology,* 39 (1955): 330–333.

Stewart, Paul, *Job Enlargement in the Shop and in the Management Function* (Iowa City: University of Iowa, Center for Labor and Management, 1967).

Susman, Gerald, "Job Enlargement: Effects of Culture on Worker Responses," *Industrial Relations,* 12 (1973): 1–15.

Turner, Arthur, and Laurence, Paul, *Industrial Jobs and the Worker* (Cambridge, Mass.: Harvard Business School, 1965).

Turner, Arthur, and Michlette, A., "Sources of Satisfaction in Repetitive Work," *Occupational Psychology*, 36 (1962): 215–231.

Vroom, Victor, *Some Personality Determinants of the Effects of Participation* (Englewood Cliffs, N.J.: Prentice-Hall, 1960).

Walker, Charles, "The Problem of Repetitive Jobs," *Harvard Business Review*, May-June 1950, pp. 54–58.

Walker, J., and Marriott, R., "A Study of Some Attitudes Toward Factory Work," *Occupational Psychology*, 25 (1954): 181–191.

Walton, Richard, "How to Counter Alienation in the Plant," *Harvard Business Review*, November-December 1972, pp. 70–81.

Weinberg, Arthur, "Six American Workers Assess Job Redesign at Saab Scandia," *Monthly Labor Review*, September 1975.

White, op. cit.

Wyatt, S., et al., *Fatigue and Boredom in Repetitive Work* (London: Industrial Fatigue Research Board, 1937).

Job Enrichment Strategy

Carlson, Elliot, "Job Enrichment: Sometimes It Works" *Wall Street Journal*, December 13, 1971.

Davis, Louis, et al., *Supervisory Job Design* (Berkeley: Institute of Engineering Research, 1964).

Davis, Louis, and Valfer, E., "Intervening Responses to Changes in Supervisor Job Design," *Occupational Psychology*, 39 (1965): 171–190.

Frank, Linda, and Hackman, J. Richard, "A Failure of Job Enrichment," *Journal of Applied Behavioral Science*, 2, no. 4 (1975): 413–436.

Ondrack, D. A., "Energy Occupational Values," *Academy of Management Journal*, 16, no. 3 (September 1973): 423–432.

"Job Redesign on the Assembly Line: Farewell to Blue Collar Blues," *Organizational Dynamics*, 2, (1976): 51–56.

Paul, William, et al., "Job Enrichment Pays Off," *Harvard Business Review*, March-April 1969, pp. 61–78.

Schwartz, Howard, and Gruenfeld, Leopold, "Psychological Assumptions and Utopian Asperations: A Critique of *Work in America*," *Administrative Science Quarterly*, 20 (March 1975): 126–130.

Whitesell, David, and Winslow, Erile, "An Analysis of Studies Critical of the Motivation Hygiene Theory," *Personnel Psychology*, 20, no. 4 (1967): 391–415.

Work in America, op. cit.

CHAPTER 15

ORGANIZING AND COORDINATING WORK UNITS

15

Learning Objectives

1. To understand what organization and coordination are and why managers are involved.
2. To learn the mechanisms used to organize and coordinate.
3. To understand various organizations and coordination styles.

Chapter Outline

ORGANIZATION

Organization is the process by which people and the tasks they perform are related to each other systematically to help achieve the enterprise's objectives. Organization includes dividing up the work among groups and individuals (division of labor) and linking the subparts together (coordination).

Note some of the crucial elements of organization:

1 *Objectives:* We organize to achieve our objectives. We often hear people complaining about how disorganized they are. Stores will sell you little cards that say "Some day we have to get organized!" This is a typical problem of business enterprises. Organization helps clarify the objectives of the enterprise as they apply to work units.

2 *Formality of relationships:* A second characteristic of organization is the establishment of relationships so that each person knows what must be done and how his or her job relates to other jobs. The first step in organizing is effective job design and job descriptions. But without formal relationships no one knows who is supposed to do what and how each person is supposed to work with others to get the job done.

3 *Stability/duration of relationships:* Effective organization requires some stability over time in relationships at work. A firm cannot claim to be organized if each time you try to get a part for a machine you have to go to a different person located in a different department. This is chaos. Effective organization requires reasonably long-lasting relationships among jobs even if the employees in the jobs change.

In Chapter 14 you learned how to organize a group of duties into a job. In this chapter we will discuss how to group a set of jobs into a unit (department, etc.). This process is called *division of labor.* Then I will describe how these units are linked together so they will work together. This process is called *coordination.*

WHY STUDY ORGANIZATION?

We study organization because well-organized enterprises are more effective and because employees are more satisfied if the enterprise is well organized. Note that I did not say that managers spend a great deal of time organizing. Managers do spend some of their time organizing. If they do a good job at it, it does not take a great deal of their time. If it is done poorly, much more time is spent dealing with problems that arise because of poor organization.

Organization is a cyclical kind of activity, not a regular daily occurrence. In general, what happens is that symptoms of organizational problems appear. The manager studies the symptoms, makes an organizational adjustment, then checks to see if the problem has been solved. Organization then recedes into the background until dysfunctional symptoms arise again or the manager decides to make strategy changes that will necessitate changes in organization.

The amount and types of organizational problems faced by managers vary with the kind of enterprise. This is related to the evolution of the enterprise from a small entrepreneurship to a large company.

ALFRED P. SLOAN JR. (1875–1966)

Henry Ford's dominance of the auto industry was overthrown by the first and greatest of a new breed, Alfred Pritchard Sloan Jr., who reconstituted General Motors in the 1920's so successfully that most large U.S. corporations, including Ford, have come to run on principles that Sloan developed. An M.I.T.-trained engineer, Sloan sometimes referred to his system as "scientific management," but a better term would be "rational structure of the decision-making process." He had built the Hyatt Roller Bearing Co. to the point where William C. Durant, the brilliant assembler of G.M., was glad to pay $13.5 million for Hyatt. Sloan liked and respected Durant, whose own operating style was intuitive. But too many decisions crowded in haphazard fashion on Durant's desk with its ten busy telephones. Sloan in 1920 produced a twenty-eight-page memo on how the management should be restructured, and he was about to resign when Durant was forced out by his largest stockholder group, the du Ponts. Sloan was soon at the top because he demonstrated an ability to marshal facts around the points of decision. His 1920 memo recognized that in so large an enterprise a high degree of operating authority must be left in the divisions. But he built a strong central staff and a system of forecasts against which performance was measured. Sloan, in short, dealt effectively with one of the fundamental problems of modern life: how to achieve cooperation among men who were—and needed to be—too individualistic to be commanded in the old sense, but who would accept an orderly framework of policymaking.

THE THEORETICAL BASIS FOR ORGANIZATION

Much of what follows in this chapter and in Chapter 16 is based on a field of study called *organization theory*. This is a subject that appeals to many disciplines all over the world, although it was suppressed in the Soviet Union for over fifty years. Organization theorists are found in management, psychology, sociology, political science, anthropology, education, engineering, economics, public health and hospital administration, and other fields. The amount of literature in this field is unbelievably large, but as in many other areas, there is much more descriptive work than research that tells us how to organize effectively.

For many years management experts and sociologists talked about organization structure in general terms. But it took a group of British sociologists, psychologists, and management specialists at the Industrial Administration Research Unit at the University of Aston in Birmingham, England, ten years of work to describe organization structure *empirically*.

They selected certain aspects of organization such as specialization and formalization and developed valid and reliable scales to measure them. They then developed a data bank on 52 industrial and industrially-oriented government units. Their research will be referred to frequently in this chapter. Before discussing division of labor or coordination, however, it is important to understand that the organizational problems faced by managers and entrepreneurs change as the organization evolves.

ORGANI-ZATIONAL PROBLEMS CHANGE OVER TIME

The word *organization* often conjures up images of vast, highly organized bureaucracies like General Motors, the Department of Defense, the State University of New York, and Veterans Administration hospitals. In fact one of the characteristics that set our society apart from so-called primitive civilizations is the number of formal organizations that touch all our lives.

Our society is dominated by a few large organizations. But there are millions of small and medium-sized enterprises as well. The organizational problems of an entrepreneurially operated Colonel Sanders chicken franchise and those experienced by the Pentagon are significantly different. Although we are very aware of the impact of organizations like the Pentagon, there are relatively few such large organizations. And they rarely began that large.

Figure 15.1 portrays an enterprise that began as a small toy-manufacturing firm. Initially the entrepreneur assembled games that he had designed, with the help of his wife and children, in his basement. As sales grew, he rented an empty store building and hired high school students to work after school. Soon he had 5 full-time employees, then 10, then 15. At this point the enterprise had "primitive" structure: a boss and several employees. In this structure the boss tells everyone what to do. Everyone turns to the boss to organize the enterprise's activities (and do all managerial jobs).

As the enterprise developed further the boss could not do all the managing. So he informally began to ask one employee to help him with sales (probably calling on the smallest customers), another to help schedule employee time, another to hire people. They became his assistants. Eventually this structure became formalized; that is, the assistants became full-time specialists and the enterprise developed the *functional* structure shown in Figure 15.1. This structure lasted until the firm became very large (with thousands of employees) and after the entrepreneur had entered another business. When his strategy changed and he diversi-

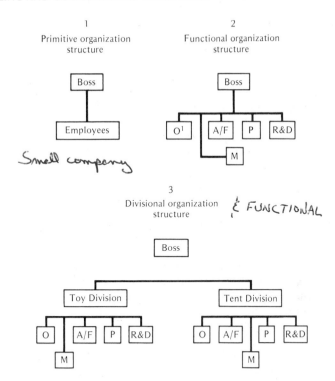

Figure 15.1

Evolution of an organization.

[1]O = operations; A/F = accounting/finance; P = personnel; R&D = research and development; M = marketing.

fied into tents, he changed his organization accordingly. This resulted in a *divisional* organization structure (again, see Figure 15.1).

There are more "advanced" forms of structure such as adaptive and innovative structures. They divide the enterprise into project management units or current business and innovative business units. But they are rarely used.

The evidence is that most enterprises are characterized by primitive structure. This is because most enterprises are very small. The most popular structure for enterprises that have been in existence more than five years is the functional structure. As for the largest enterprises, a majority have shifted to the divisional form. For example, more than 80 per cent of the *Fortune* 500 firms are organized on a divisional basis.

A major point of this section is that the number and types of organizational problems faced by managers vary, depending on the enterprise being managed. For example, the organizational problems of smaller enterprises center on division of work, establishing responsibilities, and determining spans of control. Middle-sized enterprises run into more problems in the use of functional organization and in staffing and coordination. Larger firms begin to have problems of decentralization.

A major problem for the manager of a small enterprise is to organize and operate a team of managers; for managers of larger firms the problem is to interrelate the different divisions as the enterprise grows. This distinction will become clearer as more details are given later in the chapter.

HORIZONTAL DIVISION OF LABOR

Division of labor can be done along two dimensions: horizontal and vertical. In horizontal division of labor the work to be done at one level is divided among units or departments. For example, at the level of the smallest plant there are scheduling, personnel, and maintenance departments. Vertical division of labor divides up the work from the bottom level (e.g., the plant) to the top level (corporate headquarters).

Horizontal division of labor is done in three ways: formalization, specialization (departmentation), and standardization.

FORMALIZATION

> **INFORMAL ORGANIZATION**
> In informal organizations the manager verbally explains organizational relationships to employees and changes these relationships as needed.
>
> **FORMAL ORGANIZATION**
> In formal organizations the manager describes the organizational relationships in written and graphic form as precisely as is practical. Changes thereafter can be made in formal or informal ways.

In a smaller enterprise, if you ask the manager or entrepreneur how the unit is organized, he or she will tell you in general terms. If the organizational structure is well thought out and clearly communicated to and understood by the employees, this is a good way to organize. As we have seen, managers prefer verbal communication. For what is most vital to effective organization is a thorough understanding of the relationships involved. And this can be effectively communicated verbally (with supportive nonverbal cues).

Almost all small enterprises and a great majority of medium-sized ones organize informally. Some medium-sized and most large enterprises formalize their organizational structure with organization charts and manuals. They do this because, as you will recall from Chapter 9, it is difficult to communicate effectively to large numbers of people verbally. And it is more efficient to communicate information of this nature in written form.

Few smaller and medium-sized enterprises formalize their organizational structure because they rarely need to. But there is another reason: Formal organization documents can make power relationships clear to all. As we shall see shortly, organization charts and manuals can spell out who has power, the limits of their power, and the results for which they are responsible. Things can be pleasantly muddled and status differentials less clear in informal systems. This is why some people resist formalizing the structure: it often causes as many problems as it solves. So if the structure is to be formalized, it is vital that great care be taken in drawing up the charts and writing the manuals. The people represented on the charts and in the manuals should be consulted before these documents are distributed. Where differences exist on how to draw the chart or write the manual, management must reconcile these differences.

But this is a very general description of formalization. The Aston group measured formalization by determining the extent to which communications and procedures are written down and filed in an organization. Procedures include statements of procedures, rules, and roles (contracts, agreements, etc.), and the operation of procedures that deal with decision making (applications for employment, etc.), instructions (requests), and feedback. The documents can include present, past, and future orientations. Formalization was measured by how much is written down and how many documents are filed and why (e.g., legal reasons, organization preferences). The Aston scale included about fifty measures of formalization.

The Aston group found a wide range of differences in degree of formalization, but larger organizations were much more likely to be highly formalized. And they found American firms *50 per cent more formalized* than British firms.

The most frequent and important means of formalization are organization charts and manuals. Let us look briefly at each.

Organization Charts

If the organization is formalized, an early document to appear is the organization chart. Several guidelines are used in the preparation of this chart:

1 The unit to be charted is usually represented by a rectangle (occasionally by a circle or some other geometric figure).

2 The most powerful unit is normally represented at the top of the page. The distance below the top unit indicates the power of each lower unit. Variations on this standard are the horizontal chart (where the power is to the left) or the circular chart (where the power is at the center.)

3 Organizational relationships are shown as lines between units showing who reports to whom.

4 When a power relationship is partial, it is represented by a dotted line. For example, if a personnel unit reports to a plant manager but the vice president for personnel at the home office is responsible for the technical expertise of the unit, a dotted line runs from the vice president to the unit. This is called *functional authority*.

5 If the firm distinguishes home office staff authority from line authority (see Chapter 7), staff units are shown to the side of the line organization structure.

Several examples should help you understand organization charts. All are based on the same company. Figure 15.2 is an example of a standard vertical organization chart showing the line executives (president; vice presidents for finance, operations, and marketing). The vice president's report to the president, and regional managers report to each vice president.

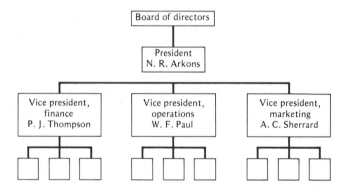

Figure 15.2
A line organization chart.

Figure 15.3 adds the staff vice presidents (for simplicity, only three are shown). Note that staff units are shown to the right of the line hierarchy. In advising the line executives the personnel department would begin at the vice presidential level and proceed down the hierarchy.

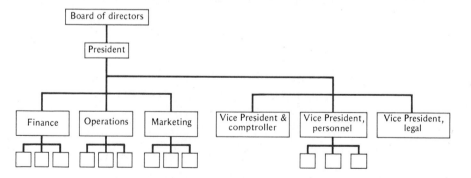

Figure 15.3
A line and staff organization chart.

Figure 15.4 shows a more likely possibility: The personnel manager at plant 3 reports to the plant manager, but personnel at headquarters tells him or her which tests and performance evaluation methods to use and provides the necessary technical training. This relationship is indi-cated by the dotted line.

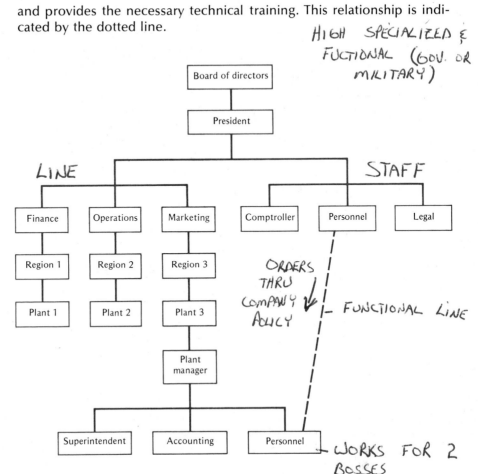

Figure 15.4
A line and staff
(functional)
organization chart.

Figures 15.5 and 15.6 show the less frequently used horizontal and circular organization charts. It is very important to be accurate in showing power and responsibility relationships on organization charts, especially when they are first drawn up.

Organization Manuals

Some very large organizations develop their formal organization struc-ture further by means of organization manuals. These usually contain the following information:

· organizational objectives
· organizational policies and procedures
· organization charts
· job descriptions for key executives
· guidelines for executive titles

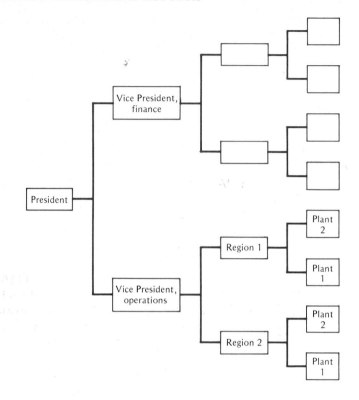

Figure 15.5
A horizontal
organization chart.

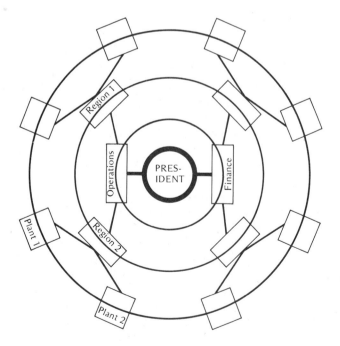

Figure 15.6
A circular
organization chart.

Organization manuals are expensive to develop and maintain. Many managers do not like them. They prefer verbal communication and feel that manuals limit their freedom. Manuals are found primarily in very large organizations. Top managers usually delegate the preparation of these manuals to planning executives.

When top executives are asked for their organization charts and/or manuals, they usually answer with some variation of A or B:

A "You know, we don't have them here, although we probably should."

B (Very reluctantly) "Here they are, but they aren't up to date. I've been meaning to update them but haven't had a chance."

These responses lead to the conclusion that enterprises really operate on the basis of informal relationships developed interpersonally from day to day. They do not need formalities like charts and manuals to operate (except in the case of an employee learning a new job). The informal relationships are not shown on these charts, and at times they are more important than the formal relationships. But charts and manuals do provide a beginning point for understanding how an enterprise is organized, especially a large enterprise.

Specialization and Departmentation

Specialization operates at several levels. It operates at the job level, as discussed in Chapter 14. It also operates at the organization level, where it is often called *departmentation*.

> **DEPARTMENTATION**
> Departmentation is the way one groups jobs or divides up the work of the total enterprise. The result of departmentation is the creation of subunits, often called *departments*.

Process departmentation results when jobs with similar technical content are grouped together into single-function units. An example of a process department is given in Figure 15.7.

The second approach to division of labor is grouping by purpose. In this approach departments are designed according to client, location, product or service, or time. Examples of these forms of departmentation are given in Figures 15.8–15.11. (Note: Usually you will find the process units [operations, finance, accounting, personnel, etc.] as the next level below the purpose units, [e.g., mid-Atlantic]. Very large enterprises might

2 WAYS TO ORGANIZE: 1. FUNCTION
                      2. PURPOSE

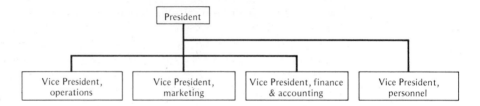

Figure 15.7
An enterprise divided into departments by process (function).

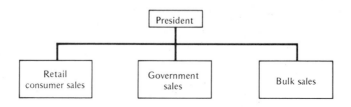

Figure 15.8
An enterprise divided into departments by purpose (client).

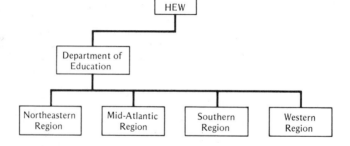

Figure 15.9
An enterprise divided into departments by purpose (location).

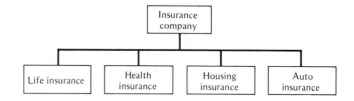

Figure 15.10
An enterprise divided into departments by purpose (product/service).

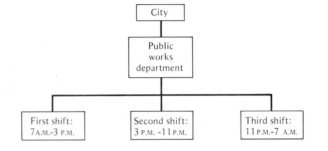

Figure 15.11
An enterprise divided into departments by purpose (time).

use purpose departmentation in some divisions and process departmentation in others.)

The third approach to departmentation is the matrix organization. In this kind of division of labor the organization is divided into process (technical, functional) groups and purpose (program) groups. People are assigned from process to matrix groups for the duration of a project. Matrix organizations can be illustrated in several ways; Figure 15.12 shows Jay Galbraith's approach.

LARGE SCALE COMPLEX PROBLEM (AEROSPACE)
- REQUIRES MUCH COORDINATION

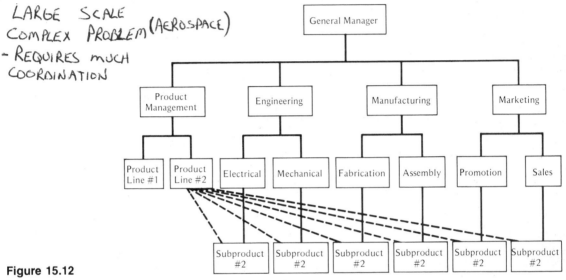

Figure 15.12
Standard's pure matrix organization (Galbraith).

- - - - = Technical authority over the product
———— = Formal authority over the product (in product organization, these relationships may be reversed)

Measuring Specialization

The Aston group measured degree of departmentation (specialization) by several criteria:

1 The degree of specialization of positions in the enterprise.

2 The ratio of line to staff positions.

3 The degree of specialization *within* the line or staff department.

The third criterion is the chief determinant of whether the firm has a process, purpose, or matrix type of organization. The Aston group counted 16 specialist-staff groups (see Table 15.1) and studied the degree of specialization within both staff departments and the line organization (Table 15.2 shows specialization in a maintenance department). They then computed indexes of specialization and classified organizations on the basis of those indexes.

Table 15.1 Specialization of Functions (Aston)

No.	Specialization Example of Title	Activities
1	Public relations and advertising	Develop, legitimize, and symbolize the organization's charter
2	Sales and service	Dispose of, distribute, and service the output
3	Transport	Carry outputs and resources from place to place
4	Employment	Acquire and allocate human resources
5	Training	Develop and transform human resources
6	Welfare and security	Maintain human resources and promote their identification with the organization
7	Buying and stock control	Obtain and control materials and equipment
8	Maintenance	Maintain and erect buildings and equipment
9	Accounts	Record and control financial resources
10	Production control	Control workflow
11	Inspection	Control quality of materials and equipment and outputs
12	Methods	Assess and devise ways of producing output
13	Design and development	Devise new outputs, equipment, and processes
14	Organization and methods	Develop and carry out administrative procedures
15	Legal	Deal with legal and insurance requirements
16	Market research	Acquire information on operational field

Mean item analysis value:
Range obtained = 0–16; Mean = 10.19; S.D. = 5.19.

Advantages and Disadvantages of Departmentation Styles

A number of advantages and disadvantages have been listed for both the process and purpose methods of departmentation. The advantages for process departmentation are disadvantages for the purpose approach. They are summarized in Table 15.3.

A quick look at the table shows that there are advantages and disadvantages to both styles. But they are not always of equal weight, and they are relative, not absolute. So a manager must choose the set of advantages that are vital and the disadvantages he or she can live with.

Table 15.2 Degree of Specialization *Within* Functions (Aston)

Specialization No. 8: Maintenance (*n = 49, scale no. 51.09*)

Engineer
Machine maintenance
Building maintenance
Electrical maintenance
Machine maintenance specialized by process, etc.
New work force
Surveyor or architect
Instrument maintenance
Research into maintenance
Electrical maintenance specialized by process, etc.

Mean item analysis value:
Range obtained = 2–10; Mean = 4.29; S.D. = 1.89.

Table 15.3 Advantages and Disadvantages of Process and Purpose Approaches to Departmentation

Factor	Process Departmentation		Purpose Departmentation	
	Advantage	Disadvantage	Advantage	Disadvantage
A. Efficiency of resource use, production/ operation	+			−
B. Coordination cost		−	+	
C. Willingness to adapt and change		−	+	
D. Ease of measurement of output and results	+			−
E. Preparation of broadly trained managers and employees		−	+	
F. Preparation of well-trained specialists	+			−
G. Interdepartmental conflict		−	+	
H. Client satisfaction		−	+	

There is very little research evidence that these supposed advantages and disadvantages always hold true. Arthur Walker and Jay Lorsch examined two plants that were alike in external and internal factors except that one used process, the other purpose departmentation. They found that

· the plant using process departmentation was more efficient.
· the plant using purpose departmentation was better coordinated and its communication was better.

·the plant using purpose departmentation solved problems more quickly and adapted to changing conditions more readily.
·the plant using purpose departmentation trained generalists better.
·job satisfaction was higher in the plant using process departmentation.

Arthur Kover's study of an advertising agency resulted in the following findings:

·Purpose departmentation led to greater client satisfaction.
·Purpose departmentation improved coordination.
·Communication patterns changed when the organization shifted from process to purpose departmentation. Communication with clients went up, but communication between specialists went down.

Studies by Galbraith generally confirm the advantages and disadvantages just listed.

The matrix structure is an attempt to get the best of both worlds (and somehow eliminate the worst). It has been used in a few volatile industries like defense. Andrew Grimes and his associates have analyzed the matrix approach in 826 task units of 18 plants of a single company. The results were complicated, but in general they found that elements of both process and purpose departmentation were present.

In sum, managers should choose the form of departmentation that is critical to their success. Are efficiency and cost crucial? Use process departmentation. Are coordination and getting the job done within narrow time limits crucial? Use purpose departmentation. If a mixture of these needs is present, a matrix structure might be useful. The following propositions summarize these aspects of departmentation.

Proposition 15.1.
When low cost and efficiency are the keys to successful goal achievement, the effective enterprise will use process departmentation.

Proposition 15.2.
When coordination and reaching objectives at a specific time is crucial to success, effective enterprises will use purpose departmentation.

Proposition 15.3.
When the environment is complex and the critical variable is exact meshing of output times, matrix structuring is effective.

Standardization

The final aspect of horizontal division of labor is *standardization.* Standardization of an organization's procedures and roles (jobs) means that the enterprise examines the events occurring regularly and establishes within the enterprise approved ways of handling them. These standards are used in hiring, training, and evaluating employees and running the organization.

Organizations vary in degree of standardization from very little to a great deal. The Aston researchers measured standardization on a scale consisting of two dimensions:

1 The extent to which the enterprise prescribes job definitions, qualifications for office, titles, rewards, and measurement of performance.

2 Standardization of procedures—how decisions are made and how jobs are done. Procedures are highly standardized when there are rules or definitions that cover *all* circumstances and when they *invariably* apply.

VERTICAL DIVISION OF LABOR

In Chapter 2 you learned that there are three kinds of managers: top, middle, and supervisory. These three kinds of managers exist within the same enterprise and actually are on a scale ranging from the supervisor up to top management.

Now we will look specifically at this dimension of organization: the vertical dimension. We just examined how enterprises organize horizontally into departments. As we go up the organization the power tends to increase. This phenomenon is called a *hierarchy* or *chain of command.*

In this section we will discuss the following three aspects of vertical division of labor:

1 *Number of levels in the hierarchy.* An enterprise can be classified as flat, medium, or tall, depending on the number of jobs in the longest "line" from worker to top executive (excluding assistants and secretaries).

2 *Span of control.* A manager's span of control is the number of subordinates directly reporting to him or her.

3 *Degree of centralization.* Centralization is present when decision making is concentrated at the top of the structure. This concentration is accomplished by assigning the decisions to top managers, designing rules that limit the discretion of middle and supervisory managers, and setting up review and control mechanisms to enforce these limitations.

Height of hierarchy and span of control are inversely related. Suppose an enterprise employs 1000 people and chooses among three spans of control: 10, 20, or 100. It can easily be seen that the height of the hierarchy depends on this choice. In the case of a large span, each supervisor has 100 employees reporting to him or her and these 10 supervisors report to the president. This results in two levels of managerial hierarchy: the supervisors and the president.

With a small span of 10 employees, the firm needs 100 supervisors. they in turn, must be supervised in groups of 10, so there are now 10 middle managers reporting to the president. This makes three levels, so the structure is taller.

Span of control influences centralization, too. With 100 employees reporting to each manager, the manager cannot make all the decisions for them, so he or she is forced to delegate decision-making power. With a small span, it is possible for the boss to centralize. But as the hierarchy grows taller the top managers are farther from the shop floor, and in fast-changing businesses they may have to decentralize to speed up the decision-making process. These relationships may be diagramed as follows:

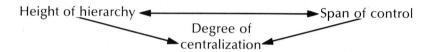

Span of control and centralization are also related to control and leadership styles (see Chapters 7 and 17).

Height of the Hierarchy   The flatness or tallness of an enterprise is relatively easy to measure. There have been a few good studies of the number of levels in various enterprises. We will look at these before examining the effects of a number of levels on performance and satisfaction.

In general, these studies show that as an enterprise grows in size it gets taller. Richard Hall and his associates studied 75 enterprises and found the following percentage of employees at various levels:

Study by Richard Hall and Associates			
		No. of Employees	
No. of Levels	**100**	**100–999**	**1000**
2–3 levels	55%	14%	10%
4 levels	35	43	40
5 or more levels	10	43	50

These differences were found to be statistically significant.

McNulty studied 30 southern California growth companies over a

10-year period and found the levels increasing with time and growth, as can be seen from the following data:

Study by McNulty

No. of Levels	1947	1955
9 and over	0	1
7–8	1	3
5–6	9	13
3–4	15	13
1–2	4	0

Ernest Dale studied several hundred large and medium-sized companies and compiled the following data on number of levels:

Study by Ernest Dale

No. of Levels	Company Size Large	Medium
2	0	1
3	0	3
4	4	6
5	9	12
6	20	18
7	19	11
8	19	6
9	5	1
10	2	0
11	2	0
12	1	1

He believed these differences resulted form such factors as company size, complexity, and top-management preferences.

Aston's study of 52 British enterprises found the levels varying from 4 to 11, with the mean about 6. This variety in height could be caused by many factors, as Dale indicated. Joan Woodward and Derek Pugh found some support for the notion that increasing technological complexity causes an increase in the height of the structure.

There are two types of research on the effects of height on structure. One relates to differences and similarities between jobs at different levels. This was discussed briefly in Chapter 2. Stanley Nealey and Fred Fiedler recently reviewed the research in this area and drew the following conclusions:

·There are no major differences in preferences for job conditions (such as pay, security, and esteem) between managers at different levels.
·Managers' job satisfaction increases with the level of their jobs.

The second research area is the relationship between job satisfaction and performance and the height of the hierarchy. Several individuals have influenced the research in this area. James Worthy studied Sears, Roebuck and its 100,000 employees over a 12-year period. He concluded that in larger and taller organizations the number of managers proliferated, which resulted in centralization and overspecialization. This in turn led to lower job satisfaction and performance. He strongly argued for flatter organization structures.

Elliot Jacques argued similarly. He believed most organizations are unnecessarily tall. No organization needs more than seven levels. He measured managerial spans of control to support this theory.

Harry Triandis hypothesized that

·an increase in managers' abilities will result in flatter structures.
·when managers believe workers are stupid, lazy, and unreliable, they will adopt a tall structure.
·when there is a large number of managers with a high need for power, the organization will tend to become taller.

Table 15.4 presents the evidence from these studies in summary form. As you will note, Kaufman and Seidman question whether organizations can be evaluated effectively on this criterion, since the structure has a different number of levels for staff than for line functions.

The evidence does not entirely support the "flat is good" hypothesis. It appears reasonable to conclude that the job satisfaction of top managers in tall organizations and supervisors in flat organizations is greater than that of supervisors in tall organizations and top managers in flat organizations. There are few studies of the satisfaction of *employees* in tall or flat structures. As for performance, the results are mixed here, too.

Span of Control   Span of control—the number of people reporting to the manager—influences the height of the hierarchy: the smaller the span, the greater the height. This in turn increases the direct costs of management: the more managers are needed, the greater the total amount of management salaries.

Theorists have argued about whether span of control should be small or large. But what actually happens in the real world? A series of studies have been done to determine actual spans of control. They are summarized in Table 15.5. Among the conclusions that may be drawn from these studies are

Table 15.4 Research on the Effect of Height of Structure on Performance, Satisfaction, and Attitudes

Author	Setting	Degree of Sophistication	Findings
Worthy	Sears, Roebuck	Sophisticated	Flatter Structures (and decentralization) create the potential for greater job satisfaction, autonomy/responsibility, and initiative.
Richardson and Walker	Single-company case study	Moderately sophisticated	Enterprise shifted from tall to flat with improved costs and no loss in job satisfaction
Jones	Lab experiment: groups of business administration students	Moderately sophisticated	Flat structures are less effective in goal achievement, moderately slow in communication, accuracy, slightly higher in satisfaction; tall structure is slow but very accurate in communication and more profitable.
Carpenter	120 teachers in 6 public school systems	Sophisticated	Teachers in flat structures have greater job satisfaction than in medium or tall organizations.
Ghiselli and Siegel	442 managers in the United States	Sophisticated	Firms with flat structures reward managers for sharing information and MBO. Tall structures reward managers who do not share information or use MBO procedures.
Ivancevich and Donnelly	295 salespersons in 3 organizations	Sophisticated	Flat organizations lead to greater satisfaction, self-actualization, and autonomy, lower anxiety, and more efficient salespeople than tall or medium enterprises.
Carzo and Yanouzas	Lab experiment: four 15-person groups of business administration students	Moderately sophisticated	No significant differences in efficiency of decision making, but tall structures are more effective in profit performance.
Porter and Lawler, Porter and Siegel	1500 managers, 5000 managers	Sophisticated	Managers in large firms are more satisfied in tall structures; managers in small organizations are more satisfied in flat structures. Tall structures satisfy more security and social needs, while flat structures satisfy more self-actualization needs.
Kaufman and Seidman	25 federal government (nondefense) agencies and 4 county health agencies	Sophisticated	Hierarchy pyramid works in line units but not staff units. Conclusion: Span of control ↔ height relationship might not be accurate in staff units.

· Most studies consider only top managers' spans of control.
· Many studies indicate that spans of control increase as enterprises get larger.
· Most top managers supervise five or six middle managers.
· There is insufficient evidence on lower and middle managers to judge their spans of control.

Table 15.5 Studies of Actual Spans of Control

Study	Setting and Characteristics	Findings
Dale	Questionnaire survey of 100 large and 46 medium-sized businesses' top managers' spans of control (1952)	Large businesses: range 1–24; median 9; only 26 had spans of 6 or less. Medium-sized businesses: range 1–17; median 6/7.
Healey	Questionnaire to 620 middle and supervisory business executives (1956)	The span of control of the majority of these executives was 8 or less.
Janger and Stieglitz (NICB)	Questionnaire to 81 large businesses' top executives (1960)	The span of control of the top managers was 5.
Entwise and Walton	Questionnaire to 20 college presidents, 20 small manufacturing company presidents, and 20 auto dealer presidents (1961)	Businesses (top executives): range 2–20; mode 5. Colleges: range 4–31; mode 5. Positive correlation between size and span of control.
Simonds	16 businesses over 8-year period (1958–1966)	Span of top executive increased over time. Range increased from 3–9 to 3–11; median increased from 4.87 to 5.56.
Pugh (Aston)	52 British businesses and government agencies (1968)	Spans of chief executives ranged from 2 to 14; mean 6.
Woodward	100 medium-sized British businesses (1965)	Spans of supervisors: range 20–80; median varied by technology.
Viola	221 middle-management insurance executives (late 1960s)	Middle managers' spans of control varied from 1 to 70, with 71% under 19; mean 6.75; superiors had larger spans of control. Span of control was related to the size of the firm.

Many researchers believe that prescribing spans of control for all enterprises at all levels is not intelligent in view of individual differences among managers.

What factors influence the span of control, then? There are many. But the major factors are the people involved, the jobs involved, and the environment.

Personal Factors

Two personal variables could influence the span of control. The first is managerial preferences. If the manager has a high need for power, he or she may prefer a larger span of control. If the manager has strong social needs, he or she may prefer to interact with more rather than fewer subordinates. Since managers usually have some discretion over their span of control, this could result in larger spans. Unfortunately, there are few studies on this subject.

The second personal factor is competence. A more competent supervisor may be able to supervise a larger group, so his or her span of control may be larger. Employee competence may also result in larger spans of control. Studies do not always support this relationship, and at least two have found that the higher the competence, the *lower* the span of control.

Job Factors

The first of these factors is the nature of the *manager's* job. Does the manager spend all his or her time in supervision or half of it? If the former, the span is likely to be larger. Few studies have been done on this aspect of management.

Other factors relate to the employees being supervised. The first is the relative importance of the job and the need of the subordinate to consult with the superior. In studying the reorganization of the state of Michigan in 1965, I noted a lot of talk about the governor's span of control—40—being too large. Some of the department heads needed to see him daily, others once a year. (The chairman of the Apple Commission posed with the governor and the Apple Queen every year when the governor declared "Eat Michigan Apples Week.") Little research has been done on this factor, but it appears that the span should be computed on the basis of a weighted importance index, not sheer numbers.

Another factor is the degree of similarity and standardization in the employee's work. Researchers have found that the lower the variety in the job, the larger the span can be.

An important variable, similar to importance, is the degree of interrelatedness in the department's work. If there is a high degree of interrelatedness among the jobs in the department, this requires more supervisory time and thus will lead to a small span of control. Little empirical research has been done on this subject, however.

Behavioral scientists have investigated a phenomenon similar to span of control: group size. The general conclusions are that groups of five and seven are excellent. Larger groups lead to clique formation and conflict, more problems of coordination, and lower participating and job satisfaction.

Environmental Factors

Technology also influences span of control. Studies have found that effective mass production companies have larger supervisory spans of control. The optimum for craft work is five and for automated work six. The optimum for mass production is 40–60.

Spans of control increase as volatility and dependence increase. They also increase as employees move farther apart geographically.

Managerial Implications

Much of the confusion in these research results is due to the fact that the researchers are defining span of control differently. But some reasonable conclusions are the following:

·The span of control of the top executive is different from that of the supervisor.
·The optimum span of top managers is probably 5–10, the larger span probably allowable at the very top management level.
·At the supervisory level span of control depends on technology and similar variables.
·It is difficult to make much sense out of all these variables in the aggregate. The best approach is to measure the variables in your enterprise and compute weighted index. Lockheed, for example, used variables similar to those discussed earlier, as can be seen in Table 15.6. Each supervisor is given a "supervisory span of control index" that adds up the points to determine the size of the supervisor's work group. Lockheed claims that it has experienced substantial savings in managerial costs by establishing larger spans of control.

In sum, span of control is a complex factor. The evidence favoring any particular span of control is equivocal, since there are many variables.

Degree of Centralization

Centralization is a measure of where decision-making authority is located: centrally (in the home office) or in local units. The Aston group measured centralization according to where decisions were made and whether they dealt with control of resources or control of activities.

As indicated previously, an enterprise can place decision-making power entirely (or mostly) at the top (centralization), or it can parcel it out downward with appropriate controls by a process called *delegation*.

Some contend that decentralization develops better managers, results in quicker decisions, and allows managers to satisfy their self-actualization and recognition needs. Conservatives point to the very real costs of developing decentralization controls.

Frankly, I do not know enough to tell you which approach is better. Later I will give you my ideas about the conditions in which each approach works well (and they both do), but the evidence is very contra-

Table 15.6 Weighted Index of Span of Control at Lockheed (Stieglitz)

Span Factor	Point Values for Each Factor				
Similarity of functions	Identical 1	Essentially alike 2	Similar 3	Inherently different 4	Fundamentally distinct 5
Geographic contingency	All together 1	All in one building 2	Separate building, 1 plant location 3	Separate locations, 1 geographic area 4	Dispersed geographic areas 5
Complexity of functions	Simple, repetitive 1	Routine 2	Some complexity 3	Complex, varied 4	Highly complex, varied 5
Direction and control	Minimum supervision and training 2	Limited supervision 4	Moderate, periodic supervision 6	Frequent, continuing supervision 8	Constant, close supervision 10
Coordination	Minimum relationships with others 3	Relationships limited to defined courses 6	Moderate relationships, easily controlled 9	Considerable close relationships 12	Extensive mutual nonrecruiting relationships 15
Planning	Minimum scope and complexity 2	Limited scope and complexity 4	Moderate scope and complexity 6	Considerable effort required; guided only by broad policies 8	Extensive effort required; areas and policies not chartered 10

dictory. In 1960 John Pfiffner and Frank Sherwood said that accepting decentralization amounts to accepting a philosophy of life. Many companies use it—including General Motors, Du Pont, and Sears. But since the evidence does not clearly favor one approach over the other, it probably makes a lot of sense for an enterprise to use a mixture of centralization and decentralization. That is, it should centralize key policy decisions and staff services, which probably yield economies of scale (e.g., research and development, legal functions, some purchasing). Centralization would also be beneficial if it is legally necessary to have uniform policies throughout the enterprise.

COORDINATION   Division of labor serves the purpose of assigning jobs to people. But what it amounts to is a division of the enterprise's whole operation into parts. How do the parts get linked back together? This is where coordination comes in.

> ### COORDINATION
> Coordination is the set of human and structural mechanisms designed to link the parts of the enterprise together to help achieve its objectives.

A great deal has been written about division of labor, but precious little about coordination. For example, the extensive 10-year Aston research project did not develop significant coordination scales or measures. However, there is greater emphasis on coordination today than in the past, as the systems approach evidences.

The Need for Coordination   It seems obvious that there is a need for coordination, but let us look for a moment at relative needs. These are described in Propositions 15.4 and 15.5.

> ### Proposition 15.4.
> The greater the division of labor, the greater the need for coordination.
>
> ### Proposition 15.5.
> The greater the interdependence of the subunits, the greater the need for coordination.

With regard to Proposition 15.4, it is clear that if all the work is done by two people in one unit, there is little need for coordination. If the enterprise's work has been divided into 1000 units with thousands of employees, the need for coordination is much greater.

Proposition 15.5 can be understood better by examining James Thompson's typology of interdependence. Thompson pointed out that units can be linked in any of three ways:

1 *Pooled interdependence*   Subunits linked by pooled interdependence make contributions to the total enterprise but are not directly related. Purina Dog Chow plants in California and New York both contribute to Purina's profits, but they are not directly interrelated. The coordination between them is minimal.

2 *Sequential interdependence*   In this kind of linkage later units depend on earlier ones. In Chapter 11, I described a beer company. You may recall this sequence:

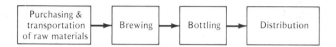

Greater coordination is necessary in sequential than in pooled interdependence, especially for later stages such as brewing, bottling, and distribution.

3 *Reciprocal interdependence*   In this relationship the inputs of one unit becomes the outputs of the other and vice versa. The airlines provide an example of this kind of relationship:

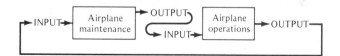

When maintenance finishes servicing a plane, the plane is an output of maintenance. The serviced plane then becomes an input to operations. When operations sees that a plane needs maintenance, the plane is an output of operations and becomes an input to maintenance. Obviously this close interrelationship leads to the strongest need for coordination between maintenance and operations.

Thompson recommends that the enterprise use nonhuman, standardized coordination for pooled interdependence. He recommends planning (human and nonhuman) for serial interdependence and mutual adjustment (by individual and group coordinators) for reciprocal interdependence. These mechanisms are discussed more fully in the next section.

Basil Georgopolous and Floyd Mann studied the coordination mechanisms used in a number of community general hospitals. They found four kinds of coordination to fit four coordination needs:

> ·*Preventive:* coordination designed to anticipate problems and difficulties.
> ·*Corrective:* coordination designed to correct a dysfunction in the system after it has occurred.
> ·*Regulatory:* coordination designed to preserve existing arrangements.
> ·*Promotive:* coordination designed to improve the system's operations or arrangements without specific problems.

There is not a great deal of evidence on this point, but most management experts would agree that promotive coordination is the least likely form. Corrective and regulatory coordination are the most frequent forms, with preventive in between.

Coordination Mechanisms   There are four mechanisms of coordination: informal/unprogramed, programed nonhuman, programed human (individual coordination), and programed human (group coordination). Enterprises can use one or several of these methods to achieve coordination.

Informal Unprogramed Coordination   VERY   POWERFUL

A great deal of coordination comes about voluntarily, informally, without programing by the enterprise. It is impossible to anticipate, plan for, or coordinate all activities. So all enterprises rely on voluntary coordination to some degree.

Essentially, informal coordination is based on reciprocal understanding, shared attitudes, and powerful psychological mechanisms to work together and cooperate. Extensive division of labor leads to problems when voluntary informal coordination is used, but unprogramed coordination exists in spite of this difficulty.

For voluntary coordination to work, the following factors must be operating:

> ·The employee must know his or her objectives and those of the unit.
> ·The employee must have a clear idea of what his or her job entails.
> ·Most of all, the employee must identify with the enterprise and its objectives. If the enterprise really means something to the employee, he or she will want to cooperate in attaining its objectives.
> ·This identification can be reinforced if the work groups identify with the enterprise.

Strong enterprise identification is often found in enterprises like churches, hospitals, charities, and arts organizations, and is sometimes found in business and government organizations, especially in times of crises like wars, disasters, and economic malfunctions. A "let's pull together to get us through" attitude develops at such times.

Strong identification is often a result of careful selection and orientation (socialization) and is strongest in employees who have undergone a lengthy training process before entering the enterprise. Examples of such groups are priests, ministers, nurses, and elite military groups (e.g., commandos). Voluntary cooperation has been shown to work in some hospitals and some hospital procedures such as operations.

As enterprises get larger, or if the employees or the situation do not fit these characteristics, informal coordination needs to be supplemented by programed coordination. But no enterprise can operate at all without *some* voluntary coordination.

Programed Nonhuman Coordination

If not all the conditions for unprogramed coordination are present, or if the organization is getting too complex or large for informal communication to be effective, the manager may develop programed methods: standard operating procedures, rules, and what Thompson called standardization. These can save the manager time if he or she spells out how to handle repetitive coordination problems in the form of a procedure, plan, or policy. Scheduling deadlines are an example of this approach. Of course policies have other purposes besides coordination (such as communication).

Programed nonhuman methods of coordination are used in all medium and large enterprises and in most small ones.

Individual Coordination

Policies are not always understood by two parties in the same way. We tend to interpret them the way we want to. So what happens to coordination? There are two ways to handle this problem with individual coordinators.

The Hierarch The most typical approach is to have the coordination problem decided by the manager who supervises the two units with coordination problems. This assumes that the same superior supervises both units.

What happens here is that the "hierarch" hears out both sides. He or she sits in judgment and uses all the available sources of influence to get the two units to work out their problem. If this fails, the manager falls back on his or her authority and establishes a procedure for future interactions. To the extent that the decision is viewed as fair and workable, this solves the problem of coordination.

The Coordinator/Integrator In especially difficult areas the job of coordinating is large enough to be a separate position like the following:

·*Product manager:*   an individual who serves as liaison for all functional areas and promotes improved sales and profits.
·*Project manager:*   an individual who serves as liaison to all units for the duration of a project (e.g., Apollo).
·*Customer coordinator:*   an individual who serves as a liaison to all functions for a major customer.
·*"Metropolitan Desk":*   a unit to coordinate all information for clients or customers (e.g., HUD's Metropolitan Desk).

Table 15.7 Division of Labor, Coordination, and Management Style

Liberal	Middle of the Road	Conservative
	Horizontal Division of Labor	
	Formalization (degree to which documents, organization charts, manuals, and forms are used.	
Nonexistent or used very little		Extensive documentation charts, forms used
	Departmentation	
Departmentation by purpose; not too specialized	Specialization	Departmentation by process function; much specialization
	Standardization of policies, procedures, and rules	
Nonexistent or not used		Extensive standardization
	Vertical Division of Labor (Chain of Command)	
Liberal	Middle of the Road	Conservative
	Height of Hierarchy	
Flat	Medium	Tall
	Span of Control	
Large	Medium	Small
	Degree of Centralization	
Low	Careful delegation	High
	Coordination	
Informal/nonprogramed; group coordination; some nonhuman techniques	Individual coordination and nonhuman techniques	Individual hierarch and nonhuman techniques

This mechanism is expensive: It increases direct managerial costs. It is frustrating for the coordinators, since they have little formal authority yet are responsible for results. They have only certain influence mechanisms available to them. This approach is used rarely, but can be effective when timing is crucial and when costs are not a major factor.

Group Coordination

In Chapter 6 we discussed several mechanisms that can be used for coordination. Enterprises set up staff groups to help in coordination and for other purposes such as control. The difficulties of line-staff relations were also discussed in Chapter 6.

Coordination can also be handled through group meetings, whether the groups are committees meeting regularly or ad hoc groups. Chapter 6 indicated the conditions under which committees are effective at jobs like coordination. But these are not easy tasks. The members are torn between their personal preferences, the group's preferences, and the objectives of the organization.

Which Way Is Best?

Little research has been done to answer this question, but results so far favor the contingency approach. Georgopoulous and Mann studied coordination in ten hospitals. They found that coordination was better in smaller hospitals where policies and rules are clearly defined, when people coordinate voluntarily, and when conflicts are handled promptly in group meetings. In effect, they say all methods of coordination should be used. Other studies have found that coordination techniques vary according to the characteristics of the enterprise's environment.

DIVISION OF LABOR, COORDINATION, AND MANAGEMENT STYLE: A CONTINGENCY APPROACH

It is useful to learn about such organizing mechanisms as spans of control and standardization. But most managers really want to know *how* to organize well—how to arrange tasks and employees so the tasks are done efficiently and the enterprise's objectives are attained. This question has been approached in two ways:

1 "There is one right way to organize":
  a conservative, bureaucratic style
  b liberal, participative style
  c middle-of-the-road style
2 "There is no single 'right' way to organize."

Table 15.7 profiles the conservative and liberal organization styles.

The first approach follows the traditional natural science model: You study an object and determine the way it operates. Two groups of researchers feel that they have found the right way to organize an enterprise in all cases (with some quibbling over exceptions). The conservative organization style has been described and advocated by two groups of writers: classical management theorists and advocates of bureaucracy in sociology.

The liberal style is in effect the opposite of the conservative style. The liberals argue that their style taps the motivations of today's men and women and can better cope with the complexities of modern technology. Their focus is on leadership style, especially as it affects control systems, goal setting, communication, and decision making.

A third style (and probably the one most frequently adopted) is the middle-of-the-road style, which says, "Sometimes the liberals are right, sometimes the conservatives, and most of the time one should pick and choose among their systems and apply parts of each to management. This approach makes some sense, but it does not tell you when to use the liberal style and when to use the conservative style.

Other managers believe that there is no single "right" way to organize. Effective organization depends on factors such as the enterprise's environment (volatility, technology, dependence) and its present characteristics (complexity, size, people). This is the contingency or situational approach and is described in detail in Chapter 16. Those who take this position follow the behavioral science model or systems approach, which says, "In changing systems with changing components, one specifies the conditions under which the conservative style, the liberal style, or a mixture of both will work." In fact one of the early contingency theorists titled his book *It All Depends.*

Although it is early to say this, the thrust of most recent research is that the contingency approach is the right one. Most of this research has tried to specify when to use the conservative model, the liberal model, or a middle-of-the-road mixture, although not everyone agrees with this approach.

The first aspect of horizontal division of labor described in this chapter was formalization. It should be easy to see how conservative bureaucracies can become fully formalized. Conservative orgainzations tend to move in that direction. Liberal organizations try to eliminate as much formalization as possible. Middle-of-the-road managers might formalize about half of the Aston items, or fulfill half the scales. Actually there are a number of stages between the liberal and conservative styles, as illustrated in Figure 15.13. The Aston group found a number of middle-of-the-road enterprises between full bureaucracies (conservative) and implicitly structured organizations (liberal).

Although Aston researchers found a high correlation between size and formalization, very few studies have shown that formalization itself leads to effectiveness. Still, it is usually present to a large extent in conservative organizations.

Two propositions seem to be in order here:

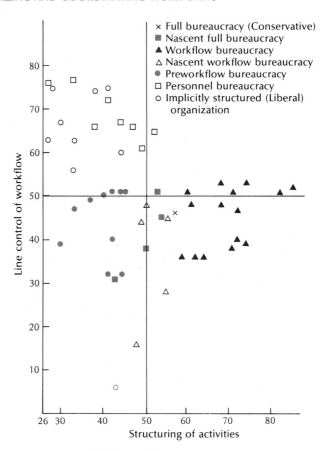

Figure 15.13
Relative
formalization.

Proposition 15.6
As an enterpise grows larger, it will tend to use more formalization.

Proposition 15.7.
If it is large and operates in a stable technological and market environment, an enterprise will tend to formalize its organization structure.

There is little research to substantiate these propositions at present, but they appear reasonable.

The second measure of horizontal division of labor is departmentation/specialization. Although there are variations, in general departmentation by process is characteristic of the conservative organization, departmentation by purpose is characteristic of liberal organization, and the matrix approach is characteristic of the middle-of-the-road style. Again, little contingency research has been done in this area.

The final measure of horizontal division of labor is standardization. There is little direct research that specifies when standardization is effective. It is based on the same studies that argue that the conservative (or liberal) approach is best.

Selwyn Becker and Gerald Gordon describe the conservative and liberal approaches to standardizing procedures as follows: "Procedures are self determined (liberal) when humans are given general instructions to achieve an organizational objective but not specific instructions on how to achieve it. Procedures are organizationally determined (conservative) when the humans are given both organizational objective and detailed instructions on how to attain the objective." They propose as a measure of standardization the ratio of self-determined to organizationally determined procedures.

The conservative organization tries to standardize as much as possible because standardization is efficient and serves as a form of control. The liberal organization takes the opposite approach because standardization tends to reduce employee creativity.

There are different styles of vertical division of labor, too. The first measure of vertical division of labor is the height of the hierarchy or chain of command. The main thrust of the arguments on the issue, as described earlier, is that a flatter structure is best for productivity, satisfaction, and employee development. But the research results on this argument are mixed. This is probably because few studies have tried to take a contingency approach. It appears reasonable to believe that when research begins to test the contingency theory described in Chapter 16, the results will be less mixed.

The second measure of vertical division of labor is span of control. Conservative organization theorists have argued that spans of control should be small because this allows the manager to control the job better and spend more time coordinating with other units. It also gives employees greater access to the superior.

Liberal theorists contend either that the span of control is unimportant or that it should be large. Large spans are cheaper in terms of managerial costs, and they allow employees to make more decisions and thus participate more. This in turn leads to greater job satisfaction and enhanced self-development.

The final vertical measure is centralization. As in the case of height of hierarchy, the research results are mixed. Again, I believe this is because researchers should be testing the contingency approach: When the conditions are right for conservative organization, centralization works; in a liberal management environment, decentralization is appropriate.

Finally, let us briefly review the managerial styles as they apply to coordination. There are four mechanisms or means of coordination: unprogramed informal, programed nonhuman; individual human (individual hierarch; individual coordinator), and group coordination mechanisms. Table 15.8 shows how these relate to organization styles as shown in Table 15.7.

Table 15.8 Coordination and Management Style

Liberal		Middle of the Road		Conservative
Informal/ nonprogramed	Group coordinators	Individual coordinator		Individual hierarch
			Nonhuman ———— coordination mechanisms	

The conservative organization will tend to place the responsibility for coordination in the hands of the line executive (hierarch) in charge of the units with coordination problems. This approach can be supplemented by nonhuman mechanisms like SOPs and rules. The middle-of-the-road organization will use an individual coordinator or liaison, and the liberal organization will use informal mechanisms or group decision making.

SUMMARY Organization is the process by which people and the tasks they perform are related to each other systematically to help achieve enterprise objectives. This includes division of labor (dividing up work horizontally and vertically). Coordination is the set of human and structural mechanisms that link the parts of the enterprise together. Enterprises organize in order to be more effective and to achieve greater employee satisfaction.

Division of labor can be accomplished along both horizontal and vertical dimensions. Horizontal division of labor takes the form of relative formalization, relative standardization, and departmentation. Vertically, the mechanisms of organization are height of the hierarchy, span of control, and decentralization or centralization.

Coordination is accomplished through four mechanisms: unprogramed/informal personal mechanisms, policies and SOPs (programed nonhuman), programed human (individual coordinators like the hierarch or individual coordinator), and group coordinators.

The chapter's final objective was to demonstrate that there are many styles of organization and coordination. For simplicity's sake I described only three. The conservative or burearucratic, approach involves more formalization, more standardization, and departmentation by process or function. It favors tall hierarchies, small spans of control, and more centralization, and coordinates by means of hierarchs, SOPs, and policies. The liberals coordinate by informal methods or use group coordinators and prefer decentralization, large spans of control, and flat hierarchies. All organization have some degree of formalization and standardization, but liberals try to minimize them and departmentalize by purpose. And there are many combinations of styles in the middle-of-the-road approach.

Questions for Review

1. What is organization? Why do managers organize? How does organization relate to job design?
2. What are the three major characteristics of organization?
3. What is organization theory? What is the significance of the Aston studies of organization structure?
4. How do organizations evolve over time? What is a primitive structure? a divisional structure? Why is this evolution important?
5. What is formalization? What are the differences between formalized enterprises and informal enterprises?
6. What are organization charts? Draw an example of a circular, a horizontal, and a vertical chart. On the vertical chart show line, line and staff, and line and functional staff relationships.
7. What is product departmentation? process departmentation? When is each best? Which is used the most? When?
8. What is matrix departmentation?
9. What is standardization? How does it differ from formalization?
10. What three mechanisms are used to accomplish horizontal division of labor? vertical division of labor?
11. What is a tall organization? a flat one? How do flat organizations become tall and vice versa?
12. Which is best, a tall organization or a flat one?
13. How are height of hierarchy, span of control, and degree of centralization related (if at all)?
14. Is height of hierarchy related to the age of the enterprise, the size of the enterprise, or managerial preferences for flat or tall hierarchies?
15. What is a small span of control? a large span? Which is best? Under what conditions?
16. What is a weighted span of control? How would you design one?
17. What is decentralization? How does it relate to organization?
18. Why do enterprises need to coordinate? How much coordination is best?
19. In what ways do enterprises coordinate?
20. Which coordination mechanisms are best?
21. How do coordination and organization relate to management style?

22. What is a conservative way to organize? to coordinate?

23. What is a liberal way to organize? to coordinate?

References

Why Study Organization?

Brown, Fred, and Chitwood, Stephen, "Highlights from the Literature on Organization," Monograph 2, Program of Policy Studies in Science and Technology (Washington, D.C.: George Washington University, July 1968).

Gorelik, George, "Reemergence of Bogdanov's TEKTOLOGY in Soviet Studies of Organization," *Academy of Management Journal,* 18, no. 2 (June 1975): 345–357.

Perrow, Charles, "The Short and Glorious History of Organization Theory," *Organizational Dynamics,* no. 2 (Summer 1973): 2–15.

Pugh, Derek, et al., "A Conceptual Scheme for Organizational Analysis," *Administrative Science Quarterly,* 8, no. 2 (1963): 289–315.

Scott, William G., "Organization Theory: A Reassessment," *Academy of Management Journal,* 17, no. 2 (June 1974): 242–254.

Starbuck, William, "The Current State of Organization Theory," in Joseph McGuire, ed., *Contemporary Management* (Englewood Cliffs, N.J.: Prentice-Hall, 1974), pp. 123–149.

Organizational Problems Change over Time

H. Igor Ansoff and Richard Brandenburg, "A Language for Organizational Design," *Management Science,* 17, no. 12 (August 1971): 717–731.

Dale, Ernest, *Planning and Developing the Company Organization Structure* (New York: American Management Association, 1952).

Glueck, William F. "An Evaluation of the Stages of Corporate Development in Business Policy," *Proceedings, Midwest Academy of Management,* 1974.

———, *Business Policy,* 2nd ed. (New York: McGraw-Hill, 1976), chap. 7.

Thain, Donald, "Stages of Corporate Development," *Business Quarterly,* Winter 1969, pp. 33–45.

Horizontal Division of Labor/ Formalization

Hinings, C. R., and Lee, Gloria, "Dimensions of Organization Structure and Their Context: A Replication," *Sociology,* 5, no. 1 (January 1971): 83–93.

Holdaway, Edward, et al., "Dimensions of Organization in Complex Societies: The Educational Sector," *Administrative Science Quarterly,* 20 (March 1975): 37–58.

Inkson, J. H. K., et al., "Organization Context and Structure: An Abbreviated Replication," *Administrative Science Quarterly,* 15, no. 2 (September 1970): 318–329.

———, "A Comparison of Organization Structure and Managerial Roles: Ohio (U.S.A.) and the Midlands England," *Journal of Management Studies,* 7, no. 3 (October 1970): 347–363.

McMillan, Charles, et al., "The Structure of Work Organizations Across Societies," *Academy of Management Journal,* 16, no. 4 (December 1975): 555–569.

Pugh, Derek, "The Measurement of Organization Structures," *Organization Dynamics,* no. 2 (1975): 19–34.

Pugh, Derek, et al., "Dimensions of Organization Structure," *Administrative Science Quarterly,* 13 (1968): 64–105.

———, "An Empirical Taxonomy of Structures of Work Organizations," *Administrative Science Quarterly,* 14, no. 1 (March 1969): 115–125.

———, "The Context of Organization Structures," *Administrative Science Quarterly,* 14, no. 1 (March 1969): 91–114.

White, K. K., *Understanding the Company Organization Chart,* AMA Research Study (New York: American Management Association, 1963).

Specialization and Departmentation

Delbecq, Andrew, and Filley, Alan, *Program and Project Management in a Matrix Organization,* Monograph no. 9 (Madison: University of Wisconsin, Graduate School of Business, 1974).

Galbraith, Jay, *Designing Complex Organizations* (Boston: Addison Wesley, 1973).

Galbraith, Jay, "Matrix Organization Designs," *Business Horizons,* 14 (1971): 29–40.

Grimes, Andrew, et al., "Matrix Model: A Selective Empirical Test," *Academy of Management Journal,* March 1972, pp. 9–31.

Hinings, C. R., et al., "An Approach to the Study of Bureaucracy," *Sociology,* 1, no. 1 (1967): 61–72.

Kover, Arthur, "Reorganizing in an Advertising Agency," *Human Organization,* 22 (1963): 252–259.

Morse, J. "Organization Characteristics and Individual Motivations," in Paul Lawrence and Jay Lorsch, eds., *Studies in Organization Design* (Homewood, Ill.: Richard D. Irwin, 1970).

Pugh, op. cit.

Pugh, et al., "Dimensions of Organization Structure," op. cit.

Reimann, Bernard, "Dimensions of Structure in Effective Organizations," *Academy of Management Journal,* 17, no. 4 (December 1974): 693–708.

Shull, Fremont, et al., *Organizational Decision Making* (New York: McGraw-Hill, 1970).

Walker, Arthur, and Lorsch, Jay, "Organizational Choice: Product Versus Function," *Harvard Business Review,* 46 (November-December 1968): 129–138.

Vertical Division of Labor

Carpenter, Harrel, "Formal Organizational Structural Factors and Perceived Job Satisfaction of Classroom Teachers," *Administrative Science Quarterly,* 16, no. 4 (1971): 460–465.

Carzo, Rocco, Jr., and Yanouzas, John, "Effects of Flat and Tall Organization Structure," *Administrative Science Quarterly,* 14 (1969): 178–191.

Dale, Ernest, op. cit.

Ghiselli, Edwin, and Siegel, Jacob, "Leadership and Managerial Success in Tall and Flat Organization Structures," *Personnel Psychology,* 25, no. 4 (1972): 617–624.

Hickson, David, et al., "Operations Technology and Organization Structure," *Administrative Science Quarterly*, 14, no. 3 (1969): 378–397.

Jacques, Elliot, *Equitable Payment* (New York: John Wiley and Sons, 1963).

Jones, Halsey, "A Study of Organization Performance for Experimental Structures of Two, Three, and Four Levels," *Academy of Management Journal*, 12, no. 3 (September 1969): 351–365.

Kaufman, Herbert, and Seidman, David, "The Morphology of Organizations," *Administrative Science Quarterly*, 15, no. 4 (December 1970): 439–451.

Meltzer, Leo, and James Salter, "Organization Structures: The Performance and Job Satisfaction of Physiologists," *American Sociological Review*, 27 (1962): 351–362.

Nealey, Stanley, and Fiedler, Fred, "Leadership Functions of Middle Managers," *Psychological Bulletin*, 70, no. 5 (1968): 313–329.

Porter, Lyman, and Lawler, Edward, "The Effects of Flat and Tall Organization Structures on Managerial Job Satisfaction," *Personnel Psychology*, 17 (1964): 135–148.

Porter, Lyman, and Siegel, Jacob, "Relationships of Tall and Flat Organization Structures to the Satisfaction of Foreign Managers," *Personnel Psychology*, 18, no. 3 (1964): 379–392.

Pugh, et al., "Dimensions of Organization Structure," op. cit.

Richardson, F., and Walker, Charles, *Human Relations in an Expanding Company* (New Haven, Conn.: Yale Labor and Management Center, 1948).

Triandis, Harry, "Notes on the Design of Organizations," in James D. Thompson, (Pittsburgh: University of Pittsburgh Press, 1960).

Woodward, Joan, *Industrial Organization: Theory and Practice* (New York: Oxford University Press, 1965).

Worthy, James, "Organization Structure and Employee Morale," *American Sociological Review*, 15 (1956): 169–179.

Span of Control

Bell, Gerald, "Determinants of Span of Control," *American Journal of Sociology*, 73, no. 1 (July 1967): 100–109.

Blau, Peter, "The Hierarchy of Organizations," *American Journal of Sociology*, 73, no. 3 (1968): 460–470.

Dale, op. cit.

Davis, Ralph, *Fundamentals of Top Management* (New York: Harper and Brothers, 1951).

Entwisle, D., and Walton, J., "Observations on the Span of Control," *Administrative Science Quarterly*, 5, no. 4 (1961): 522–533.

Fayol, Henri, *General and Industrial Administration* (New York: Pittman, 1949).

Graicunus, V. A., "Relationship in Organizations," in L. Urwick and L. Gullick, eds., *Papers on the Science of Administration* (New York: Institute of Public Administration, 1937).

Healey, James, *Executive Coordination and Control* (Columbia, Ohio: Ohio State University, Columbia Bureau of Business Research, 1956).

House, Robert, and Miner, John, "Merging Management and Behavioral Theory: The Interaction Between Span of Control and Group Size," *Administrative Science Quarterly,* 14, no. 3 (1969): 451–465.

Janger, Allen, "Analyzing the Span of Control," *Management Record,* 22, no. 1 (1960): 7–10.

Lawrence and Lorsch, op. cit.

Likert, Rensis, *The Human Organization* (New York: McGraw-Hill, 1967).

Ouchi, William, and Dowling, John, "Defining the Span of Control," *Administrative Science Quarterly,* 21, no. 3 (September 1974): 357–365.

Pugh, et al., op. cit.

Shull, Fremont, et al., op. cit.

Simonds, Roland, "Is Organization Structure Reflecting New Techniques and Theory?" *MSU Business Topics,* 17 (1969): 65–71.

Streglitz, Harold, "Optimizing Span of Control," *Management Record,* 24, no. 2 (1962): 25–29.

Suojanen, Waino, "The Span of Control: Fact or Fable," *Advanced Management,* 20, no. 11 (1955): 5–13.

Udell, Jon, "An Empirical Test of Hypotheses Relating to Span of Control," *Administrative Science Quarterly,* 10, no. 4 (December 1967): 420–439.

Urwick, Lyndall, "The Span of Control: Some Facts About the Fable," *Advanced Management,* 21 (1956): 5–15.

Viola, Richard, "The Span of Management in the Life Insurance Industry," *Economic and Business Bulletin,* no. 1 (1975): 18–25.

Woodward, op. cit.

Degree of Centralization

Baker, Helen, and France, R., *Centralization and Decentralization in Industrial Relations* (Princeton, N.J.: Industrial Relations Center, 1954).

Baum, Bernard, *Decentralization of Authority in a Bureaucracy* (Englewood Cliffs, N.J.: Prentice-Hall, 1961).

Blau, Peter, et al., "The Structure of Small Bureaucracies," *American Sociological Review,* 31 (April 1966): 179–191.

Chandler, Alfred, *Strategy and Structure* (Cambridge, Mass.: MIT Press, 1961).

Child, John, "Organization Structure and Strategies of Control," *Administrative Science Quarterly,* 17, no. 2 (June 1972): 163–177.

Dale, op. cit.

Donaldson, Lee, "The Aston Findings on Centralization," *Administrative Science Quarterly,* 20, no. 4 (September 1975): 453–460.

Hage, Jerald, and Aiken, Michael, "Relationship of Centralization to Other Structural Properties," *Administrative Science Quarterly,* 12, no. 1 (June 1967): 72–92.

Lawrence and Lorsch, op. cit.

Litzinger, William, "Entrepreneurial Prototype in Bank Management," *Academy of Management Journal,* 6, no. 1 (1963): 36–45.

Maier, Norman, and Thurber, J., "Problems in Delegation," *Personnel Psychology,* 22 (1969): 131–139.

Mansfield, Roger, "Bureaucracy and Centralization," *Administrative Science Quarterly,* 18, no. 12 (1973): 477–488.

Negandhi, Anant, and Reiman, Bernard, "Correlates of Decentralization," *Academy of Management Journal,* 16, no. 4 (December 1973): 570–582.

Starkweather, David, "The Rationale for Decentralization in Hospitals," *Hospital Administration,* 15 (Spring 1970): 27–45.

Woodward, op. cit.

Yin, Robert, and Lucas, William, "Decentralization and Alienation," *Policy Sciences,* 4 (September 1973): 327–336.

Coordination

Georgopoulos, Basil, and Mann, Floyd, *The Community General Hospital,* (New York: Macmillan, 1962).

Thompson, James, *Organizations in Action* (New York: McGraw-Hill, 1967), chap. 5.

Informal Unprogramed Coordination

Coser, Rose, "Authority and Decision Making in a Hospital," *American Sociological Review,* 23 (1958): 56–64.

Hall, Richard, "Some Organizational Considerations in the Professional Relationship," *Administrative Science Quarterly,* 12, no. 4 (1967): 461–478.

Wilson, Robert, "Teamwork in the Operating Room," *Human Organization,* Winter 1954, pp. 9–14.

Individual Coordination

Aleshire, Robert, "The Metropolitan Desk: A New Technique in Program Teamwork," *Public Administration Review,* 26, no. 2, 87–95.

Avorts, Ivars, "Why Does Project Management Fail?" *California Management Review,* 12, no. 1 (Fall 1969): 77–82.

Egloff, William, "Product Management: Status of the Art: 1969," *Proceedings, Academy of Management,* 1969, pp. 95–110.

Wilemon, David, "The Project Manager: Anomalies and Ambiguities," *Academy of Management Review,* 13, no. 3 (September 1970): 269–282.

Group Coordination

Filley, Alan, et al., *Managerial Process and Organizational Behavior* (Chicago: Scott, Foresman, 1976), 380–410.

Zander, Alvin, and Wolfe, Donald, "Administrative Reward and Coordination Among Committee Members," *Administrative Science Quarterly,* 9, no. 1 (June 1964): 50–69.

Which Way Is Best?

Georgopoulos and Mann, op. cit.

Jasinski, Frank, "Adapting the Organization to Technology," *Harvard Business Review,* (1959): 484–496.

Lawrence and Lorsch, op. cit.

Division of Labor, Coordination, and Management Style: A Contingency Approach

Albrook, Robert, "Participative Management: Time For a Second Look," *Fortune,* May 1967.

Barnard, Chester, *Function of the Executive* (Cambridge: Harvard University Press, 1938).

Becker, Selwyn, and Gordon, Gerald, "An Entrepreneurial Theory of Formal Organizations," *Administrative Science Quarterly,* 11, no. 3 (1966): 315–344.

Bennis, Warren, *Changing Organizations* (New York: McGraw Hill, 1966).

———, "Organizational Developments and the Fate of Bureaucracy," American Psychological Association, Division of Industrial and Business Psychology, (1964).

Child, John, "More Myths of Management Organization," *Journal of Management Studies,* 7, no. 3 (October 1970): 376–390.

Davies, Bryan, "Some Thought on Organizational Democracy," *Journal of Management Studies,* 4, no. 3 (October 1967): 270–281.

Fayol, op. cit.

Koontz, Harold, and O'Donnel, Cyril, *Principles of Management* (New York: McGraw-Hill, 1976).

Korman, Abraham, and Tanofsky, Robert, "Statistical Problems of Contingency Models of Organizational Behavior," *Academy of Management Journal,* 18, no. 2 (June 1975): 393–397.

McKelvey, Bill, and Kilman, Ralph, "Organization Design," *Administrative Science Quarterly,* 20, no. 1 (March 1975): 24–36.

Moberg, Dennis, and Koch, James, "A Critical Appraisal of Integrated Treatments of Contingency Findings," *Academy of Management Journal,* 18, no. 1 (March 1975): 109–124.

Mooney, James, and Reilly, Allan, *Onward Industry!* (New York: Harper and Brothers, 1939).

Powell, Reed, and Schlacter, John, "Participative Management: A Panacea?" *Academy of Management Journal,* 14, no. 2 (June 1971): 165–173.

Sherman, Harvey, *It All Depends* (University-University of Alabama Press, 1966).

Steinmetz, Lawrence, and Greenidge, Charles, "Realities That Shape Management Style," *Business Horizons,* October 1970, pp. 23–32.

Strauss, George, "Participative Management: A Critique," *ILR Research,* 12, no. 2 (1966): 3–6.

Weber, Max, *The Theory of Social and Economic Organizations* (New York: Oxford University Press, 1947).

CHAPTER 16

A CONTINGENCY APPROACH TO ORGANIZATION AND COORDINATION

Learning Objectives

1. To understand the factors that influence the choice of organizational style.
2. To learn how to be a more effective organizer.

Chapter Outline

Introduction to the Contingency Approach
Internal Factors in the Choice of Organizational Style
Size of Enterprise
Employee Characteristics
Environmental Complexity
External Factors in the Choice of Organizational Style
Dependence on External Forces
Technology and Organizational Structure
Volatility/Uncertainty and Organizational Structure
Strategy and Organizational Style
Summary

INTRODUCTION TO THE CONTINGENCY APPROACH

This chapter completes our three-chapter unit on organization and coordination. Chapter 14 described how to design and organize jobs: the basic unit of work. Chapter 15 moved up one level to organizing and coordinating groups of jobs into units. This chapter looks at the organization as a whole and at the organization's interface with its environment.

The subject of this chapter is the contingency approach to organization and coordination. That is, we will try to answer the question, When is it effective to organize and coordinate using a conservative, liberal, or middle-of-the-road style? The answer is that all styles can be effective. But one style is more effective than the others when the conditions for that style are right.

Figure 16.1 specifies the conditions that determine when each organizational style is best. From time to time I have touched on these or related factors. In Chapter 2 you learned that enterprises differ along such dimensions as size, purpose, strength, and technology. And in Chapter 7 you learned that leaders prefer different organizational styles. I will elaborate on this point now.

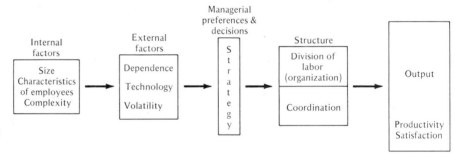

Figure 16.1
Factors determining organizational style.

INTERNAL FACTORS IN THE CHOICE OF ORGANIZATIONAL STYLE

The first set of factors determining whether organizational style should be conservative, liberal, or middle of the road is a set of three internal factors: characteristics of the organization as a whole. Just how these factors indicate which style is most likely to be effective is shown in Table 16.1 and explained in the sections that follow.

Size of Enterprise

ENTERPRISE SIZE
By enterprise size we mean the number of employees working for the organization in a single location. Although these numbers are somewhat arbitrary, small enterprises employ 1–250 people, medium-sized organizations 251–1000, and large organizations over 1000.

Table 16.1 Internal Factors Determining the Effectiveness of Organizational Styles

Liberal	Middle of the Road	Conservative
Size		
Small	Medium	Large
Employee Characteristics		
Education		
High PARTICIPATI UE	Moderate	Low
Rearing Style		
Nonauthoritarian PARTICIPATIVE	Moderate	Authoritarian
Location of Rearing		
Urban RURAL	Surburban	Rural URBAN
Intelligence		
High	Moderate	Low
Experience		
Wide	Moderate	Narrow
Complexity (No. of Products/Services)		
High	Medium	Low

Some might argue that you should measure size by amount of assets or sales (or the equivalent in nonbusinesses—revenue flow). But the correlation between these measures of size is over .95 in most studies. The exceptions are a few capital intensive organizations like oil refineries.

Note that the measure of size is the number of *people* at a location. The relevant variable here is how many people relate on a face-to-face basis.

Size has other important effects on enterprises. For example, there is strong evidence that as units increase in size, job satisfaction decreases and absenteeism, turnover, and accidents increase. The size of support staff increases as a percentage of the total staff and then declines.

As size increases, the unit has a tendency to become more conservatively organized. Why? For two reasons. Larger numbers of people find it difficult or impossible to relate informally as the liberal style requires. Ten to fifteen people can relate to each other rather informally;

500 cannot. As the number of people increases, the amount of formality increases to cope with the complexity of employee interrelationships and communication problems.

The other reason larger enterprises tend to become conservatively structured is that large size provides a greater opportunity to utilize the economics of specialization and thus encourages conservative structuring.

Are all large enterprises necessarily conservatively organized, then? No. Consider two firms: Ralston Purina and McDonnell Douglas. Both are large firms. Ralston's employees tend to work at one of a large number of plants, all of which are small. McDonnell has essentially only two locations and concentrates large numbers of people at these locations. But the relevant factor is the size of the local unit. For example, Ralston subdivides a large number of people into smaller units and then the smaller units can organize liberally at the unit level. Or it could organize so that only the top executive at each location needs to relate to a conservative structure (at the home office) and he or she can organize the plant liberally since the number of employees there is relatively low.

Another way to deal with size is to make strategic changes. The company can merge (and increase size) or divest (and reduce size). Still, is it likely that McDonnell would break up its St. Louis complex of over 10,000 employees and assign them to 15 medium-sized plants all over the country? It is possible, but not too likely. Is Ralston likely to consolidate all its plants into a single large one? The technology and economies of scale tend to prevent major moves of this type. So we treat size as a "given" in the organizational situation and therefore as an influence on structure.

Table 16.2 presents a sample of the studies that have examined the relationship between unit size and organizational structure. The conclusion we can draw is that size does influence structure: In general, larger size leads to conservative style. But there is inadequate evidence to say that conservative style is *always* effective in larger organizations.

Size alone does not dictate organization style. As will be indicated later, five factors—people, complexity, dependence, technology, and volatility—also influence structure.

Employee Characteristics   The next internal variable influencing organizational structure is the "stock" of personnel employed at the enterprise. Many enterprises require employees with specific abilities. Oil refineries need chemical engineers; insurance companies need actuaries; the Securities and Exchange Commission needs lawyers. Organizations also vary in their percentage distribution of professional/technical, managerial, clerical, and operative employees. Obviously each of these groups contains some college graduates, but in almost all cases professional/technical and managerial employees have more education than operative employees. Thus certain departments or units are more likely to show particular educational patterns.

Table 16.2 Research and Theory on the Relationship Between Unit Size and Organizational Structure

Study	Site	Degree of Sophistication	Findings
A. Child; Child and Mansfield	82 British firms in six industries	Very sophisticated	Effective and profitable large firms use conservative style; effective smaller firms use liberal style. Size is a more important predictor of structure than technology.
B. Aston studies (Hickson)	52 British firms and government agencies	Very sophisticated	Large enterprises organize conservatively, smaller ones liberally. Size is a more important factor than technology in forecasting structure.
C. Khandwalla	79 American manufacturing firms	Very sophisticated	Technology and size are about equally important in influencing structure in effective firms.
D. Pfeffer	80 American manufacturing firms.	Sophisticated.	As a firm gets larger, it increases the number of directors in order to cope with larger size; and it becomes more conservatively organized.
E. Hrebiniak and Alutto	338 in-patient psychiatric departments	Very sophisticated	As departments increase in size, they become more conservatively organized.
F. Blau and Schoenherr	53 U.S. state (and territory) employment security agencies (including their subunits: 387 major divisions and 1201 local offices)	Very sophisticated	As enterprises increase in size, they organize more conservatively, although the degree of conservatism does not increase linearly forever.
G. Meyer	194 city, county, and state departments of finance in 2 different years	Very sophisticated	As enterprises increase in size, they organize more conservatively. Size is the key determinant of structural style.
H. Hall, et al.	75 organizations (business and government)	Sophisticated	Size is one of the factors that leads to conservative structure.
I. Woodward	100 British businesses	Very sophisticated	Technology is more powerful than size. (Opponents point out that Woodward did not study enough large organizations to come to a scientific conclusion.)

There is much evidence that work attitudes and preferences correlate with education. One possible modifier is child-rearing practices. But, in general, education and intelligence are correlated with a preference for a liberal organizational style, as may be seen in the following excerpt from Table 16.1:

Liberal	Factor	Conservative
More	Education	Less
High	Intelligence	Low
More	Experience	Less
Nonauthoritarian	Child-rearing style of parents	Authoritarian
Urban	Location of upbringing	Rural

The studies in the reference list provide some evidence for these predictions. But one can conclude from the data in Chapters 4, 5, and 7 that people with more experience and education prefer more autonomy and responsibility and thus prefer the liberal style. There are individual differences, of course. An authoritarian or rural upbringing would reduce this preference. Several negative experiences might reduce the preference for the liberal style too. But, in general, unit whose employees are highly educated, intelligent, experienced people are likely to be more effective if they are organized liberally. This variable needs much more research support to back it up, however.

Environmental Complexity   Complexity is the final internal variable and the one on which the least research has been done. So much of this section is speculation.

> **ENVIRONMENTAL COMPLEXITY**
> An enterprise or unit is said to exist in a complex environment if the number of factors it must deal with is large; if the number of factors is small the enterprise faces a simple environment.

A marketing department of a business firm may have to perform its functions (personal selling, advertising, pricing, sales promotion) using few or many media (TV, radio, newspapers, magazines); it may have to perform these duties for a short product list or a large product list and through a single channel of distribution or several channels. Thus I would call the environments of Departments 1 and 2 in Table 16.3 simple and complex, respectively.

Robert Duncan has devised a more specific measure of complexity—a complexity index:

Complexity index = no. of decision factors (F) × no. of components (C)^2

$$I = (F) \times (C)^2$$

Components are a measure of similarity and dissimilarity between factors.

Table 16.3

	Marketing Department 1	Marketing Department 2
No. of products	3	320
No. of sizes per product	average 1	average 3
No. of channels used	1	4
No. of advertising media used	1	89
No. of salespeople	10	1000
No. of sales districts	1	50
No. of price lists	1	174
No. of sales promotion mechanisms (other than advertising)	0	5

Duncan combined this simple/complex variable with the volatility factor (static vs. dynamic) and came up with the matrix in Table 16.4. He argues that perceived uncertainty ranges from low (Cell 1) to high. He then proposes that the higher the perceived uncertainty, the greater the need to use a liberal style. In his study of 22 decision groups in 3 manufacturing and 3 R & D organizations he found that this statement was generally correct.

David Murphy studied 37 U.S. and Canadian breweries. He found that the higher the complexity, the greater the tendency toward middle-of-the-road or liberal styles.

EXTERNAL FACTORS IN THE CHOICE OF ORGANI-ZATIONAL STYLE

Table 16.5 summarizes the ways in which external factors influence the choice of organizational style. We will examine each of these factors in turn.

INDEPENDENCE
Independence is freedom to choose a strategy and organizational structure independent of the pressures of resource providers (suppliers, unions, stockholders, etc.), regulators (government, community), and clients or customers.

Table 16.4 Environmental State Dimensions and Predicted Perceived Uncertainty Experienced by Individuals in Decision Units (Duncan)

	Simple	Complex
Static	**Cell 1:** low perceived uncertainty (1) Small number of factors and components in the environment (2) Factors and components are somewhat similar to one another (3) Factors and components remain basically the same and are not changing	**Cell 2:** moderately low perceived uncertainty (1) Large number of factors and components in the environment (2) Factors and components are not similar to one another (3) Factors and components remain basically the same
Dynamic	**Cell 3:** moderately high perceived uncertainty (1) Small number of factors and components in the environment (2) Factors and components are somewhat similar to one another (3) Factors and components of the environment are in continual process of change	**Cell 4:** high perceived uncertainty (1) Large number of factors and components in the environment (2) Factors and components are not similar to one another (3) Factors and components of environment are in a continual process of change

Table 16.5 External Factors Determining the Effectiveness of Organizational Styles

Liberal	Middle of the Road	Conservative
Dependence		
Lower	Moderate	Higher
Technology		
Nonroutine	Some routine, some nonroutine	Routine
Volatility		
High	Moderate	Low

Dependence on External Forces

> **DEPENDENCE**
> Dependence is the relative loss of flexibility in choice of organizational structure or enterprise strategy.

> **Proposition 16.1**
> The more dependent an enterprise is on an external force, the more it must respond to its wishes. This can affect the design of the organization's structure.

Table 16.6 provides a few examples of companies that are relatively dependent on or independent of external forces. With its diversified ownership, AT&T is not as dependent on the wishes of the owners as Hallmark's management is on the wishes of the Hall family.

Table 16.6 Relatively Independent and Dependent Enterprises

Relatively Independent Enterprise	Dependence Factor	Relatively Dependent Enterprise
Resource Suppliers		
AT&T	Stockholders (business)	Hallmark
IBM	Unions	Chrysler
Ace Hardware Retailers	Suppliers: subparts	Jack's Paving
Regulators		
Ace Hardware	Government	New York Life
New York Life	Community	Small clothing manufacturer
Clients/customers		
General Foods		Lockheed
Competitors		
IBM		Small clothing manufacturer

It appears reasonable that if an external force has concentrated power and wishes to dictate structural arrangements or strategy, the enterprise has a tendency to respond. If the enterprise is shielded from this problem, its strategists can base structural choices on other factors. The other side of dependence is independence, when the organization can be structured the way management feels is best.

There is not a tremendous amount of research in this area (see Table 16.7). And what there is tends to be as much theorizing as research. More studies have been made in nonbusiness than in business sectors. But all show how the enterprise accommodates itself to dependence pressure through various mechanisms, including adjusting its organizational structure to the force on which it is most dependent. Choice of structure is not always voluntary. If the firm is subject to government regulation and the government requires a strict control bureaucracy, its managers cannot take a liberal approach even if they want to.

James Thompson's theoretical work provides some useful (and generally untested) propositions:

Proposition 16.2.
The greater the firm's dependence on only one supplier, the more the supplier can affect the enterprise's structure if it chooses to.

Proposition 16.3
Enterprises seek to reduce dependence by maintaining alternative sources of supply.

Proposition 16.4.
When dependence is concentrated, the enterprise tries to equalize power through cooptation, coalescence, or contracting out.

Proposition 16.5.
Organizations too dependent on suppliers may coopt them through vertical integration.

Proposition 16.6.
Enterprises too dependent on a few clients will try to increase the number of clients they serve.

Table 16.7 Research on Dependence and Organizational Style

Dependence on Resource *Users*

A. Densmore and Klein	Describes how hospitals are now creating patient responsibilities (ombudsmen) and "patient bills of rights"
B. Maynes	Describes businesses' reactions to organized consumer groups

Dependence on *Regulators*

Boddewyn	Describes the role of government relations executives who serve as liaison between businesses and regulators/legislators

Dependence on Resource *Providers*

A. Aiken and Hage	Describes conditions under which health and welfare organizations cooperate instead of competing (thus reducing dependence)
B. Assael	Describes dealer dependence on a supplier (General Motors) and its effect on structure
C. Baty, et al.	Examines how faculty move between universities; one university is dependent on the other for faculty
D. Blankenship and Elling	Describes how hospitals respond to the power of large givers and important doctors by accommodating them on the board and in structural arrangements
E. Elling and Halebsky	Describes how hospitals' (city sponsored and community general) structures are a consequence of their sponsorship
F. Hage	Describes methods of creating interdependence (instead of competition) between welfare agencies
G. Khandwalla	Describes how the degree of competition a firm faces affects organizational structure: the more competition, the more decentralization
H. Kochen	Describes how the dependence of unions affects their organizational structure
I. Litwak and Hylton	Describes conditions under which government agencies are cooperative and when they are competitive
J. Martin and Kearney	Describes how trade associations become powerful and individual companies become dependent on them and on their competitors
K. Pfeffer and Leblebici	Like Khandwalla: the more competitiveness, the more central controls (and other structural impacts)
L. Pfeffer	Like Blankenship and Elling, describes how owners influence board membership, size, and structure
M. Schermerhorn	Describes conditions under which hospitals cooperate (instead of competing)
N. Warren	Describes conditions under which metropolitan agencies work together rather than competing

Hans Thorelli also provides several useful propositions:

Proposition 16.7.
The greater the intensity of competition, the greater the degree of decentralization.

Proposition 16.8.
The greater the diversity of customer needs, the greater the diversification of the organization.

Proposition 16.9.
The greater the power of customers, the greater the degree of centralization in the enterprise.

Proposition 16.10.
The greater the relative power of customers, the stronger the tendency to organize by client (not by function).

These hypotheses can only indicate in general terms how dependence affects structure. The more dependent it is on external forces, the more the enterprise adjusts its structure to meet the needs of those forces. If the external forces are pulling in opposite directions, the enterprise responds most fully to the most powerful force. Thus external forces lead to dependence, which, in turn, affects structure. The lower the dependence, on the other hand, the more likely we are to find a liberal organizational style.

Technology and Organizational Structure

The second external factor that influences organizational structure is the technology of the enterprise. Of course once the technology is applied inside the enterprise, it becomes an internal variable as well. Here we will treat it as primarily an external variable.

The research on the relationship between technology and organizational structure is more sophisticated than most organization research. But not all researchers define *technology* the same way. I will define it as follows:

TECHNOLOGY
Technology consists of the techniques (such as equipment, computers, forms, etc.) used on the inputs to the enterprise (such as money and materials) to accomplish the enterprise's objectives.

For example, the technology of an office could include a computer, standardized forms, typewriters, and the like.

Before summarizing the results of the research relating technology to structure, I will give a brief summary of the most influential work in this area. This is the research done by Joan Woodward between 1953 and 1971.

Woodward studied the relationship between technology and effective organizational style in British firms employing over 100 employees. 40 percent of the businesses she studied employed from 100 to 250 employees; another forty percent, 251-1000; and twenty percent, 1000–8000.

Woodward used a combination of research methods, including interviews, observation, and analysis of documents. Her measures of technology were sophisticated, her measures of structured and of organizational effectiveness less so.

At the time of Woodward's study England had a system of night and correspondence schools run by professional associations that taught management to people holding management jobs. They taught a conservative style of management. Woodward set out to see if what they were teaching was correct. But her results were confusing until she hit upon the idea of classifying the firms according to their technology.

The firms were classified into three groups: unit/small batch/job shop (produces units to customer's requirements, makes prototypes, or fabricates large equipment in stages); mass production/large batch (produces small or large batches on an assembly line); and process automation (chemicals in a multipurpose plant; continuous flow production of items like gases, liquids, and crystalline substances). Woodward found that

1 structure was related to the technology of the firm:

a Chain of command (number of levels of authority) increased as the firm went from small to mass batches and then to automation.

b Ratios of managers to employees increased as the firm went "up" the technology ladder.

c Span of control was low for small batches and automation, high for mass production.

2 organizational success was correlated to the median structural characteristics in each technological group. In general, successful mass production firms used a conservative organizational style. Other successful enterprises used a liberal style.

She also found that the two "extreme" technology groups (small batch and automation) were alike in that they used a liberal style, including mostly verbal communication.

In summary, Woodward found that the routineness of the technology influenced organizational structure. In mass production the technology led to specialization because of the routineness of the output; in such cases the conservative organizational style was used most frequently. But more than that, the more the enterprise followed the conservative model's median structure (narrow span of control, strict chain of command, etc.), the more successful it was. This pattern is found in most of the research.

Two interpretations could be drawn from Woodward's work: Technology influences structure in such a way that enterprises with routine technology *must* organize conservatively ("the technological imperative"), or technology is an influence on structure, especially at the level where the technology is used (the shop floor of a factory, the welfare processing office). Most of the research since Woodward (see Table 16.8) agrees with the second interpretation, and in the last years of her life she herself indicated that she had shifted to this interpretation.

Some conclusions of the research on technology and structure are as follows:

1 Technology has a tendency to influence organizational structure. Routine technology tends to lead to conservative structure, nonroutine technology to liberal structure.

2 Technology is not *equally* influential on all organizations and parts of organizations. It exerts the strongest influence on small, production-oriented units. It is least influential on upper levels of enterprises and on nonproduction units like staff services.

3 This is so because many factors influence structure, and sometimes they exert opposite pulls.

4 There is not nearly enough research to support a firm conclusion that if technology matches structure, the firm is more effective. But it seems clear that there is a general correlation between the two.

Volatility/ Uncertainty and Organizational Structure

VOLATILITY
Volatility is the degree of change in the marketplace and in the enterprise's technological environment.

Volatility can be measured as the percentage of change and/or the predictability of the changes faced by the enterprise. For example, as mentioned earlier, manufacturers of washboards have not experienced unpredictable changes in market or technology since the introduction of the wringer washing machine. The market environment of fashion goods manufacturers changes all the time, but the managers know that

Table 16.8 Research and Theory on the Impact of Technology on Organizational Structure

Researcher	Setting and Sample	Level of Sophistication	Findings
A. University of Aston studies (Pugh, Hickson, et al.)	52 British firms and government divisions in Birmingham, England	Very sophisticated	A. Technology influences structure directly mostly in smaller firms. The patterns found by Woodward generally held in small firms. When you look at levels higher in the organization, the structure is not significantly influenced by the technology of the shop floor.
B. Khandwalla	79 medium-sized U.S. manufacturing firms	Very sophisticated	A. Profitable mass production firms follow the conservative model, especially in decentralizations and control methods. B. Technology influences structure less than Woodward would conclude but more than Aston found to be the case.
C. Grimes and Klein	9 American plants with 828 departments	Moderately sophisticated	Technology is related to structure, but more at the shop level than above (agrees with Hickson-Aston researchers).
D. Child and Mansfield	89 British businesses in 6 industries	Very sophisticated	Technology is a less important influence on structure than size even in production. It is very unimportant in higher levels and service and staff groups. Successful companies use conservative structure in routine technologies in their production units.
E. Harvey	43 small and medium-sized American firms	Sophisticated	The greater the routinization of technology, the more conservative style is used. (No measures of effectiveness were used in this study.)
F. Keller, et al.	44 Pennsylvania plants of automated enterprises	Somewhat sophisticated	Consistent with Woodward's findings: automated employment leads to liberal style. But the "right" organizational style was not related to success.
G. Zwerman	55 Minnesota businesses	Sophisticated	Successful small-batch and continuous process firms use liberal style; mass production is successful if conservative style is used.
H. Mohr	144 work groups in 13 American local health departments in large cities	Sophisticated	The relationship between technology and structure is present but is not strong because technology and structure are both complex entities.
I. Hage and Aiken	16 small American health and welfare organizations	Somewhat sophisticated	Routine tasks in government and voluntary agencies lead to conservative model. (No measures of effectiveness.)

these changes will affect either the spring line or the fall line. The most difficult kind of volatility is wide market swings whose timing cannot be predicted.

One way to measure technological volatility is to check the expenditures for research and development of various industries. These data indicate that the most volatile industries are communications equipment; aircraft and missiles; the least volatile are textiles; lumber, wood products, and furniture; and food and kindred products. But this approach focuses mostly on technological change.

Ramon Aldag and Ronald Storey have computed an index of volatility based on variation in sales over the past ten years plus the average amounts of R&D and capital expenditures relative to total assets. They came up with the categories of volatility shown in Figure 16.2.

Volatility of Industries (Aldag and Storey) (Modified by the author)

		Technological volatility	
		Low	**High**
		Middle-level volatility	**Most volatility**
High		Construction—special	Drugs—ethical
		Plastic products—miscellaneous	Drugs—medical and hospital supply
		Machine tools	Chemicals and chemical preparation
		Real estate	Office and business equipment
		Retail—variety stores	Electronics
		Metal work—miscellaneous	Photographic

Market volatility

		Least volatile	**Middle-level volatility**
Low		Vegetable oil mills	Chemicals—major
		Machinery—specialty	Tire and rubber goods
		Auto parts and accessories	Flat glass
		Confectionery	Steel—minor
		Food—meat packers	Electrical and electrical leaders
		Retail—department stores	Aerospace

Figure 16.2 Market and technological volatility (Aldag and Storey, modified by author).

F. E. Emery and Eric Trist tried to indicate how the environment (dependence plus volatility) would influence the organization and its operations. Table 16.9 shows how they categorize the environment. Their categories may be described as follows:

· A *placid, randomized* environment is a lot like the economist's world of many competitive firms with no big ones dominating the market place. These firms operate in a low-volatility environment (routine). This is the ideal environment for the conservative firm.

·A *placid, clustered* environment is like imperfect competition, with a low rate of change. It is rather easy to predict the future (i.e., watch the change makers). Again, conservative organizations will work well under these circumstances.

·A *disturbed, reactive* environment is like oligopoly in a changing environment. Such an environment dictates some liberalization, probably modified decentralization.

·A *turbulent* environment involves so many unknowns that it requires a liberal structure.

Table 16.9 Relationship of Environment to Structure and Operations (Emery and Trist)

Environment:				
Volatility	placid	placid	disturbed	turbulent
Dependence	randomized	clustered	reactive	turbulent
Structure	conservative	conservative	middle of the road	liberal

Thorelli provides the following hypotheses:

Proposition 16.11.
The greater the volatility of the environment, the more decentralized the organization is likely to be.

Proposition 16.12.
The greater the volatility of the environment, the more flexible the organization is likely to be.

My own predictions follow this line of reasoning: As volatility goes up (as change accelerates) it is harder to effectively systematize (and thus organize conservatively) because things change too fast and because conservative organizations react too slowly. Table 16.10 summarizes the evidence in support of this position. And my conclusions are as follows:

·In general, the prediction that stable conditions lead to conservative structures and volatile conditions lead to liberal ones is supported.

·There is more evidence for the preceding statement than for the

Table 16.10 Research on the Relationship Between Volatility and Organizational Structure

Study	Site	Methods	Findings
A. Burns and Stalker	20 British firms or divisions	Moderately sophisticated	Successful firms in highly volatile industries use liberal style; those in stable industries use conservative style
B. Lawrence and Lorsch	6 American firms in plastics, food, and container industries	Sophisticated	Firms whose environments are volatile and that organize according to the liberal model are successful; stable, successful enterprises use the conservative model; subunits whose environments are more stable (e.g., production) should use a conservative approach; volatile units like R&D should use a liberal approach.
C. Child	86 medium-sized British companies in 6 industries	Very sophisticated	Firms in volatile industries do tend to use liberal style, though the most successful firms do not use it exclusively. Size is a more important predictor than volatility.
D. Downey, et al., Tosi, et al.	Theoretical	Sophisticated	Both warn that the Lawrence and Lorsch and Duncan volatility scales should be used cautiously.
E. Pennings	40 branches of stock brokerage firms in the U.S.	Sophisticated	Evidence does not support the volatile-liberal relationship, but volatility measure used included other factors such as dependence.
F. Harvey	43 small and medium-sized American firms	Sophisticated	The greater the volatility in the market, the more likely the use of a liberal style.
G. Khandwalla	79 American firms that varied in profitability	Very sophisticated	This research defines volatility to include competitive dependence conditions. As predicted, volatility leads to liberal structures (in general) in profitable firms but not necessary in unprofitable firms.
H. Keller, et al.	44 automated plants in Pennsylvania	Sophisticated	Supports Woodward (disagrees with Harvey) in arguing that automation requires liberal structure. Also finds that volatility *alone* is not a good enough predictor of success in automated plants using liberal style.
I. Negandhi and Reimann	30 manufacturing firms in India	Moderately sophisticated	Some minor adjustments need to be made to achieve effectiveness in India, but generally supportive of the volatile-liberal relationship.
J. Duncan	22 decision units in 3 manufacturing and 3 R&D organizations in the U.S.	Sophisticated	Supports the stability = conservative, volatility = liberal relationships.

proposal that this correlation leads to more effective enterprises.

·Some of the inconsistencies probably are due to differences in the measures used.

·None of the data demonstrate that volatility *alone* leads to liberal structure.

STRATEGY AND ORGANI- ZATIONAL STYLE

We began by saying that three sets of factors affect the choice of organizational style: internal factors, external factors, and strategy (managerial preferences and decisions). In fact, strategy is the decision process that considers internal and external factors (as well as other factors) and creates the strategic plan that guides the enterprise. This plan (see Chapter 11 for further detail) then determines the enterprise's organizational structure.

Why does strategy affect structure?

First of all, if your organization is a mutual benefit association it is unlikely that a purely conservative structure would be effective. Rather, a middle-of-the-road or liberal structure would reinforce the voluntary character of the organization.

In the second place, the six external and internal variables by themselves do not determine strategy. The strategy chosen by the manager is the primary explanatory variable for organizational structure. Alfred Chandler's work is the best research to date on this subject. Using historical methods, Chandler showed that of the hundreds of firms he studied, only those that adjusted their structure to fit their strategy were effective.

We can summarize these findings in the following proposition:

Proposition 16.13.
Organizations that implement the organizational style appropriate to their strategy will be more effective than those that use an inappropriate style.

I hasten to add *again* that organizational style contributes its part to success along with planning, good employees, communications, and so forth.

But what if you get mixed signals? That is, what if it is not clear which style is appropriate?

Unfortunately, there are few research studies that answer this question. However, the following suggestions might be helpful:

1 If five or six variables point to a single style, adopt that style.

2 If four or more variables point in one direction and the others in the other direction, then examine the first four. If three of them are the "strong" variables as shown in Table 16.11, stay with the predominant style.

3 If the "strong" variables are mixed, structure your organization according to the middle-of-the-road style, trying to match the strong variables with the relevant aspects of structure. For example, if the "people" fit the liberal characteristics, leadership style and control methods should be liberal.

Table 16.11 Estimates of the Relative Strength of Predictor Variables

Very Strong	Moderately Strong	Somewhat Strong
People Size Volatility	Technology	Dependence Complexity

Table 16.12 is intended to give you some idea of how to compute these trade-offs. You calculate the direction of the predictor, weigh it by the strength of the predictor, then structure accordingly.

Chapter 16 describes in more detail how to handle the subparts of structure: specialization and departmentalization, standardization, coordination, and others.

Table 16.12 Relationship Among Six Predictor Variables and Structure

HORIZONTAL DIV. OF LABOR

Factors	Specialization	Standardization	Formalization	Vertical Division of Labor	Coordination	Control Mechanisms
Dependence	0	0	0	0	+	+ +
Technology	+ +	+ +	0	0	+	0
Volatility	+ +	+ +	+ +	0	0	0
Complexity	+ +	+	+	0	+	0
Size	+ +	+ +	+ +	+	+ +	+
People	+	0	0	0	+	+ +

FAST PACE

Go TOGETHER

Key:

+ + very important
+ important
0 not too important

SUMMARY   This chapter completes the three-chapter unit on organization. Its purpose was to make you a more effective organizer through an understanding of how the three internal factors (size, employee characteristics, and complexity) and three external factors (dependence, technology, and volatility) are combined with the manager's preferences into a strategy that, when matched to the right structure, leads to effectiveness.

The amount of present research to support this contingency theory varies, depending on the factor. As indicated, the effects of size, dependence, technology, volatility, and strategy are rather well documented. More research is necessary, however, especially on the relationships of employee characteristics and complexity to choice of organizational style.

Questions for Review

1. What is the contingency theory of organization? Does it make sense to you?
2. What factors determine the choice of organizational style?
3. In what ways does enterprise size affect the choice of organizational style?
4. How do employee characteristics affect the choice of organizational style?
5. What is complexity? How does it affect organizational style?
6. What external factors are important in the choice of organizational style?

References

Introduction to the Contingency Approach

Neilson, Eric, "Contingency Theory Applied to Small Business Organizations," *Human Relations,* 27, no. 4 (1974): 3–329.

Internal Factors in the Choice of Organizational Style/Size of Enterprise

Blau, Peter, "A Formal Theory of Differentiation in Organizations," *American Sociological Review,* 35, no. 2 (April 1970): 201–218.

Blau, Peter, and Schoenherr, R., *The Structure of Organizations* (New York: Basic Books, 1971).

Child, John, "Managerial and Organizational Factors Associated with Company Performance," *Journal of Management Studies,* 11 (1974): 175–189; and 12, no. 1 (1975): 12–28.

Child, John, and Mansfield, Roger, "Technology, Size, and Organization Structure," *Sociology,* 6 (1972): 369–393.

Hall, Richard, *et al.,* "Organization Size and Organization Structure," Ohio State University, 1964 (Mimeograph).

Hickson, David, et al., "Technology and Organization," *Personnel Management,* February 1970, pp. 21–26.

Herbiniak, Lawrence, and Alutto, Joseph, "A Comparative Organizational Study of Performance and Size Correlates in Inpatient Psychiatric Departments" (Buffalo: State University of New York at Buffalo, 1970), Mimeograph.

Khandwalla, Pradip, "Mass Output Orientation of Operations Technology and Organization Structure," *Administrative Science Quarterly,* 19 (1974): 74–97.

Meyer, Marshall, "Size and the Structure of Organizations: A Causal Analysis," *American Sociological Review,* 37 (1972): 434–441.

Pfeffer, Jeffrey, "Size and Composition of Corporate Boards of Directors," *Administrative Science Quarterly,* 17, no. 2 (June 1972): 218–228.

Weber, Max, *Essay on Sociology* (New York: Oxford University Press, 1946).

Woodward, Joan, *Industrial Organization: Theory and Practice* (New York: Oxford University Press, 1965).

Employee Characteristics

Allutto, Joseph, and Belasco, James, "A Typology for Participation in Organizational Decision Making," *Administrative Science Quarterly,* 17, (1972): 117–125.

Esser, Norbert, "Rule Interpretation as an Indicator of Style of Managers," *Personnel Psychology,* 15 (1962): 375–386.

Lorsch, Jay, and Morse, John, *Organizations and Their Members* (New York: Harper & Row, 1974).

Seiler, John, *System Analysis in Organizational Behavior* (Homewood, Ill.: Irwin Dorsey Press, 1967), esp. pp. 23–31, 51–72.

Environmental Complexity

Duncan, Robert, "Characteristics of Organizational Environments and Perceived Environmental Uncertainty," *Administrative Science Quarterly,* 17, no. 3 (1972): 313–327.

Murphy, David, "Decentralization: The Effects of Complexity," *Southern Journal of Business,* 7, no. 4 (1972): 79–86.

External Factors in the Choice of Organizational Style/Dependence on External Forces

Aiken, Michael, and Hage, Jerald, "Organizational Interdependence and Intraorganizational Structure," *American Sociological Review,* 33, no. 6 (December 1968): 912–930.

Assaiel, Henry, "Constructive Role of Interorganizational Conflict," *Administrative Science Quarterly,* 14, no. 4 (December 1969): 573–582.

Baty, Gordon, et al., "Personnel Flows as Interorganizational Relations," *Administrative Science Quarterly,* 16, no. 4 (1971): 430–443.

Benson, J. Kenneth, "The Interorganizational Network as a Political Economy," *Administrative Science Quarterly,* 20 (June 1975): 229–249.

Blankenship, L. Vaughn, and Elling, Ray, "Organizational Support and Community Power Structure: The Hospital," *Journal of Health and Human Behavior,* 3 (1962): 250–260.

Boddewyn, Jean, "External Affairs," *Organization and Administrative Science,* 5, no. 1 (1974): 67–111.

Densmore, Max, and Klein, Donald, "Health Care's Response to the Consumer: Patient Representatives," *Proceedings, Academy of Management,* 1975.

Elling, Ray, and Halebsky, Sandor, "Organizational Differentiation and Support," *Administrative Science Quarterly,* 6 (1961): 185–209.

Emery, F. E., and Trist, Eric, "The Causal Texture of Organizational Environments," *Human Relations,* 18, no. 1 (1963): 20–26.

Evan, William, "The Organization Set," in James Tompson, *Approaches to Organizational Design* (Pittsburg: University of Pittsburg Press, 1966).

Hage, Jerald, "A Strategy for Creating Interdependent Delivery Systems to Meet Complex Needs," *Organization and Administrative Science*, 5, no. 1 (1974): 17–43.

Hall, Richard, and Clark, John, "Problems in the Study of Interorganizational Relationships," *Organization and Administrative Science*, 5, no. 1 (1974): 45–65.

Hicks, Herbert, and Goronzy, Friedhelm, "A Survey of Certain Economic Concepts Relevant to the Study of Management and Organization," *Management International Review*, 8, no. 2-3 (1968): 55–67.

Jacobs, David, "Dependence and Vulnerability," *Administrative Science Quarterly*, 19, no. 1 (1974): 45–59.

Khandwalla, Pradip, "Effect of Competition on the Structure of Top Management Control," *Academy of Management Journal*, 16, no. 2 (June 1973): 285–295.

Kochen, Thomas, "Determinants of the Power of Boundary Units in an Intraorganizational Bargaining Relation," *Administrative Science Quarterly*, 20 (September 1975).

Levine, Sol, and White, Paul, "Exchange as a Conceptual Framework for the Study of Innerorganizational Relationships," *Administrative Science Quarterly*, 5 (1961): 583–601.

Litwak, Eugene, and Hylton, Lydia, "Interorganizational Analysis: A Hypothesis on Coordinating Agencies," *Administrative Science Quarterly*, 6 (March 1962): 395–420.

Macaulay, Stewart, "Noncontractual Relations in Business," *American Sociological Review*, 28, (1963): 55–69.

Martin, Desmond, and Kearney, William, "External Policy and Control in Large-Scale National Trade Associations," *Journal of Business Administration*, 1, no. 1 (1969): 29–37.

Maynes, E. Scott, "The Power of Consumers," *Business Horizons*, June 1972, pp. 77–86.

Mindlin, Sergio, and Aldrich, Howard, "Interorganizational Dependence," *Administrative Science Quarterly*, 20 (September 1975): 382–392.

Pennings, J. M., "Interdependence and Complementarity," *Human Relations*, 28, no. 9 (1975): 825–840.

Pfeffer, Jeffrey, and Leblebici, Huseyin, "The Effect of Competition on Some Dimensions of Organizational Structure," *Social Forces*, 52 (1973): 268–279.

Rosner, Martin, "Economic Determinants of Organizational Innovation," *Administrative Science Quarterly*, March 1968, pp. 614–625.

Schermerhorn, John, "Determinants of Interorganizational Cooperation," *Academy of Management Journal*, 18, December 1975.

Terryberry, Shirley, "The Evolution of Organizational Environments," *Administrative Science Quarterly*, 13, no. 4 (March 1968): 590–613.

Thompson, James, *Organizations in Action* (New York: McGraw-Hill, 1968).

Thorelli, Hans, "Organization Theory: An Ecological View," *Proceedings, Academy of Management*, 1967, pp. 66–84.

Van de Ven, Andrew, et al., "Frameworks for Interorganizational Analysis," *Organization and Administrative Science*, 5, no. 1 (1974): 113–129.

Warren, Roland, "The Interorganizational Field as a Focus for Investigation," *Administrative Science Quarterly,* 12, no. 3 (December 1967): 346–419.

**Technology and
Organizational
Structure**

Blauner, Robert, *Alienation and Freedom* (Chicago: University of Chicago Press, 1964).

Child and Mansfield, op. cit.

Fouraker, Lawrence, research described in Paul Lawrence and Jay Lorsch, *Organization and Environment* (Cambridge, Mass.: Harvard Business School, 1967).

Grimes, Andrew, and Klein, Stuart, "The Technological Imperative," *Academy of Management Journal,* 16, no. 4 (December 1973): 583–597.

Hage, Jerald, and Aiken, Michael, "Routine Technology, Social Structure, and Organization Goods." *Administrative Science Quarterly,* 14, no. 3 (1969): 366–376.

Hall, Richard, "Intraorganizational Structural Variation," *Administrative Science Quarterly,* 7, no. 2 (1962): 295–308.

Harvey, Edward, "Technology and the Structure of Organizations," *American Sociological Review,* 33 (1968): 247–258.

Hickson, David, et al., "Operations Technology and Organization Structure," *Administrative Science Quarterly,* 14, no. 3 (1969): 378–397.

Hickson, et al., "Technology and Organization," op. cit.

Hrebiniak, L. "Job Technology, Supervision, and Work Group Structure," *Administrative Science Quarterly,* 19 (1974): 395–410.

Hunt, Raymond, "Technology and Organization," *Academy of Management Journal,* 13, no. 3 (September 1970): 235–252.

Keller, R., et al., "Uncertainty and Type of Management System in Continuous Process Organizations," *Academy of Management Journal,* 17 (1974): 56–68.

Khandwalla, op. cit.

Leavitt, Harold, "Unhuman Organizations," *Harvard Business Review,* July-August 1962, 90–98.

———"Management According to Task," *Management International Review,* 1 (1962): 13–22.

Mahoney, Thomas, and Frost, Peter, "The Role of Technology in Models of Organizational Effectiveness," *Organizational Behavior and Human Performance,* 11 (1974): 122–138.

Mohr, Lawrence, "Organization Technology and Organization Structure," *Administrative Science Quarterly,* 16, (1970): 444–459.

Perrow, Charles, "Technology and Organization Structure," *Proceedings, Industrial Relations Research Association,* 1966, pp. 156–163.

Perrow, Charles, "A Framework for the Comparative Analysis of Organizations," *American Sociological Review,* 32, no. 2 (1967): 194–208.

Revans, R. W., "Hospital Attitudes and Communications," in Ann Cartwright, ed., *Human Relations and Hospital Care* (London: Routledge and Kegan Paul, 1964).

Sayles, Leonard, *The Behavior of Industrial Work Groups* (New York: McGraw-Hill, 1963).

Scott, W. Richard, "Organizational Structure," *Annual Review of Sociology,* 1 (1975).

Thompson, op. cit.

Thompson, James, and Bates, Frederich, "Technology, Organization, and Administration," *Administrative Science Quarterly,* 2, no. 3 (December 1957): 325–343.

Trist, Eric, and Bansforth, K. W., "Some Social and Psychological Consequences of the Longwall Method of Goal Getting," *Human Relations,* 1951, pp. 1–38.

Udy, Stanley, *Organization of Work* (New Haven, Conn.: HRAF Press, 1959).

———"Technical and Institutional Factors in Production Organization," *American Journal of Sociology,* 67, no. 3 (November 1961): 247–260.

Woodward, *Industrial Organization: Theory and Practice,* op. cit.

Woodward, Joan, *Industrial Organization: Behavior and Control* (New York: Oxford University Press, 1970).

Zwerman, William, *New Perspectives on Organization Theory* (Westport, Conn.: Greenwood Press, 1970).

Volatility/ Uncertainty and Organizational Structure

Aldag, Ramon, and Storey, Ronald, "Environmental Uncertainty," *Proceedings, Academy of Management,* 1975.

Bell, Gerald, "Formality vs. Flexibility in Complex Organizations," in Gerald Bell, ed. *Organizations and Human Behavior* (New York: Harper & Row, 1970), pp. 97–108.

Burns, Tom, and Stalker, G., *The Management of Innovation* (London: Tavistock Institute, 1961).

Child, op. cit.

Downey, H. Kirk, et al., "Environmental Uncertainty: The Construct and Its Application," *Administrative Science Quarterly,* 20 (1975): 613–629.

Duncan, Robert, "The Implementation of Different Decision Making Structures in Adapting to Environmental Uncertainty," *Proceedings, Academy of Management,* 1971.

Emery and Trist, op. cit.

Harvey, op. cit.

Keller et al., op. cit.

Khandwalla, Pradip, "Uncertainty and the Optional Design of Organizations," *Administrative Science Quarterly,* (Montreal: McGill University, 1975, mimeographed).

Lawrence, Paul, and Lorsch, Jay, *Organization and Environment* (Cambridge, Mass.: Harvard Business School, 1967).

Negandhi, Anant, and Reiman, Bernard, "A Contingency Theory of Organization Re-examined in the Context of a Developing Country," *Academy of Management Journal,* 15, no. 2 (1972): 137–146.

Pennings, Johannes, "The Relevance of the Structural Contingency Model for Organizational Effectiveness," *Administrative Science Quarterly,* 20 (September 1975): 393–410.

Thorelli, op. cit.

Tosi, Henry, et al., "On the Measure of the Environment: An Assessment of the Lawrence and Lorsch Environmental Uncertainty Subscale," *Administrative Science Quarterly,* 18 (March 1973): 27–36.

Strategy and Organizational Style

Blau, Peter, and Scott, W. Richard, *Formal Organizations* (San Francisco: Chandler Publishing, 1962).

Chandler, Alfred, Jr., *Strategy and Structure* (Cambridge, Mass.: M.I.T. Press, 1962).

Child, John, "Organization Structure, Environment, and Performance: The Role of Strategic Choice," *Sociology,* 6 (1972): 1–21.

Cyert, Richard M., and March, J. G., *Behavioral Theory of the Firm* (Englewood Cliffs, N. J.: Prentice-Hall, 1963).

Glueck, William F., *Business Policy* (New York: McGraw-Hill, 1976).

Kaplan, Berton, "Notes on a Non-Weberian Model of Bureaucracy," *Administrative Science Quarterly,* 13, no. 3 ( ): 471–497.

Rosengren, William, "Organizational Age, Structure, and Orientations Towards Clients," *Social Forces,* 47, no. 1 (1968): 1–11.

Selznick, Phillip, *Leadership in Administration* (Chicago: Row Peterson, 1957).

Thompson, James, and Bates, Frederick, op. cit.

CHAPTER 17

CONTROL
AND CONFLICT
MANAGEMENT

17

Learning Objectives

1. To understand the purpose and methods of controls.
2. To learn when controls are effective and when they are ineffective.
3. To understand conflict and how to manage it.

Chapter Outline

Control: Definition, Explanation, and Justification
Control and Other Managerial Skills
Control and Managerial Style
Tools of Control
The Budget as a Control Tool
Other Control Devices
PPBS
Control and Enterprise Effectiveness
Effects of Control on Employees
Positive and Neutral Reactions
Negative Responses
Making Controls Work
Conflict Management
Attitudes Toward Conflict
Causes of Conflict
Kinds of Organizational Conflict
Conflict and Management Style
Summary

**CONTROL:
DEFINITION,
EXPLANATION,
AND
JUSTIFICATION**

CONTROL
Control is the managerial skill that attempts to ensure effective use of the enterprise's resources and achievement of its objectives. It includes at least three elements:

· Establishing standards for measurement
· Developing measurement procedures to determine progress toward enterprise objectives
· Acting to reinforce successes and correct shortcomings

The subject of this chapter is not a popular one. Few people like to know that enterprises or supervisors have created systems to check up on employee performance and on the performance of the work unit. This is especially true in light of their legitimate fears that governmental units have been illegally bugging our rooms, stealing our records, listening to our phone calls, and in other ways depriving us of privacy.

If we lived in a perfect world where all managerial plans were fulfilled, control would not be necessary. But the world is far from perfect. Factors in the environment change, and these changes influence our plans. Employees make mistakes. And not all employees are motivated to achieve the results needed to keep the enterprise on its planned course; they may not do their jobs at all. So control is necessary to enable management to anticipate problems and act to adjust the plan or take corrective action when the plan is not being met.

The process of control includes the following subparts:

· *Defining the desired results* This must be done in *measurable terms* for individuals and work groups. (This was done in the planning stage if planning was done well.) MBO helps clarify the desired results of the enterprise and of the individuals and groups within the enterprise. This is the link between planning and control.
· *Looking for predictors of results* "Early warning signals" are needed in the form of feedback on what is actually happening. Effective managers do not wait for a specific time to find out whether the desired results are being achieved. They look for reliable, prompt indicators. If they are concerned with sales, weekly or monthly sales results highlighting problems by product/service and territory provide managers with the opportunity to help define problems and/or correct them. This requires an effective flow of information and communication.
· *Evaluating results against standards* When the manager sees re-

sults early enough to act on them, he or she determines which are critical, which are worth watching, and which can be ignored at present, based on the amount of divergence from standards and the significance of the item. Thus a 5 percent shortfall in the firm's smallest territory on a minor product is not the same as a 30 percent loss on its largest product in its biggest territory.

·*Acting to reinforce the positive and correct the negative*   Many people have the idea that control is only negative. This is not so, and this is where control is affected by leadership style. The effective manager reinforces positive responses to the plan on a regular basis. The manager lets the employees know how pleased he or she is with positive results and reinforces outstanding performance.

For those units and/or individuals that are performing below par, the manager controls by attending to the biggest problems first. The manager first determines what the problem is and then decides whether he or she can help improve the employee or unit's performance, applying corrective action only if the unit does not perform up to its capability after receiving help.

Thus the control process tries to *prevent* disasters by determining how the enterprise is faring relative to its plans and objectives and taking action to ensure good results.

CONTROL AND OTHER MANAGERIAL SKILLS

In earlier chapters I tried to make the point that although I would be discussing managerial skills one at a time, these skills and the interpersonal skills discussed in Part 3 are interrelated. Thus as I describe some of the tools used for control it will become clear that some were discussed earlier because they serve more than one purpose (such as planning and control).

Controls can be personal-behavioral or impersonal. We can control people and resources by personally watching them—personal surveillance, as described in Chapter 7. We can reinforce this with personal evaluation—performance appraisal, as discussed in Chapter 10. And we can control people and things personally by centralizing key employee and resource decisions, as described in Chapter 5.

The other approach is impersonal. We can control people and resources by developing policies, procedures and rules and by using tools like break-even analysis, inventory control models, and linear programing, as described in Chapters 11 and 12.

All but the smallest organizations use both of these approaches. The smallest probably use primarily the personal approach. A tool that tries to combine the two approaches is MBO (described in Chapter 12).

Which approach (personal or impersonal) is best? Few studies have attempted to answer this question. Bernard Reimann and Anant Negandi studied 30 manufacturing firms in India ranging in size from 120 to 6500 employees. They found that the impersonal control method worked well when the controls attempted to control both human and material resources. Roger Mansfield examined a number of British enterprises and found that impersonal controls worked best in large organizations, personal controls worked best in small enterprises, and neither system by itself was best for middle-sized enterprises (150–6000 employees).

In this chapter we will examine several more impersonal control mechanisms. We will not reexamine the tools described earlier, despite the fact that they are applicable to the control process.

One last point: Controls can have different time emphases. They can be future oriented or past oriented. Past-oriented controls examine what has happened in a particular period. Examples of such controls are most accounting records and school grade reports. These controls can be used to plan future behavior in light of past errors or successes. They also can be used as a basis for distribution of rewards.

Future-oriented control systems are designed to measure results *during* the process so that action can be taken before the job is done or the period is over. An example of this type of control is a missile guidance system that measures the missile's actual trajectory prior to landing and adjusts or controls its flight path.

CONTROL AND MANAGERIAL STYLE

Span of control was described in Chapter 15. As far as impersonal controls are concerned, conservative managers believe it is necessary to control most important factors in detail. Liberals trust their well-motivated subordinates to be responsible and thus control resources. Moderates are in between. Liberals expect employees to impose self-control, while conservatives exert control to see that objectives are reached. They

Table 17.1 Control Mechanisms in Three Management Styles

Liberal	Middle of the Road	Conservative
Span of Control		
Large	Moderate	Small
Degree of Control		
Few things controlled	Some things controlled	Many things controlled
General controls	Some general, some specific controls	Specific controls
Determination of Control Standards		
Determined jointly by work group and manager	Manager consults work group, then sets standards	Determined by manager

also tend to control the means by which people perform their jobs. Liberals are concerned only with attainment of objectives. Table 17.1 is an excerpt from Table 7.7.

As far as personal control is concerned, note the differences in who sets the controls. Conservative managers set control standards, check frequently, and use rules, SOPs, and personal observation. Liberals use the work group to set controls and monitor results in ways chosen by the group. The control tools (such as budget) used probably do not vary by organizational style. But how they are used and how many are used is where the differences come into play.

TOOLS OF CONTROL I will now describe several additional tools of control. The major tool used in the control process is the budget. Others include scheduling and planning-programing-budgeting systems (PPBS).

The Budget as a Control Tool

> **BUDGET**
> A budget is a statement of future expenditures and receipts of funds. It is a quantification of management's plans with a view toward control of the use of financial and other resources.

In its most fully developed form, the enterprise develops budgets for all major uses of funds. These normally include the following:
- a sales or receipts budget
- an operations or production budget
- a financial budget
- a capital expenditures budget
- expense budgets

Essentially, an enterprise begins its budgeting procedure with the projected receipts. In a business, this figure is based on the sales forecast. For other enterprises, it is a forecast of receipts from various sources of funds. For a state university, for example, the sources include the state legislature, student tuition, research grants, gifts, and profits from ancillary enterprises such as food service, bookstores, and sports. Each of these subitems must be forecast; then the totals are combined to yield gross receipts.

Subsidiary budgets are then developed. For example, the operating budget would spell out materials, labor, overhead, and other costs. Financial budgets would project cash receipts and disbursements; the capital budget would project major additions or new construction. The expense budgets would project expenses not covered in other budgets, such as marketing costs.

The summary budget (profit and loss or income statement) subtracts the totals of the subbudgets from the receipts budget. The remainder is a *profit* or *loss* (in the nonprofit sector these might be called *surpluses* or *deficits, excess revenues,* or other terms). Various other kinds of graphs, statements, and presentations can be developed.

The purposes of a budget are to preserve the enterprise's capital resources, to promote the efficient use of capital, and to help achieve the financially oriented objectives of the enterprise.

A budget is a control tool for several reasons. A budget limits the amount of resources that can be used by a unit. It is also a standard: A budgeted amount of output must be produced or explanations must be given for not meeting the standard. When your report indicates that you are not meeting budget standards, your superior takes action.

Conceptually, the budgeting process sounds easy. In practice, however, there are serious problems involved in budgeting. Estimating both revenues and costs is very difficult. In the case of an auto maker, how many new cars will the company sell? This depends on factors such as the economy, competitors' products, and how consumers evaluate its product compared to competing products. The company's pricing and market image affect this estimate, as do product quality, engineering, the aggressiveness and reliability of dealers, and other factors. In the case of a college, how does the administration know how many students will enroll (and pay their tuition), what the legislature will appropriate, how many grants it will get (or lose), how many gifts it will receive?

On the cost side, how much inflation will there be 18 months from now? What will the interest rate be? What about the cost of coal to heat the place? Accountants have developed methods to *try* to cope with these uncertainties, but this is not an easy process.

The other difficult process is subbudgeting, or allocating funds among subunits. Who gets the money to hire more people, buy new furniture or machinery, build a new building? In most enterprises resources are scarce and one can never give every unit what it wants (and says it needs).

The budget can be a powerful instrument. Selective budget cutting can have drastic effects. Loss of marketing funds for TV spots at a crucial time, for example, can wreck the results of your unit—and, hence, your career.

Other Control Devices

Besides the budget, enterprises use many other types of control devices. Space does not permit more than a mention of each at this point.

One frequently used control mechanism is scheduling: the development of times for completion of all the subparts of a job. Most managers develop work schedules. The supervisor schedules daily and weekly, middle managers monthly, quarterly, and semiannually. Top managers schedule for the long run. Schedules vary in sophistication from simple lists of the priorities of jobs to be done and who should do them to sophisticated schedules like PERT and critical path scheduling (see Chapter 12).

Once schedules are developed (and in the conservative organization copies are made for superiors and may require their approval), they help control the behavior of the work unit. Superiors can review progress relative to the schedule and determine if targets are being met.

Schedules are used almost universally in enterprises employing more than about ten people. How precisely they are used as control devices relates to how conservative the organization is.

Enterprises also develop specific functional control mechanisms such as production control and quality control. These devices have varied success rates depending on the need for the device, the effectiveness of its application to the enterprise, and the skill of the manager using it.

Some enterprises go much further. Gillette, for example, has created a vice president for quality and safety control who can halt the sale of its products, order product recalls, stop ads that are untrue or tasteless, and in other ways protect the safety, quality, and image of Gillette's products.

PPBS

Planning-programing-budgeting systems (PPBS) is the latest in a series of attempts to do a better budgeting and controlling job in government and educational sectors. Essentially, PPBS forces administrators to define the objectives of the unit (in measurable terms), identify programs that can meet these objectives, consider alternative programs to see which has the more efficient cost-benefit ratio (and effectiveness rating), and then budget the costs in relation to the outputs.

The PPBS system is a "rational" approach to control. Its advocates neglected to consider the political realities of budgets, and PPBS can be fudged just like other budgets. In many areas, defining measurable objectives or outputs is difficult or meaningless. As we saw in Chapter 12 on MBO, quantitative objectives can supersede vital qualitative objectives. What is the objective of a mental retardation rehabilitation project? If you are not careful, PPBS could define it as partially processing large numbers of patients instead of thoroughly rehabilitating a smaller number of patients.

PPBS has had a mixed success record. Until the mid-1970s most federal agencies were required to use it. This requirement was dropped recently, and most agencies stopped using it. (The Department of Defense is a notable exception.)

CONTROL AND ENTERPRISE EFFECTIVENESS

Should you develop control mechanisms if you are a manager? The logical answer would seem to be "yes." In fact a number of research studies have found that good controls lead to greater organizational effectiveness (see Table 17.2). Note, however, that although control led to effectiveness *in general,* not all effectiveness measures were always *equally* high. And the control measures used varied according to the contingency variables described in Chaper 16. Enterprises whose variables indicated the appropriateness of conservative control styles were most effective using conservative control mechanisms.

Especially critical here is the degree of volatility. The greater the stability of the environment, the greater the use of close supervision, small spans of control, continuous or frequent checks, precise standards of performance, and both behavioral and output controls. Enterprises in volatile environments should use primarily output controls and only general behavioral controls, and should involve the employees in the development and use of the control system.

To be effective, control mechanisms must be understood. This requires effective communication. They also need to be as efficient and inexpensive as possible.

Many executives have become famous for developing effective control systems. George Eastman is a good example.

GEORGE EASTMAN (1854–1932)

The quiet man with the camera stayed on his knees as the rhinoceros charged. It was only five feet away from him when the white hunter at his side shot it dead. The guide remonstrated with the camera buff for not having fled. "Well," said George Eastman, "you've got to trust your organization." Eastman Kodak was built by a man who met every threat by an effort to strengthen his organization. He hadn't been in business a year when he began to get complaints from customers that his photographic dry plates didn't work. After 472 experiments, Eastman concluded that nothing was wrong with his formula; the trouble lay in a component, a gelatin he bought from a British chemical company. Thereafter, he tried to control by integration every essential ingredient in his product. (Eastman's chemicals division now has sales approaching $1 billion.) He did for photography what Ford did for automobiles: cut costs to a level where the average man—or child—could enter the market. In 1900 his Brownie camera sold for $1 and a roll of six-exposure film for 15 cents. Eastman's most enduring contribution was in corporate research. No company has ever been better served by R and D. In the early sixties, Bell & Howell teamed up with Du Pont in an attempt to break into the color-film market. Senator Charles Percy, who was then chairman of Bell & Howell, recalls, "Du Pont film was very good but Kodak's film kept improving and sending us back to the drawing boards." When he was seventy-eight, Eastman, a bachelor, arranged that his fortune go to philanthropic projects. Next he had a doctor diagram exactly where his heart was. Then Eastman, methodical to the last, went home and put a bullet into it. His note said, "My work is done, why wait?"

Table 17.2 Research on the Relationship Between Control and Effectiveness

Researcher	Setting	Degree of Sophistication	Findings
A. Farris and Butterfield	16 banks in Brazil	Sophisticated	The greater the control, the greater the effectiveness. Effectiveness is greater if the manager at a lower level perceives the manager at the next level as having greater control over him or her than is actually the case.
B. Lawrence and Lorsch	6 American companies	Sophisticated	The greater the control, the more effective the firm. But the firms in stable industries use conservative control mechanisms; those in volatile industries use liberal mechanisms.
C. Woodward	100 British companies	Sophisticated	Effective control leads to organizational effectiveness. The control mechanisms vary, however. Effective small-batch firms use behavioral control based on single measures of effectiveness. Effective automated firms use mechanical controls (output controls). In mass production both behavioral and output controls are used, but on an infrequent (not continuous) basis.
D. Bell	204 employees in 30 departments of a Connecticut hospital	Sophisticated	Control leads to effectiveness. The more routine the job, the greater the use of behavioral control (personal supervision). The more volatile, the greater the use of output control. This confirms the Ouichi and Maguire study.
E. Khandwalla	80 large American firms	Very sophisticated	The more volatile the environment, (as measured by type of competition) the greater the control in effective business.
F. Tannenbaum	104 League of Women Voters units	Sophisticated	The greater the amount of control the greater the effectiveness.
G. Bowers	40 life insurance agencies	Sophisticated	The greater the amount of control, the greater the effectiveness as measured by job satisfaction and organization development (not by growth, sales, or turnover). Greater control costs more, too.
H. Turcotte	2 state government agencies	Very sophisticated	Higher performance is found where output measures are clear; the control-level executives are high; and the control system emphasizes and helps achieve high output. Not all measures of output are equally high.
I. McMahon and Perritt	2537 line managers in 12 plants of a large and successful mass production technology firm	Very sophisticated	The greater the control, the greater the effectiveness.

But his work went on in the organization he designed to keep moving ahead.

EFFECTS OF CONTROL ON EMPLOYEES

Control can have one of three effects: positive cooperation, neutral acceptance, or negative resentment and evasion.

Most of the research on employee responses has centered on budgets. Some of the research applies to imposed schedules and other control devices. But the findings are so systematic that it appears that these results might well apply to all types of controls.

Most of the research describes what happens when budgets are implemented. It does not describe or analyze the maneuvering that goes on in the development phase of budgeting. As indicated earlier, the question of who gets the most money from the budget has a major effect on one's career and work environment. If you "lose the budget battle," your employees will have to do more work with fewer helpers and less desirable equipment, and they will feel that you failed them and treat you accordingly.

The "budget battle" has been studied by Jeffrey Pfeffer and G. Salancik, who studied the budgeting process at the University of Illinois. They found that the powerful departments (those with national reputations and major committee appointments) got more than their "fair share" of the budget. These departments had established good peer and superior relations (as described in Chapters 7 and 8), which gave them considerable influence on the budget.

One of the manager's most important jobs is to make sure the department gets its fair share of the budget. If this process becomes too competitive, however, it is very dysfunctional for the enterprise. Cooperation and coordination may decline to zero. Some people become so used to budgets that they cannot function without them.

"Oh, it's great here, all right, but I sort of feel uncomfortable in a place with no budget at *all.*"

Source: Drawing by D. Reilly; © 1976 The New Yorker Magazine, Inc.

Positive and Neutral Reactions

Controls lead to voluntary compliance (neutral) or support (positive) when the following conditions are met:

1 *Technical competence*   The control process must be competently designed and operated. This means the following characteristics should be present:

· The information and data used in the control system are accurate and up to date. This gives the system creditability.
· The control system is not overly developed. That is, the number of standards to be met is reasonable and it is clear which are of primary and which of secondary importance.
· The feedback system is accurate and timely so that the manager becomes aware of problems in time to act if necessary.

2 *Managerial participation and communication*   A number of studies have found that controls meet with acceptance and cooperation if the subordinates participate in the design phase, understand why the standards are needed, believe them to be both fair and attainable, and are included in the communication network.

MBO and similar control systems try to fulfill both the technical and the participation-communication phases of the control process. Thus at present the evidence indicates that middle-of-the-road or liberal control mechanisms lead to positive *managerial* and *employee reactions* to controls. The evidence does *not* prove that liberal control mechanisms always lead to greater output, effectiveness, or efficiency. As should be clear by now, all the different styles can work when the style used fits the contingency variables as described in Chapter 16.

Negative Responses

Poorly designed (technically incompetent) controls or controls that are perceived as arbitrary (imposed from above) can lead to a series of negative results such as the following:

1 *Fudging the records or the system*   One of the more typical responses to poorly designed or arbitrary controls is to try to beat the system. No accountant, lawyer, or manager has ever designed a control system that could not be beaten very ingeniously by "innovative" managers. There have been many studies of this response, but one of the most fascinating is Dalton's *Men Who Manage*. This is one of the most interesting books ever written by a manager about real-life management. It is full of accounts of the ways managers get around what they perceive to be unfair controls. Here are some examples:

· "The office" put pressure on the supervisors to meet safety standards and set a maximum number for accidents. So the supervisors did not report all the accidents that occurred, and the more serious ones were listed as less serious than they actually were.

·"The office" pressured quality control to lower its reject rates. The inspectors reported only a fraction of the rejects, secretly sending most of them back to the production department.

·New control standards were devised in an effort to reduce costs. The cost figures were fudged to fit the new standards.

·Middle managers and supervisors wanted their offices redecorated. The budget would not allow it. So the maintenance department redecorated the offices and charged the expenses as a maintenance cost. In exchange, these managers did not report maintenance errors and backlogs.

·"The office" became concerned about theft of parts and excessive parts inventories. The inspectors' secretaries typed up a list of the units to be inspected. The inspectors dictated their schedules to the secretaries, knowing the units would be "tipped off."

2 *Horse trading*   If top management sets unrealistic budgets and control systems, supervisors and middle managers will begin to horse trade. If they have found in the past that their realistic budget requests were cut 20 percent, they will inflate their requests by 20–25 percent. When top management realizes what is going on, the budget is cut further, which leads to an escalation of the horse trading. This can be compounded by competition among units, which keep bidding each other up until no one knows the real needs of any unit.

3 *Cost inefficiencies*   Often, in order to meet unit budgets on time, excessive overtime is put in, quality controls are lowered, and breakdowns result. Soviet managers frequently take this route. If the controls are poorly designed and require only a certain number of units, it is cheaper for the Soviet manager to run too many shoes in size 9A than are needed. This fills the quota; if more 8B's were needed, that is too bad. Other observers of Soviet budgets have noted that quotas are often set in pounds. So the manager of a Soviet nail factory produces mostly bigger, heavier nails. It is easier to meet the quota on time this way than by producing twice the number of smaller nails.

4 *Overemphasis on the short run*   Imposed controls can lead to an overemphasis on meeting today's budget in spite of what is happening to long-run results. Salespeople often oversell a customer to meet today's budget, knowing that in the long run they will lose business. Some units sell assets in order to make short-run figures look better. Others lay off employees, knowing they will have to rehire and retrain them later. Deferring maintenance costs also makes the books look better, but it costs more when a new machine must be bought.

5 *Reduced coordination* Various studies have shown that imposed strict controls lead to tunnel vision—an overconcern with meeting standards regardless of the effects on other departments. Coordination suffers under these conditions.

6 *Feelings of tension or pressure* Various studies have indicated that imposed strict controls can lead to the feeling that controls are simply pressure tactics. This often results in tension among lower-level employees, who then react negatively to management.

MAKING CONTROLS WORK

Do these negative results mean that the enterprise should forget about controls? No. Even though some units may fudge their reports, controls still lead to improved performance. For example, in Dalton's description of the parts inspectors, even though the units knew the inspector was coming, the company theft rate went down, as did the costs of parts inventory.

Simply put, you need controls to police the worst managers and employees, those who are so inefficient or unethical that without controls they would abuse the enterprise and their peers. We may fondly desire to do away with police and armies. But this clearly cannot be done. Until all managers and employees are honest and hardworking the enterprise cannot do without controls.

There are different kinds of controls. Well-designed and carefully operated controls work better than those that are poorly designed and badly run. So the manager needs technical competence in the design and implementation of controls. In addition, many people react better and are more satisfied with controls when they help design them. Controls will work better when employees are made aware of the need for them and allowed to participate in their design.

CONFLICT MANAGEMENT

The final topic to be discussed in this chapter is conflict management. The preceeding section focused on control of resources. In a way this section focuses on control of people, particularly when they come into conflict. The enterprise "controls" people through its reward and discipline system (described in Chapter 10). But a different challenge is the management of conflict within the enterprise so that it is not detrimental to achievement of the enterprise's objectives. Satisfaction and development of the employees and managers are also applicable here.

> **CONFLICT**
> Conflict is said to exist between two or more individuals or work groups when they disagree on a significant issue (or issues) and clash over the issue.

CONFLICT MANAGEMENT
Conflict management includes all actions and mechanisms used by executives (or the parties in conflict, or independent third parties) to keep the conflict from interfering with achievement of the enterprise's objectives.

Figure 17.1 is a model that describes how conflict takes place. Here the conflict situation is called an episode.

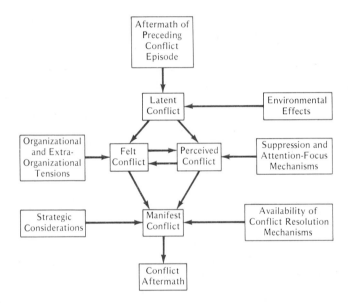

Figure 17.1
The dynamics of a conflict episode.

In his studies of conflict, Louis Pondy found that conflict is not a series of isolated incidents but a set of incidents; thus it is part of a process. The present episode is partly influenced by preceding episodes. The present episode comes about because of conditions in the environment and other forces leading to latent (or less obvious) conflict. People perceive these conditions differently (see Chapter 4), and then we get the actual incident *(manifest conflict),* which can be handled by various conflict resolution techniques. After the episode comes the *aftermath,* which includes hurt feelings on the part of the "loser" and good feelings on the part of the "winner."

Table 17.3 reproduces the part of Table 7.7 that applies to conflict in terms of attitudes toward conflict and how to manage it. In the remainder of the chapter we will discuss these topics in more detail.

Table 17.3 Conflict Management in Three Organizational Styles

Liberal	Middle of the Road	Conservative
General Attitude		
Conflict is normal and can be managed	Some conflict is inevitable and is very difficult to manage	Conflict is abnormal and must be suppressed
Managing Conflict		
Discuss the conflict fully with the parties and work it out	Solve conflict by majority rule, compromise, or hierarchial appeal	Suppress conflict by use of authority and subordinates; be competitive with peers; be persuasive with superiors

Attitudes Toward Conflict

Conservative theorists believe that conflict reflects a failure of managerial planning and control. Conflict must be suppressed and dealt with severely. Liberals contend that conflict is normal, even desirable, and can be managed so that an equilibrium state is attained. Middle-of-the-road theorists argue that conflict sometimes arises, that it is more likely in some departments than in others, and that it should be both minimized and managed.

Most managers believe that conflict is inefficient and detrimental. But some argue that it is good for the enterprise. Conflict provides the opportunity for new leaders to arise and for the enterprise to examine and possibly change its objectives and react to changing environments. Some feel that conflict relieves boredom. Franklin Roosevelt felt that deliberately designing for conflict led to more effective policy. He appointed assistants who would clash and present conflicting advice. He served as an arbitrator and felt that he got less biased advice that way.

When is conflict useful? William Evan, a contingency theorist, argues that conflict is dysfunctional in crisis organizations, such as armies, and in stable enterprises, but desirable in such volatile enterprises as R&D organizations. Claggett Smith found that conflict is undesirable in most effective businesses but useful in effective unions and voluntary organizations. Although there is not a lot of research on this subject, what there is tends to support the contingency position: Conflict is sometimes good, sometimes bad, and the manager should design a control and conflict resolution system to fit the amount of conflict that is desirable in his or her organization.

Causes of Conflict

Conflict is a complex phenomenon. It rarely develops from a single cause. The major causes of conflict appear to be the following:

1 *Differences in group objectives* The conflicting parties may be seeking quite different and conflicting objectives. Management may be seeking to keep costs down, while the unions seek higher wages. One of the objectives over which conflict often develops is power. Often the leader(s) of one faction are fighting for increased power at the expense of the other group. Perhaps (in McClelland's terms) they have a high need for power.

2 *Differences between individuals*   Conflict may result from an inability to communicate because of differences in perceptions and attitudes toward the problem. This can be compounded by differences in personalities. Some people do not like others, and this acts as an information filter, causing conflicts that are really personality conflicts.

3 *Differences resulting from job or structure*   Some jobs call for more interaction with others. This can lead to more frequent occasions for conflict. A scientist working alone in his or her lab has fewer occasions for conflict than the manager of the typing pool (as indicated in Chapter 8). Poor structural design and unclear relationships with overlapping authority patterns can also lead to conflict.

Proposition 17.1.
The greater the number of potential causes of conflict present in the situation, the greater the probability that conflict will develop.

Kinds of Organizational Conflict

There are various kinds of conflict: conflict within an individual, conflict between organizations, conflict within an organization. The latter is the focus of this chapter.

There are two kinds of organizational conflict: interpersonal conflict and intergroup conflict. Interpersonal conflict is conflict between two or more people as individuals. A boss and a subordinate can come into conflict, or two supervisors can become involved in conflict. Intergroup conflict is conflict between two or more units (e.g., sales vs. operations) or two or more groups (line vs. staff, officers vs. enlisted soldiers). Interpersonal conflict in a hospital, for example, may take the form of nurse versus doctor or dietician versus doctor on the subject of the treatment of a particular patient. Intergroup conflict may take the form of administrative sector versus medical staff or administrators versus nursing staff.

Conflict and Management Style

As indicated in Table 17.2, there are three basic approaches to dealing with conflict. Conservatives rely on dominance or power to settle the conflict: The person (or coalition) with the most power imposes the solution. Sometimes they suppress the conflict. The liberals try to work it out through bargaining, persuasion, problem solving, and confrontation. Middle-of-the-road moderates try in-between mechanisms: discussion, then vote (majority rule); compromise (each gets part of the loaf); or political mechanisms, changing the structure, or if necessary, submitting the dispute to an impartial arbitrator or hierarch.

The research evidence on conflict management (see Table 17.4) appears to support the following conclusions:

·Conflict has many causes.
·Many conflict reduction methods are effective in reducing conflict.
·Conflict does not always reduce productivity.

The best advice that can be given, then, is that there are no better or worse methods for managing conflict. The "right" method depends on the kind of enterprise. Organizations whose characteristics call for a middle-of-the-road style should try to reduce conflict by means of the appropriate conflict management techniques, and the same applies to liberal or conservative organizations.

SUMMARY   Control is the managerial skill that attempts to ensure effective use of the enterprise's resources and achievement of the enterprise's objectives. Control is interrelated with other managerial skills such as planning.

There are two general approaches to control: personal/behavioral and impersonal. Personal control methods include personal supervision (leadership style), performance appraisal, and centralized decision making. Impersonal controls include policies, procedures, planning tools, budgets, schedules, and other tools. Control methods vary according to managerial style.

Controls can have positive, neutral, or negative effects on the employees and the enterprise. To be effective, the controls must be competent and the system competently administered. Employee communications and participation in the design and implementation of the controls can lead to greater effectiveness.

The chapter concluded with a discussion of the management of conflict. Conflict exists between two or more individuals or groups when they disagree on significant issues. Conflict management is used by executives, by the conflicting parties themselves, or by third parties to keep conflict from interfering with achievement of the enterprise's objectives.

Conflict has many causes, and peoples' attitudes vary from "It's bad" to "It's natural and can be managed." The methods used to reduce or manage conflict range from the conservative use of suppression and/or hierarchical arbitration to liberal discussion, bargaining, and "working the problem through."

Table 17.4 Studies of Interpersonal and Intergroup Conflict Resolution

Study	Setting	Degree of Sophistication	Findings
Interpersonal Conflict			
A. Burke	Questionnaire to executives in a management development program	Moderately sophisticated	Managers perceive liberal conflict methods as good, conservative methods as bad.
B. Corwin	1500 questionnaires and 600 interviews in 28 public high schools	Sophisticated	Conflict is very complicated. Size, complexity, heterogeneity, cohesiveness, and other factors influence the pressure of conflict. A major source of conflict is conflict between administrators and teachers.
C. Stagner	Top managers	Moderately sophisticated	Conflict at top management level is settled by taking the conflict to the boss to arbitrate it.
Intergroup Conflict			
A. Argyris	Conflict between professionals and line management in one large corporation	Moderately sophisticated	Conflict develops between line and staff executives. Only liberal conflict management methods will really solve this problem.
B. Darkenwald	54 universities' 283 department chairmen	Moderately sophisticated	Conflict is related to size, quality, and research orientation. Conflict between administrators and department chairmen is greatest in middle-level colleges, probably reflecting disagreement over goals and objectives.

C. Lourenco and Glidewell	15-month case study of conflict between local TV stations and home office (vertical conflict)	Moderately sophisticated	Conflict is due to differences in attitudes toward legitimate power bases. Conflict is resolved by adjusting the structure to matrix structure.
D. Pugh	Study of 3 plants in Scotland; conflict between line and inspectors	Moderately sophisticated	Inspectors can get work done only if middle managers back them against line supervisors. (middle-of-the-road solution). Conflict is due to differences in perception of role of inspectors and power differences.
E. Smith	4 locals of a union; 112 units of League of Women voters; 30 units of a delivery company; 33 auto dealers; 40 units of an insurance company; 36 units of a stock brokerage firm (vertical conflict)	Sophisticated	Tested three hypotheses: (1) Better interlevel communications reduce conflict. True of business organization (not the union or LWV), although size affects this. (2) Conflict is caused by conflicts of interest in objectives and power. True in business (not the union or LWV). (3) Conflict is due to lack of consensus in personal attitudes. True of businesses (not the union or LWV). In all three cases conflict does not necessarily lead to lower productivity.
F. Sorenson and Sorenson	254 CPAs in 4 large CPA firms	Sophisticated	Conflict between CPAs and clients results from differences in structure and personal attitudes
G. Walton	4 studies	Sophisticated	Conflict is the consequence of many causes.

Questions for Review

1. What is control?

2. Why do managers need to develop control methods?

3. Distinguish between personal and impersonal control methods. Which kinds of enterprises use each?

4. Which approach to control is better: personal or impersonal? When?

5. What is a budget? In what way can it be used as an impersonal control tool?

6. What other control tools are used by managers and entrepreneurs?

7. When are controls effective? When do they have a neutral effect on the employees and the enterprise?

8. When do controls have a negative effect on the employees and the enterprise? What kinds of negative effects can they have?

9. What is conflict? Conflict management?

10. When is conflict useful?

11. Is conflict more useful in some enterprises than others? Which ones? Why?

12. How does managerial style affect conflict management?

References

Control: Definition, Explanation, and Justification

Eilon, Samuel, *Management Control* (London: Macmillan, 1971).

Gilbert, Xavier, "Does Your Control System Fit Your Business?" *European Business,* Spring 1973, pp. 69–76.

Newman, William, *Constructive Control* (Englewood Cliffs N.J.: Prentice-Hall, 1975).

Control and Other Managerial Skills

Giglioni, Giovanni, and Bedeian, Arthur, "A Concensus of Management Control Theory: 1900–1972," *Academy of Management Journal,* 17, no. 2 (June 1974): 292–305.

Mansfield, Roger, "Bureaucracy and Centralization," *Administrative Science Quarterly,* 18 (1973): 477–488.

Ouchi, William and Maguire, Mary Ann, "Organizational Control: Two Functions," *Administrative Science Quarterly,* 20 (December 1975): 559–569.

Reimann, Bernard, and Negandhi, Anant, "Strategies of Administrative Control and Organizational Effectiveness," *Human Relations,* 28, no. 5 (1975): 475–486.

Tools of Control/Other Control Devices

Greenhouse, Samuel, "The PPBS System: Rationale, Language, and Idea Relationship," *Public Administration Review,* 26, no. 4 (December 1966): 71–277.

Hirsch, Werner, "Toward Federal Program Budgeting," *Public Administration Review,* 26, no. 4 (December 1966): 259–270.

Martin, Robert, "The Watchdog," *The Wall Street Journal,* December 12, 1975.

Schick, Allen, "The Road to PPB," *Public Administration Review,* 26, no. 4 (December 1966): 243–258.

Wildavsky, Aaron, "The Political Economy of Efficiency: Cost-Benefit Analysis, Systems Analysis, and Program Budgeting," *Public Administration Review*, 26, no. 4 (December 1966): 292–310.

Control and Enterprise Effectiveness

Bell, Gerald, "The Influence of Technological Components Work Upon Management Control," *Academy of Management Journal*, 8, no. 2 (1965): 127–132.

Bowers, David, "Organizational Control in an Insurance Company," *Sociometry*, 27 (1964): 230–244.

Farris, G., and Butterfield, D., "Control Theory in Brazilian Organizations," *Administrative Science Quarterly*, 17 (1972): 574–585.

Gilbert, op. cit.

Khandwalla, Pradip, "Effect of Competition on the Structure of Management Control," *Academy of Management Journal*, 16, no. 2 (June 1973): 285–295.

Lawrence, Paul, and Lorsch, Jay, *Organization Environment* (Cambridge, Mass.: Harvard Business School, 1967).

McMahon, J. Timothy, and Perritt, G., "Toward a Contingency Theory of Organizational Control," *Academy of Management Journal*, 16, no. 4 (December 1973): 624–635.

Tannenbaum, Arnold, *Control in Organizations* (New York: McGraw-Hill, 1968).

Turcotte, William, "Control Systems, Performance, and Satisfaction in Two State Agencies," *Administrative Science Quarterly*, 19, no. 1 (1974): 60–73.

Woodward, Joan, *Industrial Organization: Behavior and Control* (New York: Oxford University Press, 1970).

Effects of Control on Employees

Argyris, Chris, "Human Problems with Budgets," *Harvard Business Review*, January-February 1953.

Becker, Selwyn, and Green, D., "Budgeting and Employer Behavior," *Journal of Business*, 35 (1962): 392–402.

Berliner, Joseph, *Factory and Manager in the U.S.S.R.* (Cambridge, Mass.: Harvard University Press, 1957).

Dalton, Melville, *Men Who Manage* (New York: John Wiley and Sons, 1959).

Henderson, Bruce, and Deardon, John, "New System for Divisional Control," *Harvard Business Review*, 44, no. 5 (September-October 1966).

Hofstede, G. H., *The Game of Budget Control* (London: Tavistock Publications, 1968).

Jasinski, Frank, "Use and Misuse of Efficiency Controls," *Harvard Business Review*, 34, no. 4 (July-August 1956): 105–112.

Miles, Raymond, and Vergin, R. C., "Behavioral Properties of Variance Controls," *California Management Review*, Spring 1966.

Pfeffer, Jeffrey, and Salancik, G., "Organizational Decision Making and Political Process: The Case of the University Budget," *Administrative Science Quarterly*, 19 (June 1974): 135–151.

Ridgeway, Val, "Dysfunctional Consequences of Performance Measurements," in Walter Hill and Douglas Egan, eds., *Readings in Organizational Theory* (Boston: Allyn and Bacon, 1966).

Searfoss, D. Gerald, and Monczka, Robert, "Perceived Participation in the Budget Process and Motivation to Achieve the Budget," *Academy of Management Journal,* 16, no. 4 (December 1973): 541–554.

Simon, Herbert, et al., *Centralization vs. Decentralization in Organizing the Controller's Department* (New York: Controllership Foundation, 1954).

Tosi, Henry, "The Human Effects of Budgeting Systems on Management," *MSU Business Topics,* Autumn 1974, pp. 53–63.

Conflict Management

Filley, Alan, *Interpersonal Conflict Resolution* (Chicago: Scott, Foresman, 1975).

Nye, Robert, *Conflict Among Humans* (New York: Springer Publishing, 1973).

Pondy, Louis, "A Systems Theory of Organizational Conflict," *Academy of Management Journal,* September 1966, pp. 246–256.

————, "Organizational Conflict: Concepts and Models," *Administrative Science Quarterly,* 12, no. 2 (September 1972): 296–320.

Rico, Leonard, "Organizational Conflict," *Industrial Management Review,* Fall 1964, pp. 67–80.

Attitudes Towards Conflict

Bennis, Warren, *Organizational Development* (Boston: Addison Wesley, 1970).

Evan, William, "Conflict and Performance in R and D Organizations," *Industrial Management Review,* 7, no. 2 (Fall 1965): 37–46.

Schmidt, Warren, and Tannenbaum, Robert, "Management of Differences," *Harvard Business Review,* 38, no. 6 (November-December 1960):107–115.

Smith, Claggett, "A Comparative Analysis of Some Conditions and Consequences of Intraorganizational Conflict," *Administrative Science Quarterly,* 10 (1966): 405–529.

Causes of Conflict

Paine, Frank, "Why Don't They Cooperate?" *Personnel Administration,* May-June 1966, pp. 15–21.

Stagner, Ross, "Resolving Top Level Managerial Disagreements," *MSU Business Topics,* Winter 1965, pp. 15–22.

Thompson, James, "Organizational Management of Conflict," *Administrative Science Quarterly,* 4, no. 1 (March 1960): 389–409.

Kinds of Organizational Conflict

Schultz, Rockwell, and Johnson, Alton, "Conflict in Hospitals," *Hospital Administration,* 16 (1971): 36–50.

Conflict and Management Style

Argyris, Chris, "Management Information Systems," *Management Science,* 17, no. 6 (February 1971): b-275-b-292.

Burke, Ronald, "Methods of Resolving Interpersonal Conflict," *Personnel Administration,* July-August 196 , pp. 48–55.

Corwin, Ronald, "Patterns of Organizational Conflict," *Administrative Science Quarterly,* 14, no. 4 (December 1969): 507–520.

Darkenwald, Gordon, "Organizational Conflict in Colleges and Universities," *Administrative Science Quarterly,* 16, no. 4 (1971): 407–412.

Dutton, John, and Walton, Richard, "Interdepartmental Conflict and Cooperation: Two Contrasting Studies," *Human Organization,* 25, no. 3 (Fall 1966): 207–220.

Gross, Edward, "When Occupations Meet: Professions in Trouble," *Hospital Administration,* 12, no. 3 (1967): 40–59.

Harrison, Roger, "Understanding Your Organization's Character," *Harvard Business Review,* May-June 1972, pp. 110–128.

Lourenco, Susan, and Glidewell, John, "A Dialectical Analysis of Organizational Conflict," *Administrative Science Quarterly,* 20 (December 1975): 489–508.

Pugh, Derek, "Organizational Problems of Inspection," *Journal of Management Studies,* 3, no. 3 (October 1966): 256–269.

———, "Role Activation Conflict," *American Sociological Review,* 31, no. 6 (December 1966): 835–842.

Smith, op. cit.

Sorensen, James, and Sorensen, Thomas, "The Conflict of Professionals in Bureaucratic Organizations," *Administrative Science Quarterly,* 19, no. 1 (1974): 98–105.

Stagner, Ross, "Corporate Decision Making," *Journal of Applied Psychology,* 53 (1969): 1–13.

———, "Conflict in the Executive Suite," in Warren Bennis, ed., *American Bureaucracy* (Chicago: Aldine Press, 1970), pp. 85–95.

Walton, Richard, "Interpersonal Confrontation and Basic Third Party Functions: A Case Study," *Journal of Applied Behavioral Science,* 4, no. 3 (1968): 327–344.

Walton, Richard, et al., "Organizational Context and Interdepartmental Conflict," *Administrative Science Quarterly,* 14, no. 4 (December 1969): 522–542.

Walton, Richard, and Dutton, John, "The Management of Interdepartmental Conflict: A Model and Review," *Administrative Science Quarterly,* 14, no. 1 (March 1969): 73–84.

CHAPTER 18

RELATIONSHIPS WITH THE ENVIRONMENT

18

Learning Objectives

1. To understand how managers and enterprises are affected by forces outside the enterprise.
2. To learn how managers influence the environment and the forces in the environment.
3. To describe how management varies within the developed world and between developed and less developed nations; to describe the role of the multinational manager.

Chapter Outline

This chapter and Chapter 19 focus on the manager's or entrepreneur's relationships with the world outside the doors of the enterprise—the environment. A few enterprises are so powerful and so self-contained that they do not spend much time dealing with the environment. But in this interdependent world of ours they are few and declining in number.

The enterprise must seek its supplies (money, people, raw materials, equipment) from other enterprises or from other sources outside the enterprise. The enterprise must be legitimized by a government. It is located in a community. It has competitors to fight with and clients to satisfy. These usually exist *outside* the boundaries of the enterprise. They can and do influence the managerial job. And managers try to influence them in order to make their enterprise more successful and their life easier.

This is not the first time I have touched on this topic. In Chapters 2 and 3 it was pointed out that managerial attitudes and behavior are influenced by the enterprise's environment. In chapters 4 and 5 we discussed how people differ in motivation and attitudes as a result of differences in culture and history. In Chapter 11 we saw how managers perform strategic planning, which is a conscious attempt to plan how the enterprise will deal with environmental opportunities and threats. In Chapter 16 I indicated how factors like environmental dependence, volatility, and technology influence organizational structure, and in Chapter 20 we will see how the environment can lead to the need for organizational change.

This chapter focuses on two managerial roles: the manager as negotiator and the manager as spokesperson. Envision the manager as facing outward from the enterprise's front door. He or she must negotiate with forces in the environment to keep the enterprise functioning—negotiate with unions for people, suppliers for equipment, governments for charters and reasonable laws. In this role the manager is in effect an information gatherer and negotiator. But managers do not just play a passive role. They try to influence these outside forces as well, and thus they are spokespersons for the enterprise, defending it, polishing its image, and protecting it.

Perhaps in simpler times the entrepreneur or manager could ignore much of what went on outside the company. But a glance at any newspaper will give you an idea of the environmental influences on enterprises today:

- OPEC shuts off oil exports to the United States.
- The UAW strikes and shuts down Ford.
- Ralph Nader attacks the safety of GM's cars.
- Oregon passes a law outlawing nonreturnable beverage containers.
- GM increases its advertising and affects Chrysler's market share.

·Stockholders of Gulf Oil revolt and get the board to fire its top management.

·A community votes not to change its zoning laws and thus prohibits a new plant from being built there.

·Church members boycott certain products produced by firms with interests in South Africa.

Further readings show how the enterprise influences the environment:

·Lobbyists for real estate interests influence congresspeople not to change depreciation rates on rental property.

·Mobil Oil sponsors TV programs to get its message across to customers.

·The Kellogg Foundation gives funds to community organizations and hospitals. The image of Kellogg cereals may benefit.

·The manager is active in trade associations and tries to influence them to police unethical competitive behavior.

In this chapter we will analyze the roles of the manager and how the manager's attitudes toward the environment have varied over the years.

THE MANAGER AS NEGOTIATOR AND SPOKESPERSON

As indicated earlier, all kinds of individuals and forces in the environment can influence the manager and the enterprise. The manager must decide how and whether to react to these influences. He or she will process the information and passively or actively react to these influences depending on his or her attitudes toward the environment.

Whether a businessperson can negotiate with the environment or try to influence it as a spokesperson is partially a result of the position of the manager or entrepreneur in society at the time. This conditions the attitudes and behavior of the manager or entrepreneur in negotiations with the environment.

The prevailing evaluation of business has ranged from "The business of this country is business"—in which businesspeople were very influential—to "Business is dull, dirty, and beneath the dignity of important people." In a society where business is revered, businesspeople can (if they choose to) negotiate with and influence the environment effectively. In an antibusiness society the businessperson is on the defensive and usually reacts to the environment rather than trying to influence it positively.

There are examples of societies at both extremes, some in between, and some (including our own) where attitudes toward business are cyclical. Examples of anti-business societies include classical Greece, imperial Rome, medieval Catholic Europe, and Ottoman Turkey. Middle-of-the-road attitudes prevailed in Byzantium, Russia under the Czars, and England from 1600 to 1800. Pro-business societies include Protestant Europe in the nineteenth century (especially Scotland, Holland, Switzerland, Scandanavia, and Germany) and the United States from 1865 to 1929.

With regard to the United States and Canada, business was most influential in good times and was given credit for the general prosperity. The periods when businesspeople had the greatest influence were 1860–1900, 1900–1929 (the high point), and 1953–1961. Men like John Jacob Astor, J. P. Morgan, Henry Ford, Thomas Watson, and George Humphrey were highly influential in society and could affect government policy.

Some writers contend that businesspeople hold consistent values, attitudes, and assumptions that influence their behavior. These include the following:

> ·*The master of destiny viewpoint:* Human beings influence human events; since we can control our future, we should act.
> ·*The independent enterprise is the basic unit:* The private sector of the economy is what makes our society work.
> ·*The quest for improvement:* If we try, we can make our society better.

But Herman Krooss, in an extended history of American business, has shown that *no* single business ideology has dominated at any one point in time, much less over time. At any point in time there are those who believe business should not try to influence the environment; that government and business should leave each other alone; that the laws of supply and demand should predominate. There are also those who try to lobby, bribe, demonstrate, and in other ways do just the opposite. There are strong advocates of both these extremes and in the middle as well.

Krooss puts it this way:

> But the truth of the matter is that there has never been any such thing as a business ideology. Webster defines an ideology as a manner of content of thinking characteristic of a group, an individual or a culture. At no time has there been a content of thinking, a set of beliefs, or a body of opinion to which all businessmen subscribed. To be sure, there have always been some opinions which the majority of businessmen shared, and it is therefore possible to generalize about modal opinions and how they changed over time. But this is not an ideology, except by the loosest of definitions.
>
> Businessmen differ from each other in too many ways to permit a solid consensus. Businessmen come in all sizes and shapes. There are big businessmen and little businessmen and "liberal" businessmen and "conservative" businessmen. The variety of differences in occupation, in function, in mental capacity, in personality, and in social background made

for massive differences in opinions on economic issues as well as on the general philosophy of life. Indeed, the differences in outlook, philosophy, and opinion were greater among business leaders than among most other groups, including farmers, workers, doctors, and teachers. . . .

With all these differences and more in outlook and approach, any conclusions about what businessmen believed should be cautiously stated and carefully qualified. When we say that most businessmen shared an opinion, we are stating a belief, not an indisputable fact. And "most" may mean anything from 50 percent to over 90 percent. There is no doubt, for example, that almost all nineteenth-century businessmen believed that the federal government should, except in time of war, always balance its budget. But probably only a bare majority of twentieth-century businessmen hold the same opinion. It should also be remembered that the only businessmen that we can talk about are the business leaders, for business leaders are the only businessmen who provide us with any data, and what they have left us is sparse enough. One final caveat: the scope of businessmen's interests on any economic issue was always limited by what they considered urgent at that time. Frequently, therefore, publicly expressed opinion was the minority opinion, for on any given issue, the majority of businessmen was more silent than vocal.

Thus at any point in history in a society like ours (which has middle-of-the-road attitudes toward business at present), businesspeople are likely to be split between those who take the activist position (that we should try to influence and negotiate with the environment) and those who take a passive or noninterfering position on negotiating with or influencing the environment.

Let us now examine the varieties of negotiator and spokesperson roles as the entrepreneur and manager face other elements in society: the government, the community, customers clients, suppliers, competitors, societal groups, education, and the arts.

RELATIONS WITH THE GOVERNMENT Government and business can have one of several possible relationships, as illustrated in Table 18.1. The free enterprise ideology calls for *complete* separation of business and government. As Peter Drucker points out, the free enterprise ideology is an economic model. The corresponding political science model is *constitutionalism.* This is an American construct that requires legal separation of business and government and arm's-length regulation of business. This position is based on the ideas of Jefferson and Jackson. Its underlying theory is "Business is too important to be left to the businessperson." The free enterprise businessperson wants business to stay out of government and vice versa. A businessperson who supports this position will not try to play the negotiator or spokesperson role. He or she will simply try to operate within the law.

One step leftward from complete separation is *indirect subsidy.* In this relationship business wants to be separate from government, but for certain major ventures it may seek subsidies or credit from the government. In such cases businesspeople try to influence the government on a specific matter and remain separate the rest of the time.

Table 18.1 Possible Relationships Between Business and Government				
Government Owns Business	Joint Ownership	Mixed Economy or Mercantilism (Government Gives Direct Subsidies to Business)	Government Gives Indirect Subsidies to Business	Complete Separation Between Business and Government
Soviet Union	Comsat	British East India Company	U.S. Railroads, 1860	Scotland, 1875 United States, 1810

Mercantilism is a philosophy in which the government actively fosters and subsidizes business, which then helps serve the government's ends. The East India Company, for example, was a major participant in Britain's colonial venture.

Next comes *joint ownership.* Comsat, for example, is owned partly by the government, partly by AT&T, and partly by the public. In both mercantilism and joint ownership the manager is very dependent on the government and must spend a great deal of time in the negotiator and spokesperson roles. In Marxist and socialist states, on the other hand, there is little or no private sector and the businessperson does not play either role. Thus it appears reasonable to conclude that the further to the left an enterprise is, the more dependent it is on government.

The United States of the late 1970s is a mixed economy. Some businesses are successful at maintaining an existence almost entirely separate from government. Others are quasi-governmental. Subsidized industries (e.g., airlines) live side by side with nonsubsidized firms like Westlake's Hardware.

George Lodge, a descendant of a centuries-old business family, has recently argued that business should give up its free enterprise ideology and recognize that "the role of government is inevitably expanding." He goes further and states that joint business-government planning would be more efficient and lead to a smaller government.

One other issue needs to be addressed here. We have been acting as if there are only two entities dealing with each other: government and business. In fact, however, in our society these entities are both quite splintered. There are small businesses whose interests may conflict with those of large businesses. There are businesses that are hurt by free trade policies that bring in "cheap imports" and businesses that would be severely hurt without free trade (e.g., agriculture, computers). Likewise, the government is divided into federal, state, and local units, sometimes with conflicting regulations and goals. Even within the federal government the Departments of Commerce and the Treasury may side with business against the Departments of Labor and Health, Education and Welfare or the Environmental Protection Agency.

So there are complex and conflicting relationships within the two "entities" and between them. Only if the public understands and helps clarify business-government relations (what Neil Jacoby calls a "new social contract") will we make significant progress in this area.

How Government Influences Business

When we speak of "government" we must realize that there are three levels of government: federal, state (in Canada, provincial), and local. In the United States federal and in Canada provincial legislation has had the greatest impact on business success. Governmental units can influence managers in many ways. Three to be discussed here are regulation, subsidization, and competition.

Government Regulation of Business

All three levels of government can regulate businesses. Cities can impose licensing requirements; zoning restrictions can prevent a firm from expanding. States or provinces can also regulate an industry or company, and of course the federal level can and often does regulate business. It takes a government charter to open a business, and various government agencies regulate almost every aspect of almost any business.

Among the recent popular movements that have changed or increased government regulation of business are the environmental movement (Environmental Protection Agency), the consumer protection movement (an agency for this purpose is under consideration), the civil rights movement (Equal Employment Opportunity Commission), and the women's rights movement (also covered by the EEOC). Between 1960 and 1975 eighty-eight *significant* laws were passed regulating business activity. A sample of these is given in Table 18.2. These laws supplement many others already in force, and all are enforced by government agencies—some new, some old.

Very often the original purpose of a law is lost in the process of administration. Studies have shown, for example, that laws intended to protect small business against big business have hampered small businesses with so much paper work that they have become even less competitive.

Murray Weidenbaum, formerly of the President's Council of Economic Advisors, points out that government regulation is costly to the consumer in two ways: the direct costs (in taxes) of those who administer it, and the indirect costs incurred when businesses have to modify their

Table 18.2 Some Significant Legislation Regulating Business, 1960–1975

Civil Rights Act of 1960
Federal Hazardous Substances Labeling Act of 1960
Fair Labor Standards Amendments of 1961, 1966, and 1974
Federal Water Pollution Control Act Amendments of 1961
Oil Pollution Act of 1961 and Amendments of 1973
Food and Agriculture Act of 1962
Air Pollution Control Act of 1962
Antitrust Civil Process Act of 1962
Drug Amendments of 1962
Clean Air Act of 1963 and Amendments of 1966 and 1970
Equal Pay Act of 1963
Civil Rights Act of 1963
Food Stamp Act of 1964
Automotive Products Trade Act of 1965
Federal Cigarette Labeling and Advertising Act of 1965
Water Quality Act of 1965
Clean Water Restoration Act of 1966
Fair Packaging and Labeling Act of 1966
Federal Coal Mine Safety Act Amendments of 1966
Financial Institutions Supervisory Act of 1966
Oil Pollution of the Sea Act of 1966
Age Discrimination in Employment Act of 1967
Air Quality Act of 1967
Agricultural Fair Practices Act of 1968
Consumer Credit Protection Act of 1968

Natural Gas Pipeline Safety Act of 1968
Radiation Control for Health and Safety Act of 1968
Cigarette Smoking Act of 1969
Child Protection and Toy Safety Act of 1969
Federal Coal Mine Health and Safety Act of 1969
Natural Environmental Policy Act of 1969
Tax Reform Act of 1969
Bank Holding Act Amendments of 1970
Bank Records and Foreign Transactions Act of 1970
Economic Stabilization Act of 1970 and Amendments of 1971 and 1973
Environmental Quality Improvement Act of 1970
Fair Credit Reporting Act of 1970
Investment Company Amendments of 1969
Noise Pollution and Abatement Act of 1970
Occupational Safety and Health Act of 1970
Securities Investor Protection Act of 1970
Water and Environmental Quality Improvement Act of 1970
Export Administration Finance Act of 1971
Consumer Product Safety Act of 1972
Equal Employment Opportunity Act of 1972
Federal Environmental Pesticide Control Act of 1972
Noise Control Act of 1972
Agriculture and Consumers Protection Act of 1973
Emergency Petroleum Allocation Act of 1973
Highway Safety Act of 1973
Water Resources Development Act of 1974

ways of doing business. For example, the new safety requirements for autos directly cost the purchasers of 1974 models $6 billion in higher prices and operating costs. Weidenbaum says that most of the objectives served by government regulation could be accomplished more efficiently in other ways.

Government Subsidy, Support, and Taxation

Governments can directly affect the profitability of an enterprise through their tax policies. Increases in taxes reduce the amount of money available to purchase goods and services. Selective tax policies (subsidies) can keep enterprises afloat or even make them profitable. The U.S. government subsidizes, directly or indirectly, airlines, railroads, and many other businesses. It can accomplish this by purchasing the output of an enterprise or giving loans to firms like Lockheed and Penn Central.

The Government as Competitor

The government can nationalize an enterprise and put it out of existence, as Britain did to British Leyland (its largest auto firm) and as several Latin American governments have done. Or the government can compete directly with private firms. Consider these instances:

Government Enterprise	Private Enterprise
U.S. Postal Service	United Parcel Service
TVA	Peabody Coal, Union Electric
U.S. Employment Service	Chusid Employment Agency
Public Broadcasting Service	National Broadcasting Company
Government arms factories	Remington Arms Company
Yellowstone National Park	Disney World
National Park Service	KOA
Military and Transport Service	Flying Tiger
U.S. Military Commissary	Safeway Stores
British Leyland Motors	Ford Motors (U.K.)
Veterans Administration hospitals	Doctors' hospitals

The list can easily become quite long. As governments move toward ownership of business they can squeeze out the private sector.

What Business Can Do to Influence Government

Influence, as you learned in Chapter 7, can be exerted in many ways. It can be exerted ethically or unethically, legally or illegally. It is the manager's responsibility to see that the enterprise's interests are represented and that regulation, laws, subsidies, and other government actions are efficient, intelligent, and fair to all concerned, including the enterprise. The political scientist Edwin Epstein has concluded, after a lengthy analysis, that business needs to influence the American political process and that this is a legitimate and useful function for business.

In larger enterprises there are specialists who engage in government relations. These people have been called external affairs functionaries. Very little research has been done on this function. Trade associations also serve this function. But managers in smaller and middle-sized enterprises must spend some of their time in this area, the amount varying according to the degree of dependence on the government.

There are essentially six ways in which managers can attempt to interact with the government. We will discuss each in turn.

Interpersonal Influence

Managers can get to know government officials, politicians, and leaders of groups that can influence legislation. They try to use the mechanisms of interpersonal influence to get government officials to like them and trust them. They socialize with these officials and provide them with information in an attempt to enlist their support. The manager may play golf with government officials, invite them to lunch, have a few drinks at the country club, and in general increase their interaction with these individuals. This can be done ethically and legally, and usually is.

It is not easy to develop such a dialog. Business and government leaders tend to talk past each other rather than to each other. Differences in terminology are a problem. So are differences in educational background and objectives. But it is vital to the survival of the private sector that managers make their case known. Of course anti-business analysts contend that business already has too much influence. They see these relationships as opposed to the people's interests.

Advertising and Image Building

A second approach—which has an indirect influence on the political process—is to advertise and try to build a good image for the company with the general public (i.e., the voters). News programs are sponsored on TV, ads are placed in magazines and on the radio to get the enterprise's point of view across. Like all ads, some are good, others poor. Many times it is hard to evaluate the costs and benefits of campaigns of this type.

Lobbying

A manager can influence proposed new legislation (or amend past legislation) by writing, calling, or visiting legislators, congresspeople, or senators and trying to influence the actual writing of the law. More frequently, the manager supports his or her trade association's efforts in this regard. The association hires a lobbyist who knows the lawmakers and the legal process. The lobbyist is there when the law is being drafted and argues for a particular version of the bill.

All elements of our society employ lobbyists: farmers, unions, teachers, environmentalists, and others. Ralph Nader is, in effect, a lobbyist. Businesspeople must see that their side is heard too. An example of how lobbyists can influence legislation may be seen in the strip mining industry's ability to influence the legislation regulating their industry.

The key question is how lobbyists are used. Ethical businesspeople take steps to see that efficient, respected, honest lobbyists are hired to plead their case.

Direct Political Action

Another form of influence is political activity. Businesspeople can be active in politics and even run for office. Many well-known politicians were prominent businesspeople when they ran for office. Examples include Senators Charles Percy (R-Illinois, formerly at Bell and Howell), Stuart Symington (D-Missouri, formerly at Emerson Electric), and Lloyd Bentson (D-Texas, formally an insurance entrepreneur). Governor

George Romney of Michigan was formerly an executive at American Motors. Many state legislators are entrepreneurs and family business executives.

The businessperson may also accept political appointments—examples include John Conner, George Humphrey, William Simon, and many others. There are dangers in direct political activity by business executives, however. The enterprise can lose the time and talents of executives in this way, and customers of other political persuasions may be antagonized.

Becoming a Government Business

In earlier periods entrepreneurs would seek to become the government's exclusive agent. The East India Company (British and Dutch) helped develop America and Aristotle Onassis ran Greece's Olympic Airways in this way.

Illegal Influences

The final method used to influence the government is to bribe, frighten, or blackmail politicians or government officials into going along with the enterprise's preferences. More frequently, these methods are used to get laws administered (or ignored) in such a way as to favor the enterprise over others. This activity is discussed further in Chapter 19. Suffice it to say here that business can be done without resorting to these illegal methods.

Comments on Business-Government Relations

The ultimate government weapon is regulation of business. There are arguments on both sides of this issue. Business claims that it is overregulated. Political scientists, economists, lawyers, sociologists, and others claim that business subverts regulation and "captures" it. One of the most objective reviews of regulation during the past quarter-century is that of Thomas McCraw. He has examined the evidence and has come to the following conclusions:

> ·Regulation has not been entirely "captured," nor is it always initiated by the government: For example, the broadcasting industry requested industry regulation. Sometimes the industry reluctantly assents to regulation (as with the Interstate Commerce Commission), and sometimes regulation is vigorously opposed (as with the SEC). Regulation never develops if the public is opposed to it, but it does come into being when the public is apathetic or there is widespread public support for regulation of a particular industry.
> ·Regulation is capable of serving diverse, even contradictory ends. Thus regulatory functions among different commissions and even within the same agency can conflict with each other. All of this con-

flict is rationalized with the rhetoric that it is in the "public interest" and that the policy of the moment will yield benefits to society.

Still, we know very little about this area, with all its overlapping interests and conflicts. In McCraw's words, there was a

shadowy zone where public and private endeavors met and merged, where regulator and regulated experienced a confusion of identity and assumed each other's roles. Seldom in American history did the goals of private groups form a perfect identity with those of the rest of society, but seldom a perfect antithesis, either. Instead, sets of goals overlapped, now finely, now amply. Within the zones of overlap, private groups plausibly claimed service to society, and "capture" coexisted in fleeting calm with "public interest." Fleeting, because each zone suffered a double indeterminacy: who made the decisions, the public official or the businessman? And what were the precise boundaries of the zone? Constantly shifting from internal and external pressures, the zones formed arenas whose only permanent qualities were confusion, controversy, and uncertainty. Did a given action by a businessman or regulator denote the presence of "public interest," or of "capture"? Did it deserve congratulation, or condemnation? Prize, or prosecution?

As McCraw points out, both sides make devils of the other. Businesspeople see regulators as consciously or unconsciously ruining business. Regulators often see businesspeople as predators. In reality, both sides are honestly trying to improve the world of work for clients, customers, and the enterprise. Businesspeople need to learn how to influence regulators so that enterprise objectives are met. They need to be effective spokespeople and negotiators.

BUSINESS AND THE LOCAL COMMUNITY

In essence, the preceding section argued that managers must interact with the government to ensure that the government helps the enterprise and does not hinder its progress. The same argument is made here: The local community can help or hinder an enterprise, although probably less significantly than the government. But remember, the local community influences the local government.

Why should the manager try to influence the local community? The enterprise and the local community are highly interdependent. The local community influences zoning and similar matters. But more important, the local community is the major source of the enterprise's labor force. Enterprises that are perceived to be "good places to work" probably attract better employees.

The local community also provides clients and customers for goods and services. And it is the firm's physical environment. Most of us would like to work in a clean, honest, stimulating locale. In return, the enterprise can help make the community a better place to work.

When Does Business Get Involved in the Local Community? The values of businesspeople range from "It's our responsibility to be involved" to "Business' business is to do its job." The degree of involvement also varies widely: Involvement in a company town would be much higher than in New York City.

The research on business involvement in the local community is summarized in Table 18.3. Note the variety of ways businesses can be involved, depending on the type of business, the interrelationships, and the kind of local community in question.

Table 18.3 Conditions Leading to Community Involvement (Rogers and Zimet)

More Involvement	Less Involvement
Type of Business	
Family	Absentee-owned
Local markets	Regional or national markets
Extractive or distributive	Manufacturing
Inter-Business Relations	
Centralization of influence	Fragmentation
Cohesion of interests	Factionalism
City Characteristics	
Small- or medium-sized	Large
Limited industrialization	Highly industrialized
Economically undiversified	Diversified
Minimal heterogeneity of population	High degree of heterogeneity
Limited unionization of blue-collar workers	Extensive unionization
One-party predominance	Two or more vigorous parties
Non-partisan politics	Partisan politics
Limited differentiation of polity from family and economic interests	High degree of differentiation
Limited organization of interests countervailing those of business	High degree of countervailing organization
South, Southwest, or Midwest	East or Northeast

How Businesspeople Get Involved The variety of ways in which businesspeople can get involved is almost unlimited. But a number of major activities can be delineated:

- direct political action
- philanthropy (discussed in Chapter 19)
- advisory services (to the city, voluntary associations, etc.)
- support of bond issues and civic improvement
- support of charity drives
- providing executives for city or voluntary agencies

The number and variety of possible community support situations are so large that the enterprise should set priorities and concentrate its support in the most fruitful areas.

How Business Interacts with and Influences the Community

In general, the mechanisms available for community relations are similar to the mechanisms useful in government relations. Direct political action and lobbying are less frequently used. The most frequently used methods are interpersonal influence and advertising and image building.

The one addition to the methods discussed earlier is encouraging managers to join civic groups and volunteer to help the community. The enterprise can provide funds for advertising in support of community actions and send letters of support to its employees.

Sometimes business takes the lead in civic improvement. For example, the Pittsburgh rejuvenation project was led by the business community. The pharmaceutical firm of Smith, Kline and French supported an urban renewal program around its Philadelphia headquarters. And Hallmark bought some slums near its headquarters in Kansas City, tore them down, and redeveloped the area for shopping and better housing units.

Some larger enterprises have set up their own community relations programs. AT&T, for example, trains its executives in community relations and then encourages them to become active in voluntary groups such as charity organizations, blood banks, the Rotary Club, the YMCA, PTAs, the Jaycees, and the United Fund. It encourages them to run for part-time offices such as positions on zoning boards and school committees. AT&T also provides the schools with free texts and training programs. It is not known how much all this costs. AT&T's New York headquarters budgeted $10 million for this work in 1975 alone, but this figure does not include the cost in time of executives released from work.

The community usually benefits from these kinds of activities, since business executives often have much to offer. The enterprise benefits to the extent that the community views the enterprise as a responsible employer.

THE ENTERPRISE AND ITS SUPPLIERS

As indicated in Chapter 16, the enterprise is dependent to a greater or lesser extent on the suppliers of its needs: people, money, and materials and equipment. Thus a business is dependent on unions, stockholders and bankers, and materials and equipment suppliers.

Obviously, if the enterprise is not unionized, direct relationships between managers and unions are not very frequent. In such cases it is useful to develop alternative mechanisms to determine employee complaints and concerns. An ombudsman is one such mechanism. Other mechanisms include elected employee committees and suggestion systems.

If the enterprise is unionized, it makes sense to relate frequently and effectively with union leaders. Otherwise the only contacts might be negative adversarial relationships at contract time and confrontations over serious grievances. If the differences between managers and union leaders in socioeconomic characteristics (social class, education, age, values, income) are not bridged, conflict between the two groups can be accentuated.

Business managers attempt to influence union members through image building, advertising, and interpersonal influence. They can try to influence union leaders through interpersonal influence. Essentially, managers should get to know union leaders socially. They should sound them out regularly on their feelings and those of their members. The steel industry's labor problems were reduced when the steel union presidents golfed with the steel company presidents. Again, what is suggested here is not unethical or illegal influences but simply getting to know and understand the other person so that working relationships will improve. This is the job of personnel managers (the local union president, business representatives, and officers), supervisors (the respective shop stewards), and company presidents and regional and/or international union presidents.

Managers, Stockholders, and Bankers

In entrepreneurial and family businesses the managers are the stockholders. These firms still need to cultivate relationships with bankers who can provide loans from time to time. Generally this takes the form of interpersonal relations. Bankers may also be asked to serve on the enterprise's board, an honor that can lead to a favorable attitude toward lending needed funds to the enterprise.

In some family businesses the managers are major stockholders. But other family members hold important blocks of stock. Again, these family members are often on the board of directors. The various objectives of these stockholders often strongly influence decisions like dividend policy, growth policy, and philanthropy. As discussed in Chapter 3, these relationships can become difficult if personal differences among family members are translated into differences among managers or board members. Sometimes the only way such differences can be settled is to buy out minority stockholders with a bank loan or some similar mechanism. Since these stockholders can combine and get voting control of the enterprise, interpersonal relationships with these individuals are often carefully cultivated. Sometimes positions in the company are created for relatives in order to influence their attitudes.

As indicated in Chapters 2 and 3, in many middle-sized and larger firms certain individuals own major blocks of stock. If one stockholder owns 25 percent and the other 75 percent is owned by several thousand people, the major stockholder *potentially* can have a great impact on the management.

Stockholders usually regard ownership of stock as an investment, not a means of controlling the enterprise. Most of the nation's 30-odd million stockholders do not either have the knowledge or the inclination to try to affect management policy. A few large shareholders do.

Enterprises try to influence most stockholders through advertising, image building, and good annual reports. Some larger enterprises have executives in charge of stockholder relations. These individuals often pay special attention to major shareholders and watch the trading in the stock carefully to see if problems are developing.

When a few large stockholders can influence a corporation (as the Mellons can influence Gulf Oil), the top managers must spend some of their time communicating with these individuals.

A newer group that could *potentially* influence managers is the top executives of financial institutions: mutual funds, pension funds, endowment and philanthropic funds, and insurance and investment companies. These institutions own almost 50 percent of all stocks and are responsible for two-thirds of the trading on the stock exchanges. The managers of these institutions, a relatively small group, could make or break a firm. If they decided to "dump" 50 percent of the company's stock within a brief period, the firm's cost of capital would skyrocket. Financial managers and top managers try to influence these individuals directly and indirectly through interaction with stockbrokers and financial analysts. It is not beyond the realm of possibility that these people might demand changes in management and threaten to dump stock if the changes are not made. To the extent that your enterprise's stock is "closely held" by such individuals, it is well to try to influence them.

Finally, most enterprises need additional funds from banks from time to time. Thus these sources of funds need to be influenced by all enterprises, big, medium, and small, through interpersonal relations, advertising and image building, exchange relationships.

Managers and Materials and Equipment Suppliers

Many managers view their suppliers of materials and equipment as dependent on them—the purchasers. In many cases they are. If there are hundreds of companies trying to sell you lumber, you may see yourself as "in the driver's seat" and expect the suppliers to cultivate you.

In fact, however, in many cases there are only a limited number of suppliers who can provide you with the equipment and materials you need at the price you can pay for the quality you need and in the time you need it. Often there are really only one or two suppliers. You need to develop good relations with these suppliers so that when you need a favor (such as an emergency shipment) the supplier will try to help. Managers need to examine the relationships between suppliers and the enterprise's purchasing agents. Like any other group, purchasing managers can be competent or incompetent, ethical or unethical, pleasant or nasty. Purchasing is an area in which unethical people can develop bribery relationships to the detriment of both the enterprise and supplier relations. Nonpurchasing managers need to visit with supplier executives at conventions and other times to see if the supplier relationship is sound.

Whether your enterprise is dependent on a few suppliers or many, effective exchange relationships can lead to better shipping arrangements, early warning of major changes in prices, and speedy information about technological or marketing developments. Thus managers make an investment toward enterprise effectiveness if they develop friendly, professional relationships with their equipment and materials suppliers.

MANAGERS AND COMPETITORS
Enterprises compete for customers or clients with other enterprises. A major variable in a firm's success or failure (and existence) is the degree to which it competes effectively.

How should managers relate to competitors? First of all, relationships with competitors are influenced by the law and by the values of top management. In most of the world and throughout history (and in most nonbusiness sectors of society), cooperation with competitors has been the norm. Competition has been viewed as undesirable. Thus guild societies like medieval Europe and the Moravians in this country gave monopolies to craftsmen to ensure quality work and "fair return." Many European societies have seen trusts and monopolies as desirable and efficient, although the Common Market now has an antimonopoly commission. It is only the teaching of Adam Smith, as operationalized in the United States' antitrust laws, that sees monopoly as bad. If two hospitals got together and agreed to divide the market, with one specializing in heart work and another in kidney work, this plan would be applauded. If two businesses agreed to do this, their executives could go to jail.

In spite of the antitrust laws, "combinations in restraint of trade" take place in secret hotel rooms and prices and territories are sometimes agreed upon by competitors. The *Wall Street Journal* reported recently on the "gypsum trust." And you may have heard about the "electrical conspiracy," in which some General Electric and Westinghouse executives were punished for price and territory fixing. The FTC has accused a series of industries of monopolistic practices. A recent case in point is the paper craft industry.

There has been concern for some time about the concentrations of power that exist in some industries. The theory—and often the practice—is that fewer enterprises can (if they choose to) keep prices high and variety low. This is often accomplished through mergers. There is much evidence that many lose in a merger—not only the customers but also the stockholders of the acquiring company. The main beneficiaries of mergers are the stockholders of the acquired company (in the short run) and the top executives of the acquiring company. It is obvious that managers in the United States must either seek to change the antitrust laws or obey them scrupulously.

How, then, can managers relate legally to their competitors? They can do so through their industry trade associations. There are many legitimate issues that can be developed in the trade association. For example, if the industry has an inefficiently large number of product types the association may seek to standardize them. The association may fund research for safer working conditions, more efficient machinery, more efficient hiring of salespeople, and similar projects. It may also lobby and attempt to influence legislation.

Managers should get to know their competitors. From time to time they can help each other. For example, if one firm has a surplus and a competitor's plant burns down, one can sell the other some merchandise. In general, some cooperation is desirable for all concerned, as long as it is legal and ethical.

MANAGERS AND CUSTOMERS

As indicated in Chapter 16, enterprises can become very dependent on one or a few customers. The major defense manufacturers sell their products to the government (or perhaps a few governments). The success of major airplane manufacturers depends on their ability to sell planes to perhaps ten airlines. Contrast these firms with General Foods, which sells Maxwell House coffee to millions of consumers and thousands of wholesalers.

When a firm has only a few clients, the methods used to influence the customers are the same as those used to influence a few suppliers or stockholders. When it has millions of customers, the individual consumer is much less influential. If General Foods loses a few customers, many more can be acquired through TV advertising of Maxwell House coffee.

Irresponsible or inefficient service and poorly designed or unsafe products have led to the reappearance of the consumer movement. In this movement, blocks of consumers join together to exert pressure on an enterprise or industry. The consumer movement has had its ups and downs. Between 1879 and 1905 the movement was strong: 100 bills to regulate the food and drug industry at the state level and the Pure Food and Drug Act at the federal level were passed. Then the movement declined. It reappeared in the Depression, retrenched in the 1940s and 1950s, and reappeared again in the late 1960s and 1970s. Major consumer groups in the late 1970s include the Consumer Federation of America, the National Consumers League, and the Consumer Union of the United States. These groups expose irregularities, sue the enterprises involved, and lobby for their causes. Ralph Nader has been very active in this area through his Center for Responsive Law.

There is also a movement to set up a cabinet-level Department of Consumer Affairs to "protect the consumers of America." It is argued that this unit would better enforce truth-in-advertising laws and product liability legislation and warranties, as well as pure food and similar legislation.

In the past, businesses have responded to the consumer movement by trying to make sure the enterprise was not guilty of deception or illegal acts. Some enterprises supported voluntary organizations such as Better Business Bureaus to alert the consumer to fraud and exert pressure on offending businesses. Although the BBB is fairly successful, it tends to operate "behind the scenes." Thus it is not generally perceived as a powerful force in protecting consumers.

How does business relate to the consumer? Business has taken several approaches to consumer relations. Some companies have created consumer ombudsmen who see to it that the consumer gets a "fair shake." Some enterprises have widely advertised a toll free "consumer hotline." For example, Whirlpool urges its customers to call about service or product complaints and promises to take action.

Strict enforcement of the laws by government would also help. Why do some people believe that creation of a Consumer Department will ensure greater compliance with the laws? Both consumers and honest businesspeople should lobby for better enforcement of the present laws before creating new laws or bureaucracies.

Business needs to try to relate to the consumer movement. Instead of hiring private detectives to try to trap Ralph Nader, General Motors would have been more effective it it had investigated his charges and made its case known to the public and Congress. Businesses should develop interpersonal relationships with major consumer groups so that they have a "pipeline" to these influential groups. They should offer to cooperate in sponsoring independent studies of the charges made by such groups as Consumers Union. Their present stance casts them in the role of selfish interests vigorously trying to protect themselves while producing unsafe or useless goods and services. This is a losing position.

MANAGEMENT AND SOCIETAL PRESSURE GROUPS

Thus far we have discussed the relationships of business to the institutions or groups it is most likely to interact with. But there are other groups in society that can have an indirect effect on the success of a business. These groups include agricultural groups, intellectual groups, environmental groups, the poor, the aged, and voluntary pressure groups like churches, the YMCA, and similar groups.

Some businesses are directly involved with agricultural groups such as the Farm Bureau, the National Farmers Organization, and the Grange. Farm implement manufacturers, fertilizer companies, and seed companies clearly have an interest in relating to these groups of potential customers.

Businesses sometimes lobby for, sometimes against the programs advocated by agricultural groups in state capitals or in Washington. There have been few direct clashes between business and agriculture in recent years.

This is not so with other groups in society. The organized pressure groups favoring environmental protection and improvement and similar objectives have lobbied, advertised, and organized against specific business actions. Their greatest impact has been auto makers (emissions), chemicals (pollution), utilities (nuclear power), airframe corporations (SST, Concorde), petroleum (Alaska pipeline, offshore oil drilling), coal (strip mining), and defense manufacturing. In general, these groups favor improvement of the quality of life and the reduction of pollution in all its forms—chemical, noise, visual (billboards), and so forth.

These issues have divided the business community. Many if not most businesspeople favor cleaner air, more beautiful land, and a quieter environment. The affected industries usually argue that they favor these objectives too, but differ on the attainable goals for economic reasons.

The businesses involved use all the influence mechanisms available to them to plead their case: interpersonal relations, image building, lobbying, and others. In some cases they have also used threats: "If you require a particular level of air purity, we will close the plant. It will no longer be cost effective."

Business needs to do a better job of stating its case and trying to influence environmental groups. Of course in some instances (e.g., Gary, Indiana, steel works) the case is difficult to make and the firm should comply with the regulations or close the plant.

Another "pressure group" that has arisen in the past ten years is the urban poor. This group has publicized the urban crisis and urged or demanded that business improve urban living conditions by helping with urban renewal, job training, minority entrepreneurship programs, and more jobs. The response from business is directly related to the "social responsibility consciousness" of managers. This issue is described further in Chapter 19.

The final group with which business can interact is the intellectuals and media influence leaders. Important television, radio, newspaper, and magazine opinion leaders can have a significant impact on the future of business. If, for example, they all coalesced behind a demand that the oil companies be nationalized, this would have a major impact on voters (who are consumers) and legislators. To a lesser extent, some intellectuals such as scientists and professors can have an effect on business, usually by influencing key people in the media.

Business managers should try to influence these groups. The most effective method is to have intelligent, persuasive spokespeople develop interpersonal relationships with them. Other methods are less fruitful. One other method that is sometimes useful is philanthropy, as discussed in Chapter 19.

PLANNING FOR EXTERNAL RELATIONS   The manager's need to influence various institutions, groups, and individuals outside the enterprise have now been described. But unless managers plan their time and programs of influence, they may find themselves spending their time trying to influence unimportant groups. The most significant groups are those on which the firm is most dependent.

Like any other aspect of the managerial job, external relations will benefit from planning. The first step is conscious setting of priorities: asking various management groups to determine where the firm should place its energies and spend its time first—that is, which areas are most significant.

The second planning aspect is determining which mechanisms of influence will be used and which managers will be involved. For example, the vice president for marketing may be assigned to relate to consumer groups, the vice president-general counsel to relate to the state legislature, the vice president for personnel and organization planning to relate to the unions, and the vice president for finance to relate to stockholders.

Although there is little direct proof that planning this aspect of management will lead to greater effectiveness, research has shown that planning has been beneficial in other aspects of management. So it seems reasonable to conclude that it would help in managing external relations.

THE MANAGER IN AN INTERNATIONAL SETTING

We turn now to a discussion of external relations in countries other than the United States and Canada. Let me say in passing that American and Canadian business practices are not identical. And I am aware of Canadian concern over loss of cultural identity and political independence through "excessive" American ownership of Canadian corporations. I use the two together here because we do in fact have very similar managerial practices. Although there are a few environmental differences (especially the Canadian bilingual requirements and certain laws affecting business practice), there are more similarities between U.S. and Canadian managerial practices than between those of any other two countries in the world. We are closely interdependent—in fact we are each other's biggest customers. So I will concentrate on differences between U.S.-Canadian managerial practices and those of other countries.

There are three possible cases requiring knowledge of the environment for more effective management of external relations:

·An American or Canadian company sets up a branch office in another country.
·Your company is a multinational enterprise; that is, it derives almost as much business and profits from operations abroad as it does from domestic activities.
·A firm from another country sets up a business inside the United States or Canada.

In all three of these cases the number of managers who will actually be involved in international business is very small. Nevertheless this is a significant aspect of management.

How Does the Managerial Job Differ in Other Countries?

Some people contend that management is the same through all ages and in all countries. And in many ways this is true. But the differences are more important than the similarities. In chapter 16, I explained how six factors (three in the external, three in the internal environment) influence enterprises in determining their organizational styles. Management practices abroad are constrained by four sets of differences:

·*Educational factors*   Examples include the number of skilled employees available, attitudes toward education, and literacy level. Educational deficiencies in some countries can lead to a scarcity of qualified employees and/or a lack of educational facilities to upgrade potential employees.

·*Behavioral factors*   Societies differ in factors such as attitudes toward wealth, the desirability of profits, managerial role, and authority.

·*Legal-political factors*   Laws and political structures differ and can encourage or discourage private enterprise. Nations also differ in degree of political stability. Some countries are very nationalistic (and xenophobic). Such countries can require local ownership or, if they are so inclined, expropriate foreign enterprises.

·*Economic factors*   Economics differ in basic structure, inflation rate, ownership constraints, and the like.

Before entering into a foreign venture managers should examine these constraints as they affect each aspect of management and prepare a matrix like that in Figure 18.1. Table 18.4 shows how this might affect their managerial practices abroad. It is obvious that not all factors are going to be different in each country. There will be some overlap in attitudes and practices. The degree of difference seems to decrease in more economically developed countries.

LOCAL ENVIRONMENT CONSTRAINTS

	Educational	Behavioral	Legal-Political	Economic
Planning	a_1	a_2		
Control				
Organization				
Staffing				
Direction				
Marketing				
Production & Procurement				
Research & Development				
Finance				
Public & External Relations				a_{40}

(FIRM AND MANAGERIAL FUNCTIONS)

Figure 18.1
The firm/environment matrix (Farmer).

Each block a_1, a_2 --- a_{40} is a potential interface problem between the firm and its environment.

Table 18.4 Environmental Factors Affecting Managerial Function (Haynes, et al.)

MANAGERIAL FUNCTIONS	ENVIRONMENTAL FACTORS			
	Educational	Sociological-Cultural	Legal-Political	Economic
Setting objectives	Technical and higher educational systems	Role of religion; View of management goals and contribution to culture	Govt. influence/regulations	Fiscal and monetary policies
Policy formulation and implementation	Educational match with requirements	Attitude toward management and managers	Political stability	Economic stability
Research and development	Scientific orientation	Acceptance of change		View of risk taking and progress
Production and procurement	Supply of eng. and technicians	Attitude toward efficiency	Govt. support: defense and other Govt. contracts, industrial zoning	Availability of resources; adequate infrastructure
Finance	Specialized training in accounting and economics	View of savings and investment	Tax reliefs, subsidies, financial restrictions	Central banking system; foreign aid and private investment
Marketing	Literacy level	Attitude toward material possessions	Import-export and foreign exchange regulations	Market size, degree of competition, per capita annual income, price stability
Planning and innovation	Technical capability for budgets, schedules and basic policies	View of time and change, use of new knowledge and statistical data, population growth	National planning by central govt.	Inflationary-deflationary tendencies
Organization	Functional specialists and type of education	View of authority; group decision-making; interorganizational cooperation	Predictability of legal actions, political influence	Division of labor Factor endowment
Staffing	Educational level	Interpersonal cohesion, class structure and individual mobility	Status of management vis à vis govt; labor laws	Labor union influence, attitude toward unemployment
Direction, supervision, motivation	Management development	View of achievement; dedication to work; language barriers to communication	Tolerance of bribes, fraud, and tax evasion	Worker participation in management; use of monetary and fringe benefit; incentives
Control	Ability to use feedback for corrective action	Attitude toward scientific method	Accounting data, reports for govt. regulation	Private property rights; quotas

We can divide the nations of the world into three economic categories: fully developed, developing, and less developed. The fully developed nations include the United States and Canada, Australia, Israel, Japan, South Africa, and most European countries (the United Kingdom, West Germany, France, the USSR, Belgium, Luxembourg, the Netherlands, Switzerland, Italy, Sweden, Denmark, Norway, Finland). In these countries the American or Canadian manager will find fewer differences in educational, behavioral, economic, and legal-political factors than he or she is likely to encounter in developing or less developed countries.

The "developing" nations are those that are well along in economic development but not yet fully developed. Examples include Brazil, Mexico, Argentina, Venezuela, Chile, Spain, Portugal, Nigeria, Saudi Arabia, Iran, Libya, India, Singapore, Taiwan, eastern Europe (Yugoslavia, Romania, East Germany, Czechoslovakia), Korea, and possibly China. These countries provide more constraints in all four categories than developed countries.

"Third World" nations—the less developed countries—are the most difficult to work in because of significant constraints in all four categories. The remaining 90 or so countries in the world are in this group. A sample list would include Egypt, Pakistan, Bolivia, Paraguay, Bangladesh, Upper Volta, and Sudan.

To be successful abroad, the manager must learn about the country where he or she will be working. There are many sources of this kind of information. Haire, et al., for example, describes managerial attitudes around the world. Harbeson and Myers, though dating back to 1959, provides a description of what it is like to manage in ten countries around the world; Massie and Luytjes give advice on effective management in 12 countries.

So knowledge of differences among nations in the four constraints listed earlier is essential for success abroad. Equally important (and more difficult to obtain) is proper attitudes toward other countries and their cultures. The United States is the most powerful and affluent country in the world. Canada has the second-highest standard of living in the world. Managers working abroad may develop a mind set like the following:

U.S./Canada	Characteristic	Host Nation
Strong	Strength	Weak
Wealthy	Wealth	Poor
Advanced	Managerial Practice	Primitive
Important	Culture	Insignificant

A manager with this set of attitudes may try to transfer North American ways of doing things directly to the host country without considering the four constraints. The more significant the differences in the four constraints, the more likely they are to cause problems for the unperceptive manager.

Effective international managers adapt their managerial practices to conditions in the host country. Just as the tools of management science do not work on very unstable problems, so leadership styles that work on educated, achievement-oriented employees may not work on uneducated, nonachieving employees. A liberal in the United States may have to become a middle-of-the-road manager in Egypt.

The willingness to adapt managerial practices to the needs of the environment or culture joined with knowledge of the legal-political and economic factors is likely to lead to success overseas.

Management in the Multinational Corporation

A small number of firms are *multinational;* that is, much of their business and/or profits may come from overseas. These firms have regional headquarters for whole areas of the world (e.g., ABC Europe, ABC Asia, etc.). They develop worldwide strategies in order to survive and grow. It is estimated that 15 per cent of gross world product is produced by multinational corporations.

Most multinationals are owned and controlled primarily by individuals in one country. A few are transnational (e.g., Shell and Unilever): their ownership is split among individuals in several major countries.

To get an idea of the differences between a firm with branches overseas and a multinational corporation, consider these instances:

· Nestle, a Swiss corporation, does more than 98 per cent of its business outside Switzerland.
· Certain German-based multinationals have invested more capital in South Carolina than anywhere else except Germany.

Multinational corporations have existed for centuries. A number of recent works have described the evolution of multinationals in Japan (Yoshino), the United Kingdom (Stopford), and Europe (Franco, Mazzolini). In fact the literature on multinationals is large. A great deal has been written about multinationals and their strategy. Some work has also been done on how to organize multinationals and on how to develop control systems for them. In addition, courses have been developed on management in multinational corporations.

Some people worry that multinationals could take over the world. Others argue that they are a good thing and are not excessively powerful. Still others see them as greedy predators willing to sell anything to anybody. But when Daniel P. Moynihan was the U.S. ambassador to the United Nations, he pointed out that most recent changes in governments had resulted in shifts from capitalism to socialism. If his trend analysis is correct and if it continues, multinationals do not have a bright future, since they are likely to be nationalized by socialist governments.

Successful multinationals grow because they develop good managers who respect other nations and their cultures as they establish their management structures and build their marketing, financial, and operating strategies. They have learned to strike a proper balance between executives who are citizens of the host country and executives from the home office. Multinationals have been criticized, however, for not developing a global management group. The members of such a group would be on the same pay scale, evaluated on the same criteria, kept on the same management inventory, and given experience around the world. Instead, the present pattern is to have the home office staffed primarily by executives of the home country, the local branch staffed primarily by host country nationals, and very few "third country" nationals in management positions anywhere. It is argued that to be successful, multinational corporations need a core group of globally oriented executives and professionals who can work anywhere. This may be true, but knowledge of the four constraints (economic, political-legal, behavioral, and educational) is necessary for success in most overseas assignments, and this is very difficult to develop if you spend two years in Mexico followed by two years in Japan, two in South Africa, and then two in Belgium.

The multinational corporations are still evolving the most effective mechanisms of international policy and personnel development. More research is needed before we can say much more about effective multinational management.

SUMMARY   If the enterprise operates in an environment that can have a significant impact on its activities—as is usually the case—the manager is often cast in the role of negotiator or spokesperson for the company.

The most important forces in the environment affecting the enterprise are the government, the local community, and suppliers of people (unions), money (stockholders, bankers), and materials and equipment. Managers must also interact with customers, competitors, and societal pressure groups.

The means of influence available to the manger vary according to the sector of the environment he or she is dealing with. For example, in dealing with the government a manager uses interpersonal influence, advertising and image building, lobbying, direct political action, and other methods. In dealing with the local community the entrepreneur or manager uses interpersonal influence, direct political action, and advertising and image building; he or she may also provide advisory service. The entrepreneur or manager allocates time so that he or she interacts most frequently with the most crucial forces in the environment.

The enviroment of the manager conducting business overseas is different and more complex. Less developed nations do business and relate to businesspeople differently than developed nations like Canada. Managers must adjust their operating methods to the overseas environment to some degree if they wish to be successful.

Chapter 19 continues the discussion of environmental relations. Specifically, it describes how managers' values (toward social responsibilities, ethics, etc.) and those of the enterprise affect their managerial roles.

Questions For Review

1. Why do managers become negotiators and spokespeople?

2. How are these relationships affected by the society's prevailing attitudes toward business?

3. What are some of the possible relationships between government and business?

4. What means of influencing the government are available to an entrepreneur or manager?

5. When does a manager or entrepreneur try to interact with the local community? How does he or she do this?

6. Which suppliers does an entrepreneur or manager try to influence? How?

7. Can managers legally relate closely to competitors? How? Why?

8. How does a manager relate effectively to consumers? to pressure groups?

9. How does doing business abroad differ from doing business in the United States and Canada?

References

The Manager as Negotiator and Spokesperson

Gordon, Robert, *Business Leadership in the Large Corporation* (Berkeley: University of California Press, 1966).

Krooss, Herman, *Executive Opinion: What Business Leaders Said and Thought 1920–1960* (New York: Doubleday, 1970).

Macmillan, David, *Canadian Business History* (Toronto: McClelland and Steward, 1972).

Mintzberg, Henry, *The Nature of Managerial Work* (New York: Harper & Row, 1972).

Monsen, R. Joseph, *Business and the Changing Environment* (New York: McGraw-Hill, 1973), chap. 5.

Nash, Gerald, *Perspectives on Administration: The Vistas of History* (Berkeley: University of California, Institute of Governmental Studies, 1969).

Newman, William, "Cultural Assumptions Underlying U.S. Management Concepts," in Joseph Massie and Jan Luytjes, eds., *Management in an International Context* (New York: Harper & Row, 1972).

Waldo, Dwight, "The Novelist on Organization and Administration," University of California, Institute of Governmental Studies, (Berkeley, 1968).

Relations with the Government

Drucker, Peter, *Management* (New York: Harper & Row, 1974), chap. 27.

Eels, Richard, and Walton, Clarence, *Conceptual Foundations of Business* (Homewood, Ill.: Richard D. Irwin, 1974), chap. 14.

Jacoby, Neil, *Corporate Power and Social Responsibility* (New York: Macmillan, 1973).

Lodge, George, "Business and the Changing Society," *Harvard Business Review,* March-April 1974.

How Government Influences Business

Bagge, Carl, "The Changing Regulatory Scene," in *Business & Society in Change* (New York: American Telephone and Telegraph Company, 1975), pp. 143–154.

Clark, Lindley, Jr., "Speaking of Business," *Wall Street Journal,* January 30, 1976.

Seelye, Alfred, "Societal Change and Business-Government Relationships," *MSU Business Topics,* Autumn 1975, pp. 5–11.

Weidenbaum, Murray, "The High Cost of Government Regulation," *Business Horizons,* August 1975, pp. 43–51.

Government Subsidy, Support, and Taxation

Connally, John, "The Case for the L-1011 Lockheed Transport Loan Guarantee," in *Hearings Before the Senate Banking, Housing, and Urban Affairs Committee on S1891,* 92d Cong., 2nd sess., June 1971.

Proxmire, William, "The Lockheed Bail Out: A Threat to Free Enterprise," speech before the National Federation of Independent Business, Washington, D.C., May 18, 1971.

What Business Can Do to Influence Government

Bauer, Raymond and Greyser, Stephen, "The Dialogue That Never Happens," *Harvard Business Review,* November-December 1967.

Boddewyn, Jean, "External Affairs: A Corporate Function in Search of Conceptualization and Theory," *Organization and Administrative Science,* 5, no. 1 (1974): 67–111.

Cole, Arthur, *Business Enterprise in its Social Setting* (Cambridge, Mass.: Harvard University Press, 1959), Section 5.

Epstein, Edwin, *The Corporation in American Politics* (Englewood Cliffs, N.J.: Prentice-Hall, 1969).

Gannon, James, "Business Blitz," *Wall Street Journal,* August 5, 1975.

Hamilton, Walton, *The Politics of Industry* (New York: Alfred Knopf, 1957).

Hunt, Raymond, and Ruben, Ira, "Approaches to Management Control in Interpenetrating Systems: The Case of Government-Industry Relations," *Academy of Management Journal,* 16, no. 2 (June 1973): 296–311.

Moremont, Arnold, "The Dangers of Corporate Activity in Politics," *MSU Business Topics,* Winter 1960, pp. 7–17.

Powell, Reed, and Hostwick, K. Tim, "The Business Executive's Role in Politics," *Business Horizons,* August 1972, pp. 49–56.

Final Comments on Business-Government Relations

McCraw, Thomas, "Regulation in America: A Review Article," *Business History Review,* 49, no. 2 (Summer 1975): 159–183.

Business and the Local Community

Davis, Keith, and Blomstrom, Robert, *Business and Society* (New York: McGraw-Hill, 1975), chap. 17.

Litwak, Eugene, and Meyer, Henry, "A Balance Theory of Coordination Between Bureaucratic Organizations and Community Primary Groups," *Administrative Science Quarterly,* 16, no. 1 (June 1966): 31–58.

Rogers, David, and Zimlet, Melvin, "The Corporation and the Community," in Ivar Berg, ed., *The Business of America* (New York: Harcourt, Brace and World, 1968), pp. 37–80.

Warner, W. Lloyd, and Low, J. O., "The Factory in the Community," in William Foote Whyle, ed., *Industry and Society* (New York: McGraw-Hill, 1966).

The Enterprise and Its Suppliers

Kochen, Thomas, "Determinants of Power of Boundary Units in an Interorganizational Bargaining Relationship," *Administrative Science Quarterly,* 20 (September 1975): 434–452.

Kuhn, James, "Business and Unions," in Ivar Berg, ed., *The Business of America* (New York: Harcourt, Brace and World, 1968), chap. 9.

Managers and Competitors

Conti, John, "A Profitable Delay: FTC Paper-craft Dispute Renews Doubts About Effectiveness of the Anti-Trust Laws," *Wall Street Journal,* December 2, 1975, p. 40.

Eichner, Alfred, "Business Concentration and Its Significance," in Ivar Berg, ed., *The Business of America* (New York: Harcourt, Brace and World, 1968), pp. 169–200.

Jacoby, op. cit., chaps. 2, 4, 6.

Martin, Desmond, and Kearney, William, "External Policy and Control in Large Scale National Trade Associations," *Journal of Business Administration,* 1 (Summer 1969): 29–37.

Martin, Desmond, and Kearney, William, "Who Makes the Decisions in Trade Associations," *Atlantia Economic Review,* 19, no. 9 (September 1969): 10–13.

McClintick, David, "Busting a Trust," *Wall Street Journal,* October 3, 1975.

Managers and Customers

Brunk, Max, "Consumerism and Marketing," in George Steiner, ed., *Issues in Business and Society* (New York: Random House, 1972).

Maynes, Scott, "The Power of Consumers," *Business Horizons,* June 1972, pp. 77–86.

Monsen, R. Joseph, *Business and the Changing Environment* (New York: McGraw-Hill, 1973), chap. 3.

Management and Societal Pressure Groups

Davis and Blomstrom, op. cit., chaps. 18, 19, 22, 23.

Drucker, op. cit., chaps. 24, 25.

Jacoby, op. cit., chaps. 10, 11.

Monsen, op. cit., chaps. 1, 2, 7.

Steiner, op. cit., chaps. 7, 8, 10.

The Manager in an International Setting

Abegglen, James, *The Japanese Factory* (Glencoe, Ill.: Free Press, 1958).

Ehrmann, Henry, *Organized Business in France* (Princeton, N.J.: Princeton University Press, 1957).

England, George, et al., *The Manager and the Man* (Kent, Ohio: Kent State University Press, 1974).

Farmer, Richard, "International Management," in Joseph McGuire, ed., *Contemporary Management* (Englewood Cliffs, N.J.: Prentice-Hall, 1974).

Gordon, Paul, "Organizational Strategies: The Case of Foreign Operations by Non-U.S. Countries," *Journal of Comparative Administration,* 2 (May 1970): 81–108.

Haire, Mason, et al., *Managerial Thinking* (New York: John Wiley and Sons, 1966).

Harbeson, Frederick, and Myers, Charles, *Management in the Industrial World: On International Analysis* (New York: McGraw-Hill, 1959).

Hartmann, Heinz, *Authority Organization in German Management* (Princeton, N.J.: Princeton University Press, 1959).

Haynes, W. Warren, et al., *Management,* 3d ed. (Englewood Cliffs, N.J.: Prentice-Hall, 1975), chap. 27.

Lauterbach, Albert, *Enterprise in Latin America* (Ithaca, N.Y.: Cornell University Press, 1965).

Litvak, I. A., and Maule, C. J. "Branch Plant Entrepreneurship," *The Business Quarterly,* Spring 1972, pp. 44–53.

Massie, Joseph, and Luytjes, Jan, *Management in an International Context* (New York: Harper and Row, 1972).

Richman, Barry, *Soviet Management* (Englewood Cliffs, N.J.: Prentice-Hall, 1965).

Schollhamer, Hans, "The Comparative Management Theory Jungle," *Academy of Management Journal,* March 1969, pp. 81–97.

Management in the Multinational Corporation

Bradley, Gene, and Bursk, Edward, "Multinationalism and the 29th Day," *Harvard Business Review,* January-February 1972), pp. 37-47.

Fouraker, Lawrence, and Stopford, John, "Organizational Structure and Multinational Strategy," *Administrative Science Quarterly,* 18, no. 1 (June 1968): 47–64.

Kuin, Peter, "The Merger of Multinational Management," *Harvard Business Review,* November-December 1972, pp. 89–97.

Lebel, Don, et al., "Small Scale Industries and Developing Countries," *California Management Review,* 17, no. 1 (Fall 1974): 32–40.

Mason, R. Hal, "Conflicts Between Host Countries and the Multinational Enterprise," *California Management Review,* 17, no. 1 (Fall 1974): 5–14.

Perlmutter, Howard, "Some Management Problems in Spaceship Earth: The Megafirm and the Global Industrial Estate," *Proceedings, Academy of Management,* 1969, pp. 59–93.

Perlmutter, Howard, and Heenan, David, "How Multinational Should Your Top Managers Be?" *Harvard Business Review,* November-December 1974, pp. 121–134.

Robbines, Sidney, and Stobaugh, Robert, "The Bent Measuring Stick for Foreign Subsidiaries," *Harvard Business Review,* September-October 1973, pp. 80–88.

Rose, Sanford, "The Rewarding Strategies of Multinationalism," *Fortune,* September 15, 1968.

Rutenberg, David, "Organizational Archetypes of a Multinational Company," *Management Science,* 16, no. 6 (February 1970): B337–349.

Schollhammer, Hans, "Organization Structures of Multinational Corporations," *Academy of Management Journal,* 14, no. 3 (September 1971): 345–365.

Sethi, Prokash, and Holton, Richard, "Country Typologies for the Multinational Corporation," *California Management Review,* 15, no. 3 (Spring 1973): 105–117.

Youssef, Samir, "Contextual Factors Influencing Control Strategy of Multinational Corporations," *Academy of Management Journal,* 18, no. 1 (March 1975): 136–143.

CHAPTER 19

MANAGERS AND THEIR VALUES

19

Learning Objectives

1. To understand how managers' attitudes toward social responsibility affect the enterprise's relationship with its environment.
2. To learn how managers' ethical values affect their behavior toward the environment and toward employees.
3. To understand how managing a nonbusiness enterprise is similar to managing a business, yet different, and how it is different.

Chapter Outline

Social Responsibilities of Managers and Entrepreneurs
The Profit Ethic
The Social Ethic
The Pros and Cons of Social Responsibility
Social Responsibility Projects
The Poor, Minorities, and the Urban Crisis
Environmental Improvement Projects
Philanthropic Activity
The Planning and Operation of Social Responsibility
Managers and Ethics
Recent Examples of Unethical Behavior
Are all Managers Unethical?
Ethical Behavior and Legal Behavior
What Are the Sources of Ethical Problems?
Action to Improve Business Behavior
Ethics in Business—Old Hat?
Managing Public and Nonprofit Enterprises
The Public Manager
The Hospital Administrator
The University Manager
Arts Management
Managing Voluntary Organizations and the ''Third Sector''
Summary

As we discussed external relations in Chapter 18, reference was made to two issues: ethical relationships and the degree to which an enterprise involves itself in philanthropy, urban renewal, and the like. The latter is social responsibility, the former a personal moral value. These values can have a significant impact on managerial decisions and behavior. Later in the chapter I describe how the values and environments of managers in nonbusiness enterprises are similar to, yet different from those of business managers.

SOCIAL RESPONSI-BILITIES OF MANAGERS AND ENTRE-PRENEURS

In Chapter 4 we defined a *value* as a type of attitude that evaluates a stimulus in a positive or negative way. Values are learned from family, peers, church, and school. They help a person make sense of the stimuli coming in from his or her environment. Values are an important part of personality.

The particular value described here is an important predictor of how managers will respond to requests that the enterprise help solve societal problems such as poverty and urban decay. It amounts to this: Do private enterprises have improvement of the human environment as one of their basic objectives? Those who answer "yes" hold social responsibility among their values. Those answering "no" are opposed to social responsibility. The pragmatic manager says "sometimes."

At present all three of these values are held by managers. Historically, however, one of these values has been typical of most managers in a given period. Before 1100 A.D., businesspeople tended to hold social responsibility or "trusteeship" values. From 1100 to about 1800, they shifted toward pragmatic attitudes. Adam Smith's *Wealth of Nations* ushered in the anti-social responsibility period (from about 1800 to 1930). Since then there has been a move back toward pragmatic or pro-social responsibility values. But in most periods all three values have existed together. Thus Robert Owen, Oliver Shelden and others in the 1800s were clearly in favor of social responsibility in an era when most businesspeople were opposed —an era notorious for its robber barons. Other examples could be cited for other historical periods.

Joseph McGuire argues persuasively that social responsibility will become an objective of business and/or enter the decision making processes of managers and entrepreneurs when (1) social responsibility becomes an important value of managers and entrepreneurs and (2) when environmental forces pressure the manager to accept these premises.

Let us be more specific about these views. The "anti" position has been called the profit ethic, the "pro" position the social ethic. I will use these terms here.

The Profit Ethic

The profit ethic holds that the primary objective of a business is to maximize profits and serve the interests of its owners. The business of a business is to make money. If the enterprise pays out some of its profits to socially responsible ends, this is a tax on profits, and only the government should tax. Of course individual managers should be socially responsible, but with their own money, not someone else's. The followers of Adam Smith argue that when each business maximizes profits, this lowers the cost of everything and improves the economic well-being of all.

The Social Ethic This position holds that a business is responsible to many groups besides owners—including employees and customers. Therefore profit maximization is not the only objective of a business. Some profits should be diverted to social responsibility projects in the short run; this will lead to greater ability to survive and satisfactory long-run profits.

The Pros and Cons of Social Responsibility

The "Anti" Argument

Those opposed to social responsibility give six reasons why business executives (not entrepreneurs) should follow the profit ethic:

1 The enterprise's profit is not the executive's own money. It is the stockholders' money. Executives should be responsible as *individuals*. As managers, however, they are only the agents of the stockholders and have no legal right to spend money on social responsibility projects, notwithstanding the desirable ends of these projects. The money spent on such projects lowers the dividend and/or price of the stock. This denies the stockholder the use of this money, which is a rightful return on invested capital.

2 If one enterprise spends money on social responsibility projects and its competitors do not, this increases the costs of the socially responsible firm and, thus, its prices, and it will lose business. If the socially responsible firm is economically marginal, it will put itself out of business. It can also cause balance-of-payments problems if its prices are higher than those of its overseas competitors.

3 The spending on social responsibility projects increases prices to all customers. In effect this is a tax, since customers lose the opportunity to spend this money on other goods.

4 Managers are not trained in, nor competent at, judging which of the many socially desirable projects they should fund. Those trained in this kind of decision making are government officials, politicians, and voluntary organization specialists. Thus many businesspeople's social responsibility decisions are inefficiently made.

5 Social responsibility puts too much power in the hands of business executives. The perennial fear of political theorists has been a condition in which economic and political-social power is concentrated in a few hands. A fundamental ideal of a democratic society is *pluralism,* that is, a condition in which power is widely distributed among individuals and institutions. In effect social responsibility concentrates political-social power in the hands of those with economic power.

6 Social responsibility is a movement toward socialism. People have progressed economically and socially under free enterprise regimes and have lost economical and often political power under socialist regimes.

It is important to note that most of these arguments do *not* hold for entrepreneurs and many family business executives. These executives can spend the enterprise's money as they please, if they spend it out of profits and do not pass it on as a cost to the consumer. Argument (4) may still hold, however.

The "Pro" Argument

People who hold the social responsibility ethic advance five reasons why executives and entrepreneurs should make social responsibility an objective of business and a part of the decision-making process:

1 Times have changed. People *expect* institutions (including business enterprises) to be socially responsible. Those that refuse will not survive the wrath of their clients or customers.

2 If business is not socially responsible, the public will press for more government regulation, which in effect will lead to socially responsible behavior. So it makes sense to be socially responsible in order to prevent further government regulation of business.

3 In the long run a business' profits will be higher if it is socially responsible. For example, if a business in a ghetto goes not hire members of the local minority group, it will lose business and suffer pilferage; it may even be burned down. Therefore it makes more sense to be socially responsible even if it costs more in the short run.

4 Business should become involved in socially responsible projects because it has the financial resources to do so. Besides, business executives are efficient. After some initial training, business can do a better job of improving social conditions than other institutions.

5 The findings of social science research in the past twenty-five years have shown that all organizations have multiple objectives, including businesses. Short-run profit maximization must be tempered by social responsibility.

Both sides make good points. Maybe this is why many executives wind up being pragmatists on social responsibility—"pro" when profits are exceptionally good or social conditions very bad, "anti" when the enterprise is up against the wall or when social conditions do not warrant a great deal of concern.

SOCIAL RESPONSIBILITY PROJECTS

What are "social responsibility projects"? Although several such projects have been mentioned earlier, some examples of these projects may clarify what we mean by this term. Two of these may be called *indirect philanthropy;* the third is *direct philanthropy.*

The Poor, Minorities, and the Urban Crisis

One of the most frequently cited projects for business is to try to ameliorate conditions in decaying urban centers populated by poor, untrained individuals who are often members of black, Spanish-surnamed, and other minority groups. Business has been asked

· to hire and train ghetto dwellers to do productive work.
· to set up and run job retraining centers to channel these people to other employers (e.g., Motorola's Chicago Industrial Skills Center).
· to provide public health information and education (e.g., Metropolitan Life Insurance).
· to clean up the ghetto and help rebuild it (e.g., Georgia's Citizens and Southern Bank).
· to locate new plants near these potential workers.
· to purchase supplies from minority-owned businesses.

These and many other projects would improve the lot of the poor, especially the minority poor. Some businesses have responded to these and similar requests. Such projects often amount to subsidies at the expense of profits and therefore can be considered indirect philanthropy. In some cases, of course, they may be good business.

Environmental Improvement Projects

Governmental units and agencies—city-run power plants, city sewerage systems, the Atomic Energy Commission, nuclear programs, military poison gas projects—are often the most polluting enterprises in America. Nevertheless the environmental protection movement has asked for and received governmental support actions designed to get business to "clean up the environment." Some of these projects include

· Elimination of the billboard industry.
· Reduction of noise from transportation (especially airlines) and other businesses.
· Reduction of water pollution and destruction of fish through discharge of chemicals, hot liquids, and similar materials into streams and the water table.
· Reduction of air pollution from auto emissions and particle discharges from metals, mining, chemicals, and similar enterprises and from utilities.

In many cases businesses have voluntarily reduced the pollution they cause. In other cases, when they have considered the standards imposed to be too strict and/or uneconomical, managers have opposed pollution control. To the extent that companies have voluntarily reduced pollution or positively improved the beauty of their buildings and land, this is a form of indirect philanthropy.

Philanthropic Activity

Education

Businesses (and of course businesspeople as individuals) have a long tradition of giving large sums of money (and sometimes goods in kind) to education, the arts, and churches and similar voluntary groups.

With regard to education, businesses have donated funds for student scholarships, research, endowment funds, and capital improvements. Many businesspeople feel that business will benefit from a more knowledgeable society and workforce and that this will result from gifts to education, to vocational education at the secondary level and both vocational and other areas of education at the university level.

It is estimated that 2 percent of business income *before* taxes is allocated to philanthropy. Two-fifths of that amount goes to higher education. One study found that of 167 firms, 25 percent gave funds to secondary and teacher education. Business also provides indirect aid by accepting field trips, sending speakers, and helping with curriculum and student travel programs.

The Arts

The business community has also given money to the arts. Business philanthropy has extended from libraries and museums to the performing arts to TV specials. An estimated 5 percent of corporate gifts go to the arts, not counting individual gifts by business executives.

In other countries the primary support for the arts comes from the government. For example, the city of Vienna's total art subsidies amount to *more* than the total art subsidies of all levels of government throughout the United States.

Generally, executives will argue that support of the arts leads to better and more satisfied employees. So U.S. business supports the arts, although less than the arts would like and probably more than most stockholders desire.

THE PLANNING AND OPERATION OF SOCIAL RESPONSIBILITY

If an enterprise takes a pragmatic or pro-social responsibility position, it needs to determine its priorities. Since a goodly amount has been written on this issue, only a few words need be added here.

There are several ways in which an enterprise can respond to the social ethic if it chooses to. Among them are the following:

Public relations response: use of press releases and advertising about the enterprise's social concern.
Legal response: the minimum compliance required by law.
Bargaining response: negotiating with the group that is demanding social responsibility.

An enterprise moving toward social responsibility may go through three stages:

Token behavior: A few gestures are made to indicate concern or a liberal position.
Attitude changes: The enterprise goes beyond gestures because its managers support social responsibility.
Substantive changes: The enterprise makes structural or behavioral changes to implement social responsibility. Some of the structural mechanisms used include setting up task forces, committees, or special departments or executives to handle social issues (see Figure 19.1).

Figure 19.1
Continuum of responses to social responsibility (Duncan).

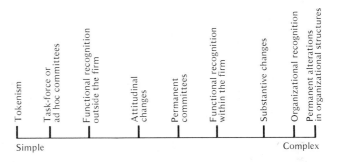

Robert Ackerman has studied the responses of large corporations to the social ethic for ten years. He points out that there are three factors that hinder social responsibility implementation in large corporations:

1 Corporate and division responsibilities are separate. Thus a decision at the top does not easily filter down to the "firing line."
2 The financial reporting system used for measurement does not include social responsibility.
3 The performance evaluation and reward system does not reinforce social responsibility.

The existing social responsibility patterns are summarized in Table 19.1. Ackerman has observed that enterprises go through three phases in their response to social responsibility (see Figure 19.2). The first phase begins when the top manager gets involved, makes speeches, maybe even gives money from corporate headquarters (with no impact on the operating divisions). The next step occurs when the president appoints a staff executive responsible to the president to coordinate the firm's efforts in this area. The result may be almost no response or a token response. In the final phase the president builds social objectives into the firm's reporting and reward system. This produces results.

Table 19.1 Existing Management Patterns and Social Issues (Ackerman)

Existing Management Patterns	Problems in Responding to Social Issues
Allocation of Responsibilities	
Corporate level: secures division performance commitments and monitors the results, while fostering operating autonomy.	A corporatewide responsibility is implied, with the demand or desire for a corporatewide response. But that response involves operations, and implementation is possible only at divisional levels.
Divisional level: formulates strategy for the division's business and accepts responsibility for achieving the results.	
Executive Performance Evaluation	
Performance of assigned responsibilities—often measured through the financial reporting system—is reinforced by incentive compensation and is the determinant of career paths in the organization.	Benefits of social responsiveness may appear in time frames longer than the manager's tenure in his job.
	Current expenditures of time and money may penalize the financial performance to which the organization is committed.
	Trade-offs are required which involve values and judgments on which managers may reasonably differ.
Management through Systems	
Division performance is monitored by financial reporting systems that are:	Social costs and benefits are often not amenable to financial measures or planning.
related to division commitments	Current expenditures are real; long-run benefits are uncertain.
amenable to corporatewide aggregation	Benefits may be general and not related to the spending unit.
reasonably simple to communicate and understand.	

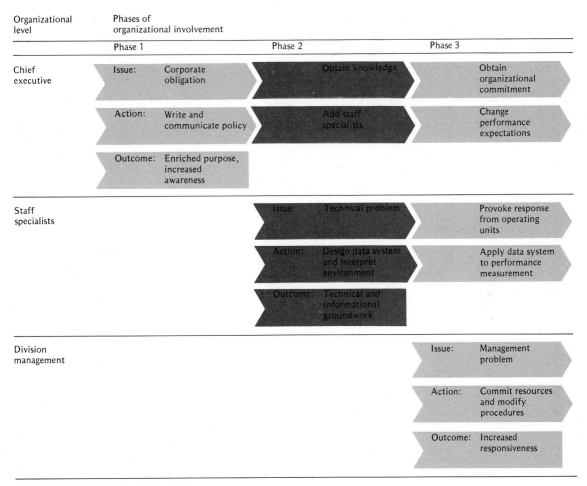

Organizational level	Phases of organizational involvement		
	Phase 1	Phase 2	Phase 3
Chief executive	Issue: Corporate obligation	Obtain knowledge	Obtain organizational commitment
	Action: Write and communicate policy	Add staff specialists	Change performance expectations
	Outcome: Enriched purpose, increased awareness		
Staff specialists		Issue: Technical problem	Provoke response from operating units
		Action: Design data system and interpret environment	Apply data system to performance measurement
		Outcome: Technical and informational groundwork	
Division management			Issue: Management problem
			Action: Commit resources and modify procedures
			Outcome: Increased responsiveness

Figure 19.2 Conversion of social responsiveness from policy to action.

Ackerman observes that a test case or confrontation will speed the movement from phase 1 to phase 3.

The cost of social responsibility varies, depending on the organization's response (and so do the benefits). This is illustrated in Table 19.2. The direct costs of things like pollution control programs are very difficult to estimate.

One movement that has tried to enlist both the financial reporting system and the reward structure in support of social responsibility is the development of the social balance sheet and social audit. Figure 19.3 presents the social balance sheet of Abt Associates. The purpose of social auditing or social accounting is to formally consider social responsibility using the kinds of statements managers are used to. At present, however, this approach is not widely used.

Table 19.2 Advantages and Disadvantages, Costs and Benefits of Responses to Social Ethic (Duncan)

Response Category	Advantages	Disadvantages
Tokenism	Least expensive; adaptive; fast	Ineffective, inefficient
Functional reorientation	Relatively inexpensive; provides supportive expertise and specialization; relatively adaptive	Can result in organizational expansion; potential for conflict
Structural change	Visibility of commitment; specialization of labor; meaningful representation	Expensive; produces additional value conflicts in decision making

In sum, enterprises vary in their degree of acceptance of the social ethic, the profit ethic, or a profit ethic modified by a social ethic when economically possible. If the social ethic is accepted, it must be planned for and managed effectively.

MANAGERS AND ETHICS

Many historians believe that whether a society survives or falls depends on the moral, ethical, and legal conduct of its citizens and institutions. As a result institutions like churches and synagogues have tried to impart respect for the law and for moral and ethical codes such as the Ten Commandments.

Many business associations have drawn up codes of conduct to try to guide their members into ethical business practices. Business schools try to infuse ethical values into their students in each course they teach and in special courses devoted to ethical and socially responsible business practices. Most families try to teach their children to be honest both within and outside the family.

Until now it has been assumed that in the long run "honesty is the best policy" and that respect for the law pays off. But recent events make us pause and ask the question, Has our society moved so far away from the ethics of the past that parents, churches, and schools are doing a disservice when they encourage ethical and legal choices? Are ethical managers at a competitive disadvantage in the America of the late 1970s? We will address this question in the following pages.

Recent Examples of Unethical Behavior

Sometimes it is hard to define ethical behavior. Perhaps the point can be made more clearly by discussing some recent news reports of "unethical" and/or "illegal" conduct.

Abt Associates Inc. Social Balance Sheet
Year ended December 31, 1971 with comparative figures for 1970

Social Assets Available	1971	1970
Staff		
Available within one year	$ 2,594,390	$ 2,312,000
Available after one year	6,368,511	5,821,608
Training investment	507,405	305,889
	9,470,306	8,439,497
Less accumulated training obsolescence	136,995	60,523
Total staff assets	9,333,311	8,378,974
Organization		
Social capital investment	1,398,230	1,272,201
Retained earnings	219,136	—
Land	285,376	293,358
Buildings at cost	334,321	350,188
Equipment at cost	43,018	17,102
Total organization assets	2,280,081	1,932,849
Research		
Proposals	26,878	15,090
Child care research	6,629	
Social audit	12,979	—
Total research	46,486	15,090
Public services consumed net of tax payments	152,847	243,399
Total social assets available	$11,812,725	$10,570,312

Social Commitments, Obligations, and Equity		
Staff		
Committed to contracts within one year	$ 43,263	$ 81,296
Committed to contracts after one year	114,660	215,459
Committed to administration within one year	62,598	56,915
Committed to administration after one year	165,903	150,842
Total staff commitments	386,424	504,512
Organization		
Working capital requirements	60,000	58,500
Financial deficit	—	26,814
Facilities and equipment committed to contracts and administration	37,734	36,729
Total organization commitments	97,734	122,043
Environmental		
Government outlays for public services consumed, net of tax payment	152,847	243,399
Pollution from paper production	1,770	770
Pollution from electric power production	2,200	1,080
Pollution from automobile commuting	10,493	4,333
Total environmental obligations	167,310	249,582
Total commitments and obligations	651,468	876,137
Society's Equity		
Contributed by staff	8,946,887	7,874,462
Contributed by stockholders	2,182,347	1,810,806
Generated by operations	32,023	8,907
Total equity	11,161,257	9,694,175
Total commitments, obligations and equity	$11,812,725	$10,570,312

Source: *Business Week,* September 23, 1972.

Figure 19.3
Social balance sheet, Abt Associates, year ended December 31, 1971, with comparative figures for 1970.

Reading the newspapers, *Time,* and the *Wall Street Journal* has been an unpleasant experience lately, especially for those who believe that the future of our free enterprise system depends on ethical behavior. Recent news stories about illegal or unethical acts fall into three categories: illegal political donations, political payoffs, and unethical behavior in general.

Political "Gifts"

Although there are laws in the United States that prohibit corporate gifts to politicians or their committees, some businesspeople have clearly violated these laws. Often the violators are the same people who can be heard complaining about the decline of the work ethic and morality in America or about how unions bribe politicians. Their illegal actions usually include falsifying documents and reports in order to cover up the gift.

The list of offenders is long; a few examples will suffice:

1 *Ashland Oil:* Illegal gifts were made to the Nixon campaign and to Republican and some Democratic candidates in Kentucky amounting to about $800,000.

2 *Gulf Oil:* $10 million was illegally given to politicians after being sent through a Bahamas subsidiary.

3 *Minnesota Mining:* A $635,000 political fund was kept in the financial vice president's safe.

Recently the Internal Revenue Service, the Securities and Exchange Commission, and shareholders have been pressing for more information on these gifts. Perhaps the most depressing recent headline in *The Wall Street Journal* was this one: "IRS Investigates 111 Companies on Political Gifts." Before you object that "only a few executives can spoil things for everyone," note that most of these "gifts" involved *most of the top executives of the companies involved,* who received phantom bonuses to "contribute." They created schemes to falsify expenses or get phantom bills sent, or served as "bag men," bringing money back from Europe or stashing it in secret safes in their offices.

Even when political gifts are legal, some corporations still get into trouble. Often foreign parties do not want it known that they are taking American corporate cash, so under-the-table dealings are used.

Political Payoffs

Political gifts differ from political payoffs in the directness of the payment. A gift is usually indirect: It is assumed that if an oil company gives money to a campaign, when it gets in trouble it will have a "friend" in Washington or the state capital. A payoff is direct: If you want an order from the government or a regulation changed in your favor, you bribe the politician to get what you ask for. Here are some recent examples of political payoffs:

1 Gulf Oil admitted paying $4,200,000 to stay in business in "a foreign country." Its board of directors fired the president and several other top executives.

2 Northrop admitted spending $450,000 to bribe two Saudi Arabian officials to buy its planes and goods. Its president resigned but may be reinstated.

3 United Brands (Chiquita Banana) admitted bribing Honduran officials $4,250,000 to lower taxes on its bananas. It also admitted paying a bribe of $750,000 to Italian officials. Its president committed suicide just prior to this revelation.

4 Lockheed Aircraft has admitted to bribing foreign officials (so far the figure used is $22 million in Japan, Holland, Indonesia, and other countries). Lockheed's chairman actually claimed that the company had a right to bribe in these cases. Japan canceled $2 billion in orders when this came out.

Unethical Business Practices

The previous two categories of illegal actions are fairly clear-cut: illegal campaign contributions to politicians or political parties and bribes to government officials. This third category of unethical behavior is a catch-all that includes a variety of practices. Here are some examples:

1 *Braniff Airways*   Braniff admitted before the CAB that it had given 21,600 free tickets worth $750,000 to travel agents to promote Braniff travel. This is illegal. The travel agents sold the tickets or used them themselves.

2 *General Motors and "Motor Gate"*   General Motors discovered that a number of its Chevrolet dealers in the eastern United States were bribing their managers to defraud it of funds. The dealers reported that they had performed repairs on Chevrolets covered by warranties and billed GM for them. They in fact did no work and defrauded GM of large sums of money (original estimate: $600,-000). GM fired 43 managers in the New York and New England area and canceled a number of dealerships. One GM employee who was ready to report the fraud was murdered and found floating in the Boston River. A dealer was charged with murder. The managers were responsible for checking that the warranty work was done. GM claims that its employees allowed themselves to be bribed and looked the other way.

3 *Grain thefts*   A number of grain inspectors at ports like New Orleans are under indictment for falsifying grain reports in order to cheat U.S. customers abroad on the quantity or quality of grain they had bought. Bunge, for example, is charged with shorting buyers of 1 million bushels of wheat and covering up the shortage by means of an elaborate fictitious reporting scheme. Bunge is the third-largest firm in the grain-exporting business.

Are All Managers Unethical?

Earlier I mentioned the "robber barons" of the nineteenth century. They are evidence that unethical business is not a new issue. But are all business people unethical? Is *The New York Times* right in suggesting that "in business, ethics is not a big seller"?

The answer is no, not all businesspeople are unethical. As Jacqueline Thompson points out, while some corporations have made illegal gifts to political campaigns, others have refused. Among them are Eastern Airlines, IBM, General Motors, W. R. Grace, American Motors, Eli Lilly, Gulf and Western, Allied Chemical, Union Oil, Litton, Iowa Beef Processors, General Electric, American Express, Firestone, Georgia Pacific, and Greyhound-Armour. Some of these firms are in the same industries as those that have violated the law and/or ethical business practice. They are subject to the same pressures and the same governmental "recriminations." Recent reports have shown how Ingersoll Rand carefully avoids any bribes or semblance of bribes overseas, how IBM turns down business in Latin America if it has to bribe to get it, and how Caterpillar's business is booming although it is known to be scrupulous in dealing with potential bribery situations. So although the newspaper reports are gloomy at times, remember that those who are *not* in the news probably are not there because they follow the law and/or ethical constructs.

Ethical Behavior and Legal Behavior

Consider the following definitions:

LEGAL BEHAVIOR
Legal behavior consists of acts that are not prohibited by the laws of the jurisdiction in which the behavior takes place.

UNETHICAL BEHAVIOR
Unethical behavior is the set of acts that the society considers wrong.

There is an important distinction here. Actions can be legal but unethical; they can also be ethical but illegal. For example, campaign contributions by corporations are legal in Canada, though some Canadians may consider them unethical. Consumption of alcoholic beverages in the United States was illegal in 1923, but most citizens considered it ethical. Discrimination against Jews was legal in Germany in 1943, but unethical. So laws can be passed that violate the ethical codes of citizens, and unethical acts may not be covered by existing laws.

Most normative ethicians would argue that to be ethical a business person must obey the law. If he or she feels that a law is unethical, the executive must work to have the law modified. The ethicians would also argue that an executive must avoid acts that are unethical (but not covered by any law) or must perform acts that are not required by law (but necessary from an ethical standpoint).

What Are the Sources of Ethical Problems? Some researchers have studied the question of where ethical problems come from. Archie Carroll asked 238 randomly chosen executives from *Standard & Poor's Executive Register* to respond to a questionnaire about ethical problems in business today. He tried to determine whether executives feel under pressure to compromise their standards to achieve company goals. Sixty-five percent felt such pressure, especially the supervisors and middle managers.

Other interesting questions asked by Carroll (and the responses) include the following:

Is it possible to have sound ethics throughout the structure but pressure for results leads to unethical behavior "down the line"?	78% yes
Is social responsibility of business an ethical issue?	76% yes

The most interesting question was

The junior members of Nixon's reelection committee who confessed that they went along with their bosses to show their loyalty is just what young managers would have done in business.

The responses were as follows:

Response	No.	Percent
Disagree	58	24.6%
Somewhat disagree	38	16.1
Somewhat agree	84	35.6
Agree	56	23.7
Totals	236	100.0%

Carroll concluded that

> Almost 60 percent of the respondents agree that young managers in business would have done just what the junior members of Nixon's reelection committee had done. Coupled with [my] earlier findings, the result adds support to the belief that managers are under strong pressures to adhere to their superior's expectations of them. An examination of responses by managerial level reveals an interesting schism between the opinions of top management and those of middle and lower managers. Sixty-three percent of the top managers disagree with the above assertion, while 61 percent of the middle managers and 85 percent of the lower managers agree with it.

In a study of 3000 British managers' moral and ethical concerns Simon Webley found that the major sources of ethical problems lie in dealing with customers and employees. With regard to the latter, the major problems arise in times of conflict and layoffs. Webley found that ethical standards had declined in Britain. Fifty-two percent of top managers and 69 percent of middle managers knew of unethical practices in their industry, and higher percentages indicated that there are regularly occurring situations in which what needs to be done to be efficient and profit conscious conflicts with ethical principles.

John Newstrom and William Ruch studied 121 southwestern U.S. executives' attitudes on ethics. They provided them with a list of behaviors that they considered unethical and asked them if they themselves and/or their peers performed unethical acts. Figure 19.4 is a summary of their findings. They concluded that

> · what is perceived as ethical varies, depending on the individual.
> · some managers will act unethically if they believe no punishment will be forthcoming.
> · Managers perceive their peers to be more unethical than themselves.

This can lead to the "everyone's doing it" rationale for unethical behavior. Newstrom and Ruch believe it is important to establish ethical standards to guide behavior. So do most authorities on the subject. For unethical acts lead to a credibility gap. When the attitudes of many business people become unethical, this can lead to lower productivity from honest employees.

Action to Improve Business Behavior

Of course some people may feel that this whole section is irrelevant—that ethics is outdated. Others, however, believe there are several answers to the problem. Webley found that executives perceived the following factors as influencing their behavior:

	Middle Managers Ranking 1st or 2nd	Top Managers Ranking 1st or 2nd
Formal company policy	25.1%	19.5%
Your own personal code of behavior	35.8	39.9
The behavior of your equals in the company	1.4	1.6
The reputation of your company	29.6	36.0
The behavior of your superiors in the company	8.1	3.1

Several approaches to improvement of business behavior have been suggested. Some encourage increased efforts by the churches to produce the "religious manager." This approach would increase ethical behavior, and there is some evidence of a general resurgence of religion as an important force in personal life. This would help, but it may be a long-run process.

A second approach is for top management to set a good example itself. And a set of policies—a code of conduct—should be established and enforced by top management and the board of directors. United Brands is trying it. Bank of America is doing it, and so is Bendix.

The third method is rigorous enforcement of the laws by the SEC, the IRS, and other government agencies. Ralph Nader and Mark Green suggest that the Justice Department set up a Division of Corporate Crime to combat internal offenses and to take more vigorous antitrust action on bribery both here and abroad. In addition, they argue, bigger fines and jail sentences for offending executives are necessary to prevent illegal and unethical acts.

Ethics in Business—Old Hat?

We are now back where we started: Do we do businesspeople a disservice in urging that they behave ethically and legally? My answer is no, for if they do not behave ethically, business institutions will not survive. They cannot: Comsumers and employees will retaliate. There have always been ethical and unethical business executives. There have also been periods in which honesty has been the rule and others in which it has gone into a decline. The 1920s in Chicago was not an ethical period, nor was the Boss Tweed period in New York City. Reform movements in business and government normally followed these periods. But perhaps we have reached a nadir today. What is the answer?

Some argue that a code of conduct will work. But if executives violate laws with penalties, will they hesitate to violate codes of conduct? Most argue that both laws and codes of conduct should be rigorously enforced and the penalities swift and severe. In some cases, when unethical and illegal behavior is discovered (Gulf Oil) the culprits are fired and required

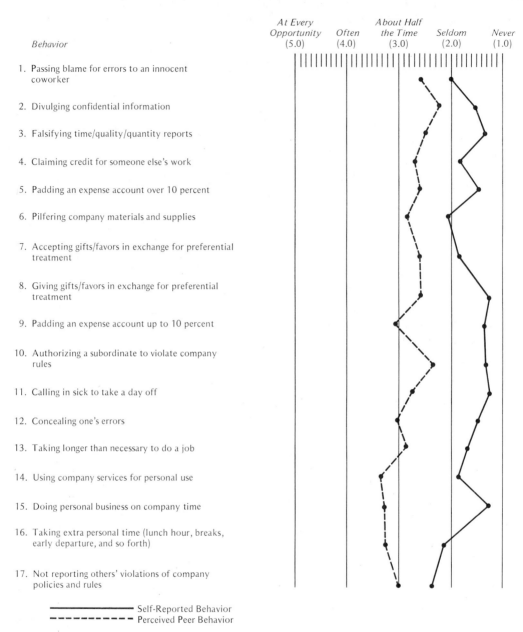

Behavior	At Every Opportunity (5.0)	Often (4.0)	About Half the Time (3.0)	Seldom (2.0)	Never (1.0)

1. Passing blame for errors to an innocent coworker

2. Divulging confidential information

3. Falsifying time/quality/quantity reports

4. Claiming credit for someone else's work

5. Padding an expense account over 10 percent

6. Pilfering company materials and supplies

7. Accepting gifts/favors in exchange for preferential treatment

8. Giving gifts/favors in exchange for preferential treatment

9. Padding an expense account up to 10 percent

10. Authorizing a subordinate to violate company rules

11. Calling in sick to take a day off

12. Concealing one's errors

13. Taking longer than necessary to do a job

14. Using company services for personal use

15. Doing personal business on company time

16. Taking extra personal time (lunch hour, breaks, early departure, and so forth)

17. Not reporting others' violations of company policies and rules

——————— Self-Reported Behavior
- - - - - - - - - Perceived Peer Behavior

Figure 19.4 Frequency of self-reported and perceived peer behaviors (Newstrom and Ruch).

to pay the money back. In others (Ashland Oil) such actions are not taken.

The government and corporate boards of directors must make the penalties for illegal acts clear: You will be fired, you will pay *large* fines, and you will go to jail if you violate laws and ethical precepts. Too often we read of a thief who stole $50 being sent to jail while executives who stole millions go on living in luxury and status. The punishment must fit the crime or law and ethics become a joke.

Auditors must become more aggressive in order to learn about bribes and other illegal behavior. The government must strengthen the penalties, and those who break the law must go to jail for their crimes. The Ralph Naders of the world must be encouraged to seek out and find the thieves. And employees must be rewarded for turning in thieves who stick up the store *and* "white-collar criminals" who, as described earlier, steal indirectly.

Stockholders must sue the offending corporate officers when their unethical behavior becomes known (as is happening more often now). All these pressures must be brought to bear if our business society is to survive. Unions will not allow a person with a criminal record to hold office. *Businesses should do the same.*

To put this in perspective, it should be noted that most businessmen are honest, a few dishonest. Some marginally honest executives will be tempted to become dishonest if they feel that this is the way to get ahead. Soon they influence others to participate in unethical behavior. The only way to prevent this is to punish the offenders *severely;* also, society must shun these people so it will not appear to be "smart" to be dishonest. They must be punished for their crimes against stockholders, customers, and employees.

We began this section with the question, Do we do businesspeople a disservice by encouraging legal and ethical behavior? The answer is no, *if* the guilty are punished. If not, we may in fact be sending ethical sheep to compete with immoral wolves, and this would be tragic for us all.

We turn now to a different issue: In what ways are managerial values, objectives, and behavior different in a nonbusiness enterprise from their counterparts in a business enterprise?

MANAGING PUBLIC AND NONPROFIT ENTERPRISES

Some of you, by chance or choice, may wind up as managers in a nonbusiness setting. Do the principles of management set forth in this book apply to the managers of the employment security office of the government? or the postal service? or the administration of Greenlawn Hospital? Do they apply to the vice president for finance of Tulane University? the business manager of the Seattle Opera Company? the business vice president of the Episcopal Diocese of Southern Ohio?

I believe the answer is yes—for the most part. Most of what was said in Chapters 4, 6–10, 12, 17, and 20 applies. In fact most health care facilities, universities, churches, and similar organizations are run like small or middle-sized-businesses. The federal government is similar to a large business; state and local government services are like small and middle-sized businesses.

People are similar in all organizations. Small groups exist in all organizations. Leadership styles vary in all organizations. Planning, organization, and control need to be performed in all enterprises. Job enlargement is the same in a university machine shop as in a private sector machine shop. A laundry worker's job in a hospital probably is not much different from working in a business-run laundry.

Note, however, that I left out Chapters 5, 11, 18, and 19. Chapter 5 discussed the motivation of people. It is *possible* (though there is little evidence here) that some employees working for some nonbusiness enterprises are more dedicated to the objectives of the enterprise than the employees of some businesses. For example, church secretaries may receive more satisfaction from helping others than they would from working for a foundry. So they may work for less pay. In other words, the motives people have for working for an enterprise like a church, an opera company, a hospital, or a university might be different from the motives of business employees. The jobs must be designed to satisfy these needs. This difference could also affect leadership style, control style, and so forth.

A second difference may lie in the objectives of the enterprise. This was pointed out in Chapter 11. Thus the Orthodox Church in America does not have the same objectives as Mattel Toy Company. Moreover, the nonbusiness enterprise may not be as profit oriented as a business. This will depend on the ranking of objectives by the enterprise. It is true that there are hospitals that are operated for profit, but many nonprofit hospitals will improve the quality of patient care even if it means no net surplus is added in 1977. Such differences in objectives can have an effect on reward systems, on job development, and on how the manager spends his or her time.

A third difference may be found in the environmental forces faced by nonbusiness enterprises (internal forces may differ too.) In this final part of the chapter we cannot discuss all these differences. But a few words will be said on how these differences affect the life of the manager in the public and nonprofit sectors.

The Public Manager   The public manager is an individual who manages an enterprise whose primary source of revenue is local, state (provincial), or federal taxes and similar flows of funds. In what ways does the managerial job differ in the public sector from the equivalent job in the private sector? First of all, the public sector enterprise can seek different objectives and, usually, more objectives than the private sector enterprise. And most of these objectives are very hard to measure. It is more difficult to design planning and control systems if objectives are broadly defined.

Secondly, the public manager faces more uncertainty more frequently than the private manager. This is a consequence of the environment in which he or she operates. Thus the public manager must seek resources and support from the hierarchy. But the hierarchy can include a split between the executive branch (President, governor, city manager) and the legislative branch (Congress, the legislature, the city council.) These groups may choose to have a political fight over your program. Then there is the press or the media, whose business it is to expose the "useless, inefficient bureaucrat." And out-of-office politicians are continually feeding the media information to expose the misdeeds—past or present—of public managers.

Politicians can interfere with the public manager's operations, and the remnants of the spoils system found in the "merit system" often lead public managers to prostitute their procedures in order to keep the politicians happy and/or off their backs.

Thus environmental forces have a much stronger impact on the job of the public manager than on that of most private managers. The public enterprise's "suppliers" (executive and legislative branches) and customers and pressure groups are highly interrelated, with the public manager in the middle, often subject to close scrutiny so that the press can sell papers or the politician can get elected. Business managers, by contrast, face neither of these threats. This greater dependence on a complicated and conflicting environment provides the major difference between the public manager and the business manager.

In addition, just as there is diversity in the jobs of business managers, so there is variety in those of public managers. Some technical jobs are little affected by the political process. A technician in the Weather Bureau or a researcher in a government lab are examples. I would hypothesize that successful public managers who must deal with the political environment need more leadership ability, greater ability to deal with peers, and more tolerance for ambiguity and change than most business managers. The difficulties of the public manager's job may help explain Bruce Buchanan's findings that businesspeople are much more involved in their work and identify more strongly with their company than public managers.

Some private managers are involved in joint public-private projects where they become exposed to the political process itself. Comsat is an example of such a project. I once studied a steel company that was owned half by private sources, half by the government. The board was half private and half public. It operated fairly well, but its members had different expectations. For example, the government directors pressed for more profit than the private sector directors felt was appropriate for the safety of the workers. Public managers need to be more skilled in dealing with complex environments and with a situation that involves greater dependence on the outside environment.

The Hospital Administrator There are over 7000 hospitals in the United States, employing well over 2 million people. About 15 per cent of these hospitals are proprietary (for profit) hospitals. About half are nonprofit community hospitals, and the rest are run by governments at several levels: federal (Veterans Administration and military); state (mental hospitals), and local (city-run hospitals). In my opinion hospitals are *the* most difficult enterprises to manage.

First of all, none of the hospital's "customers" really want to be there. By definition most are not well, and therefore they can be difficult to handle. The hospital's employees are quite different in background, varying from the poorest-trained and paid employees in America (food service, janitorial, housekeeping) to some of the best-trained people employed anywhere. Large numbers of hospital employees are professionals (nurses, medical technicians, occupational therapists, dietitians, etc.) who identify with professional objectives that sometimes conflict with the objectives of other groups in the enterprise. The objectives of the hospital are many and hard to measure. Frequently cited are quality patient care, creative health research, effective training of physicians and other health professionals, financial solvency, growth in size, and variety of health care. The trustees' objectives may include prestige in the community.

In no other institution that I can think of can outsiders come in, use the facilities for their own business, and not be financially responsible to the hospital. Yet physicians are not employees of hospitals. They have the highest status of all the people involved in hospitals, use the facilities to cure their patients, yet may be on the staffs of several hospitals.

The hospital's "suppliers," in addition to suppliers of materials, can include donors, the state, and "third-party" groups—Blue Cross, insurance companies, Medicare/Medicaid (government bodies)—which can question and withhold payments if hospitals "violate their contracts." The hospital is also subject to suits for improper care as well as competition from the plush new hospital down the street.

At the center sits the hospital manager (or administrator). He or she is responsible for the survival and prosperity of the hospital and patient care. The successful hospital administrator must understand the work motivations (and status needs) of professional employees, deal with sick customers, fend off third-party payees, raise money from trustees and friends of the hospital, manage volunteers who want to help (and often get in the way) and keep physicians from leaving the staff. And if the hospital fails a customer, it does not mean a return order but pain, suffering, and sometimes death.

Hospital administrators too must be able to deal with more ambiguities than most business managers. They must be able to get conflicting groups to work toward common objectives and stay financially viable. The leadership qualities needed are *extraordinary*.

Health care is a "growth industry" in our society. We need to produce more health care administrators capable of staffing these challenging (and rewarding) jobs.

The University Manager There are about 3000 colleges, junior colleges, and universities in the United States, with about 6 million students and somewhat less than 1 million faculty. They range from small colleges with fewer than 500 students and a faculty of about 30 to vast multicampus systems like the State University of New York, the University of California, and California State Universities and Colleges, with budgets of hundreds of millions, students in the hundreds of thousands, and faculties in several college organizations.

The official objectives of colleges and universities include teaching and dissemination of knowledge, research (creation of new knowledge), and service to society. But the more complex institutions of higher education also

·counsel students on personal problems.
·provide for the health needs of students and the community.
·provide job placement services.
·run cultural programs.
·provide intercollegiate athletic programs that gross hundreds of thousands of dollars on football weekends.
·run "hotels" (dormitories) for students.
·provide food service for students and the college or university community.
·operate buildings and grounds services.
·run museums, radio stations, and newspapers.
·provide for the religious needs of students and the community.

The major elements in higher education are the following:

·The board of trustees, representing the people of the state (in the case of a state-supported institution) or the alumni, donors, church, or similar supporting groups (in the case of a private university).
·The faculty, who see themselves as independent professionals attached to the college; they are responsible for curriculum, granting degrees, and academic counseling.
·The students, who spend two to four (or more) years at the college until the degree or program is completed. The student is there to learn and develop himself or herself socially for the transition period between childhood and adulthood.
·Academic administration: a set of officers who are responsible for the use of the college or university's resource.
·Professional support staff: people who help the faculty educate students and do research. This group includes librarians, audiovisual aids specialists, lab technicians, extension specialists, and counselors.
·Business staff: people who run the "business side" of the university—dormitories, food service, development, sports, ancillary ser-

vices, admissions, personnel, buildings and grounds, maintenance, etc.

The ultimate power in a university lies with the board of trustees. The president's job is to see that the university survives. He or she needs to get enough money from tuition, gifts, grants, foundations, the legislatures, and alumni to keep the university open. The president must see that the business side of the university is efficient and the academic side effective. This includes recruiting and holding good students and competent faculty.

You may choose some day to enter university management—as a controller or personnel officer, for example. The higher administrative offices in a college or university are usually held by former faculty members. Some day colleges may change this policy and hire professional managers as presidents (the way hospitals are headed by administrators, not physicians). The problem with academic administrators is that most of them have *no* professional training as managers. Yet they are asked to manage very complex, fragile organizations. The provost, vice president, or president may have been a good (or satisfactory) Milton scholar, research biologist, theologian, or anthropologist. But he or she may know nothing about administration, or only what he or she has learned through "on-the-job training" as a department chairman or dean. In the long run I expect many of the positions now held by academics to be held by professional managers. Only academic matters (curriculum, degree approval, faculty recruiting and development) will be held by academics.

Colleges and universities are exciting institutions to manage. They have had a lot of problems recently. For example, in the 1960s they had to deal with riots. In the 1970s, seas of red ink appeared in the account books. The differences between business and university management include

·different objectives, and hard-to-measure objectives at that. (What is quality research? How much "service" should be done—and which kind? What is good teaching?)
·different powerful environmental forces: "suppliers" that include politicized legislatures or governors. The legislature may fight budget battles with the governor, with the university in the middle. Donors may want their names perpetuated. Alumni may be dissatisfied with the way the college is being run. An old joke has a new college president asking his predecessor, who was retiring after a very successful career, "How do you get to be successful in this job?" The retiring president answers, "Really, you just have to try to satisfy the important groups and remember what they want: Give the alumni a winning football team; allow the student rules to be flexible

enough so they can have sex and beer; and give the faculty enough parking places."

Thus university managers must deal with a volatile budget situation, changing student demands and a generally dissatisfied faculty. Most faculty are trained to be critical of students, their peers, and society as a whole. This critical attitude leads to dissatisfaction with the present and to creative new approaches. So faculty usually are critical of university administrators.

Still another group has started to put pressure on universities: the federal government. Universities get large amounts of federal money to fund research, student loans, and scholarships, to build buildings, and for other purposes. Therefore universities are subject to federal pressure to hire and promote members of minority groups, among other things.

In sum, universities are complex enterprises to run, but this makes their management more challenging.

Arts Management

Another set of smaller enterprises that can benefit from effective management are arts organizations: ballet troupes, symphony orchestras, opera companies, theater groups, museums, and similar enterprises. Museums are usually among the smallest of these enterprises. Musical and theater groups can employ several hundred people, but still are relatively small enterprises. General Motors, by contrast, employs 600,000 people. A large hospital (1500 beds) may employ 4500.

Arts organizations derive their funds from donations, foundations, government grants, and ticket sales or admission charges. Almost all have continuous money problems as they try to balance their budgets while inflation eats away at their endowments.

The employees of musical and theater groups generally are professional artists, 98 per cent of whom are dedicated, underpaid people who are in the job because they love it. Museum employees are headed by professionally trained curators who purchase and arrange their collections. Artists are not normally employed by museums.

Many arts organizations survive because of the dedication of volunteers who work for the institution for nothing, helping to raise money, sell tickets, and the like. In some communities these volunteer groups have high social status.

Managers have a lot to offer an arts organization. First of all, management tools can improve the efficiency of the operation if the manager is sensitive enough to know where he or she can cut costs without impairing the quality of the performance. Marketing skills are desperately needed by most arts organizations. Additional sources of revenue can be generated. For example, the Smithsonian Museum started a magazine; it "franchises" its collection for royalties; textile firms make sheets using its patterns; toy firms make replicas of old toys; and so forth. Most museums now have "stores." Many run TV auctions. Especially for the individual who loves great art, ballet, music, or theater, the job of business manager of an arts organization might be the right career choice.

Managing Voluntary Organizations and the "Third Sector"

There are many other nonprofit enterprises in our society that need managers: churches, community groups, consumer groups, public and private elementary and secondary schools, libraries, political parties, unions, charity organizations, social groups, country clubs, and so forth. Some authors refer to these enterprises as the "third sector."

In each case the manager must determine how the enterprise differs from a "main line" business in employee motivation, enterprise objectives, and environmental forces. The manager can then adapt his or her leadership practices, communications, planning and control, organizational style, and other management tools to the setting.

SUMMARY

Two opposing positions and a middle position are taken on social responsibility. The profit ethic argues that managers (and entrepreneurs) should be socially responsible as individuals but that they have no legal right to spend stockholders' money on social responsibility projects. The social ethic argues just the opposite: For our current institutions to survive, managers must include social responsibility as a significant, meaningful objective of the enterprise. The middle-of-the-road, pragmatic manager takes no position on the issue but occasionally engages in social responsibility projects that appeal to him or her or can enhance the enterprise's image. I described some social responsibility projects such as urban renewal and corporate philanthropy.

We went on to address the issue of ethical and unethical behavior of managers and entrepreneurs. Examples of unethical and in some cases illegal acts such as political gifts, political payoffs, and unethical business practices were given. The issue of how many managers are unethical was discussed, as was the question of how to keep businesspeople ethical.

In the final section of the chapter we examined the similarities and differences between business managers and managers in the public sector and the third sector. Most of what was said in Chapters 4, 6–10, 12, 17, and 20 applies to both types of managers. Differences may exist in motivation (Chapter 5), objectives (Chapter 11), and the external environment (Chapters 18 and 19). There may be slight or major differences in the areas covered in Chapters 12, 13, 14, 15, and 16, depending on the enterprise.

Chapter 20 completes Part 4 describing how organizations change, sometimes in reaction to external events.

Questions for Review

1. What is social responsibility?

2. Define the social ethic and the profit ethic for a manager and for an entrepreneur.

3. What arguments are given for and against social responsibility? Which side makes the best case? Why?

4. What are the major social responsibility projects of the past ten years? Suppose you are the president of a large manufacturing firm in Minneapolis, an insurance company in Newark, New Jersey, a hardware wholesaler in Miami, or an aerospace firm in Los Angeles. Which projects would you support in each case?

5. On what basis would the presidents in question 4 decide to give corporate money to various fund drives?

6. What is ethical business behavior? How can ethical behavior be illegal and legal behavior unethical?

7. Are all businesspeople unethical? What can we do to encourage ethical behavior?

8. In what general ways is management similar in business and nonbusiness settings? How is it different?

9. Contrast the job of a business manager with that of a government manager.

10. Contrast the job of a business manager with that of a hospital administrator or the business manager of a university, museum, or church.

References

Social Responsibilities of Managers and Entrepreneurs

Carroll, Archie, "Corporate Social Responsibility: Its Managerial Impact and Implications," *Journal of Business Research,* 2, no. 1 (January 1974): 75–88.

Davis, Keith, "The Case For and Against Business Assumption of Social Responsibilities," *Academy of Management Journal,* 16, no. 2 (June 1973): 312–322.

Davis, Keith, "Five Propositions for Social Responsibility," *Business Horizons,* June 1975, pp. 19–24.

Duncan, W. Jack, *Decision Making and Social Issues* (Hinsdale, Ill.: Dryden Press, 1973).

Drucker, Peter, *Management* (New York: Harper & Row, 1974), chap. 26.

Friedman, Milton, "The Social Responsibility of Business Is to Increase Profits," *New York Times Magazine,* September 13, 1970.

Hay, Robert, and Gray, Ed, "Social Responsibilities of Business Managers," *Academy of Management Journal,* 17, no. 1 (March 1974): 135–143.

Hayes, Douglas, "Management Goals in a Crisis Society," *Michigan Business Review,* 22 (November 1970).

Levy, Lawrence, "Doing Well by Doing Good Can Be Both Risky and Difficult," *New York Times,* August 10, 1975.

McGuire, Joseph, "The Social Responsibility of the Corporation," *Proceedings, Academy of Management,* 1964, pp. 21–28.

Monsen, R. Joseph, *Business and the Changing Environment* (New York: McGraw-Hill, 1973): chap. 4.

Moore, Robert, "Business Philosophy," *Business History Review,* 10, no. 3 (December 1950): 196–209.

Social Responsibility Projects

Byars, Lloyd, and Mescon, Michael, *The Other Side of Profit* (Philadelphia: W. B. Saunders, 1975).

Luthans, Fred, and Hodgetts, Richard, *Social Issues in Business* (New York: Macmillan, 1972).

———, *Readings on the Current Social Issues in Business* (New York: Macmillan, 1972).

Education

Ayers, Albert, "How Business and Industry are Helping the Schools," *Saturday Review,* October 17, 1964.

Council for Financial Aid to Education, *Aid to Education Programs for Some Leading Business Concerns* (New York, 1964).

Davis, Keith, and Blomstrom, Robert, *Business and Society* (New York: McGraw-Hill, 1975), chap. 20.

Freeman, Marcia, "Business and Education," in Ivar Berg, ed., *The Business of America* (New York: Harcourt, Brace and World, 1968), chap. 12.

Hill, Karl, "Business and Science," in Ivar Berg, ed., *The Business of America* (New York: Harcourt, Brace and World, 1968), chap. 8.

The Arts

Davis and Blomstrom, op. cit., chap. 21.

Eels, Richard, "Business and the Performing Arts," in Ivar Berg, ed., *The Business of America* (New York: Harcourt, Brace and World, 1968), chap. 14.

Wilson, Robert, "Business and the Creative Arts," in Ivar Berg, ed., *The Business of America* (New York: Harcourt, Brace and World, 1968), chap. 13.

The Planning and Operation of Social Responsibility

Ackerman, Robert, "How Companies Respond to Social Demands," *Harvard Business Review,* July-August 1973, pp. 88–98.

———, *The Social Challenge to Business* (Cambridge, Mass.: Harvard University Press, 1975).

Adizes, Ichak, and Weston, J. Fred, "Comparative Modes of Social Responsibility," *Academy of Management Journal,* 16, no. 1 (March 1973): 112–128.

Andrews, Kenneth, "Can the Best Corporations Be Made Moral?" *Harvard Business Review,* May-June 1973, pp. 57–64.

Bauer, Raymond, and Fenn, Dan, Jr., "What is a Corporate Social Audit?" *Harvard Business Review,* January-February 1973, pp. 37–48.

Carroll, op. cit.

Cooper, S. Kerry, and Raiborn, Mitchell, "Accounting for Corporate Social Responsibility," *MSU Business Topics,* 22, no. 2 (Spring 1974): 19–26.

Dierkes, Meinolf, and Bauer, Raymond, eds., *Corporate Social Accounting* (New York: Praeger Publishers, 1973).

Dilley, Steven, "External Reporting of Social Responsibility," *MSU Business Topics,* 22, no. 3 (Autumn 1975): 13–25.

Duncan, W. Jack, *Essentials of Management* (Hinsdale, Ill.: Dryden Press, 1975), chap. 17.

Henry, Harold, "Policy and Planning Impacts of Environmental Protection in Major Corporations," *Proceedings, Academy of Management,* 1973, pp. 73–80.

Lowes, B., and Sparkes, J. R., "Social Responsibility Accounting," *Journal of Business Policy,* 3, no. 4 (Summer 1973): 43–49.

McAdam, Terry, "How to Put Corporate Responsibility into Practice," *Business Society Review,* 6 (Summer 1973): 8–16.

Narver, John, "Rational Management Responses to External Effects," *Academy of Management Journal,* 14, no. 1 (March 1971): 99–115.

George Steiner, "Institutionalizing Corporate Social Decisions," *Business Horizons,* December 1975.

Wilson, Ian, "Reforming the Strategic Planning Process," paper delivered at NACBS Symposium, University of California at Berkeley, Graduate School of Business, November 10, 1972.

Managers and Ethics

Adams, Kenneth, *Exploring the Business Ethic* (London: St. George House, Windsor Castle, 1971).

Baumhart, Raymond, *Ethics in Business* (New York: Holt, Rinehart and Winston, 1960).

———, "How Ethical are Businessmen?" *Harvard Business Review,* July-August 1961.

Brown, Terry, "Ethics and Earnings: Bendix," *Wall Street Journal,* November 18, 1975.

Byrne, Harlon, "What Recession?" *Wall Street Journal,* April 19, 1976.

Carr, Albert, "Can an Executive Have a Conscience?" *Harvard Business Review,* July-August 1970.

Carroll, Archie, "Managerial Ethics: A Post Watergate View," *Business Horizons,* April 1975, pp. 75–80.

Clark, Lindley, Jr., "Innocents Abroad?" *Wall Street Journal,* April 14, 1976.

Davis and Blomstrom, op. cit., chap. 10.

Eels and Walton, op. cit., chap. 19.

Flory, Charles, and Mackenzie, Alec, *The Credibility Gap in Management* (New York: Van Nostrand Reinhold, 1971).

Glueck, William F., "Ethics in Business: Have They Gone Out of Style," *Survey of Business,* University of Tennessee, January-February, 1976, pp. 8–12.

Griffith, Thomas, "Payoff is not 'Accepted Practice,' " *Fortune,* August 1975, pp. 122–125, 200–206ff.

Hogan, Robert, "Moral Conduct and Moral Character: A Psychological Perspective," *Psychological Bulletin,* 79, 4 (August 1973): 217–232.

Jolson, Marvin, "Consumers as Offenders," *Journal of Business Research,* 2, no. 1 (January 1974): 89–98.

Lippitt, Gordon, *Value Implications in Organizational Reward: Ethical Guidelines for Leaders* (Washington, D.C.: Project Associates, 1971).

Mann, Andrew, "The Ethics Puzzle," *The MBA,* September 1974.

Mason, Edward, ed., *The Corporation in Modern Society* (Cambridge, Mass.: Harvard University Press, 1960).

Nader, Ralph, "A Code of Professional Integrity," *New York Times,* January 15, 1971.

Nader, Ralph, and Green, Mark, "What to Do About Corporate Corruption?" *Wall Street Journal,* March 12, 1976.

Newstrom, John, and Ruch, William, "The Ethics of Management and the Management of Ethics," *MSU Business Topics,* Winter 1975, pp. 29–37.

Senger, John, "The Religious Manager," *Academy of Management Journal,* 13, no. 2 (June 1970): 179–186.

Stone, Christopher, *Where the Law Ends* (New York: Harper & Row, 1975).

Tarnowieske, Dale, *The Changing Business Ethic* (New York: Amacon, 1973).

Wall, Jerry, "What the Competition is Doing: Your Need to Know," *Harvard Business Review,* November-December 1974.

Walton, Clarence, *Ethics and Executive* (Englewood Cliffs, N.J.: Prentice-Hall, 1969).

Webley, Simon, "Business Policy and Business Ethics," *Journal of Business Policy,* 3, no. 3 (Spring 1973).

Managing and Nonprofit Enterprises/The Public Manager

Buchanan, Bruce, "Government Managers, Business Executives, and Organizational Commitment," *Public Administration Review,* July-August 1974, pp. 339–347.

Cayer, N. Joseph, *Public Personnel Administration in the United States* (New York: St. Martin's Press, 1975), chap. 1.

Golembiewski, Robert, and Cohen, Michael, *People in the Public Service* (Itasca, Ill.: F. E. Peacock, 1968), chap. 1.

Henry, Nicholas, "Paradigms of Public Administration," *Public Administration Review,* July-August 1975, pp. 378–386.

Levine, Robert, *Public Planning: Failure and Reduction* (New York: Basic Books, 1971).

Murray, Michael, "Comparing Public and Private Management: An Exploratory Essay," *Public Administration Review,* July-August 1975, pp. 364–371.

Otten, Alan, "Politics and People: On Managing," *Wall Street Journal,* February 12, 1976.

Shafritz, Jay, "Political Culture: The Determinant of Merit System Viability," *Public Personnel Management,* January-February 1974, pp. 39–43.

Wamsley, Gary, and Zald, Mayer, "The Political Economy of Public Organizations," *Public Administration Review,* January-February 1973, pp. 62–73.

Warren, Earl, "Value and Quality of the Career Public Service," *Public Administration Review,* July-August 1974, pp. 390–394.

The Hospital Administrator

Blakenship, Vaughn, and Elling, Ray, "Organizational Support and Community Power Structure: The Hospital," *Journal of Health and Human Behavior,* 3 (1962): 257–269.

Densmore, Max, and Klein, Donald, "Health Care's Response to the Consumer: Patient Representatives," *Proceedings, Academy of Management,* 1975.

Etzioni, Amitai, "Alternative Conception of Accountability: The Example of Health Administration," *Public Administration Review,* May-June 1975, pp. 279–286.

Forrest, Christopher, et al., "The Changing Role of the Hospital Administrator," Proceedings Academy of Management, 1976.

Georgopoulous, Basil, and Mann, Floyd, *The Community General Hospital* (New York: Macmillan, 1962).

Gordon, Paul, "The Top Management Triangle in Voluntary Hospitals," *Academy of Management Journal* (1961).

Makowski, Robert, "Hospital Planning: Synthesis and Restatement," *Hospital Progress,* 54, no. 11 (April 1973): 24–28.

Wilensky, Harold, "The Dynamics of Professionalism: The Case of Hospital Administration," *Hospital Administration,* Spring 1962.

Managing Voluntary Organizations and the "Third Sector"

McGill, Michael, and Wooten, Leland, "Management in the Third Sector," *Public Administration Review,* September-October 1975, pp. 444–455.

O'Connell, Brian, *Executive Leadership in Voluntary Organizations* (New York: The Associated Press, 1976).

Reimnitz, Charles, "Testing a Planning and Control Model in Non-Profit Organizations," *Academy of Management Journal,* 15, no. 1 (March 1972): 77–87.

CHAPTER 20
MANAGING CHANGE

Learning Objectives

1. To understand the causes of change.
2. To learn how organizations and people change.
3. To understand how to cope with varying responses to proposed changes.

Chapter Outline

The Dimensions of Change
Some Causes of Change
Mechanisms of Organizational Change
Structural Change Mechanisms
Technological Change Mechanisms
Behavioral Change Mechanisms
Combination Change Programs
Environmental Differences in Organizational Change
Conclusions
Positive, Negative, and Neutral Responses to Organizational Change
Negative Responses
Neutral Responses
Positive Responses
Summary

In this chapter we will look at changing organizations and the people in them. Change results from stimuli from both outside and inside the enterprise. Observers of modern organizations have found that

> ·change·takes place in all organizations, but at varying rates of speed and degrees of significance. As was indicated in the discussion of volatility in Chapter 16, change is a fact of life in some enterprises (e.g., high-technology electronics firms) more than in others (e.g., lumber mills).
> ·change takes place in all parts of an organization, but at varying rates of speed and degrees of significance. The marketing department may face much more change, and more significant change, than the quality control department.

So while change is important, it is necessary to keep the varying rates of change in perspective. And in some organizations stability is so crucial to enterprise effectiveness that a strategy of no change at all is not only feasible but mandatory.

THE DIMENSIONS OF CHANGE

> **CHANGE**
> To change an enterprise is to make the enterprise different in some way in order to better achieve its objectives.

Obviously, the enterprise can be changed in several ways: Its technology can be changed; its structure, its people, and other elements can be changed. But technology, structure, and people are the major foci of change in an enterprise.

Change comes in several varieties and can be scaled as shown in Table 20.1.

Whatever its causes, organizational change has several dimensions. The first dimension of organizational change is the planned–unplanned continuum. This is an old one in sociology, where it is called the rational model and the systems model. Henri de Saint-Simon stressed the importance of the rational model, whose assumption is that people can better plan what changes they should bring about than if "nature took its course." Auguste Comte felt that the system itself would find its own best equilibrium, and planning would follow naturally. Perhaps the essential differences between the systems and rational approaches is simply the assumption by the rationalists that their intervention can speed up the organization's adjustments. This chapter will focus on *planned* change.

Table 20.1 Dimensions of Organizational Change

Change Factor		
Degree of Planning		
Unplanned change		Planned Change
Size and Scope		
Small changes		Large changes
Minor change		Major change
Initiation Point		
Supervisor or employees		Top management
Time Dimension		
Experiment and change over time		Change all at once
Elements to be Changed		
	Structure	
	Behavior	
	Technology	

The second dimension of organizational change is the size and scope of the change. Obviously, minor rearrangements of the functions in the corporate legal department at IBM will not have as much impact on organizational structure and behavior as its complete reorganization by changing from centralized to decentralized structure in 1956.

Source: © King Features Syndicate, Inc. 1976.

The third dimension of organizational change is the point at which the change is initiated. Does the change originate at the bottom of the structure with employees or supervisors, or at the top with the president? Organizational change comes about either by restructuring from the top down or by beginning at the bottom and restructuring upward. My hypothesis is that the more the organization perceives itself as being in a crisis, the more likely it is to restructure from the top down; the less compelling the cause, the more likely it is to restructure from the bottom up.

A fourth dimension of organizational change is the extent to which the proposed change is tested for effectiveness prior to implementation: the time dimension. On one end of this continuum is incremental change. In this approach the organization first tests the effectiveness of the change by means of one or several "pilot study" changes. If these prove out, then the planned change proceeds step by step through the other parts of the organization. On the other end of this continuum is change that occurs throughout the organization simultaneously. I hypothesize that the more the proposed change is perceived as crucial to survival, the more likely the organization is to change all its parts simultaneously.

The final dimension of change is *what* is to be changed: the enterprise's structure, its attitude and behavior patterns, its technology, or some combination of these.

Several of these dimensions have been summed into liberal and conservative patterns by Larry Greiner. At one extreme (the conservative approach) he finds unilateral power: the *decree approach* (top managers announce the change and pass it on to supervisors); the *replacement approach* (top managers replace key individuals in their jobs); and the *structural approach* (management changes the structure to fit its new plan).

The middle-of-the-road approaches (what Greiner calls *shared power*) use either of two mechanisms:

·The group decision approach (the group involved in the proposed change discusses several alternatives).
·The group problem-solving approach (the group discusses the alternatives and suggests solutions).

The liberal approach also uses two mechanisms:

·The data discussion approach (the change agents and the group involved gather data to determine when and how change should take place).
·The sensitivity training approach (managers are trained to be sensitive to changes in individuals and work patterns and to adjust the organization accordingly).

More will be said about these mechanisms of change later.
Change involves several stages or steps:

·Detecting disturbances or deviations (the causes of change).

·Assessing the significance of the deviation.
·Considering corrective or stabilizing action.
·Analyzing the data for recurring or continuing sources of deviation or stress.
·Choosing the change and implementing it.
·Validating the change (to see if it is working).

Greiner diagrams the process in more detail in Figure 20.1.

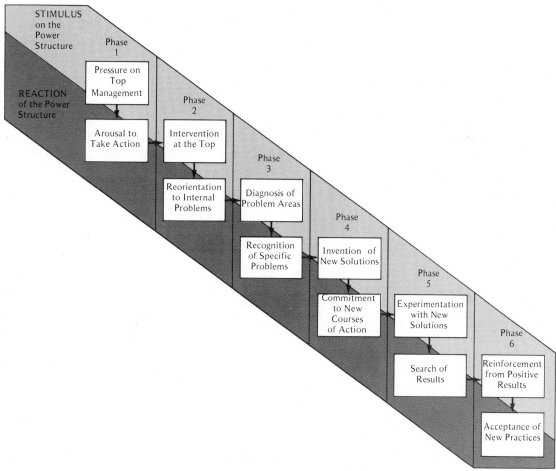

Figure 20.1 Phases of organizational change.

SOME CAUSES OF CHANGE Recall our discussion of environmental factors in Chapters 18 and 19. Each element (government, community, customers and clients, suppliers, competitors) can and does change. Competitors can increase advertising, cut prices, increase in number. Customers' attitudes toward the enterprise's products or services can turn negative. Suppliers' technology can change radically. The government can begin regulating the industry of which the firm is a part. In other words, the enterprise operates in an open system and thus is affected by what other institutions do.

In addition to responding to external influences, organizations grow, differentiate internally, and experience an organizational life cycle. In John Gardner's words, "like people and plants, organizations have a life cycle. They have a green and supple youth, a time of flourishing strength, and a gnarled old age. . . . An organization can go from youth to old age in two or three decades, or it may last for centuries." Whether this description is accurate or not is yet to be tested. But as organizations grow in size and especially in complexity, organizational change receives impetus from internal adjustments, conflict over roles, lack of adaptation to external changes, and other causes.

The people employed by the enterprise also change (as was indicated in Chapters 4, 5, and 6), both as individuals and as groups. They change in their abilities, attitudes, and behavior. These "internal" causes of change can significantly affect the enterprise and the achievement of its objectives.

MECHANISMS OF ORGANI- ZATIONAL CHANGE

Organizational change may be accomplished through three mechanisms, as illustrated in Figure 20.2. These three mechanisms can be used alone or in conjunction with each other. We will examine each of them in the following sections.

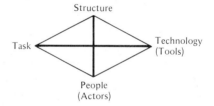

Figure 20.2
Relationships among mechanisms of change (Leavitt).

Structural Change Mechanisms

The structural approach to change is advocated by classical organization theorists. The first structural mechanisms (widely used by organization planning departments and management consultants) is to try to solve organizational problems by clarifying and defining jobs, changing job content or relationships, establishing coordination mechanisms, dividing functions logically with minimal overlap, and establishing small spans of control. The second structural mechanism (called the social engineering approach) tries to improve task performance by modifying the flow of tasks to fit the flow of work. This may involve transfer of people to fit the new structure. The social engineers argue that you will modify the organization's structure when you modify the behavior of people in order to improve structural task performance.

The third structural mechanism is to modify the structure to fit the communication needs of the specific type of task (e.g., centralized communication structures for repetitive tasks, open systems for unstructured tasks). The fourth structural mechanism is decentralization to (1) reduce the cost of coordination and increase the controlability of subunits and (2) increase the motivation of goal-oriented behavior through the use of smaller centers of decision, power, and information, giving greater flexibility and speed of response through local autonomy.

D. Ronald Daniel reports that *at least* two out of every three large firms make major structural changes. His data indicate that the typical large firm makes a major structural change every other year. The bigger the firm, the more likely it is to change. For example, 9 out of 10 of the largest firms made a major change in the late 1960s, and 16 of the next 25 did so. Management made these changes because it felt that they would make the organization more effective.

Jeremiah O'Connell reported on a major structural change in a large insurance company. The company had not grown. A consulting firm was brought in to recommend and implement structural changes. Control procedures were tightened, new job descriptions written, spans of control made smaller, and the hierarchy increased by two levels of supervision. Communication patterns were changed as a result. More formal compensation patterns were developed, and even the office layout was changed to reflect status changes more directly. Supervisors were given more status in terms of organization charts and offices as well as salary. The short-run results were dissatisfaction and higher turnover. The long-run results were improved growth and profitability.

Structural change has been the major method of change used in state, local, and federal governments. This is usually called administrative reorganization. In the federal government these changes took place under President Taft (1910–1912) and were repeated in 1920–1922 under President Harding. More changes occurred in 1932 under Hoover, in 1937–1939 under Roosevelt, in 1947–1949 (Hoover Commission 1) and 1953–1955 (Hoover Commission 2) under President Truman. Usually the states reorganized shortly after each of these federal reorganizations and followed the federal lead in methods used.

Technological Change Mechanisms
A second approach to organizational change is to change the task (not the structure or behavior). The management theorist Frederick Taylor's use of the industrial engineering tools of work simplification and task redesign is one example. Its modern equivalent (operations research and operations management) can have similar effects. If one installs new computers and new punch presses, this is a way of changing the organization in terms of job content, working conditions, social relations, and the like. Of the three approaches to organizational change, the technological approach has been studied the least.

One example of this approach is William Whyte's study of restaurant organization. Whyte showed how as the restaurant grew in size and business, the problems of coordination between subgroups (waitresses, cooks, supervisor, bartenders, pantry runners) increased, as did problems of customer relations. Whyte indicated that sometimes a technological change can reduce conflict and status problems. Thus installation of a spindle in which lower-status waitresses could insert the "orders" to higher-status cooks reduced status problems and improved coordination.

Similar studies have shown how the installation of new machinery changed organizational structure and behavior patterns in British coal mines; how the transition from individual craftmanship to machine tending to mass production to automation affected structure and behavior; and what happened when paper work departments were computerized in the late 1950s and 1960s.

Behavioral Change Mechanisms

The final mechanism of change is behavioral change. Whereas the previous methods attempt to bring about change in the behavior of the enterprise by changing inanimate objects like structure or task technology, behavioral change methods attempt to *directly* influence the people in the enterprise.

The advocates of the behavioral approach to organizational change contend that organizations are changed by modifying the values, attitudes, and beliefs of the people in the organization. The people will modify the structure and improve task performance after their values have changed. One behavioral approach is power equalization and client-centered applied group dynamics. This approach encourages human growth and attempts to redistrubute power. Programs such as group goal formation, participative decision making, two-way and "authentic" communications, and mobilizing group resources in problem solving are used. Specific techniques involved range from unstructured T-groups (sensitivity training, transactional analysis, confrontation meetings) to structured training techniques (e.g., the managerial grid). The behavioral approach can be utilized at several levels. First, one can attempt to change the individual's perceptions, attitudes, motivations, learning, or maturing mechanisms. Those working at this level tend to draw upon the developmental psychology of Allport, Maslow, and Rogers, and on psychoanalytic psychology.

The second change level is the interpersonal level, and the clinical psychology of Carl Rogers can help change two-person relationships such as superior-subordinate relationships. Behavioral change methods can operate at the small-group level; the social psychology of Kurt Lewin and group dynamics, T-groups, and structured T-group training have been used at this level.

Finally, several of the behavioral methods (or all of them) can be combined to try to change the whole organization. When management tries to change the whole organization at once, the program is called *organization development* (OD). Although OD has become very popular, its scientific support is less than overwhelming.

All the behavioral change methods tend to rely on Lewin's model. Lewin believed that for a change in attitudes (and then perhaps behavior) to occur, the person needs to go through these stages:

· Desire to change—dissatisfaction with the present.
· Unfreezing—removal of support for present values or behavior patterns.
· Conversion—exposure to the new behavior pattern and attitude set, as well as strong evidence that the new attitude or behavior pattern is better.
· Refreezing—reinforcement of the new attitudes and behavior pattern and integration of these into the person's psychological constructs.

The structuralists contend that structural change is adequate to bring about organizational change. They criticize behavioral change methods as taking too long, costing too much, tending to "fade out," and leading to ethical problems. (Does the organization have a right to attempt to change an employee's personality)? The behaviorists contend that real long-term change comes only through the use of their methods. They contend that technological or structural change alone leads to results that are more apparent than real and are neither lasting nor effective.

The main difference between these two approaches is the *direction* of the change relating the task and the people involved. For example, Eliot Chapple and Leonard Sayles (structuralists) expect that changing the structure will change the people and thus improve task performance. The behaviorists, on the other hand, seek to change the people so that they, in turn, will change the structure and technology to improve task performance and provide more satisfying and meaningful work.

Combination Change Programs

For ease of presentation I have discussed the three change mechanisms separately. It is obvious, however, that any two or all three can be used simultaneously. For example, some organizational changes utilize both the structural and behavioral approaches. They attempt to improve goal achievement by changing the people's attitudes, values, and beliefs *and* the organization's structure as well.

A recent piece of my own research may illustrate this point. I studied the process of change at two organizations using the participant observer method. The first change was the reorganization of the executive branch of the State of Michigan in 1965–1966. The other was the reorganization of a large firm (which I will call the Forest Products Company). The events will be briefly summarized, and then similarities and differences between the two will be analyzed.

Michigan had elected George Romney governor and had changed its constitution in 1961, at least partially in response to a financial crisis. Newspapers were running headlines that Michigan was bankrupt before Romney's election. One requirement of the new consitution was that the executive branch be reorganized into not more than 20 departments. At the time it had 160 departments. In 1965 the legislature and the governor attempted to bring about the particular organizational structure that each wanted. Finally a compromise bill was agreed upon. During the next seven months the organizational change was implemented and all departments were reorganized by executive order from the governor, using structural change methods.

The stated goals of the organizational change were increased efficiency, increased power and responsibility for the governor, and greater responsiveness and vitality in the state government. The results included reclassification of several clerks and elimination of a few (usually low-level) positions. The 160-odd bureaus were organized into 19 large departments. Several organization analysts were hired at $16,000 per year, and the new department heads got raises (e.g., from $16,000 to $25,000), since they now had more responsibilities. Some top positions were reclassified as appointive (not civil service); the governor's staff was enlarged. The civil service employees had to be reclassified for promotion purposes. Although the proponents of the changes claimed that they had resulted in greater efficiency, when they were pressed for specifics their explanation shifted to "long-term savings." There was also some question about whether the governor's position had been strengthened. For although he now dealt with nineteen agencies, the realities of the line item budgeting system were such that the former agency heads could still undercut administrative control through liaison with the legislators.

The second organizational change studied took place in the Forest Products Company (FPC), which employs 30,000 people and has assets of approximately $385 million. FPC had been the market leader but had dropped to third place because of a loss in market share by its major consumer products line. Profits had gradually slipped much below the industry average. The president felt that an organizational change might contribute to a turnaround. Therefore he asked the organization development department to do an extensive organization study and propose changes. He asked a management consulting firm to make a parallel study and proposal.

On the basis of these studies a proposal for organizational change was made. Drastic changes in structure and authority relations were suggested. The organization development department proposed that the change be made incrementally. It would convince each plant manager of the desirability of the change, and behavioral change methods would be used along with the structural change. The first plant organized under the new structure was a new plant. It was significantly more successful than the older plants. When the news of this success was passed along, the managers of the older plants asked to try the structure used in the pilot plant. Then, one by one, the other plants were changed, with generally very successful results.

Similarities in the Organizational Changes

Both organizations' inadequate goal achievement (FPC's slippage in market leadership and profit; Michigan's financial crisis and loss of industry and employment) were thought to be solvable through organizational change. There is also a similarity between the primary goals of the reorganization. Both were seeking improvement in administrative effectiveness, which is the major goal of most government reorganizations.

Formally, the process of change was not too different in the two organizations. FPC's president received approval for the change from the board of directors. The state received the approval of the Constitutional Convention. Two studies and proposals were made in both organizations. At FPC, an inside study was made by the president's staff and an outside study was also done. In Michigan, one study was made by the governor's staff and one by the legislature.

Finally, there were other similarities in that the leaders of the reorganization mobilized support from the membership. After all, people do not automatically accept or encourage organizational change. At FPC, the top management (or at least the president) encouraged the change. Some other top managers and many middle managers opposed the change or were skeptical at best. Had the pilot program been less than successful, they would have mobilized to oppose the change. At the plant level the change agents "sold" the program before putting it into effect. Once a plant had been reorganized, its members supported the change. The greatest resistance came from middle and upper middle management. Strong support from the top was necessary.

In Michigan, some citizens' groups enthusiastically supported the change. The governor strongly favored it. The legislature, especially the opposition party, opposed the specifics of the plan. Most of the departments affected by it were skeptical or opposed it, for they were losing their autonomy and had little to say about the change. The six or seven departments that substantially gained from the change favored it.

Differences in Organizational Changes

In addition to the similarities in the two cases, several differences come to mind. The first is that the goals of reorganization were substantially achieved at FPC but not in the State of Michigan. An examination of the differences in the methods of organizational change used and in the types of organizations involved may help explain the divergence in achievement. First, Michigan was attempting to centralize the power structure. The change was made without using participative decision-making techniques. Also, Michigan used only structural change methods. There is now much evidence that in some circumstances "mature" Americans prefer the responsibility that can arise from a decentralized structure. But they would resist the loss of this motivator, especially after it had become part of their role expectations.

Next, legislators, with relatively little real understanding of the operations of the various departments, restructured the organization after brief testimony by the bureau heads, using criteria that are at best hard to explain, much less justify. Researchers have not proved that participative methods of organizational change are more effective in government reorganization, but there is some evidence that this is so in industrial reorganizations.

FPC "proved its case" by demonstrating the benefits of the change, changing units incrementally, and mobilizing support and/or desire for the change in the process. It was also able to adjust the changes to differences in culture, technology, economic conditions, and personnel among FPC's divisions. The State of Michigan took none of this directly into account, and the reorganization was done almost simultaneously in all departments.

Finally, FPC was aware that the structure and the people in it are interrelated. The company felt that it would be easier to achieve change if both structure and behavior were dealt with. The state's actions indicate that it assumed that the people would adapt to the structural change without the reverse adjustment.

Michigan's organization was changed by the use of structural methods. Activities were regrouped, reporting relationships changed, and authority relationships modified to strengthen the governor's powers. At FPC, structural changes were also made. The firm was decentralized in terms of line and staff; jobs were redesigned with different authority relationships; and evaluation methods were changed. At the same time, behavioral change methods were used to reinforce the structural changes. People's attitudes toward authority were changed, and their motivations were also changed. It is felt, then, that some of the differences in success are attributable to the use of simultaneous structural and behavioral changes in FPC's case. It is also felt, however, that even if Michigan had wanted to use structural and behavioral methods, its environment might have prevented it from doing so. In my opinion some of these differences in organizational change are caused by differences between government and business organizations.

ENVIRON-MENTAL DIFFERENCES IN ORGANIZATIONAL CHANGES

That government and business are quite similar is the opinion of many who have worked closely with both business and government organizations. Herbert Simon, once a professor of public administration and now a professor of industrial administration, has said,

> Large scale public and private organizations have many more similarities than differences. . . . In actual administration, there is often a greater

difference between small and large organizations than there is between public and private organizations.

Simon illustrates this point by discussing the conversion of the Chicago transit system from private to public ownership. He contends that all that changed was that different people received interest on the bonds and different people managed the organization.

Harvey Sherman, head of the organization department for the Port of New York Authority, a public corporation, has wide experience in public administration but much contact with business administrators. He says,

> In my judgment, the difference between public and private enterprise has been grossly exaggerated, at least insofar as organizational consequences to particular governmental agencies or private companies are concerned.

He compares the organization and administration of private and public airlines, private and public universities, private printing firms and the U.S. Government Printing Office, private insurance companies and insurance programs for veterans, and finds more similarities than differences. I am not sure, however, that the examples given by Simon and Sherman are representative comparisons. Transit companies, airlines, and insurance companies are examples of regulated industries, and universities are from the nonprofit segment of the economy. It has been pointed out that regulated industries have significant differences from completely privately run firms in terms of pricing, goal formation, and even the salaries paid to executives. Better examples might be given, perhaps comparing the military arsenals and the Remington Company or a government-run shoe firm and a privately run shoe firm (in Argentina, for example).

In fact there is one difference affecting the reorganization process in government that makes it more difficult if not impossible to reorganize as FPC did. This difference is the traditions and/or law that require governments to define their organization structure in detail by statute. Thus when a major change is needed it must be done through the political process, usually involving a provision for judicial review. There are power centers inside all organizations that may oppose organizational change. They can frequently be neutralized by surprise moves. But when (as in Michigan) all parties must be formally notified of the change, this provides an opportunity for the enemies of change to mobilize groups within the government and client groups outside it (e.g., the public) to oppose the change. When one adds the tradition of balance of power, the bureaus can mobilize public support and legislative support against the governor (for example), as happened in Michigan. Perhaps this is why Sherman advocates change all at once rather than incremental change.

But organizational change of this type is slow, involving judicial review, amendments, and the like. In any case, this limits the variety of approaches to organizational change available and may suggest why so few government reorganizations are successful. Several of these points were made in Chapter 19, of course.

CONCLUSIONS

Thus far we have discussed the dimensions of organizational change and two approaches to it: structural and behavioral. The organizational changes at FPC and the State of Michigan were described. Comparisons and contrasts were delineated and at least partially explained by differences in the political environment of business and government. One conclusion that may be drawn from these and other studies is that organizational changes that proceed incrementally, from bottom to top, involving participation in the change by those affected and using behavioral as well as structural methods, are likely to be more effective than those using only structural methods, announced all at once from the top and without employee participation. I believe the organizational change process in government would be more successful if the detailed organizational structure did not have to be incorporated in statutes. This would allow flexibility and change to develop as needed.

Many organizational changes fail to achieve their objectives because they result from arbitrary decisions without adequate planning. Many would be considered failures if evaluations were made afterwards. What is needed is a prior assessment of the degree of goal achievement by the organization. Measures of the effectiveness of the organization should be made regularly. For a government department, for example, the extent of satisfaction of clients, other departments, and the legislature with the department's services could be determined in terms of speed, quality, and cost. As these indicators became negative, proposals for change will be made. The changes would use the guidelines listed earlier, and then continued evaluation of the service would be made. After the change has been made, the organization would determine whether it had any significant effect. Evaluations of the direct and indirect costs of the change would also be made. This strategy could help in evaluating whether changes are necessary, whether they are effective, and whether they are needed at all. Further research and experimentation is needed to determine how effective this approach would be.

Let us now try to summarize the conditions under which change is received positively, negatively, and neutrally by those affected.

POSITIVE, NEGATIVE, AND NEUTRAL RESPONSES TO ORGANI- ZATIONAL CHANGE

There are three possible responses to a proposed change. One is a positive response, which means the change is likely to be successful in receiving the support of the employees involved if it is directed at the *real* cause of the problem and *is an effective solution* to the problem. The second is a neutral response, which is probably the most frequent response. In this case the employees "wait and see" about the change and do not oppose it.

The third response is negative (i.e., a resistance to change). In this case the employees either actively or passively oppose the change. Most managers view resistance as bad. But is it? What if the employees see problems in the change that the manager has overlooked? Is management always right? When resistance is found, management might first reexamine the proposed change to see if it is *in fact* an improvement. If it is, then management must try to "work it through" with the employees.

Negative Responses

There are many reasons for negative reactions to change. They include the following:

1 *Ignorance of the need for change.* The need for change must be crystal clear to the affected employees because most people perceive most change as painful and threatening. Management needs to make the reasons *manifest* and these must be perceived as *real.* The ignorance may be due to poor management communication, actual ignorance on the part of the employees, or both.

2 *Reaction to the change agent* Employees can resist the change if the source of the proposal (manager, consultant) is viewed as incompetent, unpleasant, both. This indicates a lack of interpersonal skills, leadership, communication skills, or all of these abilities.

3 *If the employees are going to lose* Some people who talk about change imply that it is possible for everyone to win through change and that it is "modern" to go along with the change. The facts are that in many changes, for economic or technical reasons, many of those affected by the change *lose.* You cannot expect people to support changes that will cause them to lose some or all of their need satisfactions. Physiologically, they can lose their job or get lower pay; they can lose job security; they can get lower social interaction (and thus lower satisfaction of social needs). The change can lead to less status and power (recognition needs), require less ability (lower self-actualization), or require them to do jobs in areas where their abilities are limited. Thus the change can result in *lower* need satisfaction. Not surprisingly, people fight change if they are going to lose as a result of the change.

4 *Poorly planned changes* Finally, people fight poorly planned change—change that comes too frequently because of poor planning (or none at all), poor communication of the change, or adverse consequences of the change.

Often people who are resisting change give *technical* reasons: "It won't work—we tried it before," "the machine can't do that," and the like. The *real* reason might be that they feel they will lose from the change. Just as people may quit because of a poor supervisor and say they wanted better pay, so they may say they are resisting change for technical reasons when their reasons are actually personal ones. After all, some people do not want to admit that they are trying to protect their job—they appear too selfish. Besides, those who resist change are often perceived as "old fogeys" or reactionaries. So the employee gives technical shortcomings as the reason for opposing a change.

Neutral Responses   An employee is likely to respond neutrally to a proposal change if it is not too threatening to his or her personal interests and some positive methods are used to offset the negative response.

Positive Responses   Gene Dalton has modeled effective change methods that he believes will lead to positive responses from employees and to successful change. In effect, Dalton is describing the liberal approach to change (see Figure 20.3). That is, employees participate in all phases of change:

- Analysis of the data to see if change is needed.
- Consideration of alternative solutions.
- Choice of method and implementation of the change.

In effect, too, the change is slowly and experimentally introduced. It follows the pattern described in my study of FPC. But there is not enough evidence to prove that this method is best. The conservative approach *may* work better when

- the employees expect or prefer the conservative approach.
- the employees are not particularly well trained or able.
- top management or the consultant are more familiar with the conservative style than with the liberal style.
- the purpose is knowledge change, not attitude change.

For example, if you use the liberal style with uneducated employees, you pool ignorance. In such a situation the participatory approach would be dangerous.

To these reasons I would add the following:

- The conservative style works best when the affected employees lose too much if one of the better choices is accepted. It is asking a lot of employees when they are expected to willingly fire themselves or severely cut their own reward structure.

SUMMARY   The purpose of this chapter was to help you understand the causes and methods of organizational change. To change is to make the enterprise different in some way in order to better achieve the enterprise's objectives.

Change has several dimensions. It can be planned or unplanned

	Phase 1	Phase 2	Phase 3	Phase 4
Overall pattern of successful change effort	tension experienced within the system (unfreezing)	intervention of a prestigious influencing agent	individuals attempt to implement the proposed changes	new behavior and attitudes reinforced by achievement, social ties and internalized values—accompanied by decreasing dependence on influencing agent (refreezing)
Subprocess 1		generalized objectives established	growing specificity of objectives—establishment of sub-goals	achievement and re-setting of specific objectives
Subprocess 2	tension within existing social ties	prior social ties interrupted or attenuated	formation of new alliances and relationships centering around new activities	new social ties reinforced—altered behavior and attitudes
Subprocess 3	lowered sense of self-esteem	esteem-building begun on basis of agent's attention and assurance	esteem-building based on task accomplishment	heightened sense of self-esteem
Subprocess 4		external motive for change (new schema provided)	improvisation and reality-testing	internalized motive for change

Figure 20.3 Dalton's model of change.

and can vary in scope from major to minor changes. Change can be initiated from the top or bottom, all at once or incrementally, and the elements to be changed can be the enterprise's structure, technology, or employee attitudes and behavior. Change can be caused by environmental change or by internal readjustments.

The structural, behavioral, and technological mechanisms were described and illustrated with empirical studies. A combination of two or more change mechanisms seems to be a very effective way to bring about organizational change.

Employees can react positively, neutrally, or negatively to proposed changes. The liberal approach to change seems to reduce resistance to change most effectively.

This completes our discussion of management of the organization's resources. But what lies in store for the manager of tomorrow? We turn now to a discussion of the problems managers are likely to face in the future.

Questions for Review

1. What is change? To what extent is it a universal experience in enterprises today?

2. What are the major dimensions of organizational change?

3. What are the most frequent causes of change?

4. What are the major mechanisms of structural change? behavioral change? technological change? combinations of these kinds of changes?

5. Which mechanisms are best?

6. What are the major negative responses to proposed organizational changes?

7. How can we avoid unnecessary resistance to change?

References

The Dimensions of Change

Gardner, John W., "How to Prevent Organizational Dry Rot," *Harpers Magazine,* October 1965.

Glueck, William F., "Organizational Change in Business and Government," *Academy of Management Journal,* 12, no. 4 (December 1969): 439–441.

Greiner, Larry, "Patterns of Organization Change," *Harvard Business Review,* 45, no. 3 (May-June 1967): 119–130.

Mosher, Frederick C., ed., *Government Reorganizations* (Indianapolis: Bobbs-Merrill, 1967), p. XV.

Mechanisms of Organizational Change

Chandler, Alfred, Jr., *Strategy and Structure* (Cambridge, Mass.: M.I.T. Press, 1962).

Chapple, Eliot, and Sayles, Leonard, *The Measure of Management* (New York: Macmillan, 1961).

Daniel, D. Ronald, "Reorganizing for Results," *Harvard Business Review,* November-December 1966, pp. 96–104.

Lawrence, Paul R., *The Changing of Organization Behavior Patterns* (Cambridge, Mass.: Harvard University Press, 1958).

Leavitt, Harold, "Applied Organization Change in Industry," in James March, ed., *Handbook on Organizations* (Chicago: Rand McNally, 1965), pp. 1144–1167.

Technological Change Mechanisms

Blauner, Robert, *Alienation and Freedom* (Chicago: University of Chicago Press, 1964).

Taylor, James, "Some Effects of Technology on Organization Change," in Jun and Storm, eds., *Tomorrow's Organizations* (Chicago: Scott, Foresman, 1973).

Trist, Eric, and Bomforth, K. W., "Some Sociological and Psychological Consequences of the Longwall Method of Goal Getting," *Human Relations,* 4 (1951): 3–38.

Whyte, William, "The Social Structure of the Restaurant," *American Journal of Sociology,* 54 (January 1949): 302–310.

Behavioral Change Mechanisms

Allport, Gordon, *Personality and Social Encounter* (Boston: Beacon Press, 1960).

Argyris, Chris, *Organization and Innovation* (Homewood, Ill.: Richard D. Irwin, 1965).

Bennis, Warren, *Organization Development: Its Nature, Origins, and Prospects* (Reading, Mass.: Addison Wesley, 1969).

Hodgson, Richard, Levinson, Daniel, and Zalesznick, Abraham, *The Executive Role Constellation* (Cambridge, Mass.: Harvard University, Graduate School of Business, 1966).

Kahn, Robert, "Organizational Development: Some Problems and Proposals," *Journal of Applied Behavioral Science,* October-December 1974, pp. 485–502.

Lewin, Kurt, "Group Decision Making and Social Change," in T. M. Newcomb and E. C. Hartley, eds., *Readings in Social Psychology* (New York: Holt, Rinehart and Winston, 1958).

Likert, Rensis, *Human Organizations* (New York: McGraw-Hill, 1968).

Margulies, Newton, and Wallace, John, *Organization Change: Techniques and Applications* (Chicago: Scott, Foresman, 1973).

Maslow, Abraham, *Motivation and Personality* (New York: Harper & Row, 1954).

Mosher, op. cit.

Rogers, Carl, *On Becoming a Person* (Cambridge, Mass.: Riverside Press, 1961).

Environmental Differences in Organizational Change

Ginzberg, Eli, et al., *The Pluralist Economy* (New York: McGraw-Hill, 1965).

Sherman, Harvey, *It All Depends* (University: University of Alabama Press, 1966), pp. 23, 87.

Simon, Herbert, et al., *Public Administration* (New York: Alfred Knopf, 1962), pp. 8–9.

Conclusions

Short, Larry, "Planned Organization Change," *MSU Business Topics,* 21, no. 4 (Autumn 1973): 53–61.

Tichy, Noel, "Current Trends in Organizational Change," *Columbia Journal of World Business,* Spring 1974, pp. 98–111.

Positive, Negative, and Neutral Responses to Organizational Change

Coch, Lester, and French, John Jr., "Overcoming Resistance to Change," *Human Relations*, 1 (1948).

Dalton, Gene, "Influence and Organization Change," in A. Bartlett and T. Kayser, eds., *Changing Organizational Behavior* (Englewood Cliffs, N.J.: Prentice-Hall, 1973).

Filley, Alan, et al., *Managerial Process and Organizational Behavior* (Chicago: Scott, Foresman, 1976), chap. 21, 22.

Greiner, Larry, "Red Flags in Organization Development," *Business Horizons* (June 1972), pp. 17–24.

Hershey, Paul, and Blanchard, Kenneth, "The Management of Change," *Training and Development Journal*, January 1972, pp. 6–10; February 1972, pp. 20–24; March 1972, pp. 28–33.

Kaufman, Herbert, *The Limits of Organizational Change* (University: University of Alabama Press, 1971).

Lorsch, Jay, "Managing Change," in Paul Lawrence, et al., *Organizational Behavior and Administration* (Homewood, Ill.: Irwin Dorsey Press, 1976).

CHAPTER 21

MANAGEMENT AND THE FUTURE

21

Learning Objective

To understand the problems managers may face in the future.

Chapter Outline

Changes in the Manager's Environment
Changes in Managerial Skills
Changes in People and Interpersonal Skills
Changes in the Managerial Task

In this chapter we will discuss some predictions of what management may be like in the future. Then I will make a few comments on managerial effectiveness and wish you well in your new career as a manager, family business executive, or entrepreneur.

A number of writers have had a lot of fun lately. They have dug out past predictions of the future ("Management in the Soaring Sixties," etc.) and pointed out the wild differences between what the experts predicted and what really happened. In fairness to the futurists, their job is not easy. It is not as bad as weather prediction, when everyone knows when you were wrong and forgets when you were right. But almost.

A look back at the Organizational Model at the beginning of Part 4 illustrates some of the predictions we will be discussing. But since this is the end of the book, I will reverse the order of discussion so we can wind up at the beginning—the managerial job and what it will be like in the future. Let us begin with the changes some futurists see coming in the environment in which managers work.

CHANGES IN THE MANAGER'S ENVIRONMENT

The manager's environment includes the community, the government, customers and clients, competitors, and suppliers. Most futurists contend that the community and the government will have a greater impact on the manager's world, primarily through new laws and regulations that will constrain the manager and entrepreneur even more than today.

This would mean more restrictions at all levels—local government restrictions, state and federal regulation. To the extent that this becomes true, managers will need to know more about law and regulation either directly (through training) or by consulting specialists. To the extent that this becomes true, top managers will have to spend more time as negotiators and spokespeople. This will tend either to move "inside" operating decisions further down in the organization or to increase the size of the top management group. It will also make decision making more difficult and/or complex.

I do not know what the probability of this increase in government and community influence is. At any one point in time there are always crosscurrents of opinion favoring and opposing this attitude. In the mid-1970s, the climate is not particularly pro-business. Yet there is a group of people who are unhappy with the lack of efficiency and effectiveness in the government. The general disgust with the Post Office's operations is an example. Many are unhappy with the operation of the welfare program, too. On the other hand, many people feel that the privately run railroads have done a poor job. Many feel that the health care enterprises in the "third sector" have done poorly. One can also cite examples from all sectors of generally efficient and effective enterprises: AT&T, IBM, the Federal Reserve Board, the Agricultural Extension Research and Service, the Kaiser Permanent Health Program, and others.

So it is difficult to predict this aspect of the future. It is quite probable that government, the community, and business and the third sector will be more closely related than they were twenty-five years ago. But the form this relationship takes will no doubt vary at any one point in time from one subunit to another. Fewer businesses will be isolated from the government and the community. It is quite possible that the government may offer more services, but contract them out to businesses or the third sector. It does not follow that whenever the government takes on new responsibilities it will administer the program itself.

What of relations with customers and clients? It is hard to predict whether the consumer movement, which is moderately influential in the mid- to late 1970s, will increase in importance. From past patterns one would predict that the movement will increase in influence in the near future and then decline. This is so because voluntary organizations with changing memberships due to aging and death are very difficult to hold together and mobilize on a continuing basis. It is probably too soon for managers to stop worrying about these groups. But the near-term prospects are not very threatening compared to potential governmental impact.

The amount of threat from competitors varies greatly by industry. There has been a tendency for large firms to become increasingly vast. The government's antitrust activities have not been successful in preventing oligopolies and have been enforced only on rare occasions. These activities may have influenced some firms to diversify in their merger growth so that they could avoid the Justice Department.

Some industries (e.g., appliances) are very competitive, and their price rates show it. Others are dominated by a very few firms (e.g., glass, nonferrous metals, autos), and the results have been as predicted—less innovative administration, higher prices, and so forth.

In many industries the evidence is that most new ideas and new products come from small enterprises or newcomers to the industry. If firms continue to grow, especially through massive mergers like Marcor, their innovativeness may decline. Mergers also concentrate tremendous economic and social power in a few hands. Yet as it is currently applied, antitrust legislation is difficult to administer and costly to litigate. The simplest and fairest approach to this problem would be to pass a law that any firm with sales and/or assets of $100 million or more could not merge with any other firm for any purpose. Then growth could come internally for the large, efficient firm, and smaller and middle-sized firms could grow through merger if they wanted to instead of being subject to predatory forced mergers to make a less effective giant's balance sheets and records look better.

Relations with materials suppliers may see some changes too. The suppliers are the sources of much of the technological change we see in some fields. This may also lead to an explosion of information and data to keep up with; the computer has helped a great deal in coping with the latter. Some contend that the vast technological change occurring in some sectors will mean fundamental changes in how enterprises plan, organize, control, and so forth. They foresee a withering away of the systems currently used to do these things. They may be right, of course. But Marx predicted the withering away of the state after socialism and/or communism took hold. But if anything, the state became more onerous in such cases.

At least for the foreseeable future, employees are still trying to find order in chaos and systematize what they are doing. There has always been change, and enterprises have adjusted to it. The only difference is that in some sectors the changes are coming more frequently. Instead of new structures evolving, I foresee cycles: an opening up of the enterprise at certain times and a process of readjustment and resystematization until new changes come. If that is a sluggish process, then enterprises will develop units at their boundaries that search for change and translate it into needed internal changes. These boundary units may be much more liberal than the enterprise proper. But the main line units will be operating quite similarly to the way they operate now, though perhaps a little more liberally, just as factory managers today treat people differently than some of them did in 1915.

An important "supplier" (of people) is the unions. The union movement has not increased the percentage of the workforce it represents because it has not unionized the white-collar, service, professional, and technical employees, which have grown as a percentage of the labor force, while their stronger area—blue-collar workers—has been declining in percentage terms. Moreover, the unions are weaker in the faster-growing parts of the country—the South, Southwest, and West—and stronger in slower-growth areas like the East and Midwest.

The unions have had some success among white-collar, service, professional, and technical employees—especially in the public and third sectors. But they have a long way to go before they have the impact they do in, say, the trucking industry, the auto industry, or the mining industry. I expect the union movement to be about as influential in the year 2000 as it is now.

CHANGES IN MANAGERIAL SKILLS

In Part 4, I concentrated on the managerial skills of planning, decision making, design of jobs and organizations, control, and conflict management. How likely are these areas to change in the near future? I sincerely believe that planning will be more in evidence than it is at present, just as we see more now than we did in the past. I believe this will be true in enterprises of all sizes and in all sectors. Planning will not be easier to do—it will just be recognized as more important. The tools and techniques used probably will become *somewhat* more sophisticated than at present. I still do not foresee widespread effective use of computerized simulation, for this still amounts to modeling—even in a very sophisticated way—the unknown, and assigning probabilities to unknowns by computer is not necessarily more scientific than doing it manually.

Will job design tend more toward job enlargement and job enrichment? It probably will to some extent, but I doubt that a revaluation of job design lies ahead. I believe much more flexible work scheduling—four-day weeks and especially flexitime and multiple careers—will be more widespread than job enlargement and job enrichment, though I do believe that this is the trend of job design.

More liberal organization and control methods? Because our society is having so many control problems today in the schools and in the political sector as well as in business, I believe that, if anything, control systems will become more conservative and more stringent. The organizational methods used may become somewhat more liberal in some cases. The mechanisms will probably be used to deal with problems of coordination and conflict more effectively than in the past.

CHANGES IN PEOPLE AND INTERPERSONAL SKILLS

Parts 2 and 3 dealt with people's attitudes, abilities, perceptions, and motivation and the interpersonal skills of leadership, influence, and communication. Much has been written about the new employee—the *now* employee, who wants satisfaction *now*—hard to manage except by liberal methods.

It does appear that the percentage of employees *desiring* a liberal management style increases with education. In the late 1960s some students were demanding the freedom to dress as they felt, talk as they pleased, study or not study, and were expected to be rewarded for this behavior. The crunch of the early and mid-1970s came along and hair shortened, voices became subdued, and students studied business, not "The Sociology of Star Trek."

Does this mean that a new "Fifties generation" is here? That "Happy Days" is the way America is? No, what it shows is that attitudes, values, and motives change as conditions change. I doubt that there ever was a generation of people who wanted to be autocratically or extremely conservatively led (should I say bullied?), and chances are most people in the United States and Canada would prefer to be treated with dignity than with disrespect. They would rather feel that their opinions are valued and their talents utilized than the reverse. But some of them may still take jobs that do not offer these rewards. Thus the job seeker still encounters a cafeteria of offerings—aspects that fulfill his or her needs and others that do not. You will still have to search until you find the job that satisfies enough of your needs so that you will say, "This is it, recognizing that there are good and bad days, good and bad aspects to *all* jobs. The bad parts are compensated for by the good parts and by your life off the job.

It does appear that some of you will not spend your life with one enterprise or even in the same type of job, because the job and/or the enterprise will cease to be. How widespread this phenomenon will be is hard to say, except that it is more likely to occur in fast-changing sectors than in slower-changing sectors.

This prospect is at once exciting and frightening. Would you really like to do the same job for the rest of your life? What if you are a purchasing agent? Most of us would say no. But what if you knew now that at age 42 you would have to start all over again in a new career—which may not even exist now? That would be a bit frightening.

Multiple careers have always existed, but they are more frequent today than some years ago. Your predecessors adjusted. Farming played out and your grandfathers moved to town and took up a trade. What happened to the ice men when refrigerators took over? to door-to-door grocery peddlers when supermarkets came in? to chimney sweeps? to comptometer operators? Multiple careers have been with us a long time, but a majority of people have not experienced this phenomenon. Your generation may be the first in which a majority of people willingly or unwillingly have several careers in succession.

CHANGES IN THE MANAGERIAL TASK

This brings us back to the beginning: What will the managerial task be like in the future? At the risk of sounding totally cynical, an easy way to get an article published is to write about what management will be like in the future. This is especially true around the beginning of the decade. I should start writing one entitled "What Management Will Be Like in the Exciting Eighties," timed to appear in January 1980. After all, who can claim that *whatever* I say is wrong before 1989? (And by then everyone will have forgotten what I said.)

A different type of predictor concentrates on the skills a manager must have to "survive" the future. Usually these authors make the point that future managers will have to be smarter, better trained, harder working, and more highly motivated—that they must be equally well trained in the use of computers, management science and mathematical models, behavioral sciences like psychology and sociology, and several foreign languages. Chances are that only about half of one percent of future managers, family business executives, and entrepreneurs will fit the specifications these writers say they will need to "survive."

Peter Drucker has been one of the best predictors of the future managerial sphere. He sees the future manager as

· more accountable for the quality of life—this applies to managers of *all* institutions, not just businesses.
· more involved in entrepreneurial innovation to cope with new challenges and changes.
· more involved in trying to make resources and knowledge more productive.

·working with as much management art as management science—now and in the future.

·a leader in economic and social development.

In other words, the future management job will be as exciting and challenging as management jobs today. Management is where the action is and where rewards of all kinds may be found.

Our journey through management is now over. I hope you learned some things that will help you become a better manager. As I explained in Chapter 1, I have tried to present the systematic or "science" part of management. I wish you the best of luck in the "art" of management: applying management "science" to the challenging job of management.

References

Ansoff, H. Igor, and Brandenburg, Richard, "The General Manager of the Future," *California Management Review,* 11, no. 3 (Spring 1969): 61–72.

Athos, Anthony, "Is the Corporation Next to Fall," *Harvard Business Review,* January–February 1970, pp. 49–61.

Drucker, Peter, "Management's New Role," *Harvard Business Review,* November–December 1969, pp. 49–54.

Foss, Lawrence, "Managerial Strategy for the Future," *California Management Review,* 15, no. 3 (Spring 1973): 68–81.

Jacoby, Neil, *Corporate Power and Social Responsibility* (New York: Macmillan, 1973), chap. 12.

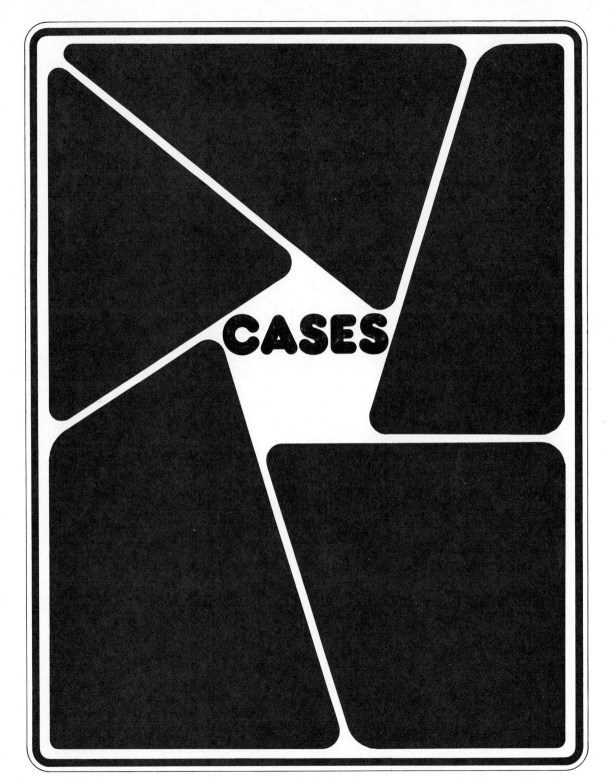
CASES

Cases for Part One

HARTLEY FOODS

James Hartley III (Jim) joined the family firm three years ago after graduating from Emory University. He spent two years in the Army between high school and college (to get away from home and to "become a man"). He majored in business at Emory and graduated in the top 10 percent of his class.

James Hartley, Sr., Jim's grandfather, is president of the firm. Uncle George is treasurer. Uncle Errol is sales manager. Jim's father was killed in an accident several years ago. The firm, a food wholesaler, employs 100 people.

Jim has done all kinds of jobs. While he was in school he worked on the loading docks, filled orders, drove a truck, and took telephone orders. Since joining the firm he has done bookkeeping, pricing, purchasing, and advertising. He has tried very hard to do a good job, but his grandfather and uncles have not given him much feedback on his performance.

Jim knows that Uncle George has two sons in college, and both have told Jim that they plan to enter the firm. Uncle Errol has a daughter who plans to go to work for Hartley when she finishes her M.S. in accounting at the University of North Carolina.

Jim is single. His salary is below what his college classmates are making. Recently he overheard several nonfamily department heads talking. One said he feared that he was going to be fired to make room for Jim. As he put it, "Jim's OK, I guess, but we all know that he's only getting ahead at Hartley because of his name." The others agreed. Jim wonders if he really has a future at Hartley and why he is staying on there.

Requirement You are a friend of Jim's from Emory days. He has asked you for your advice on what he should do. Give Jim your advice and an explanation or justification for it.

MADMAN MUNTZ

Nobody has ever accused Earl Muntz of being subtle.

When Muntz was selling television sets in 1948 and Congress was hunting reds and radicals in Hollywood, he asked his advertising manager: "Do you think I'd make the front pages if I joined the Communist Party?"

Politics meant nothing to Muntz; he just wanted the publicity to help sell merchandise.

But Muntz didn't choose anything as offbeat as joining the Communist Party. Instead, he used more dignified sales tools—such as hiring 400 disc jockeys around the country to plug Muntz TV, and printing ad slogans—"Stop staring at your radio"—on the back of street car transfers in Chicago.

That's Earl Muntz, the salesman.

Muntz, the tinkerer, is another person: the guy who developed a car stereo system on his kitchen table, and pioneered in the recorded tape business to supply music for his own stereos.

To anybody who lived in Los Angeles during World War II, Earl Muntz' real first name is "Madman." Radios blared out 176 commercials daily about the eccentric car dealer who was a soft touch for his customers. Mike Shore, a high-powered young advertising man, created the "Madman Muntz" personality with commercials and billboards that boasted, "I buy 'em retail and sell 'em wholesale—it's more fun that way," and complained, "I want to give 'em away but my wife won't let me—she's crazy."

Muntz was quick to recognize a successful gimmick. He gave Shore 20 per cent of the gross for advertising and a free hand. The "madman" tag has stuck to Muntz throughout his business career, sometimes to the anguish of public relations advisers trying to create a new, staid image for the high school dropout from Elgin, Ill.

Muntz' wanderings through the halls of business have paralleled the growth of America's consumer society in recent decades. He sold cars in the 1940s, with a peak of $72 million in a single year; television sets in the '40s and '50s, with a one-year gross of $55 million; and car stereos and tapes in the '60s, enjoying a best year of $37 million volume.

Those were the successes. Muntz also recorded notable failures trying to keep up with changing tastes; the Muntz Jet sports car (he built 394, lost money on each one); the Muntz dream house (he built 11 all-aluminum homes, but lost interest); the Muntz motorcycle park in Simi Valley (Calif.) and the Muntz rental motor homes (he lost customers, who kept driving the motor homes off the road and into accidents).

Now, the 61-year-old entrepreneur is deep into another venture, manufacturing giant screen television sets. The picture is projected on a special 40-inch by 30-inch screen, equal to the combined viewing areas of four 25-inch sets.

Muntz started the business late in 1974, and says he has sold 2,200 of the sets, priced at $1,595 apiece. Sales have been doubling each month for the past four months. Production should reach 750 units this month, and 1,000 sets in November.

At an age when most men are dreaming of golf games and fishing trips during retirement, Muntz is aiming at building another big company. The old salesman is still in there. "Things are going red hot," he says. "The dealers are driving us crazy yelling for more sets. Everybody wants it."

In his Van Nuys factory headquarters, Muntz points to a wall map, where red and blue battle flags denote the location of dealers who sell the Muntz home theater television. "Is Louisiana gone yet?" he yells to someone in the office. "Yes, it is," the response comes back.

Muntz works a full day in the office, then goes home to suburban Encino at night for meetings with visitors from out of state who are thinking about selling his big screen sets in their stores. Dealers must pay cash up front before getting the sets.

For Muntz, "there's nothing as much fun" as getting a business started, and building it into something of substance. He likes being the boss. "Somebody's got to rule the roost."

A man who started his first business at age 11, buying Model-T Fords for $5, fixing them up, and selling them for $10, doesn't care for the idea of being someone else's employee.

"I wouldn't want to work for a big company. They have too many rule books and regulations about how things should be done. The business I'm in now will be a big success; but I'll tell you that it wouldn't do nearly as well run by some big corporation."

Muntz' current business partner, Sy Weintraub, says, laughing, "I don't care if we're the giant company, I just care if we make the most profit."

Competition for Muntz' new venture comes from the giant Sony Corp., and Advent Corp., of Cambridge, Mass. Both the Sony and Advent big screen sets are more expensive than the Muntz model.

Muntz isn't worried about battling Sony; after all, he was once the fourth biggest TV manufacturer in America.

But his inability to become an organization man has cost Muntz a lot of money.

Danny Elman, who first bankrolled Muntz in the car stereo business and provided initial financing for the current big screen TV venture, remembered when a big Eastern company wanted to buy the stereo firm. Muntz would have been paid a fat retainer, with the other company getting control of the board of directors, making Earl just another worker.

"Earl said no," Elman remembers. "He would have wound up with several million dollars."

Elman admires Muntz as an inventor and a salesman. "But he's just not a good businessman, in my opinion."

Elman brought inventory-industrialist Bill Lear (the Lear jet) to meet Muntz, hoping the two men could collaborate in the car stereo field. "They didn't get along at all because they're both the same type," says Elman. Lear devised the eight-track stereo cartridge, which ultimately became standard, wiping out the four-track system developed by Muntz.

Muntz the capitalist doesn't quite match Muntz the inventor and salesman. He never amassed the wealth that might normally be associated with the big companies he developed.

The "Madman" Muntz of the 1940s sold acres of used cars, and was the biggest single dealer for Kaiser-Frazier, not the most notable success in automotive history.

He sold the car business for $400,000 or $500,000, a hefty profit in those days, and entered the embryo TV business in 1948.

Muntz television exploded into marketing success. More than 4,500 sets were sold in a single weekend one year. Disaster struck in 1953 when RCA chief David Sarnoff promised color television by Christmas. People stopped buying black-and-white sets; Muntz was out on a limb, operating factories and warehouses, paying rent on 73 stores that sold nothing but Muntz TV sets.

Muntz television never recovered fully; creditors forced it into bankruptcy reorganization in 1955. Muntz left the company in 1957, getting about $200,000 for his stock, which had been worth $6 million in the firm's better days.

Muntz never regrets the money he didn't make in the stock market. "I suppose I had a bad sense of timing, but you don't worry about it. If you did, you wouldn't do anything else. That's like worrying about yesterday."

In 1962, he began selling car stereo systems based on a model he put together in his home after four years of tinkering with electronic components. He arranged contracts with 60 different record labels for music to fill the 30,000 tape cartridges pouring out of the Van Nuys factory every day.

The business peaked in 1968, with a volume of $37 million, about 60 per cent from the sale of car stereo units and the rest from the tapes. But a 1969 fire temporarily wiped out tape production, and other manufacturers cut deeply into the marketing of the stereo units.

Volume dropped 40 per cent. He sold the business in 1970 for $1 million in cash and notes.

The next two years were occupied with a futile struggle to make money by renting motor homes. "I don't even want to talk about that," Muntz says.

Then he talks about it. "You rent one out and you may have to tow that son-of-a-bitch 300 miles." One trailer broke down in Yellowstone Park. Muntz had to fly the customers back to Los Angeles, and pay a $1,100 towing bill for the vehicle.

About $2\frac{1}{2}$ years ago, Muntz began tinkering with lenses used in aerial photography.

From this came his new product. The picture, produced by a 15-inch Sony television set modified in the Muntz factory, travels through the lens to a mirror, and is reflected onto the big 1,200-square-inch projection screen. The apparatus is housed in a single cabinet 68 inches high, 49 inches wide, and 22 inches deep.

The "madman" image will be used to sell the big television screens just as it promoted cars in 1942. The Muntz emblem—a cartoon man wearing red flannel underwear and Napoleonic hat—will soon be stamped on each shipping carton along with the line about "I want to give 'em away, but . . ."

Muntz has just returned from a trip to Japan, where he arranged for the manufacture of his latest product—a color videotape television camera for home use.

"There's a great need for a color camera," Muntz says with absolute sincerity and belief. "We're gonna sell a hell of a lot of cameras. Everybody's been waiting for a low cost color camera."

Questions

1 Is Muntz an entrepreneur?

2 Is he successful?

3 How could he be more successful?

4 How does Muntz' personality influence his behavior as a businessman?

Cases for Part Two

A SUPERVISOR'S DAY

Arthur Moment, aged 24, is a supervisor at a large glass manufacturing plant in an eastern U.S. city. Arthur graduated from Cornell's business school, spent two years in the Peace Corps, and then entered the company's management training program. This supervisory job is really his first significant work experience.

Arthur has been a supervisor for three months. Recently his superior, David Thrasher, pointed out to him that the production of his units is dropping.

> Thrasher: I think I know why, too, Moment. Recently I passed by your Unit 1 when you weren't there and there was some goofing off going on. Later that day I passed your Unit 2 and it was the same there.
>
> Moment: I'll look into it at once, Mr. Thrasher, and we'll get the production back up, you'll see.

What Arthur did not want to admit was that he knows there is goofing off but does not know what to do about it. Arthur's area of supervision includes two buildings. As the company grew, it added a small unit away from the main building, so Arthur's employees work in two places (see Figure 1). There are no windows in Unit 2's building and none near Unit 1's walls.

Unit 1 is composed of 15 employees who are very similar in ethnic background, age, education, and experience. The employees are unionized and have worked for the company about 7–10 years each. Unit 2 consists of 10 employees with 12–15 years experience with the company. They belong to the same union as the Unit 1 employees and are similar to each other in age, ethnic background, and education, although they are not the same age or from the same ethnic background as the Unit

1 employees. The workers at the two units do not get together at work.

When Arthur catches someone goofing off, the person usually passes it off as a brief interlude or makes remarks like "When the cat's away, . . . Besides, we do our fair share." When Arthur tried to crack down, he found that the employees were using "lookouts" to warn the others when he was coming. Arthur is wondering what he should do next.

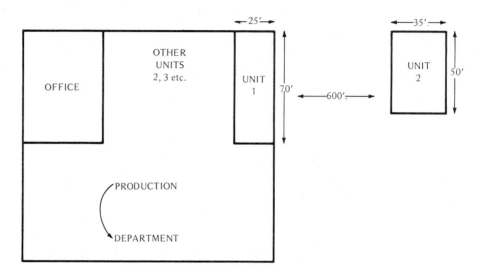

Figure 1
Location of Units 1 and 2, XYZ Glass Works.

Requirement You are Arthur's friend Sally Wurtzlebacher. Sally has years of supervisory experience at Arthur's Enterprise. Advise Arthur on how to improve productivity and avoid future problems with Thrasher.

FRED MENGEL An office of the Tennessee State Department of Revenue is located in Memphis, Tennessee. This unit is responsible for the collection of Tennessee taxes for the region and for enforcement of the tax laws.

One of the employees of this office is Fred Mengel. Fred, a civil service employee, is 51 years old. He has worked for the State of Tennessee for twenty years. He could not afford to go to college, but he has taken all the training the department offers and has occasionally attended night courses at Memphis State University, especially when the state paid for the course and if it raised his pay grade.

Fred was divorced some years ago. Between his job and his alimony he has more than enough money to live and retire on. He has no children and his parents are dead. His wife moved to California after the divorce.

Fred likes television. Every Thursday night he plays cards with friends. On Saturdays he usually has a date to go dancing or to a movie. Fred feels that life is quite pleasant, especially when nobody pushes him.

The preceding is a preliminary description of a problem employee to the casewriter by his superior, Bernie Lovell. Bernie is 38 years old, a graduate of Memphis State with a Masters degree. Bernie has been Fred's boss for a year. He has discussed "the Fred problem" with his two previous supervisors, Walter Rogers and Forrest Quigley. Their analysis is the same as his.

As Bernie sees it, Fred is a classic case of the ineffective employee that you cannot do anything about. But he pulls morale and performance down. He says,

> Fred is the twenty-year civil service veteran. You really can't do anything about him. He slides through his job, never straining himself for anyone or anything. He drifts in about on time. He fiddles around his desk for half an hour or so. He starts the 9:30 coffee break early and stretches it late. He does the same at lunch and at the afternoon coffee break. He starts getting ready to leave 45 minutes early with the going to the rest room and straightening up his desk routine. He has never, *never* left late. He has a good time with a circle of friends at breaks and lunches. He calls them during the day too, though I've never caught him at it.
>
> Fred knows how to work the system. He does just enough so you can't do anything about him. Have you ever tried to discipline a civil servant, much less a twenty-year veteran?
>
> I've tried to talk to him. His attitude, never spoken, is: I've seen bosses come and go and I'm still here. I'll listen, appear hurt, may even agree to try harder, but there's nothing you can do and we both know it. We're playing a game.

Fred's job involves routine checking of tax payments. He has never received either a bad performance evaluation or a good one. It is always average, slightly above, or slightly below.

But Bernie is perturbed because the other employees tend to emulate Fred after a while. Even if they are enthusiastic and hardworking at first, pretty soon they begin to follow his behavior patterns.

Requirement You are Bernie's personnel staff adviser. He has come to you for suggestions about improving the performance of the employees in the unit, especially Fred.

THE FOUR-DAY WORK WEEK

Sandy Jones is the manager of a regional insurance company office. Recently the company began a set of experiments to test the usefulness of a 4-day work week.

Traditionally, insurance offices work 36-hour weeks. So the home office recommended that some of the regional offices try out a 4-day week composed of 9-hour days. The bulletin from the office said that the approach that had been shown to be most effective was 8:00 A.M. to 6:00 P.M., with a half-hour for lunch and two fifteen-minute coffee breaks.

The office must be open five days a week. It is up to the supervisor to determine the hours of work at his or her office. A description of Sandy's employees is given in Table 1.

Table 1 The Four-Day Work Week

Employee Name and Job Title	Age	Sex	Marital Status	No. of Dependents	Time With Company	Other Experience	Education	Personality
1. Tom Jones, asst. manager	34	M	divorced	wife (alimony)	3 years	military	high school	introvert
2. Mary Mifflin, clerk typist	19	F	single	none	6 months	none	high school	extravert
3. Aimee Moore, clerk typist	24	F	married	invalid husband, 2 children	4 years	none	high school	introvert
4. Sammy Embry, claims adjuster	35	M	married	wife, 1 child	3 years	10 years with another insurance company	2 years college	introvert
5. Richard Schroeder, claims adjuster	23	M	single	widowed mother	1 year	2 years Army	3 years college	extravert
6. Sally DeWeese, claims processor	39	F	widow	3 children, her mother	6 years	none	high school	introvert
7. Lyn Peters, file clerk and typist	18	F	single	none	1 month	none	3 years high school	introvert

Sandy has been a manager six months. She graduated from State U ten years ago with a degree in business, and previously was a claims adjuster and assistant manager at the same branch of the company. She likes working for TIC.

Sandy, who is 31 years old and single, lives at home with her father, Tom. She and Tom are discussing the pros and cons of taking part in TIC's experiment.

Sandy: I think I'd like to have the group decide whether they want to participate or not. And if they decide to go along, let's let them help decide on the hours and schedule too. What do you think?

Tom: Are you crazy? You couldn't get this group to agree on anything. They are so different. Besides, you're the boss. TIC pays you to make decisions, not kick them down to the group to make up their minds.

Requirement Do you believe this is the kind of decision this group can make? (Your instructor will give you more information if you ask for it.) What should Sandy do?

Cases for Part Three

ALBERTA MOBILE HOMES, LTD. Alberta Mobile Homes, Ltd., is a small manufacturer of mobile homes and modular homes located in Calgary, Alberta, Canada. The firm has about 250 employees.

Alfred Butkus, president of AMH, recently attended a seminar on personnel administration in Calgary conducted by Professor Warren Simpson of the University of Calgary's business school. After the session was over, Butkus approached Simpson and asked him if he'd be willing to come to his place and provide consulting help for several personnel problems.

"Sure, I'd be delighted," replied Simpson. A few days later, he went to AMH to begin the project.

Butkus introduced the problem this way: "Look, Warren, we seem to be having problems with our promotion and evaluation system here. Let me describe two incidents that have come up just in the last two months. We're in a growth industry. We've doubled our work force in the last year and a half. This means we need to move some people up, but we are having the darnedest time with it.

"Recently, George Drester, the head of our plant, came to see me. He said he'd been wrestling with this problem for months. He'd promoted Jay Gilbreth to supervisor about six months ago. Jay was good at his job before, but he's not a good supervisor. His employees don't like or respect him. Jay himself seems aware of the situation. George is wondering what he can do about Jay.

"Then there's the case of Ed Bankhead, the head of marketing. He needs to recommend someone for promotion to sales manager. I've been asking him to do so for weeks, and no recommendations yet. See what you can do about it, will you?"

With this send-off, Simpson went to meet Bankhead. After some preliminaries, he came to the point. "Look, Ed, I'm here to see about establishing some policies about promotion. Frankly, Al gave you as a case in point. He's wanting to know what you've done about the sales manager's job."

Bankhead shifted around in his chair. He then described in some detail the men he was thinking about:

1 James Prior: ten years' experience in construction sales, lots of personality, no supervisory experience, high school graduate.

2 Harley Cortney: four years' sales experience for AMH, the best salesman of the bunch, college degree in business, no supervisory experience, very quiet, almost introverted.

3 Matt Dotler: older, 12 years' experience selling, 5 of it for AMH, outgoing personality. He did supervise two men with his previous company.

"Frankly, Warren," Bankhead said, "I'm leaning towards Harley. I figure the best salesman is bound to make the best sales manager. But I really don't have a lot of facts and figures to back up my choice. How should I go about this, anyway?"

Simpson said he would make a recommendation on this shortly. Next he visited Drester. "What am I going to do about Jay?" asked Drester. "He's not cutting it."

Simpson pressed Drester and asked him how he "knew" that Gilbreth's employees didn't like or respect him. "How wasn't he cutting it?" he asked. He quickly determined that these were just Drester's general impressions, not based on a lot of evidence. He also learned that Drester had not tried to discuss the issue with Gilbreth or try to counsel or help him.

Requirement You are Professor Simpson. Write the report to Butkus, copies of which will go to Drester and Bankhead. The report should include recommendations on:

1 How to decide on a sales manager and if possible whom Bankhead should recommend.

2 What to do about Drester and Gilbreth.

3 Recommendations for improving promotion, evaluation, and counseling at AMH.

1 Go to a work area where the noise is so loud that people cannot talk to each other easily (auto factory, lumber mill, punch presses, etc.). List the ways in which employees communicate nonverbally or get around this problem of communication. Rate these methods on a scale from ineffective to effective.

2 Keep track of all the nonverbal messages you respond to tomorrow. Identify those that had the greatest and the least effect on your behavior. What conclusions do you draw?

3 What nonverbal messages do your instructors send? During one week observe carefully and write down the messages sent to you by each of several instructors through their nonverbal behavior.

4 With a friend, and over a period of several days or a week, play the game "What you wear says to me . . ." Each day note what your partner wears, then write down what messages you received about your friend's mood, purpose, feeling, and the like. Have your friend do the same with you. Exchange your written notes and talk about why you got the messages you did.

5 List things that distract you most from listening. Then discuss the list with others to see if there is a pattern of distractions.

6 After reading a case in this book, ask a colleague what the case was about. Then repeat what you think you heard. Evaluate how well you listened.

**LIBERTY
SAVINGS AND
LOAN**

Liberty Savings and Loan is a medium-sized savings and loan firm head-quartered in the Los Angeles area. Its president is John Barnesely, age 55, who has spent twenty years with the firm. His experience is on the lending side of the business.

About five years ago Liberty decided to formalize and centralize some of its marketing activities such as advertising premiums. Among other things, Barnesely wanted to enlarge the marketing area (a staff function for a savings and loan firm) to include contact calls on builders, realtors, and potential large depositors.

Barnesely hired his first marketing director, Jim Johnson, from the marketing department of California's largest savings and loan company. Johnson did a good job setting up the department and getting it organized. Then, after 3½ years on the job, Jim left to head the marketing department of another savings and loan.

John then hired Sonia Ramirez, a 35-year-old MBA graduate of USC. Ramirez had worked in the marketing department of a large savings and loan firm in Los Angeles. She is married, has no children, and is the daughter of a successful entrepreneur in East Los Angeles.

She described her situation to the casewriter as follows: "I've been on the job a year now and I'm very frustrated. I have developed four major marketing programs that I know would be successful. But only two branch managers have cooperated. Four others won't help."

The branch managers are

Arthur Steiner: 25 years old, B.S. California State at Long Beach, 4 years with Liberty. He cooperated.

Ralph Paul: 33 years old, B.S. San Diego State, 8 years with Liberty. He cooperated.

Ernesto Oliva: 36 years old, B.S. California State at Fullerton, 7 years with Liberty. He refuses to cooperate.

Willson Bolton: 47 years old, B.S. UCLA, 10 years with Liberty. He makes many small criticisms of the programs and does not follow through.

Juan Roderiquez: 42 years old, 2 years at East Los Angeles College, 18 years with Liberty. He agrees to cooperate and then "forgets."

Vincent Kybal: 28 years old, 2 years at California State University at Los Angeles. He loses the plans and does not follow through.

Requirement You are Art Burns. You work for Ramirez and she has asked for your advice on how to increase her effectiveness with the branch managers. What are your suggestions?

THE MANAGER'S DILEMMA I

Gary Hulse is the manager of one of the larger departments of the Forbes Broadcasting Corporation. Forbes owns a chain of radio and TV stations in a number of cities in the United States. The flagship station and corporate headquarters are located in Dover, Delaware.

Gary has always viewed himself as a very democratic manager. Essentially, he believes in employee participation. He tries to develop employees' capacities to their fullest. He does this by involving them in decision making and goal setting. His preferred leadership style is to explain to an employee the major purpose of a project, ask for his or her suggestions, then tell him or her when the project is due. Then he leaves the employee alone, although he makes it clear that he is there to help if the employee runs into stumbling blocks. This has worked well for the employees he has dealt with at Forbes and in previous jobs in his twenty-year career in broadcasting.

Recently Gary hired a new MBA from a major midwestern university, Carroll ("Buzz") Kanatza. Buzz had a good grade record (3.5 as an undergraduate, 3.7 as a graduate student on a 4.0 scale) in business school. He was very active in extracurricular activities and was well known at college. He was a star end on the football team. In his senior year he went to the Rose Bowl.

Buzz is also "Mr. Personality": very good looking, confident to the point of being cocky. In fact several female employees had their eye on Buzz, and Gary felt that he had to remind him of the company policy against dating other Forbes employees.

After the orientation-management training program Buzz was assigned to Gary's section. Gary treated Buzz as he did all the other employees. He discussed the project he wanted done, set a target date, offered help, and sent him on his way. Yet the first three projects were not completed on time, and their quality was not good. Gary told Buzz about these shortcomings, but results do not seem to be improving.

Requirement What would you do to try to improve Buzz' work performance?

THE MANAGER'S DILEMMA II Gary thought about Buzz. The third project was not half what it should have been and it was late, too. It should have been simple for a person with an MBA and Buzz' obvious brains to handle. Gary was thinking of transfering Buzz or letting him go, something he had had to do only once before in his entire career.

Gary decided to confront Buzz. He asked him to come in at 5:30 on Friday night. He explained his feelings about quantity and quality of work and how he had even thought of termination. He said, "Buzz, I'm not one for hiding things. I believe you should get it out in the open. What is your problem?"

Buzz sat looking at Gary with a stunned look on his face. For once, he was speechless.

Requirement Do you think this was the right way to handle the situation? What would you as personnel manager at Forbes advise Gary to do instead?

THE MANAGER'S DILEMMA III Finally Buzz got up his courage. He said, "Gary, I like you, but this has been the strangest experience of my life, working for you. I'm sorry, but you asked me to lay it on the line. I guess I've really only had two jobs in my life. I worked in my Dad's hardware store and I worked for Coach Meador. In both these cases they told me what they wanted me to do and I did it. With Meador, it was play by play. With Dad, it was two or three times a day. I liked that and it was good for both me and them.

"But I flounder working for you. I sometimes don't know what to do next. It takes me longer. If I could benefit from your experience by having you tell me each day what steps to take next, I'm sure things would work well. What do you say?"

Gary just sat there. If he had to take ten minutes each morning to tell each of his employees what to do that day, it would take more than three hours to talk to them all. He would never get his work done. He did not know what to say.

Requirement You are Forbes' personnel manager. Gary has asked for your advice. Can these two people work together? How should each be counseled? What would you recommend that Gary do: transfer Buzz, fire him, try to change him, or try to work with him?

VANCOUVER CONTAINER COMPANY

Vancouver Container Company is a medium-sized manufacturer of metal cans located in Vancouver, British Columbia, Canada.

The situation takes place in the operations section of the firm. W. A. (Walt) Polen is a foreman in this department. He reports to Henry Knotts, a department manager. Walt described his situation to an investigator from the business school of the University of British Columbia as follows:

> My problem, the major problem I have, anyway, is the authority a foreman has at this company. Really, it's the lack of authority, that's the problem. I'm responsible for what results come out of this section. Yet I have so little authority to get these results. Let me give you a couple of examples. A foreman is only as effective as his manager will let him be, and my manager, Mr. Knotts, likes to do everything. When it comes to hiring a new employee for my section, I don't even get to meet him or her until afterwards. The people I train and supervise are not always the people I would have hired. I have no idea what wages they are paid and I don't have access to their personnel files. He keeps these as confidential information.
>
> Secondly, he encourages my people to come to him with their complaints without telling me. Then he confronts me with their complaints and doesn't even give me a chance to explain my side of the issue. The employee is right! So I don't really know how to describe what my job is. It sure isn't management as I understand the job. I've been a foreman for three months and am seriously considering going back to an operator's job. It just isn't worth all the problems working for Knotts.

Mr. Knotts is 56 years old. He has been with the company for 27 years, 10 of them as a supervisor and 5 as department head. The investigator from UBC is there to try to determine the causes of heavy turnover in foremen at VCC.

Questions

1 Why does Knotts behave the way he does?

2 Is it possible to get Knotts to change?

3 If you were Walt, what would you do?

YOUR CAREER PLAN

Complete this career planning guide for yourself.

Your Career Objectives Are

Title	by year
Salary	by year
No. of people supervised	by year
Colleagues	

Your Comparative Advantages Are

1 Education
   Courses (which ones)
   Grades (be specific)
   Skills developed

2 Experience

Jobs Held	Time in Job	Skills Developed
A		
B		
C		
D		

   Summary: variety, relevance of jobs to job sought

3 Personality
   A Interpersonal skills (be specific)
   B Ambitions
   C Leadership

4 Contacts/references by level
   A
   B
   C
   D

Job You Want

1 Size of enterprise   small   medium   large

2 Location

3 Sector   profit   nonprofit   public

4 Industries   *Future of Industry*

	Good	*Average*	*Poor*	
A				(1st preference)
B				
C				
D				
E				

5 Manager   Entrepreneur

6 Amount of responsibility desired   great   average   low

7 Amount of variety desired   great   average   low

8 Amount of money desired   great   average   low

9 Others

List Enterprises That Fit Your Desired Characteristics

1
2
3
4

List Kind of Job at These Enterprises That You Can Realistically Fill Now
1
2
3
4

Finally, prepare a job-seeking strategy to get Job 1 at Enterprise 1.

Cases for Part Four

ACME OFFICE FURNITURE (AOF)

AOF is a medium-sized manufacturer of office furniture. The firm, located in an eastern Canadian province, has been growing fast in recent years, although profit margins have not kept pace with sales increases and increases in employment.

The president of AOF is Gideon Fletcher. Fletcher was brought in from a larger firm when the previous president retired and the board felt that an outsider was needed to rejuvenate the firm, especially in terms of profitability. When Fletcher asked about some other success indicators, he found that absenteeism and turnover were up, quality was down, and the new-customer ratio was weakening.

The number of problems Fletcher faced was large, for most of the financial ratios had been weakening and production costs were increasing relative to past performance. Fletcher knew he could not run the

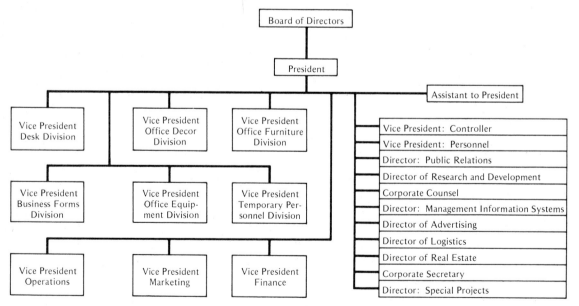

Figure 1 Organization chart: Acme Office Furniture.

firm the way his predecessor, Noel Lincoln, had. Lincoln had built up the business for the widow of the founder, Ed Upton, after Upton died. Essentially a salesman, he had let the organization take care of itself. "Just get enough orders—that's what keeps a firm going" was his belief.

Fletcher looked at the organization that Lincoln had left him (see Figure 1) and was not sure he could live with it. It had a large span of control. Fletcher felt that this was the time to centralize some of the decisions that had been left to drift. Yet he knew he could not make all the key decisions himself (nor did he desire to). He began to think about what he should do to make the organization easier to handle, yet not overly centralized.

Requirement You are a consultant hired by Fletcher. Recommend
·a better organization to deal with the firm's problems.
·the right span of control for this situation.
·justify your recommendations.

AJAX FOUNDRY   Ajax Foundry has a large plant in Arizona. Each worker's job has been analyzed using time and motion study. Each worker therefore is responsible for a certain amount of output. The company also uses a common recording and control device: the time clock.

On one particular job some of the employees, who had been selected on the basis of their skill, were getting the job done an hour and a half before quitting time. So one worker would stay around and punch the whole section out on the time clock at the end of the shift. This "job" was rotated among the members of the section.

One day the plant manager caught one worker punching out all the workers in the section. The next day he met with them. He reminded them that this action justified firing them all. But in this case he would just warn them that if it happened again he would have to fire them. At this point John Sikes, the informal group leader, spoke up: "Look, Mr. Paul, we do good work. We do all our work. Why not put this job on a 'get the work out, then go home" basis?"

The plant manager said, "I wish I could do that, but as you know, you guys are unionized. If I put the job on that basis the senior men could apply for your jobs and bump you from them. The contract says they have that right, and you know this would happen because many would like to leave early. Frankly, many of the senior men are not as skilled as you guys and production quality would drop."

The men continued to work fast. But since they had to stay around, they tended to wander around the plant, distracting other workers, reducing their productivity, and lowering their morale ("those guys must have cushy jobs"). And as they started messing around, the accident rate increased by 5 per cent.

Requirement You are the assistant plant manager. What recommendations would you give Mr. Paul on this control and morale problem?

American Hardware Supply (AHS) is one of the largest wholesale hardware firms in the United States, with headquarters in a large eastern U.S. city. About two years ago, to help cover an area not previously represented in its chain, AHS bought a smaller wholesale hardware company in the Northwest.

The results reported by this division have been less than great, so top management sent a team of executives from headquarters to gain better insight into the operations of the division.

The setting of this case is the conference room. Top management is listening to what the investigative team has found out. The purpose of the meeting is to design plans for improvement of the division's operations. The team leader is delivering the report.

As you know, we purchased Northwest Supply two years ago. The top management of the firm stayed on per our request and consists of Ike Farmer, 63 years old. He blames most of Northwest's current problems on us. He contends that if we easterners would just leave him and his team alone, they'd be doing fine. He sees us tying his hands with our admittedly rather complete policy manual, forms, and reports, none of which he'd ever had before two years ago. The rest of his team consists of guys who have worked for Ike for an average of 15 years, mostly high school educated, up-from-the-ranks boys who learned "the hard way."

Here are some of the specific problems we found at the division:

Sales: The sales curve of the division has started to flatten. Sales grew 27 per cent in the 5-year period prior to our purchase and only 14 per cent in the last two years. This partly reflects heightened competition in the area.

Profits: Profits have been declining and are now in the lowest 20 per cent of the industry. Last year the operation approached the break-even point.

Warehouse: The warehouse is the oldest in the company, and it is inefficient. It is a multistory job, which requires a lot of elevator trips to fill orders. It is also 20 per cent below the recommended size for the volume of business it handles. It would take $2 million to replace it.

Dealer Relations: The division has longstanding, close relations with dealers in the area. But it is not adding new dealers. Competitors are getting to them sooner. The division seems satisfied with its share of the market.

Finance/Accounting: The accounting department is only now adjusting to our accounting policies. The division is solvent, but with declining profitability. Without an addition of funds soon, its ratios will not look good.

Relations with Home Office: The division resists most incentives from the East, whether they have to do with advertising, accounting, or training. This causes a problem in view of our decentralization philosophy.

Overall Effectiveness: In general, the division is not meeting the objectives of the company, although it seems to be one of the leading wholesalers in the Northwest; that is, its results are as good as those of competitors in the area. Its turnover and absenteeism rates are better than average.

Requirement You are the president of AHS.

1 Which of these problems is the most important?

2 What additional information do you need to set your objectives and make your decisions?

3 What would you do about the Northwest Division?

4 Design an MBO system for AHS that will help deal with the division's problems.

APPELBAUM FURNITURE

Appelbaum Furniture, located about 35 miles from a major southern U.S. city, manufactures a variety of products at different price levels. The "Kingston" line is high-quality furniture that is very expensive. Kingston pieces are made of good wood with some hand carving and hand-rubbed finishes. Kingston represents 15 per cent of Appelbaum's sales.

The middle-of-the-line "American Beauty" items represent 60 per cent of sales. These items are produced in large batches with no hand carving or hand rubbing, but solid wood and good veneer are used.

The "Econoline" is the lower priced line. The materials used include plastics and pressed woods. To compete, these items must be produced on the assembly line.

Several years ago Appelbaum employed a firm of industrial engineers to reduce its production costs. The firm redesigned all the jobs to fit the work simplification model. The results have been mixed. Direct labor costs have been reduced. That is, fewer skilled employees are needed. And through attrition direct worker wages have been reduced by 3 per cent (after adjustment for inflation, wage increases, etc.) over the years.

Appelbaum pays average wages (time based, not incentive based). Employee distribution is as shown in Table 1.

The quality of work, as measured by rejections by inspectors and returns by stores for poor workmanship, has been dropping. Reruns for quality purposes have risen from 1 per cent of payroll to 1.7 per cent in the past three years.

Joseph Appelbaum, son of the founder and recent graduate of the University of North Carolina Business School, has suggested that the firm consider job enlargement and/or job enrichment. He recently prepared an attitude survey that dealt with this issue. The results are given in Table 2.

Appelbaum's technology does not prevent job enlargement. Appelbaum is not unionized and has average fringe benefits. Joseph Appelbaum, Sr., is considering several strategies in response to his son's suggestion:

Table 1 Appelbaum Furniture

		Daily Absenteeism Rate			Turnover		
Employees	Age	Year 1	Year 2	Year 3 (Now)	Year 1	Year 2	Year 3 (Now)
Under 25 male	16%	3	4	5	7	10	12
Under 25 female	5	2	3	2	4	5	6
26–35 male	18	4	5	4	6	7	8
26–35 female	3	3	4	4	4	4	5
36–45 male	19	3	4	5	5	6	7
36–45 female	3	1	1	1	2	2	3
46–55 male	21	3	2	2	2	3	4
46–55 female	0	0	0	0	0	0	0
Ovfr 56 male	15	2	2	2	1	1	1
Over 56 female	0	0	0	0	0	0	0

Table 2 Appelbaum Furniture

	Kingston Employees			American Beauty Employees			Econoline Employees		
	Agree	Neutral	Disagree	Agree	Neutral	Disagree	Agree	Neutral	Disagree
Under 25 male	70	20	10	70	10	20	60	20	20
Under 25 female	65	30	5	60	20	20	50	35	15
26–35 male	60	20	20	55	25	20	45	25	30
26–35 female	50	30	20	45	40	15	45	55	0
36–45 male	55	35	10	50	40	10	50	0	50
36–45 female	60	30	10	50	30	20	40	20	40
46–55 male	75	10	15	70	10	20	50	0	50
46–55 female	0	0	0	0	0	0	0	0	0
Over 55 male	80	15	5	70	20	10	60	0	40
Over 55 female	0	0	0	0	0	0	0	0	0

Strategy 1: an incentive compensation system tied to quality and slightly increased quantity.

Strategy 2: management development program to upgrade the supervisors' leadership skills.

Strategy 3: job enlargement throughout the plant.

Strategy 4: combination of strategies one and three in one or several parts of the plant.

Strategy 5: Combination of strategies 1 and 2 in one or several parts of the plant.

The Appelbaums are neither for nor against any of these strategies.

They are wondering whether they should accept one of them or wait a bit longer to see if clearer trends emerge.

Requirement What do you as a management consultant suggest that the Appelbaums do in view of current trends in their firm?

HONEST EMPLOYEES

Recently a fast food retailer that was concerned about robberies installed television cameras on an experimental basis. They were focused on the cash register. The chain explained the purpose of the experiment to its employees and said it did not know if it could justify the expense for the full chain.

A few months after the installation one of the accountants pointed out an interesting phenomenon. The accountant had compared the cash register receipts before and after the installation of the cameras and found that the number of small sales rung up after the installation was substantially higher than before. "It seems to me that some of the employees were taking some sales as "tips" before we installed the cameras. Now they think we're watching. This should help profitability."

At the same time, the personnel manager began to get complaints about "Big Brother" in the exit interviews of some of the employees who quit. He followed this up and found that a number of employees felt that they were being watched by the bosses and were really upset about this.

The security specialist pointed out that not one of the outlets with the cameras had been robbed. The stores had prominent signs warning thieves about the cameras.

But the cameras are very expensive. The additional cash in the cash registers covered 10 per cent of the cost of the cameras. At the stores without the cameras (used as "control" stores) there was one robbery. The total "savings" from additional cash and "lack of robberies" equaled 25 per cent of the cost of the cameras.

Requirement You are the manager in charge of this firm. Since the three-month trial period is over, should you
  ·remove the cameras (they are leased)?
  ·continue the experiment another three months?
  ·expand the experiment?

Explain your answer.

MBO: A FAILURE?

Recently Frank Siemers, president of a medium-sized machine tool manufacturing company, attended an industry convention. One of the major topics was management by objectives. Frank had heard about MBO but did not know much about it. The session consisted of a main speaker who briefly described what MBO was and how it was implemented, and then a panel of industry executives who spoke about five minutes each praising MBO's results in their companies.

On the flight home Frank reflected on that session. It seemed to be describing his company's problems: declining achievement of objectives, people whose responsibilities overlapped, less than fully motivated employees, and the like. The speakers all seemed satisfied with how MBO worked at their companies. Frank decided to try MBO.

Frank called the usual Monday executive coordinating meeting to order. He spent ten minutes summarizing some of the news he had picked up on new products, personnel changes, and so forth. Then he launched into a fifteen-minute description of how MBO could help the company. He made it clear that MBO would be their next major project.

As the other executives spoke up, it became clear that serious problems had arisen while he was gone. Some important operating decisions had to be made about the new plant in Australia; there was the issue of the reorganization of the regional sales offices; and a decision had to be made on whether to offer to buy back the million shares of company stock as recommended by the treasurer.

So Frank took the vice president of personnel aside and told him he was making him the MBO officer and that he wanted MBO operating in the company within three months.

The personnel vice president, Nat James, rushed out, bought some books on MBO, chose a set of forms to be used, and sent out a letter stating that MBO would be the new policy and directing that each department adopt it within 60 days.

Frank has heard rumbling from the ranks about "this MBO joke." He does not understand what happened and has called Nat in for a meeting.

Requirement What advice would you give to Frank and Nat about what probably went wrong and how it might be corrected?

MODER AIRCRAFT, INC.

Moder is a medium-sized company that supplies subassemblies for major aircraft firms. It ships its parts to all the major airframe manufacturers as well as firms that make executive aircraft and similar products. Its president is Jason Fleming.

Recently Fleming has seen many articles about affirmative action for women and minority groups. He wondered how his company would be evaluated on this issue. So he asked the personnel vice president to prepare a report on Moder's employees. Table 1 is that report.

After looking the report over, Fleming called the personnel vice president, Elling Takover, into his office. The following is an excerpt from their discussion.

Table 1 Moder Aircraft, Inc.

| Level of Employees | Employees by Sex | | | Employees by Ethnic Group | | | | | |
	Male	Female	Total	White	Black	Hispanic American	American Indian	Asian Pacific Islanders	Total
Top management	100%	0%	100%	100%	0 %	0 %	0%	0%	100%
Middle management	99	1	100	99	0.5	0.5	0	0	100
Technical	93	7	100	97	1.5	1.5	0	0	100
Supervisory	89	11	100	94	2	4	0	0	100
Clerical	1	99	100	79	11	10	0	0	100
Operative	92	8	100	61	28	11	0	0	100

Fleming: "El, tell me the truth. If a government guy came in here, what'd happen?"

Takover: "We'd be in trouble, boss."

Fleming: "It's not like we discriminated. We hired minorities long before others did. But most of our managers are engineers or ex-engineers. How many female engineers are there? Blacks?"

Takover: "I'm not sure that'd cut much ice. We really have an affirmative action problem, I think. Maybe we haven't been as socially responsible as we thought."

Requirement Takover is asked by Fleming to recommend some preventive action. You are Takover. What do you recommend?

THE RESTAURANT QUESTION

You are Justin Orman. You have just inherited $25,000 (after taxes) from your grandfather. You graduated from a good business school and have thought of entering the restaurant business because you like it. You would like to move to a warm climate, so you are considering several smaller California cities.

Your present first choice has a population of about 100,000. The city is not contiguous with others. You have heard that the population is about one-fourth upper class (incomes over $20,000), one-third lower class (incomes below $12,000).

At present there are 12 restaurants of the quality you would like to run in this city. Their characteristics are presented in Table 1.

Four of these restaurants have changed management in the past year. Three others (nos. 2, 7, and 9) previously went bankrupt. You have heard that several of the restaurants are barely making it.

Table 1 The Restaurant Question

Type of Restaurant	Seating Capacity	Liquor License	Years in Business
1. Chinese	100	yes	4
2. Chinese	75	yes	1
3. Steak	160	yes	8
4. Italian	60	yes	2
5. Steak/seafood	150	no	1
6. Vegetarian	50	no	new
7. German	100	yes	1
8. General	150	yes	3
9. General	100	no	1
10. General	125	yes	2
11. Barbecue	100	yes	3
12. Mexican	75	yes	2

You would like to run a very nice, rather expensive restaurant and cocktail bar with Greek decor. You are wondering if you should go ahead.

Questions

1 What kind of planning should you do before you decide to go ahead on this project in this city?

2 What additional environmental search should you carry out?

3 What objectives should you set up? Can MBO be used here?

4 Can you ever make a decision like this on the basis of premises and studies alone?

SCIENTIFIC DECISION MAKING

Bob Bates is the president of a company that makes subassemblies for large auto firms. Bates' firm is located in the upper midwestern United States. One thing that Bates has learned in business is that committee meetings are a big waste of time. So he always schedules them so that "natural stopping times" will keep them reasonably short. For example, he schedules them at 3:30 or 10:30 so that lunch and quitting time will cut the chatter. He has also found that Friday afternoon is a good time, since many people like to go away for the weekend.

At a recent Friday afternoon meeting it was 4:50 P.M. There was one more item on the agenda: a proposal by the production department for new machinery. The vice president of production, Oscar Slusher, presented the proposal, which claimed that the new machinery would "pay for itself" in five years in labor cost savings. The machinery would cost $1 million.

The vice president of finance, Sam Donaldson, was opposed to the plan.

Donaldson: Wait a minute. Our rate of return is not good right now. We don't have much cash on hand. I'd have to borrow that money. The banks aren't happy with our balance sheets and income statements right now. I'm not sure they'd give us the money at all, and if they would, it would cost us 2 per cent above the prime interest rate. I don't believe we should borrow any more money until we get our ROI up. Besides, where are the figures to support this labor cost saving figure?

Slusher: This is a chicken-and-egg thing, Sam. How can we increase our ROI with the lousy machinery we've got? Our labor costs are killing us, and with competition the way it is, to get GM and Ford's business sales can't raise prices. We've got to get our costs down.

Donaldson: Yea, but where are the figures to prove labor costs would go down $200,000 a year?

Bert Smith (sales vice president): Figures, figures, figures! We've been here four hours now. I've got an important engagement shortly. I'm with Oscar. I heard the sales presentation from the machinery company and it sounded good to me.

Donaldson: "Important engagement," eh? Is she a blond or a brunette? And did you give your wife that line about a conference in Houston again?

Smith: Sam, watch it!

Bates: It's getting late. Let's get back to the issue.

Donaldson: This is a lot of money. It *is* late. This can wait until next Friday's meeting, when I'd like to see the figures on where the cost savings will come from and I can check what the banks will . . .

Bates: All in favor say aye. . . . The proposal passes. Meeting adjourned.

Requirement Evaluate the approach used to make this decision.

AERONAUTICAL SYSTEMS CORPORATION

The Aeronautical Systems Corporation has experienced rapid growth in the past decade. Its current annual sales are approximately $250 million. The company employs 10,000 employees, a large proportion being highly talented engineers, technicians, and scientists. The company designs and manufactures complex custom-built electronics systems for the government, aviation firms, and other types of industrial organizations. Much of this work is done on a contract basis, where a number of companies are involved in the manufacture and construction of one major end product such as a missile, rocket or booster, or a new type of aircraft. This company also has standardized product lines that are produced and distributed by six United States divisions, a Canadian division, and an International division.

A basic company objective is constant product and systems innovation of a highly technical and complex nature in fields where there are few competitors. Top management believes in a highly flexible organizational structure, which—in large part—entails organizing activities around highly talented personnel, rather than fitting men to an "ideal" organizational structure.

Following is an outline of the major manufacturing and distributing divisions and their major product lines:

1 Systems-Manufacturing Division, Los Angeles
  a Space-Life-Support Systems
  b Missile Systems
  c Fluid Systems
  d Flight-Electronics Systems
  e Heat-Transfer Systems
  f Environmental-Control Systems

2 Systems-Manufacturing Division, Phoenix
  a Space-Power Systems
  b Air-Pumping Systems
  c Gas-Turbine Power Plants
  d Pneumatic and Fluid-Control Systems

3 Research-Industrial Division, Los Angeles
  Manufactures and markets a line of industrial exhaust-driven turbo-chargers and specialized valves.

4 Research-Aviation Service Division, Los Angeles
  Conducts airplane modification work—including structural and system changes—and distributes several lines of turbine-powered executive aircraft in the Western states.

5 Electric Division, New York
  Manufactures a line of specialized industrial generating equipment.

6 Air Cruisers Division, New Jersey
  Manufactures fabricated products, aircraft-escape devices, missile-recovery systems, etc.

7 Systems Manufacturing, Ltd. of Canada
  Manufactures avionic systems such as temperature controls and static inverters.

8 Aeronautical Systems International, with head offices in Geneva
  Controls a series of technical sales offices in Europe, and is also the holding company of subsidiaries in Japan, Great Britain, and West Germany.

On most major contracts, more than one of the company's divisions are involved in the design, manufacture, and distribution of the systems or company end product. Divisions I and II, in particular, are highly interdependent and interrelated in much of their work. Divisions V and VIII are the most autonomous in terms of their product lines and operations. All of the divisions, however, have some standardized products or systems, over which they have considerable operating autonomy.

Divisional organization

To quote a current company manual:

> Each manufacturing division is responsible for its own financial statement and, therefore, enjoys a great deal of autonomy. The divisional manager, assisted by an assistant manager, has a complete organization of managers to control the operation of such departments as Engineering, Manufacturing, Quality Control, Quotation Administration, Accounting, Sales, and various service departments such as Personnel, Administrative Service, and Plant Engineering and Maintenance. In addition to this basic functional organization, Divisions I and II are further divided into product-line organizations. Hence, the chief engineer, for instance, has a chief-product engineer over each product line. Similarly, the sales manager has complementary product-sales managers over each product line, and so on.
>
> The history of the Aeronautical Systems Corporation is one of deliberately planned internal growth through continuous investment in research and development of new products to supplement and complement existing products and systems capabilities. This policy has resulted in an unusually wide product mix, with uniquely complementary characteristics, that enables the development and production of complete, comprehensive accessory systems from components of various divisions and product lines. This practice has been exercised repeatedly and has established firm, practicable lines for inter-product group and inter-divisional collaboration in the creation of multiproduct systems.

Corporate organization

To quote the company manual:

> The corporation or head-office management consists of a board of directors, a chairman of the board, a president and an executive vice-president. All divisional and subsidiary managers report to the executive vice-president. He is assisted in his task by several corporation vice-presidents and directors who are responsible for policy direction to the divisions relating to matters such as law, finance, accounting, public relations, industrial relations, contract and quotation administration, engineering, material, product planning, manufacturing, quality control, and sales and service. The vice president of Sales also has a complete Corporation-Marketing Organization, which is responsible for the sale of the corporation's products from offices throughout the free world.

Some additional comment on the corporate-level marketing organization is warranted here. Under the vice-president of Sales there are a number of sales forces organized on a customer basis; and within some of the customer groupings, there are also territorial breakdowns. For example, the following sales managers report to this vice-president:

1 Field Sales: Throughout the country, there are district sales offices, whose salesmen call on industrial customers.

2 Government Relations: This sales force deals with government contracts.

3 Airlines: This sales force deals only with airline companies; it consists of a number of regional offices.

Also reporting to the corporate vice-president of Sales are the manager of Engine Sales, whose sales force calls on both the airlines and government customers, and the manager of Special-Systems Sales (mechanical, electrical, etc.), whose sales force calls on all types of company customers. A director of Marketing Services also reports to this vice-president.

The head-office salesmen are the customer-contact men for those systems and product lines that require joint developmental and manufacturing operations involving more than one division. These salesmen are the key disseminators of information between customers and those parts of the company concerned directly with the system or product being produced and sold to the customer. The divisional salesmen directly contact customers primarily where standardized products are involved and where the systems and products are under the autonomous control of a particular division.

Program organization

To quote the company manual:

For the development of larger systems involving components of various types and requiring the coordinated efforts of several product-line organizations and more than one division, some form of program organization is used. The extent and exact composition of the program organization will vary with the size and complexity of the program involved.

A complete program organization consists of the following major positions:

Program Manager
System-Project Engineer
Contract Administrator
PERT Coordinator
Reliability Coordinator
Maintainability Coordinator
Value-Engineering Coordinator
Quality-Control Coordinator

Support-Service Coordinator
Manufacturing Coordinator
Material Coordinator

The subdivisions within the program organization follow the functional-line organizational structure in each Manufacturing Division. They draw on the strength, skill, and experience of existing line-organization people, combining it into a highly specialized group with a program of centralized responsibility and authority that comes directly from division and corporate management. This program structure has proven highly successful on many major programs such as the recent F-111 aircraft, Gemini, Apollo and SPUR space programs, and many others.

Program manager

To quote the company manual:

> The program manager has complete responsibility for the development of the systems in the program and complete authority to implement all activities necessary to insure contract compliance. He has overriding authority to alter decisions and to recommend alternate action, if such will enhance contract compliance, improve product reliability or quality, reduce development of fabrication costs, or reduce the time to develop the systems. The program manager reports any conflict between programs, regarding utilization of manpower or facilities, to the appropriate division managers. The division managers take appropriate actions to resolve such conflicts. The program manager must resolve all internal program conflicts involving compromise of costs, performance, product quality or reliability, or program scheduling. He has authority to request such action as is required to resolve any conflicts. The program manager represents the primary liaison and coordination point between the manufacturing division(s) involved and the customer. He authorizes all personnel conferences and correspondence at the technical and administrative levels between the division(s) and the customer. The program manager participates in all personnel-performance reviews for all key program members. He may recommend personnel changes when and if he deems such action necessary to the successful accomplishment of program tasks. He continually keeps abreast of all program developments, significant accomplishments, and important problems. He reports general program progress to division management on a biweekly basis and is responsible to the customer for all contractual reporting.

Questions

1 On one or more organization charts, depict the key organizational relationships discussed. You may make any assumptions you wish regarding specific titles of the personnel involved in cases where such titles have not been given.

2 What types of authority relationships does the program manager have with other company personnel (e.g., line, staff, functional, informal, formal)? Illustrate with examples.

3 Given this company's organizational structure and relationships, what significant organizational problems do you think are likely to arise? Illustrate with some examples involving personnel at different levels and in different departments or divisions.

4 In spite of any organizational problems that you might envision, do you feel that the overall organizational structure and authority relationships depicted are the most effective and practical for this particular company? Why or why not? If your answer is no, what are some of the more significant organizational changes that you would recommend?

5 How important do you feel technical as opposed to managerial skill is in effectively staffing the following positions in this company: (a) program manager, (b) divisional general manager, (c) corporate vice-president of Sales, (d) corporate manager of Special-Systems Sales, (e) corporate manager for Government Relations, (f) divisional chief engineer, (g) divisional manufacturing manager, (h) executive vice-president, (i) president?

6 Discuss some of the advanced and more sophisticated planning and control techniques that may prove effective in the Aeronautical Systems Corporation.

7 Do you envision any serious directional, leadership, motivational, or communication problems in this company on the basis of the information provided? Illustrate with hypothetical examples in order to justify your answer if it is in the affirmative.

FALLER AND BROWN

Jack Faller, Superintendent of the Screw Machine Department of Acme, apprehensively entered Mr. Brown's office.

"Jack, your department's in a terrible mess," Mr. Brown, the Factory Manager, roared as soon as he entered. "Look at this." Brown gestured to a pile of correspondence on his desk. "Rejections and more rejections! And this! Two weeks behind on the Navy order! What am I supposed to tell the Captain? That I have a slob of a superintendent who doesn't know how to get his work out?"

"Mr. Brown, I . . ."

"What is going on down there, anyhow? Here I give you complete authority to run your shop the way you want. . . I treat you like a son . . . I spend half my time down there in your department, trying to unscramble the mess you have . . ." Brown paused to wipe his glasses. "Jack, what is the trouble?"

Jack felt that he might as well speak up. He'd probably get fired anyhow. "Do you really want to know?"

"Do I want to know! For gosh sakes, Jack, tell me!"

"Can I fire Joe?"

"Of course not!" Brown was aghast. "You know he's the son-in-law of the Chairman of the Board!"

"He causes 90 per cent of the trouble in the department," Jack said. "A fine quality-control specialist he is! Where'd he learn to do statistical work? In a course in non-Euclidian geometry? I try to get him to cut off at the 5 per cent confidence level, and he cuts off at the 30 per cent level. No wonder we have so much trouble with quality control!"

"Now, Jack, be reasonable. You have complete authority down there, but after all . . . the Chairman of the Board . . ."Brown shivered and mumbled to himself.

"Can I give the boys in Heat Treating a raise?"

"Of course not! Personnel says that that would be unfair!"

Jack sighed. "The last wage agreement we made had that loophole in it, remember? Those five boys receive about 10 per cent under what they should be getting relative to the rest of the men. Shoot, they're about 20 per cent under the market, too. Two of my best men have already tried to quit, but so far, I've talked them out of it. I wish the others would quit." He shivered. "What a crew!"

"Jack, you know that wage policy is determined by Personnel."

"Yeah, and I wish that some of those characters would come down and try to justify their great policies to the guys who get the paychecks. If they'd get out of their ivory tower once in a while, they might find out that their theories don't always work out so well."

"Jack, you're just passing the buck. Here you are, with complete authority to do whatever you want, and you keep passing the blame on to others."

"Can I get rid of those old Brown & Sharpe shapers and buy some decent equipment? That machine line costs us more than it's worth. Remember, those machines were purchased in 1923, when we got our first GM contract. They were good machines then, but times have changed. I spend more time maintaining those things than I do getting work out on them. That's why your Navy work is so far behind."

"You know we can't do anything about that, Jack. We've been over this before." Brown sighed. "First, the engineering committee has to approve the new machines—and old Fisher just loves those shapers. He was the one who bought them in the first place."

"I know," Jack said. "Just oil them a bit and treat them right, and they produce." He snorted. "Maybe that was true in 1925, but it sure isn't now."

"And besides," Mr. Brown added, "the budget committee would have to approve the new purchase. You know how that works."

"I know," Jack said. "I spent four weekends last year working out the request—you helped me on it, remember? We proved that we could get a 30 per cent return on the new machines, but the budget committee turned the request down."

"Well now, you can't blame the committee for that. They have lots of uses for limited funds."

"OK, OK. But you wanted to know why we weren't getting the work out."

Brown sighed again. "Jack, you're just evading the issue. If you can't produce, well . . ." he paused ominously.

Jack stood up to go.

"By the way, Jack," Mr. Brown added, "I just got a note from the traffic manager. You shipped the last Navy shipment by truck, in direct contradiction to his instructions. You know that material is to go out by rail. It's a lot cheaper."

"It's a lot slower, too."

"Well, we all have to follow our basic directives."

"Sure," Jack said. "Sure."

Questions

1 What management considerations are involved in this incident?

2 What should Faller do?

3 What should Brown do?

HARRISON, INC.

Harrison, Incorporated, is a small firm in Milwaukee, Wisconsin. Its business at present involves the installation of flooring, walls, and ceilings in commercial buildings.

The company historically has been well run and profitable. Founded by the late John Harrison, Sr., in 1960, the company then concentrated on installation and sales of floor tile. Harrison would approach potential buyers, acquire installation contracts, and then hire workers to install the tile.

Noting the increased interest in acoustical tile, Harrison diversified his business by adding to his product-service mix in 1962. This decision was wise, for by 1970 new-product sales exceeded sales of floor tiles.

Always on the alert for new products that would fit into the company's line, Harrison added wall partition products to its list of installation services in 1969.

A family firm

Harrison had been a tile salesman for another firm, but he longed for the pleasures and pains of his own business. Psychologists have not often studied the motives of people who form their own firms. This decision often means that they will work longer hours for less money and with a high risk that they will lose all their investments and have no job at all. The failure rate of new small businesses is high. William Henry, analyzing the thematic apperception tests of successful entrepreneurs, concluded that the firms were mother substitutes for men with oedipal complexes. But some people do have a desire for the independence and success that entrepreneurship can bring, and Harrison seems to be one of them. He knew the construction business, and by watching cash contracts and careful bidding for jobs, he avoided the bankruptcy that most similar businesses experience.

In 1975 Harrison became ill, and he died in June 1976 after a lengthy illness. He was succeeded in the presidency by his 26-year-old son John. The younger Harrison had received a bachelor of education degree from Wisconsin State University at Whitewater and had spent three years in the Air Force before entering the business during his father's illness. His experience in the business was limited to part-time work while in high school and college.

The casewriter interviewed young Harrison and asked him what the outlook was for his business. He replied:

> This has always been a profitable business, but in the last few years we've suffered setbacks in sales and profits. But some of this is due to slowdown in the construction industry in the last 5 years. I think we're just about over the slump period. We should see a reversal in the sales situation over the next few years.
>
> I'm more concerned about other aspects of our operations. It seems like a lot of inefficiencies and poor practices have crept into our work in recent years. Dad was in poor health much of that time, and I guess he just didn't realize what was happening.
>
> One main problem is that our jobs are poorly coordinated. We usually have three crews working on large projects: a floor crew, a wall crew, and a ceiling crew. Changes in work procedures and work schedules for one crew can completely wreck the plans of the other crews. Yet, in most instances, none of the crews know what each of the other crews is doing. Sometimes it's like we're three different companies working on the same job.
>
> Another problem is a lack of good supervision. Often times I find workers just loafing around, waiting for some types of material or just waiting for further instructions. Invariably, the supervisor in charge is up to his elbows in another job—doing things that the foremen should be doing. This sort of thing may have been permitted in the past, but we're simply too big now. We need supervisors who will be supervisors.
>
> Yes, I'm anxious to get a few things straightened out—to really shake things up around here. The trouble is, any time I mention changes, I meet with resistance. For example, I met with the supervisors last week to try and iron out the problem I was just telling you about. They agreed to do a better job of supervision, but the last on-site visit I made revealed that the problem is worse, if anything.
>
> At first I thought that such resistance was due to the fact that I am fairly young and inexperienced. People seem to resent being told what to do by a newcomer. But now I'm beginning to think that some people around

here are just plain stubborn. I can tell you one thing: a few heads are going to roll unless things improve pretty soon!

The casewriter then asked Harrison to describe briefly the business as he saw it in view of its history and possible future. He described it as follows:

In the past, Harrison served both residential and commercial customers. Presently, the company limits its business to commercial customers. You see, it is difficult to compete in the residential market, since the small contractors selling in that market are not unionized and are therefore able to do the job cheaper. And we didn't want to spread ourselves too thin. Typically, we lay the floor, put up wall and ceiling work for medium-to-large stores and office buildings. We try to work out a "package" deal with our customers. That is, we prefer to do all the basic interior work—floors, walls, and ceilings—ourselves. These three jobs require a certain amount of coordination, and it is usually better to have one outfit doing them rather than many. We do, on occasion, contract to do just a portion of the interior work. Profitwise, these jobs have not been as satisfactory.

Harrison continued:

We offer a total interior service, you see. The floor line consists of vinyl tile, carpeting, and other resilient coverings. The ceiling line includes acoustical board material, illumination panels, and suspension hardware. We do some plastering work, but most of the wall work involves installation of drywalls. The company has developed its own line of drywalls, which features metal studs and channels rather than the more common wood studs and bases. These light and nonpermanent wall partitions have been especially popular in remodeling.

How the firm evolved

When the company began operations, Harrison, Sr., performed a wide range of tasks himself. He did all the selling, ordered materials, scheduled and supervised operations, and handled all bookkeeping and accounting routines. He employed a secretary and four or five workers. More workers were added as the business grew. Then, as the company began taking on simultaneous projects, it became necessary to hire foremen for each project, and supervisors to supervise the foremen. Salespeople were hired to help Harrison find new business.

Presently, the organization consists of about 110 employees, 65 of whom are skilled or semiskilled laborers. At the management level there are two vice presidents, an accountant, and three production supervisors. Figure 1 shows what the organization presently looks like.

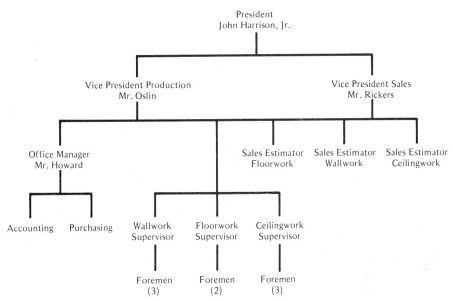

Figure 1
Organization chart:
Harrison, Inc.

Thomas Oslin is the vice president in charge of production and also serves as general manager. Forty-eight years old, Oslin began working for Harrison in 1966. Before that, he worked for a firm which manufactures acoustical ceiling material. Besides having responsibility for all production activity, Oslin is in charge of the main office and accounting department. Mr. Howard reports directly to him.

Reporting to Oslin are three production supervisors. One is in charge of drywall construction, another supervises ceiling operations, and the third is responsible for floor installation. These persons schedule and control all production activity. Each supervisor assigns work crews to their jobs, ensures that needed supplies are on hand at the work sites, and coordinates work activities with the other two supervisors. The foremen working on specific projects report to these men. All three supervisors have worked for Harrison for many years and have "risen through the ranks."

The vice president of sales is Glynn Rickers. Rickers worked in the construction business for 18 years before coming to Harrison. He started as a sales estimator and was promoted to vice president in 1973. Rickers is knowledgeable in all aspects of the company's business and works closely with Oslin in planning and scheduling jobs.

Four sales estimators work directly under Rickers. They are responsible for locating new business and for preparing price estimates for bids. They also assist customers in selecting materials and color schemes. All four have had considerable experience in the interior finishing business. One man previously owned an acoustical tile company.

The firm's operations

Jobs at Harrison are obtained either by bids or by negotiated sales. Most Harrison business is a result of bid jobs. Typically, a job is announced in a trade magazine, or in a construction service bulletin to which the company subscribes. When a potential job is announced, Rickers sends sales estimators to review the plans with the building owners and architects. Guided by the blueprint plans, the sales estimators compute the costs for materials and labor. Estimates of cost are made as close as possible to actual direct costs, with overhead, error allowance, and profit margin added on.

Rickers emphasized the importance of accurate cost estimation: "Most firms lose their shirts because they underestimate costs," he said. "A good estimator can determine almost exactly what the labor and materials needs will be from a good set of plans. A poor set of plans can throw estimates off seriously. We give ourselves a large error margin if plans are not specific. Overall, we've done a pretty good job of bidding most projects. Sometimes we're caught off guard by unforeseen hikes in wages or materials prices, but this is unusual."

Rickers said that the firm tries to make a 13 percent operating margin on most projects. He added that it was not always possible to obtain such a margin, particularly if a number of other firms are anxious to obtain a given project. Profits for most companies have been generally lower during the construction decline of recent years.

A small proportion of jobs are obtained through direct negotiation with general contractors. In most such instances, contractors have worked with Harrison in the past, or desire a specific skill or material available only from Harrison. Some interior materials businesses have salespeople who solicit sales by calling on architects and contractors. Rickers does not feel that this marketing approach is worthwhile, particularly since most of Harrison's work involves rather large projects for which bids are necessary.

There are dozens of firms in the Milwaukee area that install floor, wall, or ceiling material. However, only four firms engage in all three types of activities on a large commercial scale. Harrison, Jr., said that his company has about 25 percent of the commercial market, and that this market percentage has remained fairly constant for the past 5 years. Harrison presently limits its market to the immediate Milwaukee area.

The other three firms are Bischoff Construction Company, Arrighi Services, Incorporated, and Pulaski Interiors. Bischoff is the leading firm, having about 35 percent of the commercial market. But in addition, it has as much residential business as commercial. An old, well-established and respected firm (founded in 1925), it originated as a family concern but is no longer dominated by the family. Its bids are always competitive, yet it stresses quality workmanship as well. It does not do as much wall business as Harrison.

The third firm, Pulaski Interiors, was founded in the Depression and has about 20 percent of the commercial business. Its share of market has been declining. Pulaski, whose son was killed in the Korean War, seems to have lost interest in the business as he nears retirement in about 1981. Pulaski's business is about the same size as Harrison's.

The newest entry is Arrighi Services. At present it gets only 5 percent of the commercial business, but it has a fairly large residential business. It also offers wider services, including painting and decorating. The business is about two-thirds the size of Harrison but growing fast. Harrison feels that Arrighi cuts a few corners and has been getting more bids than he should of late.

Like other firms tied to the construction business, these firms find that their business fluctuates considerably. Construction activity is both seasonal and cyclical. Seasonality does not affect firms doing interior work as much as it does firms doing outside work, since workers inside are afforded protection from the elements. Nevertheless, most companies like Harrison do a greater amount of work during the warm months. All construction activity is dependent upon a number of political and economic variables, including interest rates, rate of business growth, employment rates, etc. Recessions in construction activity are often rather prolonged, and marginal companies are sometimes forced to go out of business during such periods. The level of manpower in this labor-intensive industry fluctuates in proportion to the level of construction activity.

Once the job is obtained, a sales ticket and work ticket are filled out. The sales ticket is sent to the accounting office, and the work ticket is sent to the production department. As soon as the production supervisors receive the work ticket, they begin planning operations. Materials for the job are ordered, and manpower assignments are tentatively made. The production supervisor must keep in close contact with the general contractor to determine the exact date when the job will begin. When the job is ready for Harrison to begin operations, the material is sent to the job site from the warehouse and labor is scheduled.

The accounting office records job expenses as they accrue. Actual material costs and labor costs are compared to bid cost estimates on a weekly basis. Wide variances between bid and actual costs are reported immediately to Oslin, who investigates the discrepancy and takes corrective action, if necessary.

To explain more about his operations, Harrison took the casewriter on a visit of several work sites. He explained what he considers the production problems to be. He said:

> For one thing, our work crews can never seem to follow schedules. You see, work crews for the three basic operations—wall work, ceiling work, and floor work—are scheduled so that the needed workers are available for each successive phase of a project. But if one crew gets behind, this delays the starting time for the next crew. For example, if the wall crew

is delayed in finishing a job, the ceiling crew cannot begin on time.

Since there is often no more work for the ceiling crew to do, they are temporarily idle. This is not because of a lack of planning, but subsequent changes in work assignments throw projects off schedule. What happens is that the wall superintendent sees that he's getting a little behind on one project, so he shifts men over from another. This delays work on the other project, and throws everything off schedule. Mr. Oslin and I have talked over the problem a great deal, but haven't come up with any workable solutions. He claims that you just have to expect so much slack in the work schedule.

On a later day, the casewriter visited with the production vice president, Oslin. Earlier a worker had told the casewriter that he should talk to Oslin, since "he runs the whole place, anyway."

The casewriter asked Oslin about the production problem mentioned by Harrison. He replied rather sharply:

No, I don't think we have poor supervision or poor work conditions. John seems to think that something is wrong when every single man is not working every single minute of the day. But this just isn't always possible. Things happen which upset even the most carefully planned schedules. I try to keep in touch with the production supervisors about scheduling and work assignment changes. We work things out the best way we can.

But I'll tell you one thing, we do have a supervisor problem. Our three supervisors are spread too thinly. Right now, for instance, we have four major projects under way. It's impossible for each supervisor to be everywhere at once, although sometimes it's almost necessary for him to do so. We need more supervisors. That's the only solution.

The casewriter asked several other questions and at one point commented that a worker had said he really ran the Harrison company. Oslin replied:

Oh, sure, I guess you might say that I did run the place for quite a while. Mr Harrison, Sr., became so sick that he even stopped coming to work. He left everything in my hands. The business would have gone to pieces if someone hadn't taken over. But now that John, Jr., is here, things are different. There's only room for one man at the top, and right now that's him. I'm careful not to infringe on his authority. Sometimes that's difficult, because many people still look to me for instructions and guidance. I discourage this. I'm trying to help John, Jr., all I can.

Asked to comment on Harrison's abilities as president, he said:

Well, you can't learn everything there is to know about this business overnight, but John is working hard and learning fast. He's interested in the business. Sometimes, though, I think that there could be better communication between John and the rest of us. He makes a lot of decisions without talking them over with anyone. Some guys resent this. But I'm not going to say anything. As I said before, he's running this show, not me.

Financial management

Mr. Howard, the company's accountant, told the casewriter about the financial problems that are unique to the business.

> For one thing, we must pay for materials and labor long before we receive payment from the customer. Furthermore, the customers retain a certain amount to assure the completion of a job. Usually, 10 to 15 percent of our accounts receivable consists of such funds. Because of these factors, we must manage our money more carefully. This involves sound financial planning. Also, it's imperative that we maintain a good relationship with the bank. Since there are relatively few fixed assets to serve as collateral in this business, most banks want prompt payment. Yes, many firms in this business fail because they lack financial management capabilities.

Harrison recently investigated the possibility of computerizing such operations as accounting, inventory control, cost estimation, and profit planning. He decided that there is not enough work to justify the purchase of a computer but feels that it may be worthwhile to contract with an outside computer service in the future. Presently, the office force handles the bookkeeping, payroll, and job-cost records. Mr. Howard personally keeps track of delinquent accounts receivable. Entries to all accounts are made by hand and checked by machine.

Mr. Howard's department also handles purchasing functions. Purchases are made for inventory and in response to specific job requests. All materials are stored in a new warehouse building having rail access. Mr. Howard explained that since there is ample storage space, he usually goes ahead and orders materials as soon as he finds out that they will be needed.

> Sometimes we have all the materials for a job as much as 3 months in advance of the time they are needed. This way we avoid the possibility of work stoppage due to the late arrival of materials.
>
> I think we've done a good job managing our assets. You're welcome to look at our financial records if you wish.

Harrison has had nearly a 40 percent sales decline from 1974 to 1975. Much of this is no doubt due to bad economic conditions. But not all.

Profitability has declined. The ratio of net profit to sales has been falling and deficits appeared in 1975 and 1976. Some of the losses are due to a rise in variable costs and increases in selling and administrative costs. The costs of materials and labor have also risen at the same time that competition for bid business has intensified. All of this has put serious pressures on the firm's financial health.

Some final comments

As the casewriter was getting ready to leave, he was pondering the challenges and problems at Harrison. Running through his mind were some of Harrison's earlier comments about his dream for the firm. He had said:

> I want to get things shaped up around here first—make the most of what we have now. But my real hopes are far beyond that period. I dream of a firm that is growing and expanding. We've entrenched ourselves—cut out our share of the pie. But we've been standing still—we still think of ourselves as a small outfit. It's about time our managerial thinking caught up to our size and we did some long-range thinking instead of operating only on a day-to-day basis.

The casewriter wondered if Harrison was capable of fulfilling those dreams.

Requirement You are a consultant called in by Mr. Harrison. Analyze this case and make suggestions to Mr. Harrison for improving the managerial effectiveness at Harrison, Incorporated.

THE HOEPPNER COMPANY

Hoeppner is a closely held, family-managed manufacturer of hospital beds and allied products sold to hospitals and nursing homes in the United States. Founded in 1897 by a German immigrant, Morris Hoeppner, it still bears the imprint of this patriarch who strongly influenced its policies until 1952 when he died at the age of 78. Hoeppner began operations as a partnership. But because of a personality conflict between Morris Hoeppner and Clarence Estill, Estill went into the furniture business and Hoeppner took complete control of the company in 1903.

Morris Hoeppner was very frugal, conservative, and hard working. He never took a vacation or time off. He believed in plowing back every penny of profits into the business. "Yes, much of what we do today at Hoeppner is a legacy of my father's philosophy," explained Morris, Jr., the president. "Firms like ours have the character and the values of strong and good men like my father."

The firm is located in Greenville, Kentucky, a small and somewhat isolated town. The firm's location has an important influence on company policy. Morris Hoeppner, Sr., used to say, "Whatever is best for Greenville is best for Hoeppner." Hoeppner, Jr., strongly agrees with this assertion.

The majority of people in Greenville work for Hoeppner, and many have worked there all their lives. Hoeppner, Sr., personally knew most of the families in the area. He knew the names of most employees, their wives and children, and where they lived. The older employees who knew him still joke that "Father Hoeppner tucked us into bed at night." He was interested in seeing that the community was a desirable place to live, and was primarily responsible for the construction of schools, public facilities, and the town's only park. Morris, Jr., doesn't have the intimate relationship with the townspeople that his father did, but he does share his father's concern for community affairs. Last year, for instance, he was instrumental in planning and financing a new elementary school.

When the older Hoeppner died, the new president felt that it was his obligation to see that the company continued to provide a livelihood for the family and community. He viewed continued growth as being necessary, but felt that rapid expansion or diversification was too risky. Thus, the company has grown slowly to meet an expanding demand, but has done little experimentation with radically different products or markets. In 1976 the company had assets totaling over $24 million and sales of about $19 million.

Hoeppner's place in the industry

Hoeppner competes for business in the health care industry, which has been growing for years. The industry represents 5–6 percent of gross national product and employs about 4 million people. It includes over 7,000 community general hospitals with over 850,000 beds. Hoeppner also sells its products to mental hospitals, which have about 700,000 beds. Then there are the nursing homes, which have over 550,000 beds. How fast the industry develops, and in what ways, will depend to a great extent on what the government does about the proposal for national health insurance.

Hoeppner produces hospital/health care beds (manual and electrical), tables, cabinets, chairs, hospital davenports, and bedside communication and control devices. It competes with about eleven other firms that make hospital beds and is one of the largest in the industry. Its beds are higher priced. A Hoeppner bed is viewed as the Rolls Royce of the industry.

Most companies sell their output to hospital equipment supply houses, who in turn sell the beds to the customer. Hoeppner still sells the products to the hospital or nursing home through direct salesmen. "By doing this," said Hoeppner, "we are able to maintain a high level of customer confidence. We don't just 'wash our hands' of a unit when it leaves the plant. We consider a Hoeppner bed to be our responsibility from the time it is built until it is no longer in use. We feel that the quality of hospital equipment is only as good as the service that goes along with it." The major facets of what the company calls their "Perpetual Service Plan" are as follows:

1 Beds are shipped to customers only by company-owned trucks.

2 Every bed delivered is set up and inspected by a salesman before being put into use.

3 Hospital engineers and servicemen are given the training and equipment they need to properly care for Hoeppner beds.

4 All parts are guaranteed against defective workmanship and will be replaced free of charge as long as the bed is still being used by the original hospital.

A Hoeppner executive explained that they experimented with the use of common carriers for delivery and it had proved to be unsatisfactory. Beds and equipment were not packed properly, and were damaged as a result. And the customers had to set the beds up themselves. By running its own delivery fleet, the company is able to train drivers to pack, deliver, and assemble beds. The company makes it a point to deliver an order on the exact date requested. "When you order a bed and want it to be here by June, don't order it in April, expecting it to be late. We'll check back with you before we send it and make sure you really want it. After a certain point, you're going to get it anyway," said a Hoeppner executive.

A 3-day course in the proper care and maintenance of a Hoeppner bed is given once a month for hospital engineers. The engineers are flown to Greenville, with all expenses paid by the company. Here they learn how to completely disassemble and assemble a bed, and do repair work. Hoeppner has determined which parts are most likely to wear out and when they can be expected to need replacement. For about $75 a hospital can purchase a packet containing these parts. It is recommended that one packet be purchased for every 10 beds in use.

The Hoeppner Company employs 37 salesmen who cover nearly the entire United States. The size of a salesman's territory is governed by the population density of the area. Some salesmen, for example, are assigned to two or more states, whereas several salesmen are assigned to a state such as New York. All salesmen report directly to William Hoeppner.

A job as salesman is about the highest position to which an employee outside of the Hoeppner family can aspire. The salesmen are carefully selected from a large number of applicants, many of whom have college degrees. They are then given an intensive training course, in which they learn everything from how to assemble and disassemble a bed, to designing a complete hospital room.

Much of the salesman's time is spent in servicing old accounts. This includes taking care of the hospital expansion needs and keeping the administrator informed of new types of equipment. "We work around the needs of the customer," said William Hoeppner. "Other companies make several lines and go to the customer and say, 'Here's what we've got—which one do you want?' We use a 'custom' approach. Our salesmen try to work with the hospital and make suggestions and recommendations concerning his equipment needs. Often they work with planners in setting up a whole new wing. Recently we did all the designing work in setting up rooms for a nursing home chain."

An important part of Hoeppner's promotion effort is the "customer party." Hospital administrators, or other persons involved in purchasing hospital equipment, are invited to spend 3 days at the company headquarters in Greenville. Here they are entertained royally at the Hoeppner ranch, and are given tours of the plant. The Hoeppner tradition of quality is emphasized throughout the stay. The "party" is well known and much talked about in the hospital field. It is said that whenever hospital administrators get together, the question always comes up, "Have you ever been to Hoeppner's?" The company entertains from 25 to 75 persons a week in this manner. Hoeppner pays all expenses, including travel costs.

The management team

In 1952 Mr. Hoeppner died at the age of 78, leaving the company to his four sons. By this time, the company had grown to be one of the largest producers of hospital beds. At the time of his death, his four sons ranged in age from 20 to 44 years. In his will, Mr. Hoeppner specified that the four sons would become the owners of the company, and that the oldest son, Morris Hoeppner, Jr., would become president of the firm. Forty-year-old John Hoeppner became executive vice-president, and William Hoeppner, who was 27 years old, retained his job in the production department. The youngest son, Samuel, was completing college at the time. In 1962, Samuel Hoeppner was brought into the firm as a salesman. In 1965 he became assistant production manager, and in 1968 was promoted to vice-president in charge of production.

The top management can be described as being very "tightly knit," with the four Hoeppner brothers controlling every aspect of the company's operations. Known simply as "The Brothers," they have indicated a reluctance to turn any part of the company over to an "outsider." "We have grown up with the company, and the company has grown with us," said Morris Hoeppner, Jr. "It's part of the family itself, and no one else could possibly devote to it the time and effort that we have." It appears that the family will be able to fill the top positions for some time to come. The four men have a total of six sons, ranging in age from 2 to 26 years, and 3 daughters age 12 to 20.

Morris Hoeppner, Jr., has been the dominant force in shaping the company's policies over the past 18 years. He has been involved with the company in some way or another for nearly 48 of his 62 years. Mr. Hoeppner worked part time performing various tasks while in high school, became production manager after completing college, and later became sales manager. He was promoted to executive vice-president 5 years prior to his father's death. Employees often joke that "Brother Morris is watching you," and the line contains more fact than humor. Mr. Hoeppner is familiar with virtually every aspect of production, and spends much of his time supervising operations. He feels that by getting close to the workers, he is able to instill within them "the Hoeppner tradition of quality and workmanship." Mr. Hoeppner is becoming increasingly involved in state politics, and estimates that he spends about one-third of his time in state and local affairs.

As executive vice-president, John Hoeppner is concerned primarily with office management and purchasing. Described as being less outgoing and less of a "wheeler-dealer" than his brothers, he is considered to be indispensable when it comes to taking care of routine administrative details. He has made it known that he does not wish to be president of the firm and that he will pass up the opportunity should it ever occur.

William Hoeppner was recently made vice-president in charge of sales, after having served as production manager for nearly 20 years. In his present capacity, he coordinates all sales activities, including field sales and customer "parties." Reporting directly to him are the company's 37 salesmen. Well-liked by both customers and company personnel, the third-oldest brother is considered by many to be the person most likely to succeed Morris Hoeppner, Jr., as president.

The youngest brother, Samuel, is vice-president in charge of production. Samuel Hoeppner was at first reluctant to join the company, and upon graduating from college, had a brief career as a math teacher. At the age of 29 he decided to join the Hoeppner firm. He began in the sales department, and was later promoted to production manager. Samuel Hoeppner calls himself the "maverick" because he is constantly pushing new ideas and exploring new areas for operation. He admits that he is seldom able to obtain approval for his proposals, but he has had a few successes. For example, it was his idea to enter the electronic control field.

Morris Hoeppner, Sr., was very concerned with preserving family unity. In his will, he stipulated that all four sons and their families spend the entire summer at a recreational ranch owned by the family. Here they relax, get to know each other better, and have time to "think about the company." The relationship between the brothers must be described as being "very intimate."

A formal organizational chart had not yet been devised. When asked a question regarding channels of communication, Samuel Hoeppner replied, "Everyone around here knows what his job is, what he's supposed to do, and what he's not supposed to do. As far as my brothers and I are concerned, we're in touch with each other all the time. We run things rather well on a day-to-day basis as we see fit. Any unusual decisions to be made—anything at all out of the ordinary, and we talk to Morris. We generally meet every afternoon and talk over all problems we might have. Getting back to your question, I think most companies as complex as ours would require that formal lines of communication be established. Here, we work together so closely that I don't think it's really necessary."

One of the unique characteristics of Hoeppner is its strong commitment to quality products. "The Brothers" want to be known as the best in the business. Some of this quality emphasis becomes evident in the tour of the plant given all visitors. Hoeppner manufactures 98 percent of its own components, from the smallest coil spring to the wooden headboard. Raw materials arrive in basic form, consisting mainly of metal and wood stock. Morris Hoeppner, Jr., explained that the company follows this practice to ensure that quality standards are met. "The only way we can keep adequate control of quality is to make the product ourselves, from start to finish," he stated. "When it comes to hospital equipment, we want nothing but the best. You'll see a lot of things being done around here that may not appear to be too efficient, but for the sake of quality, we do them." About the only items that are not made at Hoeppner are the electrical components, including electric bed motors and control units.

Quality of raw materials is only one aspect of the intense need for quality products. Of equal or perhaps even greater importance is quality workmanship. Morris Hoeppner, Jr., emphasized that only the most skilled and dedicated workers were promoted to the woodshop. Here, time and patience are the most important ingredients in producing what are generally regarded as the finest headboards in the industry. "If we wanted to, we could just about double our output in this area using the same workers and facilities that we have now," he said. Only the best woods are used. The company actually owns its own forest, and has control over the wood from the time it is selected and cut until it is used in making the finished product. The headboard consists of a core section covered with veneer. The core is composed of high-grade hardwoods, placed in cross layers to avoid possible warpage. The veneer is selected from the most attractive and durable woods, and is finished in a special process that makes it extremely hard and durable.

The beds on the assembly line are suspended on gimbals. As a worker completes his particular task, he slides the bed to the next worker. The time required for each operation has been computed so that the line will flow smoothly. Management does not want the individual worker to feel rushed, and employees are told to spend as much time with each bed as necessary to do the job "right." Many of the tasks on the assembly line involve welding together metal parts. Again, it would be cheaper to use bolts or rivets, but welds are used because they are stronger.

After a bed leaves the assembly line, it is completely tested to see if it meets quality standards. Every electric bed, for instance, is placed in a room with about 500 pounds on it and run in every possible position for 30 minutes. Every fiftieth bed is completely disassembled and closely examined for defects. One of the main concerns is to see that each electric bed is completely safe. In years past, there have been instances of patients being electrocuted by other brands of electric beds. Since that time, Underwriters Laboratories has imposed rigid standards on makers of electric beds. Hoeppner in all instances meets or exceeds these standards. For example, UL suggested that all metal parts be insulated so that they would not carry an electrical current. This was only a suggestion, as the process is fairly expensive. Hoeppner complied with this without question.

Visitors to the plant are impressed by the spaciousness, cleanliness, and apparent efficiency of the production facilities. The aisles are extremely wide, and there is absolutely no clutter in any of the working areas. An elaborate system of air ducts is used to carry off wood shavings and sawdust. There are no "dirty jobs" in the plant. Every worker, regardless of his particular task, wears an immaculate white smock and is expected to maintain a neat and clean appearance. The company's philosophy is that if the workers take pride in the appearance of both themselves and their work areas, they are more likely to take pride in the quality of work performed.

A small laboratory is maintained to improve product quality and design. The department is under the supervision of Philip Stern, a mechanical engineer who has worked for Hoeppner since 1956. Besides performing tests on beds coming off of the assembly line, the department investigates customer complaints and makes corrections in design or assembly techniques whenever necessary. For example, maintenance problems were reported about a certain bearing in the company's electric bed. Mr. Stern substituted a self-lubricating bearing, and the problem was solved. Sometimes customers remark that they would like to see certain features incorporated into the bed design. If Morris Hoeppner decides that the idea is worthwhile, it is given to Mr. Stern to develop. When asked what his operating budget was, Mr. Stern replied, "There's a budget, I'm sure, but I don't know how much it is. If I'm overspending, I'll find out about it."

The plant is in operation 8 hours a day, 5 days per week. Production capacity is rated at 145 units per day. Of some concern to Hoeppner's quality emphasis are some recent developments in the craftsman worker's part of the quality equation. Thomas Hoeppner, the 26-year-old son of John Hoeppner, heads the personnel department. He began working for the company after completing college and serving in the military. Thomas Hoeppner discussed several aspects of the company's concern. One of the main problems concerns the shortage of available manpower in the area. Greenville, with only 3,500 inhabitants, is not able to supply the nearly 800 employees which Hoeppner needs. The nearest large town is Owensboro, which is 45 miles away and has a population of about 50,000. Because of difficulties in obtaining sufficient numbers of personnel, the company has encouraged women to come to work. As a result, nearly 40 percent of the total work force is female. "For the most part, they are able to do the same kinds of tasks as the men, and our experience has shown that they perform them as well or better than the men do. We don't discriminate against the girls when it comes to pay. We feel that if they do the same work, they are entitled to the same pay," Thomas Hoeppner said.

Union problems have also been a cause for concern in recent years. In 1971 a strike lasting 4 months resulted in some violence, and the homes of the owners as well as the plant were damaged. Because of this, a high, electrified fence has been placed around the plant, with television cameras placed in areas both inside and outside of the plant. "Our troubles began when we hired a large number of unemployed coal miners," Thomas Hoeppner explained:

> Several years ago we were looking for a large number of employees. The government suggested that we bring in some coal miners from another part of the state, so we did. Not very long thereafter, a representative of the United Upholstery Workers' Union came in and tried to organize these people. Previously, our employees had seen little need for a union, since their pay and benefits were comparable to unionized plants. The union was a way of life to the miners, however, and they were easily swayed. Thus, nearly 50 percent of our work force became unionized. I'm not certain what actually caused last year's strike. We offered an increase in pay and benefits comparable to what we had in years past, and most of the workers generally agreed to these increases. There were a few agitators, though, that were pressing for an even better contract. Morris wouldn't discuss their demands with them, and many of the other workers got upset about this. At any rate, they managed to get enough support to bring off the strike. By the time the strike was over, union membership had dropped to about 25 percent. Many people left the union because they needed the money and had to come back to work before the strike was over. Others were rather upset by all the violence and wanted to disassociate themselves from the union.

Fourteen men were fired as a result of violent incidents that occurred during the strike. One of the union demands was that a federal arbitrator come in and determine whether or not these men should have been fired. This was done, and it was decided that the workers were justifiably fired.

Hourly wages range from $2.00 to $4.75 per hour. The average pay is about $3.40 per hour. Most of the workers receiving the higher wages are welders. The personnel manager emphasized that pay policies are completely fair and objective. The casewriter noticed that on a payday all the workers carried their checks in their shirt pockets, with the amounts in plain view for anyone to see. Employee benefits include group hospitalization insurance covering the worker and his family, a retirement plan, and a 1-week paid vacation annually. Morris Hoeppner stressed that the benefits the employees received were not brought about by union pressure, but were part of a personnel policy developed years ago:

> Before the union came along, we had no formal life or hospital insurance benefits, but the employees knew that if they became sick or disabled, they would be taken care of. We would pay all medical expenses and make sure that the family was able to pay its bills. Or, if an employee died, we would send money to his widow as long as she needed it. There was never a contract. Everything was based on mutual trust. When the miners came, it was a different story. These people feel that they are entitled to whatever they can wheedle out of the company. Then, when they get what they want, they decide that they want more. If they did their work properly, I wouldn't mind. The trouble is, they take no pride in their work. You have to keep after them and make certain that their work meets our quality standards. The people who grew up around here are different. The company has been an important part of their lives ever since they can remember, and they do their best to carry on the Hoeppner tradition of quality. It seems like we're running out of this kind of worker.

On weekends, the Hoeppners' recreational ranch is open to employees and their families. The ranch features picnic grounds, playgrounds, pony rides for the children, and a small zoo. Every year on July 4th the company sponsors a barbecue and fireworks display at the ranch.

The company is proud of its nondiscriminatory hiring policy. While visiting the plant, the casewriter noticed that there were no blacks present. He asked a foreman if any did, in fact, work for the company. The foreman replied, "Have you seen any? Well, you probably never will." An estimated 22 percent of Greenville's population is black at the present time.

The future for Hoeppner

Recently, William Hoeppner explained that the firm has experienced some flattening of the sales curve. Some salesmen think this is because of slower expansion of hospitals, but others say that for the first time they are experiencing resistance to Hoeppner prices. Samuel Hoeppner feels that perhaps the firm ought to diversify. He asked rhetorically: "Where are we going in the future? We've passed the point where rapid growth is possible in this business. Increasing our market share significantly is out of the question. Our competition has us hemmed in. No, in order to really grow, we've got to diversify."

He went on to say that he was trying to convince his brothers that they should go into the nursing home business. The nursing home industry was given a shot in the arm by recent government actions which amplified the benefits given to those in extended care facilities. At the same time, the over-65 population continues to explode. As a result of these factors, an already apparent shortage of beds has become even more acute. Most estimates place the present need at between 250,000 and a half-million beds. Many firms are getting into the act, building new homes, and in some instances, starting nursing chains. Despite this activity, the needs still outpace construction.

"We're definitely in a position to take advantage of the situation, especially since we're already involved in the design of nursing home facilities and equipment," Samuel Hoeppner said. He estimated that Hoeppner could build nursing homes at a cost of around $5,000 per bed, which is considerably less than the industry average of nearly $8,000 per bed. Profits in the nursing home business fluctuate widely. Last year, one firm made 28 percent pretax profit, and many were in the 15 to 20 percent range. Many homes, however, had low profits or deficits. Many new homes had deficits, especially where the owners and operators were lacking in experience.

Samuel Hoeppner continued:

> The only problem right now is that I can't seem to convince anyone around here that we should go into the nursing home business. Bill agrees that we should probably look into the idea of diversifying, but is not certain that nursing homes will suit us. Morris can't figure out why we should want to risk what we have on one of my "wild schemes." John won't even discuss it. I wish I could encourage them to talk about it. I'm worried about our current demand situation.

Information about the company's financial position is closely guarded. Stock in the company is held entirely by the family. Only the four brothers have access to the company's financial statements. No one else—not even other members of the family—knows how much the assets of the company are worth.

Samuel Hoeppner has repeatedly tried to sell his brothers on the idea of a public stock issue. He indicated that his had to be done if the firm is going to make a serious venture into the nursing home field.

In a final conversation Samuel told the casewriter:

> I think you'll have to admit that things are pretty well in order around here. We're a tight and sound company, from just about any angle you want to look. This is precisely why I feel we're in a position to broaden our interests. We have a strong foundation on which to grow. Perhaps going into the nursing home business isn't the right thing for us to do. I don't know. But I'm sure you'll agree that we should start thinking about branching out into some other area. I'll be looking forward to seeing your recommendations.

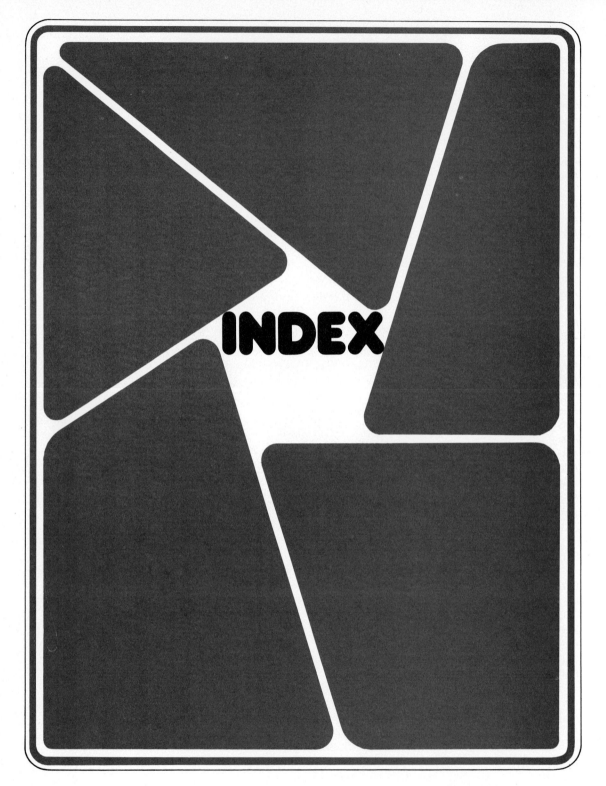

Acknowledgments and Copyrights

Chapter 2 Table 2.1, p. 24, reprinted by permission of the publisher from Stewart, Rosemary, "The Manager's Job: Discretion vs. Demand," *Organizational Dynamics,* Winter 1974, ©️ 1974 by AMACOM, a division of American Management Associations.

Table 2.2, p. 25, reprinted by permission of the publisher from Stewart, Rosemary, "The Manager's Job: Discretion vs. Demand," *Organizational Dynamics,* Winter 1974, ©️ 1974 by AMACOM, a division of American Management Associations.

Table 2.3, p. 26, after Robert Guest, "Of Time and the Foreman," *Personnel* 32 (1955/1956), pp. 478-486. Adapted by permission of the publisher from *Personnel* 32 (1955/1956), ©️ 1955/1956 by American Management Assn., Inc. Also after Frank Jasinski, "Foreman Relationships Outside the Work Group," *Personnel* 33 (1956/1957), pp. 130-136. Adapted by permission of the publisher from *Personnel* 33 (1956/1957), ©️ 1956/1957 by American Management Assn., Inc.

Table 2.4, p. 27, after D. L. Marples, "Studies of Managers: A Fresh Start? *Journal of Management Studies* 4 (1967), pp. 282-299. Reprinted by permission of Basil Blackwell & Mott Ltd.

Table 2.5, p. 28, after D. L. Marples, "Studies of Managers: A Fresh Start? *Journal of Management Studies* 4 (1967), pp. 282-299. Reprinted by permission of Basil Blackwell & Mott Ltd.

Table 2.6, p. 28, after D. L. Marples, "Studies of Managers: A Fresh Start? *Journal of Management Studies* 4 (1967), pp. 282-299. Reprinted by permission of Basil Blackwell & Mott Ltd.

Quote, p. 29, from Lyman Porter and Edwin Ghiselli, "The Self Perceptions of Top and Middle Management Personnel," *Personnel Psychology* 10 (1957), pp. 397-406. Reprinted by permission.

Quote, pp. 30 and 32, from "Dynamo at Work: At W. R. Grace and Co., It's Tough to Keep up with the Chief Executive's Pace," Wall Street Journal, April 2, 1975. Reprinted with permission of the Wall Street Journal, ©️ 1975 Dow Jones and Co., Inc. All rights reserved.

Figure 2.1, p. 31, from Diana Pheysey. "Activities of Middle Managers: A Training Guide," *Journal of Management Studies* 9 (May 1972). Reprinted by permission of Basil Blackwell & Mott Ltd.

Photo of Royal Little, p. 32, Donald L. Miller, *Fortune Magazine,* ©️ Time Inc.

Article about Royal Little, p. 32, *Fortune,* Hall of Fame, January 1975. Reprinted by permission.

Article about Catherine Cleary, p. 32, *Fortune,* April 1973. Reprinted by permission.

Chapter 3 Figure 3.1, pp. 57-59, after John Komives, "Are You One of Them?" *MBA Magazine,* reprinted with permission from the June/July 1973 MBA. Copyright ©️ 1973 by MBA Communications Inc.

Article about Walt Disney, p. 61, *Fortune,* January 1976. Reprinted by permission.

Table 3.1, p. 61, data from 1970 Census.

Article about Tillie Lewis, p. 63, *Fortune,* April 1973. Reprinted by permission.

Quote, pp. 64-65, from Studs Terkel, *Working* (New York: Pantheon, 1974). Reprinted by permission of Pantheon Books, a division of Random House.

Fig 3.2, p. 66, from Frederick Webster, "A Model for New Venture Interaction," *Academy of Management Review* 1 (January 1976), pp. 26-37. Reprinted by permission.

Photo of Walter McIlhenny, p. 71 courtesy of Walter McIlhenny.

Article about Walter McIlhenny, pp. 71-72, reprinted with permission of The Wall Street Journal, ©️ Dow Jones & Company, Inc. 1975. All rights reserved.

Photo of Paul Smucker, p. 72, courtesy of Paul Smucker.

Article about Paul Smucker, p. 72, reprinted with permission of The Wall Street Journal, ©️ Dow Jones & Company, Inc. 1975. All rights reserved.

Drawings of Bill and Mel Lane, p. 72, reprinted with permission of The Wall Street Journal, ©️ Dow Jones & Company, Inc. 1975. All rights reserved.

Article about Bill and Mel Lane, p. 72, reprinted with permission of The Wall Street Journal, ©️ Dow Jones & Company, Inc. 1975. All rights reserved.

Photo of Thomas John Watson, Jr., p. 73, John Marmaras from Woodfin Camp & Associates.

Article about Thomas John Watson, Jr., p. 73, *Fortune,* January 1976. Reprinted by permission.

Chapter 4 Quote, p. 102, from Leslie This and Gordon Lippitt, "Learning Theories and Training," *Training and Development Journal* 20 (April 1966), pp. 2-11, and 20 (May 1966). Reproduced by special permission from the April and May 1966 *Training and Development Journal.* Copyright 1966 by the American Society for Training and Development, Inc.

Photo of Leo Garrett, p. 107, courtesy of Columbia Missourian. Photographer Dave Rees.

Article about Leo Garrett, p. 107, *Columbia Missourian,* December 7, 1975.

Chapter 5 Quote, p. 118, from Studs Terkel, *Working* (New York: Pantheon, 1974). ©️ 1974 by Pantheon Books, a division of Random House, Inc. Reprinted by permission.

Photo of Abraham Maslow, p. 126, courtesy of The Bettmann Archive.

Photo of David McClelland, p. 129, courtesy of David McClelland.

Chapter 6 Figure 6.1, p. 149, after Leonard Sayles, *Behavior of Industrial Work Groups* (New York: John Wiley & Sons, 1958), p. 39. Reprinted by permission of the author.

Quote, pp. 158-161, from Donald Roy, " 'Banana Time': Job Satisfaction and Informal Interaction." Reproduced by permission of the Society for Applied Anthropology from *Human Organization* 18 (4), 1959-1960.

Chapter 7 Figure 7.1, p. 189, from Mason Haire et al., *Managerial Thinking* (New York: Wiley, 1966), appendix. Reprinted by permission.

Listing, pp. 194-195, reprinted from "What Managers Think of Participative Management," by Larry Greiner, *Harvard Business Review* 51 (March/April 1973). Copyright © 1973 by the President and Fellows of Harvard College; all rights reserved.

Figure 7.2, p. 195, after Rensis Likert, "New Patterns in Sales Management," in *Changing Perspectives in Marketing Management* edited by Martin R. Warshaw, *Michigan Business Papers* No. 37 (Ann Arbor: Bureau of Business Research, Graduate School of Business Administration, 1962), Fig. 7, p. 24. Also after Rensis Likert, *The Human Organization* (New York: McGraw-Hill, 1967), Figure 4-10.

Figure 7.4, p. 197, reprinted from "How to Choose a Leadership Pattern," by Robert Tannenbaum and Warren Schmidt, *Harvard Business Review* (March/April 1958), pp. 95-101. Copyright © 1958 by the President and Fellows of Harvard College; all rights reserved.

Table 7.3, p. 199, from *A Theory of Leadership Effectiveness* by Fred Fiedler. Copyright © 1967 by McGraw-Hill. Used with permission of McGraw-Hill Book Company.

Table 7.4, p. 200, reprinted from *Leadership and Decision-Making* by Victor H. Vroom and Philip W. Yetton by permission of the University of Pittsburgh Press. © 1973 by the University of Pittsburgh Press.

Table 7.5, p. 201, reprinted from *Leadership and Decision-Making* by Victor H. Vroom and Philip W. Yetton by permission of the University of Pittsburgh Press. © 1973 by the University of Pittsburgh Press.

Figure 7.5, p. 202, from *Managerial Effectiveness* by William Reddin. Copyright © 1970 by McGraw-Hill. Used with permission of McGraw-Hill Book Company.

Chapter 8 Quote, p. 215, from Studs Terkel, *Working*, © 1974 by Pantheon Books, a division of Random House, Inc.

Chapter 9 Figure 9.2, p. 242, from George Porter, "Non Verbal Communications," reproduced by special permission from the June 1969 *Training and Development Journal.* Copyright 1969 by the American Society for Training and Development, Inc.

Figure 9.3, p. 243, from George Porter, "Non Verbal Communications," reproduced by special permission from the June 1969 *Training and Development Journal.* Copyright 1969 by the American Society for Training and Development, Inc.

Fig. 9.4, p. 244, from Raymand Ross, *Persuasion,* copyright 1974. Reprinted by permission of Prentice-Hall, Inc., Englewood Cliffs, New Jersey.

Figure 9.6, p. 247, from C. Ogden and I. Richards, *The Meaning of Meaning* (New York: Harcourt, Brace & World, 1956). Reprinted by permission.

Summary, pp. 252-254, from Mortimer Adler and Charles Van Doren, *How to Read a Book,* copyright © 1940, 1967 by Mortimer J. Adler, copyright © 1972 by Mortimer J. Adler and Charles Van Doren. Reprinted by permission of Simon and Schuster, Inc.

Figure 9.8, p. 259, from *Human Behavior at Work* by Keith Davis. Copyright © 1972 by McGraw-Hill Book Company. Used with permission of McGraw-Hill Book Company.

Figure 9.9, p. 260, from Keith Davis, "Management Communication and the Grapevine," September-October 1953 *Harvard Business Review,* copyright © 1953 by the President and Fellows of Harvard College; all rights reserved.

Chapter 10 Figure 10.1, p. 276, from National Industrial Conference Board, *The Expanded Personnel Functions,* Studies in Personnel Policy 203 (New York, 1966). Reprinted by permission.

Listing, pp. 295-296, from Meyer Friedman and Ray Rosenman, *Type A Behavior and Your Heart* (New York: Knopf, 1974). Reprinted by permission.

Figure 10.4, p. 298, reproduced with permission from *How to Get the Job That's Right for You* by B. Greco (Homewood, Ill.: Dow Jones-Irwin, 1975 ©).

Chapter 11 Table 11.1, p. 322, from *Principles of Management* by Harold Koontz and Cyril O'Donnell. Copyright © 1976 by McGraw-Hill. Used with permission of McGraw-Hill Book Company.

Table 11.3, p. 330, after James Dent, "Organizational Correlates of the Goals of Business Managers," *Personnel Psychology* 12 (1959). Also after George England, "Organizational Goals and Expected Behavior of American Managers," *Academy of Management Journal* (June 1967). Reprinted by permission.

Photo of David Sarnoff, p. 332, Steve Shapiro, Time-Life Picture Agency. © Time Inc. Article about David Sarnoff, pp. 332-333. *Fortune,* January 1975. Reprinted by permission.

Photo of Theodore N. Vail, p. 339, courtesy of American Telephone and Telegraph Co.

Article about Theodore N. Vail, pp. 339-340, *Fortune,* January 1975. Reprinted by permission.

Chapter 12 Article about George Washington, p. 354, *Fortune,* January 1975. Reprinted by permission.

Table 12.1, p. 355, from Bruce A. Kirchhoff, "MBO: Understanding What the Experts Are Saying," pp. 17-23, *MSU Business Topics,* Summer 1974. Reprinted by permission of the publisher, Division of Research, Graduate School of Business Administration, Michigan State University.

Table 12.3, pp. 362-363, from Allen Slusher and Henry Sims, "Commitment through MBO interviews," *Business Horizons* (August 1975), pp. 5-12. Copyright, 1975, by the Foundation for the School of Business at Indiana University. Reprinted by permission.

Table 12.5, pp. 370-373, from John C. Chambers, Satinder K. Mullick, and Donald D. Smith, "How to Choose the Right Forecasting Technique," *Harvard Bsuiness Review* (July/August 1971), pp. 45-74. Reprinted by permission.

Chapter 13 Figure 13.1, p. 390, from Richard Tersine, "Organization Decision Theory: A Synthesis," *Managerial Planning* 21 (July/August 1972), pp. 18-24, 4Off. Reprinted by permission.

Table 13.1, p. 391, from Robert Duncan, "Characteristics of Organizational Environments and Perceived Environmental Uncertainty," *Administrative Science Quarterly* 17 (September 1972), pp. 313-327. Reprinted by permission.

Table 13.2, p. 296, from Henry Mintzburg, "Strategy in Three Modes." © 1973 by the Regents of the University of California. Reprinted from *California Management Review,* volume XVI, number 2, p. 49, by permission of the Regents.

Chapter 14 Table 14.1, pp. 414-415, from U.S. Department of Agriculture, *Dictionary of Occupational Titles*, 3rd ed. (Washington, D.C.: Government Printing Office, 1965).

Figure 14.2, p. 427, from J. Richard Hackman et al., "A New Strategy for Job Enrichment." © 1975 by the Regents of the University of California. Reprinted from *California Management Review,* volume XVII, number 4, p. 60 and p. 62, by permission of the Regents.

Table 14.4, pp. 428-429, after William Reif and Robert Monczka, "Job Redesign: A Contingency Approach to Implementation." Adapted by permission of the publisher from *Personnel* (May/June 1974), © 1974 by AMACOM, a division of American Management Associations.

Figure 14.3, p. 430, from J. Richard Hackman et al., "A New Strategy for Job Enrichment." © 1975 by the Regents of the University of California. Reprinted from *California Management Review,* volume XVII, number 4, p. 60 and p. 62, by permission of the Regents.

Chapter 15 Photo of Alfred P. Sloan Jr., p. 441, courtesy of General Motors.

Article about Alfred P. Sloan Jr., *Fortune,* January 1975. Reprinted by permission.

Figure 15.12, p. 451, from Jay Galbraith, "Matrix Organization Designs," *Business Horizons* 14 (1971), pp. 29-40. Copyright, 1971, by the Foundation for the School of Business at Indiana University. Reprinted by permission.

Table 15.1, p. 452, reprinted by permission of D. S. Pugh, London Graduate School of Business Studies.

Table 15.2, p. 453, reprinted by permission of D. S. Pugh, London Graduate School of Business Studies.

Table, p. 456, from Richard Hall, "Organization Size and Organization Structure." Reprinted by permission of the author.

Table, p. 457, top, from James McNulty, "Organization Change in Growing Enterprises," *Administrative Science Quarterly* (June 1962), pp. 1-21. Reprinted by permission.

Table, p. 457, bottom, reprinted by permission of the publisher from *Planning and Developing the Company Organization Structure* by Ernest Dale, © 1952 by the American Management Assn., Inc.

Table 15.6, p. 463, from Harold Stieglitz, "Optimizing Span of Control," *Management Record* 24 (1962), pp. 25-29. Reprinted by permission of The Conference Board.

Figure 15.13, p. 471, reprinted by permission of D. S. Pugh, London Graduate School of Business Studies.

Chapter 16 Table 16.4, p. 490, from Robert Duncan, "Characteristics of Organizational Environments and Perceived Environmental Uncertainty," *Administrative Science Quarterly* 17 (1972), pp. 313-327. Reprinted by permission.

Figure 16.2, p. 498, from Ramon J. Aldag and Ronald G. Storey, "Environmental Uncertainty: Comments on Objective and Perceptual Indices," *Proceedings,* Academy of Management, 1975. Reprinted by permission.

Chapter 17 Photo of George Eastman, p. 518, Paulus Leeser, Time-Life Books, courtesy of Eastman House, Rochester, New York.

Article about George Eastman, pp. 518 and 520, *Fortune* January 1975. Reprinted by permission.

Figure 17.1, p. 524, from Louis Pondy, "Organizational Conflict: Concepts and Models," *Administrative Science Quarterly* 12 (September 67), pp. 296-320. Reprinted by permission.

Chapter 18 Quote, pp. 538-539, from *Executive Opinion,* copyright © 1970 by Herman E. Krooss. Reprinted by permission of Doubleday & Co., Inc.

Table 18.2, p. 542, from Alfred L. Seelye, "Societal Change and Business-Government Relationships," pp. 5-13, *MSU Business Topics,* Autumn 1975. Reprinted by permission of the publisher, Division of Research, Graduate School of Business Administration, Michigan State University.

Quote pp. 545-546, from Thomas McCraw, "Regulation in America: A Review Article," *Business History Review* 49 (Summer 1975), pp. 182-183. Copyright 1975. Reprinted by permission.

Table 18.3, p. 547, from "Business and the Local Community" by Rogers and Zimet in *The Business of America* edited by Ivar Berg, copyright © 1968 by Harcourt Brace Jovanovich, Inc., and reproduced with their permission.

Figure 18.1, p. 556, from Richard N. Farmer, "International Management" in *Contemporary Management: Issues and Viewpoints,* by McGuire, © 1974, p. 300. Reprinted by permission of Prentice-Hall, Inc., Englewood Cliffs, New Jersey.

Table 18.4, p. 557, from W. Warren Haynes et al., *Management,* 3rd. ed. Copyright 1975; reprinted by permission of Prentice-Hall, Inc., Englewood Cliffs, New Jersey.

Chapter 19 Figure 19.1, p. 573, from *Essentials of Management* by W. Jack Duncan. Copyright © 1975 by The Dryden Press, A Division of Holt, Rinehart and Winston. Reprinted by permission of Holt, Rinehart and Winston.

Table 19.1, p. 574, reprinted from "How Companies Respond to Social Demands," by Robert Ackerman, *Harvard Business Review* (July/August 1973). Copyright © 1973 by the President and Fellows of Harvard College; all rights reserved.

Figure 19.2, p. 575, reprinted from "How Companies Respond to Social Demands," by Robert Ackerman, *Harvard Business Review* (July/August 1973). Copyright © 1973 by the President and Fellows of Harvard College; all rights reserved.

Table 19.2, p. 576, from *Esssentials of Management* by W. Jack Duncan. Copyright © 1975 by The Dryden Press, A Division of Holt, Rinehart and Winston. Reprinted by permission of Holt, Rinehart and Winston.

Figure 19.3, p. 577, from *Business Week*, September 23, 1972. Reprinted by permission.

Questionnaire, p. 581, from Archie Carroll, "Managerial Ethics: A Post-Watergate View," *Business Horizons* (April 1975), pp. 75-80. Copyright, 1975, by the Foundation for the School of Business at Indiana University. Reprinted by permission.

Figure 19.4, p. 583, from John W. Newstrom and William A. Ruch, "The Ethics of Management and the Management of Ethics," pp. 29-37, *MSU Business Topics*, Winter 1975. Reprinted by permission of the publisher, Division of Research, Graduate School of Business Administration, Michigan State University.

Table, p. 584, from Simon Webley, "Business Policy and Business Ethics," *Journal of Business Policy* 3 (Spring 1973). Reprinted by permission.

Chapter 20 Figure 20.1, p. 603, from Larry Greiner, "Patterns of Organization Change," *Harvard Business Review* 45 (May/June 1967), pp. 119-130. Reprinted by permission.

Figure 20.2, p. 604, from Jarold J. Leavitt, "Applied Organizational Change in Industry: Structural, Technological, and Humanistic Approaches," in James G. March (ed.), *Handbook of Organizations*, © 1965 by Rand McNally College Publishing Co., Chicago, Figure 1, p. 1145.

Quote, pp. 610-612, from William Glueck, "Organization Change in Business Government," *Academy of Management Journal* 12 (December 1969), pp. 439-441. Reprinted by permission.

Fig. 20.3, p. 615, from Gene W. Dalton, "Influence and Organizational Change," in Avant R. Negandhi and Joseph P. Schwitters (eds.), *Organizational Behavior Models*, Comparative Administrative Research Institute, Kent State University. Reprinted by permission.

CASES Case about Madman Muntz, pp. 629-633, from "'Madman' Muntz Rides Again," by Robert A. Rosenblatt. Copyright, 1975, Los Angeles Times. Reprinted by permission.

Case about Alberta Mobile Homes, Ltd., pp. 637-638, reprinted with permission from Glueck, William F., *Personnel: A Diagnostic Approach* (Dallas, Texas: Business Publications, Inc., 1974).

Case about communications exercises (adapted from Keltner), p. 639, adapted from *Interpersonal Speech Communications*, by John Keltner. © 1970 by Wadsworth Publishing Company, Inc.

Case about Aeronautical Systems Corporation, pp. 653-658, from *Incidents in Applying Management Theory* by Richard N. Farmer, Barry M. Richman, and William G. Ryan. © 1966 by Wadsworth Publishing Company, Inc., Belmont California 94002. Reprinted by permission of the publisher.

Case about Faller and Brown, pp. 658-660, from *Incidents in Applying Management Theory* by Richard N. Farmer, Barry M. Richman, and William G. Ryan. © 1966 by Wadsworth Publishing Company, Inc., Belmont California 94002. Reprinted by permission of the publisher.

Case about Harrison Inc., pp. 660-668, adapted from *Business Policy* by William F. Glueck. Copyright © 1976 by McGraw-Hill, Inc. Used with permission of McGraw-Hill Book Company.

Case about Hoeppner Company, pp. 668-677, from William F. Glueck, *Business Policy* (New York: McGraw-Hill, 1972). Reprinted by permission.